CW00821684

DIARIES FROM **HELL**

DIARIES FROM HELL

CHARLES BRONSON

My Prison Diaries

y Lolfa

First impression: 2009

Cover design: Nina Camplin

ISBN: 978 1 847711 168

Published, printed and bound in Wales
by Y Lolfa Cyf., Talybont, Ceredigion SY24 5HE
website www.ylolfa.com
e-mail ylolfa@ylolfa.com
tel 01970 832 304
fax 832 782

I dedicate this book to my 'landlady',
The one and only Queen of the land.
God save our Queen!
Without being rude or ungrateful,
Don't you think it's time you kicked me out, Mam?
In 3 ½ decades I've never paid you a penny!
It's time to let me go!

CONTENTS

DING DING... ROUND 1

ROY 'Pretty Boy' SHAW

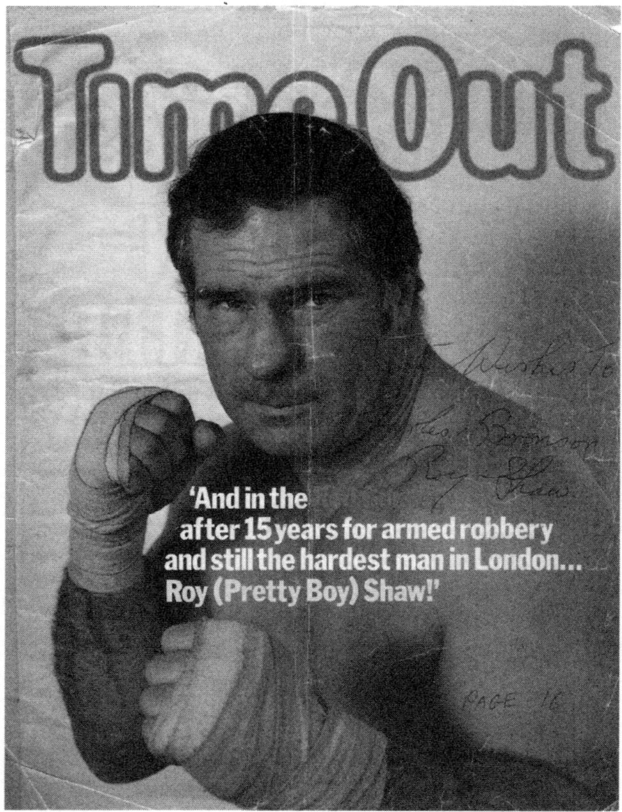

Time Out
'And in the
after 15 years for armed robbery
and still the hardest man in London...
Roy (Pretty Boy) Shaw!'

If you know me, then you'll know that I haven't exactly been an angel during my life. I've done time for robbery and for violence. Am I proud of it? No I'm not! What I am proud of is that I've been given a chance to prove to myself and others that I can turn my life around and live without being considered a threat to society. This I have done successfully.

Give Charlie Bronson the same opportunity as I had. Let him prove to whoever it needs proving to that he is no threat to society. Let him prove to the public and the media that his word is true when he says he intends to live an honest life.

At Luton Crown Court I approached Charlie, shook his hand and said, "Keep yourself calm. Fighting the system does you no good. Give yourself an opportunity to gain freedom by showing who you really are." Charlie has shown who he really is: an artist, a charity fund raiser and an asset to anyone needing advice on physical fitness.

I know there is a future for Charlie outside the prison walls. Free him and let many others reap the benefits of his knowledge.

DING DING... ROUND 2

BILLY COOPER

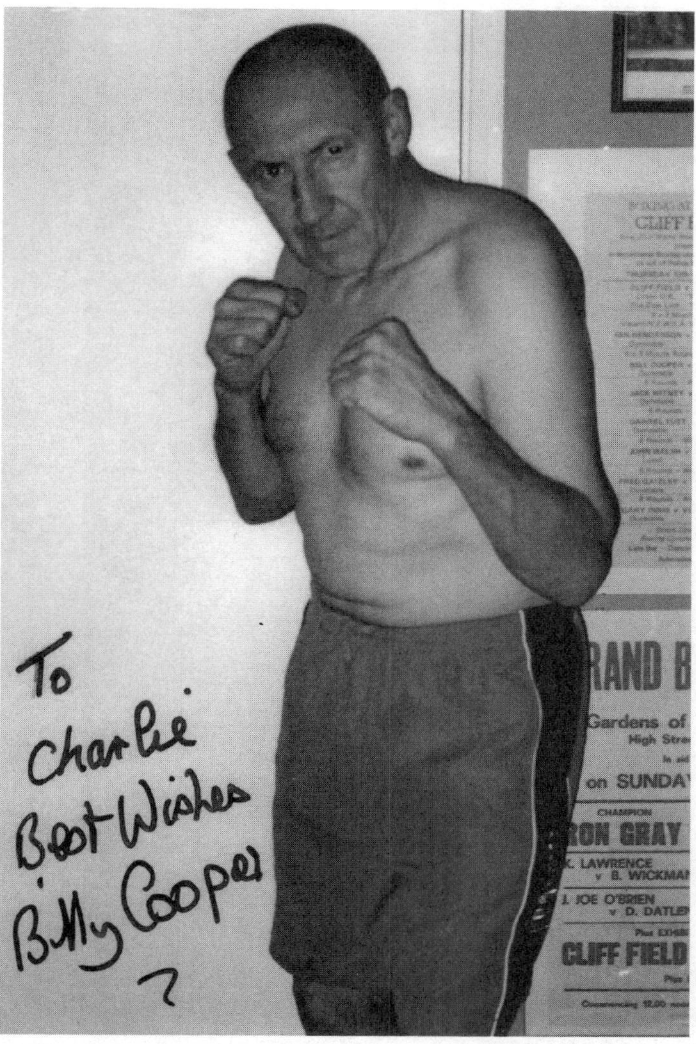

14 unlicensed fights
Won 11, Lost 3
After serving more than eight years of a life sentence in isolation, Charles Bronson should be allowed back into mainstream prison so that he can prove he is a changed man and can live and mix with other people. This is the perfect opportunity for the prison system to show it can rehabilitate a long-term prisoner.

I've known Charlie and his family for a number of years, and from the feedback I've received he is ready for this move.

DING DING... ROUND 3

GARY 'The Hammer' DELANEY

Former undefeated Southern Area light-heavyweight champion
Former undefeated Commonwealth light-heavyweight champion
Former WBO Intercontinental light-heavyweight champion
Former undefeated British Masters cruiserweight champion
Former undefeated Southern Area cruiserweight champion
Former two-time world cruiserweight title challenger
"I coulda been a contenda, Charlie."

I can relate to Charles Bronson since I also reside in one of Her Majesty's establishments. I regularly hear stories from people who are innocent – how they were hard done by and how it was a miscarriage of justice. Most of the time it's a load of bollocks. I can never understand why these 'gaffs' are so overcrowded when everyone in prison is innocent! I haven't met a guilty convict yet. A lot of the time they deserve everything they get and more, much more, believe me.

Charlie, on the other hand, is a man who has done 34 years at Her Majesty's pleasure, 30 of them in solitary confinement. Does Her Majesty really get pleasure from that? She's a sick bitch if she does! This is a man who has never killed anyone (the recommendation is only 15 years for murder) and who will be drawing his pension and collecting his bus pass soon (sorry Charlie).

The question you've got to ask yourself is this: is Charlie really a danger to the public? The system says he is, but this is the same system that allows rapists and nonces to freely walk our streets. Is that a system you can trust? A system like that is more of a danger to the public.

Charlie would be a great asset if they allowed him to be and if they worked with him. He'd keep a lot of the younger generation on the straight and narrow. I personally think that if he lectured and spoke out about life behind bars he'd have a major impact on prison overcrowding within a generation. Who'd want to risk going to prison after hearing of the horror Charlie's experienced while inside?

Charles Bronson, 34 years in prison, 30 of those years in solitary confinement. Now that's a man who's been hard done by. That's a real miscarriage of justice. I think the system's had its money's worth and has taken its pound of flesh (and more). It's time to let him go; the joke's over now.

Free Charles Bronson.

Tuff times don't last but tuff people do!

JOE EGAN

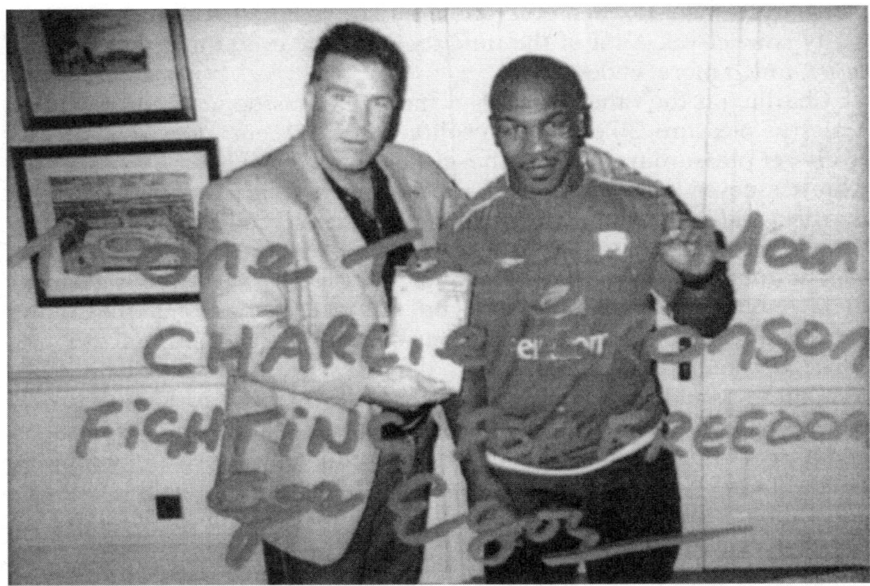

My name is Joe Egan. I was a seven-time Irish boxing champion and a sparring partner to Mike Tyson. I have never met Charles Bronson but I've read about him many times. I look forward to shaking his hand one day when he is a free man – soon I hope. I served two years in prison and that was hard enough. Charles has served 34 years, 30 of them in solitary confinement. That's wrong for a man who's never killed anyone.

Being a boxer is a hard life. The psychological side is even more difficult to cope with than the physical one. The walk to the ring before a fight is so scary that some boxers are beaten before the first bell rings because they are not mentally prepared.

Boxing tests a man's character. What Charles Bronson's endured shows he is a man of strength with a character second to none.

Good luck and God bless you, Charles Bronson.

DING DING... ROUND 5

MICK LEAHY

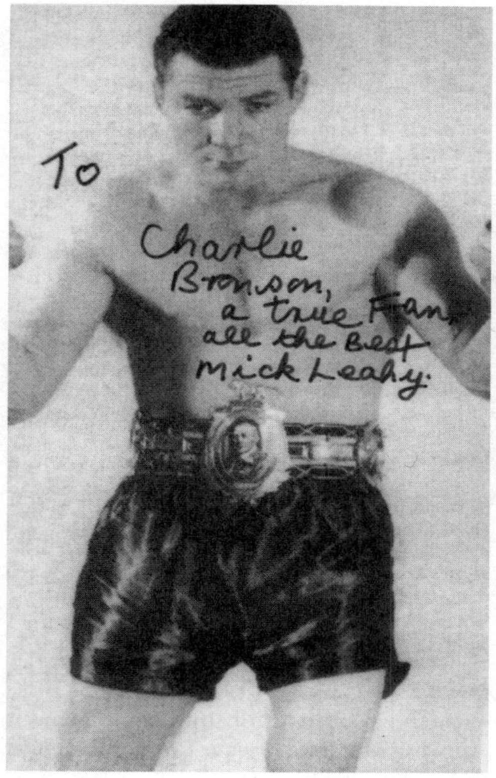

Middleweight
Won 46, KO 16, Lost 19 (KO 5), Drawn 7
I'm Mick's wife Teresa, writing on his behalf. I'm sorry to tell you that Mick now has Alzheimers due to a terrible road accident he had 40 years ago involving an articulated lorry that was parked in the dark. The driver was asleep with no lights on and Mick went through the windscreen of his car when he crashed into it. Glass entered his brain, severing the nerves at the back of his left eye and his ear. As a result he is now partially sighted.

Mick is a former British middleweight champion, holder of the Lonsdale Belt and the last fighter to beat the man who was regarded as the greatest 'pound for pound' fighter of all time, Sugar Ray Robinson. Mick also fought some other greats of the division such as Nino Benvenuti, Laslo Papp and Gomeo Brennan. At the time of the accident he was due to fight the legendary Emile Griffith for the middleweight championship of the world.

My family and I are so pleased Charlie remembers Mick's career and was a true fan. I believe Charlie is a kind and thoughtful man who does so much for various charities. He also did a lovely piece of art for us. We wish Charlie all the very best for his freedom and liberty. Be lucky, Charlie.

DING DING... ROUND 6

SAMMY McCARTHY

Lightweight
Won 44, KO 26, Lost 8 (KO 1), Drawn 1

When I was asked if I could do a piece for Charles Bronson's book, I said it would be a pleasure. Me and Charlie go back a long way; I remember him as good ol' Mickey Peterson before he changed his name.

Charlie loves boxers and boxing and always took an interest in my career. People have often said to me that the fight game is a violent sport and I agree with them. But some have used it as an avenue to improve their lives, to escape from ghettos, to make some money and earn some respect. And that's why Charlie has so much heart and respect for boxers.

Charlie would do so much good if he was on the outside, talking to youngsters in schools and young offenders' units about the harsh, brutal reality of adult prison life. Some youngsters in London and in every town and city up and down the country seem to think it's 'cool' to be part of a knife and gun culture. Charlie would be the ideal man to help prevent these youngsters killing each other and to steer them away from a life of crime and imprisonment. Why this man is still incarcerated is beyond me. Charlie is a very affable and kind lad, not the thug that the media portray.

I wish Charlie all the best in his fight for freedom and hope he can touch base here in east London when he gets out for a well-earned pint with his pal. My heart goes out to you Charlie.

God bless,

Your old pal, Sammy

DING DING... ROUND 7

CLIFFY FIELDS

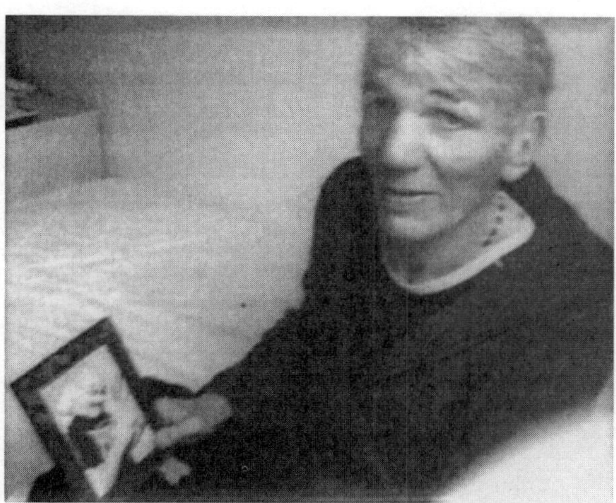

'Charles Bronson BT1314, Britain's most dangerous prisoner.' It must be difficult for Charlie to try and shake off that image when he's in solitary confinement and the media are free to carry on calling him what they want.

I've been on the boxing circuit as a professional and as an unlicensed fighter. During this time I've met many people who have spoken to me about Charlie's short time in Civvy Street. These conversations were usually about his time in the ropes and in the gym – his ability to fight, not as a street thug but within recognized rules in a legal organization.

Our paths crossed one day in a pub on the border of Luton and Dunstable where we didn't come to blows or rob the till – we chatted of boxing. He was respectful and had a good knowledge of the noble art. I felt then and still feel today that Charlie has a lot to offer. Foolishly, he ended up in jail when he was a young boy. Now a man, leaving his past behind, he spends a lot of his time writing to various people with solid words of advice. He frequently assists charities through his artwork and physical feats. For some reason the media ignore this side of the man, choosing instead to project the image of a monster to the general public.

His sentence is way past its sell-by date, whereas the real beasts around him take early releases, usually to reoffend and return. Charlie, when released, will never return to his hellhole. His destiny is to encourage people to live respectfully, to stay away from the path of wrongdoing and appreciate their lives. One thing is for sure: keeping him in that cage is denying a lot of people a good future.

DING DING... ROUND 8

MARK 'Del' DELANEY

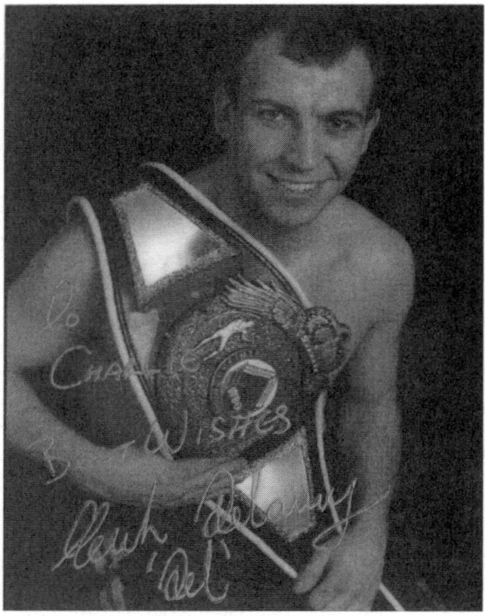

Light heavyweight
Won 26 (KO 16), Lost 3 (KO 2)
My name is Mark 'Del' Delaney. I am the former WBO Intercontinental super middleweight champion and former British title challenger from London's Canning Town.

As a kid I was always aware of 'Charlie Bronson – the most dangerous man in Britain' through the media. He was caged 24 hours a day and was said to be too violent to ever be released. This seems to be a far-fetched description of the man I have come to know and respect.

I received my first letter from Charlie shortly after fighting Joe Calzaghe for the British title in 1996. He said I'd fought like a lion and had done my fans, family and most importantly myself, proud. He told me to carry on fighting for what I wanted and because of this I carried on chasing my dream and gave it another go.

Over the years I have got to know Charles Bronson and believe him not to be the lunatic or thug that people accuse him of being. He has shown intelligence, thoughtfulness and true friendship to me. He doesn't deserve to be incarcerated any longer than necessary. If we are considered to be part of the human race, then why treat someone like a caged animal?

Charles Bronson wants to see the world, live a normal life and see as many sunrises and sunsets as he can before he dies. Would this be a danger to society?

Tough times don't last, but tough people do. Proud as a peacock.

DING DING... ROUND 9

JOEY GIAMBRA

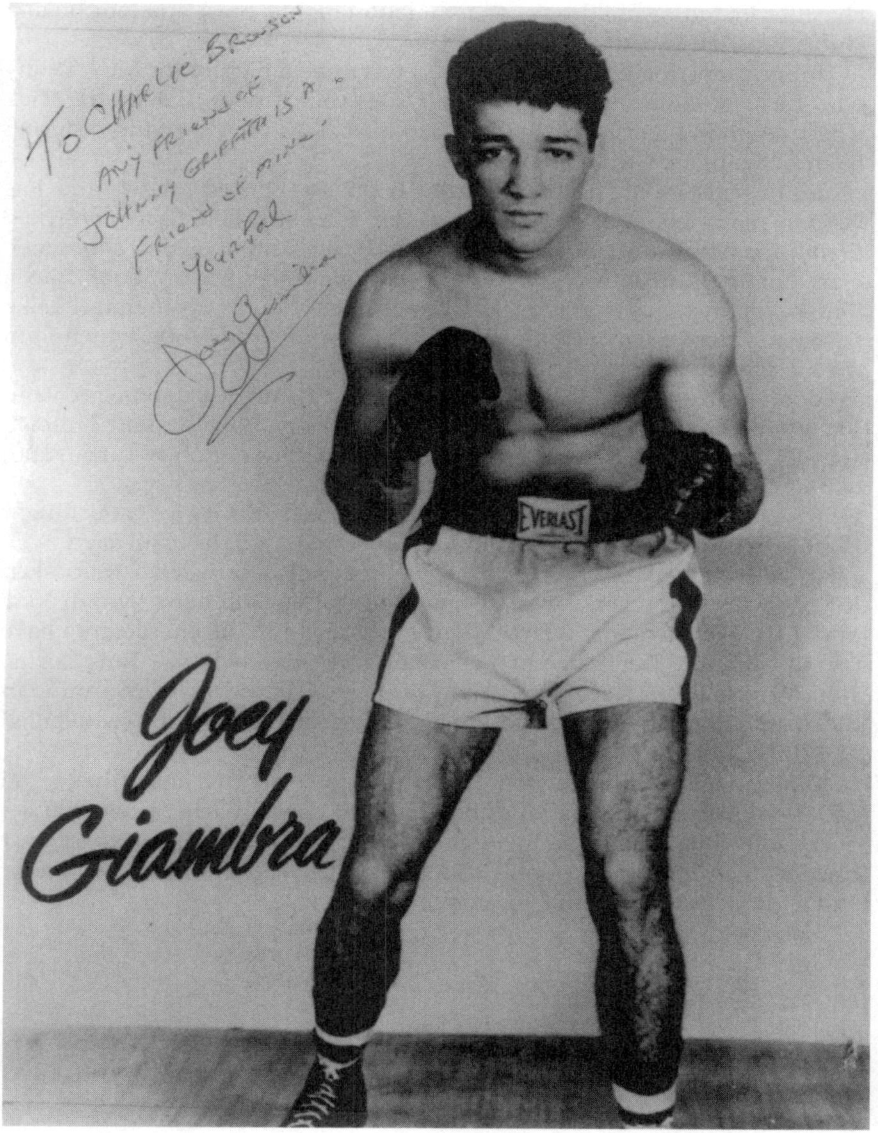

Middleweight
Won 65 (KO 31), Lost 10, Drew 2

When my pal Johnny Griffiths from the UK asked me to do a write-up for Charles Bronson, I honestly thought he meant the movie star of the same name! To tell you the truth, I'd never heard of Charlie but Johnny filled me in about him and his life in incarceration. Gee, I thought Rubin

Carter had it rough when he was in Trenton Penitentiary! But Charlie sure is one tough *hombre*. This man has really been through it in the 34 years he has been away and yet Johnny says he is a man of many talents. Not only is this guy a fantastic artist but he also donates his pictures to various charities including children's cancer auction nights, boys' amateur boxing clubs… the list is endless.

Johnny informed me that Charlie's even done a picture for Mick Leahy who I was going to fight here in the States (but it never came off). Mick was a tough kid and I was saddened to hear he is poorly and is suffering from Alzheimers. Get well, Mick.

Johnny also told me that Charlie is an established author and has written many books. I have also written a book called *The Uncrowned Champion* about my life as a prize fighter and a number one contender. I am currently in talks with a movie company to turn my book into a film. Colin Farrell is to play me, with Jack Nicholson as my manager Mike Scanlon. I hope Charlie's film is a success when it comes out, which I am sure it will be.

Boxing was good to me, and in my era there truly were some greats in the middleweight division with the likes of Carmen Basilio, Gene Fullmer, Joey Giardello, Dick Tiger, Emile Griffith, Bobo Olsen, Randy Turpin and, of course, the legendary Sugar Ray Robinson.

I fought Joey Giardello three times and beat him twice, and fought Bobo Olsen for the world title but lost on points – a fight I still say I won. Jake LaMotta was my hero and I was on cloud nine when I was asked to spar with him when I was 19 years old in Lou Stillman's gym in New York City. I could go on and on about my career and the characters I have met like Sinatra, Dean Martin, Peter Lawford, Sammy Davis, Tony Curtis, John Wayne, Ricky Nelson and many of the mob guys who were around in those days like Blinky Palermo, Frankie Carbo and Jack Ruby (who killed Lee Harvey Oswald).

I sure hope Charlie gets out. He sounds a swell guy, and if he's a pal of Johnny's then he's a pal of mine, that's for sure. Charlie, when you get out, buddy, make sure you invite me to your party and we can toast your freedom with the finest bubbly. Good luck, Charlie. It's been an honour and a privilege to write this for you.

Your pal,
Joey Giambra

DING DING... ROUND 10

PHIL GOODSON

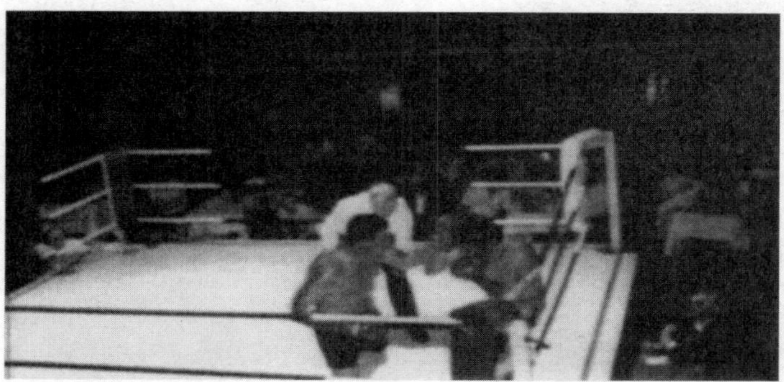

Heavyweight
Amateur 32, lost 11
Professional 23, lost 8

Charlie, it's a long time since we met at Luton High Town Boxing Club run by Jack Lindsey, and lots of things have changed. The club has closed down due to council cut-backs along with political correctness, health and safety issues, etc. But we still find places to train and keep fit.

I have followed your progress over the years, and as an ex-prize fighter, businessman and regular member of society with a family, I'm often shocked at how harshly you've been treated – your punishment seems disproportionate to your crime. I won't compare you with others in the system as I am sure every case should be looked at individually. But I would like to see the authorities starting to work on a way to get you back into society and mixing with people.

We all need a second chance to allow us to live a normal family life. We mellow as we grow older. Our problems, anger and anti-social behaviour fade away. Let's hope the prison service remembers this.

Best wishes,
Phil Goodson

DING DING... ROUND 11

NOSHER POWELL

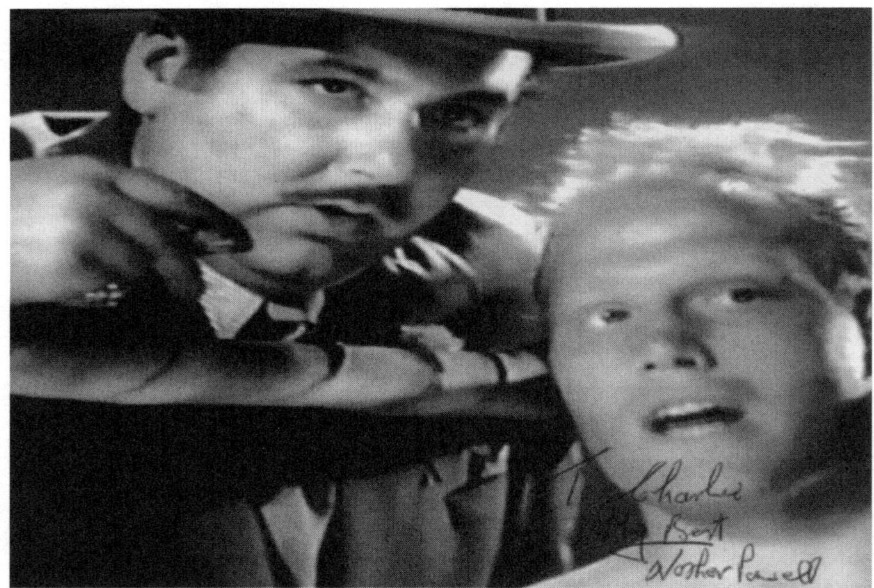

Boxer, film star and author

What does it take to become a great warrior and champion? That's an easy one: GUTS!

Charlie had plenty and proved it time and time again. Why the hell they still have him in custody when they seem to set free sex perverts to rape and abuse young kids and then set them free later to offend again and again is beyond me. When I think of all the charities that Charlie has supported and the thousands of pounds he has helped to raise for them, I cannot think of what or who makes these decisions. Perverts themselves, possibly.

I sparred with Tommy Farr and Randy Turpin – both great fighters. They don't make them like that anymore, do they? I was very lucky to be able to spar with some of the all-time greats like Joe Louis, Don Cockel, Joey Erskine, Henry Cooper, Ingemar Johansson and Nino Valdez. What Nino would do to the current crop of top heavies doesn't bear thinking about.

My boxing career enabled me to break into the film game and I went all over the globe making epics with stars such as Errol Flynn, Sean Connery and John ('Duke') Wayne. Both my sons are now top stunt artists, sought by top directors to arrange and carry out big stunts. Gary, my youngest son, is currently in Mexico working on the new James Bond movie and Greg is at the studios as an advisor on many films.

All the best,

Nosher Powell

DING DING... ROUND 12

PAUL HODKINSON

Former world featherweight champion

"Seconds out!"

Charlie Bronson is a massive boxing fan and was a great fan of mine throughout my career.

I have never met Charlie but have heard so much about him through fellow boxers who know him well. They all say what a really nice fella he is and talk of his endless charity work for the boys' boxing clubs all over Britain.

Boxers are all part of one big family and are gentlemen in and out of the ring. My dream was always to be a world champion. Whatever I've wanted to achieve in my life, I've always studied those who did it well, memorized what I had learned and believed that I could do it too. Then I went out and did it. That was the attitude I had to have to be a world champion.

Boxing is known as 'the noble art' and Charlie is a very noble man for donating his art to worthy causes. Keep up the good work, Charlie, and I wish you all the very best for freedom and the future... Keep punching.

Your pal,

Paul Hodkinson

DING DING... ROUND 13

MATT LEGG

FREE CHARLIE BRONSON

I have known Charlie and his family for a few years now and I believe he should finally be freed.

It is terrible how he is portrayed in the media as the most violent man in the prison system. Since I have known Charlie, he has not only made me laugh almost every time I receive mail from him, but he also sent my wife and myself a very comforting letter after we had lost our twin boys just before they were born. This is a side of Charlie that I wish more people would be able to see.

He has served more than enough time; he deserves freedom at last.

Friend of Charlie,

Matt Legg

DING DING... ROUND 14

CRAWFORD ASHLEY

BRITISH LIGHT HEAVYWEIGHT CHAMPION
WON 19, DRAW 1, LOST 6

I have spoken to Charlie over the phone a few times and have visited him once.

We hear a lot of talk about protecting human rights, but this man has had his taken away from him. Don't you think it's about time he was free?

Ask Charlie to go into schools and talk to the kids about the price you have to pay if you follow his path. He could be one of the saviours of today's troubled youth culture.

Crawford Ashley

DING DING... ROUND 15

AUDLEY HARRISON

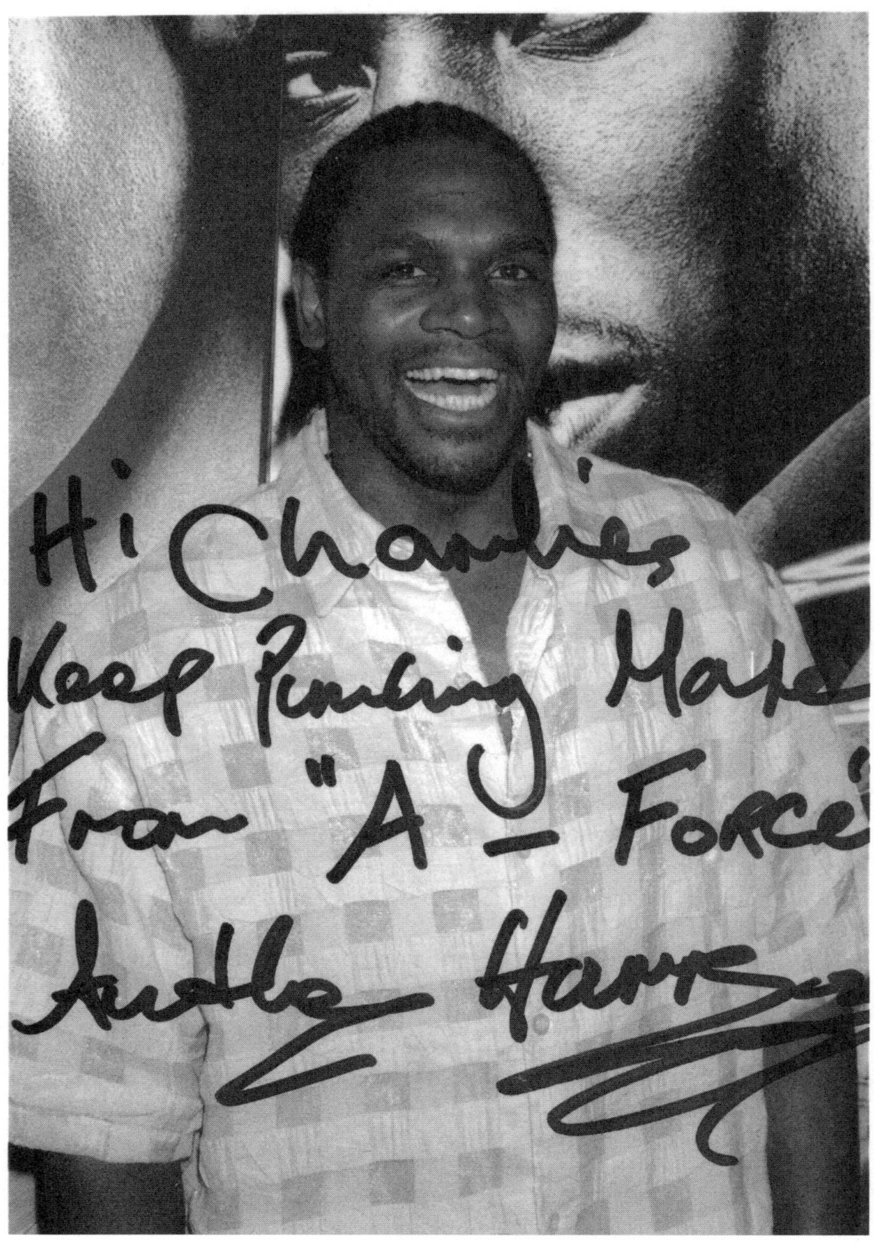

Hi Charlie
Keep punching mate
From 'A-Force' Audley Harrison

DING DING... ROUND 16

GEORGE CHUVALO

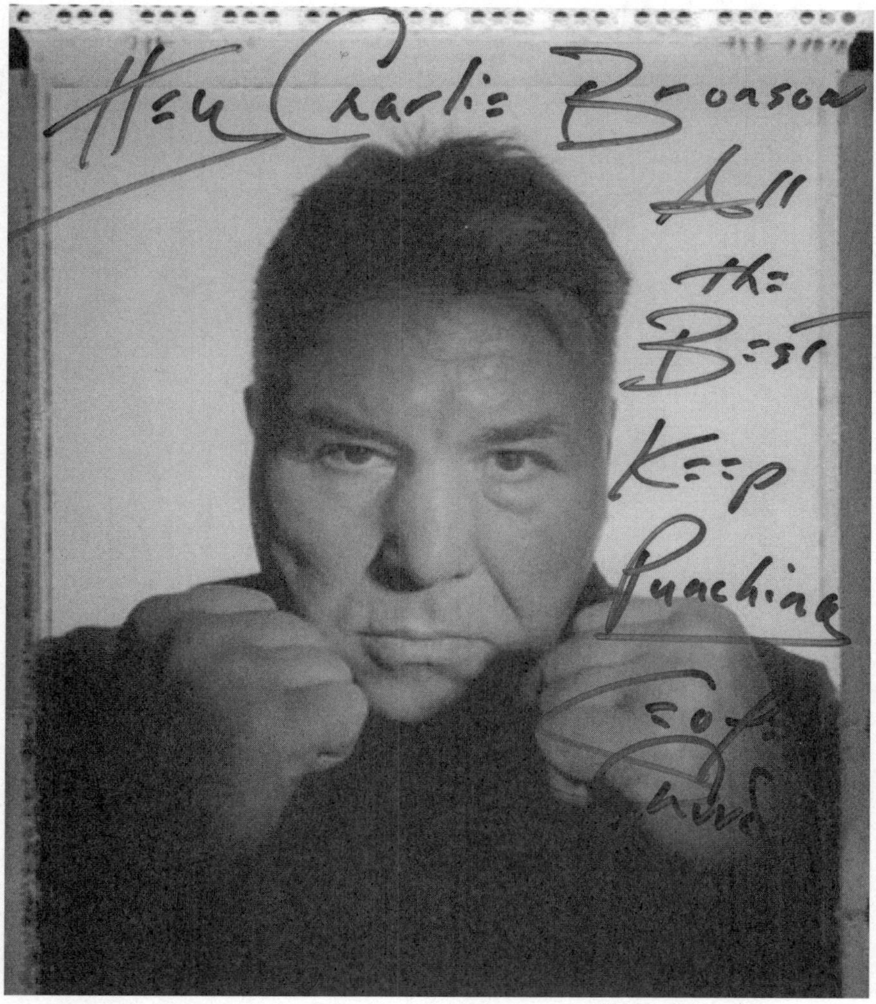

Hey Charlie Bronson
All the best. Keep punching.
George Chuvalo

DING DING... ROUND 17

RUBIN 'HURRICANE' CARTER

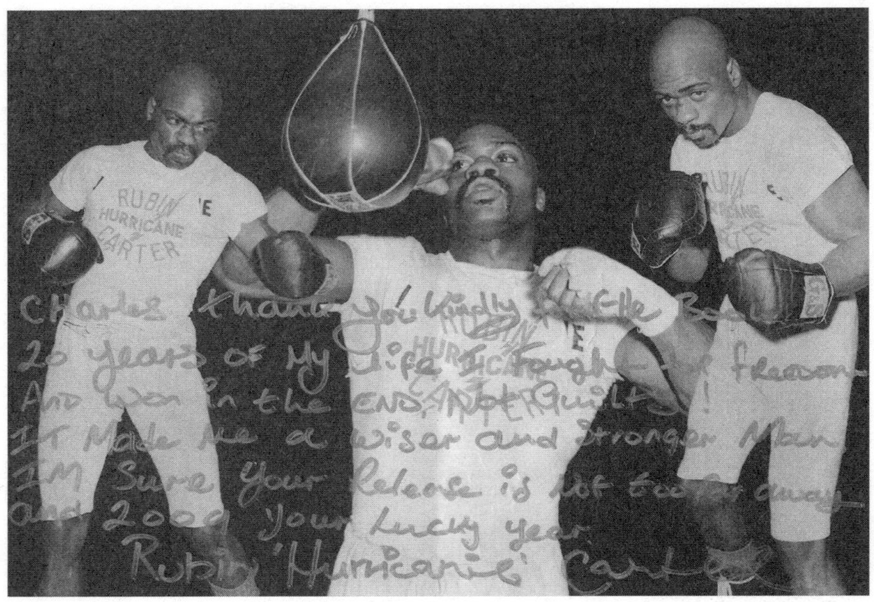

Charles

Thank you kindly for the book. 20 years of my life I fought for freedom and won in the end, Not Guilty! It made me a wiser and stronger man. I'm sure your release is not too far away and 2009 your lucky year.

Rubin 'Hurricane' Carter

DING DING… ROUND 18

SUGAR RAY LEONARD

SUGAR RAY LEONARD

To Charlie
Best Wishes
Sugar Ray Leonard

DING DING... ROUND 19

JOHN CONTEH

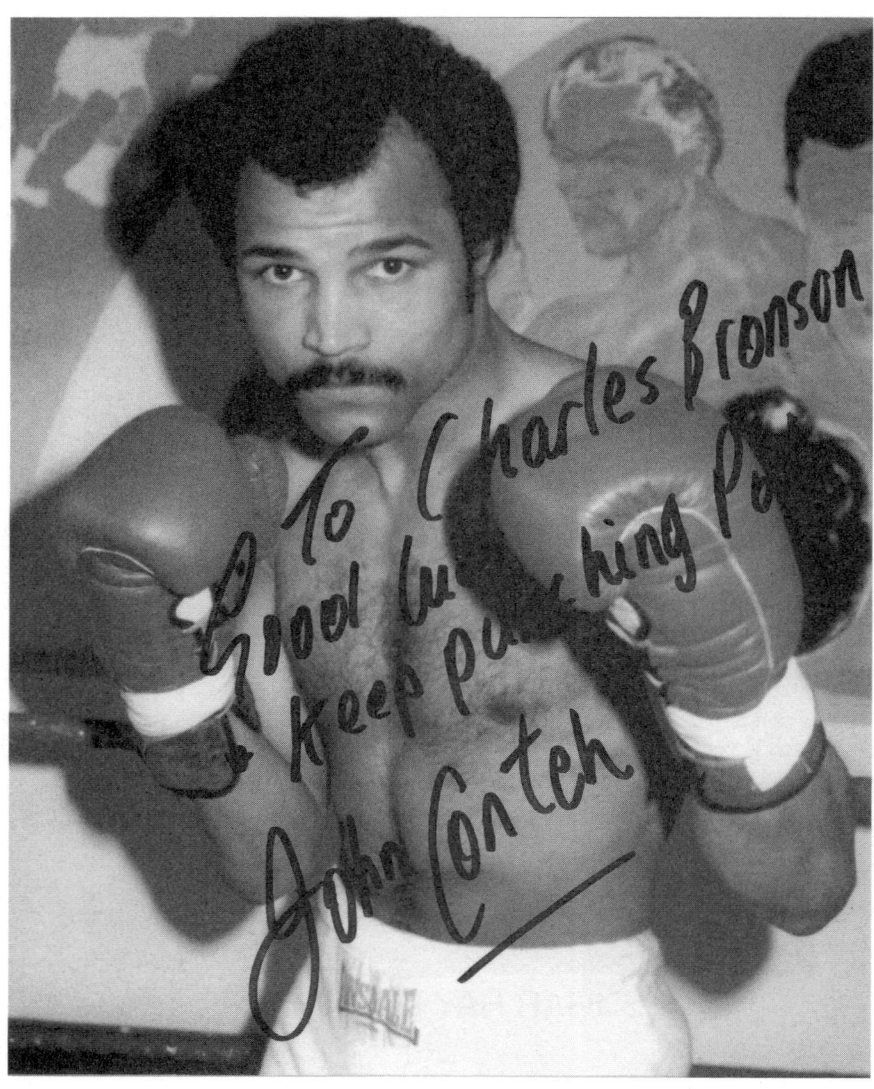

To Charles Bronson
Good luck. Keep punching pal
John Conteh

DING DING... ROUND 20

FRANK BRUNO

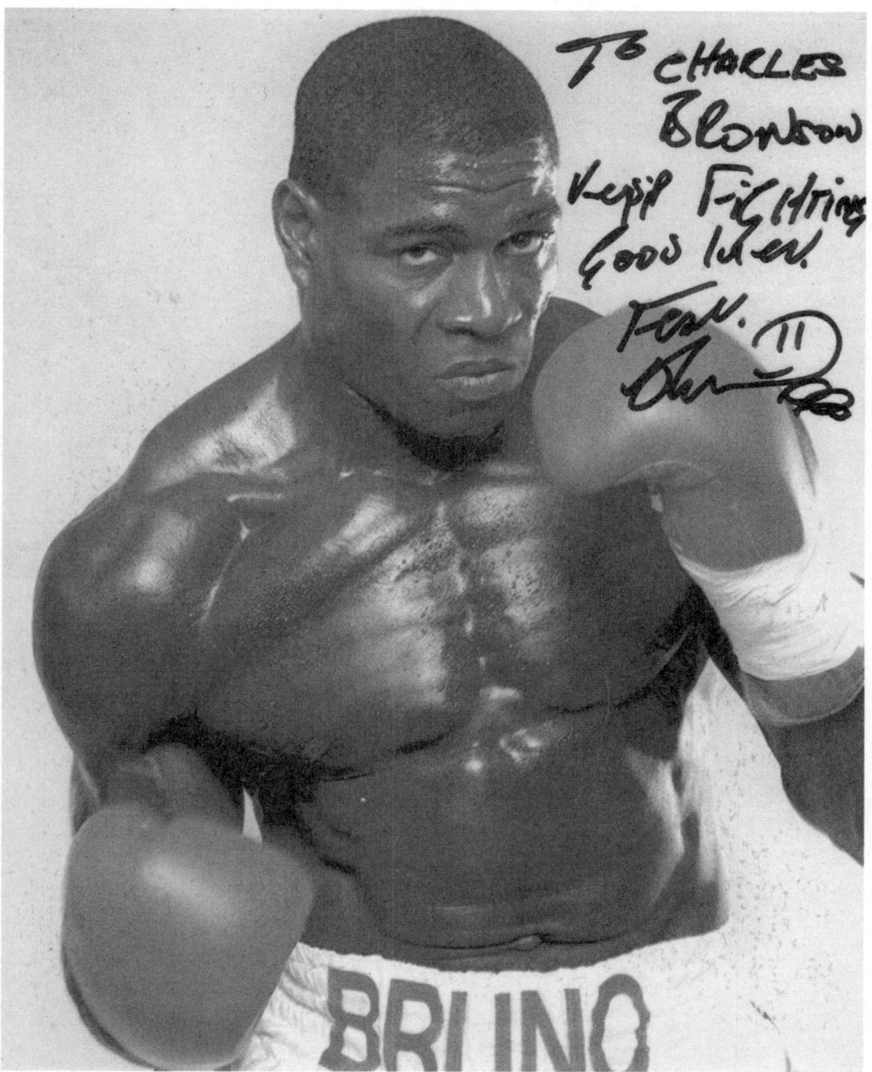

To Charles Bronson
Keep fighting. Good luck
Frank Bruno

PAUL HODKINSON

To Charlie
Best wishes
Paul Hodkinson, WBC World Champ 91-93

DING DING… ROUND 22

JOHN H. STACEY

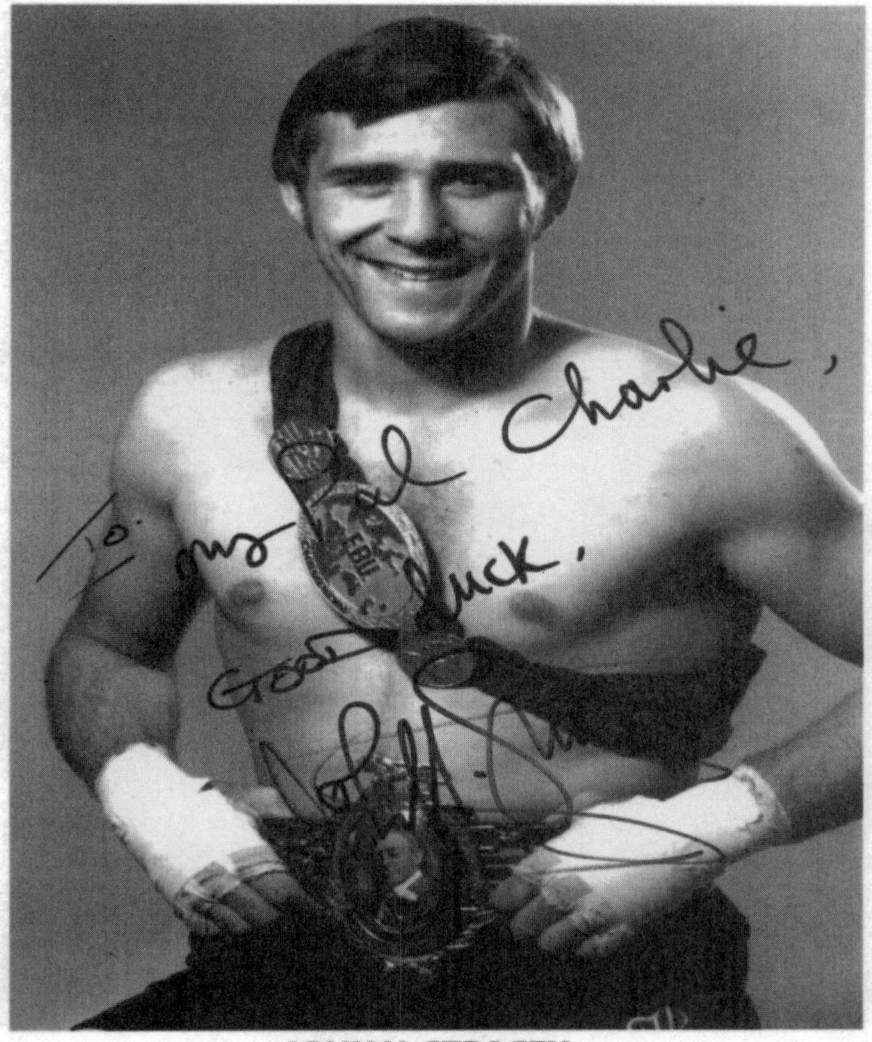

JOHN H. STRACEY
Undefeated British Welterweight Champion 1973 - 74 - 75
Undefeated European Welterweight Champion 1974 - 75
Welterweight Champion of the World 1975 - 76
WBC Boxing Hall of Fame Inductee 2005

To my pal Charlie
Good luck
John Stacey

DING DING... ROUND 23

DON KING

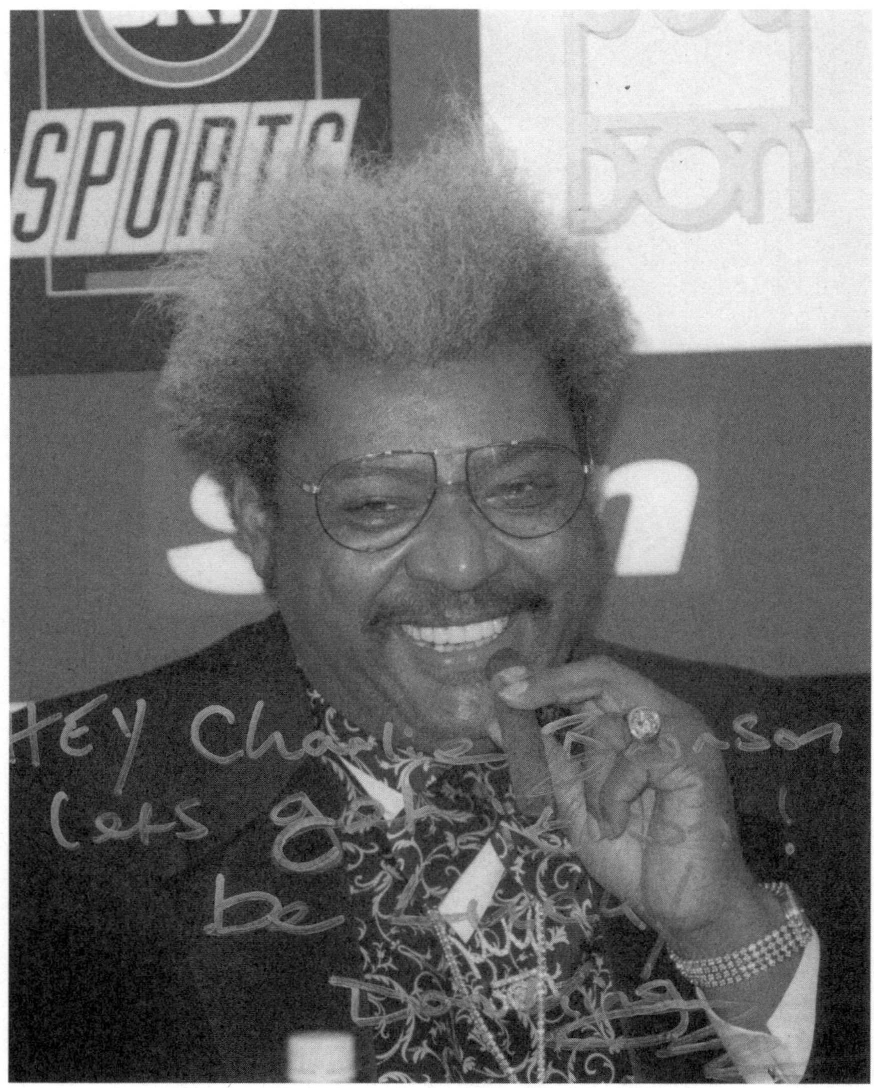

"Hey Charlie Bronson

Let's get it on!

Best wishes

Don King"

DING DING... ROUND 24

RICKY HATTON

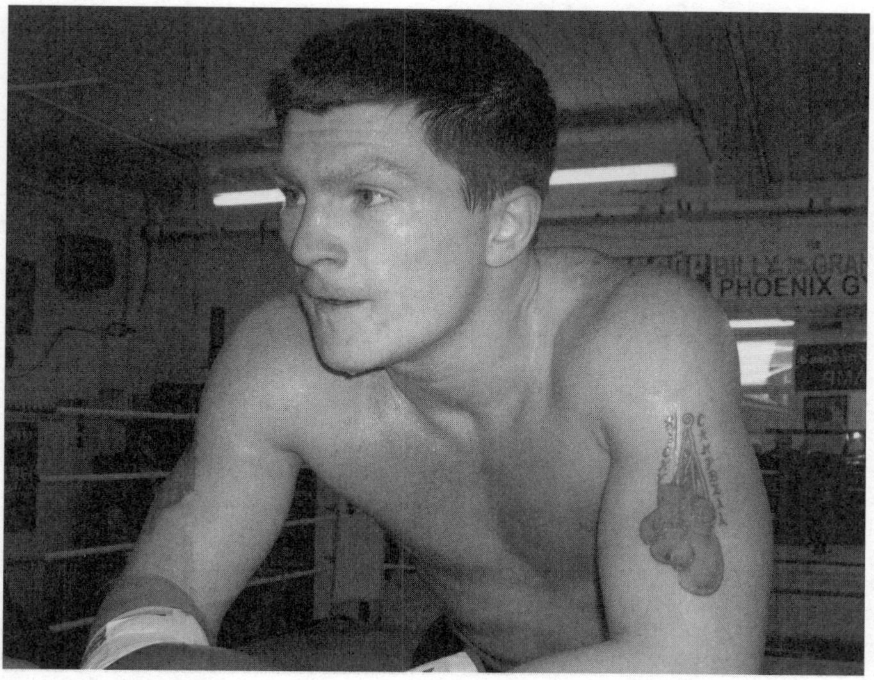

Best wishes, Charlie
Ricky Hatton

CHAPTER 1

Turn the light off on the way out!

In the darkness I come alive.
You'll see me in your nightmare!
I'll give you a wave!
One moment of insanity can obliterate a lifetime of normality.

Dead Dreams

Rocking in the graveyard
They're dying to get in there
The last stop
Final destination
The end of time
This is it
What we all feared
Death
Parked up for all time
No way out
Nothing left
Just darkness
There to rot
Dreamless
Soul – less
Blown away
A hole of bones
All chewed up
One dies – One born
A life – A death
"Let go"
Time for sleep
It's all behind
Inside your mind
The inner darkness
Time to reflect
Time to understand
Just what went wrong
What the fuck went wrong?
Why me?
It wasn't my time
It wasn't my turn
Who turned the light off?
Where did it all go wrong?
Why did it have to end?
Was it all worth it?
Why the fuck me?
Why now?
What now?
Dead Dreams
Black rainbows
Dried-up wishing wells
It all dies with your dream
Senseless
Worthless
Totally fucked away
A burnt-out soul
A melted heart

Empty
Bottomless
Hollow
An empty tortoise shell
Homeless
Dull and cold
A great big fucked-up lonely hole
Rotting bones
It's goodbye time
Loonyology time
Insanity gone mad
The shows over
Curtains
Dead dreams
Good night
Sleep forever

SO WHO WANTS some good news? Anybody? I know you do, so here it is: the biggest, ugliest monster in UK, John Straffen, finally died up in Frankland Prison, Durham on 19 November 2007. Yipppeeeee, yarhhhooooooo – party time! Straffen killed three little girls back in the 1950s. He served a total of 55 years as a Category A prisoner under maximum security. He was 77 years old. Let it be a lesson to all you would-be child-murdering bastards. You will die in hell even before you go there!

I'm glad the old nonce died inside, but he should've died years ago really. If anyone's neck should've been stretched and snapped it was Straffen's. He was actually sentenced to hang but was later reprieved on mental health grounds and sent to Broadmoor criminal lunatic asylum. Guess what? He escaped and killed another little girl. That about sums this system up in a nutshell: Loonyology.

It was in Long Lartin jail in the late 1980s that I covered Straffen with a bucket of shit and piss. Fond memories. I'm glad the old cunt's dead; it's one less nonce to feed.

I'll tell you who's an evil fuck-faced twat: Dave 'Pervo' Beech. For 23 years he was sexually assaulting kids. He's a right old dirty nonce, a serious predator of children and the worst type of monster you can imagine, but at Sheffield Crown Court he copped his just deserts: a life sentence rammed up his fat arse. By the time he hits the streets again he will be on a Zimmer frame and there'll be flying cars and day trips to Mars. Hopefully a gang of yobs will kick him to death. Better still, let's have a Straffen ending. Burn in Hell, you beast.

Did you know insects outnumber humans by one billion to one? One fucking billion of them to one of us! Can you believe that? Doesn't that just blow your socks off? Those creepy-crawly little fuckers are about to take our planet over. Mad or what? One billion to one… that's fucking mental!

Come on, who remembers Wayne Fontana? Way back in the 'Swinging Sixties' he was lead singer with the Mindbenders. Their No. 1 hit was 'Groovy Kind of Love'. Anyway, on 9 November 2007 Wayne copped an 11-month prison sentence for setting fire to a bailiff's car. Good old Wayne, that's how to handle the bailiffs. I bought his record in the '60s and I often wondered what had become of him. You old jail bird rocker!

Get on this for a pucker story; it's fucking brilliant. In 1977 Debbie Gavin got a seven-year sentence for armed robbery in Georgia, USA. She was only 20 years old. She served just a year then escaped and remained free until she was 53 years old and a settled, happy wife and mother of two with a nice home. Nobody knew her past, not even her husband – that is until armed cops smashed in their door and dragged her away screaming. What an unfuckingbelievable nightmare! Imagine it.

I think the police should give her a medal and the courts should free her since she's proved she can live and survive as a decent woman for 33 years. Let's face reality here: Debbie Gavin was a real-life Bonnie without a Clyde in her youth, but time has changed her. She's now a good mother and a lovely wife – an inspiration to us all I think. A leopard has changed its spots before our very eyes. Respect to Debbie and I hope you're soon free. One thing's for sure: I can see a great movie on its way – a blockbuster!

I can never work out how the prison bosses' minds work; they are a funny lot. Here's a classic example of Loonyology. Last year in Wakefield Prison, 62-year-old 'lifer' Clive Spinks died of cancer. He had been very sick for years, so why didn't they parole him? They could have freed him on compassionate grounds and allowed him to end his days in a hospice with dignity. Why keep him in prison? What danger would he have been to anybody? I thought the whole point of prison was to lock up dangerous people in order to protect the public. Or am I wrong?

Clive Spinks got his life sentence at Leeds Crown Court back in 1996 for stabbing Andy Knowles to death. It happened during a fight and it's sad Andy lost his life, but in a fight anything goes. It's the law of the jungle: some live, some die. This was not the 'crime of the century' – nor was Clive a gangster or some notorious villain. Nobody has ever heard of him. Have you?

A year before the tragic fight, Clive was diagnosed with colon cancer, so he was a sick man even before he ended up with a life sentence. But he fought it and survived 12 years inside, which can't have been easy with a colostomy bag and a life full of pain. So why couldn't they have slipped him out the back door to die a free man? I'll tell you why – it's simple: the system is run by faceless, spineless, gutless, stinking, low-life parasites. It beggars belief. These are cruel, evil people. Cunts, that's all they are – cunts. You only have to look at what they did to Reggie Kray. You fucking heartless dogs. It was inhumanity at its lowest.

Why do they do it? How are they allowed to do it? It's going on all the time. They're piss-takers. It winds me up just to write about it. It sickens me to think about it because it's pure bollocks. Now you know why I've pulled off so many prison and asylum roofs – it's the only way to expose the cunts! Even the screws are disgusted over a lot of decisions. It's all a big farce, it's Loonyology! It's a bit like *The Muppet Show*.

Who fancies getting me a nice watch for my birthday? The Zenith Grande Class model only costs eight grand. Come on, somebody, you know I want one! Pop into Harrods and treat me to one. What's 8K between friends? If you love me, you'll get it. If you're skint then nick it. Just get me one... It's my birthday so someone spoil me!

All you dog lovers, why not spoil your dog with a special diamond-encrusted collar? It's only 500 grand in Harrods, so go rob a bank and get your dog a treat! Your dog's worth it; spoil it!

I do love a mad story, don't you? Like the one about the knife mugger in South Africa who mugged an elderly couple then ran off into the night. They found him the next day – or what was left of him after the fucking lions ate him! Is that brilliant or what? You can't make up stories like that. Some would call it poetic justice; I call it hungry lions. Loonyology at its very best.

Crime really is crazy at times. Take James Elliot for example. He held up a store in Long Beach, California with a .38 calibre revolver. He pulled the trigger for a warning shot but it didn't go off. He pulled it again and nothing happened. So he looked down the barrel and pulled again – this time it goes off: 'BANG'. He blew his brains out of the back of his skull. That's crime for you... Some robbers are just not meant to be robbers and James Elliot was one of them. He was born to lose. It's a world of Loonyology and guys like Elliot make our life worth living. Loonyology is the gift of life, so accept it graciously and learn to value madness for what it is. It's wonderful – it's fucking priceless.

I'll tell you what else is wonderful: a freshly-cooked home-made apple pie. That's Heaven – that amazing smell, that delicious taste. Who said there's no Heaven? You lying bastards.

Cops in Holland arrested James Hurley in November 2007. James escaped from a prison van 13 years ago whilst being transferred from Whitemoor jail to Wandsworth. Oh well, he squeezed 13 years of freedom so he's done himself proud. I was in Brixton with him in 1989. He got nicked with my buddy Charlie Magee on a bit of work where a hero cop got shot. They both got 'lifed off' – it's all part and parcel of the criminal world! Some you win, some you lose, and it's the ultimate gamble of life. No doubt they will extradite him and make him get on with his remaining sentence. He knows it too...

Here's a new meaning to the word 'knob-head'. Gary Ashbrook from East Sussex was found dead in his bedroom with a condom pulled over his head. A fucking condom; can you believe it? What a mad way to leave the planet. I can think of three million better ways. The coroner's verdict was 'misadventure'. He was only 33 and it's obvious it was a 'sex stunt' gone wrong. Imagine your wife or mum walking in on that! "Cup of tea, love? AARRRRGHHHHH. Oh my God... HEEELLPPPPPPP!" Loonyfuckingology at its maddest. What a sad, pathetic, lonely old death. Who the fuck gets their rocks off by pulling a condom over their nut? Oh well, it takes all sorts. Fucking knob-head.

Did you know that if all the bees in the world were to become extinct, the world would die within no time? That's because most food crops rely on bees to pollinate them. Now see how precious bees are? They're nature at its very best. We need the bees, they don't need us – remember that. It's wonderful, it's nature, so respect our bees. Nature is brilliant. Love it. Pass the honey!

The Irish cops have just found a houseful of seriously hardcore sex videos made by the 'little people'. It's called 'Lepraporn'.

Barbara Dainton died in 2007 aged 96. She was one of the last survivors of the Titanic. She was only a nipper at the time of the tragedy, but she's one of life's true survivors. We salute you Babs... R.I.P. Don't we just love a real survivor? They sort of warm your heart.

They said the Titanic was unsinkable. Fucking idiots. Nothing is unsinkable, nothing is unbeatable, nothing is indestructible. Nature is the strongest force on the planet and if nature wants you then nature will get you. It's basically that simple and you haven't got a snowball's chance in Hell. Against nature you're a snowflake in a furnace – bye bye.

Did you know that 68,000 people are diagnosed with bowel or lung cancer in the UK each year? Doesn't that send a shiver down your spine? Cancer just eats you up – sad but true. Very few ever beat it; it nearly always gets you in the end.

Here's a frightening thing: malaria kills almost two million people every year – that's a death every 30 seconds. Think about it: two million a year. Awesome... it's fucking insane.

I was so sad to hear my old buddy Dave Croke hanged himself in Whitemoor jail last year. What a sad way to leave the planet. I first met Dave in the 1980s up in Frankland max secure; he copped a 20 stretch for armed robbery and it was a beautiful bit of work. Unfortunately for Dave, he did it with a fucking snake called Don Barret. Barret was born a grass and he cost Dave 20 years of his life. But he survived and made it out, only to end up with a life sentence over a contract killing that I don't believe he did. Dave wasn't a killer.

I last bumped into Dave in 2006 when he looked old and worn out with that prison look of no hope. He was only 60 years old but he looked beaten – a man with no dreams left. I think he woke up in Whitemoor and thought, "No more. I'm out of here, enough's enough. Fuck this for a life, it's time to leave it all behind. Fuck the system. Bye bye."

Why the fuck can't Huntley do that? I'll tell you why: he's a cunt. He doesn't want to do it; it's all attention seeking with him. Dave Croke meant it. Rest in peace, Dave, you were a good old-fashioned blagger – a dying breed; one of the best. I salute you.

The sweetest tears are the tears of happiness, so die laughing.

Did you know that 144 people were beheaded in Saudi Arabia in 2007? Can you believe that? 144 heads rolled into the basket. How mental is that? Human rights? Fuck me; they had none!

Did I ever tell you about the time I was lying on the cold stone floor in Wandsworth strong box all wrapped up in a strait jacket? Believe me, you've never lived till you've been in a strait jacket. So there I was, all wrapped up like an Xmas turkey, when a little mouse ran under the door and stopped a foot away from my head. He looked at me, wiggled his nose, then shot off. You never forget amazing memories like that. They make life worth living. That mouse lifted me up and made me feel happy. He had more bottle than the ten rats who had just bashed me up and strapped me up. It was beautiful and I drifted off into a lovely sleep. Things like that help keep a man sane. Thanks, little fella.

Let me tell you about surviving in a big black hole. It's not easy; you have to work at it to overcome it. To survive you have to become a part of it, you need to switch off from the outside and switch on to the inside – become part of the hole and fill the hole. You dig deep inside yourself and fuck everything else. It doesn't matter what's outside – it's all gone. It's what's inside that counts. You have to search and find yourself. It may take a week, a month, a year, but who gives a fuck how long it takes? Time doesn't mean anything. What matters is your sanity and your survival. Never give up. Work on your inner self, find a dream and don't let go. The pain soon passes and the dream takes over – it's wonderful. Life in a hole can be a special time, so see it as a test. Use it to your own advantage. You're not alone. There's always something: a spider, a fly, a mouse, a moth, silver fish, cockroaches; they come to you, they're all part of the dream. And dreams don't last forever. When you wake up, the hole's gone and you've survived it.

They say 'crime doesn't pay' but the Mafia makes 17.5 million bucks a year from public and private contract in Italy. 'Crime doesn't pay' – what a laugh.

Did you know the second Harry Potter movie grossed £100 million in its opening weekend? Can you fucking believe that? Who said pigs don't fly?

Razor wire around your neck
Forever in your face
Satan whispers in your head:
"Soon you will be mine."
No escape from the wishing well
It dried up long ago
No more sunshine in the sky
Tomorrow is wet and dry
Wake up to a pot of shit
To a world of make believe
Fuck you, I'm out of here
I'm back to the empty hole
A place where I can think
A tortoise in a shell
Hid away from all the crap
In a world I only know
Solitary is a heavenly place
The man behind the door
The man behind the mask
Four walls and a concrete floor
A place where dreams are free
Alone to think
Razor wire around your neck

The world is made of stone
The days creep into years
Water turns to ice
Food starts to smell and rot
Maggots fly off laughing
A journey gone mad
I look in the mirror
My eyes are dead
My skin is grey and flaky
The brain's shrivelled
A body riddled with pain
The darkness sucks me dry
A blood-soaked face
Tears of blood
Nothing, No more is real
Sweet Baby Turned Sour
Watch me fly.

In 2007 more than 50 youngsters were killed on our streets, all shot or stabbed to death. In London alone there were 24 body bags. How sad is that? This is England, our 'great country'. What's so great about it? Nobody is safe, not even our kids.

Dale Little from Southampton was 15 years old, he was stabbed to death.

Martin Dinnegan was 14 and from North London, he was stabbed to death (a 15-year-old boy has been nicked).

The pain and misery goes on for all, families torn apart.

Abukar Mahamud was 16 when he was shot dead in South London.

Paul Erhahon from East London was 14 when he was stabbed to death.

Why? What's going on? The world's lost the plot. What a waste of life. These are all kids being wiped out. It's senseless.

Adam Regis was 15 when he was stabbed to death in East London. (Adam's uncle is John Regis, the Olympic athlete.)

Kamilah Peniston, 12 years old, shot dead in Manchester.

Billy Cox, 15, shot dead on Valentine's Day in South London.

Michael Dosunmu, 15, shot dead in South London.

Rhys Jones, 11 years old, shot dead in Liverpool.

Jonathan Matondo, 16, shot dead in Sheffield.

James Andre Smartt-Ford, 16, shot dead in South London.

Doesn't it make you feel sad? Doesn't it break your heart? These are just a few. Wake up world! There are kids dying on our streets from bullets and knifes – a waste of humanity. It's not just sad, it's bloody tragic and it breaks my heart, it really does. What will 2009 bring us? I wonder. I bloody wonder, don't you?

Some people are just born evil like this cunt Chris Jewell, a fucking cowardly baby-killer. His beautiful four-month-old daughter Demi suffered eight broken ribs and brain damage – she died before she lived. Her dad pleads guilty to manslaughter and gets eight poxy years. This cunt should have got 38 years – in fact he should have hanged. How the fuck can a man kill a baby and only get eight years? It doesn't make any sense; it was murder. He will be out in four years. What a farce. Dirty baby-killing bastard. It makes me sick.

I've got to take my hat off to Malcolm Edwards-Sayer, he got a ten-year stretch in 2007 for fraud on the VAT – 51 million quid's worth. I just love to see the tax man getting fucked; that's what I call crime. He even bought himself a title: Lord Houghton. He lived it up for real, ten years of the good life, but nothing lasts forever. I salute you mate, you did well.

I met an old silver-haired con in Parkhurst years ago (who will remain nameless). He had so much dosh that he did a deal with the prosecution and copped a seven-year sentence when he was looking at a 20 stretch. Three million quid changed hands and saved him 13 years. If you don't believe it goes on, then fuck off back to Disneyland. It's been going on forever. Judges, QCs, barristers and lawyers are no different from the rest of us; in fact they're worse. You'd better believe it, their lifestyle needs a lot of dosh and three million bucks is a nice earner for 13 years knocked off. When you're loaded you get a good deal!

Did you know the Spanish 'flu killed more people in 1918 and 1919 than Hitler killed in the entire Second World War? Hitler left school with no qualifications and still came close to ruling our planet. Did you know he was born without a left testicle? I thought he walked funny!

Here's one for your heart strings: Emma Hart was 27 and had a five-year-old son called Lewis. She was diagnosed with cancer in 2007 and only given six months to live. It would be her last Christmas alive and she couldn't cope; it was too much for her to accept. She loved Lewis so much that she couldn't leave him, so she gave him all her cancer drugs and then cut her wrists. They went together – a double funeral. How sad can it get? When I heard this story I thought to myself, how cruel can the world get? And then I thought: it's a mother's love! She just couldn't die without him; in birth and death they were one. I just hope there is a heaven, I really do, and I also hope the family left behind can forgive Emma. It's just one of those cases that breaks your heart. It's bloody tragic. Everybody lost! Nobody won! R.I.P.

On 12 December 2007 *The Sun's* front page news was about how Rose West's guinea pig had been murdered. How fucking sad is that? How pathetic, who really gives a flying fuck about her guinea pig? Here's a woman who let her husband rape her kids and then bury them under the garden patio. Rose herself was convicted of ten murders and she's got more compassion for a fucking pet guinea pig. And to top it all, how the fuck is she allowed pets? I'm not! I'm the one in a cage. I'm the system's fucking pet guinea pig. HMP Bronzefield, where Rose is kept, must be some sort of asylum but the lunatics have taken over for real. It's Loonyology at its best; you can't make it up. All the world's problems and the front page is about a guinea pig. Pass me a cup of tea!

Did you know that avocado has the most calories of any fruit? Not a lot of people know that. (Now you do.) You learn a lot in Loonyology. It's not all mad you know – it's an education.

When it comes to nutters, this twat takes some beating. Rob Stewart takes the biscuit. Weirdo Stewart got caught bang to rights last year having sex with a bicycle. A fucking bike! How the fuck can you have sex with a bike? This nutter did. He got caught in a hostel room when two cleaning ladies walked in as he was shagging it doggy-style. Imagine walking in on that! What a sight. Fucking hells bells; it's mind boggling. He copped three years probation and was put on the sex offenders list. This lunatic is still out there on your streets. Be warned now: your bike could be next. I still can't believe it myself. How can a bike turn a man on? And how do you go about shagging a bike? I wish I could've seen those two cleaning ladies' faces. I bet they will never forget it. Would you? It really does give a new meaning to 'riding your bike'. Rob Stewart, you have got to get the Loonyology badge for 2007 as the nutter of the year, you old nonce. Good riding.

Did you know that Aids has killed 25 million people since it was first recognized in 1981? In 2005 it killed an average of 8,500 people in a single day. There are an estimated 40 million people living with the HIV virus. Does that scare the shit out of you? Well it should do, because you may well have it! It's food for thought. Who was your partner last night?

I see that fat, four-eyed twat of a nonce Ronald Castree copped a life sentence in 2007, finally getting his just deserts. It was back in 1975 that he killed 11-year-old Lesley Molseed but it's taken 32 years to put the cunt behind bars. Sadly, poor old Stefan Kiszko got blamed for it and spent many years inside when he was a totally innocent man. Kiszko won his case at the appeal court and walked free, only to die soon after. He didn't even live to enjoy his compensation. How fucking sad is that? Imagine serving life for a child murder you didn't commit. Castree, the cunt, is now 55 years old and has got life, so that's him buried. Thank fuck for DNA evidence, because it trapped this snake after more than 30 years and put him where he belongs. If he ever passed me on a landing I would nut him on sight. I would do it for Kiszko, for what he put him through. He stole 17 years of his life. Castree, you're a cunt – a child-murdering dirty paedophile. You're on a one-way ride to Hell; no return ticket.

Stefan Kiszko, without being nasty about it, was a bit 'simple' – you could describe him as the village idiot and that's basically all he was. The police had to nick somebody over the murder and he would do. That's how it was. But in prison, Kiszko had 17 terrible years of Hell. He was, after all, a convicted nonce, and a nonce is a nonce. He got special treatment: piss in his tea, spit in his food, a slap, a punch, verbal, old smelly clothes, shit-stained bed sheets. He got it all, even off the screws! People forget that screws are only human and they have children, so what do you expect them to do with a child rapist or killer? Some screws are as violent as the cons. I've seen them headbutt a nonce in the face and kick them in the bollocks (especially in reception). Cons and screws all love a nonce arriving from court. It's the highlight of the day. The word goes out that there's a baby-killer on the way. We know who they are and what they are before they arrive (especially with a high-profile case). Someone like Kiszko was easy meat: a big, fat, useless, simple nonce. From day one until the day he cleared his name, he was a nonce.

How sad is that? Could you have survived all that? What about his family? How did they cope? People forget about the families. Fingers point and the gossip starts: "Her son's that child killer. His son is a pervert. His brother is a child rapist." They get all the hate and bitterness from the neighbourhood: bricks thrown through windows, verbal abuse, threats – they got it all when all the time he was innocent! How tragic is that?

The question you need to ask is: how many more Kiszko's are there in the system? Fucking hundreds, I bet! Frightening or what?

I'll tell you who and what's mad. Have a butcher's at this; if this isn't Loonyology then what is?

Pop souvenirs, sold under the auctioneer's hammer:
Frank Sinatra's wig – £2,000.
Elvis Presley's coat hanger – £7,500.
Madonna's bra – £1 million. (What sort of muppet pays a million quid for a used bra?)
Geri Halliwell's Spice Girls Union Jack dress – £41,000.
Get on this one, this one takes the biscuit: George Harrison's dandruff – £6,500.
Justin Timberlake's toast (with one bite out of it), highest bidder on eBay – £1,500. Tell me, is this world insane or is it me? What sane person pays £1,500 for a bit of toast? It's fucking bollocks. Who paid that? He/she should be in a padded room. Why? Somebody please tell me why!
Britney Spear's chewing gum – £270.
Lock of John Lennon's hair – £24,000.
Ozzy Osbourne's dog bed – £1,150.

If somebody put a turd on eBay, believe me, some fucking idiot would buy it. What's wrong with these people? The world's gone mad.

What is it about Christmas number ones? We all remember them; they stick in our minds for all time.

1968: Scaffold, 'Lily the Pink'. I was on a building site in Luton carrying the hodd for some brickies. The whole site was singing it because it was so cheerful. It was fucking brilliant, if not the best Xmas No. 1 of all time. Mike McGear was in this band; he's Paul McCartney's brother (not a lot of people know that).

1969: Rolf Harris, 'Two Little Boys'. This was the same year as the Parkhurst riot and the year I got put inside for nicking a furniture lorry. I never did like this song, it sounds a bit pervy to me. A bad Xmas.

1971: Benny Hill, 'Ernie (The Fastest Milkman in the West)'. Who can forget this classic? It was brilliant. Incidentally, Cherri Gilham, one of Benny Hill's 'angels', used to visit me. She was the blonde bombshell he used to chase around the set. Cherri's a good soul, a nice woman.

1973: Slade, 'Merry Xmas Everybody'. I remember this blaring out in the Bull's Head, Ellesmere Port. I ended up having a right punch-up with three Hells Angels. It was a blinding Xmas: the fight broke out in the bar and ended up in the car park and it was fucking snowing. Happy Crimbo everybody.

1974: Mud, 'Lonely this Christmas'. I had just copped a seven-year stretch and that one I'll never forget. Fuck me, was it lonely. I had a wife and son outside and it tore me up.

1976 was Johnny Mathis' 'When a Child is Born'. I was in Parkhurst and I can remember it coming on *Top of the Pops* in the TV room like it was yesterday. At the time I was on C-Unit with Ronnie and Reggie Kray, Chilly Chamberlin, Dougie Wakefield, Colin Robinson, Ray Gilbert and Jako. We were all watching it and having a mug of hooch (our moonshine). We always had a good piss-up on *Top of the Pops* night; it was one of the highlights of our week.

1978 was Boney M with 'Mary's Boy Child'. I was in Rampton Asylum for this one and all the loonies were jumping around singing it. I had landed on Mars.

1980: St Winifred's School Choir, 'There's No-One Quite Like Grandma'. I was in Broadmoor for this one. We were all singing it and to top it all the lunatic in the next cell to me had strangled his grandma. You can't make it up. As we all sang it he was shouting and banging on his door all night; we drove him mad. Well, I should say madder than he already was.

1984: Band Aid, 'Do They Know it's Christmas?' I was in Ashworth Asylum for this one, soon after I smashed a sauce bottle in a lunatic's face and cut him up. Merry Christmas.

1985: Shakin' Stevens, 'Merry Christmas Everyone'. I was in the segregation block in Walton jail after taking their roof off a few months earlier. It wasn't a merry Christmas for me.

1988: Cliff Richard, 'Mistletoe and Wine'. I was up on Leicester jail's roof and all I got was a good kicking and plenty of porridge. How old is Cliff? He must be at least 140. You've got to give it to him though; he keeps knocking out the hits.

1993: Mr Blobby. I was in Winston Green for this one, what a load of shit. I was so bored that I took the prison doctor hostage. That livened the Xmas up.

1994: East 17, 'Stay Another Day'. I was in Hull special unit for this one. Unfortunately, I fell out with Governor Wallace and took him hostage. That fall-out cost me an extra seven years on my sentence, but it was a great Xmas…

2000: Bob the Builder, 'Can We Fix It?' I was in Woodhill CSC Unit for this one. They needed a builder after I wrecked the place.

2002: Girls Aloud, 'Sound of the Underground'. Anything these girls do is No. 1 with me; they're all deliciously lovely. I was in Wakefield cage for this one.

Yeah, these Xmas number ones have a lot to answer for. Every one's a winner. Lovely memories. I wonder who will have the Xmas No. 1 when I'm free? Whoever it is, it will be one to remember. I'll drink to that! Cheers!

Welcome to Loonyology! Pass the Vaseline and bend over…

Did you know there's a frog in South America that leaks out poison from its skin which can kill a man in 30 seconds? Can somebody post me one in so I can have it put in Huntley's bed?

Life is a giant canvas. Throw all the paint on it and create your own beautiful rainbow.

Rhys Totterdell just copped a four and a half year stretch for biting a man's nose off in a fight. I've got to ask: what's wrong with that? As cruel and barbaric as it sounds, in a street fight anything goes – there are no Queensbury rules. Sure it's naughty to bite off a man's nose but it's even worse having your own bitten off. Bite or be bitten. It's so easy to condemn this chap and label him an animal, but nobody knows the true situation he was in or how he was feeling. Maybe he was fighting for his life.

I was once in a pub fight and I had half a dozen on top of me. One cunt had his fingers in my mouth trying to rip my lips off my face, so I bit two of his fingers off. What else could I do? What would you do? What would anybody do? In a fight like that you act on impulse and the survival instinct kicks in. You can't predict what's about to happen in a street fight. A knife, a gun, a knuckle duster, a bottle – anything can be used, and if you're on the floor you must get up and fight and do anything to win. You have to survive.

I don't believe Rhys Totterdell is a bad man. I actually see him as a survivor because I've been there. I've seen men lose a kidney and I've witnessed men get seriously busted up. It only takes a few seconds to hurt or even kill a man, in a split second your whole life can be taken away, all over a fight. There will always be fights. Nine out of ten fights are over women, so be careful or you too could easily lose a nose. Animals do it all the time; are we not animals? We all shit and piss, we all have to survive the best we can, and if that means chewing a nose then that's how it is. So be warned now: it's best not to get involved in fights. It could be your nose next!

I see some drunken bird mugged Jimmy Saville a while back. She ran at him and grabbed his specs off his face and legged it away. That eBay has a lot to answer for! I suppose Jimmy Saville's specs would fetch a nice few quid.

I met Jim in Broadmoor years ago; all the loonies loved him. He used to be on the entertainment committee and come in every so often. He once brought in Acker Bilk to do a show. Jim's a decent fella and he's got a good heart. He must be 170 now. You wouldn't believe the marathons he's run and the millions of pounds he's made for charities. A top geezer in my book; max respect. He once gave me one of his cigars and I've still got it. That must be almost 30 years old. I may smoke it at my freedom party with a nice brandy, but I sure won't be selling it on fucking eBay. Some cunts have even sold my letters and cards on there. Fucking low lives, they would sell their arses for a fiver – probably already have. No fucker is safe today, eBay will sell your soul! You soulless parasites.

I see big John King, one of Ricky Hatton's ex-minders, copped a life sentence in December 2007 – all six feet six inches and 18 stone of him. He's a filthy triple rapist. It just goes to show you never know who's about to rape your daughters. Ricky would never have had this nonce on the firm if he had known what he was like. Fuck all amazes me anymore. I've seen it all.

I'll tell you who was a fucking wanker: 'scouser' Roy Grantham. In the early 1970s he was giving it the large in Parkhurst but he came unstuck with the Krays and they made sure he needed sewing-up big time. He was a typical bully. He served his 12-year stretch and got out, only to turn a grass. He put half a dozen scousers away for big bird, but being the cunt he was he hanged himself. Best thing he ever did, but he should have done it before he made all the statements and put all those lads inside. It must have been his last act of evil. Reg Kray described him as a “reptile”. Ronnie just said, “He's a cunt that needs chopping up.” But that sort always cops it in the end. He just couldn't live with himself anymore, and that's how it mostly ends up for a grass. There's no lonelier end than a cell death, believe it. As a grass, even your own shadow hates you! Anybody thinking of grassing, think again. That's all I'll say to you. Be a man, not a mouse, and take what's coming. Stand tall.

On 15 November 2007 Jane Tomlinson's ten-year-old son Steven went to Buckingham Palace with his dad to collect a CBE on his mum's behalf. What a great day, what a proud day. She had fought and lost her battle against cancer two months earlier. She raised two million pounds for charity; what a great achievement, what a great lady, a true legend. Her husband and son must be so proud of her, as we all are. We salute her. R.I.P.

Cop a load of this nutter: Ross Watt was fined £100 for having sex with a shoe. A fucking shoe! Can you believe this shit? You can't make it up. There's nothing madder than real life. How can you get horny with a shoe? This mad fucker is out there on the streets eyeing up your shoes. He could be clocking your shoes right now. If a geezer is near you wanking off while looking at your shoes, it's only Ross Watt, just kick him in the nuts. He's harmless.

What about Karl Watkins? He copped 18 months for bonking a pavement in 1993. He was shagging the street and he loves a pavement. How the fuck can a sane man fuck a pavement? Please will somebody tell me? And why send him to prison? Should he not be in the cuckoo house, or am I missing something here? A shoe is one thing but a pavement is something else. Imagine walking down your street and seeing that. The mind boggles. Personally, I would give him a good old-fashioned kicking and probably cut his cock off. Fucking pervo, and he's out there amongst you sane people. My fucking head hurts.

Did you know that the first mobile phone was the size of a briefcase and it cost two grand? That's a fact! Did you know Europe's largest roundabout is the Arc de Triomphe in Paris? It's fucking awesome. Get on this one: the Barbie doll is 50 years old this year!

World War I hero Harry Patch celebrates his 110th birthday in 2008. He won five gallantry medals. What a fucking legend Harry is; a true survivor. The landlord of the Rose and Crown in Stoke will give him free beer till he pops off; let's hope it's another 110 years before that happens. Cheers to Harry and respect to the landlord.

I bet you wonder where I'm going next. You have to admit it's impossible to know – even I don't know and I'm writing the fucker. It's Loonyology at its very best!

Big tough karate teacher Paul Rudwick copped 14 years for raping a 13-year-old girl. Let's see the beast chop his way out of that. Also, let's hope the father of the girl will bump into him later. Cunts like Rudwick give sport a bad name; it leaves a bad taste in the mouth. This is a sports teacher trusted to teach kids, and what does he do? He rapes one. 14 years is not enough; he will be out in seven and the girl will be 20. This cunt got let off lightly for now, but who knows what's in the future for him? These nonces always get their just deserts in the end. A double helping, too!

Do you remember Gillian Gibbons, the teacher who got jailed in Sudan over a teddy bear she called Mohammed? Fuck me, they wanted to behead her. The Islamic faith was insulted so they wanted her dead. Can you believe that? But it all ended sweet – she flew back home to good old England and made a fortune from her story. But what I want to know is, what about the teddy? Who gave a fuck about the bear? Where is Mohammed? Or is it a case of Gillian's safe and fuck the teddy? Cruel bastards, I bet teddy got beheaded!

Here's a few outrageous dressing room requests from some pop stars, superstars, celebrities, big heads and flash fuckers:

James Brown – Two 21-year-old girls and a hair dryer.
Paul McCartney – Nineteen six-foot leafy plants.
Rolling Stones – HP sauce, shepherd's pie, paint brushes and a snooker table.
Nirvana – Macaroni cheese.
Madonna – A new toilet seat and 25 cases of Kabbalah water.
Barbara Streisand – Rose petals in toilet.
Led Zeppelin – An ironing board.
Janet Jackson – Ten black roses, marmite and all-male catering staff. (Er, isn't that sexist?)
Sammy Davis Jnr – Assortment of hot sexy chicks. (You've got to give it to Sammy! He was a black Jew with a false eye and was one of the famous 'Rat Pack' – a true legendary superstar.)
Oasis – Loads of booze.
Will Young – Pink champagne and pink towels. (That about sums him up.)

Who would be a superstar? It's all Loonyology. I won't even bother with Elton John!

Who can ever forget the wife of a prisoner at Stanford Hill open prison on the Isle of Sheppey in Kent, who broke in and spent the night with her husband in his cell but got caught in the early hours trying to smuggle herself out. What a wife, what a legend; brilliant or what? So what would your old lady do to prove her love to you? Why the fuck can't I go to an open jail so some hot chick can break in and ride my cock all night? It's just not fair! Come to think of it, why didn't he break out and fuck her?

A geezer walks into his psychiatrist's office wearing only cling film. The doctor says, "Well, I can clearly see you're nuts."

The ugliest fucker I ever came across was Crazy Horse. All the cons in Parkhurst in the 1970s will remember this nutter. He was black as the ace of spades and he never walked – he skipped and danced about. Crazy Horse was not just physically ugly, he was mentally and spiritually ugly too. He was just born ugly, like the elephant man. He could have joined a travelling freak show and made a nice living. He got a serious reputation as a lunatic in all the jails he was in, and I bumped into him in several. He was a fighter and he loved a punch-up, but I honestly can't ever recall him winning one. He got knocked out, cut and slashed but he still came back for seconds. Looking back on it, I think he must've been insane or else he just loved getting smashed up.

Imagine this: it's 7.30am and all the cell doors unlock for slop out. Scores of cons are marching down the landing with piss pots full of shit to empty down the sloosh and it fucking stinks. It's the worst time of day in prison life. Slopping out is soul-destroying and inhumane. There are all types of cons – gangsters, terrorists, armed robbers, psychos – and none are in the best of moods. All are feeling fed-up. This is life at its most tense: the smell of shit, piss and stale body odours; and to top it all, Crazy Horse is in your face at start of a new day – all six feet of him, with bulging eyes and mad gorilla features. He's jumping up and down shouting, "Give me a match, give me a fag paper, give me a tea bag." Give me, give me, give me! Right in your face: give me, give me! It's a nightmare; who needs it?

"Fuck off!" someone screams. "Piss off, Crazy Horse." A fight breaks out. Pots of shit fly about. Blades come out. Violence explodes! Alarm bells... the riot mob steams in, insanity takes over. This is Parkhurst life in the 1970s and cons like Crazy Horse love it.

Imagine this: Crazy Horse walks into a con's cell and says, "Give me some tobacco." The con replies, "Fuck off, get the fuck out of my cell." Crash! Bang! Wallop! More violence, more madness. This is a normal day for Crazy Horse; he will get hurt again and become even uglier!

Cons like Crazy Horse become legends but remain dangerous bastards. They're fearless, they have no fear of the consequences and a fight is all in a day's work. He would rip your eye out. You had no choice but to bash him up and hit him hard – fast and hard. Crazy Horse wouldn't just attack cons, he attacked anybody at any time he liked. He's the only man alive who could have got a part in the movie *Planet of the Apes* without any make-up. I used to study him out on the exercise yard – the way he moved, his posture, his facial expressions, those mad eyes... believe me, he was insane.

I wonder what happened to him. Surely he can't still be alive, can he? I hit him once with a PP9 battery in a sock. Crash! Why break my knuckles on his head? A good crack with my PP9 did the trick. But he was a fucking character and he livened the jail up. Crazy Horse was a legend in his own right. I think a lot of his problems were down to the 'wacky baccy'. I don't think he realised half of what he said or did, or how offensive he could be. Surely he must be dead. No mad-man can survive all that, can they? Crazy Horse, you ugly old fucker, where are you? We all love you. Three cheers for the lunatic! HIP HIP – HOORAY! HIP HIP – HOORAY! HIP HIP – HOORAY!

Life is not a race and the winner is not the one who finishes first.

It's not going to be easy for Kenny Richey, the geezer who's been let out of death row after 22 years of sitting and waiting to fry. Imagine that! He got sentenced to death in 1986 for the murder of a two-year-old kid but he claimed from day one that he didn't do it. Now it seems he didn't and the cops knew he didn't. That's American justice for you! So they freed him on Friday 21 December 2007 and flew him back to the UK (he's a Jock). What an Xmas, what a new lease of life, what a dream. Can he ever rebuild his life? Could you? Could anybody? Two years back he was one hour from execution; they had shaved his hair off and prepared him for old sparky, only for him to be reprieved again. Imagine the mental torture of preparing to die then being given another break… it's inhumanly cruel! It's like leading a cow into a slaughter house then leading it back out again.

Kenny Richey's life has been inside a concrete coffin – airless and empty. You sleep but you never wake! Everything is bitter, even your dreams are stale, it's Hell. What can he do now after 22 years of death? Write a book? Make a movie? Whatever he does he will always drift back into Hell. This guy has lost his soul; only his heart got him through. Good luck, mate, for what's facing you. You deserve some luck!

Talk about Loonyology, this story takes the biscuit. It's unfucking-believableamazing. I do love a good counterfeiter, and they come no better than Marcus Glindon. He flooded the market with 14 million £1 coins. Tons and tons of the little fuckers. Sadly, he got nicked and ended up with a five-year stretch. Five years for 14 million quid. He will serve two and a half. Wouldn't you serve two and a half years for 14 million? Not bad, eh! 'Crime doesn't pay' – don't make me laugh! That's a right fucking touch! I bet he had a bad back lumping that lot about. Fuck me. 14 million quid! Lovely jubbly.

I was so sad to lose my old buddy Ron Greedy. He died on 1 December 2007. Let me tell you about my old friend. I first met Ron in 1978 in Broadmoor asylum; he was a legend and a man of dignity, one of life's survivors. Sadly, the years he spent inside institutionalized him. He spent well over half a century locked up. Imagine that: 50 long, hard years. Ron had survived some tough years in the asylums, and I mean tough. Broadmoor in the 1950s, '60s and '70s was no picnic; it was cold, cruel and brutal. Ron had his share of brutality and not just from beatings. He also had the 'liquid cosh' (drug control) and long periods of isolation in empty cells with nothing but dreams. Broadmoor was a hell-hole in that era, but men like Ron Greedy fought it and turned it around. Today's lunatics have a lot of comfort and privileges thanks to men like Ron! I pulled their roof off three times to expose the inhumane treatment. We fought to change it and we bled trying – a river of blood, tears and misery, but we did a good job! I salute men like Ron Greedy. I loved him as a brother. We were brothers of madness and he stood loyal till the end! A true brother. Fifty wasted, stolen years. But he had the heart of a lion.

In loving memory. Ron Greedy 23.7.1933–1.12.2007. Never forget. Respect.

Another death in 2007 was that of Harry Marsden. It's no secret that Harry and I had a falling-out a couple of years back, all over bollocks. We couldn't work the problem out and it just got bigger. With Harry being a proud man and me a stubborn old fucker, we cut off, even though our respect for each other never died. Our friendship went back almost 40 years. I first met him in Armley jail in the 1970s and we spent a long time together in the notorious punishment block there. It was the era of serious brutality. Screws used to run Armley with a fist of steel and boots to match. Harry and I were forever battling the bully screws and there wasn't a week that went by without one or both of us being smashed up or being put in a strait jacket or body belt. He was only a short guy but he was fast, super fast. He wasn't scared of anything or anybody. He was fearless, much like Frank Fraser! All Harry loved to do was fight this muggy system. He was the ultimate jail bird, a real con. They don't come like Harry anymore, his type are a dying breed. He never once backed down and still fought even when the odds were 10/1 against – that's ten screws with sticks against him. It's why I loved him.

God only knows how, but Harry got out and changed his life around. He changed into a great chap helping under-privileged kids. He opened up a boxing gym and trained the youngsters. The respect just grew. There really was only one Harry Marsden and he proved how a man could change. He was an inspiration. Nothing could beat this man except cancer, but he even fought that and got the better of it for several years.

I won't even bother to say why we fell out after 30 years of brotherhood, but rest assured I'll be giving him a hug in the next world. Let this be a lesson to people who've fallen out. Don't be silly. Make it up before it's too late! 'Max respect' to Harry Marsden! Well missed.

Did you know that all polar bears are left handed? Not a lot of people know that.

Life is a journey where the destination is unknown.

Pedro Rios, the international drug smuggler who's serving 22 years in max secure Long Lartin, has just become a dad. Guess who the mum is? Go on, guess. It's a screwess – a woman prison guard. I should say ex-prison guard, since she's been sacked. I wonder why. I wish I was out of solitary and mixing. I wouldn't mind a couple of kids myself.

I see there was another trigger-happy nutter in America. It's now so often that we read or hear about a mass shooting out there. This time, 19-year-old Robert Hawkins opened up in a shopping mall and turned it into a blood bath before blowing his own brains out. He killed nine and injured seven others. What for? All because he lost his job in McDonald's. Fucking insane or what? (Sack me you fuck-faced fuckers. Stamp on my face you cock-suckers, I'll show you who the daddy is. McDonald's kiss my butt.) Before his sacking he was just a normal 19-year-old lad. Now he's a stiff in a bag on the way to the crematorium along with nine innocent shoppers. How fucking mad is that? Loonyology at its very maddest!

Who remembers back to 1976 with the break-out of the two lunatics from Carstairs asylum? (Carstairs is known as the 'Broadmoor of Scotland' as it houses the criminally insane.) Robert Mone and Thomas McCulloch smashed their way straight out from Hell and terrorized the planet. First they killed a fellow inmate, then they killed a male nurse. Once out, they killed a cop and drove off in the police car. Hell on wheels. In all it was nine hours before they were stopped and the lunatics were put back in a cage. Since 1976 they have both spent most of their time in isolation in the Peterhead cages, but guess what? Come on, guess what's coming next! You've got it in one: they're now both in low security jails and about to be freed. Me? I remain in a cage. (Will somebody please wake me up when it's time to die?) Maybe Scottish law is different, but surely human rights come into this. What makes me so evil and dangerous that I can't be freed when these two can? Somebody tell me!

I've just finished a cracking book: *The 16th Round* by Rubin 'Hurricane' Carter. It's kept me alive for three days. What a fucking read. All the people who think they've had a bad deal in life, think again. You fuckers don't know what a bad deal is. You fuckers don't know you're born.

The Hurricane geezer is the daddy and I salute the man. You lot must read his book. It's powerful stuff – one of the best books I've read in years. He's a true survivor, a born fighter, a black man fitted-up, a man with fire in his heart, a man whose soul is ablaze. This guy went from No. 1 boxing contender of the world to prisoner number 45472. Read it and wake up! It's no wonder Bob Dylan wrote a song about him. Respect to the Hurricane.

Remember: the most difficult step in any journey is the first. Good luck.

I see Hollywood star Kiefer Sutherland spent an Xmas inside LA's Glendale city jail after he copped two months for drink-driving. (It'll do him good.) He once played a part in a prison movie called *Last Light* about a con on death row. That's how insane life can be; it has a way of turning things around. It's Loonyology, it's fucking magical. Good old Kiefer. Just be thankful you're not on death row.

Life

It's not an act
Life's for real
You only get one go
It's not a rehearsal
Or a game
It's one shot and then you're dead
It's priceless
It's precious
It's fucking beautiful
It's like a hot, wet pussy
That's what life is
One big pussy
Chill out
Be happy
Be free
Be comfortable
Is it a problem?
Or a pain in the nut?
Stick a Colt 45 in your ear
That will sort it out
A nice big Magnum in your face
And I don't mean ice cream.
So how's your life ticking?
Sweet?
Like clockwork?
A nice routine?
A good regime?
Or is it just another day?
Is it boring?

Is it shit?
Pure fucking crap
From the time you awake
Till the time you sleep?
A problem
The tax man
The rent man
The gas man
The milkman
Bills on bills
Debt on debt
A mountain high
Who's that banging on the door?
Who's that shouting in my head?
Who's come to take me away?
First come, first served
Pay up or die
Pay now or bleed
Debt collectors
Loan sharks
Big men with bald heads
Tough guys with baseball bats
Pay up or scream
A blacked-out van
With dodgy number plates
The last ride
It's come to an end
Life's journey
What a fucking story
It all turned insane
A one-way ride
The road to the graveyard
The crematorium
The hottest seat on the planet
Tea and toast
The last supper
Pass the marmalade.

Did you know Bobby Charlton made 759 appearances for Manchester United? What a fucking player he was – a legend. But who remembers his shit hairstyle with that bit of hair trying to cover up his bald patch? A bit of wind and it flew up like a flag! It made us all laugh though. Good old days.

Did you know the average laying hen produces 257 eggs a year? They must have a sore arse!

Some crimes are beyond belief and some criminals are just insane. Take Malcolm Green for example. Back in 1971 in Cardiff he butchered a prostitute like you do a cow in a slaughter house and he got sentenced to life. He served 18 years and they freed him on parole. One month later, out comes the axe. The mad butcher is at work again and this time he chops up a man and stuffs him in bin liners. Guess what? He got lifed off again. He's now served another 18 years. Watch this space. Just don't back against it. My bet is that he gets out.

Get on this lunatic. Paul Brumfitt copped two life sentences at the Old Bailey in 1980 for the murder of a shopkeeper and a bus driver. You would have thought that's the last of Brumfitt – throw the keys away, case closed – but 20 years later he's freed. Yeah, you know what's about to come! This time he rapes a 19-year-old girl, cuts her up and burns her in a scrap-yard. She was Marcella Davies, a beautiful young girl from a loving family. Prison HQ helped to kill her, so her family should sue the fuckers and the parole board for letting Brumfitt out. It's fucking insane. Why let the cunt out? Marcella would be alive today if they hadn't let him out. Now tell me who's mad? It's the system every time...

Another Loonyology case is evil copper Gary Weddell. He was a police inspector of the Metropolitan force. He killed his wife and they gave him bail! Why give him bail? Oh! He's a copper! Let's give him bail. (Nobody on a murder charge gets bail.)

HELLO? Is anybody listening to me?

So Gary goes home awaiting a murder trial and then he kills his mother-in-law.

HELLO?

Too late... he then blew his own brains out! This cunt had a license to kill. The system let him out to kill the witness!

HELLO?

Here's a blinder; you'll love this one. Scott Davidson should get a medal. The North Wales Police arrested him in St Asaph and threw him in the cells for the night, but even though they strip-searched him they failed to see his mobile phone. So he was banged up with his phone! It gets better. Scott called up the police station and said, "Evacuate! There's a bomb on the premises." Unfortunately the Old Bill can't take a joke. Miserable cunts.

I see old Jimmy James died aged 92 on January 2007. He was a squadron leader in the RAF in World War II and was one of 76 men to escape from Stalag Luft III, a Nazi prison camp, in 1944. That's who Jimmy James was: a legend. The movie *The Great Escape* was based on Jim's escape. I salute the old rascals; those men were made of rock. In fact, Jim escaped 13 times, risking death each time. We just love a legendary character. Movies are just for actors; men like Jimmy James were for real. R.I.P. my old china.

18 January 2008.

I copped a Xmas card off Sue May (it must have come by snail mail). Sue spent 11 years in prison for a murder she didn't commit. Another miscarriage of justice. But what's new? It goes on and on...

20 January 2008.

Great visit today with Al Rayment and his beautiful wife Natalie, we always have lots to discuss. Alan's a top buddy of mine, 'the best'. I'm blessed to have so many good friends; it's like a big family, 'brothers and sisters'.

This month is flying by.

Did you hear about the blind circumcisionist? He got the sack.

Did you hear about the Russian dancer with five cocks? His tights fit like a glove.

George Leigers was an evil fucker. In 1986 he killed his wife and got sent to a funny farm. 17 years later (hello?) they freed him, only for him to stab 19-year-old Sarah Jane Couglan to death with a bayonet. Fucking idiots. Why let the nutter out? Who's insane here, the criminals or the system? Would you put your head in a lion's mouth or play cricket with a grenade? It's all Loonyology to me...

Did you know that in the last 20 years, 30 convicted killers have been freed only to kill again, and I can't even get a day out to attend a funeral? What am I doing so wrong?

22 January 2008.

I got a strange letter today from a Geordie inmate up in Durham jail who's serving eight years. He's asking me what I think of Steve Wraith, the so-called 'boss of the Geordie Mafia'. Well, what can I say? He's a cunt! A total fucking snake. I'd sooner be-friend a cobra! I get word that he's a grass, he's this, he's that. If I believed half of what I heard about Wraith then he would be the world's biggest slug! But I'm not interested in rumours, only facts. So here are the facts for all to see.

Wraith sold the Krays out but he waited till they were all buried. He taped their final phone calls then sold them on CD. He called it *The Krays' Final Word* (you two-bob fucking Geordie rat). He also photocopied all the Krays' funeral service sheets and sold them for £3.50 each. You cunt.

So how did Wraith even know the Krays? I'll tell you: he was a teenage autograph hunter – that's how it all began. He visits Ron in Broadmoor and next thing, the 'boss of the Mafia' myth is born. He does a bit of bizz here and there, he dresses the part, acts the part and some actually start believing the myth he's spread. The 'real' chaps laugh at him and some use him, because they all know he's a cunt!

Wraith was at one of my shows that Tel Currie put on. A taped message from me was being played and the entire audience were silent – all but him and a few of his mates. It all got back to me. The disrespectful cunt. He's not a villain! He's done no bird but he's a fucking good actor.

You'll love this one: in his book Wraith claims to have been on a visit with Ron Kray when Ron asked him to do a contract killing. Now bear in mind that Wraith was a young lad at the time and Ron had contacts all over the world to do a 'hit' for him. Would Ronnie Kray have asked an innocent lad to do such a thing? (Would he fuck.) I was later told by a good friend of the twins (who shall remain nameless) that Ron was having a laugh with him and that it was Wraith's arse he was interested in. Well, isn't that what gay men like? Ron was gay, and proud of it, but he was also a top gangster and he didn't go around asking 19-year-old boys to kill somebody for him. It just did not happen. So, Wraith, why say it when Ron can't answer back? Why didn't you say it when he was alive? I'll tell you why you didn't, you cunt: because a contract would have been put on your head.

The truth be known, Wraith probably gave Ron a wank under the table and then Ron gave him his autograph. Cunt. Why do people believe this gangster shit? It's all Loonyology to me. I've taken a personal dislike to Wraith as he's insulted the Krays and all they stood for. Two of my pals have actually pulled him and told him I hate his guts. He knows my feelings about him. A cunt's a cunt in my book. Look at my life: even with all I've done and all I've been, even I'm not a gangster. I'm nobody special; I'm just me. I tried, I fought my guts out and lost three and a half decades and I'm still in a coffin. So what has this cunt ever done to be a gangster? I'll show you what a gangster he is if I ever bump into him.

FULL STOP! CUNT!

I got four more letters today and I had a good work-out and jog on the yard. But the letter about the 'Geordie Al Capone' spoilt my day. Why can't people write me nice letters? Be happy! Life's wonderful.

I'll tell you who's a raving fucking lunatic schizophrenic: Tommy Owen. He rushed into his parents' bedroom and attacked them with a carving knife. After stabbing them both he started to drink their blood. Fortunately they both survived and Tommy went to Rampton top secure asylum (for the criminally insane, need I add). Whilst he's in Rampton let's hope he sucks all the blood out of that fat lunatic Beverley Allitt. She went to Rampton for killing all those babies. Who said there's no Hell? Rampton is Hell, believe me. I had a year there back in 1978. Fuck me; 30 years ago. Doesn't time fly when you're having so much fun!

You all remember Harold 'Dr Death' Shipman. When he was up in Frankland prison he was the captain of the boxing team and he had a lethal jab. Get it? Lethal jab! Ha! Ha! Ha! Ha! OK, fuck off. I'm only trying to cheer you up. I'll not bother, OK?

23 January 2008.

I've got an exclusive. Cuntley (ooops, sorry – I mean Ian Huntley) got moved out of monster mansion today and was driven under police escort to Frankland. Fucking good job too. It couldn't have happened to a worse nonce. It's the wake up call he needs. The cunt's had it too cushy here: TV, curtains, carpet, CD player, radio, lots of goodies from the canteen, and on top of all that he got his cock sucked in the shower. It's fucking disgusting.

Frankland is a tough old northern jail; even the screws are a tough bunch. I've been up there a few times. It's the nearest English max secure jail to Scotland. I was once up there in the winter when it was snowing and fucking freezing and the screws were walking about in short-sleeved shirts. The cold doesn't penetrate that mob and they love a punch-up. Huntley won't get his own way up there!

Frankland's a good nick for the hooch. I've had some good brews up there. We did six buckets of what we called 'Bronco punch' one weekend. A dozen of us were pissed; it was like rocket fuel. One con got stabbed up that weekend. I don't remember too much about it but my cell looked like a fucking slaughter house. Another time I had a punch-up on the yard with a load of London lads. We all stood firm and some screws copped it. It was like an old cowboy film with screws flying all over the place. Good old days, I wouldn't change them for the world. It was brilliant.

Only recently an Islamic terrorist got scalded with burning cooking oil in Frankland. It's always been a violent jail and it's full of real life tough nuts. For a nonce like Cuntley it's going to be terrifying. I saw a con lose an eye up there. I've seen them cut, stabbed and burnt. A burning con is not a nice smell, but if it's a grass or a nonce it's party time. I predict Cuntley will be attacked within two months. I also predict he will end up on the hospital wing as a cleaner.

Cuntley will die in jail so he may as well cut his own throat. It's really that simple. He's an arrogant fucker and he deserves all he gets! Double helpings. He's only into his fifth year inside and he's already six stone overweight and fucked up physically, mentally and spiritually. And that's with cushy treatment!

Let me explain about prison: it's designed to break men slowly. The solitary, the isolation and the punishment is all a form of torture. Cons crack up in a day, a week, a month, or ten years. It will, if you allow it to, dehumanise and degrade you into submission – first physically, then mentally. The system caters for us all. They have all the time in the world to beat you! Their time is your life. It's a game to them; your life is a game, so play to win.

I've had my doom and gloom and moments of despair. I've actually gone insane (so they tell me). The 1960s, '70s and '80s really weren't nice times to be inside if you were weak minded. But I actually enjoyed the battle and I turned it around. I overcame it all. I chose to put myself through the challenge and I think I've done a good job because I'm the fittest, strongest 55-year-old man you'll ever meet in jail anywhere in the world. I wouldn't change my past because it was fucking wicked. Superdoopertrooperfantasticallymagical. Fucking awesome! Cunts like Huntley haven't got the inner strength or self belief you need. His sort crumble and take overdoses then shout, "Please help me." The screws are bored of his attention-seeking behaviour and 'poor me' syndrome. Well, fuck him. Watch this space.

Who remembers that monster Jeffrey Dahmer, the cannibal mass killer in America? He wasn't even safe on death row; a con beat him to death. That's how it is in prison – nobody is 100% safe. Ask the wingful of nonces in Strangeways about the riot that kicked off there. They shat themselves, doors got smashed in, there was a river of blood and broken bones, and you could hear their screams half a mile away. One got a table leg rammed up his fat arse (with no Vaseline). "AAARRggghhhhhh…" He walks like a crab now. Fucking good job.

I called Mum up tonight; we always have a good laugh. She's a good soul, my mum. I do miss her at times, especially her cooking.

Jack Hazen, 61 years old, went on the run 33 years ago on an armed robbery charge. They've just caught up with him in Las Vegas. Poor sod's got cancer too…

Life's a bitch, so is Goldilocks! Did you know that slag Goldilocks got caught giving daddy bear a blow-job, filthy bitch? I've got it in my porno collection. Some women are just animals – they don't care. They're heartless souls. Snow White was no better. What she got up to with those seven lucky bastards is unfuckingbelievable; you wouldn't believe a tart could take so much cock. Those little dwarfs are known for their large cocks. Why do you think Happy was always happy? The fucking size of his bell-end, you would be happy too.

I see a Luton man hanged himself in Bedford, my local jail, on 30 April 2006. Mark Beagarie was 43 years old and on remand for ABH. He tore up his bed sheet and swung off the cell bars. If he had been convicted he was looking at a silly sentence. Why the fuck do people take their own lives? Don't they realise the misery they leave behind? So what makes them do it? Depression, anxiety, fear, mental breakdown, or is it just 'I've had enough, time to leave'? I always feel sad for the families, I really do. Oh well, that's Mark Beagarie's worries all over. R.I.P. mate.

Talking of Bedford nick, it may be my local but in 40 years of prison life the cunts have never accepted me. If that's not victimization then what is? CUNTS.

Did I ever tell you about the time I was stopped by the Old Bill on a snowy night carrying a fully-grown deer over my shoulder with a fucking big hole in its head? In fact, half its head had been blown away! The Old Bill said, "Where did you get that from?"

"I found it in the road," I said.

"How did it get that hole in its head?" they said.

"Fuck knows," I said.

"Who are you?" they said.

"Who are you?" I said.

"Where are you going?" they said.

"Home," I said.

This shit went on and on till I said, "Why don't you pair of cunts get back in your car and fuck off and arrest some burglars and stop harassing us innocent members of the public?" Fuck me, they only fucked off! So I leapt over a hedge to find the shotgun I had just slung over when I saw them coming. Well, better be safe than sorry I say! Cunts.

You can't beat a deer. A man has got to eat or he dies. Veggies... do me a favour. Our teeth are there for a reason: chewing meat. Fuck off, you vegetarians, you're all Martians to me.

Did you know female fleas drink 15 times their own body weight in blood every day? I know some women like that, don't you?

Here's a sad old story, reach for your tissues... 30 years ago when Duncan Gibb was an 18-year-old lad, he got attacked in the street and ever since he's had a serious phobia that destroyed his whole life. He was afraid of leaving the house and became an agoraphobic – a man afraid of open spaces – so for 30 years he never left his mother's house. He became a hermit. How sad is that? Well, it gets even sadder. In January 2008 he left the house for the first time since the attack three decades earlier. Nobody saw him for 11 days until his dead body was found in a shed. What a crazy life! What a mad ending! It's Loonyology... Amen!

28 January 2008.

Called Mum tonight and she had some sad news: Tel Currie (Snr) passed away last Thursday. He was one top geezer, pure old school, a great guy. I'll bloody miss him. R.I.P.

My friend Sandra Gardner's mother also passed away. It's tough to lose a mum. It's got to be the toughest part of life but it sure as hell comes to us all. And when it does, I think a part of your soul goes with her. So love your mums, spoil them, because they won't be around forever! I may be in a concrete coffin but I still look after my old duchess. You can bet your arse on that! My mum doesn't go short.

I also called up Mark Fish today and it's all great news on the bizz front! Mark never lets me down...

Here's a blinder! Get on this one. Dave Pearce, who's serving five years in Ford open prison, has just been nicked for having a mobile phone. It had photos on it of Sarah Murphy. Who? Yeah, you may well ask. Sarah is a screwess at the jail and the photos were of her flashing her tits (a fine pair too). You can't make this up! Sadly, Sarah's been sacked. A large box of Viagra was also found in the same jail! Fuck me. Please, please, can I have some of Ford? It sounds like my sort of nick...

Did you know Dalmatians are the only breed of dog that gets gout? It's because they're the only mammals other than us humans who produce uric acid. (Not a lot of people know that. Loonyology is about learning!)

I've had a letter today from Danny Hansford telling me Tom Hardy has just flown in from Hollywood and will be visiting me on Wednesday 30 January. Fucking brilliant. He's going to play me in *Bronson* – the film about my life which will come out in 2009.

Did you know fleas have killed more people than all the wars put together? In the 14th century they wiped out a third of the population of Europe with Bubonic plague. Fucking evil little fuckers. I hate fleas, they're little bastards.

Did you know slugs have four noses? Four fucking noses! What for? Why four noses? The world's gone insane. Why did God create a slug with four noses? It doesn't make sense to me. What's it all about?

Here's a fact, you'll love this one... A lion can mate 50 times a day. 50 shags a day without Viagra. No wonder they're called the 'king of the jungle'. Imagine that... It's not bad is it? Surely the bitch must have a sore pussy? I bet the male has a sore bell-end too! 50 fucks a day...

Hey! Did you know a bee has five eyes? Three small ones on top of its head and two large ones in front. It must be great to have so many. You would never get caught shoplifting.

Here's a sad story for you. James Bedell was 81 and Hilda his beloved wife was 76 when they both had a glass of whisky and put plastic bags over their heads. Time to move on. Some old couples just decide to go together. It's their decision and it's so sad, but it's their way of saying, "We love each other in life and in death." Actually, you have to admire them, you really do, it's bloody heart warming. Old James was a proud man and an RAF veteran (a hero in my book).

Did you know that 1% of all adult deaths in the UK are suicides? They just wake up and say, "That's it... it's time to fly." God bless our old folk. Where would we be without the rascals?

Did you know a bee must visit 4,000 flowers to make just one tablespoon of honey? You have to respect the little chaps, you really do! Nature is wonderful. Those bees work their bollocks off for us. All we have to do is unscrew the honey jar lid and eat it. Are we lucky or what?

Did you know a fully grown grizzly bear can run faster than a horse? Without a rifle you're in big trouble; believe me, you're fucked. It will probably fuck you before it eats you! Those bears mean bizz, believe it.

Oh well, I've got 200 sit-ups to polish off before lights out. If I don't do them, no-one will do them for me.

30 January 2008.

Tom Hardy visited today. He has put on one and a half stone of muscle for the movie. He looks awesome and I'm so fucking proud of him. You wouldn't want to meet him down a dark alley at 3am; you'd shit yourself. Tom looks more like me than I look like me! He got me four banana milkshakes and four muffins – a great visit.

Yeah, I had a great day, I enjoyed it. And to top it all we had pizza, chips and beans for tea. They do a nice home-made pizza here, with cheese, tomato and onion. It's not bad for prison but you'll still get some cons moaning. Some cons are never satisfied and the biggest moaners are the ones who haven't got a pot to piss in. It's true. I'm telling you, it's a good pizza! I could eat six of them in one go.

No call tonight; the phone's bust. Such is life.

I got nine letters today. One was from a 19-year-old girl from Doncaster who has read my solitary fitness book and wants to know a good exercise to tighten her buttocks up. I'll write back as I always like to give good advice. It's obvious this one: plenty of shagging, get that arse pumping and get a good sweat on. Burn up those calories, get that pussy flowing and go for gold. Did you know a good shag can burn off 3,000 calories, girls? It's true, it's good for your hips and your waistline! Did you know there's more protein in a teaspoon of spunk than there is in a 14oz steak? Come on girls, get it down your neck. Don't waste all that goodness; a good gobble a day will do you the world of good.

Friday, 1 February 2008.

I love the first day of the month; there's something magical about it – it just feels lucky. Fuck knows why. I had a good jog on the yard in the rain and wind. There was a crow on top of the cage roof watching me and squawking. I squawked back and it flew off. I must've said, "Fuck off, this is my cage," in crow language.

I had a chicken curry today. It wasn't too bad, either. Mark Emmins and his wife Lisa have booked up to see me on the 23rd of this month; that will be a laugh. And Billy and Rachel Bristow are up to see me on 12 February. I told you it's a lucky day! I got six letters and a few quid sent in by some pals. Magic!

Saturday, 2 February 2008.

I awake at 6am, freezing. It's fucking snowing big flakes and it's settling. I watch it fall and the memories from my boyhood flood back. Kids in my era had plenty of snow, it always snowed! Who doesn't like the snow? We all love it! Not too much, but enough to have some fun. It's lovely to watch it fall and drift back into some lovely memories where I'm not in jail, I'm free in my boyhood memories. See? No fucker can take away the good times, they're with you forever.

Amir Khan fights tonight. He's a legend in the making, believe me.

England got beaten by Wales at rugby. Wankers. We never deserved to win!

I got a card off my son Mike. He's moved in with a woman with four kids. I'm sure he's nuts. Playing dad to four kids is some feat! Good luck, son, you'll need it. Once I get out (not if – when), I'm going away with Mike for a spell to have some quality time together. We both need it. A good piss-up would break the ice. I love Mike to bits, I really do. We are just on different planets for now.

Yeah! He's done it again! Amir won! I'm telling you now, we are watching a future boxing legend on his journey to a world title. He is mustard! Double strong! Three cheers for Amir Khan! HIP HIP – HOORAY! HIP HIP – HOORAY! HIP HIP – HOORAY! Fucking brilliant! He won every round, all 12 of them. Pucker. Mad people always seem to have lots of energy; it pays to be mad.

I'll tell you who's an evil bastard: Scott Harman. He was found guilty at Lewes Crown Court in January 2008 for killing his eight-month-old daughter. She suffered 15 broken ribs. What a big brave fucker this bag of shit is! And guess what, he only got found guilty of manslaughter and not murder. He got a poxy seven-year sentence, so he'll be out in four and a half. Little Jessica will never get out of her coffin! How can anybody kill a little baby like he did? I hope he gets tortured by the cons and they break 15 of his ribs. It's an injustice that he only got seven years – a fucking disgrace and an insult to baby Jessica's life. It makes me feel angry, the dirty low-life cunt. I'll remember his name because I need a new punch bag.

Here's an article out of a Welsh paper that was actually written in Welsh but I've had it translated into English. My mother was interviewed for it just before Christmas 2007. It's a rare interview for Mum as she doesn't normally entertain journalists, not after all the shit they write about me.

GOLWG
December 13, 2007

Cover headline: A "dangerous" man – but for Eira it is Christmas without her son.

Main story: A mother talks of her "dangerous" son.

Christmas without Michael – again.
A mother from Aberystwyth will spend Christmas without one of her children – according to the tabloid press, he is the most dangerous prisoner in Britain. But to her, Charles Bronson is Michael, her son.

Eira Peterson is preparing for Christmas once again, knowing that there will be a spare place at her table. By now she has grown used to it.

Only once during the past 34 years did her son, Michael, come home to Aberystwyth to celebrate. Thirty-four is now almost 35.

To the tabloid press, that son is Britain's most dangerous prisoner; to her he is a son that has been punished far beyond reason. Eira, who is now 76, is worried that she will never see him again a free man.

Michael Peterson, aged 55, is the man known as Charles Bronson. Despite the fact that he has never murdered anyone, he is a Category 'A' prisoner at Wakefield Prison, Yorkshire and is locked up in solitary for 23 hours a day.

Eira's flat is spick and span with photographs of her three sons on the walls and shelves. She is sipping Gaelic coffee. Surrounding her are books and videos of her middle son, Michael.

He was first incarcerated for seven years for armed robbery back in 1974, and since then he has been held in 120 different prisons. His latest sentence was life, but the parole board has had the right to consider releasing him after only three years. Up to now, they have not done so.

His mother feels 'terrible' when a story about him appears in one of the tabloid newspapers. 'I do not go out for two or three days,' she says. 'People will look at me through their windows thinking, "There she goes".'

'I have never broken the law. I cannot help what he has done. He had a loving mother and father, nice houses, nice furniture and a good life. He has never wanted for anything. People would stop me in the street and tell me, "Your boys are a credit to you".'

Eira Peterson and her husband Joe were once stewards at Aberystwyth Conservative Club. Michael was raised in Luton and Ellesmere Port before his parents moved back to Aberystwyth in 1978.

The eldest son, John died in 2001, but Michael was refused permission to attend the funeral. The same was true when his father and grandmother died years previously.

The iconic photograph of Charles Bronson is that of him sporting a huge black beard and pebble-lens dark spectacles – this is the one shown repeatedly in newspapers, and his mother hates that photograph. She would rather see the photo of him looking like a film star, his hair short and neat with a long, striking moustache. He resembles his distant relative, Richard Burton. To her here is a big difference between Michael and Charles Bronson.

Her son changed his name on the advice of his boxing instructor, and stories of his violent nature soon spread – newspapers would refer to his physical feats noting that he could complete 2,000 sit-ups daily. Others would put the figure at 3,000.

The ten books he has published have fed some of the myths. But they also offer a glimpse of the other side of his character – the torture he has endured, the beatings that turned his flesh black and blue, and the use of drugs to subdue him.

Ever since that first offence, his family stress, almost all his troubles have been the result of his long struggle with the prison authorities. He has taken hostages and has caused more than £1 million damage during protests. He says that he has been on more roofs than Father Christmas.

Charles Bronson celebrated his 55th birthday last Thursday at Wakefield Prison, Yorkshire. Over the years his mother has visited him – from Walton to Wandsworth, Winchester to Wormood Scrubs.

'I have sent him a card,' says Eira, in her warm English accent, almost Cockney. 'I cannot write, "Hoping you have a nice day". But he is fine now. Years ago, when I would visit him, I would feel so sad and would cry all the way home. Now, when I see him, it is completely different. He is full of fun and has accepted his life. At Wakefield, the authorities are very good to him.'

Usually, Eira will send off a present of a book of stamps and drawing paper. This year she sent him a book of drawings made by people who paint using feet or mouth. For Christmas she will send him a card, as well as a packet of cards for him to send, although he makes his own cards.

Among the family's complaints – especially Eira and her cousin Graham Jenkins – is that the newspapers have ignored Charlie's kinder side. Both of them refer to the fact that profit from his books are sent to a children's charity in Manchester, Zoe's Place. He also sends money to his mother.

'Every time I walk in to see him he will say, "You are looking very nice today – I like that suit". Or, "that colour suits you". He is full of kind words.

'Should you ever meet him, you would think – what a nice man. It is seven years now since he has done anything wrong. I would love to see him being released. He has done his time. He has broken the law and has paid the price. He has never done anything really bad.

'At one time I would never talk of him being inside. I have no shame over it, but it causes me pain. People know only what they read – that he has taken a hostage, or is protesting on a rooftop. They do not say, "He is not a killer, he has never killed anyone".

'He has spent more than his prescribed time inside. Why was he sentenced to life? I have no idea. I simply don't know.'

Even at his last court appearance, when he was refused the right to appeal against his conviction for kidnapping a teacher at Hull Prison, the Judge suggested that he was a different man.

According to his mother, he is now decorating the walls of his cell with pictures of spiders, flowers and birds. His earlier pictures would depict images of blood, torture and madness.

'Now, I can talk about him,' says Eira Peterson. 'Once, I couldn't. I would love to see him out, before I leave this world to join my husband.'

Seeing Ian Huntley and children

Before she can reach her son's cell, Eira Peterson has to be searched and has to go through a dozen or more doors.

In his cell, he is behind iron bars, almost like Hannibal Lecter. There are four chairs and a table, fixed together.

He shares the same area as murderers and rapists. One of his neighbours is Robert Maudsley, who murdered four people and ate the brains of one of his victims.

The family's constant complaint is that Michael Peterson is in prison for life while paedophiles are released after only a few years. Once, on her way to her son's cell, Eira passed Ian Huntley, who murdered two children. He was in an open visiting room.

'There were two children with him,' she says, 'a boy and a girl. He was lounging in his chair, laughing and grinning. I just couldn't believe it – I am sitting here now while my son is behind bars. He has never raped, killed, and never has he hurt a woman.

'Yes, he has demolished jail roofs. But what he has done has always happened inside prisons, not outside.'

A dangerous man, or a victim of injustice?

In the Appeal Court in 2002, some of Charles Bronson's offences were listed – they included violent theft, three cases of injuring, blackmail, offences relating to guns, threatening to kill and kidnapping.

As well as kidnapping his teacher, he once detained three prisoners from Iraq who had hijacked a plane. They were given a three year sentence; he was given a seven year sentence.

His books are full of raw and remorseless descriptions of his offences and his boxing feats. He admits that the prison system has created within him a paranoid attitude.

But the assaults he has suffered tell another story. He has been the subject of regular beatings by more than a dozen guards. His kidneys were badly damaged following a kicking. He was also administered the liquid cosh, doses of chemicals to subdue him.

No-one denies that Charles Bronson has committed serious offences; his supporters maintain that the responsibility for committing them lies within the system.

End

What about Steve Smith winning 19 million quid on the Lotto in January 2008? He's a 58-year-old retired hospital porter. The interest alone will earn him three grand a day, 21K a week, 84K a month... Fuck me. Good luck, mate, enjoy it. He lives a stone's throw from my town, Luton. If anybody wants to be a mad hatter then move to Luton – it's famous for its hats, see! That's why Luton Town football fans are known as the 'mad hatters'. (There's a bit of history for you.)

If you own a piece of land, do you own it down to the core of the earth? To what depth do you own it? Does anybody know?

A cement lorry smashed into a prison van that had six prisoners in it. They all escaped and the police are looking for six hardened criminals. Ha Ha Ha!

Why do triangular sandwiches always look and taste better than square ones?

I see the £53 million blaggers got sentenced on 30 January 2008. Four got 15 years, one got 20. To be honest, that's not a bad sentence. Even the great train robbers in the 1960s got 30 years. Out of the £53 million only £23 million has been recovered! Cor blimey, what a fucking raid. Imagine being on that bit of work – what a dream. They had to leave behind £100 million as it wouldn't fit in the lorry. Can you fucking believe that? 100 million bucks. Fuck me, I need a lie down, I feel a bit dizzy!

Did you know a butterfly tastes with its hind feet? Now is that Loonyology or what? Did you know an elephant weighs less than a blue whale's tongue? Can you fucking believe that? A snail can sleep for three years. Lazy fuckers.

I know a big fat convict who's not far off a slug: fatso Peter Simmons! I last saw him in Parkhurst back in 2001. What a lazy, idle fucker – all 28 stone of him. He doesn't walk, he waddles. People like that should be in a fat museum or a zoo for fatties so we can all go and throw bricks at them. What good are fat people? All they do is stuff their faces, fart and sleep. And they smell of stinking, stale sweat! Some of the huge ones can't even get out of bed or wipe their own arse. What fucking good is that? They're not humans.

What about this monster Dean Galley? He was on a hospital ward, one of those mixed wards with both sexes on, and he's been convicted of a string of sex crimes. Guess what? (Well, it doesn't take much guessing, does it?) He creeps out of bed and sexually assaults an old lady of 82. What a fucking animal. Hang the bastard. That old lady is somebody's mother, somebody's grandmother; how the fuck can this piece of shit do such a disgusting act? He got life but he can apply for parole after two years and go on the sex register. Two fucking years. This cunt has been molesting women all his life, but a woman of 82 must be his vilest act yet. Why not just lock him up and forget him? (Anyway, who really wants to be on a mixed ward? Do you? I fucking don't! It's not normal, is it? Or is it? Maybe I'm old fashioned.) If that was my mother he'd sexually assaulted, I wouldn't be able to sleep till I hunted him down, the dirty low-life animal. Believe me, a nonce is always a nonce. Remember this cunt's name because I'm sure we haven't heard the last of him.

Did you know a jellyfish is 95% water and that a bluebottle fly can smell shit from four miles away? Doesn't that just blow your socks off? This world is just a dream, it's got to be!

If you enjoy riddles then you must enjoy life, because life's one big riddle.

Remember: you don't always have to go forwards; you can go sideways, upwards or downwards – just don't go backwards!

A true heart is a happy heart, it really is.

CHAPTER 2

Who painted the rainbow black?

You cruel, wicked bastards… why did you do that?

4 February 2008.

A big event today: I chopped off the most infamous tash in the UK, if not Europe – maybe the world. Yeah, my moustache has gone and it's going to end up going through Tom Hardy's letter box. Maybe the make-up artists on the film set can stick it on his lip. If not, Tom can stick it in his pocket for luck. Then at least part of me will be on the film set! I told you all, there's a method in my madness; there's a reason for everything I do.

I had a brilliant work-out today. I felt so good, fit and fast. I was running around the yard like a young deer – agile and alert. How good it is when you feel like that. I knew at 6am it would be a great day by the shit I had. It was one of those shits where it slides out hot and glossy and it felt like giving birth to a new day. A good shit is a good day. You feel light and free of all the poison in your body.

By the time the screws unlocked me at 8am for breakfast I had polished off 500 sit-ups, 500 press-ups and 500 squats! A cool one and half thousand exercises. I was fresh, alive and feeling good.

Breakfast was silly Rice Krispies and four bread rolls. I made a pint of tea – three tea bags with three spoons of honey and milk. I'm alive and kicking. I then created an A4 art. That took me up to 11.30am. Dinner is served at 11.45.

I got seven letters, two of which were from Mum and Aunty Eileen; those two are so loyal to me. My aunty Eileen is a unique and special lady, there's nothing she wouldn't do for me. I love her dearly.

It was 4pm when I decided to chop the tash off. I called Tom Hardy and Mark Fish. The good news is that my lawyer has found an old case that's similar to my own which was won at the appeal courts. Things are looking good for me but it all takes time and I've plenty of that!

What about ex-Radio 1 DJ Kevin Greening being found dead in his flat? He was found hanging upside down in a studded bondage harness in a room that was converted into an S&M dungeon. You know the sort: nipple clamps, harnesses, ball-breakers, masks, boots, chains, hooks and plenty of Vaseline. Kinky fucker. It takes all sorts! He was only 44… what a crazy way to leave the planet. I think it's sad when a geezer needs all that just to get his rocks off. If a nice juicy pussy can't do it for you then you're a sad fucker. Stay away from my party!

Did you know one pair of rats can produce 2,000 baby rats in one year? There are an estimated 80 million rats in Britain and only 61 million humans. (Be warned.) Prisons are full of rats and there are plenty of two-legged ones too. I'll tell you who's a rat: Kenny Thompson. He copped a five-year stretch back in 1976 for a robbery down in Kent. He robbed a blind woman who was 87 years old. Five fucking years. I chinned him in Wandsworth mail bag shop. Even the screws turned a blind eye on it for once. They told me later, "Well done." See? Even screws are human. We all hate a rat!

Oh well, at 2pm tomorrow, I'll be standing to attention in my cell for a two-minute silence for my old buddy, Tel Currie Snr. He gets buried then and I'll not see him again on this earth. Hopefully I'll bump into him somewhere else. Who knows!

I see the former Rhino's rugby league international player Darren Fleary has become a prison screw at Armley jail in Leeds. You just know he's going to play for the prison team. Strange old move that, from rugby to a screw. I can think of a thousand and one better jobs.

Here's a bit of good news: Wiadimir Dektereff has just been sentenced for raping a young girl and carrying out 19 sexual assaults on young girls under 12 years old. These crimes were committed 20 years ago, but this piece of shit fucked off to Portugal. Anyway, he popped back and got nicked! Guess how long he got? Come on have a guess? I bet you can't guess it. Seven poxy years! Can you believe it? I can. The only good news is that he's got prostate cancer and he's now 74 years old. This nonce will die inside for sure; fucking good job too. Those little girls he abused are now all probably mums and I bet they're buzzing. Throw a party, girls!

Thursday, 7 February 2008.

I got a book sent in today! It's *Wild Thing* by Lew Yates and Bernard O'Mahoney and I read it in four hours. I had to laugh because this guy Lew Yates reckons he was the real governor of the unlicensed fight game in the '80s. There's no doubt about it, he was a tough cookie, but he was never the governor (take that on me). He spent years on the doors and he's broken more jaws than Rocky Marciano! All through his wild life with all those fights on the doors and clubs, he never ended up in a police cell, has never been nicked and has never done a day's bird. How lucky must he be? But having said all that, I respect the bloke – a true fighter! But get real, you were never the governor!

8 February 2008.

A prison guard got lemon with me today (through my caged door). He's one dirty low-life cunt and a typical coward. He's got a set of keys and 10 screws behind him and he has to get lemon through the bars and mesh on my inner door. I spat through the mesh and got him a blinder – '180' right in his eye! My next blob of spit got him in the other eye! What a fucking shot; Eric Bristow would have been proud of that.

Anyway, the cunt said to me, "Bronson, we know about your movie coming out but the only way you're getting out is in a body bag. My brothers in the POA will see to that." What a nasty cunt. The prick doesn't even work on this unit! This is what Charlie Bronson has to put up with! Spit on him? I would sooner pour acid in his eyes, the fucking coward. I'm now nicked with spitting on him, but the cunt can threaten my life and get away with it.

Saturday, 9 February 2008.

The governor's just given me two weeks' loss of canteen and two weeks' loss of spends. My lawyer has been sent all the details; it's far from over. This cunt may be a bully to the weaker cons but he doesn't threaten my life and get away with it. Cunt. Even the screws say he's a cunt. Ask yourselves why would I spit in his eyes twice. There must be a logical reason, I didn't just do it for fun. It's obvious – it's because he said what he said. Anyway, watch this space, it could get good! But it proves what he is. What sort of man is going to stand there and be spat on? He's got the key to my door, he's got 10 screws to help him and I'm all alone! I rest my case – he's a cunt. You wouldn't want him next to you in the trenches in World War III.

It's pricks like him who have been responsible for my problems over the years. The sad fact is that when it kicks off it's sometimes good screws that end up in the way. It ends up like a cowboy punch-up with fists and boots flying all over the place. But with me it's always me on my own against a mob of this lot. It's just madness and the truth of it is, I'm getting fucking sick of it. There really is no escape from it.

Do you know something? I think of solitary as a kind of partner. I just take the madness as it's dealt out. What's the point in arguing with the inevitable when it's going to happen anyway? Fuck it; deal it and fucking let me play my hand.

A lot of people want to know how prison adjudication works, so here are the rules. This is how it goes on. If you ever end up in prison, report any abuse. Now you know how to handle it. Or just plead 'by reason of insanity' and jump on the duty governor and bite his nose off!

F1127 C **What happens when you are put on report**

1. The Prisoners' Information Pack and the Adjudication Manual (Prison Service Order 2000) give guidance on report procedure. You may ask to see a copy. If you think you need more advice, ask an officer. You will find paper attached to this page. Think if you want to call any witnesses. You may also ask to see any statements submitted in evidence.

2. The person hearing the report (adjudicator) will ask you if you have received this form showing the charges against you and if you understand what will happen during the hearing.

3. The adjudicator will read out the charge(s) and ask if you understand them.

4. The adjudicator will then ask you:

- if you have made a written reply to the charge(s) (see over the page)
- if you want any additional help at the hearing. This could be legal representation, legal advice or a friend. The adjudicator decides whether or not to allow you to have any of these. If s/he refuses the hearing will go ahead and you should be ready for this. If s/he agrees the hearing will be adjourned while you contact a solicitor. The Legal Services Officer can help you;
- if you want to call any witnesses, and if so whom. You can ask for witnesses later but if you give names now the adjudicator will have more time to find them and call them to give evidence. Remember that other prisoners cannot be compelled to give evidence.

5. The person who reported you will give evidence. You can ask relevant questions.

6. Any witnesses in support of the charge will then give evidence. You can question them. Do not argue with witnesses. If you cannot ask the right questions to bring out your point ask the adjudicator to help you.

7. The adjudicator will ask you to explain your behaviour. You can do this by speaking to him and you can also read out any written statement or ask the adjudicator to read it out.

8. If you wish to call witnesses, ask to do so and say who they are, even if you have already named them. Say what you believe their evidence will prove. If the adjudicator thinks they will be able to help to explain what happened they will be called.

9. You and other present can ask the witness relevant questions.

10. Whether or not you have called witnesses, you can now say anything further about your case, comment on the evidence and point out anything you think is in your favour.

11. The adjudicator will tell you if s/he finds the charge proved or is going to dismiss it.

12. If the adjudicator finds the charge proved (guilty) s/he will then ask you why you think you should be treated leniently. You can ask for someone to support your plea for leniency.

13. A report on your behaviour in prison and your adjudication record during this time in prison will be read out. The adjudicator will ask if you have anything to say about the report and any questions.

14. The adjudicator will announce the punishment(s) for each charge. If you do not understand how the punishment will affect you ask the adjudicator to explain.

15. The adjudicator may adjourn the hearing or bring it to an end at any time, for example, to await the results of a police investigation or for a key witness to be present. You will be told why.

16. You will be handed a form F256D at the end of the hearing or soon after. This will give you details of your punishments and tell you how you may ask for a review if you think you have not been treated fairly. You will then be returned to normal location unless you are being segregated under Prison Rule 45 or YOI Rule 49.

I bet you're even more confused now! I am and I've had it for four fucking decades. Insanity will always find a way, day or night! No doors or walls can keep it out. If you can love your madness you will be free forever! Does that make sense to you? Think about it… it will. Give it a chance!

There was a horrible, nasty, little fat screw in Armley jail in 1975 who we called 'Porky'. That's what he was – a pig with two legs. Every time the cunt was near me I used to grunt and even the other screws used to laugh. He pulled me one day going out on the yard and said, "Oi, Peterson, what's your problem?" (Mickey Peterson was my name in those days.) I said to Porky, "Look, mate, why don't you fuck off back to the farm?" He cherried up and spluttered out, "You're nicked." So I nutted him and said, "Now nick me for something, Porky." That little pig cost me 120 days remission and a good kicking off his piglet mates.

What a bloody life. What a journey. I'm sure I got off at the wrong stop! I sometimes ask myself if my mum dropped me on my head when I was born, or if the midwife smacked my head instead of my arse. Something must have gone wrong but I wouldn't have it any other way. Would you?

Sunshine and blue skies
Please fuck off
Let's have some rain
Let's have some snow
Let's freeze Hell
Why not?
Sunshine's skin cancer
Wake up
Get real
You're burning away
A slice of toast
A fucking lobster screaming in a pot
It's hot
It's roasting
Rain you bastard
Cool us down
Put out the flame
Turn off the light
Come in close
Nobody gets that close
Not to me
I'm a snowman
Don't melt the daddy
Just love me
Sunshine and blue skies
Please fuck off
I'm too young to die.

I dream of lying on a beach, I really do, I just can't ever see it. It's always a fucking dream. Some bird's rubbing cream onto my body. She's got massive tits falling out of her bikini and I can see her pussy lips dripping sweat. I'm on fire, I'm a candle burning. I'm a man, I've got desires, I've got feelings. You can laugh but it's true. I'm on the beach with a can of beer and a cheese and onion roll; her hand slips into my trunks. I've not had a hard-on like this since I chinned the governor in the Scrubs, but that was then, this is now. My dream is so fucking close… I can't take this heat anymore, so I push my cock into her ice cream. Cool, I'm so cool… I'm even cooler as she licks it off. That's living, that's the snowman!

A dream's a dream. I'm tired of dreaming, it gives me a headache. I wake up depressed. There never was an ice cream and all it ever does is fucking rain. What a cunt – it makes you feel bad, angry, moody and fucking mental.

Some con in Wandsworth once got lemon with me on the exercise yard. He called me a 'mentalist'. Cheeky cunt. I stuck his head through the window in the toilet. That's a funny thing: all the old jails had toilets built on the yards. What happened to our toilets? None of the new jails have toilets in the yards. We have to walk around for an hour bursting for a piss. What's that all about? It's a fact, a prison fact.

Everything's changed, even me. I'm no longer me and I don't know who the fuck I am anymore. My soul's twisted around my heart, it's strangled my senses. I'm well and truly fucked up.

Who am I?
What am I?
Where have I been?
What have I done?
Did I miss the revolution?
What happened?
Where are all the old faces?
Why is everybody so fucking serious?
I saw a young guy crying
On his knees begging
Praying
Bleeding
Drowning in tears and misery
What happened to the fight?
When did the war stop?
Why did I carry on?
Why is it me who's alone?
Am I a prisoner of war?
Or a political pawn?
Who the fuck am I?
Why can't some cunt tell me the truth?
How many more years do I have to give?
I'm running out of time
I'm running out of blood
My body aches
I ache for some loving
Some humanity
Wrap me up in a blanket of love

Some tenderness
Suck my cock whilst you're at it
It is clean
I wash it six times a day
I shine it on a Sunday
My helmet sparkles
You can see it in the dark
It's true
Who the fuck am I?
What's left?
What's next?
I wish I knew
Loonyology can't go on and on and on
Can it?
Will it?
Loonyology Volume 3
Volume 4
Volume 5
It's going to end up like Rocky
Fuck me
I can't do it no more
Can I?
Do you want me to?
Somebody put me out of my pain
My brain's leaking on my pillow
Take a good long hard look
This is not a joke
I'm off to bed
Nighty night.

I really am a poet – when I want to be, that is. Poetry just flows out of the pen, it never stops, and it's Loonyology at its best. Dig deep! Open up! It's pure imagination; at times it's lust. Once I dig deep I become invisible. I can smell it, taste it, at times I can actually eat it. Hell, I'm eating fresh air, that's all that's there, but my visions are beautiful. Seeing is believing. God, you really are a freaky fuck-face… go to sleep!

Get on this dirty nonce. 59-year-old Billy Wild has copped a life sentence for raping an 11-year-old girl. He put a knife to the girl's baby sister's throat who was one year old. Get your clothes off or the baby gets it! What a low-life cunt! What good is this piece of shit to humanity? And the parents of the girl and baby knew him as a friend. How must they feel? He'll be here at monster mansion in a week or two. This hell-hole welcomes cunts like Wild! It's full of them. Fuck me… I'm a celebrity, get me the fuck out of here!

This cunt Wild will fly through the system. He'll do all the sex case courses, he'll be the screws' tea boy and the governor's pet. He'll be crying to the probation and do one-on-one with the psychologists. This cunt won't even be on 'Cat A' and all his reports will be excellent. Mark my words now: life for him will be seven years, if that, because the system really doesn't see these nonces as a danger to the public. Well they can't, can they, as they keep releasing the fuckers! Why? They're a danger, they're predators, they're hungry for kids! They can only get their kicks out of kids. A few years' good behaviour in jail doesn't stop them. How can it? They're like little mice inside: yes, sir... no, sir... three bags full, sir.

Fucking wake up, public – you're being hoodwinked, you really are. They're letting the worst of the worst out! It's your kid next that gets it – or your elderly mother, your wife or your sister. They're monsters on the prowl. Be warned, be told, do something about it. What's your MP for? Use them! Demand that all child abusers serve no less than 20 years. Or better still, stick them in my cage. I'll see to it. Trust me, they won't want to see another kid once I've finished giving them some serious therapy the Bronson way.

12 February 2008.

Brilliant visit today from Billy and Rachel Bristow. They always give me a good laugh, they're salt of the earth friends. As we were chatting, Robert Maudsley was in the cage gym. I said to Rachel, "Have a peep through the observation window at your first cannibal." To see her eyes light up was a picture. She couldn't believe it. Well, it's not every day a young lady gets to see a cannibal is it? Maudsley is a frightening character to most men, let alone a woman.

Yeah, a good visit. I showed them my speed press-ups, chair press-ups and my famous crocodile press-ups. Seeing is believing: seeing me, you believe. Most guys dream it and talk it; I do it.

I heard on the news today that Roy Scheider died aged 75, after losing his battle against cancer. He was the police chief in *Jaws*. What a lot of people don't know is that he was also a good boxer in his early years. Yeah, a top geezer was Roy Scheider. Rest in peace.

Did you know *Jaws* was the first movie to earn a million bucks? The best film Scheider was in was *French Connection* with Gene Hackman. Can you believe that was back in 1971? I saw that film for the first time in 1974 in Hull jail and a con got stabbed whilst we were watching it. He was only a grass so no one saw it happen. That's how it was in jail in the 1970s: nobody ever saw anything. That's how it should be now days, instead of a dozen cons running to the office to make a statement for early parole.

Get on this. If this doesn't make you puke, nothing will. Saheed Hasmi and Jan Yadgari both admitted selling unfit food from their pizza take away in Cardiff. The customer smelt something bad so he sent the pizza away to be analysed. Shit! There was shit – human shit sprinkled on his fucking pizza. They got fined £1,500 each but both claimed they didn't know how the shit got on there. (Yeah, pull the other one.) The pizza gaff now has a new owner. Thank fuck for that! What sort of cunt would do that? What would you do if it was your food? I know what I would fucking do: Hasmi and Yadgari would both be living in the sewer, chained to the wall. The dirty bastards. Watch what you're eating out there! It really could be shit...

I got a sad letter today from Tony Hunt's daughter Michelle, letting me know her dad passed away on 4 January. He was a good man and a friend to me. I'll miss the old rascal. There's another mate that I won't be having a pint with. How many more will die before I get out? You just don't know when your time's up! It could be today, it could be tomorrow, it could have been yesterday… One sure thing: it's going to happen one day, so enjoy yourself while you can.

I got eight letters today: one from my mum (that's worth ten to me), one from Ray Kray, one from Mark Sharman, one from Sandra Gardner and three from people I don't know, but who all wish me well.

I had a lovely hour on the yard. The sun was out but it was fresh and I enjoyed a jog. It's time to reflect, time to think and time to plan… but plan what? It's all a big waiting game. Mind games. They lock me up but don't even know why or for how long! How many more fucked-up years have I got to jog around a yard? Does anybody know? Does anybody care? I fucking do. What a waste!

13 February 2008.

Valentine's Day tomorrow and I can't even get a blow job! It's all a big wind-up to me. This is not living, it's just existing. I'm like a spider with three legs ripped off, going around and around and getting nowhere, seeing nothing. I forget what it's like to walk on grass, lie on the sand or swim in the sea. I only know one sure thing: I'm a survivor, that's all I am…

I had a fry-up for tea (it wasn't too bad) and a nice mug of sweet tea to wash it down.

The governor did his rounds and stuck his head in. "Everything OK, Charlie?" he asks. "Yeah," I said, "I was happy till I saw your ugly mug!" That's it: 24 hours before I have to see that prat again. How would he be, spending year after year in a cage and not allowed to mix with anybody? I'll tell you how he would be: he would top himself! He couldn't survive a week of my life. He knows it too. Deep down he has a lot of respect for me. They all do, because they know they couldn't do what I do. It's that simple.

I'm going to create a 'tribute art' tonight for my late buddy, Tony Hunt. Rest in peace, my friend. I'll catch you up later…

I wonder who's shagging my two ex-wives on Valentine's tomorrow? Good luck, you're gonna need it… Me? I prefer a plate of chips. Good night.

If there was ever a case to bring back the death penalty it's this one. In fact, I would hang the cunt myself! Little Jessica Randall was only three months old when she was sexually abused, tortured and killed by her dad! Randall, you filthy, twisted, evil, sicko cunt. Die of cancer you scum bag, with no morphine. A life sentence is too good for you. It's just too sick to think about. Guess what, he's up here on the wing in monster mansion with all the other beasts, playing ping-pong and watching videos. He should be in a cage, getting some of what I've had for 30 years. Cunt. Human rights should not exist for monsters!

A 1740s 'Guarneri Del Gesu' violin was sold at Sotheby's yesterday for £1.8 million. Wow, that's what you call going for a string. Fuck me.

CREATED BY MY SON, MIKE

HEADED FOR CELL
BANGED UP, BRUISED UP
FLAT ON CAGE FLOOR
H... IS FOR HURT
M... IS FOR MADNESS
P... IS FOR PAIN
HMP HAVE DONE EM ALL
ANGER INTO DANGER
SMALL MINDS CLASSIFY
YOU WAS PUT ON THE WRONG PATH
ON CATEGORY "A"
YOU DONE IT YOUR WAY
ROOF PROTEST TO PROTEST
I CONFESS, I GET IN A MESS
IT'S INHUMANE, JUSTICE AT ITS BEST
SO DAD, YOU'RE ALWAYS IN MY DREAMS
AND SILENT SCREAMS
THE PATH WAS BUMPY
BUT THE END'S IN SIGHT
YOU'VE DONE YOUR FIGHT
OUR DAY WILL COME
BOTH WILL BE FREE
TO START OUR FLIGHT...

Mike Peterson 30/01/08

That's my son's poem, that's for real. He doesn't just look like me, he thinks like me too! We are the same, believe it! Mike and I will one day do some travelling and have a laugh together. You better believe it.

14 February, Valentine's Day.

I got seven cards, not bad for an old git! One smelt lovely; I'm sure she had rubbed it on her pussy lips. The only problem is, I don't know who sent it! That's the Loonyology with Valentine's cards: you're always wondering who they're from. Think about it: it could be a mad stalker, a nutter on day release from the asylum. Well, it could be! They could have put a few £50 notes in the cards...

I called Mark Emmins today. It's always great to have a chat with him. Top geezer.

A shit old day today. Miller stinks. Every time the cunt walks past my cage I can smell the rat. Why don't they just gas these nonces? The food was shit too, everything's been shit today. It must be this smelly pussy card reminding me of what I'm missing. Fuck Valentine's Day, it's for muppets! Red roses and chocolates? Do me a favour, give me fish and chips any day. I'm a man, not a fucking puppet. Pass the sick bag.

"Roses are red
Violets are blue
A face like yours
Belongs in a zoo."

I'm off...

15 February 2008.
Governor Thompson is no more! Today he moved on, I don't know where and I don't care! I don't think anyone – screws or cons – will give a flying fuck. So let's have three cheers now he's gone. HIP HIP – HOORAY! HIP HIP – HOORAY! HIP HIP – HOORAY! Fuck off.

Today's been one of those days (boring), so I'm off to bed… fuck 'em all.

I see a former Nazi death guard known as the 'Beast of Bolzano' has been extradited from Canada to serve a life sentence for his atrocities in Hitler's SS. Michael Seifert is now 83 years old, so he won't be serving much of a life sentence will he? Why don't they just shoot the old bastard? Who gives a fuck about him? After what he did to the Jews in the death camps he knows the next stop is Hell: a one-way ticket with no stops. Burn, you Nazi pig.

Get on this. Mark Farren, a sex offender, a nonce and a pervo, was freed early on 7 January 2008 because of prison overcrowding. You just know what's coming next! Four fucking hours after being freed from Exeter jail he assaulted a woman on a train. He has 27 previous convictions so why fucking let the nonce out? Why? This system is putting you women and girls at risk, and the woman he assaulted should take legal action against the Home Secretary for allowing this piece of shit to be freed early. How could the woman lose? He shouldn't have been freed early since he's a danger to the public. What nonce isn't?

This is why you're reading Loonyology: I'm exposing this hypocritical system. They're releasing scores of nonces every day! They don't give a fuck about your wife or daughters who get attacked by these nonces on a regular basis. Believe me: a nonce can't change and everybody knows it. This cunt Farren couldn't survive for four hours without getting the sexual urge. Cut his bollocks off and hang him upside down by his cock! End of story.

I see there was another USA school massacre on Valentine's Day: five shot dead and 18 wounded. Crazed killer Steve Kazmierczak opened up in Northern Illinois University in Chicago, then blew his own brains out. Good old USA – the 'land of opportunity'. I don't think so. This is happening every week over there and it always seems to happen in schools! Why? It's always innocent kids getting blown away. And the Yanks wanna rule the world! Ha ha! They can't even rule their own country. It's pure Disneyland over there. Get a mask and an AK-47 and you're on your way.

What a mental old world we all live in, eh? It's full of mentalists, loonies and crazy bulging-eyed psychos! Pass me the pop corn because that's all it is now: a fucking true-life horror movie and we all play our own parts. Frightening or what? What's next? Who's next to get a hole in the crust? It could be you! It won't be me; I'm double safe in my concrete coffin and you can't catch me. I'm like the man in the iron mask: untouchable – unless the screws kick me to death, poison my food or slip in mob-handed then hang me and make it look like suicide. Unless they do that, I'm the safest man on the planet. Now I've said that, a fucking plane will crash into the jail and kill us all. When it's time to go, it's time to go. Switch the light off on the way out. Good night.

"Hey, Tom," Billy said, "I've just moved to a bloody tough old estate. Fuck me it's rough: Myra Hindley is the Avon lady, Fred West is the road sweeper, Rose West is the baby-sitter and Harold Shipman is the GP. Gary Glitter runs the playgroup and Sidney Cooke is leader of the Boy Scouts!"

It's fucking Loonyology, it's a fucking nightmare…

Did I tell you about the time a mate of mine was walking through Soho in the pissing rain and took shelter in a peep show called the 'Peek-a-boo Paradise'? He paid his £50 and was confronted by three doors which said 'Blonde', 'Brunette' and 'Black'. He chose the blonde, only to be confronted by three more doors saying 'Small Tits', 'Medium Tits' and 'Big Tits'. He chose the big tits, only to be confronted with three more fucking doors: 'Small Cunt', 'Medium Cunt' or 'Wet Cunt'. He chose the wet cunt and found himself back out in the rain. What a cunt…

That was tragic about the Irish family who were all found frozen to death outside the Belfast Odeon Cinema. They had been queuing for three weeks to see 'Closed for winter'.

Life's a big fucking joke. I go to sleep laughing. I can't help it, it's fucking crazy. It should be a crime to be so happy…

Come on, cheer up!

Did you know mice hate cheese? So much for Tom and Jerry.

Here we go again… Gavin John was released from jail in September 2007 and on that very same day he raped a 25-year-old woman. He pleaded guilty in February 2008 and copped five years. Five poxy years! He will be back on the street in two. Watch out girls, you could be next! The judge praised him for pleading guilty. How nice of him. He didn't really have a lot of choice when faced with DNA evidence, an ID and witnesses! It's a fucking disgrace, it really is, and it makes a mockery out of British justice. I bet he'll rape again. Remember his name: Gavin John from around the Bradford area. I'll put all I've got on it happening again. Cunt.

I'll tell you about another cunt, Mick Dickinson. He's serving four years in Wymott jail up in Lancashire and he's put in an official complaint over the prison's films being too violent or too sexy. He prefers *Mary Poppins*. What is fucking happening to our jails? Where are the real cons? Why do we have to put up with these cunts? Soon it will be kiss chase, daisy chains, pink uniforms and screws in slippers with plastic truncheons. Mary fucking Poppins… pass the sick bag!

Am I missing something here or is it me? He should be grateful to be seeing a movie, not moaning about it. What's the big problem with a good old violent gangster movie or a red-hot sex film? What is the problem with this cunt Dickinson? You're in jail, wake up. Get real, smell the shit…

I just can't believe it. I don't belong inside anymore. I'm lost… Somebody please tell me it's not real and that it's all a dream. It can't be reality, can it? *Mary Poppins*. The prison psychologists will love that! Hardened cons all watching *Mary Poppins* and crying! It will be the new therapeutic regime for us all! Fuck me. Please shoot me! Please…

What next? Just what can come next? The mind boggles… It's all starting to depress me now; it's a form of brainwashing. I don't want to be a part of this madness. It's embarrassing me, it's taking away my identity. I'm a man, not a robot. I can't be going down this road. What real man can? Men don't cry about a sex film or moan about a violent film. It just doesn't happen in my world. Do me a favour: fucking wake up! How the fuck could we ever win another world war? We couldn't! That's the whole truth of it. It's now gone too far and we've been taken over by wimpy fuckers, the cucumber sandwich mob and the pansy brigade. Our jails are Wendy houses run by prats. It's all true, it's all Loonyology. The lunatics have taken over our asylums, they're painting the walls pink with flying elephants and crying, "We want Mary Poppins, we want Mary Poppins, we want Mary Poppins!" Armies of lunatics in Mickey Mouse costumes all sucking lollipops and marching unto love. That's what it's come to.

Once we were strong and proud, the real villains of the planet. We could take our punishment like men and fight back if needed. We fought for our rights and lost teeth on the way. Now look at us: sad, pathetic victims of political correctness, and I'm stuck in no man's land having to survive all this shit. Why not fly me to Mars and let me start again on my own? That would be fine. Or I can do you all a big favour and let Mary Poppins come with me. Fuck the films, I'll make my own!

Who saw that bit in *Last Tango in Paris* when Brando stuck his fingers in some butter and ended up doing his lover up the 'deaf and dumb'? That started a lot of the bum fun off. Did you know in a recent survey 85% of women said they've experienced bum sex and 75% said they'd enjoyed it? It's a big thing now: up the bum, have some fun! At least it cuts down on babies. It's a funny old world. You can't take it too seriously, can you? If you did, you'd be insane: one step away from the funny farm, a slip in the shower and a sore arse. It's all Loonyology to me… it's brilliant. Madness is the gift of God. He must be pissing himself laughing at our world. He must be!

19 February 2008.

Fuck me, it was freezing last night. I woke up about 5am and my toes were cold. I needed a piss but I stayed in bed till 5.45 when I was bursting and my bladder was in agony. I made it just in time to the bog and had one of those never-ending pisses like an elephant. How good does it feel as you flick the last few drops out? Beautiful, free and alive.

It's snowing! There's snow on my outside cage. It's also settled on the exercise yard and it looks like Christmas. Reg Wilson was first out on the yard for his hour's exercise. (We all exercise alone here, one at a time.) He drew my face with his hand in the snow! He's a fucking genius artist. I've got to admit (but I don't like to) that he's better than me! Reg is just one of those talented cons who can draw anything. When he came back in I saw my face looking up at me from the snow. I'm sure it was laughing at me. I went out after dinner. The snow had gone by then but it was still fucking freezing.

Did you know that in 2005 Blair Lazar refined 500g of capsaicin from chilli peppers to create a sauce? It was the hottest sauce ever made – it was like having your tongue dipped in petrol and set alight. Blair said, "It felt like my tongue was hit with a hammer."

I see Radio 1 DJ Ray Bingham just copped four years out in Dubai. He got nicked with a tenth of an ounce of marijuana. Four fucking years for a tenth of an ounce. That's a couple of spliffs! That's how it is out in Dubai – the law's fucking mental. He's lucky he didn't get his head chopped off! Four fucking years for two spliffs. I bet that's put him off drugs for life.

Hey! Did you know the world record for juggling balls is 12? So if you can do it with 13 balls then you're the daddy! You don't 'arf learn stuff with my books! The hardest punch ever thrown in a boxing ring was by Max Baer back in 1931. Ernie Schaff hit the canvas like a sack of spuds and never recovered. He died six months later. Max could hit, seriously hit! There were some tough fighters around in that era. They make the likes of Tyson look like pussy cats.

I'll tell you who's a true legend: Fidel Castro. Did you know Fidel's bodyguard Fabian Escalante once said there had been 638 attempts on Fidel's life? What a leader, the Cuban survivor. I fucking love the geezer. Do you know why? I'll tell you: he stood up to the Yanks. Nothing and nobody frightened him, not even death! Now he's an old man and very poorly, but to me he's still a true legend.

It was back in 1962 that the Cuban missile crisis nearly resulted in a nuclear war. In April 1961 a sea, air and land force of 1,500 CIA-trained Cuban exiles invaded Cuba. 68 were killed and the rest captured. All were sent down for 30 years for treason. Castro then allowed the Russians to stick their nuclear missiles on Cuba, all pointing at the USA. Eventually a deal was done with President Kennedy whereby he agreed to remove all American missiles from Turkey in exchange for the Russians removing theirs from Cuba. How fucking close was that? That was the closest we've got to a nuclear war up to now. So when will one really kick off? Who will start it? Who will finish it? Who will live to tell the story? It's got to happen one day; you know it! And when it does, none of us will know a lot about it. Our eyes will melt and our brains will boil in our skulls while our hearts explode. Fuck me, I bet it comes on the day I win my freedom. Just my fucking luck that would be!

I salute Fidel, a real leader of mankind. Respect.

Did you know a spider will spin 30 miles of web in its lifetime? If I had 1,000 spiders I could have a rope for Xmas!

22 February 2008.
I really do have the best lawyer on the planet.

STUDIO LEGALE INTERNAZIONALE

Via Di Villa
Emiliani 24
00197 Roma

LARGO G. TARTINI 3-4
00197 ROMA
ITALIA
TEL: +39 06 85203516 FAX: +39 06 80692652
E MAIL: GDS1955@TISCALI.IT
WWW.STUDIOLEGALEINTERNAZIONALE.COM
+39 340 1537770

Via T. Salvini 15
00197 Roma

Reference: DM/GDS
In reply to: T.Salvini

GDS/DM/SM/BRON887

18 February 2008

Mr. Charles Bronson
HMP Wakefield
NO. BT1314
Love Lane,
West Yorkshire
WF2 9AG
England

Dear Charlie,

Re: Parole

I am pleased to inform you that I have instructed MR DAVID MARTIN SPERRY counsel of over 30 years call to represent you at the parole hearing. Our firm has paid his fees as we are of the view that you should have the very best of representations. He will attend the hearing and all material prepared by ourselves.

I send you my kind regards,

Yours sincerely,

STUDIO LEGALE INTERNAZIONALE
Giovanni Di Stefano

Now do you see why I think he's the best lawyer on the planet? What a man, what a legend! Am I lucky or am I lucky? Win or lose, Giovanni is mustard. He's so fucking hot his pen melts when he writes. That's a real lawyer for you, and he won't stop till I'm free!

I got a sack load of mail today: 12 letters. That's 12 more than monster Miller and cannibal Maudsley get in a year. It's been a great day today and to top it all the news from Giovanni put the cherry on the cake. If every day was so good it would be a crime to be so happy.

I see Steve Wright got a guilty today over the five prostitute murders down in Ipswich. DNA trapped that cunt and he will be here soon. Still, after 40 years of the shit he will get used to it. He's one reptile who will leave jail in a zip-up bag. Fuck him, he's not even worth my ink. He's like the Ripper: he needs blinding. Cunt.

I called my brother Mark today. He's just back off to the oil rigs. He does three weeks on and three weeks off.

I had a nice beef stew and a lemon sponge pudding with custard. Bloody lovely it was. It reminded me of Warrington House Detention Centre back in 1970. Fuck me; that was 38 years ago. I was serving three months at the time; me and my old buddy Johnny Bristow got three months each! They used to give us some good grub in there. We were only young lads but we were hungry men! We trained hard and they fed us good. Their sponge puddings with pink custard were the best! There's something about pink custard, it's fucking lovely. I wish I was only serving three months now! Cor, nor 'arf. Oh well... maybe soon.

"The road to freedom always begins in your mind."

How *true it that?*
But who really is free?
Is anybody free?
"Freedom"
It's all one big fucked-up dream
It's not real
Nobody's free
How can we be?
Don't do this, don't do that
That's against the law
This is a 30 mile limit
Slow down or pay the price
Watch out...
The tax man's about
Where's your pooper scooper?
Put that dog on a lead
You can't walk on the grass
Can't you fucking read?
Put that sweet paper in the bin
Did I just hear you swear?
Freedom
Who the fuck is free...
Freedom is only a myth
Wake up
You're only free when you're dead
Death is freedom...
Life is a trap
Watch out... here come the cops
Those pretend ones
The ones who think they're cops
Community plastic puppets
They walk like cops
They talk like cops
It's all a dream
Even the milkman's late
Freedom
Don't make me laugh
I'm pissing myself

It's a zoo
A human zoo
CCTV
Welcome to this is your life
"Our life"
Everyone's a number
National insurance
Pin number
Bank cards
Credit cards
You're being raped
Abused and used
Freedom
You're as free as a circus horse
Keep on performing
Nobody or nothing is free!
It's all a big act
You know it
But you don't want to face it
The dream is better
Why rock the boat!
Pretend to be free
Like the sheep
Walking into the slaughter house
They can smell death
Look in their eyes
"Fear"
They know it's all over
They know it's time
The pasture's gone
Freedom awaits
They follow each other for our Sunday roast
Freedom?
Don't make me laugh
Don't make me scream
Who the fuck is really free?
You?
Him?
Her?
Us?
Tell me who's truly free?
Only the graveyard bones are free!
Freedom is another dimension
Another world
Outer space
The unknown
That's freedom
It awaits us all.

All these years I've spent in the can I feel like I've been preserved. I'm like a pilchard: I'll still be fresh when they open me up. That's how I see my life. I'm not like any normal man of my age and I don't think I'll ever be like them. How can I be? Plus, I don't wish to be. No disrespect to the old chaps of the UK but your lifestyles fucking bore me to death! I'd sooner walk into the lion's den and fight my last fight than live a boring existence. I really don't know how a man can clock on and off for 40 years and pay the tax man half his wages. How is that sane? You work your bollocks off and the tax man spends it! Fuck that. Then there's some cunt telling you, "You can't park there. You can't walk your dog there!" Pick that up, do this, do that! Fuck all that for a game of bollocks. A model citizen? What's that? Baa baa, black sheep. Walk me to the abattoir. I don't think so.

Life to me is about the buzz, it's a gamble. For me to get one over on the State is a result; it's cause for a drink, a party, a celebration. The dreamers only ever dream about it but I do it. I was born to fuck the system up. I've got my own system, my own rules and my own self-awareness. I don't need no fucker to motivate me! In jail or out of jail, I'm my own man and my destiny is freedom… or maybe a hole in the head! Bang!

David Martin had to be the most complex criminal I ever met. He really was fearless. I first met Dave in Wandsworth chokie block in 1976 or '77. I think it was '76 but I won't put my arse on that. Whatever, he was a fucking good blagger, a proper villain and a master key maker. He could make a key out of a plastic knife. At this time he was one of three top key men; another one was Cyril Berkett and the third will remain nameless, but all the old cons know him.

Dave was a one off and the screws hated him. The system tried so hard to crush him owing to his unique and unusual ways. He had long hair and Wandsworth was a very military-style jail, run by an iron fist and size 10 boots. Even the governors were nasty fuckers. Dave was a thorn in their butt, and feminine cons like him were not accepted in those days, not in Wandsworth. This was the flagship prison, so you can imagine the shit they put Dave through. "Slop out, poofter. Do that button up, faggot. Exercise, homo…" Dave just spat at the clowns. I don't know if he was gay or not, but he was into the feminine way. On some of the jobs he did he dressed as a woman and he even got nicked in a dress! He looked sexy and you wouldn't know he was a geezer!

Dave was one of 12 cons who escaped from Brixton in the early 1970s in a dustbin lorry. But it was his key making that he was famous for. Those Dave Martin keys got many a con out of jail, and Dave himself escaped several times. His best escape was from the Old Bailey cells – a classic. Sadly, he copped a 25-year sentence over shooting a cop in the late '70s and he hanged himself in Parkhurst – or did he? Why would he do that? Would he not have escaped again somewhere down the line? Why would he give up? Was he hanged? Who hanged him? It's the million dollar question nobody can answer! But my view is: why wouldn't the system want him dead? They feared him because they didn't want another embarrassing escape. What better way than a suicide? Problem solved.

Dave, to me, was a legendary character and one guy I would have loved to meet outside, simply because he was so unique. I would have loved to have done a blag with him. Imagine it: driving off nice and easy, man and wife! What cop is gonna stop you? You just look like a normal couple! Imagine walking into a top jewellers as a couple shopping for a £100K ring then saying, "Pass the tray, you cunt," with a .38 in their face! That's what I call a partner in crime. A Bonnie and Clyde without the Bonnie! A Clyde and Clyde.

What a tragic ending to a top villain, a man I respected. They should make a movie of David Martin; some of you will remember the man-hunt when the cops shot a guy in a car thinking it was him. The poor sod got five bullets in him but he survived. Believe me, they wanted Dave dead; they don't just shoot a man in a car for fun!

Yep, he sure made his mark in the criminal history books. And for what it's worth, I salute the man! R.I.P.

Where have all the legends and great characters gone? I don't 'arf miss them, I really do. Like 'Fred the Head' (Freddie Mills from Newcastle) – what a character. He nutted a screw so hard in Parkhurst that the screw 'retired'. He was never the same again. Fred's nutted off a cell door. You don't want a 'nut' off Fred! Bosh! You only need the one. He's broken more noses than any man on the planet. The last time I bumped into him was up in Durham jail in the 1980s. He sorted me out a big bag of fruit and sweets. Top geezer, the best! I did hear he got a serious bashing outside in the 1990s over selling boxes of TV sets with no TV in them. That's Fred for you: always trying something. Still, if somebody is silly enough to buy a boxful of wood thinking it's a telly, then more mug them.

In Broadmoor, I remember Fred selling bags of 'Mexican laughing grass' which was only mown grass off the football pitch dried out in a large plastic jar. He was selling little bags of it to the lunatics for chocolate and sweets. Well, it is an asylum… what do you expect? It's Loonyology at its best! And guess what? The lunatics were smoking it and laughing!

I remember a lunatic in Ashworth asylum who we called 'Shithead'. He used to dry his shit out on a radiator, crush it up into dust, mix it up with tobacco and smoke it. Fucking lunatic; it used to stink. The 'shit spliff'. But he was always happy and you can't buy happiness – happy people are blessed. Who was he hurting? His madness was his joy! Fucking nutter…

There was another one who used to buy a pound of raw liver and eat it raw. Dirty bastard. But it takes all sorts to fill up our asylums; we can't all be geniuses. Some of the maddest loons I ever met in our asylums were the psychiatrists. Please believe that.

I hear Paul Gascoigne (Gazza) has just been sectioned under the Mental Health Act. Anybody – even you – can have a breakdown! Until you've spent a bit of time in a nut house you haven't lived. It's fucking brilliant. Even Britney Spears loves it. You go in crying and come out laughing. It's another world, it's Loonyology.

My dad was a painter and decorator in the 1960s and 1970s before he went into the pub bizz. He once worked in a lunatic asylum up in Cheshire and the stories he told me were straight from Mars. Here's one I'll always have a smile about. He was painting this ward and a female loony kept giving him Turkish Delight. Dad loved a Turkish Delight (who doesn't?) but a nurse came over and said, "Don't take any chocs or sweets off her."

"Why not?" Dad asked.

"Coz she puts them up her fanny!"

That put the old man off Turkish Delight forever! That's Loonyology at its very best. Magical. Fucking mental.

I see Jennifer Lopez has just had twins. Good on her. There's something magic about twins. I honestly believe if I was to have a shag now, it would end up as triplets or quads – it's that long since I dipped my dick. I know I would shoot out so much cream it would do the bizz. Will I ever be a dad again? Would I want to be? Let's face it, being a dad is special but twins are a dad's dream!

I see that cunt Mark Dixie just got lifed off for raping and killing Sally Anne. Fucking monster… she was only 18 years old and all signed up to be a top cat-walk star when this filthy twat wasted her. The beast is six foot three and 16 stone and has a record of sex crimes as long as your arm. Shoot the dog. Mad dogs get put down, so why not Dixie? No doubt he's on his way to monster mansion! "Your cell awaits." Crash. Slam! 39 years, you cunt! You're going out on a Zimmer with your colostomy bag, you fucking animal!

Did you know that serial killer Steve Wright has got a half brother called Mark Taylor who's also a killer? He's serving life in California for killing a gang member. How weird is that? They have the same mother. Fuck me; she must be proud! Oh well… life goes on. So does porridge.

A mental patient rushes into the doctor's office. "Doctor, doctor," he screams, "you've got to help me! They keep asking me for jewellery!" The doctor says, "Take these tablets. If they don't work then give me a ring!"

23 February 2008.

A great day today: loads of letters and a visit off Mark and Lisa Emmins. They left Devon at 5am to get up here to see me. That's loyalty for you, that's what you call 'friends'. I gave them some art and one to post to Tel Currie, it's my art tribute to his dad. It turned out a masterpiece. Tel will be proud of that. Now his dad lives on! It's the first time I'd met Lisa and she's lovely – a beautiful person. She's invited me down for a Sunday roast! I've got so many visits to make and meals to eat that I'll end up 30 stone. Yeah, a great visit. I really enjoyed it! Mark's a genius to me – he's a songwriter, a writer, a musician and a top art dealer. The guy can do anything. To top it all, he's also a great bizz man. He's my brother till the end of time and I'm so lucky to have him in my corner.

I got a postcard off Eddie Richardson, who's now in India. Where the fuck next? Mars? This guy travels. After 30 years in the can, I don't blame him. That's the life I want: on the road. 'A moving target is rarely hit.' We are all targets of life in one form or another, some bigger than others. The world's too small to stay in one place! 'Rock 'n Roll' – fucking give it some!

OH! My punishment ended today so I'll get some canteen next week. YIPPPPEeeeeee… YARRRHHHoooooo… YABADABADOOOooooo! Sweets all round. Well… not really – they're my sweets. Don't get too close to me!

I'll tell you what a nasty little bastard the botfly is. It's mostly found in

South America. You get the horse stomach botfly, the sheep nose botfly and, you guessed it, the human botfly. This little fucker lays its eggs on the back of a mosquito which then lands on a human. The larvae drops onto his/her skin and burrows deep inside. End result: a fucking wormy creature growing in your body! You're bang in trouble. Yuck! Fuck the botfly! See, you learn by reading Loonyology. This is an education. Stick with me and you'll be OK. Trust me.

24 February 2008.

Just had a lovely visit from Nina Camplin and it was the first time we met. Nina is the artist who created the front cover to my book *Con-Artist*. She's a genius, probably the greatest artist I've ever met to date! Her art just blows me away. We will almost certainly go on tour together later on and put on some amazing shows. Today's visit was an inspiration for me, full of ideas and plans. It was a pleasure and a privilege to meet her. You haven't heard the last of Nina Camplin.

Nina got me two banana milkshakes and some chocolates bars. I showed her my crocodile press-ups and gave her some art. I always give my visitors a nice art; it's my way of showing them respect and thanking them for coming to see me. Us artists are very sensitive, heart-warming souls. Stop laughing, I'm serious! We take our art seriously. Look at me: I'm serving a life sentence over my art being criticised. Fact. If you've got nothing good to say about someone's art, then don't say fuck all. Keep it fucking shut!

It was a great weekend for me – all very positive. It's only sad that prison HQ can't be as positive as I am. Cunts, evil nasty bastards, I hope you all get piles and they run out of cream, you fucking half-brain twats. Still, no love lost…

I was in the *Sunday Sport* today. They reviewed the *Bouncers and Bodyguards* book by Robin Barratt. It had the story of the toe rag who tried to bite my face off. Sad bastard. For the past 30 years he's been crapping in a colostomy bag. Fucking wanker. Bite my face off, you cunt? Still, he learnt his lesson and what went down is history. We all have to move on! It's no good crying over spilt milk. Well, in his case spilt shit!

A great weekend! Magical. Hey! I actually feel human again…

Maudsley was on a visit too – his brother was up to see him. It's very rare that we both have a visit on the same day because there is only one visiting room on this unit. They let him have his visit in the classroom. Posh fucker – he gets all the perks. Still, you've got to look after our serial killers, they are a dying breed, unique specimens. Me, I'm just an old-fashioned blagger, that's all I am (or was). You can now call me the 'art man' – the 'Con Artist'. I swapped a shooter and a mask for canvas and a brush. I'm born again and I fucking love it. Wake up prison HQ – see me for what I am today. You're all fucking living in the past. WAKE UP!

Hey! Did you know 2008's a leap year? There are 29 days in February, so that's an extra day in jail. Cunts. People born on February 29th are known as 'leapers'. I bet you never knew that. The Irish government gives out £70 to parents of babies born on leap year. It's Loonyology gone mental. Fucking leap year, fuck it! Who gives a flying fart?

Do you know why the professor invented the door knocker? To win the 'No-Bell prize'!

I see somebody sabotaged the brakes on Jimmy White's Rolls Royce. If we find out who did it, they're in for it! Jim's not just a great snooker player, he's a great bloke. Be warned now: stop.

Get on this, you won't believe it. That cunt Steve Wright (no, not the radio geezer, the serial killer who just got lifed off) wrote a letter to the press asking: "Could you please call me the 'Suffolkator' because I don't like the label 'Ipswich Ripper'." Can you believe that? How insane is that? Anyway, he's now on suicide watch because he's said he's going to hang himself. Oh, poor thing. Cunt, just do it and fuck off to Hell! I think this could turn out to be another Huntley case: full of self-pity.

Prison life in this country is a fucking holiday compared to prisons abroad. We don't know we're born; it's a fact of life. Take ADX in Colorado for example. It opened in 1994 and some say it's the new Alcatraz and the closest a man can get to Hell on Earth. It enforces repressive techniques of isolation and sensory deprivation. The cons eat, sleep and shit in a box cell called 'the concrete coffin'. (What's new there? It's all I've had for 30 years!) The bed, chair and table are made of concrete. You won't escape but even if you did, you'd be faced with hundreds of miles of desert. Welcome to Hell!

What about Mendoza Prison in Argentina? You think you've got it tough? Get on this motherfucker hell-hole! Many cons that enter don't leave alive. There are 1,600 cons but it's designed for only 600. Wow, that's serious overcrowding and a lot of sore arseholes. Amnesty International is forever complaining about the torture, brutality and the lack of medical attention. It's always flooded with sewage and there are rats as big as cats. There were 22 cons killed in 2004 and the causes of their deaths have yet to be ascertained. I wonder why? Hey, here's a thought: can't we transfer Huntley there? In fact, let's do a swap with all the rapists and child killers here in monster mansion. Send them all to Mendoza nick. It's food for thought.

Take it from me: British jails are a doddle. Pass the cucumber sandwiches.

How do you stop a woman giving you a blow job? Marry her.

It's the big day tomorrow, 23 February, when they start filming *Bronson* after three and half years of planning. Good luck, Tom! Only a few weeks ago this movie almost got stopped by a so-called friend, John Blake, the book publishing millionaire. He basically claimed he owned the copyrights to it! All the lawyers had an emergency meeting and all Hell broke loose. I said, "Hold up. How the fuck does he own the rights?" He claims that the book *Bronson* which he published is the movie script. Again, I said "Bollocks". The movie script was created through my visits, letters and phone calls to friends. It wasn't copied out of any of my books. What fucking sickens me is that Blake published the *Bronson* book 10 years ago. If Blake's so interested in a movie why hasn't he made one? It's always the same: the rich are never satisfied. They're greedy, selfish fuckers. It's odds on that all my books will again be best-sellers owing to this movie and he will still make a nice few quid, so what's his fucking problem?

This is how I see it: he stuck his nose in without caring if it helps my campaign to freedom or not. He basically doesn't give a flying fuck if I get out or stay in. I could have accepted it if he had approached me first, rather than going behind my back like a rat. Anyway, all the lawyers and directors came to an agreement and he got 10K. All that for a poxy 10K. He could have stopped my movie over that, because if an agreement wasn't made fast it would have meant a court case which would go on for years. Mind you, he couldn't have won, how could he?

So that's our friendship over. I don't have it with rats. Keep friendship out of bizz, I say. A bizz man will eventually cut your throat or suck your life away just to get a new Rolls Royce. What's 10K to a bizz man like him? Oh well... he lost, I won! Plus, I found out his true colours.

I've always said it and I always will: you don't know a true friend till the heat's on. Too many melt, crumble, or spill their bottle and they become the enemy. Real friends would back you to the hilt, not try and get a wage out of it. A cunt's a cunt in my book. It's not about Loonyology, it's about morals, principles and dignity. Even a lunatic doesn't need to lose those. Stand up and be counted, I say. Be a man, live a man and die a man. All the dosh in the world can't buy a real friend! John Blake to me is a spineless rat. I'll leave it at that – for now.

25 February 2008.

I called Mark Fish tonight and it's all systems go – the filming started! He watched it all day and the first scene was of me as a boy in school. So that's that, it's rolling! Mark will be there every day till it's finished. That's what you call a true buddy. Staunch.

The only problem is that the script has been changed in parts and I've yet to see it, which I think is a bit cheeky. Why has my lawyer not sent me a copy? I'll have a copy in the next day or two but I should have seen it when it changed. There may be something in it I don't agree with! Why do people swap and change things when they've already been agreed? Crazy people. It's like those twats who buy a new car and can't wait to get under the bonnet. Fucking idiots. Why play about with something that works properly?

I only got one letter today but it was from Mum so it's worth twenty. You only get one mother. How true is that?

Here's a bit of history for you: Oxford Street in London used to be called Tyburn Road (we are going back centuries here) and it had a tree called the Tyburn Tree which was the hanging tree. Proper public hangings! Yeah! The old Tyburn Tree. "Come on kids, bring the picnic basket, we're off for a picnic to see the hangings today." YIPPEE, YARHHOO! That's how it was in those days. Sick bastards, sad fuckers, evil, twisted people. A lot of heads were decapitated and kicked about like a football. Honestly, they were brutal folk!

Did you know in 1884 at Exeter jail they attempted to hang John Lee three times? Three fucking times. The trap door wouldn't open. Imagine that; his arse must've been twitching. In the end they committed him to a life sentence and it then became law that if the hangman fucks it up three times the prisoner will not hang. A life sentence in those days would be 10 years, but you would be lucky to survive that long on their diet and poor conditions. Believe me, it wasn't the Ritz.

Get on this complaint form I submitted last week and get on the reply. It's total bollocks. You've got to laugh – they fucking make it up as they go along! Cunts.

HM PRISON SERVICE

FORM COMP 1
PRISONER'S FORMAL COMPLAINT

Establishment
Serial no. WD24/08F.

Read these notes first

1. This form is for you to make a formal written complaint under the complaints procedures. Complaints should wherever possible be sorted out informally by speaking to your wing officer or making an application. Use this form only if you have not been able to resolve your complaint this way.
2. A written complaint should be made within 3 months of the incident or of the relevant facts coming to your notice.
3. Keep your complaint brief and to the point.
4. When you have completed the form, sign it and post it in the box provided. The form will be returned to you with a response.
5. If you are unhappy with the response, you can appeal on a separate form (COMP 1A).
6. Some subjects are dealt with only by the Area Manager or Prison Service headquarters. If your complaint is about one of these subjects, the reply will take longer.
7. There is a separate pink form (COMP 2) for confidential access complaints.

Your details (use BLOCK CAPITALS)

Surname	BRONSON	First name(s)	CHARLES
Prison number	BT1314	Location	C-S-C

Have you spoken to anyone about your complaint? Yes ☑ No ☐

If so, who did you speak to?

SCREWS. GOVERNOR.

Your complaint

I RECENTLY LOST 2 WEEKS CANTEEN.
SO WHY IS IT A SMOKER CAN BUY TOBACCO WHEN HE LOSES HIS CANTEEN. BUT A NON-SMOKER CANT BUY SWEETS??
IT'S BASICALLY DISCRIMINATION.
(US NON SMOKERS ARE BEING DOUBLE PUNISHED)

Does your complaint have a racial aspect? Yes ☐ No ☐
Is your complaint about bullying? Yes ☐ No ☐

What would you like to see done about your complaint?

STOP GIVING PREFERENTIAL TREATMENT TO SMOKERS.
AND TREAT US "ALL" THE SAME.
(THEY CHOSE TO SMOKE. I CHOSE TO EAT SWEETS)

Signed [signature]

Date 21/2/2008

Printed by Albany Print and Design. HMP Albany.

Reply: Dear Mr Bronson, thank you for your request complaint form. I have looked into this issue you raise and can inform you that the loss of tobacco and phone cards is a separate adjudication award to loss of canteen.

I'll tell you why its bollocks: I lost my canteen for two weeks – that was my punishment. Where I come from punishment is punishment, so let's not play silly games here. I was allowed to buy tobacco but not sweets. So my argument is this: a smoker on punishment who's lost his canteen can buy tobacco, so why can't I buy sweets? I don't fucking smoke. It's pure discrimination. Cunts. But that's prison in a nutshell for you. It's so full of shit and muggy rules it's more like Disneyland. It's time to wake up, governors, and get real! Either we get punishment or we don't. You can't have half a punishment. If I lose my canteen then I lose it; you won't hear me crying about it. But if you're allowing smoke—rs to buy smokes then you're just taking the piss. Why? It's enough to start me off smoking! You cunts, what a fucking insane jail this is. It's all Loonyology to me.

Did you know 30 million people in UK are on Prozac? That's a mountain of pills, that's a lot of weak people. Pack it in, wake up and be thankful for being alive. A bottle of pills won't put anything right. It's all in the mind. You don't need Prozac. The best pill is the reality of life. Wake up.

26 February 2008.

Today I found out who some of the actors are in the movie. Andrew Forbes is playing my dad, Kelly Adams is playing my first wife, Hugh Ross is playing my uncle Jack, and the beautiful and lovely Amanda Burton is playing my mum. That's all I know to date, apart from that my old mate Terry Stone is playing a screw in Rampton Asylum, so no doubt he'll be jumping all over Tom Hardy's head. Such is life. That's all life is: a kick in the head!

Get on this for madness. A so-called friend of mine, Charmaine Maeer, sent me a photo and I stuck it on my website on the 'Friends' page. All my friends are on there and are honoured to be on there! (Mark Emmins sticks them on for me.) So she goes on it and next thing she's getting her mummy and an ex-boyfriend to email Mark to get it off – even threatening legal action! Well, fuck off. It's in the bin. It's that simple, you ungrateful bitch! Some friend. I would sooner have a pet rat. Why send me the poxy photo in the first place? Mark's got better things to do than fuck about with loonies. So that's the end of that! Fuck off.

Friends today just come and go. They blow hot and cold then burn up. In the trenches they would run and leave you! Fucking traitors.

Out on the yard today it was so windy, it was brilliant – all that beautiful wind in my face and in my lungs. I felt 21 again. I was running around like a whippet and I actually felt happy! When it was time to come in I shot in the shower. Our shower has a locked iron gate on it so they just lock me in and fuck off. I do like a shower but I enjoy a bath better! I've not had a bath for years. What would I do for a good soak in a bath with a woman? God, what I would do for that? Even a session in the shower would be nice. Why not? I'm only human!

I see another dirty nonce copped life at the Old Bailey yesterday: 20-stone Levi Bellfield who killed 19-year-old Marsha McDonnell and 22-year-old Amelie Delegrange. Two cracking girls, two beauties, wiped out by the beast. He raped and bashed up other young girls too. Guess what? He will be here next week. Let's be honest, he should be on the gallows with a noose around his neck. Fucking dirty nonce! What good is he alive to anybody? It's a great shame the girls' fathers can't have 10 minutes with him in a bare cell. I wonder how he would like having his skull smashed in like a watermelon? Cunt.

Who remembers the 'Jersey Beast' – evil paedophile Edward Paisnel? He copped 30 years in 1971 for raping young boys. Thirty years in 1971 tells you how bad he was. He terrified the island of Jersey for years. No boy was safe. He ended up serving 20 years and died soon after he got out. I remember the old cunt in Albany jail; he used to walk past the seg block and we used to squirt piss at him out of shampoo bottles. Dirty bastard.

I got a load of letters today and made a phone call to Mark Emmins. All in all it was a great day. Here's me all happy and positive and all those twats in prison HQ are all bitter and negative! So who's really winning? Cunts.

Did you know in Whitemoor prison five cons have committed suicide in the last 14 months? That's a death every three months. What's prison HQ doing about that? Fuck all. Like I keep saying, it's all a big piss-take! It's Loonyology. I bet they keep dreaming of Bronson taking himself to Heaven. Fucking idiots... keep dreaming!

I see Razor Smith's just written his third book in prison: *Warrior Kings*. If it's only half as good as his last two it will be well worth a read. Good on you, Razor. It beats robbing banks, mate. They should let you out now. It's fucking obvious you can make a good honest living outside from writing. It's prison HQ again. I told you: they're a bunch of wankers. They let out the cons who everybody knows will reoffend and they keep in the cons that are no danger. Fucking idiots.

Hey! I've got a cheese roll for supper and a pint of tea with two tea bags and a spoon of brown sugar. Am I lucky or am I lucky? Come on, how lucky am I? My cell is lovely and warm, I'm clean, I've got fresh clothes and I've even got a bed! Fuck 'em all, I'm happy! I may even create a piece of art later! Why not?

Why do Kamikaze pilots wear helmets? And are people who eat alphabet soup smarter than those who don't? Food for thought!!!

Summer 1985

"What a summer
What a roof
Did I enjoy it?
Do bears shit in the wood?
Beautiful
It was wonderful
Poetry in motion
Liverpool I love you
What a roof

What a memory
A part of history
My journey of life
Destruction
Flying tiles
A flying roof
Liverpool jail
May you rot and burn in Hell."

27 February 2008.
Fuck me, there was an earthquake last night which rocked the UK. Eat your heart out, Los Angeles. It would have been brilliant if the walls of this monster mansion had fallen down. I could have crawled out of the rubble and done a runner. What a result. It would have taken them months to clear it all up and by the time they'd realised I'd gone I would have been in South American for a few weeks shagging some Brazilian beauty. One can dream. A fucking earthquake… you couldn't make it up, could you?

I've been hungry all day. I fancy a big roast with loads of spuds, chicken, Brussels and gravy, but I've got a poxy cheese and onion pie! A fucking mouse gets more than that!

It's an early night for me. I hope that earthquake comes back.

What about Kate Knight getting 30 years for poisoning her husband with anti-freeze in his curry? I've always said you never know what's in a 'Ruby Murray'. Stick to a good old English dish. Anyway, Kate's now fucked. Thirty years is a long time for a woman. And guess what? Her old man survived, so it's 30 years for a botched job! Her best bet is to become a lesbo. Plenty of beaver diving for you, Kate, because you're not going to see a cock in a long time, or get your hands on any more anti-freeze. Fuck having a meal with you.

Strangely enough, I had a chicken curry myself tonight, with a nice lump of chicken in it too.

It's 29 February 2008. A leap year. Surely this has got to be my last leap year inside? It must be. Fuck another four wasted years – what for? Come on, get that campaign moving and let's get me out!!

I got a big parcel sent in today from Tel Currie, who's sorted me out with some of his dad's training clobber: proper quality Lonsdale shorts and top and a tie. I'll wear them when I'm out in respect for his dad! I'll be proud to wear them. There's a cracking photo of Tel and his dad in my first *Loonyology* book – they're together like two peas in a pod.

I had a dream
A beautiful field of flowers
Butterflies and bees
Grasshoppers and ladybirds
The sun was shining
My body felt warm and glowing
I lay down and felt so happy
I could smell the freedom

The breeze on my face
The grass on my skin
I felt so relaxed
It was heavenly
Paradise
Pure serenity
So peaceful
A bird was singing
A song thrush
It was beautiful
I watched a skylark
And a pigeon fly by
How can anybody feel so free and happy?
A beautiful butterfly landed on my arm
It seemed to have all the colours of a rainbow
It's such a long time since I've seen such beauty
Everything seemed so real
Even the trees were smiling at me
I had a dream
She lay beside me
Naked as the day she was born
I could smell her on my lips
The smell of love
I could taste her
But I could never touch her
It was only a dream
I awoke in a padded room
My head hurt
The smell turned to shit
There was no butterfly
There was no skylark
There is only emptiness
A room full of pain
An asylum full of shame
This strait jacket itches me
It's not good for the skin
It's not good for humanity
It's ripped out my soul
I'm lost in a dream
I want to bite some fucker's throat out
Some bully boy guard with a bunch of keys
They're all dehumanising me
Degrading me
Humiliating me
Why?
Coz I'm Charlie Bronson
They don't need any other reason
This is Loonyology at its very best
Pushed off the edge like Humpty Dumpty

Lost in time
Floating in space
This is the mad house
The big house on top of the hill
This is the place of broken dreams
Welcome to the dream…
It died so long ago
It's now history
A fucking life mare…
Wake up and scream
Wake up and die
This is real
Broadmoor.

Did you know a flea can jump the equivalent of a human jumping over the Empire State building? That's what I call a jump. And here's one for the ladies: there's a geezer in South America with a 14-inch cock. Now if that doesn't hit the g-spot then nothing will. I bet that would make all the gay lads' eyes water.

CHAPTER 3

Loony letters to Uncle Charlie

What a fucking laugh…
I love you all!

It's time for the 'Agony Uncle' chapter. You know you all love it. By the way, there's talk about my own page in the *Sunday Sport*. What a job!

Dear Charlie,
Q – I read your book *Loonyology: In My Own Words*. Is it true you once knocked a cow out?
Danny from Doncaster

A – Danny, it's not something I like to go on about! But I'll tell you who I will knock out: Frank Cook, from your neck of the woods. He wrote a book called *Hard Cell* and said I'm gonna kill him on sight. Fucking idiot. I don't believe in killing people. I prefer to torture the fuckers, especially cunts like Cook.

Chaz,
Q – I've read all of your books and I think you're an ace bloke. I'm 18 years old and still a virgin. Would you take my cherry, Chaz? Please?
Nina from Scotland

A – Any time, any place, anywhere… keep it sweet for me, Nina!

Hi Charles,
Q – My mum says you once went out with her before I was born, so you could be my dad. I'm 19 years old.
Danny from Dover

A – Danny, fuck off…

Charles,
Q – What's the best thing for a fanny rash?
Beryl from Bristol
A – Well, Beryl, you haven't really told me a lot about the rash! It could be a heat rash but maybe you're allergic to some fabric or you've caught a nasty disease. Or maybe you're just a dirty bitch in the hygiene department. It could be one of many things. But why ask me, I'm no doctor. Go and give it a good wash.

Dear Mr Bronson,
Q – I did read the first *Loonyology* book and I think you're a bloody disgrace. What gives you the right to give people advice? You're a lunatic ex-Broadmoor patient and you're pretending to be an Agony Aunt. I'm reporting you to the Home Secretary!
Mr S Jackson, London.

A – I'm an Agony Uncle not an aunt. And you're a cunt, OK? Now fuck off!

Dear Charlie,
Q – I'm a 19-year-old girl and I enjoy masturbation but I can't seem to climax! Have you any tips?
Carol from Luton.

A – I note you're from my town... maybe we can get together sometime. It would be so much easier for me to show you the best way to climax. I normally charge £75 an hour, Carol, but for you I'll do it for a bull's eye! I'll get your clitty standing up like a chocolate penguin. I'll even give it a good lick to get you started. You can count on me, sweetheart. I salute all the clitties and believe me, I've seen plenty – little tiny ones and big long fatty ones, but they all work with a little rub. Have some faith in me... and have your 50 quid ready.

Dear Charlie,
Q – I read the first *Loonyology* book and thought it was a load of bollocks. Then I met somebody you had helped with a problem – I should say a serious problem with sex. Now she can't get enough of it, so you do give good advice.
Charmaine from Bedford.

A – I try, thank you.

Hi Chaz,
Q – After sex I always have a sore helmet. Any suggestions?
Billy from Brighton.

A – Yeah Bill, this can be a problem for some of the chaps. You're probably going at it too rough. Chill out and slow down... nice easy strokes. Be gentle with your lady – or fella. After sex, give the old soldier a good rub with some oil. Look after it. Your cock is priceless, OK?

Dear Chaz,
Q – I don't think sex is all that. I find it quite boring and uncomfortable. I prefer chocolates and figs and cakes myself. What have you got to say about that?
Emma, Sunderland.

A – Not a lot, you fat cunt!

Charlie,
Q – My husband is so small it's laughable. And he comes so bloody quick it's all over before I get wet. What do you suggest Charlie?
P.S. I have considered another lover!
Liz from Luton

A – I see you're another Luton lass. Look, let's not pretend here, your old man's a freak! And it is true girls like big cocks and big cocks are better. So what you have to decide is: are you prepared to spend the rest of your life with that little prick or are you off? It's your life, Liz, don't throw it away. I bet you're dreaming of a big fat cock, you poor tortured woman. Write to me again with your mobile number as I've had an idea. I've got a big sex orgy coming up soon and I'll sort you all the cock you can dream of. OK, Liz?

Chaz,
Q – Can I catch a disease by sucking my boyfriend's willie? And if I swallow can I get pregnant?
Sophie from Cardiff.

A – Blimey... have you just landed from Mars? Yes, you can catch a disease if your fella has a dirty bell-end and no, you can't get pregnant if you swallow. OK, love?

Mr Bronson,
Q – I'm a very old lady and I've not had sex for over 30 years. Do you think I should do it again? I've got a son who's 63 and a daughter of 67. That will give you an idea of how old I am. I'm just wondering if I should go out with a bang!
Rose from Berkshire.

A – Bloody hell, you've thrown me here, Rose. I'm not sure what to say! What do you want me to say? If you go for it, good on you, girl. Enjoy it. What a way to go.

Charlie,
Q – Every time I laugh I pee myself and it's becoming very embarrassing.
Eileen from Ellesmere Port.

A – Eileen, it's the incontinent panties for you! Get 'em on and laugh yourself silly.

Dear Charles,
Q – I've been a widower for the last nine years. I'm only 42. My body's not bad, so do you think I should go for a new man?
Carol from Durham.

A – Carol, nine years is a long time to be alone! You have got to move on, darling, you really have. There is so much life left in you. Don't waste it, enjoy it. Join the Loonyology club and have a bloody good time. A good old-fashioned shag will light up your world. 42 is young. I bet you're gorgeous! So get out there and grab yourself a cock or two and show them what it's all about. Why not create your own porno film? It'll be something to look back on when you're 82! Enjoy life, Carol. You've got a pussy so use it! Don't let it dry up and crumble. Live life and be mad.

Charlie,
Q – I'm a 19-year-old student and I live with four other girls. We are all similar ages. The only problem is they're lesbians and I'm not, so I've got to watch it all. As we share a small one-bedroom flat I'm waking up to things I don't really wish to see. It's just one big sex marathon. Do you think I should move out, Charlie?
Lyn from Oxford.

A – WOW!! What would I do to watch all that! Well, Lyn, it's a tough one to answer! Look, why don't you secretly film it all and send it to me to see it? I can then analyse it and maybe come up with something. Better still, you move out and I'll move in. Another thought: why don't you get a strap-on 14-inch black mamba and give them all a good fucking? It will be a good laugh and a good experience – you could even charge other students to watch. You'll soon pay off your credit debt. Lyn, you need a good think, you really do.

Dear Charles,
Q – I'm only 22 but I'm flat-chested. Apart from that I'm perfect: pretty, slim, sexy and happy. Do you think I should have implants? My boyfriend says I should!
Cathy from Winchester.

A – Cathy, don't do it. I'll tell you why not: it's your body, not his. And let me tell you something else: big tits aren't everything. Sure they look sexy but it's the nipple that counts! And you've said yourself you're perfect!! I bet you're fucking gorgeous. There's nothing wrong with small tits. Hey! If he doesn't like them, you can always stick them in my 'boat'. Big tits, little tits, no tits! If you had three tits I'd still love you! Honestly, Cathy, start to love yourself! You're you, you're unique, you're hot and sexy! And Loonyology loves you! OK, babe? X

Dear Charlie,
Q – My dad knew you in Parkhurst back in the early 1970s. I wasn't even born then, but he told me before he died: "Charles Bronson is bloody crackers." (But he said it in a nice way, Charlie.) I just thought you might like to know!
Stella in Newport.

A – Stella, thanks! Sorry to hear the old man's dead. Move on and do him proud.

Mr Bronson,
Q – I work for the Bedfordshire Probation Service and I think what you're doing is actually illegal. You have absolutely no qualifications on giving anybody advice! For God's sake, you have been inside for all of your adult life! You have been certified insane! You're a violent thug! A dangerous armed robber! What right have you got to act the social worker?
Beryl in Bedfordshire.

A – That's very hurtful, Beryl. You sure know how to hurt a man's feelings! If people write to me for advice, what else can I do? I'm only trying to help others. What do you want me to do? I'm sorry that you feel this way about me, but it's your opinion and you're entitled to it. People do change you know. Life has a way of mellowing us all down. You obviously don't like me so I'll leave it at that! Good luck in life, Beryl. Try not to be so bitter and hateful. If you need any help, don't be afraid to ask! I'm here, Beryl, even for you.

Charlie,
Q – I've got a problem. I'm a 19-year-old lad, just a normal guy, nothing special. But every time I catch a bus I get a big hard-on, I can't help it, and it's so bad I end up staying on the bus after my stop. Sometimes I'm five

or six miles away from my stop! How can I sort this problem out, Charlie? What would you do?
Dave from Clacton-on-Sea.

A – Yeah, we've all been there, Dave! Trains, buses, taxis, planes, ships! A hard-on just comes with the rocking about. It's the motion, the movement and the thoughts. At 19 it's pussy on pussy – you dream it, you live it! You can't get enough of it. It's a constant hard-on. That's why a lot of middle-aged women grab a toy boy. Be proud of the bulge – it's sure to make some bored housewife smile or some bird cream her panties. You could carry a paper or book to cover it. It's all life's journey, Dave. Enjoy it whilst you're young. Some old chaps would kill to have a hard-on like that. Be proud, stand proud! OK?

Charlie,
Q – I loved the first *Loonyology* book! Will there be more?
Sally from Burton-on-Trent.

A – Well, Sally! Here's Volume 2… and you can bet your arse on there being a 3 and 4 and 5. Why not, I say. I used to know a bird in Burton-on-Trent who could open a bottle top with her arse, but that's another story…

Dear Charlie,
Q – My dog is getting very horny when we are together. He rubs his dick up against my leg and I'm amazed at the size of it. I'm starting to get some strange urges. Am I sick?
Anne from Rhyl

A – Anne. Look love, you won't be the first or the last to have a fuck with a pet. Look at Rose West: Fred used to take her in a field and let a horse fuck her silly. A horse! It's obvious to me the dog fancies you, so why not give it a go? You may enjoy it! Let's be honest, you could do worse! Some men are animals and will treat you like shit. A dog will always stay loyal to you! You never said what sort of dog it is – some dogs are very good looking. I get a lot of letters from the more mature ladies in their '50s and '60s who love a good dog licking. Apparently the dog loves it too. All these ladies climax with multiple orgasms, so you could be in for a treat, Anne. Good luck. (Send me some photos.)

Hi Charlie,
Q – I'm a 52-year-old man, married for 31 years with four kids (all grown up and left home). The wife and me have recently joined a nudist club and a wife swap club. The reason is I actually enjoy seeing my wife get a good shagging by a younger man. I can't help it, it just turns me on! She now laughs at me. Have I destroyed our marriage?
George from Bristol.

A – George, we all have our little 'kinky ways' but I suggest you do a bit more than watch. Your wife sounds like she enjoys a lot of sex. If you don't give it to her, what do you expect! I suggest that once a partner has given her a good seeing to, why don't you then jump on and finish her off? Give the old girl a treat! Surprise her and let the others watch for a change! Be the stallion, not the donkey!

Charlie,
My fanny dries up every time my boyfriend gets close to sex. Then when he goes to put it in, it hurts! So we don't have sex, I always end up pulling him off and my wrist aches. What can we do, Charlie?
Fiona from Manchester.

A – This seems to be a problem for a lot of young couples. I get lots of letters on this dryness of the fanny. You've got to start relaxing and your fella has got to be gentle! Lots of fingering and licking. You've got to show him how to get the clitty working and get those juices flowing; he should then be able to slip it in easily. Try a bit of lubricant. I'm sure you can work this out together. Try it in the bath, in the shower. Try yogurt. Dip his cock in it, that's a sure way, and then after he can lick you clean, in and out. I do wish you well, Fiona! If by chance you're just one of those with a very tight, dry pussy then try it up the bum. Up the bum, have some fun, lots of KY Jelly and you'll be sure to come... Good luck, Fiona.

Charlie,
Q – You really are insane! I've read all your books, you're fucking mental, totally off your rocker!
Jim from Dover.

A – Fuck off! Keep buying my books, you cunt!

Dear Chaz,
Q – I've got a big lump on my cock and my girlfriend says it's ugly! What can I do?
Sid from Grimshaw.

A – Get a new girlfriend.

Hi Chaz,
Q – My girlfriend won't stop drawing a face on my bell-end with her lipstick. What would you do about it?
Ernie from Sheffield.

A – Draw one on her fanny lips!

Mr Bronson,
Q – Is it wrong to fall in love with yourself? And is it dangerous?
Rupert from Rochester.

A – You are one freaky fucker, you are! I remember your last letter some time back wanting to know how to suck three men off at the same time with a Mickey Mouse mask on. Please don't write to me again. Go fuck yourself to death.

Charlie
Q – My mum reckons you make all these questions up yourself and nobody writes to you.
Lucy from Lincoln.

A – Lucy, your letter's here! (Tell your mum to go suck an egg!)

Chaz,
Q – I've just come out of jail after serving 31 years of a life sentence. I killed four gay men – strangled them – now I find it hard to get a partner. Oh! I am gay now, but as soon as they find out my past they don't want anything to do with me.
Cyril from Dunstable.

A – I wonder why?

Charlie,
Q – Do you believe in life after death?
Joe from Nottingham.

A – I believe in life after life!

Hi Chaz,
Q – I'm a 39-year-old married woman with two kids. I've started to read your books and play with myself. I can't help myself. Am I going mad or what, Chaz?
Sue from Bexleyheath.

A – Sue. Come on, send me a photo! Please! And don't come over my books!

Charlie,
Q – What's the best sex position to get full penetration? I say it's doggy-style but my partner says it's with me on top of him!
Jackie from Kingston.

A – Jackie! It's doggy! You're right.

Hey... that's brought back a crazy memory of mine. I was shagging a bird doggy-style once when she let rip – I mean a massive fart. It put me right off, it almost blew my balls off and it frightened the life out of me. I couldn't go on after that. In those days I didn't think birds farted! Or shat! Or had smelly feet! Or picked their nose! Love's a crazy thing, we all get hooked up in it! It's a drug. How many have died over love? More people die in love than hate! It's a fact. Don't fart, girls – it really does put a man off. It's not good for the soul. Angels never fart, do they?

Life is to be enjoyed.
Don't forget to smell the flowers as you go.
If you decide to be happy in life
Then you're halfway there.

I see Saddam Hussein's cousin, Chemical Ali, is to hang this month! He gassed 200,000 Kurds in the 1980s, or so they say... I don't believe fuck all on the Iraq War, do you? It's just like one big lie after another! Never trust a politician, they're all fucking liars!

Get on this prick, Shayne Haynes. He leaves his house with a fucking big kitchen knife and sticks it in a prostitute's neck. He gets life for murder and he must serve no less than 15 years. Why only 15 years? Why not 30 years? Was this not premeditated murder? I can never understand British law. It's total bollocks; they make it up as they go along. Haynes is 22 years old now. He will be 37 when he gets out. Geraldine Brocklehurst, who he killed, won't be getting out of her coffin will she? If the truth be known he probably only got 15 years because she was a prostitute, so who cares? I bet her family do!

Look at Harry Roberts, now in his 43rd year of a life sentence. 43 fucking years, but his life tariff was 30 years. So by law he has been held for 13 illegal years. If he had killed a few prostitutes or a couple of kids and raped a granny or two, would he still be locked up? Would he fuck. It makes a mockery out of justice!

Hey! Get on this next bit you're about to read from another ex-screw, this time a female one. What does it tell you all? What have I been saying for years? Why isn't anybody listening to us? This is a woman who used to unlock my door on a max secure unit in Woodhill prison five years ago! She knows me better than any prison HQ official or any prison governor. Was she afraid of Charlie Bronson? Was she fuck! Read it and digest it!

26th February 2008

Re Charlie Bronson

Dear Sir

My name is Mandy Quinn I am an ex Prison Officer I left the Service over 5 years ago but from time to time I look at the Prison Service web site just to see what is new and also from time to time I search the web for information on Charlie Bronson.

To date I cannot understand how the justice system operates and how society in the UK changes so much. I live in Spain and whenever I listen to the UK news it is full of stories of stabbings etc. This is sad but what also comes to light how soft the system is on these criminals when caught especially when you compare the time that Charlie Bronson has served without even killing anyone. Any open minded person must ask WHY?

When I look back at the time I spent working on the CSU unit at HMP Woodhill I often think to myself how challenging my job was working with some of the UK's non conformist prisoners.

However one of those prisoners who I worked with was Charlie Bronson. I had heard a lot about Charlie throughout my career prior to meeting him at HMP Woodhill the picture that was painted was that this man was a very dangerous person, so you can imagine my thoughts when I was aware I would be working with him!

Well all the concerns I may have had prior to meeting Charlie were in retrospect not necessary as during my time on the unit I never once felt threatened by this so called dangerous criminal!

Many times I would stand by Charlie's cell door and chat to him for half an hour or more about life in general. During this time Charlie always was polite and respectful to me. Even on the odd occasion he was unlocked from his cell he would always acknowledge me in a polite manner. Never once did I feel threatened in my job by Charlie.

This is why I ask myself what has he done that is so bad to keep him locked up for as long as he has been, especially when you see criminals today getting far less sentences for more horrendous crimes!

I am aware he has had his moments but we all mature in time and look for a more settled life and I am sure Charlie must feel the same way. I firmly believe that this man should be given a chance in life so why are they authorities not doing something about it?

In my opinion and this was at least 5 years ago when I worked with him he was a man who gave respect to those who respected him and I am sure 5 years on he will be the same. If not the same probably even better as he gets no younger.

I hope you have success in the future

Kind Regards

Mandy Quinn

Thanks, Mandy. I hope life's good for you out in Spain. Now see what I mean? Mandy sent this to my website in support of my freedom campaign. It says it all, and she's not on her own – I get sack loads of support letters and statements. It just proves everything I say to you – my incarceration is illegal and the time is long overdue for me to be freed from all this madness that's being stuffed down my neck. At times I can't breathe. I'm choking on the insanity of life!

Hey! I'll tell you who's fucking mental: Fat Joe Purkiss. Joe's a Leeds guy who copped a life sentence a good 20 years ago. He's spent all of it on max secure units. The last time I bumped into him was in Woodhill some years back. He won't mind me saying that he looks like that fat cartoon character in *Popeye* who eats all the grub. Joe's two cans short of a six-pack! He's got a good heart but a tiny brain. He once took a hostage here in Wakefield jail and demanded a fry-up and a six-pack of beer! All he got was 20 screws jumping on his head and 10 more years added to his sentence. The last I heard of Joe, he was down on the special unit in Whitemoor. I doubt if he'll ever get out and I doubt he wants to! He's happy! He loves his pot of tea and toast! He's just a happy-go-lucky guy until you upset him. He used to piss through the gap in the cell door on the screws; he was always up to something mad. Mad people are actually very smart at times; they do things that seem impossible to the sane. This is what Loonyology is all about!

I remember back in 1985 when I was slung back into prison from the asylums after nine years of Loonyology. I ended up in my old battle ground of Walton jail in Liverpool. From day one I was treated as a leper. The reception I got was amazing, it was like I was a mad tiger and the screws were just dying to cage me! I ended up being smashed to bits and slung into the hospital strong box trussed up like a Xmas turkey.

It's a fact of life: the system fears madness! Madness breeds paranoia, so they get in fast and hard. They are waiting for you, they love a challenge. It's a fight you can never win. If they don't kill you they will cripple you – mentally, physically, even spiritually. To them it's a 'problem' that will be 'resolved' one way or another. You have to be smart, bide your time and plan ahead. There won't always be 10 screws to open your door. You need to remember certain faces, smile, and play the waiting game. A lot of these screws are cowards when they're on their own and they know you know it. I've caught them with pots of shit. I got one in Wandsworth with a tin of Marvel full of shit. Bosh! Right in the face… OK, it will cost you a month's canteen, it may even cost you another kicking, but it works. That screw will take that to his grave with him! It's in his mouth, in his ears, all down his crisp white shirt! He stands there, empty in shock. You see him heave his guts up and it's fucking brilliant. It's get-back time. It does work: he becomes a different screw after that! He treads on egg shells. Every time he opens a cell door he thinks, "Could it happen again? I'd better not be nasty anymore!" That's how to handle a bully-boy in jail: dehumanise him.

Shit can be powerful armour in times of need! I've even rubbed it on my naked body to stop another beating. When you're in the strong box and you hear them all outside getting ready to come in and set about you, have a shit and cover yourself with it. They won't come in then. Would you? And shit dries with the body heat and crumbles off! Sure it sounds disgusting, it's filthy, but what else can you do in times of madness? I've even used my shit and blood to write on a cell wall to communicate with a doctor or governor. They look through the Judas hole and read it!

I wouldn't wish to go back to how it was in the 1970s and '80s but I would if I had no choice. My fear would be to go back down that road where the light goes off and I can't come back; that would be it for me. My end would be insanity, out of control. It would be like being buried alive in a coffin – a living nightmare, a man's worst nightmare. And the truth is that could really happen! I pray it never does but fate can be cruel. Who knows what backlash there will be once my movie is out? It could get a lot of young screws wanting to make a name for themselves. Jumping on Bronson's head is a medal for them, believe it. And the scary truth is that they have a licence to do it any time they get the urge.

"Yes sir, we attacked him before he attacked us! We could see it in his eyes. He had been brooding for a week, sir. We had to take him down."

"Well done lads. You did right!"

How can I win?

Hey! Get on this: that 20-stone monster Bellfield who got lifed off recently, his nickname at school used to be 'rabbit shagger' because he got caught shagging his sister's rabbit. But he's not on his own – you'd be amazed at how many people get it on with animals. Thomas and Jane Bamford made a video of themselves having sex with a pony and a dog and called it 'Dolly's Farm'. A fucking foursome with a dog and a pony and your wife. Fuck me, where do these people come from?

What about Stephen Hall? He got caught buggering a goat in a field. A train stopped and all the passengers watched it happen. He had a belt around its neck and he was shagging it silly. One of the passengers said, "The goat looked happy."

Mark Woollen got banned for life from every field in Britain for indecently assaulting a horse.

Here's a blinder, you'll love this one. One serial horse shagger out in California tried it the other way and let the stallion shag him. He died being sodomised by the horse. His colon and lower organs ruptured and burst open! Fuck me, you can't make this shit up!

There was a woman in France caught on CCTV giving a bull a wank. She didn't even realise she was being filmed. The bull loved it; so did she! She was seen tasting the bulls cum. That's not all, she sneaked back in the farm and did a lot more. Have you seen the size of a bull's dick? Yeah, it all goes on down farmer Giles farm. You bet your sweet little arse on it. (No, maybe not your arse, just in case.)

I see Mike Smith died just recently. Who? Yeah, you may well ask! Mike was in the Dave Clarke Five – a big group in the 1960s. They had smash hits with 'Glad All Over' and 'Bits and Pieces'. They were a good group in their day, if not one of the best. The Swinging Sixties, eh? Flower power, mods and rockers, beatniks, rockers, teddy boys, we had the lot. Make love not war, ban the bomb! We even landed on the moon. It was a good era… or was it? I often wonder. The Stones recorded '19th Nervous Breakdown' and every fucker was having a breakdown, but the crime scene was brilliant. That's when the villains ruled, believe it.

Heard the one about the psychic dwarf who escaped from prison? They're looking for a small medium at large!

Executioner Albert Pierrepoint used to run a pub in Oldham called Help the Poor Struggler, where James Corbitt was a regular. Guess what, Albert ended up hanging him in 1950. Fuck drinking with him, who wants to drink in a fucking hangman's boozer! I could never work out why Pierrepoint never got a visit off the 'chaps'. Everybody knew he ran the pub and everybody knew he was the state's executioner. Why didn't anybody pop in and 'serve him up'? I'm amazed about that, especially when he topped Ruth Ellis.

When Pierrepoint topped John George Haigh (the 'acid-bath killer') in 1949 in Wandsworth jail, Haigh asked a guard the day before if he could possibly have a trial run so that everything would run smoothly the next day! You couldn't make this shit up even if you tried. Haigh got convicted for six murders but he confessed to 10. Still, if it's six, 10 or 110, they can only top you the once. Once you fell through that trap door it was all over for sure. I suppose you could call it the original 'suspended sentence'! (Not a bad joke that – I just made it up!)

I wish they had hanged Ian Brady and Myra Hindley. That pair of cunts only missed it by a year or two. Be honest, don't you get fed up of reading and hearing about them? For over 40 years that pair of monsters have been in the media. If they'd been hanged, we would have forgotten about them long ago. It's a fact. As it is they're practically celebrities. How fucking sick is that? We now have Ian Huntley to take their place – that is till somebody rips his throat out. It will happen, no surer bet. Go to William Hill and see what odds they will put on that. It'd be a good bet!

Here's another monster on his way to the mansion: Colin Norris. This prick has just got four life sentences for murdering 80-year-old Doris Ludlam, 88-year-old Bridget Bourke, 86-year-old Ethel Hall and 79-year-old Irene Crookes. (I know a Billy Crookes. Norris wants to start praying Irene's not related to him because Billy would get himself nicked to come to jail and rip this fucker's throat out.) This creep was a nurse and killing old folk. Fuck me, how sick does it get? He's got to be the new Harold Shipman! When he gets here they will probably give him a job in the hospital wing. Nothing shocks me anymore. The world's gone insane, it's all Loonyology.

I see that Paul Raymond, the king of porn, has died aged 88. He owned 60 of Soho's 87 acres, that's worth a lot of dosh – £650 million. I would say he had a great journey through life. What a journey. He must have seen every type of pussy on earth! What a job, what a dream! He lived the dream! Respect to the old chap. R.I.P.

Warren Slanney arrived here a month back from Frankland jail. Ten black guys jumped him but he fought back like a good 'un. Fuck knows why they sent him here and put him up on the wing. Warren's a top geezer, I've known him for years! He was a good boxer in his day. Anyway, some cunts smashed him over the head with a pool cue. It's all fucking happening! It's a violent old world in which we live. If that was my head, I would have taken the cue off the guy and rammed it right up his arsehole. You only get one shot with me, believe it.

Warren is old school, he'll ride it and make a comeback on it. 'Ding Ding… Round 2…' He knocked a screw out in Woodhill some years back. One punch and it was good night, Mr Jailer. When Warren hits you, you stay hit.

5 March 2008.

I called Dave Courtney tonight. He's a good buddy to have in your corner and he told me my movie will be a winner. There's a big buzz going on about it outside! Every fucker's talking about it. In one scene that was shot yesterday I'm strangling John White in the middle of the day room in Rampton asylum. The room is full of lunatics all laughing as I'm choking this paedophile to death. Picture the scene. Cor, it brings back sweet memories. This piece of shit raped and mutilated a little girl, so don't ask why I took such drastic action – I just don't like monsters. Sadly, he survived the attack as the screws jumped all over my head, but it was good whilst it lasted. Can you believe that was 30 years ago? Anyway, you'll see it in the movie. Hope you enjoy it. I did.

I got a dozen letters today. Some crackers! Oh, and Sandra Gardner sent me in some shorts and a vest! That was a really nice surprise. It's a great day and the sun's out too! I saw two crows on top of the exercise yard, they were watching me run around. Crows don't miss a lot, they're very alert birds – a bit like me when I'm walking down a street, especially when I see a security van pull up outside a bank! I come alive, my senses kick in, my heart starts up with the rush… know what I mean? I don't suppose you do and it's best you don't. Keep on walking, don't look back.

The Loony Train.

Hop on, hop on, and take a ride
It's going all the way
No stops
All the way to the mad zone.
Tickets are free
Hop on. "Relax and sleep"
Take a chill pill
Sleep the ride away
Wake up in a new world
Learn a new way of life
In my world we are all the same
Certified criminally insane
One laughs, we all laugh
One cries, we all laugh
One dies, we all laugh
The loony train never stops
It's going all the way
To the end of the world
Accept it, and ride
Feel it
Hear it
Smell it
Taste it
Become it
Enjoy the ride
It's full up with characters
Legendary loons
Men of madness
Bulging eyes
Stone features
Men that lurk in the shadows
Crazy nightmare people
Exciting
Fucking scary fuckers
The loony train
No ticket… just your life
No luggage… just you
Welcome to the ride
The end of the world

It's time to step inside
Leave behind all the shit
All the pain and misery
All the broken dreams
All the lies
All those freaky 'normal people'
The rat-race
Squeaky little soulless pricks
Clock-work puppets
"Yes sir, no sir, shag my arse, sir"
Prats
"I paid more tax than you"
"I've got a new car"
"My kids are better than yours"
"We went to Jamaica for our holiday"
We done this
We done that
We've got this
What have you got?
"Fuck you"
Fuck face
I'm on the loony train
The ride to freedom
You never wake up
It's a way of life
A new living
The heart pumps
But it's dead
You don't dream
You are the dream
Everything's magically unreal
Like a blow to the skull
Like a blade in your leg
You don't scream
You laugh
You don't cry... you bleed
You flow away into oblivion
That's the end
The loony train
Strait jackets and padded cells
A blood-splattered ceiling
A pot full of shit
A rat chewing your ear
A cockroach in your face
Crawling up your nose
Crawling into your head
Laying eggs in your brain
That's the end
You're eaten alive

What a way to go
What an exit
The loony train.

They say that when you're about to die your whole life flashes past you. Fuck me – we've got to see it all again.

6 March 2008.

Mark Fish was up today so I got all the latest on the movie. Today they're filming the Broadmoor roof job – that should be a laugh… I hope Tom's not afraid of heights! Broadmoor's got one of the old Victorian roofs, the best sort of roof for a good old-fashioned protest with the real old slate tiles! They're very expensive, that's why I used to smash them to bits – make the cunts pay for my incarceration!

Yeah, the movie's doing great… only five more weeks of filming! It'll be out in March 2009 and it'll be worth seeing, I promise you that. This isn't just a movie, it's my journey through Loonyology. It's fucking mental. One blink and you're in a padded room. Two blinks and you're lost forever, buried inside your own life mare. Don't blink, stay awake, stay alert, stare back into the face of adversity, spit in the eyes of the devil. He's not so tough when you get him on his own. Grab his throat and rip it out.

I'll see you at the premiere. YIPPPEEEeeeeeeeee. Don't be late! I'll be the one in the black suit with the trilby on.

Hey, I'll tell you who's a cunt: Mick Burridge. He got life for killing a baby. He shook it to death. Big brave fucker. Somebody wants to shake him to death. What sort of dad could do that to his own baby? Cunt. Welcome to monster mansion.

I see Patrick Swayze's got cancer of the pancreas, that's one of the worst to get. If you're going to get cancer, then this is the one not to get. Pavarotti died of that, so did Magnus Magnusson and Syd Barrett of the Pink Floyd. Very few ever survive it!

See what I mean about life and death? It comes and goes like the weather. Here today and gone tomorrow. All the dosh in the world can't save you when it's your time to go, so enjoy life whilst you're alive – you just don't know what's around the corner! Hell, it could be me waiting there with a big axe just for old time's sake. Enjoy your life, it's brilliant.

Did you know the smallest gun in the world is just two inches long? The pigmy pistol is made by Paul Erard and it will cost you three grand. It fires a 4.53mm bullet at 300mph! It can be lethal. Paul used to be a watchmaker and the man's a genius. "Make my day, punk."

I'll tell you who's another cunt: Chris Hawkins. He got life for stabbing his four-year-old son to death. That's what I call a filthy monster! The judge said he must serve at least 21 years. Yeah, big deal. I'd make it 51 years. Nine times he stabbed that boy. Cunt. Why do they do it? Does anybody really know? Or are they just born evil? It's fucking senseless.

Kate Knight (who got 30 years for poisoning her husband with anti-freeze) wrote a letter to a pen-friend from HM Prison Foston Hall saying the jail's like a Travelodge without the bar. She's boasting how easy life is inside! Yeah, you won't be so full of yourself when you reach 10 years, then

20 years, then 30 years. You've got it all to come, girl. Your only 29 now, you wait till your arse can't get through your cell door. By the time you get out you will have forgotten what your fanny's for. You will probably have munched your way through three tons of pussy and you'll have a beard.

Her letter was in the papers. Take some advice, Kate: get your head down, don't end up a so-called 'celebrity con' or you will serve double the time. It's not worth it, believe me. Just become a number. Let time fly by peacefully. You can still munch your pussies and have a vibrator. Have fun.

Here's another psycho cunt: Karl Taylor. On a first date with beautiful Kate Beagley he slashed her to pieces so badly he severed her spine. Kate was a lovely girl with everything to live for before this cunt wiped her out. I bet her family would love to wipe him out. Still, they'll have to wait 30 years – this guy won't serve much less. Believe it.

Real psychos don't change till their old, and some never change! To them it's a mission! I know one psycho (who will remain nameless) who's almost 60 now. I've known him for a good 35 years and he's worse now than he was when I first met him. He was just born for Hell. He can't help it, he's just hell-bent on a life of pain. And believe me, he's had his fare share of it. A normal man couldn't have survived a fraction of what he has had to endure. Pain on pain. The pleasure of pain. Remember: one man's pain is another man's pleasure! We can't all be the same, can we?

There was good news today on the radio! Kenny Noye's got a fresh appeal. That tells me the Criminal Cases Review Commission are still breathing. Hurry up with mine!

Did you know a night in a police cell costs the tax payer £385? One fucking night! And it costs £12 a day to feed the prisoner but only £3 to feed a NHS patient. That's fucking mental. Loonyology.

There are still 355 prisoners in Guantanamo Bay in Cuba, all held illegally. How do the Yanks get away with it? People moan about the Russians, Japs and Chinks, what about the Yanks? Human Rights? It's more like 'inhuman rights' with that lot! Fuck me, they get away with all sorts. Crafty bastards. You wait till 'Arnie' becomes president, the Terminator for real. Today's movie is tomorrow's life. Believe it. It's fucking mental.

Who knows, maybe I could end up as some sort of MP. Why not? Yeah, why not? Let's face reality: most of our MPs are a bunch of headless chickens and gutless fuckers. I'll liven the place up, you know it.

There was a loony in Broadmoor who was always writing to the MPs. He used to write a letter and send out copies to all of them. I read one of his letters addressed to Tony Benn (remember this was back in 1979) who I think has always been a decent MP. He comes across as an 'old school' sort of chap with good morals and principles. The loon's letter started off like this: "I'm in the asylum and they won't let me have my push-bike. It's mine and I want it." It went on about all sorts of bollocks. I said, "You can't send that!"

"Why not?" he asked. What could I say! I just said, "Yeah, send it!" Well, it is a nut house...

There was another loony in Broadmoor who used to collect old catalogue magazines. We found out why: he loved the pages with the little kids in their pyjamas and underwear. He had a nasty accident in the kitchen when a pan of scolding hot water fell all over his crutch area. You should have heard us laugh. Hysterical laughter is a lot like a mad scream! Funny that, the dirty little paedo copped his just desserts! Yeah, life's a funny old game. I fucking love it, me. Don't you?

There was once a loon in Rampton who did ballet. He used to wear skin-tight track suit bottoms with soft slippers and prance about like a fairy. No problem, but he did it with a fucking big erection and a fucking big grin. It was insane... I was told by one of the screws: "He actually comes his lot with every dance he does." Well, it is an asylum – what do you expect!

There was another pair of nutters who used to have a friendly wrestle – or so I thought. It was actually a 'pretend' wrestle and they were giving each other a blow-job! They were famous for it!

Seeing all this is believing it. You've got to see it, it's fucking Loonyology gone over the edge, pushed into the madness of life. And I'm telling you now, I fucking loved it all. It was an experience of a lifetime. I once played a lunatic at snooker in Broadmoor. He played with a broomstick. What does that tell you? It's brilliant to be bonkers, they're all angels with razor blade wings. Fucking dangerous fuckers.

They do say when a man leaves prison, prison never leaves him. There is some truth in that. I had a lot of strange feelings when I got out for my short spell of freedom. Flashes of prison life just fly back into your mind. I suppose it's a lot like those poor sods who spent years in the concentration camps. How do they forget? How do they forgive?

I remember walking around the yard in Parkhurst with gypsy Joe Taylor and hearing all his stories of the war. Joe was in his late '60s back in 1976. He was serving 18 years for a blag in which a security guard got shot in the leg. When I met him in '76 he had served 10 or 11 years. He did his bird easy – his way. He was what's known as a man's man! We respected him, even the screws did because he was an ex-military man. He told me how he once shot a German's face off and just looked down at the Kraut and spat. That's what a war does to a man. Once the war's over, what then? Do they become humanised? Do they fuck. Lots of our lads come back to Civvy Street and lose the plot. Jails are full of ex-military men – men who were brave souls, men who fought their guts out for us. But once the war was over, so were they. Joe was one of these men. His cell was spotless and you could eat off his floor. His bedding was all folded neatly into a box. This guy was disciplined – he didn't walk, he marched! Left right, left right, for a solid hour on the yard! That's gypsy Joe Taylor. He must be in his 90s now and I bet he's still marching!

Joey Martin was another ex-military man who got lifed off over a murder on a robbery. He served well over 30 years and was released. The man is a legend. You'll be amazed at how many ex-military men have had to eat porridge over the years; brave men who lost their way!

There was an old con in Gartree jail who used to be a major in the army. He even had the tash. He strangled his wife; she was fucking the milkman whilst he was away on active service. That's how life can end up. It's not always the case of born evil: men can be driven into evil. A marriage can become a war in itself if you let it! Personally, I would've put the milkman in a chair for life; he would've ended up a 'raspberry ripple' sucking his double cream through a straw. The wife could just fuck off on the street.

Hey! Ain't it brilliant we don't know our own fate? Imagine if we did! Fuck me, we would all be at war. Life's a bitch and so were my two wives. I wonder who's fucking them now? Some lunatics. Poor sods, they'll need a brain transplant by the time that pair of witches finishes with them. Marriage is for muppets! I'll drink to that. Cheers.

There was a geezer in the Scrubs called 'Budgie'. You've guessed it – he bred budgies and he actually taught one of his birds to fly out and shit on a screw's head. Amazing or what? It sounds incredible but that's just what it did! There was another con in the Scrubs that had a big fuck-off rat. It was the size of a small cat – now that's a big rat. It bit an IRA prisoner's finger and that was the end of the rat. He killed it. Those IRA boys don't fuck about inside, believe me. You can take it on me: every riot in every jail in the UK over the past 30 years had some IRA lads in it. They just love a riot, it's that simple. I remember when four of them got up on the roof on the special security unit in Parkhurst and smashed it to bits. The Hull riot in 1976 was full of IRA lads like Martin Brady, Billy Armstrong and Sean O'Connell. That was a top-class riot! The Gartree riot, the Albany, the Scrubs, you can bet your arse on there being some IRA boys in them all, and boy did they get some stick for it! Plenty of broken bones, I can tell you.

I've always got on well with the Irish lads – we have a mutual respect. I think the Irish are lovely people! I used to work out in Long Lartin with big Albert Baker. Albert was fighting a war against the IRA but in jails in England the UDA and IRA seemed to get on. Fuck knows how or why – I think they just accepted they were all inside and fighting for freedom. Outside, they probably would've shot each other's heads off, but inside they just got on with it. Albert was a powerhouse: he could bench 500 pounds and had awesome strength. He was a great guy to train with. When you trained with Albert you were with the best!

Albert was also the No. 1 hooch-maker in the jail! Every Friday and Saturday night we were pissed out of our heads. Albert's cell was known as the 'Brewery' – he had more buckets and plastic bags than the storeroom, but he would never ever tell anybody his secret ingredients. Rumour had it he would often stick a bottle of vodka into his brew. Long Lartin had a lot of bent screws in the 1980s and they'd sell a bottle of vodka for 30 quid. They'd bring it in in squash bottles – no doubt watered down as they're a tight load of fuckers! Imagine it: if a screw was bringing in just one bottle a day, that's £210 a week tax free! That's almost 12K a year! It pays a lot of bills. All these idiots who say it doesn't happen can fuck off. Screws are no different to any working force: everybody's got a price. Show me a man who is whiter than snow. There isn't one.

There was one screw there who kept half a dozen cons in vodka and gin. He did fucking well out of it and I say good luck to him. What harm was done? Now days there's a lot of snake screws who sell drugs; greedy fuckers. They make thousands out of the 'quick hit' – they don't care about the damage it does! Even though some screws are serving sentences for it, you'll still get some saying, "No way do our officers do that!" Fucking idiots! Of course it goes on. Why wouldn't it? Well, it doesn't go on in my cell and never will either. But I'm still up for the odd bottle of drink. You know where I am, lads. Cheers.

I'll tell you who's a right dirty bastard: Kyle Lloyd. What a piece of dog shit this 20 year old is. Guess what he did, I bet you'll never guess? He raped an old lady of 81. How the fuck can any human do that to an old lady? It's beyond humanity, it's fucking sick. He climbed into her bungalow window and raped the poor woman. This is a case where her sons should see justice is done! Judge Caveli sentenced him to only three and a half years! But then again, that could be good as he will soon be out and then her sons can bump into him down a dark alley. Revenge is sweeter in the dark. If anybody ever did that to my mum, I would not be able to sleep until I grabbed him around the neck. May God strike me down dead, I would rip his head off. I would make him so fucking ugly, he would be sick every time he looked in the mirror, and I would chop his feet and hands off. He would live on in misery, the fucking beast. What sort of 20 year old could even think of doing such a vile act? Kyle Lloyd could. Cunt!

Hey, get on this for a nightmare. A pair of 'lesbian vampires' just got lifed off for murder in Perth, Australia. Valerie Parashumti, aged 19, and Jessica Stasinowsky, aged 21, killed 16-year-old Stacey Mitchell over jealousy. Fuck messing with those lesbo blood-suckers! Imagine it. What a way to leave the planet – being sucked dry. I can think of a million better ways to die!

Did you know the average married couple spend 25 years of their life together in bed and that 10 weeks of that is sex? Where the fuck do they do all these surveys? Do you believe this sort of stuff? Or do you even care? Me, I laugh at it because I know there'll be lots more than 10 weeks with me. How about you? 10 fucking weeks!! I'll be kissing and cuddling for longer than that.

Hey, the world's longest-ever kiss was 98 hours. You've got to laugh. 98 hours non-stop snogging! What were they? Frogs?

Did I ever tell you about the time I moved from Leicester jail to Brixton as a black man? Yeah, I was a black man. It was back in 1988 and I was being held in Leicester's punishment block over the roof job. One night a muggy old screw kept banging my cell door every hour on his security watch and flicking my light on and off. You always get one, it doesn't matter where you are, you'll always get one prick who wants to cause you grief. Sure it's his job to check me every hour, but he doesn't have to fucking wake me up and take the piss. At 2am he woke me up again. I shouted at him, "You fat cunt." I heard him laugh as he marched off and said, "I'll see you at 3am, Bronson." Yeah, I thought, I'll fucking see you before you see me, cunt! At 3am I was ready, standing by the door in the dark. I had broken the spy hole in the door and I was waiting for the cunt. The light shot on, the spy flap went and I squirted the cunt with piss and shit from my shampoo bottle all in his face. The bottle was Head and Shoulders, and that's where it went – it covered him! Who's laughing now, you cunt. He started heaving. He ran off being sick and I was laughing so much it hurt.

That's how to deal with a cunt, but every action brings a reaction so I had to prepare myself for the backlash I knew was coming. I covered myself in black boot polish and prepared for more madness. Why? Well, why not! It's different! It looks good! It's me, I like to be different, and what's wrong with a black man? So there I was, black as the ace of spades, bollock naked apart from my boots and a white bandana, lying on a blanket and kicking the door to bits! If I can't sleep, no fucker will… Within 10 minutes I could hear more doors kicking up above me. There was lots of shouting and screaming:

"Shut up, you cunt."

"Stop banging, you slag."

"Let's kill the fucker!"

"It's that mad cunt Bronson. He needs a bullet to his nut! Kill the fucker."

They can be very hurtful at times, my fellow convicts. Cunts. Why don't they shout at the screws like that? It's not me locking them up.

Another screw came to my door all nice and polite.

"Come on, Charlie," he says.

"Oi, cunt, fuck off, it's your mate that's caused all this bollocks," I told him.

"Come on Charlie, there's no need for this…"

I kept it up till 8am, when they rushed in and sorted me out. 10 on one is never good odds is it? I was bundled into a waiting van and off we shot out of the gate with a police escort. ZOOooommmm… sirens going… 100mph down the motorway. I was still black and naked, cuffed-up and feeling angry. I was fucking hungry, cold and getting fed-up of being jumped on and beat up. Plus, I had a headache.

We were soon in the London traffic. I said, "Right, where are we going? Scrubs? Or Wandsworth?" Nobody answered so I kicked off again.

"Brixton," they all shouted. "Fucking Brixton."

Remember this was 1988 and Belmarsh wasn't open. Plus, this was the old type 'Category A' van where we sat cuffed up to screws. Now days we are locked in a box cage alone, separated from the screws. Anyway, I was dying for a piss, I mean bursting. I just couldn't wait. (Well, I could've but I didn't.) I stood up and pissed and it went on forever. It was like a pony in a field – it just kept coming out. It was the longest piss I've ever had. It was like a river and it moved about as the van swerved or turned. The eight screws with me were sitting down and they all kept lifting their boots up as the piss ran their way. It was fucking magical; just to see their faces was a treat! One of them was an old screw who I had known for years. He said, "Fuck me, Charlie, that's some piss, mate! Fuck me, I'm glad it wasn't a shit you needed!" Everybody laughed, even me! That's how jail is – humorous.

Once we had driven into Brixton jail and all jumped out, the Brixton mob took one look at me as if to say: "What the fuck is that?" Obviously they were expecting Bronson, not a naked black man with a bandana! So it all began again – what happened in your last jail continues in the new jail. It's a never-ending roller coaster. It's party time. What do they do? What can they do? What do I do? Anything I fucking want!

Take some advice: don't go down my road. This is the Bronson journey. I do it alone, my way. Talking of which, get on my CD *My Way*. You'll love it. You can order it off my site! I did it my way, and did I fucking do it or did I do it?

Hey! You can't beat being a black guy, it feels good – cool. You come alive and even your teeth look good! Your eyes shine. Yeah, black is cool… But I bet they can't piss like us white guys! Was that a piss or was that a piss! I just couldn't stop. I couldn't piss like that again if I tried. Age does something to your bladder and you just can't piss like a young man does. Us old folk can't keep up with it. Did you know that as you age, your dick shrinks and your bollocks hang down like a sack of spuds? It's true! The good old days… Still, us old chaps can do what we do best: survive. And that's what it's all about, guys – surviving! I'm off for a piss.

Another 'mad' move I had was from Walton jail, Liverpool to Albany jail on the Isle of Wight in 1985. This one was a bit freaky – a dream – and still feels like a dream even 23 years later. '85 was for me one crazy, mental year when I was forever in the trenches having the shit kicked out of me. A lot of it I deserved, but some of it was purely evil and vindictive. The block in Walton was then on H/1 and I was being kept in the strong box, isolated away owing to my 'roof jobs'. Every time they unlocked me there were 10 screws always ready to pounce on me. I was cuffed up just to go on the yard. That's how life was for me; it's how I made it. No big deal, but it can get you down. It sort of causes a man to feel bad feelings. It made me angry that I was being turned into something that's not really me: an animal. I thought violence, I dreamt violence and I was violent. To me it was a war!

Kenny Goodhall and Tommy Curliss arrived – two solid, staunch lads. Both were 'block men' being constantly moved around the system like chess pieces from block to block. Being in the box, which is a double-door tomb, I don't know who's in the block but they spotted my name on the door and started to shout to me. The screws told them both, "Don't shout at him, he's a nutter." Both Kenny and Tommy said, "Fuck you, screw! Charlie's our pal. You're the fucking nutter." Then they both pulled the governor and told him, "If you don't start treating Bronson with a bit of humanity then we are kicking off." That did it: I was allowed out on the yard with them, but fuck all lasts.

Days later, a big team of screws came for me to move me on. It was after breakfast and I can remember it as if it were yesterday. My breakfast was the best I ever had in all my stay in Walton. Even the mug of tea was sweet. Sweet tea in the punishment block is rare; for me it's almost impossible to get. I should've known better. I was slipping and I put down my guard. I had been tranquillised – they had put something in my tea, the slippery fuckers! No sooner had I got in the vehicle than I was in noddy land and I awoke in Albany jail on the Isle of Wight.

Is it illegal to do that? Probably. Why did they do it? Why not! Let me tell you now: this sort of thing went on for years (mostly in the 1970s) – not just with me, with lots of us. It was control. It was either that or a good kicking and sit on top of us all the way. That's how it was – the liquid cosh. If I did that to somebody outside I would probably get 10 years for it. Personally, I prefer a kicking to drugs, simply because I'm anti-drugs. Drugs and me don't mix; never have and never will.

When I awoke in Albany a doctor, a governor and a dozen screws were all standing over me. The doctor said, "You're in Albany, are you OK?" I looked at him and just shut my eyes and went back to sleep.

It's a dream! It's been a dream from day one! Our whole life is a dream and it's fucking brilliant. YABADABADOOOoooooo. YIPPEEEeeeeeee! YEEOOWWWwwwwwwww. Pass me the sawn-off. It's my party, I'll knee-cap who I want! Isle of Wight kiss my arse. Believe me, the van soon arrived to take me away. "I was born under a wandering star."

Saturday, 8 March 2008.

I got a pile of mail today and some quality art card from Sandra Gardner. She spoils me. I'll do her a nice piece of art later, that will pass a few hours away. But I also got a mad letter from a loony! I get plenty of those, but this one you have got to read. It's the biscuit of all biscuits. It's from a guy in Dunstable, which is only a stone's throw away from my town. I've now got his name and address. What a cunt – when you read this you'll agree!

"I've been following up on you for some years and I don't think you're all you make yourself out to be. In fact I think you're a total wanker. You're a nobody pretending to be a somebody and when you do finally get out, I'll prove to everybody what a loser you are. Take this as a warning, Bronson. It's bang on you. You have yet to face me before you call it a day. Pepi."

That's it. I could sort a few of the 'chaps' to pop around and have a chat with him, but I'd sooner wait. I'll call on him myself – all in good time. What sort of mug writes shit like this? Like, who is he? What is he? Who the fuck does he think I am? Or, better still, why does he want to face me? He must see himself as an old-fashioned bounty hunter, some punk-faced gunslinger out to do Jesse James! Cunt. So why me? Why has he chosen me? Is it because I'm serving life? Is it because he thinks I'll die inside? Is he actually after a name, a reputation? Fucking Pepi.

In fact I do know a Pepi – Pepi Davies. He's a lifer, but he's been inside for over 20 years. It's now a fact: I draw a lot of loons to me. I'm a magnet to lunatics and they're in a big line waiting to put me in a hospital ward. But why? Cunts.

Oi, Pepi, I'll see you later. I'll creep up on you in the dark and show you what a life mare is. (It will be my pleasure.) Your name and address are safe with me! In one year or 21 years' time you'll get to look into my face, I promise you that. Cunt.

It's amazing that the prison censor lets this sort of letter through. I know some end up in the bin and some don't. Pepi was lucky that his didn't. You lucky fucker.

Jack Ruby's pistol, which killed Lee Harvey Oswald, has just sold for one million quid. The fucking things people buy. It's beyond Loonyology. Lee Harvey Oswald's toe tag with a lock of his hair is up at auction for 10 grand. Who the fuck's going to pay 10K for a blood-stained toe tag and a lock of hair off a president's killer? I'll tell you: hundreds of collectors!! Take the Superman outfit used in the first two *Superman* films – that's up for auction for 45 grand. Some rich fucker will be wearing that in the bedroom. Kinky fucker! One of Houdini's strait jackets is up for 18 grand. People will buy anything! It's how some people get to show off: "Look what I've got, it's the only one in the world, and Houdini used to escape from it! I've got it, look at it, it's mine!" Cunts.

Here's a fucking pucker story; you'll love this one. Weenus Chumkamnerd, a 52-year-old Thai geezer from Hatyai, went berserk with a gun, shooting eight dead. Their karaoke party drove him over the edge so he steamed in and shot them all. Let that be a lesson to all you would-be karaoke stars. You're not as good as you think you are. In fact, you're shit.

Hey! John Lennon's white suit! How much? Come on have a guess? Well, it's up for 88 grand.

One of the world's greatest rogues was Victor Lustig; he pulled off a blinder by flogging the Eiffel Tower to a scrap metal dealer in 1925 and he got clean away with the dosh. Victor travelled the world pulling off strokes, but he came unstuck when he tricked Al Capone out of 5,000 dollars in a share scam. His luck ran dry and he finally ended up in Alcatraz serving 20 years for all sorts of fraud and counterfeiting. And, you guessed it, Al Capone followed him on to the 'Rock'. Poor old Victor – he then had Scarface in the next cell. "Pay up or die!" We all love a con artist, just as long as it's not us that's being conned.

10 March 2008.

A great day today. I had a jog in the pissing rain! There were hail stones stinging my head and face. Brilliant! I felt alive, fresh and happy.

I got a pile of letters – one from a Nick Hayes. He's just started up a sporting site for autographed signatures: www.sportsignings.com. He's sent me in some of his merchandise! Take it from me, it's all good stuff. This guy goes out and does the bizz. Good luck to him!

I got a nice card from Di Brown with a nice photo of her; she's still looking hot and sexy. She's been a good friend to my mother over the years and we all love Di. She's a good soul. I also got a letter from my brother's girlfriend Bex Stone who wants to visit me with Mark. (I'll have to get security to pass her.) I also got a great card from Rachel Bristow giving me all the latest news. She always keeps me updated on the world outside. I got another eight letters and a boxing mag. Not bad for a Monday.

I called up Terry Turbo who's just finished his part in my movie, playing the part of a Rampton asylum screw. You will probably remember Terry in the *Rise of the Foot Soldier* – he's a top-class actor and an all-round good guy. I also got to call Leighton Frayne up. He and his brother Lindsey are playing their parts tomorrow as a couple of hoods. My movie only has the best actors, or real villains trying their luck at acting!

It was a good tea tonight: stew, and lots of it. All goodness, I can smell the goodness. I used half a loaf of bread on it. Dip in, swallow, lovely! It's good old English grub, a stew! It's filling and full of body. You can live on stew, you really can! I would love to make my own, with dumplings as big as Yorkshire puddings! I would put the lot in: mushrooms, carrots, peas, spuds, tomatoes, beans, sausages, beef, onions, garlic, turnips, swede and beetroot. I mean everything and more. I would make it in one of those witches' pots and it would last me a week. Real grub, body building nosh, proper British food. The problem today is that no fucker sticks by tradition and there's too much foreign shit. Even in jails it's all arse about face with the diets. We want real food: British.

Yeah, I had a great day today. The governor stuck his head in. "Morning Charlie," he said, "any problems?" I said, "You'd soon fucking know about it if there were!" He smiled and fucked off. Short and sweet.

I remember the governor in Armley jail once sticking his head in; I almost pulled it off. Boy, did I get a kicking for that! And the governor watched them do it, the sadistic fucker. But that's all part of the journey. The governor in the Scrubs once asked me, "Are you a masochist? You seem to enjoy getting bashed up by my officers on a regular form!" I said, "Gov… first thing: you're screws are not supposed to bash anybody up! And second, it's all worth it just as long as I get one good shot in." And that's the truth! Outside it would be a different story. It would be me against one of them! And believe me, it wouldn't be me in a hospital bed! Inside, yeah, I've lost before I've begun but I fucking loved all of it – the good and the bad. There's not a single screw or prison governor who can't say, "Bronson gave it his best shot." It's a fact!

It's about fucking time my premium bonds won! I could do with a nice windfall. I'd get a good digital radio and a watch, sort my mum out and get my son a break – a few months in the sun. I want to get a couple of Rolex kettles too, as gifts for two special friends. I like to treat my pals and show my appreciation for their staunchness. Friends are special to me, like family. Then again, some families are full of loonies! Dirty old paedo uncles, smack head aunties and faggots for dads. Some families must be like a fucking circus!

Talking of circuses, I loved a good show like Billy Smart's. They've all vanished now because they're seen as being cruel to the animals. Fucking left-wing libs, Greenpeace prats, animal lovers. Get a life, you cunts. Bring back our real circuses! That smell! That excitement! That buzz! It's all gone and it will never be back. Gone forever! Amen. Cry laughing, you piss-heads – it's true!

It's that Nick Hayes with some of his photos from the football world. I told you this guy gets out there snapping. That's him with the glasses on. Get on his site and see what he's got, or give him a buzz – 07970 982561. Tell him I said to call. If you're a football fan then Nick's your man! OK? I hope he gets me a drink later. I don't just put any Tom, Dick and Harry in my book!

Talking of Harry, whatever happened to Harry Batt? Harry copped 18 years back in the 1970s on a security van job with Sammy McArthy, both East London men. Sammy was, in fact, the British flyweight boxing champion in the 1960s. Fuck me, could he hit. He used to hit like a middleweight! Anyway, I last saw Harry in the Scrubs in 1985, so that's 23 years ago. He must have been 60 years old then! It's sad how years pass and you lose touch with friends. Harry was a real character of the East End and everybody loved him to bits. When Sammy got out, he visited me with his daughter and we had a good laugh. We really are one big family and as solid as a rock. I've met the cream of the crop. I'm blessed, I really am.

I was in the punishment block in the Scrubs in 1985. There are two yards, both covered in razor wire and CCTV. The fences are 18 feet high but in the middle of each yard is a toilet about 12 feet tall and covered in wire. One day I was on one yard with two other cons and there were three other cons on the other yard. One of the cons with me was shouting over to one of the cons on the other yard and it was actually giving me a headache.

"Oi! Come here mate," I said. "Get up on my shoulders."

So there he was, balancing on my shoulders. I walked over to the toilet so he could see his mate on the other side and it worked. Now they could have a chat, get it over with and give us some fucking peace. Next thing, my head and face felt all wet and hot. It was blood, and I was covered in it. His head was caught up in the razor wire! Fuck me – he was in a bad way! I got him down and the screws rushed him over to the hospital. That's how easy it is to get into trouble by trying to help somebody. It was a total accident.

There was an old screw in the Scrubs block called Taffy around this time. He was a diamond. Every time he was on, I got second and third helpings off the hot plate. Screws like him are so rare in a shit-hole jail like the Scrubs. Years ago in this block you were only allowed one book to read, but Taffy used to get me six. I read a lot in those days and I actually learned a lot! Plus, I used them for my work-outs as books are good for press-ups. Pile them up, the higher the better, and drop your chest! It's brilliant.

The Scrubs used to do a smashing spotted dick with pink custard; if I remember right it was on a Friday. And their Sunday roast spuds were second to none. Imagine cooking a roast for 1,500 cons… I do miss the old days. I know I keep going on about it, but I do.

I was next cell to a suicide in the Scrubs. I swear I could smell that death even before the night clocky found him hanging. The death seemed to creep through the wall. I was just feet away from a hanging stiff. It was a lovely evening and a breeze came in through the window. (My windows were smashed out.) I remember it like yesterday. I heard the screw shout, "Fuck me." His whistle blew and others came running. They were in there like a flash. It was no fault of the screws this time. It's always sad and it just makes you feel uneasy! It's spooky, a bit unreal and depressing. I didn't know him, I doubt if he even knew himself. He was a lost soul. I lay awake for weeks after that, thinking about death and trying to answer the age-old question: why? Where the fuck has he gone? Hell or Heaven, or is it all a load of bollocks? I've come to the conclusion that it's all a load of bollocks!

Hey! Once a suicide takes place inside, they're at the spy hole every 30 minutes at all doors. It's double security. I used to shout, "Oi, fuck off you pervo, what's the matter with you, trying to catch me wanking? Cunt." But today there are women screws, so you've got to be a bit more respectful. That's somebody's wife, mother or daughter. I always think of that, I'm just an old softy at heart. I don't believe in insulting any woman. It's just how I am, I can't help it. I think it's how we were brought up in our era. I know today it's 'cunt' and 'bollocks' and the women are the same as the blokes. They even sup pints and fart. It's all Loonyology to me!

Fuck it, I'm calling it a day.

Oi! Did you know there's a frog in South America that's got three dicks? Not a lot of people know that! Not a lot of people give a flying fuck anyway! I just love nature.

Knowledge can be dangerous. I bet you don't know how to make a bomb or your own bullets? I do! I'm basically a clever cunt! I bet you don't know how to make a 'Zoom era'? I do! Now you're thinking, what the fuck's a 'Zoom era'? Keep thinking. That's how I am see: cruel. I'm not saying fuck all without my solicitor present. No comment. Good night. Slam my door shut and fuck off! And don't forget my breakfast!

Blown away.

Walking across a mine field
That's what life is
A gamble
Anything… any time can happen
"Fuck me"
Even the sky could fall in
What then?
I'll tell you… "Nothing"
Just one big black hole
Bottomless
No way out
Forever buried
A world in darkness
Sucked inside out
Blown away
The end of life as we know it
Crushed to dust
No more rainbows
No more flowers
Nothing but emptiness
Even the tears are gone
Nothing to cry with
Your eyes have gone
Along with your face
Blown away
Point-blank range
"Bang"
Double-barrel 12 bore
Your head's flying
Your brain is splattered on the ceiling
What a way to go
What a waste of life
What a fucking end
Blown away
Dylan wrote it
Dylan sung it
'Blowing in the Wind'
That man's a poet
A genius
Knight Bob Dylan
Catch it before it blows
Let's have another century or two
Nobody wants to die
Be careful what you wish for

It could come true
It may choke you to death
You can't kill time alone
You're going to fuck up eternity
Think of solitary as a friend
A partner
Survive together…
Blown away.

Fuck knows where these poems come from, I just get the urge to create them. They flow out of my pen like a piss and I can't stop till I'm empty. The bladder of life, one long piss! It sure feels good though… what piss doesn't?

"If you think of peace and search for love, you're sure to find happiness." How nice would that be? Come on, how nice? Happy people are priceless people, but it's finding that level that can become costly and it may well cost you your life. But you can always die happy. That's the best way to call it a day: death by happiness.

12 March 2008.

Fuck me… Coco Pops for breakfast. What's that all about? I'm a man and they're giving me little kids' cereal. Ronnie Barker would turn in his grave! Fletcher out of *Porridge* would have a stroke! Coco Pops!!! I tell you, it's all Loonyology! You can't make this shit up.

Mum sent me in a nice few quid today that some guy owed me, so I'm getting a new radio and a watch. I'll treat myself; why not? I've sorted Mum out and my brother and a few friends, so we are all happy. One up, all up, I say. I'll drink to that…

Get on this, you'll love this, it made my day. It's in the Luton newspaper that I get sent in every week. It's a classic. Nonce Andrew Chaplen got nicked for playing about with little kids. The Old Bill arrested him at his house and guess what, they found 511 indecent photos of young boys. I told you a nonce is a nonce! But Chaplen's the worst kind because he lived a double life: he was married and pretended to live a normal life. Anyway, the judge gave him 18 poxy months. The good news is that three hours after he was sentenced he hanged himself. How good is that? He topped himself with his shoe laces! That's what I call justice: 18 months and a stiff. Burn the fucker and throw a party, I say! His poor wife can now get on with her life. You're free of the monster! It makes you wonder just how well couples really know each other. Believe it: nobody knows anybody 100%. You may think you do, but do you? You don't.

I called up Sandra Gardner tonight. It's the first time we spoke and she's a lovely soul. I'm just in the process of getting her passed to visit me! The Old Bill have already paid her a visit to check out who she is. That's what you have to go through to visit me, it really is.

Roll on Tuesday… I've a visit with the Frayne brothers to find out how their part went in the movie. Then on Thursday, Danny Hansford, the director, is up. I keep telling you all I'm lucky. I really am, and I feel I'm getting even luckier. Watch this space…

Friday, 14 March 2008.
I see ex-screw John Darwin pleaded guilty today at Leeds Crown Court to seven charges of deception involving a quarter of a million bucks. You'll all remember this guy who went out in his canoe never to be seen again. That was till he was spotted in Panama. He was declared dead by an inquest in 2002! His wife Anne copped for the insurance and pensions. By the way, she's pleading not guilty to all charges which seems confusing since she was out in Panama with him. Even their kids believed Dad had died in the canoe accident. Who said these screws are law abiding? Like I've been saying all along, some are bigger villains than the villains. I would say Darwin's got plenty of porridge (or Coco Pops) to get through. But with her pleading not guilty they may well keep him waiting till her trial's over. I'm dying to see what her defence will be! 'Loonyology' I would say…

Denman won the Cheltenham Gold Cup today. What a beautiful horse – a born winner. And what a way to end the week. The young girl Shannon Matthews has been found. Shannon went missing up in Dewsbury a couple of weeks back. She's just nine years old. It's been the biggest police search in years. Everybody expected another tragic ending, but she was found alive in a nearby house. It's a strange old world, but it's brilliant when there's a nice ending to a sad story. Let's have three cheers for the Old Bill here. HIP HIP – HOORAY! HIP HIP – HOORAY! HIP HIP – HOORAY! Well done lads… (but it took you long enough).

Hey get on this. Mark Moir, a known druggie, hit a geezer with a hammer down in Eastbourne. As he was running away, he smashed into a lamp post and knocked himself out. Fuck me. You can't make this shit up! It's brilliant. Imagine going on a bank job with this prat! God, give me strength.

Another druggie copped 30 years yesterday for shooting a pregnant woman on her doorstep. Thomas Hughes blasted Krystal Hart to death. What for? He's got 30 years to come up with a reason! He didn't just kill Krystal, he killed an unborn baby. I don't know any man who can justify that or sleep at peace. He would be better off to rip his sheet up and do a Fred West job. Look in the mirror, pal. It's there: the answer. It would be the best thing you could ever do. You're fucked! The hole's sucked you in and it's bottomless. It's all over. Turn the light off…

I got a pile of mail today. Four letters were from young prisoners; they ask me some mad things. Obviously I can't reply to them all. Fuck me, I'm in prison not a post office! The price of a stamp is the same as a Mars bar, and Mars bars are good for training. I also got a letter from some crazy bird who says she's 19, blonde with blue eyes, and has a body to die for. Yeah, sure, I've had all these nutters before. They turn out to be 22-stone freaky fuckers with no teeth. Why would a 19-year-old goddess want to write to me? That's the real question! Shouldn't she be enjoying life, clubbing it and having fun? What good am I to her? It amazes me, it really does!

Mark Emmins sent me in a load of *Con-Artist* today. If I say so myself, it's looking good. We're halfway through it! You're all in for a treat. This book will blow your socks off! I've got a good feeling about *Con-Artist*. Watch this space…

It's been one of those days when it feels good to be a part of the human race. Let's face it: us humans are an OK bunch of good souls! Come on, let's all say it together! Let's all be one. We're the dogs bollocks, are we not? Be proud to be human, I say! Be happy, be full of pride! You could have ended up being born a worm or a slug or a snake! What sort of life does a slug have? We humans are blessed, so be thankful. Imagine being a skunk, stinking your way through life. Come to think of it, I know a few humans like that. Shoot the fuckers, I say. If you can't be human then hurry up and die. Life's a party. Blow up some balloons and save me some cake.

Local city jails fill up with smelly tramps at Christmas time. A lot of them throw bricks through a shop window just to get a couple of weeks in a nice, cosy, warm cell and some hot grub. How fucking sad is that? One old tramp in Liverpool was a regular in Walton jail every Christmas. I saw him there back in 1974 but this time the old rascal got longer than he bargained for. He slung a brick at a shop window but it bounced off and smashed a woman in the face. He ended up with six months for assault. You can't make this shit up. 'Old Tom' they called this tramp. He must have been a good 70 years old. He had a long grey beard down to his chest and a mop of matted white hair – that was till the screws got hold of him. In those days everybody had to have a haircut. But the strange thing with old Tom was that you could still pick him out as a tramp by the way he walked and the things he did! Even in prison clothes he looked trampish. He would walk around the yard picking up fag ends and his tobacco tin was always full. This has been his life for donkeys' years and all over the UK tramps like him would come into jails for Xmas. Fucking magic or what? What does that say about our jails? At least they get a bed, warmth, food and clothes, and on release they get a new suit, an overcoat and a few quid to celebrate. Not a bad Xmas for a tramp, eh?

There was another tramp down in London who got involved in a robbery back in 1976 and ended up with three years. A team of blaggers raided a security van as it was delivering bags of dosh to a bank. Shots were fired, all hell broke loose and somehow the old tramp walked up, grabbed a bag and wandered off, only to have a police gun stuffed in his face. I thought three years was a bit harsh, but that's how the cookie crumbles! Every week in Wandsworth they used to physically wrestle this old tramp into the bath house, sling him in and scrub him with a hard brush. Tramps just don't like to bathe. That's how it is, they're strange people! They can sleep with rats in a sewer and think nothing of it, but in jail they stick out like a sore thumb!

Pentonville jail in London used to take in 95% of the tramps on short sentences; that's why it was called 'Skid Row' in the 1960s and '70s. Imagine the fleas and lice; imagine the piss-stained mattresses! And get on this: once a con is marched down to reception to be released, he leaves his bed roll there for the new prisoner. Some poor fucker will have that tramp's bed roll and sleep on that very same mattress! If that's not enough to turn you off crime, then what is?

Here's something for all you would-be criminals to think about. Imagine you've just been nicked and the courts have remanded you in custody. It's your first time inside. The van arrives at the local jail, you're taken to reception, given your prison number, you pick up your bed pack and some screw escorts you to your cell – your home for as long as you're inside. The door slams shut. Fuck me… there's a large black man lying naked on the bunk bed having a wank. He's got a cock on him like a table leg! Well? What are you going to do? This guy is 6 feet 5 and 20 stone, you're 5 feet 7 and 10 stone. He's a violent thug, you're a shoplifter and non-violent! Fuck me, you could be in trouble! What the fuck can you do? Isn't that enough to stop you coming to jail?

It really does happen – the screws can be cruel fuckers. They deliberately put weak cons in with hard men; it's their way of having a laugh. These so-called 'laughs' have turned cruel. Young men have died on their first night inside – raped and killed.

So what do you do then? You're in a locked room with a complete stranger and the room is tiny, airless and claustrophobic. You feel intimidated, afraid… is this not your worst nightmare? On top of it all he lights up a smoke – a joint! He's smoking drugs and you don't smoke, you're not into drugs! It stinks, you can't breathe… what do you do? It may not be a joint, it could be crack. This stranger could be a smack head. This could be your worst-ever nightmare! What the fuck can you do? He could well bash your brains in as you sleep or slit your throat! Then you try to sleep and he farts or he has a shit and it stinks. You're living in a toilet, you can't get out. There's no air. You're suffocating on his shit! Help! What can you do? Come on smart arse: what can you do?

There's a serious personality clash. It could be racial. You don't like each other! He may have mental problems. He may be gay or a transvestite, he could even be a religious freak – maybe one of those suicide bombers. He may need to pray six times a day! He may want to wank six times a day! You're stuck in his world and he's stuck in your world!

Me, I'm lucky because I'm stuck in my own world. Who the fuck would ever want to live in my room? I'm forever in solitary. Not my choice, but the system keeps me on high risk. So how would I handle it all? How would my cell partner handle me? No doubt the screws would have a laugh and put me in with some toothless, tattooed maniac who enjoys inflicting pain on others. No doubt I would have to hurt the cunt before he tried to get a name for himself by taking me out. The very thought of me being found strangled with a table leg rammed up my arse tells me there's no fucking way I'd let it happen. He would have to leave, and fast: walk out or get carried out, cunt! NOW! I would have to rip the cell door off. I'd use his head as a battering ram. I couldn't handle it, I really couldn't.

Take some advice lads: stay clear of jail. Don't come in. Do yourselves a big favour and stay free. Did you know young lads come into jail drug free and get released as addicts? It's a bloody disgrace. I wonder how many come in straight and go out gay. It's food for thought. A gay con once told me, "Charlie, you don't know what you're missing till you try it! How do you know you don't like something unless you try it? If you're into shagging a bird's arse then what's the difference with a man's arse? An arse is an arse, sex is sex. It's the same with a blow job: a mouth is a mouth!" That's what he said! But a bloke's a bloke and a bird's a bird. If it wasn't for his block and tackle then maybe I would give it a dabble. But the very thought of shagging a bloke and having the bollocks flap about sort of puts me off! It's just not nice, is it? And what about his cock – does it get hard as I'm pumping his arse? What the fuck happens? Do I really want to know? I've survived 55 years on this planet without finding out, thank you. It's just one of life's mysteries! Who knows? But I suppose the gay people are right. How do you know if you don't try it? The very thought of a cock rammed up my arsehole just doesn't do anything for me. Fuck me, I'd sooner be in a padded cell lying in a pool of blood than have some cunt shagging my arse. It can't do your piles any good, can it? Imagine his bollocks slapping into your backside. Come to think of it, can a bloke shag a bloke in the missionary position? Well, can he? Do they? Face to face? It's all a mystery to me, probably best to remain that way too! I just don't want a sore arse or a smelly dick!

Here's a blinder, you'll love this. Nothing like a good escape to get the juices flowing. Three young lads, Jason McInerney, his brother Kirk and their cousin Martin Carthy were all in the dock at Reading Crown Court, on trial for shooting a geezer. So they're all innocent till proven guilty. The court room's full of guards but that didn't stop them jumping over the dock. Some prat copper grabbed Jason, so Jason bit his nose; he soon let go. Yip, yip, yarhoo and away. Hi ho silver… The three made their dash for freedom! Jason got clean away but the others got caught. That's showbiz for you! I take my hat off to them. The lads have bottle, I respect that! Anybody who attempts that sort of thing, I salute them. I tried it once in court but sadly I was cuffed up to a guard. You can only get so far with a fat cunt on your back, but I tried my best. I ended up with a dozen fat cunts on top of me and a very sore head. Was it worth it? Bloody right it was! At least it livened their day up. Me… who gives a fuck!! Loonyology at its very best! Hey! How's your nose, copper? That will teach you to put it where it's not wanted. Stay free, Jason. Bob and weave and duck and dive because you're in for it when they catch up with you. Cor, not 'arf. So enjoy your run of freedom!

Did I ever tell you about the time I nicked a lorry load of chickens? Honest, it was full of fucking chickens. The stuff people leave in car parks is insane! Why leave a key in the ignition? You may as well leave a card saying 'Please drive me off'! It's fucking Loonyology! The world's gone mental. I'm the only sane one left…

I was in a pub in Chester one night back in 1972 – the Boathouse down by the river Dee. Maybe it was 1971. Oh well, it was one of them! I was with half a dozen of the lads when a fight broke out. We all piled outside and gave it to them big style. I hit one guy so hard he flew into the river. It was like one of those John Wayne films. Fucking brilliant.

I had some great times in Chester. It's a lovely city and the girls were beautiful. There was a club there in Forgate Street called the Silhouette. That was the place to go in the hot pants era! Those birds' arses did it for me! Thigh-length boots, hot pants and tight tops! Fuck me, was that the era or was that the era? There was T-Rex, Slade, Mungo Jerry, my beloved Tamla Motown and soul. For those of you who don't know, this was my 'skin' era, when I wore braces, Dr Martens and Ben Sherman clobber, not forgetting my navy blue crombie. I was invincible, I really was. Fuck

Superman – I was Superman. I rode home on a horse bareback once after a night on the piss. I can't even remember where the horse came from, I honestly can't. How the fuck I never got stopped is also a mystery!

What about the time I nicked a bus? Yeah! A fucking double-decker bus. I was stopping at bus stops picking passengers up! Ding ding... hold tight... here we go! Life's been a fucking gas – a laugh a minute! I've loved it. Who have I really upset or hurt? OK, a few officials on the way, but what have I really done that's evil? I'll tell you: fuck all. I'm proud of my journey up to now, and the best is yet to come!

Did you know Michael Caine is 77 years old? Not a lot of people know that. A screw called Dicko told me yesterday – he's been on this unit for a good five years. He's a top bloke, a proper good character. He drank 16 pints on a night out once, that's two fucking gallons. 16 pints of bitter in a night. I just couldn't do that in a million years. Why not? I'll tell you:

1. I couldn't.
2. I'd spend half the night pissing.
3. I'd be bloated like a frog.
4. I don't think I'd want to. Now, if it was 16 Black Russians...

After all these years without it, I'll probably only need a couple of shandies to get pissed now. How fucking sad is that? My pal Billy Bristow brews his own. His shed is full up with the stuff. He makes all sorts. He's actually made me a special brew, the 'Bronco Bottle' just waiting for me!

I've actually been offered to run a bar in Spain, but why would I run a bar for somebody else when I can run my own bar? I'm sick of making dosh for other people, it's time to make some for myself and sort my pension out for later, because I don't want to be robbing a bank when I'm 78 years old. Fuck all that for a lark: walking around the jail on a Zimmer frame! That's just not how I see my old age...

What about Reece Huxford? He's a big 6 feet 6 of shit who sold me out over a photo behind my back! I never forget, I never can, and neither will he when I crash into him. I fucking despise a traitor, I really do. This Huxford prick did a bit of door work and met the likes of Roy Shaw; overnight he became one of the 'chaps'. Good old Reece. He's a face! One of us! He's a big fella; he can have a serious row! Blah, blah, blah, blah. Bunny, bunny, bunny. Rabbit, rabbit, rabbit. He visited me in Woodhill and we had a photo done which ended up in a book of mine. Next thing he was contacting the publisher behind my back saying he owned the copyright. It got back to me that he was demanding dosh for his photo. He's free, I'm caged, and he tries to get dosh out of a book that I wrote in blood. My books are written in the struggle to survive and the life I live is a war zone, but that piece of shit tried to suck off me! He soon pulled out when he heard I had been told. It's never over with me, Huxford. This was seven years ago but it's seven seconds to me! You've forgotten it but I never can. You just became a typical cunt, a pretender! You're a fucking nobody, 6 feet 6 of piss and 18 stone of pure shit. And I'm after a punch bag, you cunt. Even a Broadmoor lunatic wouldn't attempt to do what you did. You're a fucking brain-dead twat. OK?

Who remembers the group the Foundations in the 1960s? Their big hit was 'Build Me Up Buttercup'. Peter MacBeth was their founding member and played bass. The cunt's just got six years for sexually assaulting a girl of seven. He pleaded guilty to playing around with her till she was 13. For six years he had his evil way with her! Fucking nonce. When the cops nicked him they also found a pile of child porn on his computer. He claimed he was 'researching it for a book'. Strange... that's what they all fucking say. They all seem to be writing books about it. Cunts. Dirty lying bastards. They're just out-and-out nonces, predators on your children. The good news is MacBeth has cancer so it's odds on the old pervo will die inside! That's the best ending for him. With a name like MacBeth, they should chop his fucking head clean off. Sadly, I bought their record in the '60s. Shame on me.

I see Paul McCartney had to pay Heather Mills 25 million quid. What a fucking joke. It works out at four 'mills' for every year they were wed! The law's insane... it's Loonyfuckingology.

There was a quiz recently and one of the questions was: "Can you name five people who played in the Carry On films?" Well, can you? I can do better than that. Here's a rundown of them!

Charles Hawtrey starred in 25 Carry Ons. His last was in 1972: *Carry On Abroad*.

Barbara Windsor did nine. (I actually thought she was in a lot more.)

Sid James. Did you know old Sid was the highest paid actor in the Carry Ons? He got five grand a film. That was big bucks in the 1960s but Sid was a serious gambler and drinker so it didn't go far with him. He died in 1976.

Joan Sims.

Frankie Howerd.

The great Hattie Jacques starred in 14. (Did you know Hattie was a nurse in the war?)

Peter Butterworth. (Did you know he was a prisoner of war?)

Jon Pertwee (also famous as Dr Who) had four rolls in Carry Ons.

Wendy Richards.

June Whitfield.

Phil Silvers (Sgt Bilko) – even he did a Carry On!

Kenneth Williams.

Bernard Bresslaw.

I could go on and on. How many do you know? What do you want from one Loonyology book? That's enough, I'm bored now and it's time to move on! Fuck Carry On Bronco.

Insanity takes root and spreads faster than cancer.

Hand on heart, swear to God, this is the whole truth and nothing but the truth or may God strike me down dead: in the 1960s and '70s prisons didn't have the nonces we have today. Never mind the Home Office crap they feed our media, I'm telling you the facts. We now have whole jails full up with nonces and it's starting to freak the fuck out of me! Where are all these monsters coming from? Another planet? Yeah, sure we've always had paedophiles and rapists, but not on this scale. They now outnumber villains by 10 to one. It's getting so bad that they now shout at us out of windows calling us names like we used to shout at them. They actually believe we are the monsters because we stole money!

"You nasty fucking blagger, Bronson. You fucking beast, you're a danger to society. All I ever did was fall in love with my neighbour's three-year-old girl and shag their poodle. I'm not dangerous like you are! Bronson should hang for his evil crimes!"

ER, HELLO? Am I dreaming here? Am I dreaming back all those years ago when nonces were kept isolated in shame? Even the screws spat at the fuckers and they walked about with their eyes on the ground. They knew their place! One or two slipped through but we 'sorted' them. Many ended up in serious trouble, like the one in Parkhurst in 1976 who was found in the old bath house with a chair leg rammed up his arse and all his teeth on the floor. They got what they did to the kids or the old ladies they abused. We all sorted it and we fucking enjoyed it! It was a con's job to do it. It was our duty. Now it's become pathetic. It's another planet where our prisons have become out-of-control asylums. The lunatics have finally bent the nurses over and shagged them silly… and guess what? They fucking love it. Tough jails are now Wendy houses with every fucker grassing each other up and nonces walking about 10 feet tall, proud as peacocks! What's gone wrong? Why? I want to go home.

I remember a big fat slob of a nonce in Walton jail in 1974 at Xmas time. We actually read about his case in the *Liverpool Echo* – he got seven years for buggering three 11-year-old boys. Well, you can rest assured he ended up in the hospital wing. A screw later told us the nonce was so scared he wouldn't even leave his cell. We destroyed the fat cunt. He was terrified and had seven years to serve in fear! That's how to treat them. The screws have kids, so what the fuck do they care if a nonce gets half his face ripped off? Would you? There was another nonce in Strangeways who lost four fingers in a door. 'Accidents' do happen – more so with a beast.

Risley was the No. 1 place to get them sorted. No jail in Britain sorted them out like that place, especially the young prisoners wing in the 1960s. We were like a pack of hungry hounds waiting for the fox to enter our world. Young prisoners can be very cruel and wicked, myself included. We were just like animals. Some of the things we got up to makes me amazed even now! But that's how we are in jail because it breeds violence. What else have we got to do? Violence releases all the frustrations and anger! It's why youth jails are always kicking off. Riots, murders, hostages – they get it all. Double bubble. "Who's the daddy now, cunt?" The more violent you are the higher your stakes! It's fucking mental; a crazy deluded way of life. I used to use a bed leg to crash in skulls – "Cop for that, cunt," – and I had a chain made out of bed springs which was lethal. A fight broke out once in the association room and I ended up wrapping it around a screw's head. That cost me dearly. I was black and blue for a month. They beat me silly.

But let me tell you now, if you live a violent life then expect violence back. The facts are simple: once you have a reputation for violence the system will be even more violent and cruel, and some screws are ruthless. Some are ex-military so they've seen more violence than most. They've seen their mates' limbs blown off, they've seen heads shot off, they've had mates die in their arms. A bunch of young prisoners is chicken shit to them, and once they have you in their sights they will go out of their way to break you. The psychological war begins to smash you when they start ripping your photos up, pouring water on your bedding, pissing in your tea, spitting on your food and throwing your letters in the bin. Then your phone call gets cut off, your visiting order goes missing, your light goes on and off and they bang on your door all night. You're given small portions of food and cold tea. There's pure intimidation, bullying, fit-up nickings, lies, and the good screw, bad screw syndrome. In the end it all wears you down! Some crack, some go mad, some are broken, but none will never forget it. How do you forget it? Could you? Me, I rode it all. I had so much of it I just rocked on and it became a way of life. I expected it, but it did drive me mad. In the end I fucking loved it! They gave up on me in the end! I was a lost cause. In fact I lost myself along the way.

Violence can and does change a man's perception of life. You become something that you never set out to be. Only time and maturity can save your soul. That's the case with me, believe it. I prefer a cup of tea and a fig roll these days. Talking of fig roll biscuits, are they nice or are they nice? They're great to dip in tea. They're also good for bowel movement. I do love a fig roll.

Hey! Laughter is the greatest medicine any doctor can prescribe. Happiness kills stress. Unhappy people look ill. Come on, laugh with me… Be a Loonyologist. Now that's a lovely word. I do love to create a word.

A thought.

What's this!
Give it here.
It's mine.
No it's mine.
Fuck you. It's mine.
No it's not.
Piss off, let me have it.
Bollocks.
I'm telling you it's mine.
Leave it alone.
I'll smash your face in.
Try it, cunt.
Give it to me now.
Fuck off.
Stop pulling it.
Fuck you.
It's my turn.
(Siamese twins wanking.)

Hey! What does an Essex girl use for protection when getting shagged? A bus shelter.

Talking of bus shelters, I once used one to do 100 pull-ups non-stop for a bet. Easy. That was in 1971 and I won 50 quid. Try it sometime, I bet you'll struggle with 10!

17 March 2008.

I woke up early with an itch in my right ear and I just lay there scratching it. Fuck me, I felt a long hair, it must have been a good two and half to three inches. One hair! How the fuck did that appear? How long had it been there? Where do ear hairs come from? Why do they just appear? I was trying to get a good grip on it when the light went on; night clocky doing his last round at 6am. Every hour they have to do a roll check. There is no privacy in jail. Let this be a lesson to all you would-be villains! They spy on you 24-7 inside; you can't even have a decent wank in jail without the spy hole opening.

Yank! Fuck me, that hurt! Why does one hair cause so much pain? It felt like my brain was coming out with it! That's old age, when hairs sprout out of your ears and nose. Imagine if these hairs were to grow inside. They would grow into the brain and cabbage you for real. Fucking hairs!

To top it all, it's Rice Krispies for breakfast. I just knew it was going to be a bollocks day! How can a man start a day with Rice Krispies? It should be eggs, beans, sausage, toast and half a loaf of home-made bread with real butter and a pot of tea. Fucking Rice Krispies... do me a favour.

What about Yusuf Jama who shot dead WPC Sharon Beshenivsky in Leeds? It's all come out now – he's also a dirty nonce. A week after he shot her, he was involved in the gang rape of a girl in Birmingham. There were nine of the fuckers. That sums him up in a nutshell. Fucking beast. He's just copped 12 years for it on top of his life sentence. Nine men raping one girl. Fucking monsters! What sort of human does that? Even a pig wouldn't do that! Dirty bastards.

The Frayne brothers had to cancel their visit because their brother-in-law topped himself. They are all in shock. He hanged himself in his own home. Why? What for? Who knows! All he's achieved is to give a lot of pain and misery to his family. It's really selfishness. Why do people do it, especially when they're free? He was a well-respected top geezer and he blows his life away! How sad is that? The brothers had just done their bit in my movie (their scene was the dog fight) and we were all buzzing and happy... now every fucker's on a downer! See what I mean? You never can tell what's next, who's next to kick the bucket. If it's me, fuck the appeal court and the parole board, stuff it up your big fat arses, cunts. But it won't be me, bet on that! I've not survived all this just to die before my time. Plus, I've got some serious shagging to get done before my time's up! Yeah, it definitely will not be my turn for a long time. I'm safe.

Mark Emmins did me proud at the weekend with a 'Bronson stall' at the Carlton Leech night. All the 'chaps' were there, even Freddie Foreman turned up. He shook Mark's hand and told him what a great job he does for me! Mark's a respected guy, a true brother! I'd be lost without him, I really would. It's good that all the 'chaps' respect him – that pleases me.

Remember: a useless life is an early death! Wake up and kick some arse! Kick it, I said, not pump it! You can't die from an overdose of happiness. Keep on laughing. Laugh till you drop!

Oh! I've had my parole date: August. They love sweating us! But they can't melt me, I'm unmeltable, the unmeltable man. Turn the heat up, I fucking love it!

20 March 2008.

You've just got to get on this. The front page headline of *The Sun* today says, "The paedo is landing." A 61-year-old nonce, Raymond Horne, is flying in today from Australia because the Aussies don't want the old pervo! He's served 12 years and Australia are sick of him, so he's coming home. Watch out, kids. Why the fuck didn't they just flush the old bastard out of the plane toilet? Problem solved. This piece of shit has been noncing kids all his life. He left Britain when he was five years old; now we've got the nonce back! He looks like Uncle Albert out of *Only Fools and Horses*! I'll give him three months till we hear about him noncing another kid. What a fucking country this is – even accepting that dirty bastard. The Aussies don't fuck about, and that's how we should be! If we sent all the foreign nonces back to their own country our prisons would be half empty. That's a fact.

Danny Hansford was up today. We had a good visit with lots sorted out. The movie will be a No. 1, he says. It will be the best movie in 2009.

I called Giovanni Di Stefano tonight (via the London office). He's back in Iraq. This guy is fearless: there are bombs going off all around him and he's still fighting for justice and still 200% on my side. How lucky am I to have him in my corner? Top man. I also called Mum up. My brother just got rushed into hospital because of his appendix. He just fainted, spewed up and that was it: in for the op. That's how life is – in and out of madness! One day you're up, one day you're down, next day you're on the operating table.

I got 10 letters today. One was from a bird in Cumbria who says she's 5 foot 6 with blonde hair, blue eyes and a body to die for. She's just read my book *The Krays and Me* and would like to get to know me better. She likes music, meals out and lots of sex. Yeah, yeah… She's probably 18 stone with four chins and stuffs her fat face with cakes and farts her muggy life away. Why not pop a photo in, you sad bitch? If you enjoy lots of sex then what fucking good am I for you? Just send me £500 and fuck off to Iceland. I'll get a new training kit. Lots of sex? Yeah, sure! Do me a favour: fuck off! Write to one of those death row inmates in the USA. Go marry the Ripper. I'm not into your little game. It's not my scene anymore.

It's fucking freezing in my cell. It's a cold old day today; the weather's changed for the worse.

I see William Shatner, the *Star Trek* captain, has auctioned off a kidney stone he had removed. How unique is that? It's up for 15 grand – a fucking kidney stone. See? There's always a first for everything! What prat's gonna pay 15K for that? Somebody will, there's always some nutter with more cash than sense!

I see that monster Steve Wright, the Suffolk strangler, has just launched an appeal. Well, it is nearly April Fools'. Fucking murdering bastard.

Yeah, a good day today. A visit, phone calls, letters, and the grub wasn't too bad. Life's a bowl of dates… and a good shit. You can't beat it, can you? Did I ever tell you about the time I was sitting on my pot having a shit in Wandsworth reading a book? I just lost track of time. My legs and arse went numb, I had pins and needles and even my toes were tingling. I started to get up but the fucking pot was stuck to my arse. Then the door opened! Clock this: I'm bollock naked with a pot stuck on my arse and the governor and six screws are at my cell door.

"Morning, Bronson!"

This is how prison life is: madness. It's just one big mad dream. It's unreal… it's Loonyology! You couldn't make this bollocks up even if you tried! It's magical.

I remember another occasion in Rampton asylum when I was lying in bed half asleep but I had a massive hard-on. It was that hard it hurt. I was only in my early 20s. So there I was all warm and cosy, dreaming about pussy, when the door flew open and in rushed six burly screws. They grabbed my blanket, ripped it off and jumped all over me. It was fucking mental – they dragged me out to the bath, slung me in freezing cold water and started hitting me with wet towels! Why? Fuck knows... If you find out, please tell me because I don't know! All I remember is the hard-on. It was a beauty and any man would have been proud of it! Rampton was like that in the 1970s – insane. The screws were madder than us!

James Whale's just come on the radio. It's 10pm so I'm calling it a day now and I'll be back when I'm ready. If not, then fuck it. Good night.

28 March 2008.

I've just had a right bad week with 'man 'flu'. Some sort of virus has hit me big time, like a tank. Loads of screws are off sick with it and others are coughing and have runny eyes. I think that's because they're crying; all they do is cry. It's one big moan all the time with them. If they all got a £100 raise they would still moan! It's just in them to moan. They're like the police: overpaid and underworked. Screws and police actually believe they're something they're not: a special breed. Fireman – yes, nurses – yes, screws and cops – I don't think so.

Anyway, the 'flu's killing us off! I feel like I've just smoked 40 fags and all I'm doing is coughing. I'm sweating, I'm shivering, I've got back ache, my eyes are blurry, I don't feel good! Medicine? Fuck off. I don't want fuck all of them! I fight my 'flu with my own resources: lots of fluids, a gargle with salt water, some honey and lemon in my tea and cod liver oil capsules! Apart from that, I let nature take its own ride.

Oh! My brother Mark's back home! He's a survivor but that was a close one – he could've lost that one. That's nurses and doctors for you, see! They're proper good workers who are worth their weight in gold. I salute them! It's high time the nation got behind them and respected them. Give them what they deserve: a bloody good wage for starters!

Here's a good bit of news! Berti Smalls is dead. That cunt should've died 40 years ago. But what amazes me is that he was actually living for years in the Surrey area! He was a fucking supergrass who put scores of villains away, and we are not talking for six months here! He put them away for 20 years and destroyed families. He smashed up so many dreams, all to save his own skinny neck. And there he was living in Surrey! Some fucker must have known! Anyway, the cunt's dead! Three cheers! HIP HIP – HOORAY! HIP HIP – HOORAY! HIP HIP – HOORAY! Who's next to leave our planet?

I had a good visit last week with Danny Hansford, the film producer. The film is rolling along like a good 'un! Everybody is buzzing on it. I've just sent Amanda Burton a nice art, basically saying thanks for playing my mum! Who better could a guy have to play his mum than her? How lucky am I? I keep telling you how lucky I am! But do you listen to me? Do you believe me? Do you fuck!

Maudsley and Miller have both got the 'flu! Fucking good job. I can hear them both coughing in the early hours of the night. Noise travels at night. Our unit is hollow like a submarine, but it's good to hear them coughing. I smile and say, "Choke." I suppose I've still got a wicked streak in me! But for them to choke would make my year, it really would. Call me a nasty bastard, call me what you will, but with neighbours like them who needs Hell? I shouted to one of them two nights back, "Hurry up and die, you old cunt." Maudsley shouted back, "I am dead, you cunt." That made me smile! That's a wicked sense of humour and he really does believe he's dead! Fuck me. Get me out of here!

Here's a mad one for you: one in every 100 US adults are in jail. In 1985 in America there were half a million in jail; now it's 2.3 million. That sums up the good old USA for you!

I see prison officer Adam Seamark has just pleaded guilty at Reading Crown Court to supplying crack cocaine and heroin to inmates at Woodhill jail. Is anybody amazed? It just goes to prove all I've ever said. It's all Loonyology. You may not like it, you may not like me and you may think it's all bollocks, but I've made it 100% clear from day one that this system is more corrupt and evil than any convict I've ever met. Seamark is just one of many, only most don't get caught. This cunt got greedy, he wasn't happy making an extra 500 quid a week (tax free) in his pocket. He wanted five grand – and got it. Greed got him nicked! Now it's porridge for him. Well, Coco Pops or Rice Krispies...

Old Jack Binns sent me in 50 quid this week! He never forgets his old china! That's my canteen sorted for April. Cheers, Jack.

Fuck me, as I'm writing this I've just had a massive coughing fit. I've got a fucking headache now! My chest feels like it's caved in.

Roll on a new week! A new month! It's April on Tuesday. I've got the Frayne brothers up on Wednesday so they can tell me all about their part in the movie. Then on Saturday I've got Lorraine and Andy up with Mark Fish. So it's all looking good!

YABADAABDOOOOooooooooooo!!!!!!!!

Chapter 4

Hollywood, Bollywood & Loonywood!

No photos – no autographs.
And don't fucking breathe on me!

My parole review for 2008 is almost on me! It will be exactly the same result as two years ago and four years ago: no. Why? Because Charlie Bronson can't ever be given parole. How can I? How can they parole a man who's constantly held in total isolation in a cage? How can they free a man into society when they won't even allow him to mix with anybody inside? It's basically impossible for me to be paroled and the system knows it only too well. I am a political prisoner, like Ronnie Biggs and the late Reggie Kray. The system can't be seen to show any compassion to people like us. They use my name to deter youngsters: "Don't play up or you'll end up like Bronson – in a hole till the day you die." That's why I'm treated this way; that's why they can't be seen to parole me.

It's total crap, it's fucking obvious I've changed! I changed eight years ago; my reports prove that! How can this shit really justify me even being held on a max secure control unit? It can't, and to top it all they won't even allow me in an open room for my parole review – the judge has to see me through bars. I can't even be trusted in the same room. That's why Bronson is fucked and buried!

It's actually illegal what they're doing. How can it ever be fair justice? My life tariff was only three years and I've now served five years over that tariff! Anyway, fuck them and fuck their parole. I'll win my appeal! All I've got to do is get my case back to the appeal court and get my conviction quashed. That way I'd walk out a free man with no silly parole restrictions hanging over me! Can you imagine what my parole restrictions would be like? Tagged, monitored, told where to live, who I can see, where I can and can't go. I'd have to report to the cops and probation every day – I'd have no fucking free life at all! It's all about control with the system: "Do what we say or go back to jail, buddy. We are your superiors. Do as you're told, little boy." Yeah, can you see me marching about to their tune? Put your dosh on me to win my appeal! That'll be a real victory! Then and only then can I get on with my life. The birdman flies for real…

Keep the faith, I always say. Tomorrow's just another day for us all and anything can happen. In fact, a plane could smash into this jail and blow a fucking big hole through my wall. I could be out tomorrow, I could even be dead. That's how life is for us all, you just never know. But I do know this parole is a fucking big piss-take. A snowball in Hell's got more chance than I have in getting parole. They know it! I know it! We all know it! So why do we actually play the game? Because that's all it ever can be – a game – until I'm let out of solitary, moved to a less secure jail and allowed to do my sentence in a normal way. Until then I'm just caught up in the madness of life! It's just Loonyology at its very, very best to me!

Man driving down road, woman driving up same road. They pass each other. Man shouts out of window: "Cow!" Woman yells out of window: "Prick!" Woman turns around corner, smashes into a huge cow and dies. If only women would fucking listen!

Did I ever tell you about the time I was driving a lorry full of booze from Liverpool to London and I picked up two girl hitchhikers? It was back in the early 1970s, the hot pants era. These two chicks were hot – I could actually smell their pussy juice. We got chatting and got onto sex.

They were both up for it, so I pulled into a lay-by. One straddles over me and started to bounce up and down whilst the other one was sticking her tongue in my mouth. How fucking wonderful can it get? It's memories like this that makes a man want to live on till he's 100 years old. That's how it was in those days: beautiful, exciting, electrifying, fucking magical. No sooner had you shot your load than you were up for a second helping. Now days they need coke and smack. All we needed was a good hot wet pussy. Sometimes I think, will I ever get another fuck on this planet? Am I really fucked; will I never get freed? The very thought of never having sex again depresses me! Surely I don't deserve that, do I?

2 April 2008

I had a visit today from the Frayne brothers – two diamonds. Watch out for them in my movie! They're in the dog fight scene where I kill a rottweiler! Although it happened, it's not something I'm proud of. Normally I love animals, especially dogs, but it was at a time I needed money! The challenge was there and I had to eat and live. What do you expect me to do – starve? I was not long out of jail and I was skint. Anyway, fuck it, 'dog eat dog' that's all this life is. Kill or be killed – survive.

I've not been too clever this last week. I've got a chest virus. I'm on antibiotics and all I'm doing is coughing my fucking guts up! I feel like I've smoked 40 strong fags or been eating a plate of tin. It's not good at all...

5 April 2008.

My chest is no better, in fact it's worse! Strange – Prince Phillip, the Queen's old man, is in hospital with the same thing. Did you know he's 87 years old? He looks older; I thought he was a good 100. Anyway, he's got a chest infection too. I probably got it off the old cunt! All I'm doing is coughing. That's not me, is it?

Hey! What's the first thing a battered wife does when she's out of the hospital? The dishes, if she has any sense.

I had a visit today from my Lorraine and Andy! They were on the movie set the last couple of days so I got all the latest action. Today it's all complete – the film's now finished! A big thanks to all the cast. My respects. You all did me proud, especially Danny Hansford and Mark Fish for their solid support. Oh well, that's it! We shall see it in March 2009. And if there's any justice in this world, I'll be at the premiere...

Two Irishmen find a mirror. First one picks it up and says, "I know this face but I can't put a name to it." Second one picks it up and says, "You daft bastard, it's me!"

Comply or Die won the National today. I fancied Simon myself so I've saved a few bob there. I would've bet on that if I was out! I told you I'm lucky – I've saved a nice few quid there!

Amir Khan fights tonight. He defends his Commonwealth lightweight title against Denmark's Martin Kristjansen. Kristjansen's no mug, he's only lost one of his pro fights. This Khan is going all the way, he will be a world champion soon. No surer bet.

An old woman's in a lift in a posh department store when two arrogant young women get in wearing very expensive scent. "Romance by Ralph Lauren – £100 a bottle!" says one. "Chanel No. 5 – £150 a bottle!" says the other. As the old woman leaves the lift she farts and says, "Brussel sprouts – 25p a pound!"

Talking of Brussels, we only used to get them twice a year in jail, at Xmas and Easter. Now we get them all the time. Diets really have changed for the better inside! The choice and variety is a lot better. It's not often you'll hear me praise the system, but the food really has improved – even though they stole our porridge and replaced it with silly kids' cereals.

I got a mad old letter today from a geezer up in Durham jail wanting to know if I ever fought Rocky Marciano. Hello? How fucking old do you think I am, you cheeky fucker? I don't 'arf get some mentalists writing to me, but it all helps to pass my time away. I actually received eight letters today, not bad for a Saturday.

I got a crazy card from a sad, lonely woman from Cumbria yesterday who's been on my website and thinks I'm lovely! Her words. Look love, I'm really not – I've never been lovely. I don't think I'll ever be that and I'm not sure I wish to be. You shouldn't really be writing shit like that! Now, if you'd said, "I love your cock," or "Your body is lovely," I could understand it! But why describe *me* as lovely? Maybe she's on day release from the local asylum! Who knows. I wish prison HQ would say I'm lovely!!!

Rolling on with time

It's all about time
They can't stop the clock
Nothing stops time
Nothing or nobody
You roll with it
Bob and weave
Duck and dive
That's what to do.
That's all you can do
Never let go
To let go is to die
Who wants to die?
Only a fucking loser
Grab on and hold tight
Enjoy the ride
That's what I do
I don't even pay
Fuck paying
Why pay a penny?
You can't buy time
Some have tried to
All have died
They never made it!
They never could
Time ran out

The heart stopped
No more beats
It pumped its last
Like a limp, lifeless cock
You're better off dead
What good's a limp cock?
Shameful
Embarrassing
Time's caught you up!
You're a joke
Sticks and stones
It does hurt
Words can destroy you
Laughter can kill you
Along with time
Viagra...
Fuck off.
Call it a day
Pay me what you owe
Crawl away and die
Do it for love
The love of time
The love of life
Don't die angry
Go to Heaven
Escape Hell.
Time's up
Fly.

That's got to be every man's nightmare – not being able to get a stiffy on in the bedroom. Imagine it: the shame... But it comes to us all, one way or the other! Fucking Loonyology or what? I say enjoy it whilst you can, because fuck all lasts forever, that's for sure.

Lorraine and Andy looked well today. Since they moved out to Spain they look more relaxed and stress free. It's a nicer way of life out there: sun, sea, a good diet, a slower way of life; the skin glows, the eyes sparkle. It's got to be good for you. Fuck me, I need a break, I really do.

Round seven: BANG. All over. That's another victory for Khan; this guy's going to be awesome. We are watching a boxing legend in the making. Brilliant.

Charlton Heston just died at 84. God bless you, mate. Top geezer. Oscar-winning legend. When you think about it, life's just an act. The world's the stage and we all play our parts, so we must be all Oscar winners! Well? Aren't we? Think about that one.

7 April 2008.

I love a Monday, the start of a fresh week! You never know what's about to happen. Good or bad, it's a buzz. I was jogging around the yard today and I was happy. One of the cons had a radio on in their cell and some great tunes drifted into the yard. One in particular made me laugh: 'I Just Called to Say I Love You' by Stevie Wonder. It brought back a crazy memory from Risley jail in 1985. I awoke in the early hours, 3 or 4 o'clock, and I just started singing that song. After 10 minutes other cons started banging their doors and shouting, "Shut up, you cunt. Fucking shut up and get your head on the pillow." Even the screw was kicking my door and shouting, "Shut the fuck up or you're nicked." Well, that did it for me. No fucker spoils my fun, so I just sang it louder and louder. I was singing so loud and for so long I almost lost my voice. I was sweating, fucking sky high on adrenalin.

"Shut the fuck up, you mad cunt," the whole jail was screaming by now. Doors were smashing, bars rattling and others were singing along with me. It was insanity at its very best! That's how prison is: mad Loonyology.

At 7.30am my door crashed in and six of the biggest screws steamed in, grabbed me and carted me off to the strong box. Cons were shouting through their doors: "Give him a good fucking kicking. Do the cockney cunt. Smash him up." You won't believe it – I was still singing 'I Just Called to Say I Love You'. Even when they slung me in the box and started kicking me, I was still singing!

Memories like these are priceless to me! You can't buy such beautiful memories. Every screw and con there that day will never forget it. How could they? Every time Stevie Wonder comes on the TV or radio they will smile just like I did today. That's what keeps us alive: memories. Without a memory you're cabbage, you're dead meat. Enjoy your journey of life and treasure every moment of it!

I do hope some of my stories make you smile! Imagine the one I've just told you and try to see it happening – all those cons shouting and screaming in the early hours, all those doors banging, then picture the six burly screws steaming into me and kicking the shit out of me and I'm still singing. It's really gone insane… hysteria!! So here I am 23 years later running around a caged yard smiling all over again. That's the magic of life; it's wonderful. Hey! Who's fucking winning here? Surely it's me! It should be a crime to be so happy!

I also thought about my age today; I'm not far off 60 – fucking 60! The big six-o… now that is crazy. That is scary. Me 60? I was only 21 when I came in. That's fucking madness…

I called Mum up tonight at 6pm. We always have a good laugh. She was at the movie set last week on the final day of shooting. The film crew all spoilt her and she had a great time with Lorraine and Andy.

Now clock this for a mind blower: the OASys report. It's brand new, all cons have to have one done, and even if you refuse to take part they will still do one for you. Read it, digest it, then decide yourselves what you think about it. My opinion is that it's a pile of shit! It's about as good as a chocolate soldier in the Sahara desert. It's just worthless! Pathetic! Useless! And it's a total joke to me. This now goes on file. It's all about scoring points on how dangerous we are, or can be, or have been! That's all the world is now days: guesswork and statistics. It's all psychological bollocks; one big fuck-off game. And if you don't play it, you don't get any points. Anyway, have a butcher's. I've got nothing to hide. It's all here for you to see. A pile of Loonyology…

AMEN.

Section 1 - Offending Information OASys Two BRONSON, CHARLES BT1314

	PSR/court considered offence	Number Of Offences	Code
1.1	False imprisonment	1	36/3
	Additional offences		
	PSR/court considered offence	Number Of	Code
	There are no Additional Offences for this offender.		
1.2		Resentencing for breach	○ Yes ◉ No

		Value	Score
1.3	Total number of separate offences for which convicted at this court appearance	2	
1.4	Any current or previous convictions for burglary	Yes	
1.5	Number of court appearances at which convicted aged under 18 years	2	
1.6	Number of court appearances at which convicted aged 18 years and over. Do not include current appearances.	13	
1.7	Age at first conviction (record in years)	12	
1.8	Age first in contact with police: first recorded caution, reprimand or final warning (record in years)	11	
1.9	Number of previous custodial sentences aged under 21 years	1	
1.10	Number of previous custodial sentences aged 21 years or over	3	
1.11	Any breaches of probation/parole/licence/bail or community based sentence	Yes	
1.12	Number of different categories of conviction (include previous and current)	5	

- [ ] Murder/manslaughter/attempted murder
- [x] GBH/wounding/robbery/abduction
- [x] Other violence
- [ ] Sexual offences
- [ ] Arson
- [x] Criminal damage
- [ ] Drug offences
- [x] Burglary
- [x] Theft
- [ ] Fraud and forgery
- [ ] Other dishonesty
- [ ] Driving offences

Total score for Section 1	17
Does this section require additional attention for the SSP?	☐

Section 2 - Analysis of Offences   OASys Two   BRONSON, CHARLES   BT1314

2.1 Brief offence(s) details
Mr Bronson was convicted at Luton Crown Court in February 2000 for the offences of Threats to Kill and False Imprisonment. The offences took place at HMP Hull where he was serving a custodial sentence for offences of GBH and carrying a firearm. Reports inform he took an art teacher hostage during an art class as a revenge attack for the teacher critising his painting. Mr Bronson had planned the offences by gathering together weapons such as a spear made from a pool cue and broken glass. He held the teacher hostage for around 40 hours during which time he tied the victim to a rope and made him crawl around the floor like a dog.

2.2 Did any of the offence(s) involve any of the following
- [x] Carrying/use of a weapon
  Provide a description of weapon(s)   Made a spear from a knife and a snooker cue, also used a knife, chisels, bottles and a rope.
- [ ] Violence or threat of violence/coercion
- [x] Excessive use of violence/sadistic violence
- [ ] Arson
- [x] Physical damage to property
- [ ] Sexual element

2.3 Did any of the following occur
- [ ] Were there any direct victim(s) eg contact, targeting
- [ ] Were any of the victim(s) targeted because of racial motivation or hatred of another identifiable group
- [x] Response to a specific victim (eg revenge, settling grudges)
- [ ] Physical violence towards partner
- [x] Repeat victimisation of the same person
- [ ] Were the victim(s) stranger(s) to the offender

2.4 Details of the victim(s)

Approximate age	26-49	**Gender**	(●) M ( ) F ( ) Unknown
Race / ethnicity	WHITE - British		
Victim/Perpetrator Relationship	Other acquaintance		

Victim / perpetrator relationship
The victim was an art teacher whom was known to Mr Bronson prior to the offence.
Any other information of specific note, consider vulnerability
The victim was taken hostage on a wing at HMP Hull.

2.5 Impact to the victim
Information states that the victim had to retire on medical grounds following the attack and that he has had difficulty finding alternative employment.

2.6 Does the offender recognise the impact and consequences of offending on victim, community / wider society (●) Yes ( ) No

2.7 Were there other offenders involved ( ) Yes (●) No
Number of others involved
Peer group influences ( ) Yes (●) No
If there were others involved, was the offender the leader
Mr Bronson acted alone in his offending.

2.8 Why did it happen - evidence of motivations and triggers
The victim had critised a painting that Mr Bronson had done during a previous art lesson. He interprated this as a personal attack and so wanted revenge.
Unrealistic expectations of the system.
Perceived challenge to status and identity.
Feeling threatened by others.
Perceived lack of response to requests.
Wanting to fight other peoples battles.
Talking about violence.
Situations that trigger feelings of upset, anger, disappointment, annoyance, frustration, tension, anxiety, stress.

2.9	**Please tick each evidenced motivation below** ☐ Sexual motivation ☐ Financial motivation ☐ Addictions/perceived needs ☐ Emotional state ☑ Hate motivation ☑ Thrill seeking ☐ Other Provide a description
2.10	**Did any of the following act as disinhibitors at the time of the current offence** ☐ Alcohol ☑ Emotional state ☐ Pornography ☐ Drugs ☐ Non-Compliance with medication ☐ Traumatic life event ☐ Psychiatric problems

2.11	**Does the offender accept responsibility for the current offence(s)** **How much responsibility does s / he acknowledge for the offence(s). Does s / he blame others, minimise the extent of his / her offending?** Mr Bronson accepts full responsibility for carrying out the offence. However he blames the 'system' for his violent outbursts, stating that it was his way at getting revenge.	◉ Yes ○ No
2.12	**Pattern of offending (consider details of previous convictions)** Mr Bronson has a long list of offending behaviour dating back to 1964. He began with numerous convictions for theft related offences which were mainly dealt with by way of community based sentences. Then he received a 7 year custodial sentence in1974 for offences of robbery, agrravated burglary, assault with intent to rob and possession of firearms. A consecutive period of 9 month for GBH, the in 1988 he received a 7 year custodial sentence for robbery. It was during the 8 year custodial sentence that he was serving when he committed the index offence he had accumulated additional sentences for incidents of attempted and actual hostage taking and aggressive and disruptive behaviour.	
2.13	**Are current offence(s) an escalation in seriousness from previous offending**	◉ Yes ○ No
2.14	**Are current offence(s) part of an established pattern of similar offending** Yes	☐ Disclosed
Total score for Section 2		**2**
Does this section require additional attention for the SSP?		☐
Provide evidence for ratings above and identify offence analysis issues contributing to risks of offending and harm. Please include any positive factors. Mr Bronson was originally sentenced to a tariff of 4 years; however in May 2001 this was reduced to 3 years on appeal. Given the serious nature of his offending behaviour there are links to risk of harm.		
Analysis of offence issues linked to risk of serious harm, risks to the individual & other risks		◉ Yes ○ No

Section 6 - Relationships	OASys Two	BRONSON, CHARLES	BT1314
6.1 Current relationship with close family members	No problems	☐ Disclosed	
6.2 Close family member has criminal record	Yes	☐ Disclosed	
6.3 Experience of childhood	Some problems	☐ Disclosed	
6.4 Current relationship with partner	No problems	☐ Disclosed	
6.5 Current partner has criminal record	No	☐ Disclosed	
6.6 Previous experience of close relationships	Some problems	☐ Disclosed	
Total score for Section 6		4	
Does this section require additional attention for the SSP?		☐	
6.7 Evidence of domestic violence / partner abuse		○ Yes ◉ No	
☐ Victim	☐ Perpetrator		

Provide evidence for ratings above and identify relationship issues contributing to risks of offending and harm. Please include any positive factors.
6.1 Mr Bronson has a very supportive family network, which includes his mother, brothers, sister and his son. He has regular contact with his family via letters and phone calls. His son, who is 36 years old, visits him on a regular basis. He reports they have fully supported him throughout his sentence and that they are now looking towards him moving from segregation to normal location. 6.2 Mr Bronson self reports that he believes one family member has a criminal record, although he is unsure as to the details of the offences. 6.3 In interview he described growing up in a 'good, hard working family'. He was raised by his mother and father, along with his two brothers and one sister. He reports of 'happy times' during his childhood, and stated there was no abuse within the home. He began offending at the age of 11 and reports that this was not due to his home life, more to do with peer pressure. 6.4/6.5 Mr Bronson does not have a partner at the present time. He reports that this is not an issue for him. 6.6 Mr Bronson has been married twice in the past. He married his first wife in 1970 and they separated 4 years later. They had a son together, to whom he still has regular contact with; he no longer has any contact with his ex-wife. He married his second wife in 2000 whilst he was still in prison. He met her whilst he was in custody when she began writing to him as a pen pal, their relationship developed over time. They are now divorced and he reports that he no longer has any contact with her. 6.7 There is no documented evidence of any domestic violence.

Relationship issues linked to risk of serious harm, risks to the individual and other risks	○ Yes ◉ No
Relationship issues linked to offending behaviour	○ Yes ◉ No

Section 7 - Lifestyle and associates	OASys Two	BRONSON, CHARLES	BT1314
7.1 Community integration	Significant problems	☐ Disclosed	
7.2 Regular activities encourage offending	Some problems	☐ Disclosed	
7.3 Easily influenced by criminal associates	Significant problems	☐ Disclosed	
7.4 Manipulative/predatory lifestyle	Significant problems	☐ Disclosed	
7.5 Recklessness and risk-taking behaviour	Significant problems	☐ Disclosed	
Total score for Section 7		9	
Does this section require additional attention for the SSP?		☐	

Provide evidence for ratings above and identify lifestyle issues contributing to risks of offending and harm. Please include any positive factors.
7.1 Prior to custody almost all of Mr Bronson's friends and associates were from a criminal lifestyle. He reports that the majority were involved in robberies as he was. In interview he reported that he now feels disgusted with his old lifestyle, discribing it as 'organised villany'. Whilst he was in custody before the index offence it is documented that he continued to lead this lifestyle. He aquired weapons from other prisoners on his wing to help carry out the index offence. At the current time he is unable to interact with other prisoners due to his location, although he has begun to interact more with unit staff; on the whole ina positive way. He has good contacts outside of prison from both family and friends; however he does report that his close friends do have criminal backgrounds although he reports that they no longer lead a life of crime. 7.2 Although alcohol or drugs did not play a direct part in Mr Bronson's offending, his entire lifestyle revolved around the criminal underworld. The way he has previously lived his life both prior and in custody has had a direct link to his offending. 7.3 It is documented in previous reports that he has become a 'leader' in custody, however he reports that prior to custody he saw himself neither as a leader or a follower. He stated that because his life revolved around the criminal underworld he was 'equal' to his peers. Since the index offence the media have labelled him as 'britains most violent prisoner'. Although at this stage it is difficult to ascertain as to whether he would return to his criminal ways if located on normal location in custody, it is documented that due to his profile he would be a target for other prisoners, which is concerning. 7.4 Mr Bronson's offences which were committed whilst in custody where committed against members of staff and fellow prisoners. On each occasion he took them hostage when they were alone and vulnerable. 7.5 His criminal convictions all have an element of risk taking behaviour. He self reported that his previous convictions of robbery where committed without thinking of the consequences and that he was willing to take the risk of going to prison as the financial gain outweighed the risk. With regard to the index offence he did not consider the risks of taking a hostage; instead he wanted his revenge on the victim. His previous convictions highlight a problem with his lifestyle and associates and this makes it a direct link between offending and a risk of serious harm.

Lifestyle and associates issues linked to risk of serious harm, risks to the individual and other risks	◉ Yes ○ No
Lifestyle and associate issues linked to offending behaviour	◉ Yes ○ No

10 Emotional well-being	OASys Two	BRONSON, CHARLES	BT1314
10.1 Difficulties coping		Significant problems	☐ Disclosed
10.2 Current psychological problems/depression		No problems	☐ Disclosed
10.3 Social isolation		Significant problems	☐ Disclosed
10.4 Offender's attitude to themselves		Significant problems	☐ Disclosed
10.5 Self harm, attempted suicide, suicidal thoughts or feelings		No	☐ Disclosed
10.6 Current psychiatric problems		No problems	☐ Disclosed
Total score for Section 10			6

Does this section require additional attention for the SSP? ☐

10.7 Tick any of the following reported

- ☑ Evidence of childhood behavioural problems
- ☐ History of severe head injuries, fits, periods of unconsciousness
- ☐ History of psychiatric treatment
- ☐ Ever been on medication for mental health problems in the past
- ☑ Previously failed to co-operate with psychiatric treatment
- ☑ Ever been a patient in a Special Hospital or Regional Secure Unit
- ☐ Current psychiatric treatment or treatment pending

Provide evidence for ratings above and identify any issues of emotional well being contributing to risks of offending and harm. Please include any positive factors.

10.1 In interview he reported that he was happy with his life prior custody, although he believes this maybe due to the amount of crime he was involved in, that he believed this was a 'normal' way of life. He reports that he believes he began having difficulties coping once he was convicted. He reports becoming angry with the system and authority and that his way of coping with this anger was through using violence and fighting, this is well documented in previous reports. It is documented in the court summary report that the index offence occured when he became upset at the art teacher critising his art work. He interperated this as a personal attack and immediately began to plan his 'revenge'. Due to the nature of the index offence, he has been located in the Exceptional Risk Unit of the Close Supervision Centre. During this time there has been numerous occasions where he has used aggression as his way of coping. This makes a direct link between emotional well-being and a risk of serious harm and offending. There is one documented incident on 13th November 2006 when he refused to leave the exercise yard. In the days leading up to this he had made threats to staff that he wanted to be moved within 7 days, following continued disagreements with another prisoner on the unit. He self reported that he has learnt through experience that he can't beat the system and that he now uses his writing and paintings as he way of coping with difficult situations. He has one proven adjudication 08/02/2008 for assault on a prison officer. This involved him spitting in the face of an officer who was carrying out a routine search on his cell. 10.2 There is no documented evidence that he has any current psychological problems. 10.3 He has regular contact with his extended family and he reports hehas cut off ties with his friends and aquaintances that he committed his earlier offences of robbery with; however he has spent his time in custody located in the close supervision centers within the high security estate. This means he is unable to interact with other prisoners on the unit; prisoners are unlocked one at a time to collect meals and undertake exercise. He is still located on the Exceptional risk close supervison center at HMP Wakefield due to the risk harm harm he currently poses to others if he were located on normal location. 10.4 He states he feels alienated from the rest of the prison population because of his location in the CSC unit. He feels that the media interest in him means that he is constantly portrayed as 'britains most violent prisoner'. It has been documented that he thrives on being in the media spotlight although in interview he stated that he has never spoken to the press. 10.5 There is no documented evidence to suggest that he has had any self harm issues prior to custody. He has not been on an ACCT document or a F2052sh. 10.6 There is no documented evidence of any current psychological problems. 10.7 Records indicate that in 1977 he was certified 'insane' at HMP Parkhurst and was subsequently transfered to Broadmoor hospital; where he spent the next 5 years. During this time he refused any treatment and after 5 years he was certified 'sane'. Due to his experience in Broadmoor he has concerns about engaging with psychiatrists and psychologists during this sentence. He self reports that he once was perscribed drugs in the 1970's for temple lobe epilepsy, but reports having no problems since.

Issues of emotional well-being linked to offending behaviour	◉ Yes ○ No
Issues of emotional well-being linked to risk of serious harm, risks to the individual & other risks	◉ Yes ○ No

Section 11 - Thinking and behaviour	OASys Two BRONSON, CHARLES BT1314	
11.1 Level of interpersonal skills	Some problems	☐ Disclosed
11.2 Impulsivity	Some problems	☐ Disclosed
11.3 Aggressive/controlling behaviour	Significant problems	☐ Disclosed
11.4 Temper control	Some problems	☐ Disclosed
11.5 Ability to recognise problems	Some problems	☐ Disclosed
11.6 Problem solving skills	Significant problems	☐ Disclosed
11.7 Awareness of consequences	Significant problems	☐ Disclosed
11.8 Achieves goals	Significant problems	☐ Disclosed
11.9 Understands other people's views	Significant problems	☐ Disclosed
11.10 Concrete/abstract thinking	Significant problems	☐ Disclosed
Total score for Section 11		**16**
Does this section require additional attention for the SSP?		☐

Provide evidence for ratings above and identify thinking/behavioural issues contributing to risks of offending and harm. Please include any positive factors.

11.1 Mr Bronson engaged fully for the purpose of this assessment; this is a postive move forward for him as in the past he has not engaged fully with his offender management team and assessments for the purpose of reports; he needs to continue to maintain consistant interactions and engagement in assessments. However his decline to complete recent lifer progress interviews with probation and the assessments and interventions team are disappointing considering his recent verbalisation of motivation to move forward. His overall communications with unit staff are documented as being polite and appropriate; however his previous custodial behaviour and convictions whilst in custody demonstrate his withdrawal from interactions with staff. His current location means he has no contact with other prisoners. 11.2 Whilst evidence from court reports indicate that Mr Bronson's offences were planned and not an act of impulsivity, his behaviour whilst in custody has involved a degree of impulsivity in his reactions to difficult circumstances. This is detailed in wing history sheets from the unit which outline verbal outbursts towards Governors and more recently resulted in a proven adjudiaction for assault on a member of staff. 11.3 Mr Bronson's offence of robbery indicates an element of aggressive/controlling behaviour, as he needed to display these traits in order to carry out this offence. The additional offences to which Mr Bronson has been convicted of whilst in custody (hostage taking) also have a high degree of controlling behaviour. The index offence involved Mr Bronson making the victim crawl around the floor like a dog; which was a form of punishment in Mr Bronson's mind. More recently in custody he has displayed aggressive behaviour; in 2006 he refused to come in from the excercise yard following a dispute with staff about another prisoner. It is documented he took an aggressive stance and tore his t-shirt to wrap around his head like a bandana; this is a risk parallelling behaviour trait to the index offence. 11.4 Mr Bronson's convictions are documented as 'planned' attacks in court paperwork; his recent behaviour in custody displays elements of loss of temper and poor temper control. This includes documented instances of verbal outbursts towards staff and Governors. 11.5/11.6 Mr Bronson self reports that he now understands the problems he had in the past; including his lifestyle prior custody and his behaviour in custody. However he has only just begun to verbalise this to his offender management team. During interview he had a tendancy to apprortion part of the blame for his offending in custody to his preceived treatment whilst he was at Broadmoor; holding a grudge against 'the system'. 11.7 Mr Bronson had previously taken members of staff hostage prior to the index offence; this was to achieve his 'revenge on the system'. He self reports that he has now learnt from his past mistakes and that he is ready to move on however he continues to have some outbursts on the unit. 11.9/11.10 The index offence happened due to Mr Bronson misinterpreting the comments made by the victim as a personal attack; he assumed hostile intentions by the victims critique of Mr Bronson's art work, when it was not meant in this way. Although in more recent times whilst Mr Bronson has been located in the CSC unit there has been little documented evidence of him reacting in this manner. Whilst in custody before the index offence Mr Bronson displayed this type of behaviour and received additional days added on to his sentence for taking hostages. This indicates that Mr Bronson has displayed concrete thinking in that he has difficulty in applying lessons learnt from his previous aggressive behaviours.

Thinking and behaviour issues linked to risk of serious harm, risks to the individual and other risks	◉ Yes ○ No
Thinking/behavioural issues linked to offending behaviour	◉ Yes ○ No

Section 12 - Attitudes	OASys Two	BRONSON, CHARLES	BT1314
12.1 **Pro-criminal attitudes**		Some problems	Disclosed
12.2 **Discriminatory attitudes / behaviour**		Some problems	Disclosed
12.3 **Attitude towards staff**		Significant problems	Disclosed
12.4 **Attitude towards supervision / licence**		Significant problems	Disclosed
12.5 **Attitude to community / society**		Significant problems	Disclosed
12.6 **Does the offender understand their motivation for offending**		Significant problems	Disclosed
Total score for Section 12			10
Does this section require additional attention for the SSP?			☐

Provide evidence for ratings above and identify issues about attitudes contributing to risks of offending and harm. Please include any positive factors.

12.1 Mr Bronson self reported in interview that prior to custody his lifestyle was heavily within the criminal sub-culture. He reports that he would regularly commit crimes without thinking about the consequences; believing it was his way of life. In relation to the index offence he self reports that he believed at the time that he had no option but to deal with his frustrations by using violence. He reported in interview that he believed his actions were justified at the time due to his previous experiences in custody; this is well documented in previous reports. He reports that his stance towards crime has now changed and that he has learnt from his mistakes; indicating upon his release he would like the opportunity to work with young adults to help them stay away from crime. Due to his current location it has yet to be evidenced as to whether he would revert back to his criminal behaviour if placed in challenging or difficult circumstances within the community. As evidenced above Mr Bronson holds some criminal attitudes which have enabled him to continue to re-offend. 12.2 It is documented in court paperwork that at the time of the offence Mr Bronson believed that the victim objected to parts of the healthy living poster ,he had designed, which referred to the use of condoms during homosexual acts. He believed he was critisised because the victim was a gay man and it is documemted that Mr Bronson stated the victim 'got what he deserved'. He self reports that he does not hold any homophobic or racist views however there is numerous reports in his files that he has written reponses on which he makes negative inferences to sex offenders and gay men. 12.3 The index offence involved taking a civillian member of staff hostage. He has previously took a prison Governor hostage and has made numerous threats to staff. He is currently located in the exceptional risk close supervision centre due to the high risk he poses to staff. During this reporting period it is documented that his attitude towards unit staff has improved and he has been interacting appropriately on a daily basis. However he has a recent proven adjudication for assault on a prison officer. The incident involved him spitting in the face of a member of the dedicated search team, which is concerning. 12.4 He has previous convictions for breech related offences. Due to the length of time he has now spent in custody it is dofficult to ascertain how he would react to supervision and license in the community. At the present time he has good communications and regular contact with his external probation officer. He has now begun to interact with his seconded probation officer beacuse in the past he has refused to engage. 12.5 Prior to custody his community was the 'criminal underworld' and he believed he had the right to committ crimes as his way of earning a living. Although he self reports that he has now changed his views on how he should live his live upon release, again this is an area that will not be tested untill his release. 12.6 Mr Bronson has not completed any offence related group work and refuses to engage fully with the assessments and interventions team therefore he does not understand his motivation for offending. He is therefore unable to evidence a reduction in risk. He needs to be encouraged to engage in offence focussed work to address his behaviour and increase his understanding 12.7 he has no completed any accredited programmes whilst he has been in custody. 12.8 He has now begun to enage with his offender management team as he states he now understands that without enagaging it is unlikely he will progress through the system. He needs to increase his interactions with all members of the multi-disciplinary team.

Attitudes linked to risk of serious harm, risks to the individual and other risks	(●) Yes ( ) No
Attitudes linked to offending behaviour	(●) Yes ( ) No
12.7 **Successful completion of accredited programmes**	( ) Yes (●) No
12.8 **Motivation**	Quite motivated

Family Name	BRONSON	**Forename**	CHARLES
PNC Number	70/16417J	**Prison Number**	BT1314

Summary Sheet - Risk of reconviction **OASys Two**

Section	**Raw score**		**Weighted score**	**Notional, Missing, Disclosed**	**Needs Attention**
1 + 2 Offending Information	19	0 1-2 3-4 5 6 | 7-9 10-11 12-13 14-15 16-17 **18-22** 0 2 5 7 10 | 20 25 35 40 45 **50**	50		☐
3 Accommodation	8	0 1 | 2 3-4 5-6 **7-8** 0 2 | 4 6 8 **12**	12		☐
4 Education, training and employability	11	0 1 2-3 4 | 5-7 8-10 **11-13** 14-18 0 2 4 6 | 12 15 **17** 20	17		☐
5 Financial management and income	2	0 1 **2** 3-4 | 5 6 7 8-10 0 1 **2** 5 | 7 9 10 12	2		☐
6 Relationships	4	0 1-2 3 | **4-6** 7-8 9-10 11-12 0 1 2 | **3** 4 5 6	3		☐
7 Lifestyle and associates	9	0-1 2 3 | 4 5-6 **7-10** 0 3 5 | 10 12 **15**	15		☐
8 Drug misuse	0	**0** 1 2 3 | 4 5-6 7-9 10-12 **0** 1 2 3 | 7 10 12 15	0		☐
9 Alcohol misuse	0	**0** 1-2 3 | 4-6 7-8 9-10 **0** 1 2 | 3 4 5	0		☐
10 Emotional well-being	6	0 1 2 | 3-4 **5-6** 7-12 0 1 2 | 4 **5** 6	5		☐
11 Thinking and behaviour	16	0 1 2 3 4-6 | 7-8 9-10 11-13 **14-20** 0 1 2 3 4 | 8 10 11 **12**	12		☐
12 Attitudes	10	0 1 2 3 | 4-5 6-7 8 **9-12** 0 1 2 4 | 7 10 12 **15**	15		☐
		TOTAL SCORE (max=168)	**131**		

Are there any low-scoring areas that need attention in the supervision and sentence plan.

Assessment of risk of reconviction ○ Low ○ Medium ◉ High

Summary Sheet - Risk of serious harm

	Risk in community	**Risk in custody**
Children	Low	Low
Public	High	Low
Known adult	Low	Very High
Staff	Low	Very High
Prisoners		Very High

Current concerns about:	**Yes**
Risk of suicide	☐
Risk of self-harm	☐
Coping in custody / hostel setting	☑
Vulnerability	☑
Escape / abscond	☐
Control issues	☑
Breach of trust	☐

Well, what about that then? OASys... what's your opinion? I bet it's: "Bollocks!!!" One sure thing is that they still don't know where I buried my dosh. The fuckers never will either. So what do they really know about us? Take it from me: 99% of it's guesswork! Plus the lies, plus the exaggeration. Anyway, I'm fucking bored of it now so let's move it on.

I read in the *Sunday People* that the mother of Michael Mullen (yeah, that skinny little prick who got life for the rape and murder of his brother's two-year-old daughter) says, "He should have hanged." Yeah! We all agree, Mrs Mullen. Your son doesn't deserve to continue to breathe air. He's a filthy beast. He snuffed your beautiful granddaughter out like you switch off the light switch. The little cunt's here in the hospital wing crying, full of self-pity. He should be with the worms. Cunt. The screws all hate him, the cons all hate him, his own mother and his brother hate him. No doubt they would love nothing better than to strangle him. Come on, Mullen, do what's right! Top yourself so we can all celebrate one less monster to feed. When your own mother says "hang" then that's it all over! Good night. Turn the light off on the way to Hell!

8 April 2008.

I called Tom Hardy up today! Great news, he's just become the proud father of baby Louis. See how life is like a jigsaw puzzle and the pieces fit together? He completes the movie then 'Bang!' – a new piece to life: a son. How great is that? Yeah, I'm well chuffed for the guy. I wish I could become a dad again. That would put the cherry on the cake for me. Now I'm older, I would be a great dad. Not that I wasn't a good dad to Mike, but I was just never there for the kid. I was out doing my villainy, 'ducking and diving' and smashing some fucker's head in, all in the name of Loonyology. It's the life I chose. I actually enjoyed myself, and if I say so myself some of those heads needed smashing in. Nasty bastards.

I can remember one useless fat prick who owed a friend of mine five grand. Peanuts today, but in 1971 that was a lot of dosh. Anyway, I paid him a visit! I smashed him to bits using a pick-axe handle. I actually enjoyed it too, because he was a fucking big fat slimy snake. He even begged me and cried, pleading for me not to hurt him. Oh! I forgot to mention that he was famous for beating up the local girls. One of those girls lived in my street and I saw her when she came out of hospital. I actually told her dad, "Leave it to me." So when I got the job to pay him a visit over his debt it was personal to me. More of a pleasure! Believe me, that day changed his life and a week later he paid up. I got 2K for that. That's what's called 'poetic justice'. It beats any police or courts. Sure it's a bit messy but it really does work! Respect – that's what it breeds! Morals – that's what it brings! You smash the granny out of a cunt like that! You give him what he lashes out, only double bubble. On top of the result I get a pat on the back and a drink off the girl's dad. Sweet. My way does work, believe it.

I got a lovely home-made card sent to me today from an invalid lady in York who's just read one of my books. She believes I should now be freed. You're not wrong either, lady. Thanks. I'll send her a card of respect, as things like that mean a lot to me. I never take anything for granted. I'm a man who appreciates things like that. I believe in respecting others.

I got nine letters in today, and my Luton newspaper! So it was a nice day. The soup was bloody lovely too: mushroom! I had two bowls and six bread rolls. It filled me up good style. Tea was a veg curry! Not bad, but it could've been better. I could do with one of my mum's meals. What is it about home cooking and double helpings? It's fucking cruel to keep on about it – painful and truly torturous. I love my grub, I really do. The only problem is that in jail most of it's shit! I eat it and forget what I've eaten 10 minutes later. It's fuck all to think about! Prison food is just eating to survive. I forget the last time I bit into a good piece of meat. I'd probably get a fucking jaw ache now if I had a steak. Steak's a dream I lost years ago. Jim Brookes, the landlord of the Moakes pub in Luton, used to do me a nice steak when I was in training for a fight. I would have two Guinnesses to wash it down. Lovely jubbly.

Who remembers Mick Leahy? He was the last boxer to beat the legendary Sugar Ray Robinson. Mick was the British Champion in the 1960s but, sadly, he's now got Alzheimer's. I've just sorted some of my art out to auction off for the old rascal. He's worth it! Men like Mick Leahy have earned respect 10 times over. He won the Lonsdale belt in 1963 against George Aldridge. Let's have three cheers for Mick. HIP HIP – HOORAY! HIP HIP – HOORAY! HIP HIP – HOORAY!

My opinion, for what it's worth, is that this country went downhill when they stopped dwarf throwing and the travelling freak shows. The 'PC brigade' have turned Great Britain into the laughing stock of Europe. Men have become pansies. Fuck me, dwarfs are only good for throwing and rubber men and bearded ladies should be in a show. We all need a bloody good laugh, don't we? Bring it all back, I say. Let's be great again.

Have you seen the state of our school teachers today? A fucking bunch of scruffy cunts. In my day teachers were full of pride and spotlessly dressed – not that it stopped me chinning the occasional one! If I was at school in this era I would hose them all down and give them a good wash! There's not a week that goes by that I don't read about some horny teacher having it off with a pupil. How fucking brilliant must that be? Some hot, sexy teacher with big tits taking you into the storeroom for a session, and you're just 15 years old! I swear to God I'd never play truant again! Would you?

It's obvious to me why some of these teachers end up going down this road. What woman doesn't dream of a young stud? Sex to a teenage boy is just dreams on top of dreams and some of those school boys can easily pass as 18 or 20. Kids like that don't need shit like Viagra! They're hard as a rock with just a sniff of a hot pussy, and even when they shoot their load they're back hard in seconds. And a horny teacher knows it only too well! The cat gets the cream. Greedy bitch.

It's been pissing down today but I still went out in the yard for my jog. It's the air I go out for. I love to fill my lungs up with fresh air – it makes you feel fresh and healthy, it makes you feel alive, which isn't bad considering I live in a cemetery. This is Dead Alley, you'd better believe it! It doesn't get any deeper. I just called to say I love you!

Here's a blinder. You'll love this one. This just proves what Loonyology is all about. Mark Corner, a body-building schizophrenic, attacked a woman with a blade and got nutted off and sent to Ferndale Mental Health Clinic in Liverpool. You would think that's the end of him. Personally, I think he was lucky not to go to Broadmoor for 20 years, but who am I to judge a lunatic? Now get on this. Corner's family said, "Keep him locked up. He's too dangerous to ever be let out." Most of the psychiatrists said the same but one old doctor released him. Guess what? You know what's coming. He got out and killed two prostitutes – he chopped them up and stuffed them in bin liners. Now he's in Broadmoor where he should have been in the first place. If those two girls' families ever get to read this, you should take legal action against the nutcase who signed Corner's discharge. Believe me, it's a fucking disgrace. Hanane Parry was just 19 years old and Pauline Stephen was 25 years old. Both wasted over some psychiatrist who thinks he's God... It sums it all up for me, it's pure guesswork and it's a big fucking game. It's why I don't play their silly games! They can keep me locked up forever knowing I'm not a danger to the public, but they free cunts like Mark Corner every single day! "Take your medicine, Mark, and be a good boy. Stay away from the girls." Blah, blah, blah. At the very least it's professional misconduct but my word for it is 'Loonyology' – insanity gone mental.

I met 'Mad' Eddie Clarke in Rampton back in the 1970s. He had butchered three prostitutes – I mean chopped them up into mincemeat. They found the hearts and kidneys in his fridge. Fucking monster. He was like a librarian to look at: short, skinny, softly spoken and wearing specs. "Oi, cunt," I asked him, "Why did you do that?" He looked at me with those sad puppy eyes and said, "I don't like prostitutes." What can you say to that? I just punched the cunt in the solar plexus and said, "Fuck off, cunt." What else could I do? Outside, I would have snapped his arms and legs. Fucking monster.

I truly have bumped into them all: the bad, the evil and the ugly.

9 April 2008.

Talking of ugly, I called Dave Courtney tonight. (Only joking Dave!) Top man is our Dave. He's up in court on Friday (another stitch-up). The Old Bill won't sleep properly till they put him away. They hate him. Why? Simple: they're fucking jealous of him and so are a lot of villains. Dave makes a lot of dosh legally. He lives a good life with a glamorous lifestyle, and I say good luck to the guy! You jealous cunts can drop him out and get on with your own boring existence, you nosy pricks.

I got 10 letters and some smashing photos sent in today. I won't say who sent the photos but she shaves her pussy. There's something about a smooth pussy! They're really strange looking things. Imagine if they could talk! A talking fanny... it would be worth millions!

Yeah, a nice day today but I may have overdone it with the press-ups as my right bicep is aching. I may have busted a vessel or ripped a tendon. That's my 'ham shank' gone for tonight, fuck it. I can't wank with my left arm, it feels weird and unnatural! I'll have to have an early night tonight. A bit of James Whale on TalkSport, a nice cup of rosy and a Taxi biscuit! Yeah, it's not a bad old life is it?

Oh, Miller the monster was complaining about something this morning. I shouted, "What the fuck are you moaning about, they should have hanged you over 20 years ago! Get back in your kennel, you dog." It's insane really as he's only three cells away, but if I get to see him three or four times a year that's a lot. Some years I don't see him at all. He never goes out on the yard, he never has a visit, he never makes a phone call, he never gets mail. The cunt's a zombie! They should burn the bastard, or let the parents of the boys he shagged get their hands on him. Now that would be real justice – justice at its very best. What's a cunt like that got anything to moan about?

Almost forgot the latest on 'Cuntley' – er, sorry – Huntley. A pal of mine up in Frankland wrote to me saying, "He's depressed and crying all the time in the hospital wing," and he wants to move back here to monster mansion! Guess what: he will probably get his way! That's how it is with cunts like him, they bend over backwards for them. Why? If you know why, please let me know, because after 35 years of this bollocks I still can't work it out.

10 April 2008.

Silly bollocks Hannibal Maudsley started his silly games today, whistling like a fucking demented parrot and shouting the odds, knowing I can't get to him. I said, "Cunt, I'll order you a bag of trill from the canteen."

"I'll cut out your heart, you cockney prick!" he shouts.

Nasty fucker, all I would do to him is break his jaw and a few ribs, and he wants to cut my heart out! A bit over the top if you ask me, but that's mad Bob for you...

I was sad to hear Damilola Taylor's mother died of a broken heart. Gloria collapsed whilst out walking, she was only 57! She never did get over her son's murder in November 2000. We all remember it; how do you forget it? A young lad getting stabbed to death is a total waste of a life. How does a mother ever move on from the grief? At least she is now with him. Now Richard Taylor, the husband and the father, has to go on alone. What a bloody tragic end! It's things like this that tell me Hell is on Earth. How can it not be Hell? We are all living in a cesspit. What next? 'Hannibal' eating my heart? How the fuck am I still sane! Would you be?

Here's another sad story. Gulf War vet David Bradley got sentenced to life yesterday for shooting dead four members of his family. He just shot them one by one: an aunty, an uncle and two cousins. Bang... Bang... Bang... Bang... then walked into his local cop shop with the gun and said, "Arrest me." This is a guy who is trained to kill! His head's in bits. He's got post-traumatic stress disorder, flashbacks of bodies being blown up, mates killed, heads cut off bodies. What about his mental problems? How did he get life? Should he not have got some sort of hospital order and mental health treatment? I personally think this guy needs serious help! And where is he? Prison. In 10 years' time he will be forgotten. In 20 years' time he will have forgotten himself. In 30 years he will leave in a body bag. The crematorium awaits the old war vet. That's British justice for you. Here's a guy who fought for this piss-hole of a government. A hero. They sent him to an illegal war, fucked up his mind and destroyed his whole life. He returned a mad man. Bang, all over! I bet he's now in his cell asking himself, "Why, oh why did I not shoot myself?" He's up in max secure Frankland jail, Brasside, Durham. Send him a card, tell him to survive, tell him he's not evil! It's the cunts in government who are the evil ones. How true is that?

I see that wanker Pete Doherty has just copped a 14-week stint of porridge. Fucking good job too! I've no time for smack nuts like him. He's had enough chances, fines, probation, more fines, suspended sentences and community work. Eat some porridge, cunt. Well, Coco Pops...

I got some brilliant photos sent in today from Lorraine at the film shoot last week. Classics. I'll have some put in this book! Did you know I put 125 photos in my first *Loonyology* book? Some blinders too: legends and icons and ghosts from the past. What other books have got so many photos? You get your money's worth with me, that's for sure! Everybody loves a photo; people want to see who they're reading about. A book with no photos is a bit suss to me – a bit iffy! A photo speaks for itself. It's a part of life's history – the journey of Loonyology.

Some people don't put photos in their books. Do you know why? Simple:

1. They don't want you to see them.
2. They don't know anybody worth knowing.
3. Their family have disowned them.
4. They're ugly bastards.

That's why. It's fucking obvious to me! People need to see who's who and what's what! When you pay £18 for a book you deserve only the best, right? Come on, am I right? You know I'm right.

Mum posted me in some nice cards today which were created by mouth, by artists with no arms. They're magical people – pure inspiration.

My old buddy Gary White sent me in a bit of dosh to get some canteen. Cheers Gary. He never forgets his old chap.

Oh well, let's hope Dave Courtney gets a 'not guilty' tomorrow. If anyone can win, he can!

OK! OK! I know you all love the Uncle Bronco Problem Page, so let me dip into my mail bag. As I told you, I've been approached by a national newspaper to do my own page so watch out, you agony aunts. I've not said I'll do it yet. Well, I don't come cheap – this is a bizz, not a game. Watch this space...

Dear Chaz,

Q – I'm going out with a lovely girl but she has terrible BO. In fact she wakes up stinking and it's making me feel sick. What do you think I should do?
Ed from Hull.

A – Get a gas mask. Problem solved.

Bronson,

Q – You're a joke – a total piss-taker. I bet you don't put this one in your book. You are responsible for my wife divorcing me. We had 22 smashing

years together until you started giving her advice. Now she's living it up down Soho as a pole dancer. If I ever bump into you I'll kill you.
Dave from Dunstable.

A – Dave, you're a nasty, angry, bitter and twisted prick. No wonder your old lady left you. You just don't like the truth so you take it out on good, honest people. Face facts: your wife (ex-wife) still had some mileage, she had a dream to live and she's living it away from a boring old git like you. She wrote to me and I advised her – just doing my job!! She told me you're fat, fart a lot and have bad breath. Also, you have problems getting a hard-on and when you do you're only four and a half inches. You're the fucking joke, pal. It's time you woke up and looked in the mirror! Stick your big fat head in the oven, cunt. Oh, and if you're coming to kill me, make sure you do it right, because if you don't I'll torture you so bad you'll end up living in a nightmare. And stay away from your pole dancer ex-wife. You little, fat, smelly, four and a half inch prick-faced snake. Cunt. (Readers – sorry about that, but some people deserve all they get.)

Charlie.
Q – I'm 19 and just got my first boyfriend, he's lovely and we really do have a connection. The only problem is, he's a serious Muslim and I'm a serious Christian. My parents don't like it, neither does his. What should we do?
Sue from Swindon.

A – Yes, a tough one this. I get a lot of these religious ones. It's a no-win situation, Sue, and it's all rather sad. All this God bollocks does nothing for me. If God is love, then why is everybody killing each other over religion? You two have to decide; only you two can! Personally, I would say if you love each other then why not fuck off religion and become non-believers or start up your own faith? Call it 'Loveology'. I'll join as long as I get a shag! In fact I'll get lots to join and we can all meet up on a Sunday in the Church of Loveology. Think about it, Sue. Get back to me on that and I'll get the ball rolling. This could be a worldwide 'love wish'. Peace and love, Sue. x

Bronson,
Q – You're just a fraud! That's all you are! You don't give a fuck about anything or anybody but yourself. What have you got to say about that?
Ernest from Manchester.

A – Ernest, well you certainly know how to hurt someone who's only trying to help people. It's very hurtful to read your letter. I'm sorry you feel this way. If you could only see the thousands of people I actually help… but I suppose I can't please everyone! I'm sorry, Ernest.

Mr Bronson,
Q – It's me again, Ernest from Manchester. I was quite taken aback over your reply. I was expecting to be slagged and fucked off. Maybe I

misjudged you, Mr Bronson. I do apologise. (I enclose £50 so you can get a drink.)
Ernest.
P.S. Keep up the good work.

A – Dear Ernest, cheers mate!!

Charlie,
Q – Is it true you're a qualified sex therapist?
Sandra from Wakefield.

A – Is it true you're a nosy bitch?

Charlie,
Q – My aunty knows you from years back and she has a photo of you dressed up in a maid's uniform. What's it worth to you? Otherwise I'm selling it to the *News of the World*. Get back to me fast, Charlie!!

P.S. If you can't remember it, you can actually see your bollocks hanging out of the crutchless panties.
George from Wrexham.

A – George. So you fancy a spot of blackmail, eh? Let it fly, George, because I don't give a flying fuck. But wait till you see the photos that I've got of your aunty! She's the original Welsh gang banger. You snake, I'll be in touch with you later, believe it.

Chaz,
Q – I'm a 17-year-old lad and I'm going out with a 42-year-old mother of seven kids. The problem is they're all older than me and I feel silly. What should I do?
Harry from Brighton.

A – Well, Harry, I know what I would do: fuck right off. Are you silly or do you just like big, slack, massive fannies? Come on son, get a life, wake up! She's had her life; yours has just started. This woman is just using you. Get out of it and move on and find a nice, sweet girl. That's what you need to do. OK?

Charlie,
Q – I'm 93 years old and a widow of 33 years, do you think I'm past it?
Beryl from Barnsley.

A – Right, Beryl, 93 is a great age and I don't think anybody is past it. There's somebody for everybody, believe it, love. You old folk are the backbone of our country. We salute you all. Some old fella out there would love a bit of company. Try and get out a bit. Bingo! Dance Hall! Pictures! Cafes! Parks! Life's a mystery and it's never too late to meet a nice fella. You take care, Beryl! We all love you. x

Chaz,

Q – I'm a 23-year-old divorcee with two kids. I've still got a good body but I've got a very ugly face! I was born ugly, Chaz. My ex-husband was ugly too, but our two kids are amazingly beautiful. Is there some sort of ugly club I can go to? Please let me know, Chaz, as I'm feeling very lonely.
Elsie from Ellesmere Port.

A – Elsie… bloody hell, this is a strange one! An ugly club! Fuck me, I can only think of Broadmoor. There are some real ugly fuckers there. Look, Elsie, surely you're not that ugly! Have you tried a mask? Then again you're only 23, you could be a hoodie! I don't know what to say, only that ugly people are in a sense beautiful because they're so different. Please send me a photo.

Incidentally, years ago I went out with an ugly bird, she had a dodgy eye and a hair lip, with a huge growth on her chin. But like you, she had a body to die for. I got her a Mickey Mouse mask (only for the bedroom). Some of my best memories are from that bedroom, please believe it. You cheer up, Elsie.

Dear Chaz,

Q – I've written before. You remember me: Juliet, the bored housewife from Portsmouth! You recommended a holiday, a break from my hubby. Well I took your advice and went to Jamaica for three weeks with two of my girlfriends. Chaz, you will not believe this – it was the greatest three weeks of my life and the cock was awesome. One chap had a 10-incher with balls like peaches, I've never seen anything like it. These guys know how to shag. I'm going again next year. Thanks, Chaz, it's all down to you!
Juliet x

A – Wow… I'm made up for you, but what about the husband? I take it you've fucked him off? I do love a happy ending! Well done, girl, you enjoy it! They do say black men know how to please a woman, but don't forget us white guys! We still know how to move and groove, we taste sweeter, and believe it or not the biggest cock ever was on a white guy from Sweden: 15 and a half inches of solid muscle! So don't think it's all 'black is beautiful'. You just enjoy what you're doing, Juliet. Send some snaps.

Bronson,

Q – You're a cunt, Bronson. I'm Juliet's ex-husband, it's down to you she fucked me off. You're an evil fuck-faced swine.
Bert.

A – Fuck off, Bert. You're a jealous little nobody who lost out to some seriously big cock! How could you compete against that? You lost mate, face it! Juliet finally found her Romeo and got a good seeing to. Now fuck off!

Sandra Gardner and her son at the Leeds half marathon, 1988.

Johnny 'Fingers' Burton and Mary Shaw Taylor. Two of of my lovely friends who visit me regular. When it comes to class and style, they're at the very top.

You can come in, but you may not get back out. Yours truly.

On the way home from the London Marathon. Sandra's still as fit as a fiddle 20 years later. That's why all love and respect her, a born winner.

"To Charlie, best wishes. Be lucky. Graham 'The Duke' Earl. Keep it up. Aim high, Charlie."

Charlie the Snowman! Who says I'm not free? 2009

Roy Shaw with Fingers

That's Whitter the Hitter, a true champ. Where there's a boxing party going on, you can bet your arse on it 'Fingers' will be there. Seen it… done it… been there… and got a box of T-shirts. Top geezer!

Debbie Diamond outside my house, 2008.

Carlton Leach, Conrad Hitchin, and Davey Courtney. Hear no evil, see no evil, do no evil.

Redd and Sabrina Menzies, 2006. A few more cups and medals for the shelf (it's a big shelf).

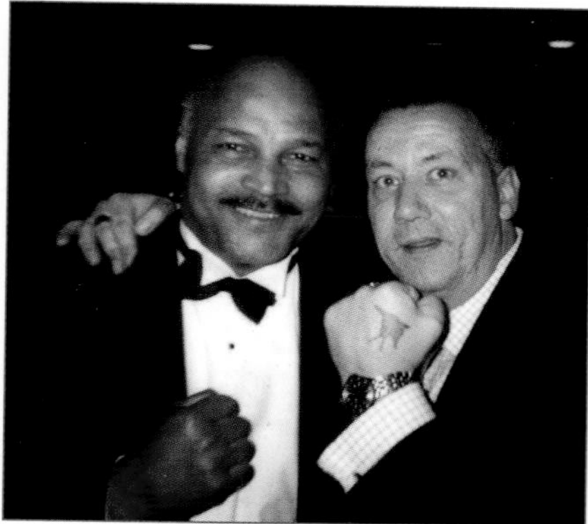

John Conteh and John Griffiths, 2006, Manchester. Nobody gets around the planet like John Griffiths does (he knows them all). Even legends like John Conteh.

Alan Minter, 2006. One of the best middleweight champions we ever had, but he was outclassed against Hagler. That Hagler was someone special.

Let's get ready to rumble. The legendary ring announcer Michael Buffer at the Hall of Fame, 2006. That's the great Alan Minter behind him.

"Thanks Charlie. Glad you enjoyed the book. Good luck in your fight for freedom. All Best Wishes, Billy Walker." Top geezer.

You can't leave Mark Fish alone for five minutes. It's the twins of Big Brother, Sam and Amanda. They should have won that. But who won it – that dopey prat Brian. I couldn't fucking believe it. I bet those twins smell nice.

Needs Swellbelly. Cheers brother.

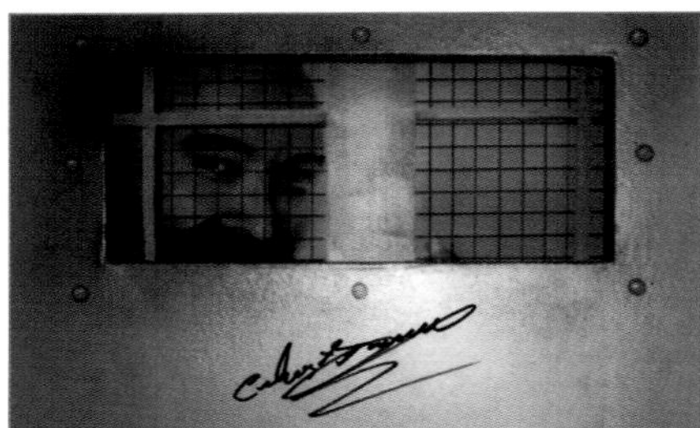

Welcome to hell.

Big George Chuvalo with his minder and driver, Bernie Slattery, 2005.

The no.1 boxing commentator of all time, Reg Gutteridge. I bet you never knew his cousin was the great wrestler Jackie Pallo. Unfortunately Jackie passed away last year.

This is a town in the USA. I'm told it's full of dickheads. You couldn't make it up, could you, even if you tried! Still… it's all loonyology.

Another town in good old USA – Shag Rock. I could do with six months there. I bet there's some serious shagging going on behind those trees and bushes.

Jed and Percy, Craig Bulger's dogs. Come on – do you really want to fuck with them? My favourite dog is a boxer! Beautiful!

Big Richard Towers (heavyweight from Sheffield), turning pro soon – watch out for him, Steven Bell, Craig Bulger, little Joe Bulger, Anthony Farnell, Jake Bulger, and Richard's brother and bodyguard. All top guys – especially Craig Bulger (we go back 30 years) lots of respect for the man. Keep on punching, lads, till the lights go out!

Mum and our loyal friend, Di Brown, on a night out. They both drink like fishes.

Eddie Clinton with my Lorraine – that's my Black Russian waiting for me out in sunny Spain. 2008. Adios Amigos!

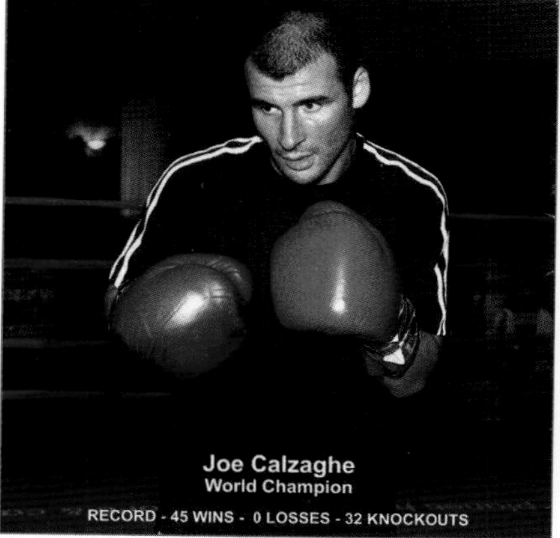

Joe Calzaghe
World Champion
RECORD - 45 WINS - 0 LOSSES - 32 KNOCKOUTS

Joe Calzaghe. "To Charlie, best wishes and thanx for book. Joe."

My Lorraine with Joe Calzaghe, Spain, 2008. What a legend Joe is, a true warrior.

Steven John Swatton. British Unequipped Powerlifting Champion Over 50's, 2007. Steve runs the Flex Fitness Gym with James Roberts down in Plympton, Plymouth. All the chaps think we have an uncanny resemblance. I'll leave that for you lot to decide. But he's a champion, so he's a winner in my book, and any man over half a century who's still winning medals is a legend to me. Max respect.

Joe Pyle, Charlie Richardson, Ray Kray.

Cliffy Field, Roy Shaw. Two of the best fighters to ever step inside a ring, and they both beat Lenny McLean. That says it all.

Margie Dempsey. I've known this lovely lady for well over 40 years. I used to go out with her daughter when I was a teenager. She treated me like a son and always was so kind to me. Even today I am still in touch with her. Our friendship is till the end of time. What does that tell you? I know what it tells me – it's just one big lovely family.

John Griffiths with Joey Singleton, former British Light Welterweight Champion, winner of the Lonsdale Belt. Joe was a big hitter, a tough guy. A man of respect.

Andy Jones made it to the film set. He owns the Crime Through Time Museum in the Forest of Dean, Gloucestershire, the only one of its kind. If you wish to see some of my greatest art, then you must pay a visit. It's there on show. You can look... but don't touch.

My little buddy Ifty keeping an eye on my old duchess at the film shoot.

Terry Stone, Loraine, Andy and Matt.

Mum, me, and Lorraine. Okay, it's Tom – we all make mistakes! Fuck me, don't forget it's *Loonyology* you're reading, not some poxy mental disturbing love story.

Andy Salvage, my cousins Stuart and Darren Godfrey, my Lorraine, and Mum. So who'se the crumpet? I'll tell you who... she's an actress who plays my girlfirnd. I don't even know her name, but I'm told she's a brilliant actress and she done the movie proud.

Tom with Mum and Loraine – my fav photo. Even my family love Tom and say how much he looks like me. He even talks and walks the same. Amazing!

Dee Morris, Tom and Rob Smith. The lovely Dee *never* lets me down and my mother loves Dee to bits (we all do).

Tom with my two cousins from Luton, Darren and Stuart Godfrey, on the film set.

My Loraine outside the Tom Hardy (Charlie Bronson) trailer on the film set. I think she could be peeping at Tom changing!

Matt Legg and Jason Marriner. Matt's in my movie – you can't miss him. They don't come much bigger than him.

Do you really wanna mess with the firm?

Nonso Anozie, Cass Pennant, Frank Bruno, Tamer Hussan, Leo Gregory, Gavin Brockter, on the set of Cass Pennant's movie, 2008. If you can get past this lot, you're a better man than most.

Matt Legg with Jamie Foreman. Jamie is one of my fav actors. He always looks the part of the character he plays. He's a great guy like his old man Fred, a diamond geezer.

I get homesick every time I look at this beautiful photo. This is Great British nosh. This is what *real* people eat – okay! A Sandra Gardner special.

Redd Menzies and Cliffy Field, 2008. Pass the salt. Lovely jubbly.

Leon Spinks arriving at Canastota Hall of Fame, 2005. This guy beat Ali and let's not forget he won a gold medal at Montreal back in 1976. That's legendary stuff. A great champion.

Gary Jones and Redd Menzies outside the White Swan in Dunstable, 2008. I wish I had a pound for every pint I've had in there. Gary is a top karate champion who's been all over the world flying our flag. Max respect.

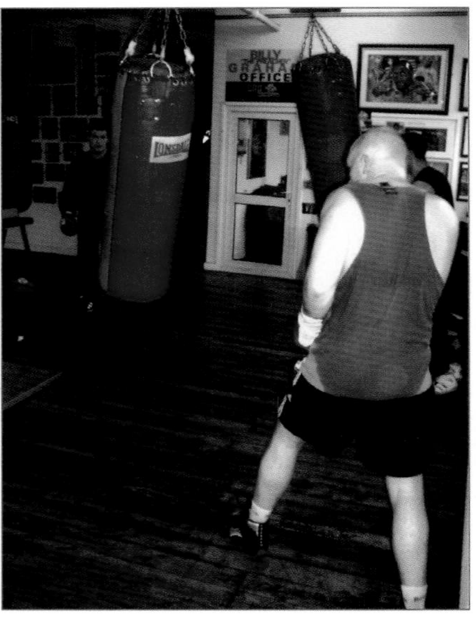

Ricky Hatton and brother Matty, training in Betta Bodies Gym in Denton, Manchester. Preparing for the Mayweather Fight 2007. If you don't sweat and bleed in this gym you're barred.

Ken Norton arriving at the Hall of Fame, 2006. This guy is one of my all-time favourites. He was a big hitter in the 1970s. Breaking Ali's jaw says it all! He went into acting and played in *Mandingo*. You don't hear a lot of him nowadays but what a boxing legend, and an inspiration to all young lads. Some guys are just born to fight. Life's journey is one big battle. Men like Ken Norton are Gladiators. Men of respect.

Sri Lanka, 2008. When my buddies, the Outlaws, put on a wedding, you just know you're in for a party. Max respect lads.

Ronnie and Reggie Kray. April 2008. They may be long gone, but I still show my respect even from this cage. Never forget.

Mark and Sandra Sharman.

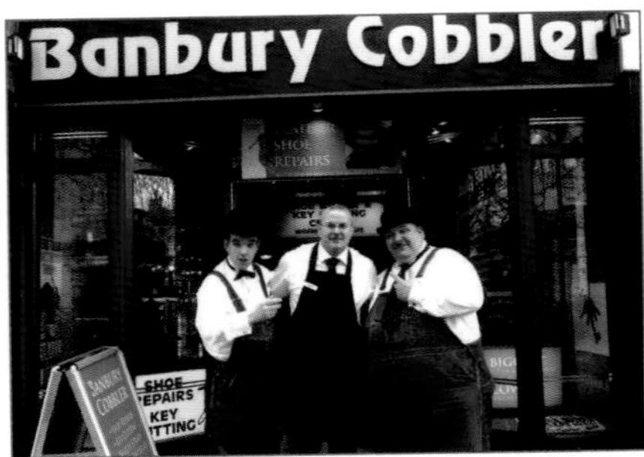

Mark and you know who! On the day of my movie being filmed, when my family and friends were needed to be on the set. Sadly Mark Sharman was opening up his new shop. Otherwise he would have been there like a bear in a honey jar. Don't forget the Banbury Cobbler – he's the No. 1 in the UK, if not the world. Plus he's a top pal of mine.

This legend's done it all. Vito Antufer Mo x middleweight champion of the planet, he even beat Hagler. So that alone makes him a legend. He was also John Gottis's minder, and he's been in the movies – *Goodfellas* for starters. What else? Yeah! He's a top geezer (one of your own). This was taken in 2005 in New York.

The black guy is the great Freddie Mack, x boxer and x manager of the Clark brothers. This guy goes back years. A true legend. Sadly just recently died.

Tony Crabb (2nd from right) being freed on compassionate grounds from his life sentence, 31 October 2008. With his wife Kim and three of his sons outside jail. On 15 February 2009, Tony lost his battle. A true legend, a top geezer and a real man! I'm gonna miss this guy. I salute the man. Max respect.

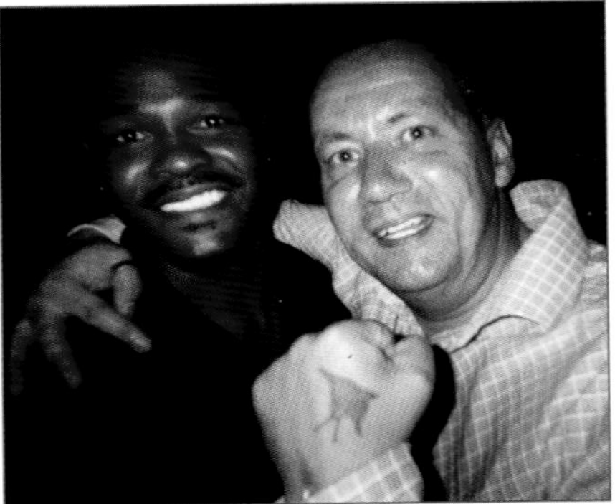

Terry Norris, former champ of the world with John Griffiths, 2005, New York.

Joe Pyle with some of the 'chaps', with the great Joe Louis belt that Joe had for years.

Andy Salvage, John Kinsella, and Loraine in 2008. This is at the Dubliners Bar in Alicante. You can see my art in the background. My art sells for thousands out in Spain (it must be the sun that does it). John turns out to be the dad of an Irish remand prisoner I met in Belmarch in the mid 1990s and he told his dad I looked out for him. I remember his son well – a good Irish rebel and a son to be proud of. It's a small world. Keep my pint cool – I'll be there one day.

Diane Brown. I've known Di for 20 years now. She's a good soul with a big heart and she's never given up on me and I'm blessed to have such amazing friends like Di, so fuck off you jealous bastards, and stop dribbling over my lovely friend.

The late Joe Pyle, Jimmy White, unknown, Ronnie Field. This photo, beliveve it or not, was taken in the visiting room in Parkhusrst in the 1990s. Jimmy went up to visit Joe and Ron. That picture in the background was painted on by a famous artist, and take it from me, it's amazing (it looks real). Poor old Joe's no longer with us, but is in our hearts forever, and photos like these are priceless.

Just recently I had a dear friend go and put some flowers and a card on Joe Pyle's grave – for me. And I'm so pleased and happy that the grave is so well looked after. My respects to a great man. We all miss you dearly.

Every picture tells a story. You'll love this one. Kelly's Bar out in Alicante, Spain. This guy Peter introduced himself to my mother, and said, "Please give my best to Charlie." She said, "Where do you know him from?" "In the nick," he said. "I was a prison officer. My job was kitchen chef." Now he's a chef in Kelly's Bar! Cheers Peter, pleased to see you. Had the brains to leave the prison service before it sucked your brain away. Good luck pal. I'll shoot out later for a pint and a steak! I hope it's better than the swill you cooked inside!

This legend for me was probably the toughest, hardest fighter that ever put the gloves on. Jake laMotta. This was taken at the Boxing Memorobilia Fair at Canastota High School 2006. We salute the man – max respect.

A treat for all the boxing fans, 2006. A legendary get-togethe from some greats (you pick 'em out). George Chuvalo, Tim Witherspoon, Chuck Wepner, Virgil Hill, Baby Joe Mesi, Carlos Ortiz, Carmen Basillio, Jose Torres. You know who they are. Men of rock.

Big John Griffiths with one of my best pals, the great Sammy McArthy, British Champion. We all keep telling Sammy to write his life story. It would make a movie. What a journey, what a life. It would blow your socks off. Sammy wasn't just a great fighter – he even enjoyed a spot of armed robbery. One fantastic man. Respect.

My old buddy Ray Williaimsm winning the Nuts Poker Championship in 2007 (I told you he's a born winner).

John Griffiths and American heavyweight fighter Freddie Mack, taken in Graziano's Bar, New York. All fight fans *must* go to this bar, as you never know who you may bump into – legends, if not icons, of the boxing world.

My lovely Aunty Eileen at 34 years old (that's 40 years ago). The swinging 60s. Believe me, that was the era when the world was rocking. Truly rocking, and I was rocking with it!

Left: Joe Coleman. One of the greatest artists alive today on this planet. All the way from the USA. He lives in a big mansion and in one of his rooms he has a lot of the world's great artists' works. And mine is amongst them. I salute you, Joe! You're an inspiration to the universe. You light up the art world.

Billy Cooper sparring with Cliffy Field in the 1980s.

Herol Bomber Graham. What a fighter. A brilliant technician, foot work, speed, power. He had it all and more! A great guy, a true Warrior. Respect.

My old buddy John Griffiths having a pint with the old bill (well, the actors, that is!). This was takin in a club in Piccadilly at the Billy Walker book launch in 2007.

Billy Cooper today, 2008. Once a fighter, always a fighter. And we all love a fighter. Max respect.

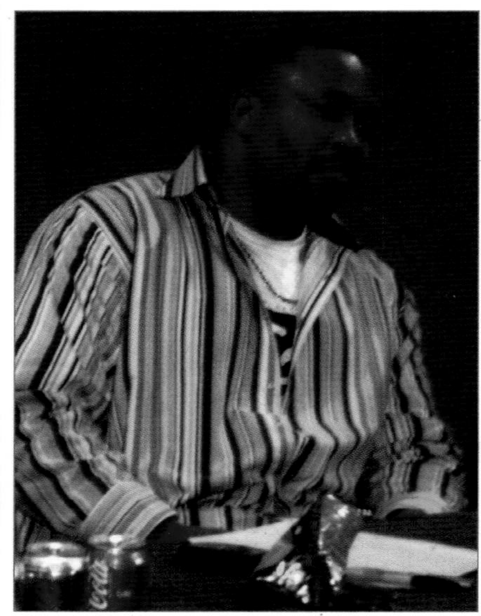

Tim Witherspoon, Canastota, New York, 2006. A great champion, great guy, great man.

Charlie,

Q – I'm a 21-year-old gay man and my partner treats me so cruelly that I'm now wondering if he loves me at all. He makes me wear a dog collar and takes me for walks in the local park which is the place where gays meet up. Last Saturday he made me bend over the slide and four men shagged me whilst he videoed it! They each paid him £100. I'm not complaining or moaning as I do like a good shag, but I feel I'm being used. What should I do, Charlie, and do you think he loves me?
Steve from Strafford.

A – Steve, he doesn't love you, he's just pimping you off! When he falls asleep, hit him with the iron and smash his fucking face in. You're worth so much more!! Fuck him off!

Charles,

Q – Hi, I'm a transvestite and I'm also a bisexual. I take it, give it, you name it, but my problem is my partner enjoys 'S&M'. He likes to do naughty things to me. One act sickens me but I put up with it coz I love him to bits. He ties me up and squats over my head and shits on me. It's bloody disgusting. Would you put up with it Charlie?
Sid from Cumbria.

A – I'd shoot the dirty bastard! How the fuck can you allow that? He is degrading you and humiliating you! He doesn't love you. Fuck him off! How's that love? The closest I've ever come to that is pouring a bucket of shit over the Parkhurst governor's head. I lost 120 days remission for that.

Charlie,

Q – My fanny is very dry and my friends all say their fannies are wet. Am I a freak?
Anne from St Albans.

A – You have not said how old you are! I've not got a lot to go on here, have I? It's a strange one to get my teeth into. I don't even know if you're a lesbian! Or anything about your partner. For all I know you could be a hooker with a dried-up snatch. Now, if you were my girl, I would give that pussy a lot of serious attention and a lot of loving. I wouldn't stop till it was flowing with juices. It'd be so wet you'd think you'd pissed yourself. You may be a slow starter or you're just not finding the right partner! Maybe you need to learn the act of masturbation! Maybe you need some help. It's difficult for me to answer a half-hearted question. You could be a 106 for all I know! I think it best if you were to write again, Anne. OK, love? Chaz.

Charlie,

Q – It's me writing back, Anne from St Albans with the dry fanny. Sorry, Chaz! I should have said I'm only 18 years old and I'm a virgin. I have masturbated with my finger and I once used a banana, but I still can't get wet. I've not really got a regular boyfriend and I only ever wank boys off or suck them as I'm too scared to have real sex. I guess I'm just a freak;

I'm known as the local gobbler. I am sad but what can I do? I enclose a photo, Charlie, it was taken last month in my parents' garden. If you look closely enough you can see I'm wearing no knickers and you can just see my fanny lips. Let me know what you think, Chaz.
Anne x (I dream about you, Charlie.)

A – Bloody hell, Anne, you're fucking gorgeous! Every man's wet dream. Yes, I can see your lips, and if I say so myself they look very beautiful. Look, I don't often do this but I want to really help you get your juices flowing. I think we need a meet up, don't you? I guarantee I'll have you wet in less than five minutes! A bloody good fingering and a bit of tongue is all you need babe, then a good old-fashioned shag. Let me be the lucky guy to turn you into a real full-blooded woman. I'll do that for you Anne, only because I feel you need it. It's more a professional decision. Would you mind if I brought my film crew? I'd like it filmed for my sexual problem file! Your case can be of help for others. Think about that, Anne. You could become a pioneer in the world of dry fannies. I could make you somebody very special – the most famous fanny on the planet. Believe me, babe, I will make that pussy flow like a mountain stream. I'll do all this for you because I believe in you. I may even be able to get a deal with satellite TV: 'pay per view'. There could be a sack of loot in it, not for us, but for future dry fannies! I'll not take a penny of it, Anne. (Only my expenses.) Trust me, I can have the contract sent to you within 12 hours. Sign it and post it back to me ASAP. (Please, God…)

Take care and leave your fanny to me, I'll sort it. You have made this old chap very happy. I feel I've finally achieved my goal, I actually feel blessed. I now know how Jesus felt: powerful. It's a miracle you've turned to me. Of all the Agony Aunts and Uncles, it's me you turn to. I feel so privileged and honoured. I think I love you, Anne. I'll be so gentle with you. God bless you, my virgin lady! Love, respect and lots of kisses, Charlie xxx

Charlie,
Q – It's Anne again. God, I love you Chaz, you're amazing. I agree to it all, you have saved me, I'm all yours, come and make my fanny flow like a mountain stream, come and do what you do. Hurry, I enclose the signed contract!
Love Anne x

A – Slow down, Anne! Thanks for signed contract but remember it's a 'bizz deal' not a fucking silly relationship. Fuck me, you'll want to be Mrs Bronson next. My job's to get your fanny wet, that's all. I'll see you soon! Chaz.

Mr Bronson,
Q – I'm a solicitor and I think you have hood-winked this Anne into signing a contract on false hopes. You should be ashamed of yourself! I'm actually reporting you to the police.
Name and address supplied.

A – Solicitor, eh? You're the biggest robbing bastards under the sun. I've done sod all wrong. What, are you jealous? Wouldn't you love to work on her fanny? You jealous cunt… fuck off!!

Charlie,
Q – I think it's marvellous what you're doing for that girl with the dried-up fanny. It proves how dedicated you really are in helping people. I couldn't see Marjorie Proops or the others doing what you do. You really do care about people. Keep it up, Charlie! Give my best to Anne!
Bert from Basildon.
(P.S. Could you send me a DVD of it?)

A – Thanks, Bert. It means a lot to me mate. I do try my best, thank you. The DVD is £15 (no freebies with me). Talking of DVDs, call Gavin Meek up. He's got CDs, DVDs, photos, art, calendars, mugs, T-shirts, all sorts! He runs the Bronson merchandise. Give him a call – 07746 781366.

Bizz is Bizz.
Pleasure is pleasure.
Don't mix it up.
That's how some prats get hurt, see!!
It's like the drinks. (Don't mix them.)
Stay in control.
Be your own daddy…
Be your own boss.
And if you've a dry fanny
Charlie Bronson's your man…
"Leave the respect to me"
Don't rely on others to show you the way
"Carry your own map"
Self-knowledge is the first step towards contentment.
Life is a riddle, a puzzle.
Learn to solve it…
So help yourself to help others to win!
And look after those dry pussies
"I'm the daddy"… "Honest" x
"Insanity is OK for breakfast!
But never OK for supper"
"You'll only have nightmares."

I'll tell you who's a living nightmare: Marc King Bromley. He recently got lifed off for smashing in his girlfriend's head with a house brick then stabbing her up. Danielle Johnson was a beautiful 17-year-old girl with all her life ahead of her. Bromley now has 30 years to ask himself why he did it. How sad is that, and he's only 18 years old himself. If that's not a nightmare then what is?

What about randy grandmother Nada Grgic in Split, Croatia? She's 75 years old and has just been arrested for threatening to kill a man of 86 if he didn't sleep with her. You can't make this madness up! It's fucking Loony-fantasticallyinsane!! God bless you, Nada!!

I see Bob Marley's mother Cedella has just died aged 81. Rest in peace Cedella! Our love to Bob! A true legend.

Filthy beast Steve Tanner's just copped a life sentence for rape, but it's a farce really because the judge only gave him a nine-year tariff. This cunt is a sex predator. He has convictions for assaulting women and kids going back to the 1980s. Why not just give him 30 years? How's nine years going to cure the predator? He's only 44 now, it's fucking pathetic and it winds me up! What's wrong with our judges? Armed blaggers get treble the sentence!! Life should mean 30 years for a nonce, no less.

I see a justice minister has just pleaded guilty to possessing dozens of indecent images of children. He worked in Jack Straw's department in Westminster. What's new? We expect it now. Fucking pervo, he gets sentenced on April 29. At least he did plead guilty! What else could he plead? He's been caught bang to rights. What happened to the old excuse: "I was doing it for research – a book I'm working on." Blah, blah, blah! "30 years, you nonce. Take him down and you prison guards make sure you give him a bloody good kicking. Next case..."

Talking of kickings, one of the worst I ever had was outside a club in Bow, East London. Sure, I'd had a few too many and I probably deserved to get slung out with a slap. I was only 20 years old but the four bouncers were all in their early or late 40s – big fucking lumps, steroid-freak fuckers. You know the sort: fucking bullies. They kicked and punched me half to death! Three weeks later every one of them ended up in the hospital emergency ward. Never let those sorts of bullies get away with it, because if you do they start to believe they're Superman! I bided my time and picked them off one by one. Two of them even cried about it to the cops! Fucking pricks.

Again, I say I probably deserved a slap, but I didn't deserve what they did to me. They deserved what I did to them, though. I actually hit one with a car jack. I smashed the granny out of him. I burst him like a water melon. There's no sound like a skull cracking open, no other sound like it. Anyway, they all learnt one thing from me: don't take liberties!

Real men always return. If you only learn one thing out of this book then learn this: revenge is wicked – it's beautiful, it's the greatest feeling, it even beats sex. Always remember, when in the jungle you kill to eat or you'll be killed and eaten. Take your pick. I know what I would do... how's about you? Only a cunt ends up as the meal.

Did you know there's a rat the size of a domestic cat that lives in the Brazilian jungle? That's what I call a rat.

Anyway... now down to some serious bizz. Read carefully:

Log on to www.dylan-foundation.com. Dylan is my cousin's little boy and he's got a very serious brain disorder called 'Lissencephaly'. Come on, support this little chap! He needs our help. Read all about him on the site and find out what you can do! I thank you, I salute you. OK, little Dylan Godfrey, the troops are out there! We are all behind you. Hold on little fella, you're not alone!

It fucking breaks my heart to see kids who are not well. It's a cruel hard life for so many youngsters. Why doesn't this so-called God do something about it? Ain't it about time he showed us who's the daddy on this planet?

Why does he sit on his big fat arse and let kids suffer... One of you sky pilots answer that if you can. But you can't, can you!!

Here's a blinder for you: old farmer Stoil Panayotou out in Plovdiv in Bulgaria has just fucked off his third wife. He swapped her for a goat. Not a bad swap if you ask me. Ain't life brilliant? Ain't the world crazy? You just never know what's coming next, especially with Loonyology.

Did you know there's a snake in South America that's got two heads? Greedy fucker, as if one head's not enough!

I remember Eric Anslow in Parkhurst back in 1976. He was a red band, a top geezer in my book, Dudley born and bred. His entire body was covered in tattoos! This guy was one of the fittest, fastest guys on the planet. He was the only con I knew who bred rabbits inside! He kept his hutches at the back of C-wing, but when he moved on some cunt made a curry out of them. I had a bowl – it was bloody lovely!! I've not seen Eric for over 30 years now. I've heard bits and bobs about him and his brother Dave, but they're two guys I want a pint with on the outside. You must understand prison life in the 1960s and '70s was a lot like the *Porridge* series: fucking mental, but there were so many colourful characters.

One con I'll never forget is 'Batman'. Parkhurst had an old bath house on the end of A-wing; it was 100 years old, with beams and joists. Each bath had a small swing door to it. The baths were the big old enamel ones with large rubber stoppers like you see in the old cowboy films. Anyway, this con called 'Batman' used to strip off and wrap his legs around the ceiling beam and hang upside down (not a pretty sight). Why did he do it? Fuck knows, I don't think he even knew why. He was just 'mad Batman' to us lads. Nobody ever bothered him. To us lot it was normal, even the screws never said fuck all. He just hung down for half an hour then had his weekly bath and that was it. Show over for another week. Crazy but true! True but insane! He was serving life and probably still is somewhere. How the fuck could they ever let him out? Imagine him doing that in his local council baths! Scary or what? Oh, and I've left out that all through his hanging upside down he had a fucking big hard-on. No women screws in those days, it was all men, it was all Loonyology. Laugh? We pissed ourselves. My memories still make me happy.

I remember once on C-unit in Parkhurst around 1985 when Neil Adamson was stoned out of his nut. He'd been on the wacky baccy for days. He came and sat in my cell, poured himself a mug of milk and drank it. My fucking milk – all I had. A pint of milk is a pint of milk inside, outside it's fuck all. I said, "Oi, cunt, what did you do that for?" He just started laughing, the maddest laugh ever. This is a guy who blew a Leeds copper away: 'Bang' – fuck off. He just walked into my cell and drank my milk. To say I was stunned is an understatement! It was madness at its very best. I could have chinned him but why bother? I ended up laughing with him for two hours! We laughed so much it fucking hurt! Top geezer! I like Neil, he's just crazy.

This was about the same time Tommy Mulligan got lemon with my mate George Heath, so I steamed into his cell and hit the cunt. Neil wanted to cut his throat, George wanted to pour hot cooking oil over him, fat Joe Purkiss wanted to stab him up.

"Fuck me," I said. "Chill out. I'll give the cunt a well-deserved slap," (and I did). That was my lot – the van arrived to take me to my next hotel. The funny thing was that not long after I moved, George nicked a bottle of medicine off the hospital nurse and drunk the lot, ending up on 24-hour watch in the hospital wing. That's prison life for you. Fond memories. Always something happening!

Here's a good tip for all you new guys in jail if it's your first time inside: always search your cell. Look for little holes in the wall, look under the lino or tiles and in the cracks of the door. Feel the mattress for lumps, check all the blanket seams, check the bed frame, the sink, the toilet. Check the light case. Spend half an hour of your life checking it all, even outside on the window sill. Why? Simple. You could find money, drugs, blades or anything else that's illegal to have. I've found all sorts and I've also lost all sorts. That's prison life for you, learn it inside out. It may save your arse!!

Most cons have a blade, a tool, a chiv. Most keep it hidden away from their cell but it's never far away, believe me, and they're not shy about sticking it in your neck. Always be aware because big, strong and shrewd men have gone home in a body bag. Violence can erupt at any time inside over the silliest things:

"Oi cunt, turn that music down."

"Bollocks."

That's all it takes! 'Crash' – that simple.

Hey! Best stay out of jail, that's the best advice I can give you. It's all Loonyology…

Sunday, 13 April, Marathon day!

Did you know the first London Marathon was won by American Dick Beardsley and Norway's Inge Simonsen? They held hands and crossed the line together in two hours, 11 minutes and 48 seconds back in 1981. Not a lot of people know that, now you do! A bit poofy for my liking, two grown men holding hands! What's that all about? I thought it was a race!! Strange people.

Did you know there have been three finishing lines since it started:

1981 – Constitution Hill.

1982-1992 – Westminster Bridge.

1993-2008 – The Mall.

Talk about moving the fucking goal posts! Are they going to move it again? There's always some prat who wants to change things! Why?

Did you know Seb Coe (OK, Lord Seb Coe) ran it in 1991 in two hours, 58 minutes? Can someone tell me why he's a Lord? What's he ever done to be a Lord? Run a few races… big deal. Ronnie Biggs should be a Lord, don't you agree?

The last British man to win was back in 1993: Eamonn Martin. I don't know what time he ran it in but I don't give a flying fuck anyway. It gets a bit boring after a while.

All these facts… I bet you're thinking this Bronson's a fucking big head, or he's making it all up. Check it out then if you don't believe me, cunt.

The slowest time was in 2003: six days, two hours, 26 minutes and 18 seconds. You'll never guess who by! Come on, have a guess... Think on, I'll come back with the answer later! See, I'm still a nasty bastard! I enjoy sweating people. I like to catch you like a fish and play with you, then pull you in slowly. Then bash your head on a rock.

The only England football manager ever to run it was Graham Taylor. He did it in five hours, five minutes and 30 seconds. Not a bad time. Well done, my old china!

Who remembers the Los Angeles waiter who ran it carrying a bottle of water on a tray? Roger Bourban was his name. He did it in 2005 in a time of two hours 47 minutes. Not bad, eh? Fucking magic. I bet you couldn't do that. Imagine your arm and the balance needed! Flash fuckers those Yanks!

Old Buster Martin runs it today. He's a 101 years old! If he finishes it he will be the oldest ever to do so. We salute you, Buster. You're a legend, mate. The current holder is 93-year-old Faija Singh, he ran it in 2003. The geezer today doing it in a nine-foot robot costume on sticks is the same geezer who did it wearing a 130-pound diving suit in 2002 when it took him five and a half days. Fuck knows how long this one will take him. This guy is Lloyd Scott, he's an amazing man who has helped raise £5 million for charity. We salute you mate, you're a star.

Did you know Paula Radcliffe's best time was two hours, 15 minutes and 25 seconds? Awesome. In 2005 Stephen Hammond from Llanelli, Wales ran it bare-footed. Ouch. I bet that fucking hurt.

OK! The guy who took six days, two hours and 18 seconds was the great Michael Watson, a living legend. This is a man with serious brain damage from boxing – a man they said would never walk again. We love you man, you're the greatest...

Kate Lawler is running it in just her underwear. She's bloody gorgeous! I wish I was running behind her, I'd have a hard-on for 26 miles. That would surely be a record. Six Masai warriors from Tanzania are running it today in full traditional dress. Fuck them running behind me with their spears. No thank you. It would be like a re-run of *Zulu*! Fuck that... That TV chef Gordon Ramsey is running it again, he does well for a big chap. Ronan Keating's doing it too. Good luck, lads.

So what about me!! Would I do it? Could I do it? I'm sure I could! Whoever wants to see me do it, write to the Home Secretary and say, "Let Bronson out to run in the 2009 Marathon, he is prepared to run it in a strait jacket so he won't be a danger, you can even put a Hannibal mask on him so he doesn't bite anybody." Well? And I will run it for a children's charity! Come on, get writing. They can also tag me! So why not, let's get it on!! Not only will I make bundles of dosh, I'll also do it in a good time. Let's do it. Sort it for Bronson. I'll run for all the loonies on the planet! If every lunatic was to chuck in £1 to support it, we'd need a lorry to collect it all in. Come on... let's do it for the name of Loonyology and to help the kids. The pen is mightier than the sword so get your pens out, but don't hold your breath. If I was a paedo or some serial sex killer they would probably allow me to do it, but I'm just a nasty, evil robber. Sorry...

I had a nice Sunday dinner today: chicken, Brussels and roast spuds. It went down well. It was a nice peaceful day and I created an art.

A fucking crow woke me up at 6.30am. Noisy fucker, what the fuck's a crow doing outside my cage? This is Wakefield, not Emmerdale. To be honest, Emmerdale's not too far away from here!!

Yeah, a lazy day today. I'm off to bed. It's 9.15pm. A guy's got to sleep; tomorrow's a fresh week and anything can happen. My motto is 'be prepared'. Good or bad, give it your best shot!

I'll drink to that.

CHAPTER 5

Reach up and kiss the sky!

Lick it till it bleeds.

"Running"

What for?
Why?
What about the knees?
The joints
The heart
Is it normal?
Or is it mad?
Can the body take it?
Will the lungs explode?
What about the air?
The pollution
Will there be enough water
What if I faint?
What if I seize up?
I could die
It could end up a suicide run
The suicide runner
Fuck me is it real?
Is it a dream?
Are we all raving mad?
Do we want to die?
What's it all about
Raising money…
Charity
Why not rob a bank
Wouldn't that be easier?
Quicker
Less stressful
Less painful
I need a lay down
It's confusing me
It may push me over the edge
I can't fly
I'm not jumping
Running…
26 fucking mental miles
That's a long way
Even in a car
That's a distance
It's forever in a traffic jam!
Should I take a packed lunch?
Maybe a crate of beer
I'll need an extra pair of socks
A good pair of trainers
I must get some Vaseline
I must look after my bollocks and thighs
A hat…
Some gloves!

A pair of shades
My boxing shorts
Yeah, I feel good
I'm just in the mood
The buzz is kicking in
The crowd will help me round
I can't let the kids down
I can't let myself down
Let's get it on
Fantastic
Us runners must stick together
I'll meet you outside the asylum
Loonyfuckingology
Yippppppeeeeeeeeeeeeeeee
Yarhhhhooooooooooooo
Yeeeeeoooowwwwww
Last one buys the beer
It won't be me
Bet your fucking fat arse on that
Bet your life on it
I would sooner shoot you than be last!
I've never been last in my life
I'm not starting now
"Runners"
That's what we are...
Running for sanity
Fuck the joints and pain
Run off the stitch
Second wind
Like a deer across a field
Like a dog at the track
A horse at Ascot
Let's run...
Keep on running
Until we die...

CONCLUSION

10. Mr Bronson is a very disturbed man who has little in life apart from what remains of his self-esteem - and this is based solely on his physical powers, his reputation within the prison system and his refusal to bow down to that system. He made contact with myself because of work he had heard I had done with other violent prisoners, and because he wanted me to read an as yet unpublished manuscript he had written, about his experiences within the Criminal Justice System. This work is quite remarkable, providing an insight not only into Mr Bronson, but into the workings of the whole system, albeit from his perspective.

11. While in the Hull Special Unit, before the incident that brings him to Court today occurred, Mr Bronson wrote another work, based on his prison experiences, which won second prize in the prose section of this years Koestler Wards. This is a great achievement for him and has brought him a considerable amount of personal satisfaction. He acknowledges the help he was given by staff in the Special Unit, in compiling this work, and takes particular pleasure in the fact that the award is signed by Judge Tumim, accompanied by very encouraging comments.

12. Charles Bronson is a man whose unpredictable impulses towards violence have meant that he has lived over half his life in custody. In all my contact with him - visits approximately every four months and correspondence that has at time been intense on his part - there has never been any difficulty in communication. He seeks advice and takes it, although clearly finds it difficult at times to maintain a consistent behaviour. He has been portrayed as a man who hates the system and will not co-operate with any member of it, but this is not at all the case and there are many prison officers around the country in whom he places great trust and whom he recognises have dealt with him in a fair and reasonable manner.

13. His life in the very recent future has been in greater turmoil than ever, following the death of his father after a long illness. Mr Bronson's relationship with his parents and two brothers - none of whom have ever been in any conflict with the law - has always been a warm one, although for many years he did not wish them to visit him in custody, feeling that the experience would stigmatise them. His father died in September, at a time when the defendant was in Wormwood Scrubs, and the following day an incident occurred which led to him incurring injuries which are presently the subject of a police enquiry.

14. Mr Bronson is under no illusion that he faces a long prison sentence for the offences with which he is charged today. He is extremely anxious as to the conditions in which he will be held in the years head. My understanding of this situation, having spoken to an official at DOC 1 on the 7th November, is that he will continue to be moved around the prison system without notice, remaining in no one establishment for longer than a matter of weeks. Undoubtedly, the disorientation and frustrations which Mr Bronson has experienced can only escalate and are likely to be reflected in the desperation he feels. The defendant is a man who, by his own admission, has been his own worst enemy on many occasions and who readily accepts that he presents difficulties for the prison system, but the treatment he has received and the conditions in which he has been held should be a cause for concern. In interview in HMP Bullingdon on the 16th November he expressed a wish to serve his sentence at either HMP Belmarsh - where he appears to have a positive relationship with staff - or in C Wing, HMP Parkhurst, a unit which caters specifically for disruptive and difficult prisoners. Given Mr Bronson's history, there can clearly be no guarantees that either of these locations would result in prolonged stability, but he expresses the wish to at least be given such an opportunity. It is accepted that this Court can have no influence on his prison location and such information is included as I understand that Judge Marshall asked for background on these matters when ordering a Pre-sentence Report at Mr Bronson's Court appearance last month.

J P Broadhead

PROBATION OFFICER

As probation officers go this guy was tops! He visited me all over the country; he says so himself. I once had 30 moves in 18 months. Imagine that! It's no wonder my head was blown away. I was waking up and having to think where I was! I was confused and disturbed beyond belief. The system was deliberately fucking me up! Visitors (family included) were booking visits and not knowing what jail I was in from week to week. It's their way of controlling us, it's their way of saying, "Fuck you, we are in charge here!" But at least guys like Julian Broadhead tried to do some good. Most probation officers are just nosey fuckers, plus they don't give a flying fuck. It's a fact of life. But I take my hat off to the 'good ones' – I really do.

The truth is that I was being brutalized and denied basic human rights. How the fuck can they justify 30 moves in 18 months? They can't, they never can. They just didn't want me to have visits and they did everything they could to fuck me up. Why? Well, why not? After all, I was a prison activist fighting for prisoners' rights. I won a few battles for the lads but I remained in the dungeons. My world was punishment and multiple moves! Fuck Bronson, he gets nothing. Hey! Not a lot's changed has it? I wonder why! Just who is the real villain here, me or them? I've changed – isn't it time they changed?

What you're about to read will blow you away; it was written and sent to prison HQ from the medical director back in 1987.

It categorically states I am not mad and I was certified 'sane' on a mental health tribunal in 1985! But the slippery fuckers were actually trying to stop my release and get me sent back to Broadmoor. I refused to speak to any doctors (prison or independent). I actually got the 'nod' off a screw in Gartree jail: "Watch it, Charlie, they're trying to nut you off again. The powers that be are trying to stop your release. They're shitting it." I wonder why? I guess it's not rocket science, is it? I was due to be released in October 1987 after 14 years away being treated like a mad dog! They were fucking scared and feeling guilty! They were afraid I might come back for revenge. A few screws in Gartree were on my side. They said, "He's done his bird, let him go." And by God they were right.

That's how the system works, the treacherous bastards were trying to stop me getting out. It's exactly what they're doing now but this time it's easy for them owing to my life sentence. I've made it easy for them. Now they don't have to lie or fit me up, or get the medical prats in on it. They've got me by the short and curlies now, and that's what fucks me up big time. I lost and they won (for now).

DEPARTMENT OF HEALTH AND SOCIAL SECURITY
ALEXANDER FLEMING HOUSE
ELEPHANT AND CASTLE LONDON SE1 6BY
TELEPHONE 01-407 5522 EXT

Rcom B306 Ext

Your reference
Our reference

Director
Prison Medical Service
Cleland House
Page Street
LONDON SW1P 4LN

MICHAEL GORDON PETERSON. 6.12.1952

I have great sympathy with your concern about this man, which was for us at a high level whilst he was in Special Hospitals and presenting severe management difficulties. I have sent for his case notes and read these through again.

He is a most difficult man who is thought to be dangerous still, after his time in prison. He has spent time in the mental health services, but throughout that time he played mainly the role of the 'convict' - and that as an adherent of the Justice System he believed that having done his bird, he had earned the deserts of freedom.

He was remanded from Park Lane to Liverpool following a serious attack on another patient in Park Lane April 1985 - He was sentenced to 3 years imprisonment, July 85. He appeared before a Mental Health Review Tribunal on 23 September 85. He was found not to be suffering from mental illness. The Tribunal also considered on all the medical evidence available and their own assessment that whilst he is abnormally aggressive and may be said to have a personality disorder he falls well short of the definition of psychopathic disorder in Sec 1(2) of the 1983 Act. There is no justification for forming the view that he needs to be liable to recall within the medical system.

Since he was found not suffering from psychopathic disorder there was no need to consider his treatability and he was absolutely discharged.

You are quite right in recognising that he cannot be detained or dealt with under mental health legislation. The matter of his release and further aftercare is a matter for the penal authorities.

I am sorry that I cannot offer any medical suggestions in this case.

Yours sincerelv

001495

Mental Health and
Illness Division

That's how dangerous – if not lethal – this game can be; it can and it will suck your life away like a straw in a can of pop. You're just a number, a nobody, you'd better believe it! And if I wasn't so well known and didn't have such a strong support group, I would be long dead by now. Nothing is surer than that, believe me. There is no limitation to these people, they will do anything to make themselves look right when it's obvious they're wrong. It took me years to realise just how ruthless they can be. It's no different to a forces 'cover up' – sweep it away, start again, dead people don't talk.

"Oh, we're so sorry he shot himself in the head!"

"What, six fucking times?"

"Yeah... it was a hair trigger!"

Like fuck it was. Murder's murder in my book. I don't play games, not when it's my life on the table!

All I know now is they're sucking me away for no other reason but 'get back time' and I can't see any change coming, can you? But they're gonna have big problems trying to nut me off again as it's in black and white in this report. QUOTE: "You are quite right in recognising that he cannot be detained or dealt with under the mental health legislation." I'm 100% sane... are they? Are you? I wonder!

The inevitable has finally happened: big fat nonce Chris Lund Yates has sexually assaulted a visitor in Wakefield Prison visiting room. This piece of shit was on a visit when he stuck his hand up a fellow con's visitor's dress. Fortunately a screw spotted it and intervened! Now get on this: Dr Al–Nufoury told the court Yates was diagnosed with schizophrenia and he has a sexual deviancy problem. Anyway, Yates has now been sent to Broadmoor where the fat cunt belongs.

But what about this poor lady visitor? Why was she put into this position in the first place? Please, lady, if you read this then sue the prison as they actually put your life in danger. It's serious neglect and incompetence; heads should roll. This case has actually been hushed up – it's only got a small piece in the *Yorkshire Evening Post* when it should have been in every national paper in the UK so all can see it. It's a fucking joke, an absolutely shameful thing to happen. I've been saying this for years: why are our visitors put into potential danger? (I would now be on a murder charge if it had happened to one of my visitors!) What was this fat cunt doing in a room full of women and kids when he's got serious problems? (Now see why it's called 'monster mansion'.) This poor lady now says she is frightened to visit the jail again. You must sue the governor and prison HQ! Expose the daft bastards, because they are putting the lives of women and kids in danger!

Read all my books from the past 10 years and you'll see I've predicted this sort of thing happening many times. It's only a miracle some kid has not been killed before now. Our families are at risk in every jail in Britain. They're sitting next to paedophiles and rapists, and the prison bosses are taking the piss. There should be special visiting rooms for monsters; this sort of thing should not be allowed to happen. The con whose lady got assaulted must be a right prat. Why didn't he at least chin Yates? I can't understand why he didn't do anything. What a total fucking mug.

It's going to happen again – and worse. All you visitors should now demand a public enquiry. The cons should also act on it. Me, I'm still on closed visits so I'm lucky. My family are safe from the monsters.

You got it from Loonyology! You heard it from me! Nobody is safe in a prison visiting room! You're surrounded by monsters eyeing up your old lady and dribbling over your kids. Wake up!! This really is the wake–up call. Tell that lady to take legal action because it's a case she can't lose. She will get thousands, plus she can put a stop to this madness and save others from being sexually assaulted. Sack the governor I say, it's a complete disgrace…

What makes me laugh is when cons start moaning about silly little things like: "My pillow is too lumpy, it's too cold, I've only got two blankets. My cell's too small and it's painted green. My boiled egg is a funny shape…" Fuck me… shut up!!! If you were in IK–10 Krasnokamensk out in Siberia you would have something to moan about. IK–10 is Hell on Earth. It was once one of Stalin's torture camps and little has changed since his time. Temperatures drop to minus 33 degrees, you piss ice, your tears are frozen, it's fucking freezing. Your balls become nuts, your dick shrinks. It's that cold your nose bleeds and the blood turns to ice. You can be put into solitary for just looking at a guard or coughing near one. You can be beaten for sniffing. Even your dreams are from Hell. It holds just 1,000 inmates and the average convict will die before he reaches 40. The food is shit and if you can't eat cockroaches, rats, worms and maggots then you're not going to survive for long. Cons have even eaten each other – raw. Fuck me… Maudsley would love that!!! We just don't realise how comfortable we have it!

Boscobel, USA, is another hell–hole. It's a new 'Supermax' jail built in 1999 to break America's toughest cons. It's said to be the harshest, most brutal jail in the country, not through beatings but through their strict isolated regime. It's cruel and barbaric. If you treated a dog like they treat their cons you'd get six months. These cons are locked up in cells without windows for month after month with no books, no TV, no radio, no mixing, no talking. They see nobody and they know nothing. It's not normal. The screws are more like robots!! The lights are on 24/7 so you don't know if it's day or night. You get just four hours a week on the yard for a walk, chained up like a mad dog. (Again you see no–one.) You get one shower and one set of clean clothes a week. There's even a CCTV camera in your cell so you can't top yourself. They're watching you 24/7, watching you shit, piss, wank! They're studying every move you make and analysing everything you do! Believe me, it's inhumane.

My life and my world is bad enough, but Boscobel makes it seem like Heaven. David Hatch, a long–term prisoner was told he was down for Boscobel. He said, "Fuck you, I'm not going to that hell–hole," and wrote a suicide note saying, "I told you I'm not going." I respect a man who lives and dies according to his word! I take my hat off to him.

One con who spent time in Boscobel said, "I prayed every night I would get cancer, I wanted to die. I wanted to go to sleep and never awake! There was nothing to wake up for, I was forever depressed. I banged my head on the door a 100 times a day, hoping it would bring on brain cancer. All it gave me was bad headaches and guards rushing in to restrain me and put me into a strait jacket… I lost my way… I felt I had walked into darkness and just lost the will to find the light. I would hear crying, sobbing, grown men begging to be moved to another jail. There was a lot of hysterical laughter; men were going mad each day. Alcatraz would have been a blessing compared to this place! They broke us with mind games, psychological torture." The person who designed Boscobel was a sadist – one cruel motherfucker! Yeah! What the fuck have we got to moan about?

Take Nairobi prison, Kenya. It was designed to hold 800 cons, now there's over 4,000. A cell built for 12 men now holds 200!! Imagine that! The fucking stench of sweat, shit, piss and dead rats! Tuberculosis is rife: 814 cons died in nine months. Fuck me, it's a slaughter house. HIV Aids is also rife and lots of arses get stabbed whether they're gay or not. If your arse is fancied then the odds are you'll get it shagged. Not a lot you can do with 10 cons on top of you with a blade to your eye! In 2000, the guards shot dead six escapees, just blew them away, and birching is a daily event! Stay out of trouble – stay well away from Nairobi prison.

Another tough old jail is Yodok in North Korea, a World War II–style concentration camp. Need I say more? You really don't want to know. It makes Wandsworth jail in London seem like a 5-star hotel, believe me. If you ever end up in North Korea, go straight or you could well die in Yodok prison – a nightmare come true. We are lucky over here, as bad as it can get. Even in the very worst conditions we face we are still well off, and that's a fact. Eat your porridge, lads...

I hear Rose 'Fatty' West is doing a college course in baby–sitting. You couldn't make that one up. And she's just got a budgie called 'Fred'. Why can't we send that witch bitch to Korea? It'd do her good. Put her on a snake diet (poisonous of course)!

Did you know sex goddess Marilyn Monroe had a nose job in 1946? See, you get all the facts out of my books. (I bet you never knew that.) After she had it done she signed up with Twentieth Century Fox.

Did you know sneezes are known as 'sternutations' in the medical world? They are actually convulsive explosions of air, and experts reckon they can come out at 650mph. What a load of bollocks... They get paid for that? Who gives a flying fuck how fast a sneeze comes out? You just make sure it's not in my face or you'll hit the floor at 650mph, that's for sure...

Turk Mehmet Ozyurek has the longest nose in the world. I won't say how long it is or you'll think he's a fucking elephant.

Here's a blinder, you'll love this one. Picking your nose is called 'rhinotillexts'. Are they fucking sure? Those medical people are nuts... King Tutankhamen of Egypt had it all sorted out. He actually had his own personal nose picker. Can you believe that? A nose picker, what a job! What sort of muppet does a job like that? Loonyology or what. Madness at its very best!

I bet you don't know what 'Hongi' means? Sounds filthy, like some sex move! It's not, it's the traditional greeting of the New Zealand Maori where they rub noses. I bet that's not all they rub either! It's all insane to me!! Nosey bastards...

Old Dickie Best was buried next to his son George yesterday. He was 88 and a good old chap who some say never got over losing his son. Dads are not meant to outlive their kids.

Did you hear about the two Indian junkies who injected curry power instead of heroin? One's in a korma and the other one's got a dodgy tikka!!

If you don't remember too much then just remember this from me:

Never take someone for granted,
Hold special people to your heart.
Because one day you could wake up,
And realise you've lost a diamond whilst you're collecting stones.

Remember I told you that – it's so true.

Did you know there's a drug rehab clinic in Hollywood called 'Pussy'? It's the No. 1 rehab clinic in the world. Even the most violent and hard prick comes out soft and humble and reduced in size to a dribbling mess. It's true, trust me!!

Saturday, 19 April, 2008.

Chris Young was up to see me today! He's a top geezer in my book. We had a great visit with lots to discuss. He got me two banana milkshakes and some chocolates, lovely jubbly.

I also got nine letters in, one from my son Mike – that's worth 1,000 letters to me. He's doing great and I'm so proud of him because he had a right pop at his mum for selling silly stories to the media about me. He told her, "Grow up and get a life, stop trying to ride off my dad, coz all you're doing is helping to keep him locked away for more years." Well done, Mike, you tell the parasite! She would sell her soul for a monkey – in fact the money-grabbing bitch already has!

My next visit is on Wednesday with Sandra Gardner. I'm looking forward to that as it's our first meet-up. She's a good soul with a good heart and she's a lovely friend. I'll fight anyone who says different.

I had a fry up today (well, that's what they call it)! We only get it once a week but it's fucking brilliant and I look forward to it. I have a nice cup of 'rosey lee', two bread rolls and a bit of brown sauce with it. Lovely.

I'm going to create Sandra a bit of art tonight, ready to give to her on her visit. It gives me something to do and keeps me active. I enjoy it. If I had a pound for every art I've created, I would be the richest con in the UK, that's for sure.

21 April 2008.

Joe Calzaghe cracked it over in Las Vegas at the weekend when he beat Bernard Hopkins. That's Joe's 45th fight, unbeaten! That's what you call a champion, a true gladiator. He could fight Roy Jones next, for 20 million bucks. That's the way to do it, Joe! We salute you mate. A living fucking legend in my book! And so say all of us.

Sadly, Tom Hardy didn't win a Bafta, but I say fuck the Bafta, get an Oscar! I called my brother today. Mum's now out in Spain for two weeks, a bit of sun will do her good. It's been one of those days today, I've been bored stiff and I just couldn't get into anything. I got 12 letters, not bad for a Monday. Five of them were from strangers who have read my books, just to wish me well and to say they hope I get out one day.

I sorted out a wreath today for a mate's grandmother's funeral, and a few quid for Ray William's son who's just copped four months in a young offenders' centre. Now he's got no excuses to not phone up his mum and dad! I'm like a bloody social worker some days, but I get a buzz out of helping youngsters. It's all about respect with me, looking after 'your own'

– the ones that count in life.

I had to laugh about 'two Jags Prescott' who claims he had bulimia when he was Deputy Prime Minister! What a load of old bollocks. What's that all about? He's got it all wrong, he stuffs his big fat face and it's the public that feels sick. Those MPs are all the same: full of shit.

You all know I love a good word so here are some 'phobia' words. Guess what 'arachibutyrophobia' means. I bet you can't! It's fucking mental – it's a fear of peanut butter sticking to the roof of the mouth. It's Loonyfuckingmentalology.

Here's a blinder: hippopotomonstrosesquippedaliophobia! That's 36 letters of crap. You'll never guess in a million years what it means. It's a fear of long words! I bet you think I'm making this up!! How the fuck can anybody fear a word?

What about this one: aulophobia. It's a fear of flutes! Fucking idiots... some people need shooting! Here's a good one: clinophobia – it's a fear of going to bed. I've got a cure for that one: don't go to bed, sleep on the couch you mad fuckers. Optophobia, that's a fear of opening your eyes. I've got a cure for that one too – die! They're all bollocks these phobias, total bollocks. Wake up and get a life, you cunts. I'm getting bored now. Soceraphobia, a fear of parents–in–law. Easy solution: shoot them (no more phobia). Yep, it's a mad old crazy world!

There was a con in Albany jail who had a fear of porridge. It wasn't long before they moved him to the padded cell in Parkhurst. If you've got a phobia in jail you're in big trouble as it's seen as a 'problem'. Problem cons soon get sorted out – normally with a size 10 boot and a truncheon across the back.

I remember a lunatic in Rampton who we called 'the lizard' because he kept sticking his tongue out for no reason and licking things – a window, the wall, a book, his hands. It was fucking insane. I can see him now; nutters like that you never forget. The criminally insane stick in your brain forever. A grown man like a lizard... I wonder what he's doing now, 30 years later. I wonder if he got out and had baby lizards?

Madness is in the genes: madness breeds madness. It may miss a generation but it always returns. That's why it's so interesting, a brilliant subject! I know more about insanity than any doctor. I remember one loony in Broadmoor who I caught in the recess banging his head into the wall again and again. The thud was sickening to hear. This loony was well into his 40s and there he was nutting the wall whilst I was having a piss.

"Oi, slow down," I said. "You'll fucking knock yourself out."

He looked at me with blood running into his eyes and he had a look of relief all over him. He said, "That's better," and walked out. To say I was blown away is an understatement. I actually felt quite sad. I've seen it all, sadness on top of sadness!

Another time I walked into a loon's cell and saw him with a knotted sheet around his neck, about to stand on a chair and tie it on the bars. I saved him, only for him to do it properly a week later. Believe me, it's not nice to see. You would have to be a cold psycho not to feel any compassion for these poor souls. It's bloody tragic. Nonces and grasses can do it all day long for me (the more the better), but when you witness genuine people in despair it's so sad to see! And you can never forget it.

Some screws are heartless and born cold. They've been in the job too long and they have to switch off. They can zip up a stiff at 10am and be in the staff tea room at 10.10am having a cuppa. Life or death doesn't matter to them, it's a job, but it's my life and it's fucking horrible at times.

Did I tell you about when my son Mike climbed onto the roof of London Zoo? He said, "My dad's not an animal, these animals get treated better than him!" That's my son – a chip off the old block! He can have a right punch-up too! Wonder where he got that from? Must be his mother – she once hit me with an iron. Fuck knows why, I never did find out, one of her mad moments, I guess. I did love Irene once, so long ago, but I love an apple pie more these days. All that love shit makes a man soft in the nut, it really does. Get a fucking life and be a real man, not a bleeding puppet. Pull my strings and your jaw gets broken in three places. Oh well… a boring old day is over, but I still did my press–ups and had a jog.

I saw big Robbo today! It's always nice to see him, I sorted his mother a book out and she loved it. Robbo is old school with good old–fashioned morals – he says something and sticks to it. He's the white version of that black dude in *The Green Mile* – an awesome man mountain and a top geezer in my book. Does his porridge good! I like that.

I heard Fred shouting in his sleep last night! It woke me up. It sounded like, "I'll strangle you, you fucker." I hope it's not me in his dream. This place is a fucking horror house – switch the light off on the way out.

Their wages were only £22.54 a week in 1973! Now can you understand why I took up armed robbery? I've never understood why they're called 'officers'. A fucking monkey can open and shut doors. What have they ever done in life to be called an officer? They're 'screws', 'guards' or 'turnkeys' to me and always will be. An officer in the forces has earned that rank; I can respect that and admire it. But a screw being called an officer? Don't make me fucking laugh. Not that I'm slagging them off, but they don't deserve to be called officers and most of them would agree. Half the prats are fucking idiots and they haven't got a clue about life in general. They're no different from traffic wardens – they're little fucking Hitlers, power–crazed rats.

'Officers' – fuck me, stop it... they're having a bubble, it's a piss-take. Wake up! Oh well, I've had my moan for the day, that's my lot. See you tomorrow. As Bruce Forsyth would say: "Nice to see you... to see you nice!"

22 April 2008.

I only got one letter today, from my old buddy Leighton Frayne (my Welsh connection). Top geezer. I was gutted to hear my old mate Tony 'Squeak' McCann copped a life sentence yesterday. I knew Squeak when he was serving time for armed robbery – a top–class blagger. (I also know his brother Pat, a good fighter in his time.) They've convicted Squeak of murder; some geezer got stabbed to death. Looks like a fit–up to me so I hope he's got an appeal in. Stabbing people isn't Squeak's game, he's more into: "This is a raid! On the floor, you cunts. Where's the loot?" He doesn't go around stabbing people. His girlfriend is Nicola Cowper who used to play Gina Williams in *EastEnders*. Yeah, it doesn't add up to me, it stinks. Get that appeal in!

I'll tell you who's an evil cunt who should have hanged: Joshua Cook. What a piece of dog shit this fucker is. He was baby-sitting 22–month–old Charlie Johnson when he sexually assaulted him and kicked and punched him to death. 22 months old!! How can anybody do that to a kid? Charlie Johnson – what a great name too, snuffed out by a piece of shit, Joshua Cook. Remember that scumbag. Should he be allowed human rights? Put him in with me, I'll look after the fucking prick. Evil bastard...

Peladaphobia – that's a fear of bald heads. My head's as shiny as a snooker ball. How can a bald head be somebody's phobia? Soon us baldies will have to wear hats so as not to scare phobia prats! What about my phobia? Phobicphobia: I'm phobic of all phobics. Be warned now, you phobic nutters: stay well away from me. You're all nuts – certified nutters. Here comes the asylum van; fuck off and don't come back.

I was reading about some bloke up in Newcastle who's got size 18 feet. What's his dad, a fucking penguin? Did I tell you I stopped wearing shoes and slippers for five years? Bare feet 24/7. Why? Well, why not! It was something different I suppose! It broke the boredom up, it was something new. My feet were rock hard after six months; I could kick cell doors all day, and did. Feet are serious weapons, believe me.

I had a cheese salad today with a nice lump of cheese which was big enough to fill four rolls! The sun was out and it was a really nice warm day. I did my session on the yard and I felt good, light and fast. I called Dee Morris up – she's a lovely sort, a good soul and a good friend to me. We go back 10 years now. I'm on a visit tomorrow – it'll be a good day with a few chocolate bars, a banana milkshake and a nice chat with Sandra Gardner. I'm looking forward to it.

Did I ever tell you about the time I had a visit in the Scrubs from Dickie Ryan? Who? Yeah, you may well ask, so I'll tell you. I've known Dickie for well over 30 years. Some call him 'Sniffer' as he had half his nose chewed off in a fight in Brixton jail in the 1970s. He won't mind me saying he's a very ugly man, but he's also a very loyal man. Dickie was once the best cat burglar I knew – he never once got caught in the act, it was always down to grasses. He was unlucky and got his collar felt more times than he should have done. Anyway, on this visit in the Scrubs in 1985 we were chatting away when he clocked a screw who he remembered from Wandsworth jail in the 1970s. He said, "See that twat over there? He gave me a good kicking with his mates in the block in Wanno." Then he walked straight over to the screw and spat in his face. It was a great shot; it went right in his eye.

"You cunt," Dickie said, "come outside now and try it on your own, cunt." The bell went and dozens came running. Unfortunately, Dickie was escorted out of the jail and our visit was stopped. But he shouted over to me, "Chin the cunt if you get the chance, Chaz." Can you believe it, I was put in the van that very same day and moved up north. Cheers, Dickie. That's how life is in jail – you have no control over what they have planned for you. They only have to think you're up to something and they will act on it. They obviously believed I would've chinned the screw for Dickie, that's how petty they are! Paranoid fuckers. Hey, who guards the guards? (Always remember that and you won't go far wrong.)

I woke up early today, about 4.30am, and I had a fucking big hard–on. It was throbbing (you know the type – pumped up like a steel rod) and I was bursting for a piss. But you have to wait for it to go down before you piss or you'll hit the fucking ceiling. Anyway, just as I got up to have a slash, guess what? Yeah, you guessed it. My light went on and the eye is at the Judas hole in my door. What a way to start a day: a fucking stranger peeping in on my hard–on. What can you say, what can you do? Fuck all. So I stood there and pissed, one of those pisses that go on forever. (For fuck's sake hurry up!) Then I got back into my pit and thought, I've got to get out and fast, prison is chewing my brain up. I started to get another hard–on, but then I thought of some horrible cunts who have pulled serious strokes on me behind my back and it soon faded away.

That's how a day in the life of Bronson starts. It's pure Loonyology, but don't we love it. (You wouldn't be buying my books if you didn't – you know you love it.) All you girls would love to wake up with a bloke like me; you'll always have a shag before the day starts. If not, you have my permission to shoot me on sight or slice my bollocks off and feed them to your cat. OK? That's a promise. My word's my bond, believe it.

The power of Loonyology is the power of life. Nobody can be you better than you. You are you: unique. Life is to be enjoyed. Don't forget to rob a bank on the way!!

One time I was in my friend Kelly Anne's Leabank flat having breakfast. (I do love a good breakfast: four sausages, four eggs, four tomatoes, bacon, mushrooms, fried bread and beans. My plate was like a dustbin lid!) I was enjoying myself when the door went: BANG – BANG – BANG. Who the fuck's that? I thought. I only had my boxer shorts on and Kelly was away for a few days. (Fuck knows where, I never ask. It's her life and her bizz what she gets up to!) I was only halfway through my breakfast. BANG – BANG – BANG! That's it, I was mad. Cunts. I went to the door and didn't even bother to look through the spy hole. I pulled it open and there was a scruffy prick in front of me.

"Is Kelly in?" he asked.

I grabbed him and said, "Sit there, cunt."

So there he was, sitting on the big chair in the lounge while I went back to my breakfast.

"Move you cunt and I'll kill you, OK?" I told him.

He sat there like a statue while I finished my fry–up and had a cuppa, then I went for a chat.

"Who the fuck are you, and why were you banging on the door?" I asked him.

"Er, I'm Kelly's friend, she's expecting me," he said.

So I told him, "Turn your pockets out, cunt."

He had a bag of weed, some coke and tablets, and about £300. I smacked him and said, "Bang on the door again whilst I'm here and I'll cut your arms off. Do you understand?"

"Yeah, sure mate, I promise I won't!"

So I said, "OK, pick your shit up and fuck off." As he was walking to the door I gave him another slap around the head and said, "And have a wash. You stink." Then I stopped him and spun him around. I looked deep into his eyes and said, "Do you know who I am?"

"Yes."

"Are you shagging Kelly Anne?"

"No."

"OK, fuck off cunt," I said, and I kicked him out of the door.

That was it; I never did see him again! It doesn't take Einstein to work out what he wanted, but it's not my bizz. When Kelly came back I didn't even mentioned it! A day or two later she asked me, "Did anybody come round whilst I was away?" I said, "Nope, nobody." It was only later after my return to jail that Kelly wrote to me saying that Luton's drug firm had a contract on my head. Big fucking deal. Don't worry boys, I won't be hard to find. All I did was give him a slap, and only because he upset my day. I didn't even take his dosh or drugs off him so what's the big deal? What are you going to do, waste me? Please believe you don't really want to be making silly threats to a guy like me. You're not in my league, my league is Loonyology. I don't need drugs or a fucking mob behind me, I'll just walk into your gaff on my own with a big fucking axe and go to work. It's 15 years ago since I slapped your smack nut, but it's yesterday to me. You're probably all fucked-up now – you fucking will be if you call it on with me.

They're strange people in the drug world, very strange. They think they're big-time gangsters and supermen when they're high, but when they come down and wake up they'll realise there's only one Superman: me. I'm on a high 24/7. Think on. In fact you pricks have destroyed my home town and it's time you cunts got a good seeing to. Be told: climb down, go to sleep, wake up real men! Then you can earn my respect.

Talking of respect, get on this. 1987 is full of good memories for me as I was free for 69 days. I would do my training on the park at the back of Leabank flats – it was pure freedom with lots of grass, a football pitch, trees, bushes, a river and a kids' park. It was beautiful and it smelt beautiful. This particular day was a Sunday and I remember it like it was yesterday; it was cold, a bit foggy, crisp, fresh and alive. My face was burning and tingling, my heart was strong and warm, and I was alive and kicking. I was wearing my boots, a tracksuit with a black jumper and a woolly hat with black gloves. (A nice day for a bank job only it was a Sunday; even us robbers have to have a day off.) So there I was enjoying myself jogging around and stopping to do my stretches and pull–ups on the goal posts when three young lads, probably 12 or 13 years old, came strolling over.

"OK mister, what you training for?" they asked.

"For life, I'm a life trainer," I told them.

One thing lead to another and before I knew it I was talking to a dozen lads all aged between 12 and 16. One had a ball and that was it – we played football and had a great laugh for the next hour. I showed them some good exercises and did press–ups with three of them on my back. I showed them some of my special moves. At the end of it all, I felt like I had really achieved something. These kids were cheeky fuckers but great lads and they needed some sort of direction in life. One said something to me that I'll never forget: "I wish you were my dad." How can I ever forget that? I shook all their hands and said, "Box it smart, lads, and stay out of trouble." As I jogged away I actually felt human for the first time in years.

I was back in Luton four days later after a bit of bizz and I'd popped into the Heron pub to see a guy, when a woman walked over to where I was sitting.

"You're Charlie aren't you?" she said. "You're the fella my son and all his friends can't stop talking about. Can I get you a drink?"

"No thanks, love, I'm off in a minute," I said.

She shook my hand and said thanks, but I said I hadn't done anything. She said, "You're joking! The kids loved it and they can't stop talking about it."

So I got up, did my crocodile press–ups across the pub floor and said, "Tell your son to practise that one."

That's how life is: a beautiful memory! Those kids are now dads with their own kids. I don't even know their names but I can see all their faces still laughing in my mind. They helped me that day more than I helped them. I found my true self: humble and filled with pure humanity. I felt 10 feet tall. Even the nastiest bastards of the world can have a soft touch, and I admit I have been a nasty fucker at times – in fact you could say I've been a nasty, nasty, naughty fucker! I don't deny it and I never will, but when it comes to kids they're safe with Charlie Bronson. I trust them and they trust me – why shouldn't they? I was a kid once, I really was! You shouldn't treat kids as kids, you should treat them as equals. If you respect their ways then they'll respect yours. But I can't or won't allow kids to get too close to me now, as my life is already complex enough! If I did there'd soon be gossip, talk and lies doing the rounds. ("Watch out, he's a jailbird, he ate two kids, he's a fucking lunatic and even Broadmoor couldn't control him. He took his own mum and dad hostage!" BLAH – BLAH – BLAH.) A man like me has to be so careful in anything he does, I'm a target wherever I go! And when the Old Bill get a sniff of me they overreact. A guy has to be realistic! Most parents would have a heart attack if they knew their kids were playing football with me. Yeah! But they'd be 100% safe!

That was a magical day and a memory I cherish. It's only sad that every day can't be so great, but a man's got to do what he does best. For me, that means surviving and making a £50 note. On the floor you cunts and don't move! You lucky people. This is your lucky day! Enjoy the moment...

23 April 2008.

Great visit from Sandra today. She looked smart in a black trouser suit with a striped shirt and a lovely waistcoat with a silver pocket watch on a silver chain that used to belong to her late mother. She looked the dog's bollocks and she spoiled me rotten with four milkshakes and some chocs. The screw that brought her over told her: "Charlie should not even be here, he should have been released years ago." They tell my visitors that all the fucking time! (Why not do something about it then? Talk is cheap: it doesn't get me out, does it?) Yeah! Great visit. I really enjoyed it!

Did you know Eartha Kitt is 82 this year? I can't believe that, she still looks in good shape and can still knock a song out. Let's face it, she is the original sex kitten, they don't come any hotter than her. Most act the part but Eartha was and still is the real thing. What a roller-coaster life she's had.

Get on this tragedy! Three months ago, 24–year–old Andrew Davis hanged himself one week before his wedding to Kerrie Lawless (also 24); now Kerrie has hanged herself as well. How sad is that? They've left behind two kids! Why? What for? What's it all about? Who's ever going to know? It doesn't come any more confusing than that! I actually see it as selfish. What a crazy world.

26 April 2008.

I bet when I disappear for a few days and there's no diary entry you all start wondering: "What's he been up to? Why has he not written anything down? What's he hiding from us? What's going on, this is only half a poxy diary! He's holding out on us! I bet the cunt's won the Lotto!" Well, I'll tell you: fuck all's happened. I just can't be bothered some days. Sometimes I even bore myself and switch off. OK?

It's Saturday today and a horse called Bronson F'sure is running at Market Rasen in the 2.20 – price 11/2. Not bad eh, let's see if it wins. (I'll come back to that later.) Roll up, roll up, lay your bets please. (I know for a fact some screws here are backing it. Why? Because they know Bronson's a winner, see!)

Hey! Did you know every 20 minutes somebody dies of lung cancer? That's three people every hour, 72 people every single day. Work that out for a year, it's frightening. Lung cancer is the worst to get. It's a killer for sure, few survive it. Stop smoking, don't take the chance, it's a mug's game and you stink.

Ex–copper Andrew Shovelar copped two years' jail yesterday. The big brave fucker kept bashing his girlfriend up. He would headbutt her, get her in lock holds, march her off to the empty bedroom and lock her in. The cunt must have thought it was a police cell. Talk about bringing your work home. Shovelar's just a typical bully cop, a fucking dog. Two years? He should have got 20 years and a good kicking to see him on his way. Cunt. 'Allo, 'allo, 'allo… who's eating porridge now! (See how you like it, copper.)

What about the 'Crawley Demon Barber'? This nonce just copped 14 years for sexually assaulting four little girls. The parents dropped the kids off for a haircut and they got a seeing to by the monster. Who can you trust today? Even the barbers will rip your panties off and have a sniff. Nobody is safe anymore, the world's gone mental. This old fucker's well past his sell–by date so let's hope his heart packs up inside and he leaves jail in a body bag, or some con gives him a good smack over the crust and turns him into a vegetable – a dribbling old wreck of a pervo. You old cunt…

Adam Nind just copped a life sentence for breaking eight ribs on his 10–week–old daughter and snapping her arms like chopsticks. What a fucking monster. He doesn't deserve to be called a dad. I just want to punch this fucker's face in, don't you? Doesn't it wind you up and make you feel sick? I bet this cunt's never hit a man in his life. I bet he's a born wimp. Believe me, I'll break his jaw if I ever bump into him, I swear to God I will (and I'll enjoy it). Watch out, Nind, I'm hunting for you and no doubt others will be too. We hate you bastards, you're dog shit.

I see Wesley Snipes just copped three years for tax evasion. ('Blade' should be able to handle that! What's three years? It's a shit and a shave.) Wesley Snipes is like Al Capone: they both got fucked by the tax man. That's showbiz for you… It's one of my ambitions in life to fuck the tax man and die owing the prick millions, just to say, "I fucked you, you never fucked me!"

Here's a little story for you to dwell on – it happened back in the Scrubs in 1992. I was about to get out and an old buddy of mine copped a life sentence weeks before my release day. He turned up at the Scrubs for allocation and ended up chinning a screw on the wing. He got dragged down to the block next cell to me, so we had some quality time together by chatting out of our windows. It turned out his best mate was shagging his wife and had practically moved in with her the day he got arrested for murder. He had spent 18 months on remand going mad over it and offered me 10K to sort lover boy out. I told him, "Fuck off, you're my mate, I'll do it for fun." So one week after I was free I paid lover boy a visit and it was fun. I enjoyed it. Cunts like him have to have some. I won't go into details but suffice to say he sucked his food through a straw for a long time afterwards, his bollocks swelled up like watermelons and his own mother never recognised him again. Let that be a lesson to all of you who are thinking of shagging a con's wife. We take that sort of thing very seriously!

I am happy to say the lifer is now free. He served 15 years and was let out on licence, so it had a sweet ending. That's how a guy wins. He's probably got a nice fresh piece of pussy on his arm and a new chapter in his life. But I'm one pal he will never forget – that's respect, you have to earn it! It often comes in blood and a lot of pain but it's very pleasurable, very rewarding. Revenge is like a bowl of strawberries and cream: delicious.

The inevitable has happened again, we all knew it was coming. Raymond Horne (the dirty old nonce I mentioned earlier, who was sent back from Australia after serving 16 years for rape and murder) has been back for just four months and is now on remand for the alleged offences of attacking a 70–year–old woman, attempted rape and two other sex charges. I have to say 'alleged' as the law states you're innocent until proven guilty. But fuck me, couldn't we all see this coming? It was written on the wall in capital letters. This old cunt should never have been freed! I wouldn't trust this monster on a farm: the animals would all be in danger. These old pervs are a danger to anything with an arsehole. This piece of shit moved to Australia in the 1960s with his family and since then all he's done is rape anything that breathed. Now he's back here, shoot the fucker! Anyway, look out for his trial and remember what I've told you all from day one:

once a nonce, always a nonce. They never change!

I got a pile of letters today. Sandra wrote and said she loved our visit. I got some signed photos from the great John H Stracey, the welterweight world champion boxer in 1975 who's now a top singer doing all the clubs and cruise ships. John's a gentleman, a living legend! I also got a letter from Robert Verkaik who's just been passed by the Old Bill to visit me. I'm a bit shocked by this as Robert's a top crime reporter for the *Independent*. I expected him to be knocked back as the system doesn't like reporters visiting 'Cat A' prisoners (especially me). I'm well chuffed and so will he be! See, they do make fuck–ups. Now he's on my visit list they can't stop him seeing me.

Terry Silk sent me in some smashing photos of the *Bronson* film shoot last month. Cheers for that, Terry. Well appreciated, mate. I also got a letter from my buddy Ifty and four from people I don't know, three of whom I don't wish to know either. Muppets – I can always smell a muppet, can't you? It's a sense, they throw off a bad vibe and I'm not a bad judge of character.

Hey! Exclusive. Get on this: Bronson F'sure won the race! What a magic day; it came in at 15/2. I bet loads of people saw that horse's name and backed it. I hope my son did. I would've put a 'monkey' on if I'd been out. Such is life!

Did I ever tell you about the time I had a bit of bizz to sort out in Nottingham? It was nothing too heavy, more of a favour for an old buddy. That's how the criminal world is. Most times it's better for an outsider to slip in and out, then the Old Bill are baffled because nobody's got a fucking clue who it was. The only risk is getting lost on the bit of graft! Taking a wrong road out, that's always the fuck–up, even more so if you're carrying a 'tool'. Anyway, it all turned out lovely. I'd done the bizz and was on my way out, only to find the motor had been nicked – some thieving bastard had nicked the car I had nicked myself only hours ago! Can you fucking believe that? You can't even park a motor now days without getting it nicked. I ended up getting a taxi to the train station. One mustn't grumble!

I knew a geezer who nicked a car and drove off with a fucking big Alsatian on the back seat. He almost had a heart attack when it licked his head. You just don't know the stress us villains have to put up with. Why leave a big fucking dog on the back seat? Have you 'honest' people got no feelings at all? (Er… I think I'd better leave it at that, don't you? Soon you'll be thinking I'm insane.)

Wasn't it magic when you were young and in love? Walking the girls home, stopping for some fish and chips, eating them on a park bench or sitting on a wall – what lovely treasured memories. Imagine doing it now at 50 or 60 years old; you'd get locked up in the local asylum. Life's journey is really magical. Those times will never come back, so you youngsters enjoy them.

I had a nice cheese salad today with a jacket spud. I touched lucky at breakfast too: I got two extra cartons of milk, a right touch. No phone calls on weekends here, so apart from the mail we are cut off from the outside world. I see it as a rest.

Chelsea beat Man U today! It's about time somebody beat the flash fuckers! But what a team United are, eh? The cream of the crop. That reminds me: I once went out with a bird who used to cover my dick in cream and enjoyed licking it all off. Yeah, that's OK, but she would do it in a packed pub under the table. I always seem to meet the nutters. Life is just insane, it really is. It's like Dave Glover – a proper tough guy from Newcastle. He can have a right fight and his old man's a top face. They're a good family of villains (respected) but what does Dave do? The heat's turned up and he grasses up good people. One he helped put away was Paddy Conroy, that was a right fucking liberty. I met Glover in Full Sutton jail a 10-stretch ago but unfortunately we were both in solitary or I would have chinned the cunt. What the fuck do they grass for? The soft twats still go down, maybe not for so long, but they could at least go down with pride. Keep your fucking mouth shut, do your bird and walk out tall.

Another Geordie I met inside was 'Big' Joe Hunt – one top bloke and a good armed blagger in his time; he was in Winson Green when I took a hostage there. He was on remand for some security van job and when they took him to court the screws all wore bullet–proof vests, the Old Bill were armed and there were choppers up in the air. They laid it all on for Joe! Do you know why they do all that? It's to scare the jury and get the media on the law's side! (Look how dangerous this man is; he must be guilty!) That's why they do it. Wake up and smell the coffee.

It's like me – during some of my trials I've been surrounded by up to 10 guards (not one of them under 6 feet and 200 pounds). What do you think the jury are thinking? "Cor blimey, Bronson must be dangerous." Even the judge thinks it, what else can they think! But the prosecutor is loving it all. How the fuck can we ever get a fair trial? Be warned now, you would–be villains who are about to pick up a shooter and a Mickey Mouse mask: it's Disneyland all the way, so stop and think before you end up like this. But I will say the first 20 years are the worst; after that it's easy – honest! You don't even miss pussy, well, maybe a bit. Every time I have fish I think of pussy, so I don't have too much fish.

Anyway, that's my lot for today! Fuck tomorrow, it may never come, and if it doesn't, do I really care? Fuck it, I really don't give a fuck!

Do you want a few nightmare true stories before I call it a day? How about Karl Denke? Who? You may well ask. Back in 1924 in Germany this guy killed 31 innocent people in a three–year run of serious butchery. He mostly chopped up vagrants and then ate them. He was known as 'Papa the axe man'. When the police kicked in his door they found two giant tubs full of human meat in brine and a killing journal chronicling his murders and cannibalism. They found 'Papa' hanging from the rafters with some lady's suspenders. Kinky old fucker. They don't make them like Karl Denke anymore, thank fuck.

What about this fruit cake, Herb Mullen. He went on a killing spree in 1972 in good old USA because he thought by killing people it would stop an earthquake from happening. Fuck me, what a barm-pot defence. From October 1972 until January 1973 he killed 13 people, some of whom were kids. He shot them, stabbed them, even used a baseball bat. Can you believe he was found sane enough to stand trial? He was sentenced to life and he's eligible for parole in 2025 when he'll be 80 years old. But what about the earthquakes? An 80–year–old lunatic is still dangerous with a gun! Fuck Herbie, keep the cunt in the slammer.

Then there's Joe 'Cobbler' Kallingher, a working–class shoemaker who really lost the plot in 1976 in America when he took his 13–year–old son on a mission to Hell. Joe believed he was a messenger from God and that God's message was to kill. (Strange, I thought God was love! Maybe he got it all mixed up.) He raped a few and killed a few, showing his son all about God's message. His plan was to kill everybody, rid the world of evil and then kill himself. They were caught in no time and charged with three murders, dozens of kidnaps, three rapes and a score of robberies. His son was released after serving 13 years, changed his name and disappeared. Joe died inside back in 1996 after choking to death on a chicken pie. It's a mad, mad old world.

Here's a living nightmare for you! At the age of 15, Edmund Kemper murdered his grandparents for fun. He said, "I just wanted to see what they looked like dead." After 10 years he was back out, killed his mum, decapitated her and then raped her headless body. This guy is fucking sick – only a freaky fucker could even think of that. What a weirdo. This nutter is 6 feet 9 inches and 300 pounds of insanity – a giant psycho nutter. To top it all, he then killed a handful of female hitch–hikers and raped their dead bodies. He's in jail till he dies. Let's hope somebody fucks his dead arse to see how he likes it. Fucking monster!

Anyway, sleep tight. Look under the bed – you never know…

You've just got to laugh at this guy Broderick Laswell. He's in Benton County jail in Arkansas, charged with murder, and he's suing the jail over losing seven stone. He was 29 stone and he's now only 22 stone. Fuck me, he should be thanking the jail for helping him prevent an early heart attack. He says the jail diet is starvation, but I say he's a fat, greedy fucker. Fuck me, 30 stone, what is he, a fucking hippo? That's America for you. Loonyology.

I was sad to read about the death of Sundeep Majhail, the 14–year–old boy who stole his mother's car and smashed it into a house at 100mph in West Sussex. How sad is that? He only reached 14 years on our wonderful world. I think that's tragic. Stop taking cars, you youngsters, it could be your last drive like Sundeep's was! Don't do it. Imagine how his family must be feeling! Think – stop and think. It's not worth it!

Hey! Exclusive news! All prisoners in the UK are to get a pay rise of 60%. It's our first rise in 10 years and it works out at £1.50 a week extra. Don't spend it all at once, lads, save a bit for your old age. Mr Michael Spurr, the Deputy Director General of the Prison Service, has ordered this pay rise, so cough up boys or we all go on strike or rip the roofs off. We want our £1.50 rise and fast! I say they should backdate it from 1998. All in favour, shout: "The Queen's a tart." If all inmates in the UK shouted that at midnight, I'm sure we could get some support from the unions outside! What about the public in general? What's your view on it being backdated? It's food for thought. I could be on to something here!

What about this Austrian monster Josef Fritzl who kept his own daughter isolated for 24 years in a cellar and knocked her up seven times to have kids by him? What sort of beast does that? Even animals don't act like that. This monster needs his heart ripping out and throwing in the incinerator. He's not even human, is he? Cunt! It beggars belief he kept it secret for a quarter of a century. (I don't believe that, do you? Some fucker must've known.)

What's coming next? Will it be me found in a box with my throat cut and a suicide note reading 'I leave all my dosh to the Prison Officers Association. Goodbye world, kiss my cock. Excuse the handwriting, I've had a drink. Signed: Charles Bronson'? Fuck me, that's got me thinking now. How easy would it be to wipe me out? It's possible, it really is! But never believe it, you know it's bollocks!!

Good old Kenny, this guy never stops. Max respect to the man.

DRAFT

News release – for immediate use

KENNY HERRIOT TO CYCLE FROM LAND'S END TO JOHN O'GROATS

Top wheelchair athlete Kenny Herriot is preparing for the charity challenge of a lifetime – cycling from Land's End to John o'Groats in the hope of raising a record £100,000 for Cash for Kids.

The gruelling 17-day challenge will see Aberdeen-based Kenny covering around 1,000 miles on a specially designed hand cycle.

Accompanied by two friends, he hopes to raise £100,000 for Cash for Kids, Northsound Radio's listener charity – which would be the most ever raised by a single supporter.

Ranked among the world's leading wheelchair athletes, Kenny also has his sights set on the 2008 Paralympics in Beijing in September and he has been training hard in Atlanta, Georgia and South Africa.

His journey will start on June 3, taking in a scenic route that will wind through Cornwall, Devon, Dartmoor, Somerset, Bristol, the Severn Bridge, Hereford, Shropshire, Cheshire, Lancaster, Cumbria and the Lake District, Carlisle, on to Gretna Green, Ayrshire, Loch Fyne and Inverary, Ballachulish, Drumnadrochit, Bonar Bridge, Altnaharra, Thurso and finally arriving in John o'Groats on June 20.

Kenny's major fundraising drive will be officially launched at a reception at the Marcliffe at Pitfodels next Tuesday evening (March 11), which is being generously sponsored by Aker Kvaerner Offshore Partner.

Companies and organisations have been invited to hear more about Kenny's challenge and to sign up to sponsor legs of the trip.

All proceeds from Kenny's challenge will be donated to Cash for Kids, which was set up to make grants towards children's groups, organisations and projects throughout the Northsound transmission area and each year hopes to raise £200,000.

All the money raised is raised locally and spent locally and goes to children who suffer from mental, physical or sensory disabilities, behavioural or psychological disorders, distress, abuse or neglect, or who are living in poverty or deprivation.

As a dad-of two himself, Kenny said the charity's work was important to him.

"Raising money for kids is very rewarding and I am hoping to raise £100,000 for Cash for Kids, which was particularly important to me as all the money is raised locally and spent locally," he said.

"I also wanted to help a charity that supports causes that mean something to me, including riding for the disabled, Aberdeen Children's Society, sports, family centres and music.

"I am looking forward to the challenge and hope to encourage and inspire as many companies and individuals as possible to sponsor me and support us throughout the 17 legs of the cycle."

After becoming disabled in 2000 as the result of a motorbike accident, Kenny has competed in marathons all over the world and broke the British record for the marathon in 2005.

John Curran, Chairman of the Cash for Kids Trustees, said Kenny's story was inspirational.

"We are absolutely delighted that Kenny has so generously decided to take on this personal challenge in aid of Cash for Kids.

"His story and determination to get back to incredible fitness after his accident are inspiring to everyone who meets him and this also reflects the positive work Cash for Kids is doing to raise money to support young people who are in need and to give them a helping hand in life.

"We are hoping that many companies will follow the lead of Aker Kvaerner and sign up to sponsor Kenny on part of his amazing trip."

Rod Buchan, Managing Director of Aker Kvaerner Offshore Partner, added: "We are pleased to be supporting Kenny as he prepares to embark on this huge challenge and would urge other businesses to get behind him and help to smash the £100,000 fundraising target.

"We wish Kenny all the best for this challenge of a lifetime and for future success at the Beijing Paralympics."

Kenny's journey will be tracked with bulletins on Northsound 1 and Northsound 2 and there will also be a blog on the Cash for Kids website.

For more information, please go to http://www.cashforkidsnorthsound.co.uk or http://www.kennyherriot.co.uk

ENDS

Issued on behalf of Northsound Radio by The BIG Partnership. For more information please contact Shona Hendry on 01224 578173 or 07739 314158 or Dave Macdermid on 01224 650406 or 07710 580148.

1 May 2008.

Some sad news today: my website is closing down! My reasons are personal and no–one else is responsible – it's my own decision and one that I've not taken lightly. I'm actually about to go back into my own world again and I'm feeling my old self coming back. Life outside for me is starting to choke me and darken my days. I'm getting unnecessary problems, headaches and cunts asking too much from me. It could well be time for a step back into the darkness, maybe a rest will do me good. But the site is now stopping, who fucking needs it? It's more trouble than it's worth, with all the silly hangers–on, Charlie this, Charlie that. Can you really do 94 press–ups in 30 seconds? Cunts, do it yourself. Wake up and live your own lives.

Top wheelchair athlete narrowly escapes death in accident while training

A top wheelchair athlete preparing for the fundraising challenge of a lifetime was lucky to escape with his life after an accident while training in Aberdeen.Kenny Herriot, who will cycle from Land's End to John O'Groats in aid of Northsound Radio's listener charity Cash for Kids, was cycling along the beach promenade when a driver sped out in front of him writing off his hand cycle and leaving Kenny with minor injuries. To add insult to injury the driver failed to take any notice of what had happened and fled the scene. Kenny was helped by pedestrians who had watched in shock as the accident unfolded. Unperturbed by the incident Kenny went on, the very same evening, to give a speech for the Bridge of Don Rotary after which he was picked up by a close friend and they embarked on a 1000 mile round trip to pick up a new hand cycle. Kenny travelled to Godmanchester to the Draft wheelchair factory where staff had worked tirelessly to put together a new machine to ensure his fundraising event was not in jeopardy. The whole event had shocked Kenny but he was unwilling to let it ruin the chance to raise money for a charity which he sees as hugely beneficial to the local community. "Immediately after it the accident I was in a state of shock and I was looking around to see if anyone else had seen what had happened. Luckily for me two people saw the incident and were able to help me."The next 24 hours were somewhat of a blur but my thanks go out to all the staff at Draft who have been incredible in the work they have done for me, to turn it around in a matter of hours was nothing short of a miracle. "My new bike is actually a combination of two bikes and I think it may take a little getting used to but now I am back on the road my training can get underway once again." Kenny will take part in a gruelling 17-day challenge - starting in June - which will see him cover around 1,000 miles on his new hand cycle. He hopes to raise £100,000 for Cash for Kids, Northsound Radio's listener charity – which would be the most ever raised by a single supporter.

Issued on behalf of Northsound Radio by The BIG Partnership. For more information please contact Shona Hendry on 01224 578173 or 07739 314158 or Dave Macdermid on 01224 650406 or 07710 580148.

Whoever was driving that motor, pray I never get a hold of you. You're nothing but a gutless fucking prick. It's cunts like you who cause men like me to end up in jail, because I would willingly lose my liberty to sort you out. I'd put you in a chair for life by snapping your cowardly spine for what you did to my mate Kenny. Start praying, cunt, because it could come back and haunt you. What goes around comes back twice as hard – no surer fact of life, cunt!

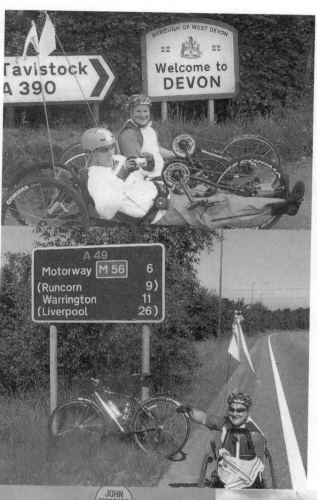

Hold up. Let's just take a snap of that lunatic.

Blimey – not even half way yet! I think Charlie hit a post office in Runcorn years ago.

The *Loonyology* book comes in handy!

A few snaps of Al Rayment and Kenny Herriott on their Land's End to John O'Groats marathon charity run 2008.

Now we know how Charlie feels! One of the oldest jails in Scotland. Trust Al and Kenny to end up in it – they probably got nicked for speeding!

Stop living mine. Sums it all up in a nutshell: Loonyology!!

I don't know why I'm feeling this way. I just feel I'm trapped and living my life for others. I'm trying to please too many when I'm really not living at all. I sense I'm coming to the end of a dream and my faith is leaving me. I see myself as an old man with a white beard and bent back, hobbling about. I picture all those lost souls in Broadmoor in my dreams coming back. If my appeal fails, that's my ending. Why live on with false dreams? Every time I speak to my mother I'm finding it difficult to even talk about how it really is, so why pretend? Two worlds can't ever be one.

It's only my appeal now that holds me together. Win it, I fly! Lose it, I fall! But I need it to come soon. Once it's come and gone I can then say how it all ends and you can all say, "Fuck him," and I can say, "Fuck you." I can then dive into myself, my world, alone and create the best stuff ever, free of all the shit. (Do it this way, do it that way! More colour. Don't do that, it will spoil your parole. They will see your anger. Think!) Well, fuck all you would-be critics, let me create what I see, how I feel! I also feel a new book bubbling up inside me, maybe a novel. I actually need another 30 years to give birth to all my inner feelings and thoughts. My brain is hurting me with so much to come out. Who fucking needs a website? Read my books for real, the best is yet to come. I'm on fire.

What a way to start the month – a fresh beginning, a new era, free of pressure with a new burning sensation in the loins and my heart ablaze. Don't rely on others, be your own destination. Be your own driver on this journey of life. Maybe my life is this? Maybe I now know it for real! Many have said it before – never to my face, but plenty behind my back. They could be right. Right now, this very day, I truly don't give a flying fuck, and you've got that from me, from the 'Hell diary' from me to you! The truth...

I got 10 letters today plus my manuscript of *Con-Artist* all typed up lovely. Mark Emmins has done me proud, he really has done a lovely job on it! Enjoy *Con-Artist* because my soul's in that book; I gave birth to it. It's the art book from Hell, but it's been humanised by Mark Emmins.

I got a lovely letter from Sarah Macleod who's an ex-prison screw. She was actually a good, decent, kind-hearted screw who took her work seriously and tried to do a fair job. But those screws are seen by other screws as weak and pathetic so they rarely last long. Some leave the job, others end up corrupted by other screws. It's very sad. I think the police force is the same: lots join up to do a fair job but they don't last long. They soon change when the shit hits the fan!

I got a letter off my old buddy Terry Smith, whose latest book is called *Blaggers Inc. – Britain's Biggest Armed Robberies*. Terry was once a top-class blagger, maybe one of the top 10 in the UK, so his books are really worth a read. They're full of facts and great insight. But all these 'top blaggers' end up paying the price: lots of porridge and lonely nights dreaming of a hot, juicy pussy that never ever comes. Years and years of mental torment driving you nuts! And it's even harder when the grass gets off scot free and the cunt's spending all the loot. That hurts.

I also got a strange letter from a stranger!

Dear Charlie,
I've just finished reading your book, *The Krays and Me*. Can I please ask you a personal question? Did you ever see Ronnie Kray go berserk? And did Reggie have a cat in jail?

Harry Jackson from Nottingham.

I've just replied: "Fuck off, Harry and get a life!!"

That's how it is: crazy people are free and living amongst you lot. That's how my life has become: a magnet for the insane. I guess I once enjoyed it as it kept me busy, but now it's boring me to death. I can no longer relate to cunts like Harry! Sure, he's probably harmless and he means well, but year after year of this shit can chew you up and spit you out. No – Reg never had a fucking cat! And Ron didn't have to go mad – he was mad! How does a madman go mad when he is already mad? (Er, hello... Broadmoor's an asylum. Mad people go there!) I also got a nice letter from Pearl Thwaite, Kate Kray's mother–in–law.

My apologies to all those I've not replied to lately. My only reason is that I'm not in the mood. A stamp is a Mars bar to me; a call is five Mars bars. I have to think of No. 1; it's me who has to survive this shit and it's me who will.

Imagine this if you can: pick up any man on the street and sling him in jail, put him in my hole, treat him like me (isolate him and brutalize him) then ask him how he feels. Then pick me up and stick me on the street and ask me how I feel. Go ahead and ask me! You'll see the answer on my face – I'm the happiest man on the planet! Put your arse on that. I bet the other man's not too happy, he's probably topped himself by now!!

Section 5 – Security Information Date Reports Due for Completion .... from Security Department		
SECURITY INFORMATION REPORTS Please provide information relating to SIR's, which would be relevant to the category A review, and evidence a continued high level of dangerousness.		**Source of Information and date** (please indicate whether information is based on evidence or intelligence)
Concerns have been raised regarding Mr Bronson attempting to give literature out during visits in attempt to by-pass censoring procedures. Also concern regarding possible abuse of Rule 39 mail. May 2007 - Mr Bronson became angry and abusive towards staff when asked to finish his visit.		Security File Security File
COMPLETED BY	M L Hollis	
GRADE/TITLE	T/SO	
DATE	03/02/08	
Prison Behaviour: Please list and describe any evidence of behaviour consistent with offending history and index offence. i.e. violence, bullying, drug dealing, stalking, etc.		**Source of Information and date** (please indicate whether information is based on evidence or intelligence)
No adjudications during this reporting period. Mr Bronson is currently interacting well with CSC staff, taking part in CSC meetings and also engaging with both probation and psychology.		Personal Officer CSC Staff
COMPLETED BY	M L Hollis	
GRADE/TITLE	T/SO	
DATE	03/02/08	

What you've just read is my 'Category A' report done by security for this year, 2008. I'm now going to prove it's a complete lie. Let me explain first about 'Rule 39' mail. When a prisoner writes to his/her solicitor he/she is allowed to seal it for legal confidentiality and the censor is not allowed to open it or read it. That also applies for incoming legal mail. The only way it can be censored is if security believes contraband is being smuggled in by mail. However:

1. My legal team do not send me anything illegal.
2. None of my 'Rule 39' mail has been opened (except by me).
3. I have never been informed of it.
4. Why haven't I been nicked over it?
5. Why have my legal team not been told about it?
6. And the million dollar question is: how would they know if I ever sent out anything in a 'Rule 39' when they can't censor it or open it? Or have they opened it? If so that's illegal! So I think I've well won this case.

On to their other allegation, that I have "attempted to smuggle out literature on visits". To whom? When? What? Again, if it's true, why have I not been told? Why did they not intervene? Why were my visitors not pulled? My visits are in max secure conditions under CCTV and behind bars; I am searched, metal-detected and watched like a hawk, so how could I smuggle anything out and what am I supposed to be smuggling in or out? It's the biggest load of shit I've ever read on a report.

So why the fuck have they done it? I don't even know this senior officer Hollis who did this report, but I'm told she's a security officer. Isn't it strange that nobody who works on this unit seems to know about it? I've put in a complaint so watch this space because I'm telling it how it is, this is a lie. But why do it? What's their reason or purpose? I'll tell you why: they've got nothing better to do than sit on their fat arses and make it all up. If it were true then they must be cunts to allow it to happen! Let me now put a spanner in the works. Some screws have a price, so if I want to smuggle something in or out I don't have to fuck about or take a chance with my family or friends, I'll use a bent screw. It's that simple.

Senior Officer Hollis wants to get her facts straight on this one: 'Rule 39' mail is illegal to open. So has she been opening my legal mail? It's possible – I wouldn't put fuck all past them. The governor can order my legal letters to be opened in front of me if he/she thinks it's being abused. So why hasn't that been done either? I'll tell you why not: because it's a load of bollocks designed to make me look a shifty character. These are the lies I have to live with and this report is now in my security file forever. It follows me on, so other jails will now believe I'm abusing 'Rule 39'! It all helps to stop me ever being de-categorised and it's all over some power-freak fucker!

I see Tom Hardy was in the *Star* yesterday. There was a full page on the movie and he looks the dog's bollocks. Hollywood, look out!

I also clocked another gun nutter went berserk in America shooting his dad, his step-mum, brother and sister. Nataniel Dickson, the gunman, is just 18. There must be something in the water over there – it's going off every fucking week. Who's next to go berserk? I bet it was an argument with Dad over a pizza or a Big Mac or some shit like that. That's what it usually boils down to: crap. I'll blow the family away, I'll teach them not to fuck with me.

I called up my friend Sandra! She's already got my art up on her wall in a frame. I also called up my brother and all's sweet out there. I'm sweet too! I'm always sweet, even my cock's sweet – so the girls have told me.

Hey! I've come up with a new word today: madopath. Not bad, eh? It's a good title for a book. It perfectly describes a freaky fucker coming out of the darkness who's probably escaped from the asylum. He's got bulging eyes and he's dribbling all over your sandwich. These words just come to me.

I was watching Maudsley on the yard walking around earlier. He's got a strange walk but it's difficult to describe; it's more animal than human. It's a dream walk like something out of a horror film – a zombie coming at you out of a graveyard, slow but dangerous. Make no bones about it, he is one freaky fucker. If we were in a room together only one of us would be walking out, and that's me. Yeah! I'll dedicate 'madopath' to Maudsley!

I had a nice drop of tomato soup today! I had two bowls with four bread rolls. I got six letters in; not bad for a Monday! One was from Giovanni, my lawyer – 'Rule 39' legal mail (unopened). Don't tell security or they will try and say it's a bomb or something like that. Cunts.

I got a letter from my Lorraine, who says my mum's having a great time in Spain with Eileen. That pleased me. Yeah, not a bad day at all, I feel good. It should be a crime to be so happy, especially in prison. I think they should birch me for being so happy, don't you? A fucking good birching would do me the world of good.

Ronnie 'the rocket' O'Sullivan made a 147-break today at the Crucible. The man's a genius, maybe the greatest snooker player of all time! I salute him.

I had a good work-out today in the rain. It was lovely and I was jumping around like a frog, so I'm going to have a good sleep tonight. A peaceful sleep is priceless. There may be a 30–foot wall around my body and a barbed wire fence around my heart, but my mind is totally free. I'm freer than most of you guys outside, I really am! It's crazy but true! What I've got is priceless and it's not for sale! I sleep like a baby and I awake as fresh as a daisy. Do you? I bet you're jealous, I bet you think, "Who the fuck does he think he's kidding?" Good night, sleep tight.

Oh! Why did the scarecrow win a noble prize? He was outstanding in his field!

Do you know something? Well, I'm gonna tell you anyway. Hell's not so bad, it just stinks of hypocrisy! Apart from that, who needs Heaven? It's probably full of fairies. Fuck that, better the devil you know than the devil you don't know.

What still baffles me about prison life is how some men are forever hounded by the press and media and forever popping up in magazines and papers decades after they were sent down for their crimes, while others seem to escape all that sensationalist shit. Take Michael Lupo, for example. Who? You may well ask! It's just a name to you, but I've never forgotten him. I'd say Lupo was probably one of the 10 most dangerous men of all time in British crime but few have ever heard of him. Why is that? You all know the Ripper, Brady and Cuntley. (Ooops sorry, Huntley, I always fuck his name up but don't you think Cuntley sounds nicer?) You all know Nielson and Ireland and the likes. But Lupo? Who the fuck's he? Well, back in 1987 he made criminal history by becoming our first-ever gay serial killer. He was convicted with four murders but many more were left on the books. Some say he probably killed a dozen more. I met Lupo in Brixton jail and then later up in max-secure Frankland. To look at him he just seemed like a normal sort of geezer – I suppose you would say a good-looking sort of chap, pretty harmless, softly spoken and a bit shy. But underneath all that armour walked a fucking nightmare.

Some say Colin Ireland was the first gay serial killer, but he came on the scene in 1993 so how could it have been him? Lupo was the first, but my question is: why do so few know of him? He only survived for eight years up in Frankland before dying of Aids in 1995. I guess you can only shag so many arses on this planet before Aids catches you up. I've always said it and I always will: arses are not designed for shagging, they're shit holes, that's all an arse will ever be! What sane man dreams of shagging another man's shit hole? I rest my case.

Another infamous con who is never talked about is Jimmy Anderson. He and Mickey Jamieson terrorized East London in the early 1980s when they went on a killing spree – a very sick one at that. Both were finally convicted of four of the most grotesque killings you can imagine! They were pure fucking evil and they sickened Londoners. There was uproar and they both got natural life. I bumped into Jimmy down in Parkhurst and Mickey up in Full Sutton. Mickey hanged himself but, amazingly, Jimmy has managed to stay out of the media for over 20 years. Have you ever heard of him? In fact he is here in monster mansion up on normal location where he has been for a good 10 years, mixing with all the shit in criminal history – child killers, serial rapists and all sorts of low-life shit.

That's something I've never understood. How does a normal man accept doing time with a wing full of nonces? Could you? Would you? Should you have to? Fuck that! I couldn't, I'd never accept it! I've not survived Hell to live amongst scum in Heaven. But men swallow it, they switch off and mix with them. Why? Probably because they think it'll help them get good reports and early parole. It's all a big act, but I'm not acting. For me to live amongst so much shit would be torture, mental pain and agony. I would only have to pick up a paper and see a paedophile's just raped a kid, and I would just grab the first nonce on the landing. Fuck that for an existence! I'm not being mentally abused by any system! A wingful of nonces should be gassed, it's that cut and dried with me. Fuck it. If it means early parole by mixing with the cunts, then you guys do it and crawl out of Hell, but you'll have to live with that till the day you die! You'll probably see them all later in the next world. Even in the next world I'll break their fucking noncy jaws if they enter my space. That's how it stays with me, I can't change that part of my life. I don't know one person outside who will accept a nonce as a neighbour.

Fuck the 'PC brigade' and human rights bollocks! A nonce is a danger to the public and your kids come first in life (not a nonce).

Yeah! You'll be amazed at how many infamous cons disappear in the belly of the system. Most are in the asylums; they just get their heads down and the world forgets them and their crimes – that is till they reappear and rip your throat out! Do psychos ever change? Would you marry Rose West? Do dogs lick arse? Do frogs jump? Has a donkey got a massive cock? Ask yourself! Be your own judge! Build your own gallows. Amen.

Who remembers Fonzi Badavi? Who? You may well ask! To us cons who knew him, he was 'Fossie' and he's the only terrorist that survived the Iranian Embassy siege in 1980. You will remember the SAS storming the building, which even today they still brag about. They shot dead five terrorists and one innocent hostage; all the terrorists threw down their guns and were shot unarmed! The SAS have a thing about bragging over their hits but, believe me, they're not always on the good side! They're not superhuman either, they just have a licence to kill when they feel it's right – but no fucker is always right. Always remember the SAS just killed them for the sake of killing. They're psychos, that's all it boils down to really – they're the Queen's Own Psycho Unit. In and out and leave a few stiffs. Bring on the body bags, boys, then let's pick our medals up after the party.

Anyway, Fossie has served 28 years for his part in that infamous siege. At the time he was only 22 years old, a young freedom fighter, and a man full of the horrors of life. The real story can now be told with no red tape or political lies as Fossie's just been freed. He's a good guy and all the cons liked him, so we all hope he will tell his side of the story!

Right, you all know me by now and that I like to prove all I say is 100% truthful. I've always said I have nothing to lie for. I let the system do that until they tell one lie too many and mug themselves off again and again. So read this next page on your right very slowly and take it all in. The lying bastards have been caught out again. Read this complaint form and their reply, then think about it. (I'll be back).

369 F2059 B- Sec

HM PRISON SERVICE

FORM COMP 1
PRISONER'S FORMAL COMPLAINT

Establishment
Serial Nº WD47/08F.

Read these notes first

1. This form is for you to make a formal written complaint under the complaints procedure. Complaints should wherever possible be sorted out informally by speaking to your wing officer or making an application. Use this form only if you have not been able to resolve your complaint this way.
2. A written complaint should be made within 3 months of the incident or of the relevant facts coming to your notice.
3. Keep the complaint brief and to the point.
4. When you have completed the form, sign it and post in the box provided. The form will be returned to you with a response.
5. If you are unhappy with the response, you can appeal on a separate form (COMP 1A).
6. Some subjects are dealt with only by the Area Manager or Prison Service headquarters. If your complaint is about one of these subjects, the reply will take longer.
7. There is a separate pink form (COMP 2) for confidential access complaints.

Your details (use BLOCK CAPITALS)

Surname	BRONSON	First name(s)	CHARLES ARTHUR
Prison number	BT1314	Location	C.S.C. UNIT

Have you spoken to anyone about your complaint ? Yes [✓] No [ ]
If so, who did you speak to ?

SCREWS.

Your complaint

S.O HOLLIS AS SUBMITTED A REPORT FOR MY CATEGORY A REVIEW ACCUSING ME OF ABUSING RULE 39A MAIL. AND ATTEMPTING TO SMUGGLE OUT LITERATURE ON VISITS.
BOTH ARE LIES AND IN 33YRS OF PRISON I HAVE NEVER DONE EITHER OF THESE.
THESE ALLEGATIONS ARE NOW IN MY FILE AND WILL BE USED AGAINST ME WHEREVER I GO.
WHY LIE ABOUT ME ?

Does your complaint have a racial aspect ? Yes [ ] No [ ]
Is your complaint about bullying ? Yes [ ] No [ ]
What would you like to see done about your complaint ?

"PROVE IT." OR TAKE IT OUT OF MY FILE.
I'VE GOT NOTHING TO HIDE.
YOU LOT OBVIOUSLY HAVE TO WRITE LIES FOR MY COMING CAT 'A' REVIEW.

Signed [signature] Date 25/4/2008

Reply: Thank you for your complaint. The information contained on your 'Cat A' report was the result of intelligence received into the security dept. I have reviewed this intelligence and decided that it is not strong enough to warrant inclusion in your 'Cat A' report, therefore it will be removed and re-submitted without that piece of information.

Now see the lies that help to keep me locked up? Now see what evil fuckers they can be? There never was any 'intelligence' – it was all made up to make me look bad. This is what they've been doing to me for years: making up lies. The truth is I could name names of 'iffy screws' who will smuggle things in and out of jail for the right price. I could do that now and prove it, but why should I? Screws like that are worth their weight in gold to me. Sure the greedy fuckers take the piss with their price, but that's life inside. Now see what I have to endure? A life of treachery! They do it to cause me shit and to fuck up my legal correspondence! This sort of shit stays on my file forever, but fortunately this time it gets taken off. I've been exonerated over a crime they tried to stitch me up with. Again I'm the target; again they are guilty but go unpunished. A cunt – that's all this lying screw is! A lying, evil, toe rag! What next? Cor, I wish I knew!! But as sure as chickens lay eggs there's more to come, lots more, bet your arse on that!

I'll tell you who's an evil bastard: Gordon Coulter. This Australian arse-wipe snuffed out three beautiful teenage girls, gorgeous girls with their whole lives to live. Molina Carter was 18, Habsa Harrington was 19 and Sally Norfolk 20 years old. This animal had an eye fetish – the sicko actually sucked out their eyeballs. Crazy but true. When he was arrested in Western Australia they found three eyes in the fridge; the other three were missing (presumed eaten). Coulter was found to be criminally insane and sent to a secure mental unit. I hope they keep an eye on the nutter! Watch out he doesn't suck yours out! Cunt. What a fucking sicko! They also found scores of websites devoted to major eye surgery on his computer. He admitted that once he sucked out the eye, he would use a pair of scissors to cut the optic nerve cord. He strangled the three girls and left them eyeless and lifeless! Shoot the evil bastard and let the vultures rip his eyes out. This planet doesn't need him.

Hey! There's a copper in New Jersey who's just been caught having sex with a cow in a field. Dirty bastard; he admitted doing it four times. Fuck me, once is enough! He claimed to be a sex addict and when his girlfriend knocked him back for a quickie, he just shot into the field to empty his sack. Who knows – maybe the cow was better looking than his partner. Still, it doesn't amaze me with a copper, they're a strange breed. Do you trust your local bobby? Yeah, I bet you do!!

Talking of cows, what about that Russian tart who got so sick of people calling her a fat cow that she went to live in a field full of cows? That was five years ago and she still lives in the field! Her local villagers have actually seen her bent over the water trough being mounted by the bull. Can you fucking believe that? She's 24 stone and looks like a monster wrestler. Fat, dirty cow, have you seen the size of a bull's cock? It's like a hose pipe. Dirty bitch, it's disgusting, it's not human! Is it?

I see Paul Gascoigne's at it again! This time he's tried to kill himself in a hotel room, so he's in hospital having psychiatric tests done. I don't feel sorry for him, do you? He's 40 years old and loaded, so what's to be sorry about? He wants to sort his nut out. Get a fucking life for fuck's sake.

4 May 2008.

I had a great visit today. Mark Jones and Mark Emmins came up to see me! They're two diamonds. Mark Jones is one of the best tattooists in the UK, if not the best. Some of his customers have a Bronson art as a tattoo and I've told him to tell them that when I'm free I'll sign their tattoo for them. How unique is that? Original or what?

My new book *Loonyology* was in the *Sunday Sport* today, a two-page exclusive that's helped to sell the first 5,000 copies. Thank you, *Sunday Sport*, I'll sort you a drink later.

Oh, get on this, about 6am this morning a flock of geese flew over the jail. What a fucking racket they make, but it sounded brilliant. I grabbed my 12-bore and fired. Three fell out of the sky – goose pie for a week! Have you ever had goose pie? It's lovely.

Oh well, a new week tomorrow, only it's a Bank Holiday Monday so no post. Another boring day but I'll make it positive and creative, you know it. I can feel a masterpiece coming on! I feel it in my loins, it's like sex but better. It's a warm sensation where my balls swell up, my bollock sack becomes tingly and my mind races. If my door burst open right now and they offered me a page 3 dolly-bird or a canvas and oils and brushes, do you know which I'd choose? Yeah, the page 3 bird! Fucking right I would; did you honestly think it would be the art? Come on, wake up. What do you take me for – a cunt? My name's Charlie Bronson not Rolf Harris. I'm a pussy lover, not some fucking art beatnik. I enjoy apple pies but I'm not a fat twat, am I? Everything has to be in moderation; only pigs don't know when to stop. Live the dream, don't let the dream live you! I'll be back, maybe…

Did you know the average adult human farts between 30 and 40 times in a 24-hour day, mostly in their sleep? Fucking amazing or what? We fart when we are asleep; I bet you never knew that! The old folk need to fart a lot or they explode – old age builds up gas. Let it rip I say, but don't do it near me. I once hit a geezer with a fire extinguisher for farting near me. I clobbered the fucker. I bet he was more careful who he farted near after that. Some people only learn manners the hard way! See how educational my books are? Every page you learn something about life!

Did you know the male adult mountain gorilla lets rip in the female's face as a romantic gesture? Could you see Peter Andre doing that to Jordan, or Prince Phillip to the Queen? Fuck me, what a romantic gesture! Nature is nuts, it's a magical moment! It's just brilliant, don't you agree? Take kangaroos and their pouches, don't you think that's brilliant? It's like a handbag on the belly! Pop in there, son, I'm taking you out for a hop. Why can't women have one of those pouches? It would save a fortune on prams and handbags. You could even put guns in there. Yeah, our women should be like kangaroos. Brilliant!

Did I ever tell you about the time I climbed on top of a lion? I was on it for three fucking hours in the pissing rain – that's how long it took the Old Bill to drag me off it! It was in Trafalgar Square. Fuck me, you didn't think I meant a real lion did you! Who do you think I fucking am, Tarzan? Do me a favour, give me a bit of credit. I may be ex–Broadmoor but I'm not that mad!

Hey! I was right, I did create a masterpiece last night. I was on it for four and a half hours. It's A3 size, black and white, with lots of shade and light. I enjoyed it; I created a man in a box of chains. His face said it all: "Shoot me, fucking blow me away!" That's what my art does, it screams out at you.

Guess what, come on have a guess. OK, don't bother you miserable fuckers. Now you'll never know.

I always wanted to be a baker because they make plenty of dough!

Hey! I'll tell you who's a sexy bird: my friend Di Brown. She's sex on legs and used to be the No. 1 Monroe look-alike. Even now she's older she's still hot – what I'd call elegant, cultured and stylish. Di Brown's a real woman, not like these paper-thin skinny, spotty, bow-legged, ugly fuckers who call themselves models. Knock-kneed muppets, that's what I call them, the lettuce leaf brigade. Women need some meat on them! A good arse with a proper body – something to wrestle with. Three cheers for the real girls: HIP HIP – HOORAY! HIP HIP – HOORAY! HIP HIP – HOORAY!

Hey! Could you have seen Richard Burton farting in Liz Taylor's face? She would have snapped his neck like a chicken bone! They married each other twice. What a crazy old world. He probably had a thing for wedding cake!

6 May 2008.

The sun's out and it's a beautiful day, my hour on the yard was like the Costa Del Wako. Beautiful, it's got to be the best day this year, with not a cloud in the sky.

Rocket Ronnie won his third world title yesterday. What a snooker player he is – a genius. Let's hope his old man is freed soon so he can party. He's served a good 16 years and it's time to let him out. It would be great to see him out to watch Ronnie win his fourth title in 2009. That would be the cherry on the cake! That nutcase streaker Mark Roberts did his act when Ronnie was just about to start playing and it's a wonder Ronnie didn't bust his jaw! But you've got to give it to that streaker – he gets everywhere. I suppose he's just a lunatic. Where would we be without these loonies? It would be a boring old planet. He should have waited until the games were all over and then ran out flapping his bollocks about, shouting, "Balls to the world!" But then again, do the women really want to see that? Think of something different, mate, something that's never been done before, because it's getting boring now.

I'm gutted that James Whale's been sacked from TalkSport radio. That's a true legend gone! He was on that station for 13 years and he's my favourite broadcaster. A top geezer, a true survivor – he even beat cancer! He got sacked over telling his listeners to vote for Boris Johnson to become London Mayor. Big fucking deal – so what if he did? Old Whale will be back on some other radio station! What else can he do? He's been doing that job for over 30 years now, that's how good he is. 30 years at the top! Three cheers for the Whale! HIP HIP – HOORAY! HIP HIP – HOORAY! HIP HIP – HOORAY! Fuck TalkSport, I won't be tuning in again. I doubt too many others will bother either!

What about Hussain Djemil, the former head of drug treatment policy at the National Offender Management Service? This is the former prison chief who claims that more than half of the 82,000 prisoners in England and Wales are hooked on drugs. And get on this, he claims that rogue prison officers smuggle most of it in. Surprise, surprise! What's he said that I haven't said in all my books for the last 10 years? Please wake up. Now an ex-prison chief is saying it, at least believe him if you won't believe me. There are bags and bags of smack coming into our jails every day of the week. If you still don't believe it then go back to sleep, you muppets. Djemil's even been backed up by David Jameson, the official chairman of the Independent Monitoring Board at Wandsworth prison who claims that at least £1 million worth of drugs are traded within the jail every year. Now you know why a lot of the screws drive big flash motors and have big paid-up houses. It's fucking obvious to me! The cunts won't smuggle in a 30-foot rope or a hacksaw blade but they'll sell a bag of smack to some junkie! (Now who's evil?)

I say the whole system needs looking into. Lock these drug slags up for life because they're bigger villains than us villains and they're making a lot of dosh out of misery. Evil fuckers. If they can smuggle in all these drugs, then why can't they get me a bit of pussy for the weekend and a couple of bottles of bubbly? Ain't my dosh good enough? You've got to be a smack head to get on in life. Fuck making screws rich – no wonder they're laughing all the time, they're taking the piss out of you smack heads. You're just paying their bills off, you mugs. You should be getting them to smuggle in some escape equipment so we can all fuck off home. Wake up.

It was nice to see Sir Bobby Robson getting awarded the freedom of Ipswich yesterday. Top man, Bobby. He's 75 now and has beaten cancer twice! He won the FA Cup in 1978 and the UEFA Cup in 1981 with Ipswich! He did that team proud. Respect the old chap because he's a legend for real!

I got six letters today and I called my buddy Mark Fish and Dave Courtney. Dave had a Russian film crew there doing a documentary about the Russian Mafia in Britain. He put the director on and I said to him, "My best to the firm, but tell them from me: stay the fuck out of Luton."

Yeah, a great day today and a crazy memory came flooding back to me! You'll love this one. (Are you sitting comfortably? Then I'll begin.) When I was out on the yard today there was a scruffy-looking pigeon sitting on the caged roof making that silly tooting noise they make. It took me back to the Hull special unit in 1994 when I was out on the yard on another sunny day and a crazy pigeon walked under the electric door into my cage. That's the only way it could get in owing to it being a large cage sealed off with razor wire and CCTV in every corner. I stood and watched the cheeky fucker waddling around me with its chest out. I slung my medicine ball at it and knocked it into next week, then I grabbed it and pulled its head clean off. As I did this some screws happened to walk out. Blood was pumping out of its headless neck and I threw the head at the first screw and said, "There's your dinner, cunt!" I then walked into the unit's kitchen, as we cooked our own food there. (There were only five of us on the unit, with about 20 screws!) So there I was plucking, cleaning and gutting it when Paul Flint walked in. I've known Paul for years; he copped a life sentence when he was a young lad and I've been in many jails with him.

"What you got there, Charlie?" he said.

"Pigeon."

"A fucking pigeon," he said.

"Yeah, a pigeon. I'm preparing a pigeon meal for supper!"

Next minute the governor and a dozen screws came marching in.

"OK, Charlie," the governor said. "What's going on?"

"I'm cooking pigeon."

"You can't do that on this unit."

"Why not?" I said.

"Well... one, it's health and safety and two, it's not allowed! Those pigeons are rats with wings."

"Yeah? That's your opinion but I'm still cooking it! Fuck off!"

To cut a long story short, I cooked it and it was fucking horrible! Prison pigeons are shit! They eat shit, they are shit, and for once the governor was right: they're rats with wings. Plus, a lot of old jails put down poison pigeon pellets, so I guess the governor was concerned that I might eat some poison! Personally, I think it was more the head incident! They probably thought, "Here we go again, he's lost the plot!"

Yeah, memories are wonderful! What would we do without our memories? Life would be so fucking dull. Imagine burying a bag of loot and not being able to remember where it was! Now that would be murder – torture! You know you buried it, but where? That's how priceless memories are!

I see that Pete Doherty got released from the Scrubs today (10 weeks early). I suppose he will be on the smack and having his cock sucked dry tonight. Lucky fucker, getting his bell-end sucked! He should have said to the media when he walked out: "I've just spent a couple of months locked up with Britain's most violent men. The cons were diamonds but those screws were psychos and a couple of them have bled me dry for my drugs. The fucking price of a bag of smack was disgusting and I'm fucking skint now." That's what he should have said. Maybe he did, I do hope so.

Prison's a funny old world and you've got to see the funny side. Failing that, you're sure to land up in the padded cell! Believe me, you won't like that. I first landed in Wandsworth's padded cell in their hospital wing in 1976. It's not a nice memory. There were some nasty screws about in those days and they used to do some horrible things to us 'activists'. Cunts. But I'm still here and where are they? I'm still alive and kicking, I'm still healthy! Are they? I bet not! They're probably retired, old and weak with sagging bollocks and bent backs – bitter and twisted! Most are probably in their coffins where they belong! Fucking bully boys, all boots and peaked caps with notches in their sticks! Still, that was then, this is now... Happy birthday, boys!!

7 May 2008.

I just knew today was going to be a lucky day. I felt it in my bones and when I had my 6am slash, I was smiling. I just felt happy. Call in intuition, call it fate, but I just knew it! I received the first copy of *Loonyology: In My Own Words* from the printers and if I say so myself it's awesome, brilliant and fucking magical. Apex Publishing has done it proud. It could not be better – the quality, the lay out – it's all spot on and professionally done. My respect to Chris Cowlin and all at Apex who had faith in me. Now in return you'll have a best-seller! So get your copies now, you know it's the book of the year!

I've just found out today that John Blake Publishing are bringing out a new edition of my *Bronson* book and the cheeky fuckers have not even asked me! It's a bloody insult really as they're publishing it in February 2009 just as my movie's coming out. So that has actually put a stop to this book coming out then. We shall now sit on this till the summer of 2009. The Blake *Bronson* book is eight years old! It's a book of the past, it's history! It's *Loonyology* that speaks of today! *Loonyology* is 200% me with no co-writer! I now call Blake Publishing the 'cheeky fuckers' as they do what they want, when they want and have no need to ask a man in a coffin. I bet they wish I was really dead! Ignorant people give me a headache.

One of the last books I did with Blake was *Heroes and Villains* and it was a joke. The whole book was disrespected! The brilliant colour photos of all the legendary characters were badly copied in black and white, and I had no say on the cover or lay out – they just did what they wanted. The real kick in the nuts was that they brought it out in a paperback when I said I wanted hardback. That to me was the last straw! Apex doesn't act that way. They discuss it all, they compromise and listen to ideas, and they come up with the goods so all are winners. Blake should take note of all this. Wake up and smell the coffee! Jaw jaw, not war war. I'll not be getting involved in the *Bronson* re-issue. I could have added an update chapter or new photos, but they're so ignorant they won't even ask. Fuck it... it's Loonyology to me!!

The food today was shit – one of those days when it's just not worth eating. All I've had today is a bowl of Coco Pops and about three cups of tea. That's it. I'm fucking starving. That's how prison life is: outside you can get some fast food – fish and chips, curry, and all sorts; inside you get what you're given. You may have a menu choice but it can still be shit! Every choice can be shit some days. But it's good for the body to go without; just drink lots of fluid.

The sun's out again and I had a lovely hour out there. It was a gutter to come back in. I got six letters today, all nice: one from Sandra, my book from Apex and four others. One guy is after Bronson art. He may get one if the dosh comes in but I don't do freebies all the time because a lot of my art ends up on eBay and I don't get a fucking tea bag for it. Tight, slippery fuckers trying to rip me off! Cunts, go rob a bank you greedy pricks!

Yeah! A great day, considering I didn't eat. I feel good, soul-deep.

Did I tell you about the time I poured a full urn of custard over a con's head in Wandsworth? Why? He was a cunt, that's why! If I'd had a shotgun, I would have gladly blown his legs off. He knows why and so do I; what more is there to say? Enjoy your custard, cunt... fuck off over the hospital where you belong.

It's about time I had a good old-fashioned moan. I'll tell you who's a cunt: Donal Kelleher – he's a total fucking wanker. He's in Cardiff Prison and he wrote me a letter that was printed in the *Wales on Sunday* paper. Quote: "I am currently serving a recall sentence where the probation service thinks they are punishing me. But in fact I would rather be in here because of the fantastic conditions." It goes on, four pages of pure shit! This geezer actually proves what I say: jail is now full of cunts, and this prick has turned our system into a nut house!

Cardiff Prison is a very old jail, built in 1827. In the year I was born

(1952) they hanged an innocent man in this shit hole. Mahmood Mattan was murdered by the state but 46 years later he was found to be innocent and his conviction was quashed. No doubt many more innocent men were hanged in Cardiff. I know of many cons who have served time in Cardiff: the Frayne brother's, Alfie Lodge, Stevie Miller and others too numerous to mention. It's jail, it's bird, it's porridge. Men don't like it, but they are men that get on with it. The dream is freedom, release. Only a cunt would write to a paper and confess to loving any jail and it's this sort of cunt that gets right up my nostrils. I've fought my guts out for three and a half decades, then I learn that Kelleher prat's doing this. Incidentally, he repeatedly stabbed up his wife so he's not exactly Al Capone – he's a twat.

How can any normal human prefer prison life to freedom? He must be a totally institutionalised prick to even think it, let alone write it. Somebody give him a slap from me and tell him to shake his head. Prison is shit, remember that! Your cell door slams shut. OK, you may have a TV or radio, but you're fucking locked in, you're away from your family and you can't have a shag. (Well, some do – the gays are spoilt for choice!) You're a fucking prisoner, a brother in chains. Wake the fuck up, Kelleher, and all you prats who think it's great to be in jail. Fuck me, I've got a headache now!

Anyway, not to worry, April 13, 2009 falls on a Friday and we are to be hit by an asteroid. This is an exclusive from the space agency, NASA. So watch out for it, Kelleher, you can watch it crash into Earth from your cell window, you cunt. I'm not a violent man but I've a strong urge to punch his face in.

Well, what about Mark Saunders, the gunman the Old Bill shot dead in Chelsea recently? It's one for the book. He was a barrister who went mad with a shotgun, blasting it everywhere! There was some sort of lovers' tiff and he just snapped. Suicide by cop. He was only 32. See how easily madness can creep into anyone's life? His girlfriend was also a solicitor and they owned a £2 million flat off Kings Road, Chelsea! They had everything to live for, but fuck all to be happy about. One argument, one fall out and 'Bang' – he's 'brown bread'. They do say the legal profession is stressful and lots turn to booze. If you ask me, they get paid too much. Greedy fuckers! Anyway, respect to the man, he chose his way out of all the madness: "Shoot me, you twats."

I've got a bit of classic sports history for you here! England's first ever football game was on 4 March 1876 against Scotland at Glasgow's cricket ground. There were 15,000 spectators and England lost 3-0. The England team was: E Field, WS Buchanan, CE Smith, FT Green, WJ Maynard, AH Savage, J Turner, H Heron, EH Bambridge, F Heron, BG Jarrett and AW Curshaw (sub). And get on this, they all had a Bronson tash. Fucking brilliant or what! Eat your heart out, Beckham. These guys were tough, they were all workers and got paid fuck all apart from expenses (probably a few pennies) but they played with pride. I fucking love 'em! God bless you boys. Respect! See how you learn with my books? Soon you'll all be right clever cunts!

I see Burma's just had a major disaster; a fucking big cyclone's hit them, killing 100,000 people. Can you believe that? 100,000 bodies piled up sky high! Let's face reality, nature can be cruel but you can't do sod all about it. The weather will crush us all if and when it chooses to do so. All this praying to God won't stop it, that prat can't even save one of those 100,000 bodies. It's a tragic disaster and it won't be the last! That's how this crazy world is… Loonyology!

The latest here in monster mansion is that the screws have formed a rock band. They call themselves the 'Screw Suede Shoes' and they're laying on a concert for the monsters. Thank fuck I'm in the cage so I don't have to hear their racket! What next, will they dig up Johnny Cash? (St fucking Wakefield.) My head's hurting again!

8 May 2008.

The sun's out again and it's lovely. I had cornflakes for breakfast, shaved my head and created a piece of art called 'Institutionalized Madness' before dinner was served – a nice bowl of mushroom soup. I said to them, "I hope they're not magic ones." I got nine letters including a cracker from Mark Fish with 30 photos enclosed from the movie shoot, all blinders. I'm actually worried now, as Tom Hardy is more like me than I am. Is that humanly possible? One snap is of him up on Broadmoor roof pissing, another is of him being brutalized by the screws. It's like looking at my life passing me by all over again – a weird feeling to say the least! With his bald head and tash, it's freaking me out. Mark and Tom will be up to see me on the 29th, so that's fantastic. Sandra Gardner sent me in some photos of her amazing garden and a lovely poem she found:

Smiling

Smiling is infectious
You catch it like the flu.
When someone smiled at me today
I started smiling too.
I passed around the corner
And someone saw me grin.
So when he smiled I realised
I'd passed it on to him.
I thought about the smile
And realised its worth.
A single smile like mine
Could travel around the Earth.
So if you feel a smile begin
Don't leave it undetected.
Let's start an epidemic quick
And get the world infected.

Come on, how fucking brilliant is that? It made me smile; in fact it made me feel good! Thanks, Sandra.

A little short-arse governor did his rounds today; he's five feet nothing with a big mouth. He said, "Good morning," and I said, "It was till I fucking saw you." He knows I despise the cunt and he probably hates me too. I knew him when he was a screw at Long Lartin and he's done some serious arse licking since then. I'll mention no names but a few of the screws say the same: "He's a total wanker." One says, "He gets his suits made from Mothercare!" Ha! Ha! Ha! You've got to laugh… it's a laugh a minute here.

Maudsley walked passed my door today. He's looking more like Catweazle every day. I gave him a good raspberry and he shouted, "You retard." I shouted back, "Rent boy." What a fucking life.

My old buddy Jock Wilson sent me in a book today, Ron Kray's *My Story*. There are some good photos in it too. I also got a nice letter from Di Brown. She's nuts but good nuts. I've known here for years now and she's a good soul. Yeah, I do like Di, she's one of us – a fucking lunatic. You can't ever get rid of a loony, they either grow on you or they die. Please don't die, Di.

I got my canteen today! I put my order in on the 5th and got it on the 8th (today). This is a double bubble one for me because I saved up for this spend up; clock the phone credits – 8 bleeding quid. All you out there who I call, I hope you appreciate it as that £8 could buy me a lot more goodies. People outside just don't understand how petty prison is. I've got plenty of dosh but they only allow me to spend so much at a time, and if I'm naughty they stop it all so I can't phone anybody. Fuck me, I've actually gone years without a phone call. I'm the sort of man that switches off if I need to. A letter does me fine.

ARAMARK
HMP Wakefield

BRONSON
BT1314

Location : S - 2 - 006
Ref : 0805000195 05/05/2006

Item	Qty	Price
Phone Credit	8	£8.00
Imperial Leather Soap 125g	1	£0.52
Signal Toothpaste 50ml	1	£0.49
H.S. NAS Orange Squash 1ltr	1	[illegible]
Nescafe Coffee Sachet One Cup	6	£0.48
UHT Whole Milk 500ml	2	£0.92
Soreen Malt Loaf	1	£0.63
Jif Lemon Juice 55ml	2	£0.82
C.Rich Salted Peanuts 300g	2	£1.94
Country Rich Deluxe Tropical 250g	1	£0.92
Cadbury's Dairy Milk 50g	2	£0.80
Nestlé Yorkie - Milk 68g	2	£0.86
Nestlé Kit-Kat Chunky Std	2	£0.68
Biro - Blue	1	£0.20
Eggs 6pk	2	£1.14

ORDER TOTAL £19.07

Clock my Signal toothpaste and soap! They're a treat I like to spoil myself with. I eat my eggs raw, that's the beast in me! I'm like a snake when I eat an egg – 'Gulp!' – now you see it, now you don't! It slips down like a cup of spunk! I've even eaten my own spunk to survive – it's 200% protein. If I'm caged up in a dungeon with shit food and small portions and no canteen, then I'll eat my spunk just to get some serious protein inside me. I'll have four or five wanks a day and top myself up. It's not kinky and it's not sexual, it's all about staying strong! Wank and eat it. It tastes like filth but it's proper food that can and will keep you solid. If you can't handle the taste then shoot it into a mug, add some water and a sprinkle of salt (or sugar if you have any), then gulp it down. Do that four or five times a day and you'll be OK – that's if you pussies have five wanks in you!

When I was a young man on my mission of Loonyology I could do mugfuls. I was wanking for Britain. King of the wankers I was! Proud of it too, with balls like plums and a dick like steel. I could kill a screw if I hit him with my cock. Well, maybe I'm exaggerating there, but I could do serious damage with it. Now I'm older I've not got so many wanks left. Plus, I don't do bad for grub so I've little to wank for. I have more wet dreams than actual wanks now; I'm actually tired of pulling it. How sad is that? I prefer a mug of tea and a biscuit. I really am a sad old fucker!

Oh, don't worry, don't think 'poor old Charlie'. Watch me do some serious shagging later on when you get my 'porno' – I'll show you dudes what shagging is all about! I'll be up for it, you know it. We birdmen are a rare breed: greedy fuckers when it comes to pussy. Why do you think the girls love a jailbird? They love us because we know how to treat them, it's that simple. Believe it, I rest my case your lordship. Fuck me, I'm off for a wank now just to see if it's working OK! I'll be back.

(Half an hour later.) Both barrels are shooting perfectly all right. It shot out like a champagne cork – fantastic. The only problem is my door's spy hole went and an eye appeared, so my privacy was interrupted. What can you do? What would you do? Me, I shouted out, "Yarhhhooooooo, YIPPPEEEeeeeeeeeee, YABADABADOOOoooooo," and they soon fucked off. (My only worry is it will end up in the *Sunday Sport*! Has the screw taken a snap? One can only hope not.) But who's the king of the wankers? Me. Anyone want to argue about it?

Well that's my lot for another day. It's been a blinder and I've enjoyed myself. How the fuck can a prisoner be so happy in a coffin? Well, I suppose it's because I know in my heart that I'll win my appeal soon and go home. If I lose it then I suppose it'll all end up nasty, the smiles will disappear and the action will start up again. Whatever, life goes on…

9 May 2008.

Great visit today from Nicola White from Tank Jowett Solicitors in Wembley. (She came up on the train.) Like all my visitors, legal and domestic, she is disgusted by the visiting conditions. Let me try to explain why it's so wrong. She is in one room (actually a cell) and I'm in another cell, with bars between us. Above both our heads is a CCTV camera but this is a legal visit which is supposed to be private and confidential. (Hello?!) On top of this we're bugged and they listen to every word and read every document through the CCTV then feed it all back to the prosecution. This is 2008! Get real and accept it happens. How can anybody think or believe it doesn't? Prison security are clocking it all. This is a max secure unit and it's fucking obvious what's going on. How the fuck can I ever put a serious case together when the enemy are spying on me? Nicola agrees it's unlawful and also agrees it's unlawful to hold my parole hearing in these secure conditions. As I've already stated, I will not be attending but my legal team will be there. Watch this space…

All in all it was a positive meet up. She's a smart cookie and has already decided on some serious work! The system is about to be exposed. I predict the governor will change his mind (like all wimps do) and agree to an open review. I've made my decision and I'll live by it. Bollocks, fuck off away from my door. If you've got something to say to me, go through Nicola and make an appointment, you fucking hypocrites. End of.

What's upset me today is that the hate preacher Abu Qatada – a serious terror suspect – has been granted bail. A poxy immigration tribunal has agreed to free him on a 'strict curfew'. Fucking wake up, Britain. This toe rag has done nothing but preach hate in our country; he was Osama Bin Laden's right-hand man in Europe. He's wanted in Jordan for terrorism and we are freeing him from max secure Belmarsh jail on bail. It's a complete farce… Why? How? Then ask yourselves this question: why can't I be freed on a curfew? Is it because I'm British? People, please wake the fuck up before it's too late. This fucking Islamic extremist is taking the piss. He hates us and he hates the West. He thinks our women are all slags, he loves the suicide bombers and he is a fanatical nutcase, and now he's freed on bail… It's fucking madness, it's Loonyology, and it's the public to blame for allowing it to happen. Now is a great opportunity to petition. Ask! Demand! Why not Bronson? Why can't Charlie be freed on a curfew? If thousands did exactly that, we may get somewhere! It fucking rips me up, it really does. Cunts like him can suck off the Social for years and get a nice few quid, then they slag Britain off and boast about their suicide bombers taking us out. They're all twats – evil, nasty fuckers. They can keep me in for years but let the real monsters out! Cunts.

Let's have a serious poll on it! Hands up I'm let out, hands up that fat cunt's let out. I win; lock him up! YEEEOooooowwwwww! Get the beer in lads! I can smell the pussy already.

I got a dozen letters today and a first from a *Loonyology* reader (yeah, already).

Dear Chaz,
I've just got *Loonyology*. I've read it in one sitting – what a great read. I've followed your case for a good 10 years. They are evil to the core what they're doing to you; me, my family and my friends are disgusted. You could of, should have been freed long ago. I wish you well Chaz… you're a good man. Please keep writing. You're the true man. Respect.
Stan Murray from Essex.

Now that says it all to me. Stan's probably a working-class guy, but he's a man of the world and he's no fool! He can see what's going on without anybody telling him. I salute you, Stan, that's means a lot to me! Thanks, mate!

You can't kid our public – the real people who matter. There's more for me than against me because people like Stan know I'm not a threat to him or his family. He knows I've been punished enough, but the cunts who run this system don't know when to stop punishing me. They're basically a bunch of evil masochists who want me on my knees, or crippled with old age, or wearing incontinence pants so they can say, "Look at Bronson, he's pissed himself again. Look at the old fucker dribbling. Kick his zimmo over. Let's give the old cunt a slap!" The system wants to see me begging on my knees: "Please, Mr Prison Boss, can I go home please, sir? You're God." Fuck you, wanker. Never! I'd sooner leave here in a zip-up bag and you know it. But guys like Stan know it too. You can't kid the real people. All you're doing is mugging yourselves off.

It's just like Gordon Brown, that fat shit twat in No. 10 with a backbone of jelly. Leader? He couldn't lead a group of Girl Guides into a sweet shop and everybody knows it. Churchill would be turning in his grave! We haven't had a real leader for so long that we don't know what a true leader is. The last with any balls was Maggie – and she had no balls. She really was the best in years. It's not that I liked her or her policies but she had fight in her veins and was fearless – even in the Brighton IRA bombing where the entire cabinet came close to being taken out. Brown would have shat himself, so would Blair. They're just gutless, spineless people.

Cheers Stan, today you made me feel a very proud man, you made my day! Respect!

I got some cracking letters today from family and friends. Thank you all.

I had curry and chips tonight with three boiled eggs and it really filled me up. I felt nice and cosy, sort of at peace with myself and free of confusion, like I was on a beach sleeping in the sun. I wish. But one day it'll be for real, you all know it. It's just a matter of time, that's all it is – time! The clock never stops; the heart does, but the clock of time goes on ticking away. Every second a birth and a death!

My friend Jenny Whittaker sent me in Rudyard Kipling's poem 'If' today. I last read it back in Broadmoor in 1979. It's a powerful poem and everyone should read it. I've never forgotten it. Today just brought back my first memory of it. Wow, old Kipling was the master for real, but right now I would prefer a Kipling cake with a china pot of tea, feet up with some old friends and a good old bunny to catch up on all the latest news! Bizz first, then pleasure. It's always nice to get the bizz out of the way first, don't you agree? Once you start mixing the two you get cunts taking liberties and trying it on. No fucker does that to me. You only do it the once, believe it. Now let's enjoy a cuppa and a cream cake – Mr Kipling of course. (If only.)

OK, OK, let's now get down to some serious prison bizz. I'm about to take you into the 'Bronson prison mail bag'. Names have been changed to protect the guilty. Plus, I have to give my patients their confidentiality; after all I'm now their official counsellor. You could even say I'm their psychotherapist. Call it what you will, let's open my bag. Enjoy!

This chapter will blow your socks off and prove to you all exactly what I am: a caring, heartfelt, tender, loving, trusting man of our times. Some call me 'Doc', some call me the 'prison Agony Uncle', others call me the 'Brother from Heaven'. Fuck it, where's my bag?

Chaz,

Q – Hi mate, I've not seen you since Parkhurst in 1985, that time you chinned that fat cunt of a screw on C Wing. I've heard through the grapevine you're now our official social and mental health worker. In fact a screw here in Wandsworth actually told me to write you with my problem. So here goes: I keep wetting the bed, I'm now 49 years old, I'm serving 12 years and it's starting to depress me. Any advice at all Chaz I'll be grateful, cheers mate.
Henry, Wandsworth Jail.

A – Henry, what a brave letter to write! It really must be embarrassing, but there's nothing I can't take on, so here goes... Get a black bin liner and some mail bag string and wrap it around your cock. It will work! Let the bag fall downwards from the bed to the floor, into the slop bucket. Problem solved. OK son, good luck! Yeah, you're spot on about that fat cunt screw I chinned in Parkhurst! But now I would sit him down and give him some therapy. I'm anti-violence now, I believe in 'jaw jaw' not 'war war'. Peace and love, man!

Charlie,
Q – I'm a lifer in Maidstone prison, I've served 14 years to date. I've only been here for three months and my problem is I think I'm falling in love with our No. 1 governor. He's gorgeous and I think he fancies me. The other day I was sweeping the yard up and he came over to me and slapped my arse and said, "Cheeky!" What should I do? What would you do?
Arthur, Maidstone Jail.

A – Arthur, blimey this is a tough one! What would I do if the prison boss slapped my arse? Er, let's just say he would only do it the once. But it's your problem not mine, so let's not go into what I would do, OK. Well, Arthur, you're obviously gay and so is he! So why don't you run into his office and throw yourself over his desk and shout, "Fuck me." What else can I say? Only, I would have thought a gay con would have better taste than a poxy governor! Your choice… get on with it. But what you could do is try and get one of your gay pals to slip in and snap a photo of him banging your arse. That'd be automatic parole with a nice wad of cash for a fresh start. Good luck. Chaz.

OK Doc,
Q – I've got a problem: my cell mate! I fucking hate him with his smelly feet, farting, wanking and snoring all night. I've put up with this bollocks for 18 months now and I'm sick of it. He's 6 ft 2 and 18 stone; I'm 5 ft 5 and 9 stone! What can I do?
Joe, Bristol Nick.

A – Joe, this is the sort of problem I enjoy solving because it's short and sweet. Hit him with the table leg – give him a good whack! Two if needed. Then put all his belongings in a pillow slip and ring the call bell. Tell the screw he fell out of his bed! They'll take him over to the hospital wing and you'll get a new cell mate. OK, son? Good luck! Doc.

Doc,
Q – It's me again, Joe from Bristol. I did what you said, but I'm now nicked with GBH and I'm looking at an extra 5 years. All down to you, Doc. Thanks for nothing.
Joe, Bristol Nick.

A – Joe, don't you fucking dare blame me, you little cunt! You ungrateful prick! You probably hit him too hard, you psycho prat. It's cunts like you who give me a bad name. All I'm doing is trying to help my brothers and sisters around Britain in all the jails. What is your problem, cunt? It worked didn't it? Cunt!

Hi Chaz,
Q – I'm serving 18 years in Frankland max secure jail up in Durham. My problem is my wife and kids live down south, so it's a hell of a journey for

them to visit me. It's really tough mate and it's causing a lot of stress for us all. I'd appreciate any advice mate.
Lenny, Frankland Jail.

A – Yeah, a tough one. But you're not on your own; a lot of us Southerners get moved up north. It's done on purpose to mess up our family contact – the system can be evil like that, believe me. It's their way of saying, "We are in control." Right... you need dosh, so get making buckets of 'moonshine' – make the best hooch in the jail. There must be 1,000 cons up there, so if only half come to you for a bottle you'll be minted. Then send the loot to the wife and problem solved. A little tip: put some honey in your ingredients as it helps it to ferment quicker and it tastes good! And when you use buckets, put in a black bin liner, tie it up and put it near the hot pipes. If you can't get the yeast from the kitchen get a bent screw to sort it (give him a bottle later). Good luck, Lenny. Cheers, Chaz.

Hi Doc,
Q – I'm a serving lass in Holloway jail, I got 3 years for ABH and drugs. My mum knows you from Luton and she said if I have a problem I must write to you! Well, I keep on crying all the time. I'm lonely and depressed and dying for some cock. It's been 6 months now without a good shag. I'm only 20 and I feel I'm drying up. There's a male screw here I fancy, do you think I should? And have you any tips on fighting the boredom?
Diane, Holloway. P.S. Mum's name is Carol! She says xxx

A – Diane, you don't want to be shagging the screw, you could catch something. Come on, pull yourself together! Motivate yourself, get into something and get your mind in gear. There's more to life than sex. Yeah, I remember your mum. Carol's a good sort, it's years since I've seen her. She was the best shoplifter I ever knew, she could fill up six bags in a morning's session. She nicked all my clothes for me: leathers, suits, shoes, the lot. She was the dog's bollocks. (Please pass on my love and respect.) Now down to you. If you shag that screw I'll be very disappointed in you. You don't want a muggy old screw in between your legs, save it for a nice chap like a millionaire's son to work on. This is Diane's time, use it to prepare for a new chapter to your life. Men later – this is now your time! Go see 'Big Bertha' on A Wing! She's a right good sort; we got back 30 years. Tell her I sent you and she'll sort you out a good vibrator and plenty of men's mags if she's any left, also one of my naked calendars. I did a photo shoot back in the 1980s – every shot naked with a big hard-on. You'll love it; it's the only hard-core calendar like it! In one shot I'm right up a sheep's arse! You've got to see the sheep's face, it says it all. They fucking love it. Well, it's better than them on a plate with the mint sauce.

Now where was I? Oh yeah! Go see Bertha! She'll put you right. You take care now, Diane. Stop crying. All that ever does is empty the heart and weaken the soul. Be strong, smile, go forward and win. Let your beauty shine and stay clear from any screw's dick. You're so much better than that! Give it a stroke from your Uncle Charlie. X

Bronson 'Dr Bollocks',
Q – I bet you won't use this letter! You don't want people to really see what you are: a cunt. All you ever do is take the piss out of people with problems. I'm only 19 years old and serving 6 years for street robbery, I could take you out in a fight. You're just an old has-been in a dream! You need to sort your own shit out before you pretend to sort others out. Why don't you just crawl up and die?
Rocky from Feltham Y/P jail.

A – Rocky, very hurtful that is! I take it you're one of the new generation street hoodies who terrorize all the old folk and rob school kids' dinner money? Big time gangster, eh? 19-year-old tough guy. I would punch you so fucking hard it'd knock you into next week, you cheeky little turd. Do your bird, you little cheeky cunt. Anyway, who's rattled your cage? Instead of taking it out on me, why don't you chin the governor, nick his keys and fuck off home? Cunt.

Readers, this is the sort of abuse I sometimes get from nasty individuals, but unlike all the other agony aunts and uncles and social workers around the country, I actually confront it and let you see these letters. Others pretend they don't get them but they do. I've actually written a few myself just to keep them on their toes! We all get them and at times they can stress us out, but it's all part of our job. We are not 'gods', we make mistakes! No-one's perfect. So I hope I've explained to you all that it's not easy doing this job! Personally, I do it for the sheer joy and satisfaction of helping people. I suppose one day I'll be put up for some award! Not that I think I deserve one but I'd not say no to an OBE or MBE or a title! Sir Charles Bronson! Lord Bronson! The Duke of Loonyology! King of the Insane! It's all good stuff, so if you wish to vote for me to get an award (best send your support too), Gavin Meek will comply all your statements and hand them into No. 10. Call him up for details on 07746 781366. Thank you.

Remember, I can't do this work without your support and trust and faith in me. I'm here for you all: black, white, yellow, brown, red, pink; you can be Jew, Muslim, Christian, anything – I love and care for you all. Gays, straights, bi's, you can even have two heads and a hump. I'll help you all. Fuck me, I'm here for you, just write to me! Let me help you dudes. Trust me.

Dear Doc,
Q – I'm an inmate here in Hull jail. I got sentenced to 7 years last month for rape. She was only 8 and everyone's being nasty to me, I feel so depressed.
Harry, Hull jail.

A – Harry, good, you nonce!

Chaz,
Q – I'm serving 14 years for arson and the screws won't allow me my lighter. Is this against my human rights? What grounds do I have to sue the jail? I'm also black and Muslim, so it could be racial and religious harassment. What's your advice?
Bonzo, Brixton jail.

A – Bonzo, look mate, let's be sensible! If I was in the cell next door to you and knew you're an arsonist, I would be happier if you had no lighter. Sorry, Bonzo, but I think the screws are right in this one. It's not about your race or religion, it's basically common fucking sense! Face facts, you're a dangerous fucker with a flame! That's it, live with it. Chaz. P.S. Sorry mate, but the screws are spot on! I don't like to go against a brother, but you're the problem here.

Doc,
Q – I'm 22, serving life in Gartree. I've served 9 years, my tariff is 14 years. My problem is my hair is falling out and the system are denying me a wig. Have I got any rights here?
Dave, Gartree prison.

A – Dave! Unusual one. You're obviously a vain fucker. What's wrong with a bald head? Right, here's how to fuck 'em. Get a mop head, dye it, trim it up and get some super glue. Problem solved. "Next please!" Doc.

Dear Charlie,
Q – I'm in Lewis jail on remand for theft! I'm 23 years old and gay. I look very girlish and the lads are all trying it on. Last week in the shower was the worst time in my life. I had a dozen men trying it on. My partner outside is the only man I love! I feel depressed and lonely. A lot of gays would love to be in my shoes, but I'm loyal to my partner. I fear for my life as one prisoner has told me straight, I'm either his bitch or I'll be cut up. What can I do, Charlie? Please help!
Ronnie, HMP Lewis.

A – Ronnie, leave it to me. I've already sorted it. My pal 'Big Bertie' is down there serving a 10-year stretch – he's a giant of a man, full of tattoos and he's got an ear missing. He will put a stop to it, so chill out. It may cost you a blow job but Bertie will sort it for you! Charlie.

Dear Charlie,
Q – It's Ronnie again, the gay from Lewis. Just to let you know me and Bertie are getting married, and it's all thanks to you, Charlie! Thanks!
Love Ronnie.

Readers, see how I sort problems? (Could the penal system have sorted it?) This gay prisoner still has a face in one piece, he's happy and full of life. On top of all that, Bertie is happy! (You really don't want to see Bertie upset.) Everyone's happy, even the system, and it's all down to me – the No. 1 agony uncle on the planet, the prisoner's helper.

Chaz,
Q – I'm Sid from Parkhurst, serving 20 years. I need a pen friend, some filthy tart to write me sexy letters and hard-core snaps, good close-up fanny shots! Can you fix it for me? Respect.
Sid, Parkhurst.

A – Sid, blimey you don't want much, do you? Fucking hell, I bet the prison social worker wouldn't sort it out for you! Leave it to me, Sid, I've someone in mind. Take it easy down there. My best to the lads! Chaz.

Doc,
Q – I've got genital warts, any advice?
Cyril, Armley jail.

A – Fuck off, who do you think I am – some sort of cunt? You're the cunt, it's cost you a 36p stamp, you mug. Doc.

Hi Charles,
I'm in Dartmoor, my name is Dixie, and I'm serving a 5-year stretch for fraud. Could you give me some advice on money issues? I made £3 million out of fraud and it's safe, but I'm worried about the tax man getting a hold of it.
Dixie, Dartmoor.

A – Hi Dixie, I'm sorting a visit for you off my best friend. Trust him and don't write anything else! Say nothing more! Your loot is safe, fuck the tax man. Mum's the word – trust your Uncle Charlie on this one! Loot is my speciality. Charles.

Doc,
Q – Fucking 'Doc' – what a laugh! You're a complete farce. You'll have that con's 3 million quid (we all know you will). You're the fraudster. How the fuck you sleep at night is beyond me, you nasty thieving bastard!
John, Scrubs.

A – John! That's libel! Expect a visit off my brief! I'll sue your arse for that. Apologise or take the consequences! Doc.

Doc,
Q – Fuck you... sue me. I'm in jail and I've got fuck all, you thieving twat!
John, Scrubs.

A – John, OK! You've had your chance! Doc.
Readers, I must add that I later found out 'John' was actually a screw out to wind me up and the 3 million quid got confiscated by the tax man. I told the cunt to keep quiet. (Some just don't listen to good advice.) Sadly, I've had some nasty threatening letters over it all! Some are even accusing me of being the tax man. Also, Dixie in Dartmoor, who had the 3 mill, has been found dead with his throat cut. Again the fingers are pointing at me! Me, me, me... I'm guilty without a trial. Yes, it is hurtful; yes, it does depress me, but I will not walk away from my responsibilities! I'm here for my family, you are my family. Never forget that! Trust me.

Dear Charlie,
Q – I'm serving 6 months in Belmarsh, it's my first time inside. I'm finding it hard, any advice?
Eric, HMP Belmarsh.

A – Eric, fuck off! 6 months? Do me a favour – I've served that in a strait jacket. You short-timers make me sick! Fuck off, cunt! Charlie.

Hi Doc,
Q – I've a little problem with my two cell mates, they both want to give me a spit roast. Well I'm a vegetarian myself and they know it, so why do they keep on about it?
George, Strangeways.

A – George, I don't think they mean a Sunday dinner here! Do you? Fuck me, George. Can't you work it out? Well, it is called 'Strangeways'. Charlie.

Doc,
Q – I've read one of your books and I've just beaten your wanking record. I shot my load nine times in two hours! My two pad mates were witnesses!
Tom, Pentonville.

A – Tom, you wanker... Doc.

OK Charlie,
Q – Its Reg on the Pen from Scotland's toughest jail, Barlinnie. I'm serving four life sentences! I think you're an English pussy who needs your arse shagged and I'm the Jock to do it! What have you got to say about that, bitch! Every time I see your tash it reminds me of my wife's Brazilian. I'm gonna fuck you big time, Charlie! Be prepared.
Reg.

A – Reg, a typical Jock, all mouth and kilt with no knickers. What can I say! Do your four lifes mate! And keep dreaming! Chaz.
Readers, see the filthy abuse I get? I get sackloads of this sort of thing! Could you take it? Would you take it? Should you have to take it? (Now can you see my dedication and my determination to become the No. 1 agony uncle in the world?)

Chaz,
Q – I'm on death row in St Quentin. I've read 4 of your books and they're brilliant. My problem is I can't seem to motivate myself. What's the point when they're gonna kill me?
Tucker, St Quentin, USA.

A – Hi Tucker, you raise a good point here but we all have to die. We are all one day nearer to death. The only difference with you is, you know how your end will be and when it will be. My advice to you is to be happy, smile, leave this fucked-up planet on a high. Shit all over the death chamber floor. Give those dog screws something to remember you by! I salute you, Tucker. Make your last day on death row special for all to remember. Do something that's never been done! Think about it, you're sure to come up with something unique! Peace brother, have a good journey! Chaz.

Doctor Charlie,
Q – I'm locked up in Rampton lunatic asylum and I've got piles. Can you help?
Benny, Rampton.

A – Benny, only the chosen few ever get piles – lucky, blessed people. We salute you, they're a gift from God. Keep taking the medication, Benny! Charlie.

Doctor Bronco,
Q – What can you do about my athlete's feet?
Danny, Broadmoor asylum.

A – Not a lot, Danny! Doc.

Charlie,
Q – My nose bleeds when I laugh.
Barnaby, Brixton jail.

A – Then don't laugh! Charlie.

Dear Chaz,
Q – Hello sexy! I've got problems with my clitty, I keep rubbing it and nothing happens. My cell mate Susan licks it and nothing happens. Any suggestions, Chaz? Please?
Yvonne, Styal prison.

A – Yvonne, blimey, this is a good question – a blinder. I do love a good problem to get my teeth into! Have you tried the prison cat? Rub some pilchards on your 'Jack and Danny' and slip one up your crack so the head's popping out. That cat's tongue is very coarse so once it's started licking that should do the trick. If not, get back to me. Yvonne, try and sort me some photos of your clitty! I'll then be able to study it in detail. OK, sweetheart? Chaz.

Hi Chaz,
Q – It's Yvonne back, enclosed are 3 photos! Can you help? The cat was useless.
Yvonne

A – Yvonne! Fuck me, you are a fatty aren't you? You must weigh 25 stone. You look like that wrestler Big Daddy. It's no wonder your clitty doesn't work, you're grossly overweight. You probably stink and it's just inhuman. You're fucking grotesque and you have actually made me feel quite ill! I've never, in 56 years of living on this planet, seen such an ugly fanny. You have to be the ugliest bird ever! I'm sending your photos to Madame Tussauds in London for the house of horrors. You make Rose West look anorexic! Fuck me, hurry up and die! Chaz.

Charlie,
Q – You were a bit strong there with Yvonne if you ask me.
Les, HMP Ford.

A – Les! I never asked you, nor ever would! Keep your face out of my bizz. In fact, stick your face into Yvonne's twat and choke to death. OK? Chaz.

Charlie,
Q – It's Susan on the pen, I'm Yvonne's cell mate. I can't stop her from crying. I thought you were very crude, rude and insulting and our No. 1 officer is taking action over your behaviour. You should not be allowed to be who you are. After all, you're just a convicted criminal and a nasty one at that.
Susan, Styal prison.

Readers, I'm so sorry to have to inform you all that my time has come to an end as the prisons' No. 1 agony uncle and consultant therapeutic social worker. Nothing lasts forever. I don't really wish to go into details on why I've retired from my post. Let's just say that some didn't accept me as a true helper (probably down to jealousy) but trust me, I meant well! Win some, lose some… The truth is that Yvonne is a fat, ugly cunt. She should be given a painless injection! If you kept a dog alive like that, you would be nicked for cruelty! Sad bitch!

Saturday, 10 May 2008.
Hey! Remember the barrister who the cops blew away the other day? They shot him five times – in the head, heart, liver and lower body. This guy was shot to pieces by the CO19 firearms unit. What a way to leave this world! A human tea bag. You know something, for what it's worth I respect Mark Saunders. He chose to die like a man! What more can a man do but die a man?

Hey, fuck sharing a pasta dish with Heather Mook; she was jailed yesterday for putting rat poison on her husband's meals. Let's hope she can slip onto Rose West's food boat and poison the fat cow. Heather's husband, John Mook, said that he was lucky to be alive. She loved to cook Spaghetti Bolognese. Fuck that. Oh well, that's Loonyology for you. Without nutters like Heather, what would we have to talk about? Don't we love a loony?

One day I'll fly out (never doubt it). I could be on the yard tomorrow and a plane could come down and crash into the jail, making a fucking big hole in the wall. You won't see my arse for smoke! I'm gone, never to be seen again. Did Bronson go up in the explosion? Or did he manage to escape? The truth be known, who gives a flying fuck?

Reflections.

"I looked in the mirror
What did I see?
An old man with a white beard
He was looking at me
Something I feared
Would happen to me
Now it's here
For the world to see."

I used to watch and study the old boys in the asylums, ancient old fuckers shuffling about. They were characters with a million stories and I loved them, but I also feared them. I always felt sad for them; I would see them as the living dead, the hopeless souls. They were a new breed of mutants

– old and insane! Some had committed murders of madness. Others had just been unlucky in life, they fell over the edge and become lost and empty! But every one of them crept into my space and there was never any escape from this madness. You smell it, you see it, you hear it, you feel it and it flows into your veins, it spreads into your bones until you become the old man with the white beard. I have become the past. It's taken all these years for me to realise I could never escape the one thing I actually feared: myself. I feared myself.

Those memories of being with the Broadmoor loonies have now returned, but it's me who's caught up in the hopelessness of life. It always was me. I am now convinced a man only becomes his true self. I'm just me and I was meant to be this way. Now I can see the truth within my own mind! Those crazy old characters were really telling me what was ahead: "Don't fight it, enjoy it, be as mad as they want you to be. They expect it. Bite the fuckers if you've got no teeth, then use a razor and make them bleed, make them scream. Live the nightmare, son. Become what you are."

They were fucking crazy. What the fuck was a young man like me doing trapped in that asylum with all those loonies? It was like a new planet, a new way of life. It's something a man can never let go of. You leave the asylum but the asylum never leaves you! It's there until you die – the big 'A' on your file. Broadmoor is carved into your heart! It's forever a part of you and so few, if any, have survived a normal life since! One or two may have done well. Crazy old men.

So that's what I now see and understand. The fear is gone and I am the old man looking at myself. I now study myself. It's become a battle against myself! How fucking crazy is that? How deep can it get? What's the solution? Is there one? The only sure thing, the 100% reality is that we all are going to die, that's the one thing we all have in common. We are waiting to die and until then we have to survive the best way we can. Have fun… I sure will!

"I caught a rainbow
I turned into a mass of colour
Everywhere I went people stared
Who is that guy?
He shines like a rainbow
Touch him
It could be lucky
Let's kidnap him
Lock him in a room
We want him
The rainbow man
If he stops shining
Kill him.
What good is a black rainbow?
Shine you motherfucker –
Shine or die."

The next time you see a rainbow, study it! Feel it! What a wonderful world, full of colour and beauty. It's one of life's beautiful things! Take a picture, paint it, wrap it around your heart. To see a rainbow is to come alive, it's freedom in colour, it's a beautiful everlasting photographic memory. One minute it's there and then it's gone, just like us. But a rainbow returns... do we?

An evil cunt like Michael Clark was born to spread evil and suck the rainbow away! He was a convicted rapist, let out of prison only to kill 14-year-old Zuzanna Zommer. 14 years old and beautiful just like the rainbow, with a smile like an angel and her whole life ahead of her. Then Clark blows her out like a candle. He got lifed off with a recommendation that he serves 35 years. That's a long ride and the odds are he won't last. But 35 years would have been nice for Zuzanna to live, to marry, to have children and be happy. All she got was a black hole, a black rainbow, because the penal system let out a monster! Surprise, surprise, how unusual. It's now becoming an everyday event. "Let's let a monster out and see if he does it again!" Some prat of a probation worker backs it, some muppet of a governor backs it, some parole judge backs it, then the Home Secretary signs the paperwork! (None of them are at the funeral service.)

The system is responsible because a monster can't help it, that's what monsters do. They're horrible, nasty fuckers who enjoy doing what they do! You can't really blame the monster, can you? But you can blame these fucking idiots who keep letting them out! Maybe they're the true monsters and we have all been taking our anger out on the wrong people? Now that's food for thought!

Talking of food, I'm starving and I've got a cheese roll to polish off with a mug of hot sweet tea. I'll be back. You know it.

12 May 2008.

Can you believe this shit? Pagan inmates are now allowed to have wands in their cells. A new law has come out saying they can keep twigs to use as wands to protect their rights and equality amongst different faiths. Justice reform minister Maria Eagle has backed it. If it was April 1st I would have laughed, but this is serious. They can debate a fucking Pagan's twig for their religious rights but they don't give a fuck about keeping me in a cage like a zoo animal for year after year! Am I being nasty here, or am I right? Pagans, Muslims, Christians – whatever a con is or chooses to be, we are all prisoners, we are all criminals and we are in jail for punishment, not for playing with a poxy twig. Fucking wake up, planet, before you awake in the cuckoo pit full of shit. It's getting madder.

OK! What about a Satanist religion? This will be next up for debate in the House of Commons or House of Lords. They will soon want a skull or a bat in their cell and a pint of blood every full moon. I say get rid of all religion in jail so we are all the same. Let's face reality, they can't be very good disciples of God to end up in jail, or am I losing the plot here? Jail is Hell, not Heaven. That's a fact, face it. A fucking wand! Abracadabra. Now you see me, now you don't. I think I'll become a pagan, get my own wand and turn all those screws into frogs. It's Loonyology gone insane!

I only got two letters today but that's more than monster Miller gets in a year. Anyone who writes to him, I'm telling you, you're as bad as him and you must be a filthy paedo. Fuck off.

So you wanna dice with death? Go chop carrots with the reaper!

Did you know life with a woman is like a pack of playing cards? You need a heart to love one, you need a diamond to marry one, you need a club to beat her and a spade to bury the bitch! Your full pack of cards.

I see Bernie Davies just copped an eight stretch over guns and cannabis. Bernie's been a solid supporter in my fight for freedom and you'll see him in the first *Loonyology* book. He's a good buddy of Dave Courtney! We respect the man. So go easy, mate, keep your nut down and get back out fast. An eight stretch... with good behaviour you'll be home in four years. Don't fucking slide down the Lucifer pole into the world of darkness like I did. My eight stretch ended up as forever! Lucifer got his claws into me good style. It don't 'arf fucking hurt; you bleed like a tap!

I'll tell you who's a muggy cunt! Wesley Crawford. He copped a 12-stretch for robbery back in 2001. They sent him to an open prison and he walked out, but after three days he banged on the door to come back in. What a prat. He'd already served seven years so he only had months left to serve. Why walk out? Even better, why come back? Now he will be back in a secure jail. All for what? Bollocks. This guy is just fucked up and institutionalized; he got out and thought, fuck this, I'm going back in! I would have been through that Channel Tunnel faster than Red Rum at Aintree. Me knocking on a prison gate to be let in? Yeah, in your fucking dreams.

14 May 2008.

Had a great visit with my old china John Griffiths. He's a top geezer and knows all the legendary boxers! He travels the world to meet them. He was with John H Stracy the other week and John's promised to sing 'My Way' at my freedom party if it ever happens!

I had three banana milkshakes and half a dozen chocolate bars. I made John a tea as he likes a cuppa rosey. He was telling me about his visits with the Krays – he used to visit Ronnie in Broadmoor asylum a lot. Ron once told him that I'm like Frank Mitchell – not as big, but stronger. I only found that out today. To me that's respect. Frank was a legend, a prison icon, even today his name and feats of strength live on and he's been dead 40 years. It's not bad for a convict to still live on in people's memories. That tells me exactly what Frank Mitchell stood for. He was a proper good guy!

Yeah! A great visit! I've another one tomorrow with Robert Verkaik, the crime journalist for *The Independent* I was telling you about. I'm amazed and still baffled about how he ever got passed by the system to visit me. I can't fucking believe it! It's obviously a blunder, a big fuck-up by this lot. Some heads will surely roll. He's the last person on the planet I expected to be passed to visit me! Wonders will never cease. But now he's passed, they have to let him in, so tough luck. It's one up on me this time! He's coming up to hear about Loonyology from me and to see for himself the madness of my world. Then he can go away and let the world know! *The Independent* is not the *Sun* or *Sport*, it's a bloody intelligent paper read by top people:

judges, barristers, prison HQ. The shit's about to hit the fan! Or better still, the fan's hit the shit. ("How the fuck did Bronson get a visit with Robert Verkaik? Who the fuck passed him? What's going on in monster mansion? This is a national disgrace! This is Loonyology gone mental!")

I got seven letters today and £150 from a mate. (I won't say who because he's probably just hit another bank. He always posts it in under an alias! My mates never forget me. It's a big family, a brotherhood: fuck with one and you fuck with us all! It's that simple. I think I'll treat myself to some fruit, nuts and honey this week. If I don't spoil myself, who else will?

Lindsey Frayne sent me in a mag full of mobile homes. I do love a home on wheels – it's the pirate in me! What would I have done in the pirate era? What a fucking magical life those guys had. I would've been the best pirate on the planet! Believe me.

Hey! My buddy is doing well in his new cobblers shop:

	High street prices	**Banbury cobbler prices**
Stiletto heels	£7.95	£3.00
Gents rubber heels	£10.95	£7.99
Gents leather sole and heels	£35.00	£24.99
Yale keys	£4.00	£3.00
Mortice key	£6.00	£4.00

You save with my buddy, and get a first-class job. He also does engraving on Zippo lighters, tankards, trophies, all sorts. Yeah, Mark Sharman's the dog's bollocks! He takes his work very seriously. He's a good professional man! Pop in and see him, tell him I sent you! Banbury, Bridge Street, opposite the Town Hall!

Get on this for a load of crap. Top female lawyer Saimo Chahal is about to take on Sutcliffe's (the Yorkshire Ripper) case. His human rights have been breached over his tariff and he is about to fight for his freedom. She claims he has been misrepresented over untrue claims about his life and crimes…

HELLO! He snuffed out 13 women; he's a murdering fucking nonce! Human rights, what rights? He's a cold-blooded fucking beast! I bet Saimo wouldn't be taking on his case if it was one of her relations he had brutalized and killed! It's a bloody joke – it's got to be. Even if he was let out, how long would he last before somebody chopped his head off? In 1981 he got put away, 27 years ago, and now they're on about a legal battle to free him! Hey! You tax payers are paying his legal aid bill, you daft fuckers. He kills your women and daughters and now 27 years later you pay for his fight for freedom! Fuck me, am I imagining this? I've served longer than this cunt! Haven't I got any human rights? Somebody please knock me out and put me out of this lunacy. I'm going mad…

I see the 22-year-old lad knifed to death in Oxford Street was Steven Bigby. He was actually on bail over a brutal gang rape when nine guys raped a 16-year-old girl (brave fuckers). All I can say is, life's full of surprises! It's not all one-way traffic; what goes around actually comes around sooner or later! Violence breeds violence! My end will no doubt be violent. Some little prick will probably stab me in the back and run off laughing. If it's a bad shot and he misses my organs, I'll chase him and snap his neck. That's how life is: lucky for some, unlucky for others. Make my day, punk.

I had to smile at this one! Robert Lee throttles his wife but she survives. He goes to court, gets bail, and guess what? Come on, guess... have a fucking guess! This time he stabs her to death! You can't make this shit up. Why bail him? Would you have freed him? Am I missing something here? Robert Lee's 51 years old and now he's a lifer. He's dead too – he will die inside for sure. It's a crazy old world, run by strange people. We are on a planet full of loons and the judges are the biggest lunatics going! Don't bet against the Ripper winning his freedom. He probably will! Cunt.

There was a nonce in Woodhill block when I was on remand there back in 1993 – a big black rapist. He must have been 6 foot 6 inches and 19 stone and they called him Winston. He raped a 13-year-old girl... One day I was on the yard when he came to the window. I prayed he would because I had a biro in my sock. Whoosh! I just missed his eye by half an inch if that and it stuck in his eye socket. I was gutted. You only get one shot at a nonce like him and I fucked it! I used to think what fear that girl would have felt with that cunt on top of her. He just wound me up so much I felt pure hatred. I said to a screw, "Why don't you just make a mistake and open our doors at the same time?" He said, "It's more than my job's worth, Charlie." I gave him my word that I'd only smash him with my fists, no tools, but would the screw do it? Would he fuck! They ended up moving Winston over to the nonce wing. Cunt. I could've and should've had his eye out that day!

It wasn't that long after that when I took the library screw hostage. That was my lot in Woodhill, they slung me in the van and I went 'on tour'. Do you know that I've probably spent six months of my bird in a prison van travelling around England? That's a fact. Maybe I should have got human rights involved for travelling expenses. Why not? It's not as mad as it sounds. They do say moving home is the most stressful thing to do! I could be in for a few quid there.

I was chatting to a screw today who shall remain nameless. He asked me, "How do you do it, Chaz?"

"Do what?" I said.

"Do your time so peaceful," he said.

"Let me tell you," I said. "Easy, I just plod on; no one fucks with me, I don't fuck with them!"

Take the governor who did his rounds today. I asked him, "When are you gonna have any backbone and get me moved so I can mix with people? How can you fucking sleep at night, cunt?" I'm right, they are cunts! Even the screws agree with me, so who's right and who's wrong? Why should I have to accept my life in a cage? I told the governor, "You're torturing me, this is psychological mental torture, cunt." They have no answer to it! Cunts.

I called Chris Cowlin tonight! Always good to have a chat with the No. 1 publisher in the UK. I bet prison HQ are now kicking themselves by passing him on my last visit too! Probably another fuck-up on their part. Chris tells me *Loonyology* is selling well and it could top the best-sellers chart! That would be nice... and why shouldn't it? Am I not the new era author? Is my writing the style? I write as I talk: raw, rough and aggressive. I don't mix my words for anybody, nor do I pretend to be the new Oscar Wilde! I'm me, yours truly, himself. Love me or hate me but you're never gonna fuck me. A million bucks won't get to fuck me. I'm unfuckable. You really don't want to enter into my nightmare because you wouldn't get back out sane.

I saw Hannibal today as I went on a visit. He's mad as ever. Those eyes say it all: "Let me come inside your brain, I'm starving."

When it comes to proud memories of times gone by, I look back with a lot of dignity and honour to people such as my old mate Del Croxen. Del was a proper old-school villain I had a lot of respect for! I first met him on the exercise yard in Wandsworth jail in the mid 1980s. In fact it was Frank Fraser who introduced me to Del; we got on like a house on fire but I soon got moved on after I'd wrecked my cell. I rarely stayed in any jail over a month in those days, I just got bored. The next time I saw Del was in the mid '90s at Belmarsh max secure unit. He was nicked on an armed blag. Sadly he died in his cell – he didn't even make it to trial! So he actually died innocent on remand! I was one of half a dozen to attend a service of respect for Del and I was so proud to be there along with Rooky Lee and Pete Pesato, two proper blaggers. Rooky and me go back to the early 1970s and he's a top man, a legend for real. At the service, I got to say my favourite bit of philosophy! I felt it summed it all up:

> *We the willing, led by the unknowning, have been doing the impossible for the ungrateful. We have done so much, for so long, with so little, we are now qualified to do anything with nothing.*

Pete then read something and we all felt the same sadness and loss together in that small room. Del Croxen was a powerful man; he could bench press 300 pounds, easy. He was born to kick arse! We all loved him as a brother. Never forgotten by so many! Respect to the guy and his family.

It's moments like that I feel our feelings and emotions prove that we are still human. We bleed and cry and feel sorrow just like anybody! Please believe that in all this steel, concrete and security we are still a part of the human race, except for the nonces and grasses – those cunts left the human race when they shot out of the fanny and screamed their first scream!

Hey! Did you know the slow worm is a legless lizard? Fucking strange or what? Remember me telling you about that con in Albany we called 'the lizard'? He had snake eyes and a face like snake scales: blotchy, spotty and scarred with acne. He got some serious stick off us all and everywhere he went we would all hiss! Watch out lads, here comes Boa! He ended up over the hospital wing after a breakdown (probably to shed his skin, really). What an ugly fucker he was! No wonder he got nicked – imagine that cunt on an ID parade; you couldn't miss him could you?

Come to think of it, there was a screw in Wandsworth we used to call 'Spotty'. Old pus face! Stay away from the hot plate at meal times, Spotty, we don't want your scabs falling in the porridge urn, you ugly fucker! He got some serious stick! I think ugly screws should have to wear a mask. Why should we have to accept a monster opening our doors or spying through our Judas holes? It's scary. Fuck me, I could be onto a claim here for post-traumatic stress disorder! The years I've suffered by having ugly screws being forced upon me must be a case for the human rights! Why should I have to be forced to face ugly screws every day of my life? It's a form of psychological torture. (I'll get my brief on this one. Watch this space…)

15 May 2008.
A great visit today with Robert Verkaik. What a nice man. I do enjoy meeting new people. He told me that the screw who walked him over to this unit said, "Charlie shouldn't be here." I told you that's what they say to all my visitors! But why don't they say it to the governor? Put it in writing. Talk's cheap, but it's still nice to hear it! It just proves all I say…

Yeah, it was a nice chat with Robert! They're interesting people, journalists. I'm still in shellshock over the system passing him. I gave him a nice big art which I created especially for him.

Hey, I got four letters today from strangers who have read *Loonyology*. All of them loved it. Here's one letter from Dave Thomas of Nottingham:

Charlie,
Just read *Loonyology*, it's the best book I've read for years. God only knows how you have stayed sane. I can't believe you're still inside. You're an inspiration to us all Charlie! You could do so much out here to help the youngsters stay out of trouble. I'm just about to write to my MP about your inhumane situation. Stay strong my friend. And keep on writing. You're a born writer. Dave Thomas. P.S. *Loonyology* is a masterpiece.

Cheers Dave, Well respected mate! Thank you.

So there you have it – my books are out there speaking for me. I'm out there on the shelves; pick me up and come inside.

I called up Mark Emmins and we did a tape interview that will find its way around the circuit. I pop up everywhere. Look under the bed, in the wardrobe – I could be there. (I wish!!) So what would you do if I jumped out of the wardrobe when your old man's banging away at you? "Hi–Di–Hi, Avon calling!"

That brings back a crazy memory for me! I did a midnight collecting call on a place in Bedford years back. It smelt like what it was: a shit house full of rats. I banged six times and then got bored of waiting, so I kicked down the door and ran in shouting, "Avon calling!" I got what I came for – I always do! I don't leave without it. I'm a professional, see. I take my work seriously – very seriously! At least, I did then. Now I'm an artist and I've got to take care of my hands! Artists' hands are gifts from God.

Oh well! I'm having an early night; I've got a lot to think about… Sleep tight.

I was born to kick arse. What's your excuse? I'm sticking to mine, OK?

CHAPTER 6

Dead man laughing

I'm sorry, I can't stop laughing!
Somebody knock me out – somebody shoot me!

16 May 2008.

It's been a fucking crazy, weird, dream-like day today – unreal, fucking mental. I'm sure I'm going mad. I feel dizzy and strange!

Get on this. Read it, digest it, then think on! Eight years ago Nazamuddin Mohammidy was one of the hijackers involved in the four-day siege at Stansted with 173 hostages on-board the Boeing 727 that had been flown from Afghanistan. On December 2001 the hijackers were convicted and on June 2003 the appeal court quashed their convictions. But Nazamuddin was recently discovered working at Heathrow as a cleaner! Am I missing something here, or is it me? Political asylum? I think the asylum has become political. The loons have taken over. Roll out the beer, let's all get pissed! Three cheers for Nazamuddin Mohammidy. Yippppeeeee, Yippppeeeee, Yippppeeeee! The world's now the asylum. I told you what was coming in *Loonyology: In My Own Words*, now here it is... Amen.

What about this geezer Willie Campbell in Dallas, USA? He's just been sentenced to 35 years for spitting in a cop's face. The guy's got Aids so he was convicted of using his saliva as a deadly weapon. Lucky he didn't shag the cop, he would have got 70 years then! It's a mad old world.

Back in 2003 in Styal women's prison a young girl of 17, Sarah Campbell, committed suicide. She was a beautiful girl with great big sparkling eyes. I remember it well because six women committed suicide in Styal prison that year. Sarah suffered from depression. She arrived at the jail on the 17th January and was dead on the 18th. The screws couldn't even look after her for one poxy, fucking day. They locked her in the segregation unit when she should have been put in the hospital wing. She died of a drugs overdose. What a waste of a beautiful girl. Five years later, her mother Pauline was found dead by her daughter's grave. How sad is that? Does it get any sadder? Pauline was, in fact, a serious campaigner for penal reform and did so much to help so many in prison. I guess it took its toll on the lady and she wanted to join her beloved daughter. Let's hope they're back together again! Respect.

I got a wedding proposal today from a lunatic who is (wait for it) a geezer! Some gay fella has written to me and asked me to marry him! It can only happen to me; I just seem to attract the loonies. It's harmless so I don't take it too seriously. Years ago I would have sent one of the 'firm' to pay him a visit and bust his legs up big time. They probably would've rammed a broom up his mad arse and swept the street with him. Nowadays I just laugh...

Mark Emmins sent me in a brilliant book called *The Bandana Republic* which is a literary anthology by gang members and their affiliates. It's published by Soft Skull Press (www.softskull.com) and it's a brilliant masterpiece book. I'm gonna enjoy this read! Thank you, my friend! These Yankee prison books are the cream! When these guys kick off, Hell arrives on a scooter of fire blazing away at the guards. They're real riots with legendary warriors. I salute you.

I was jogging on the yard today (slowly) and thinking, how many more miles, weeks, months, years of this bollocks? Just how many miles are left in my tank? One day my heart's gonna explode on this yard like that famous gorilla in London Zoo. Guy the Gorilla, that's who I am, that's me!

That's how I feel: crazy and fucking mental!

I see my old buddy Harry Roberts was bugged when he had a conversation with his lawyer recently at Channings Wood jail. It's totally illegal and unlawful but these cunts are a law to themselves! They've been doing it for years with me! It just goes on and on. I suppose it doesn't help that Harry wasted three cops. They fucking hate him and will do anything to stop his parole. He's now served 42 years and they want more. They won't stop till he's dead, that's for sure.

My old buddy Terry Vowls has just had a heart attack in Highdown jail. It's high time they let him out too, as the poor sod's not a well man. What fucking sense does it make to keep a sick man inside? Fucking idiots – they wind me up!

Did you know a goldfish only has a three-second memory? (As if we give a fuck.) Did you know a cow will lie down when it's about to rain? Why? Fuck knows; ask a farmer! Did you know a shark must keep moving or it will die? It's something to do with the gills! It's a strange old sea world, eh?

Hey! That Katherine Jenkins, what a beautiful woman she is and what a voice – she's an amazing singer. I would love to go to one of her concerts, I really would. She hits my soul and the hairs on my back tingle when I hear her sing! She's got a lovely personality and she's so happy and nice I could eat her between two slices of bread with loads of sauce (Daddies sauce). She's brilliant. Somebody please tell her I love her!

Fred Lowe (my next-door neighbour) had three bowls of mushy peas today so he will be farting and shitting all night. He's a fat greedy fucker. Some days he has four bowls of soup! He's a human dustbin.

Hey! Did you know the bill for Princess Diana's inquest cost the tax payers £4.5 million? £1.85 million went on lawyers' fees alone! Those lawyers don't do bad, do they? Greedy fuckers – they're bigger villains than the villains. I call them leeches because they'll suck you dry…

Oh well, it's Saturday tomorrow. Tom and Mark are up to see me and it should be a cracking visit. Until then, *adios amigos*. Have a good night, a nice warm bed and a good warm heart! Free your soul to live your dream. Or better still, get deep into the pussy. Hide away your fears, melt into oblivion and dance with the Devil. It's fun.

Oh, before I go, here's a beautiful story! Tune into this – switch off all the crap and switch onto this! You'll feel good inside. In 1982, Sandra Gardner lived opposite a young girl called Wendy who was a dwarf but a fighter. She needed to raise £3,000 for an operation that would make her three inches taller, which is a lot to a dwarf. (Come on, I bet you would like that much added on to your bell-end.) Three grand in 1982 was a lot of dosh (it still is today) and Sandra helped to raise two grand by running the London Marathon. Now see why I love and respect her? That, to me, is lovely! The dwarf gets her three inches and Sandra feels proud. That was the 'Wendy run'. Fantastical, I love it. I just love a great ending – it warms your cockles!

"Tap into the insanity of life"

Switch it on
Go with the flow
It don't get no madder than this
It's seeping into your skin
Rushing around your veins
This is the big house
This is Broadmoor asylum
Full of strange people
They look what they are
"Dangerous"
This is a trip to Mars
Believe it
Enjoy it
It don't get no deeper
This is bottomless
Laugh when they laugh
Cry when they cry
You'll fit in well
Don't rock the boat here
You'll only do it once
Your throat will be taken out
Your eyes popped with a pen
These guys mean it
They take their insanity serious
Deadly serious
This is their world
Their life
Till the day they die
There is no escape from within
Believe it
They are born this way
They can't change
Why should they?
This is the last destination
Terminal lock-down
The big house
For the big boys
Legendary madmen
Men without a soul
Men of rock
Heartless and cold
They would kill you for fun
Laugh as you bleed
Watch you die
Then eat you
Bit by bit
They eat you all
Every last portion

These guys are crazy
Staring, bulging eyes
Dribbling saliva
Hungry for action
Laugh when they laugh
Cry when they cry
Join in the madness
You'll be safe
Now you're one of them
Some have been here 30 years
You can tell
They smell of Loonyology
Mad men do smell
They throw off the scent of fear
A warning
Even their body language tells you
Don't get too close
Don't enter my space
You can come in
But you don't get back out
They can cut off your face
To make a mask
They can crush your windpipe
Like a bar of chocolate
Do you really want to live here?
Do you really belong here?
Can you really become one of us?
So much to think about
So little time
The years fly by so fast
The skin turns grey
The hair turns white
See the old man in the rocking chair
Watch him carefully
Soon it's you
They die in that chair
Rocking away
It awaits us all
It's all inside out
Upside down
2 steps forward, 4 steps back
No place to hide
You go around and around
A dizzy man is a confused man
Welcome to the big house
Make yourself at home
Your room awaits
Dressing gown, slippers and pipe
It's pie and chips tonight
You lucky man.

Saturday, 17 May 2008.
The little fat Mothercare bouncer of a governor did his rounds this morning. Cunt. That's the big problem in jail – a man can't escape these twats, but he's a brave fucker considering he's behind a caged door! The screw 'Dicko' was with him; he's a top geezer. But the difference between me and a screw is that I can fuck the governors off whereas a screw would be sacked if they did it. So in that sense the screws probably envy me.

I've had a bit of food poisoning and I've got the shits, so I've eaten nothing today but I've drunk gallons of water. I'll not eat anything tomorrow either. It's time for a bodily clean-out.

Tom Hardy and Mark Fish made it up. They got me cakes, chocolate – all sorts, but I didn't touch them. All I had was a banana milkshake! That's what you call 100% strict discipline.

I see Jeremy Bamber (yeah, that murdering bastard who wiped out his family, including kids) got a knock-back yesterday at the High Court for a release date! Now he's sure to serve the rest of his life inside. Good. Eat your porridge and fuck off!

My old buddy John Bowden has fled from Noranside open jail up in Scotland. John's been locked up since 1980 – almost 30 years, so no wonder he's had it on his toes. Good luck, John. Enjoy the freedom. I'm sure you will. (I know I would.)

I see the beast Bartley got released from his 20-year sentence for rapes. Yeah, you've guessed it: he's done it again and now he's got a life sentence. So keep the beast in and throw away the key.

It's 7.30pm and I'm calling it a day. Sleep time. Cut off and switch off; best place for me.

I had to laugh at Mark Fish as he walked in today. He saw Maudsley and shouted, "Fuck me, it's Santa!" The brain eater was walking out on the yard and he just grunted and kept on walking around. It's a strange old world! Don't we love it?

When it comes to evil fuckers, cop hold of this lot! Nutter Lucian Staniak was known as the 'Red Spider'. He was a serial killer in the mid 1960s in Poland. He confessed to killing 20 women but was convicted of only six murders. He was a sicko who loved to disembowel his victims and scrawl obscenities with their blood. He was ordered to be committed to the asylum for life. Let's hope the bastard's still in there.

Sid Abraham Rezela was a loony who enjoyed snuffing out his victims on trains across Europe. Nobody really knows how many he killed but police files have it down as dozens. Rezela had plans other than to stand trial, so in his cell in Lisbon he set fire to his mattress and the toxic fumes killed him. One of the guards said Rezela had the most evil eyes he had ever seen – even as he lay dead he still looked evil! Some people are just born evil, that's for sure.

I see Patrick Sureda has just been charged over an attack on the Yorkshire Ripper in Broadmoor asylum. Three cheers for Sureda: HIP HIP – HOORAY! HIP HIP – HOORAY! HIP HIP – HOORAY! Well done my old son! It's a pity a few more loonies don't attack the beast; he should be punched and kicked every day of his life! Who agrees with me? I bet most do. I rest my case!

In 2006 John Hall, a screw from Wakefield, got sentenced to life for multiple rapes. He worked here in monster mansion and he was a monster: six foot three and 20 stone of monster meat. He was a known bully, but who could have known he was a filthy serial rapist? Now he's being held in Frankland max secure jail up in Durham and he's Cuntley's next door neighbour. How crazy is that? Hall used to lock Cuntley up here, now he's locked up in the next cell! It's all Loonyology. The world's gone insane!

I see Portsmouth won the FA Cup yesterday. Well done to Harry Redknapp. He's a top manager – one of the best!

Monday, 19 May 2008.

Yesterday no grub, today no grub. I'm as light as a feather but twice as fast! That's my three-day clean-out done! Get all the shit and poison out of your body by filling it up with gallons of water. Mind you, I'd prefer a Guinness; I do love a Guinness. I got a surprise letter today from Trevor Liley. Who? You may well ask! Read his letter first.

Hi Charlie,

I know it's a long time since I wrote. You might not remember me, but I'm the one you left all your belongings to down the block in Gartree prison in 1987 just before you got released. The last time I saw you, you was on the yard doing sit-ups. You left me your radio and some personal stuff and you told me you were going to behave. What went wrong? It was a shame Reg dying. I stayed out of trouble for 8½ years, but nothing lasts. I know it's been a long time since we last met, so I've enclosed a stamped addressed envelope.

Your friend, Trevor.

How's about that for out of the blue? That made my day, if not my year. You see, when I was with Trevor back in 1987, we were in the punishment block. So with me getting out I let him have everything I had. That's what happens in jail when you come to the end of your time: you pass your stuff on to whoever needs it. Simple little things, stuff you accumulate over the years: special T-shirts, a carved shaving brush, wrist bands, jeans, trainers and your beloved radio. You give the lot away. I chose to give mine to Trevor and over 20 years later he still remembers! That's what I call a family. I've always said it and I always will: the prison world is a second family! Choose your friends well and you have many brothers. Brothers die for brothers! So that letter out of the blue today made it for me. Top geezer. I also got eight others, all just as special to me.

Did you know Billy Butlins opened up his first holiday camp in 1927? What a laugh you had in his camps. "Welcome campers!" They're probably seen as crap to this generation of spoilt brats, but in the 1940s, '50s and '60s it was the place to go. Everybody went to Butlins, even the No. 1 stars performed there. It really was the place to go for a good old knees-up… and a good shag. The Red Coats made sure of that. Plenty of 'special parties' in those days. Cor, not 'arf!

What about old Reggie Paisley? He was in his 80s and clubbed his wife Drusilla to death. Why? Who's ever gonna know? He then hanged himself next to her body. That's how it all ends for some: a fast ending of blind panic and fear. They lived in a beautiful 350K house in Sussex and were a lovely couple. Now see why I keep telling you all to enjoy your life? Some crazy fucker can snuff you out like a candle on a windy night. Enjoy your life because it's not forever.

Roll on tomorrow because I'll start eating again. It will be just my luck if it's a lousy diet day!

I didn't make a call today. I could have done but I didn't feel like it. That's how I am – it's how I feel on the day. Let's be honest: at times it bores the shit out of me. They're all getting pissed up and rushing around like lunatics; my world is a trillion miles away from that! Oh well, I'm still alive and kicking, and boy have I got a kick. Don't doubt it: one kick from me would ruin the rest of your life! I not only punch my own body weight, I kick it too! A size 10 at the side of your head with 16 stone behind it travelling at 85mph means good night sweet Jesus! Chose your grave because you won't make it back. If I catch you in the right spot on the chest, I guarantee I'll make your heart explode! You really don't want to test me, do you? If you do, chose a wood. Just us, no eyes – and bring a spade. That will do it, OK?

Oh well! Another day up the Queen's arse. All these years she's been my landlady. How mad is that? Loonyology!

A teacher asks a class of kids: "Give me a 10-letter word."

Little Johnny shouts, "Masturbate."

"Oh," said the teacher, "that's a mouthful!"

"No," said Johnny, "You're thinking of 'blowjob', but that's only got seven letters!"

Talking of teachers, there was a big fat bastard at the junior school I went to in Luton. He was nothing less than a bully who hit us boys with rulers and sticks and threw all sorts at us, slapping us about and almost shaking us silly! The 1950s and '60s were built on strict discipline. Those teachers were old war dogs and there was lots of shouting and bawling. Was it any wonder I hit him with a fire bucket? Cunt. Today he would have copped five years for child cruelty. That's how eras change. It's all crazy when you look back over your life; it's fucking mental. I need a cup of tea!

22 May, 2008.

Great visit with Danny Hansford. Lots of info on the movie side of life. There's a big buzz at Cannes Film Festival where they're showing a 10-minute trailer of my film. They fucking love it, but mum's the word. The world's got to wait for it – for the time when the shit hits the fan. Believe me, it will be worth the wait.

I got a letter yesterday from Barbara Davies, a top crime journalist who works for the *Daily Mail*. But she can't be too well informed about how to visit a high-risk prisoner as she seems to think she just needs my approval and they'll send her a visiting order to pop up here for tea and cucumber sandwiches. (Oops, sorry, not cucumber. I promised not to use that word again since *Loonyology: In My Own Words*. Why? Well fucking read it yourselves! I'm not a parrot! Just don't mention cucumber to me anymore!) Barbara, it can't happen. To see me you have to go through a rigorous check by security and the Old Bill. You should know all this, but anyway, I've got my 'firm' onto it! You'll get the details of what to do. If you do it and get passed – lovely! If you don't, then you don't. But you won't get into see me otherwise. And I'm sure your editor wants you in, as you're about selling papers, not making friends with convicts. You want the truth, so get passed and let's get it on!

Yesterday and today I got 28 letters in all. I got another one from Zac Goldsmith (yeah, *the* Zac Goldsmith) as I've just sorted him out some art for a charity auction. But the best letter was from Mum. She was in her local pub (the Tollgate in Aberystwyth) one weekend and one of my pieces of art sold for £1,100. It was in aid of a guy who's got mad cow disease. So how's about that? Another grand for a good cause! That's who Charlie Bronson is; that's the real me, not the nasty bastard the system want you to believe I am. Yeah! Sweet, that cheered me right up!

Unlike this fucker Darrell McLeish. He's being allowed out on day release only 17 months after being found guilty of killing a man by stabbing him with a screwdriver. They sent him to a secure mental hospital and now he's coming out for day trips to prepare him for release! Maureen Johnson (the mother of the buried son) said, "How can a man who put a screwdriver through my son's head get out after two years? It's so upsetting, I sobbed my heart out when I heard." I'll tell you why, Maureen, my sweetheart. The truth is:

1. They don't care about you or your lost son.
2. They're all nuts.
3. They're more interested in helping the filthy murderer!

OK... he was convicted of manslaughter, not murder, but it's all legal technicalities. The fact is your boy is dead and McLeish, who snuffed him out, is now out himself after two years. It's a bloody national disgrace and even I'm fuming over it. He should have done 10 years before he was even considered for release and your own views and opinions should be taken into account. It's a disgrace, Maureen, and you have my sympathies. I hope somebody 'bumps into' McLeish and he gets some of his own treatment, I really do, because he has literally got away with murder! I've spent his sentence in a steel box having the shit kicked out of me – for what? It's unfuckingbelieveablyinsane! It's Loonyology!

Manchester United stuffed Chelsea last night in a penalty shoot-out, so they're European champs again! That Man U takes some beating! They are the best, the cream! Chelsea's John Terry gave it to them on a plate by missing a penalty. Ha, ha, ha... 60K a week and he can't score a poxy penalty! Terry's a prat, Terry's a prat! He gave it to them on a silver tray. Here, Reds, have the cup. Ha, ha, ha! Such is life!

I see Joey Barton of Newcastle United has just been sentenced to six months' jail for some attack. A bit stiff if you ask me. Why not give him some community work? He could help a lot of youngsters. You watch, he will come out of jail and people will try to stop him playing football. Barton's got a gift, he's a great player and he's only young. He made a mistake. Cunts, why don't you crucify him or stone him to death? What a crazy world this is.

Hey! Look back over the years at how many top sportsmen have landed up in jail: Lester Piggot, George Best, Tony Adams, Sammy McArthy, Billy Williams… the list goes on and on! Ask yourselves why it happened when they had it all – gifts, talents, dosh and fame. I'm telling you now, it's in us all, it's boredom. We get fucking bored stiff of being Mr Nice Guys. Yes sir, no sir, I'll pay my tax sir… it's total shit. Wake up world and do some serious living! Tell the tax man to fucking wait till you come back from your world tour. (If you remember to come back, that is…) Get on that yacht before he does! He's gonna spend your dosh so spend some of his. Is it me? Why is it I can work this shit out and 40 million workers can't? (Or are you scared to?)

I had a wonderful session on the yard today. The cannibal came in as I went out but we don't ever pass each other because I would chin him on sight. Well, what would you do if he's made it clear he wants to rip your organs out and eat them? What am I supposed to do, pass him the salt and pepper? I'm a survivor, not a fucking meal ticket. I'll chin the cunt on sight and everybody knows it, including him. No fucker threatens to eat me! Cunt. I'm getting angry here just thinking about it!

Anyway, the sun was out on the yard, there was a bit of a breeze and a couple of birds were singing, so it was nice. My shower afterwards was good as well. Somebody had left a small bar of Camay soap in there but I couldn't use it. The very thought that it's been washing someone else's bollocks does it for me. That sort of thing makes me feel a bit sick so I stuck to my own Imperial Leather soap. Oh yes, only the best for this birdman! Camay smells nicer, I agree, but my Imperial Leather has a cleaner smell and it lasts longer. I know my soaps. For a good clean-up use Cold Tar! It's got that sort of hygienic hospital smell, a bit like Palmolive. When I'm on punishment and they stop me buying toiletries, I use the prison's white Windsor or carbolic. It's just as good but the scent is prison style! Fuck all wrong with that, but I do like to spoil myself occasionally!

I often wonder where my old buddy Colin Robinson is now days. What a complex character Colin is. I first met him in 1975 when he was three years into his life sentence; now he's 36 years into it. The last time I saw him was maybe 16 years back. I've picked up bits and pieces but I lost him on radar about 10 years ago, so he could be anywhere as far as I know! He must be 65 now. I fucking loved him as a brother.

Colin suffered terribly, especially in his first 10 years inside which were just pure fucking insanity! He went to work on two cons with a tool and cut them to pieces; he got his second life sentence for that. But he also suffered from bouts of severe depression that sent him into the darkness where he swallowed razor blades and cut himself up. They kept taking him outside to hospital to cut him up and take out the blades he'd swallowed. He swallowed bed springs, tobacco tins, even nails! Some called him 'Mr Iron Man' but I called him a cunt and told him to stop it before it killed him! I trained with him and helped him, we were good pals, but those dark clouds always came to take him out to hospital. It was Colin who smashed a con's head in at Parkhurst. (For that he went to Broadmoor.) He did it all and got a dozen T-shirts! He survived it all.

Where are you now, Colin? I often think of you! In or out, if you read this get in touch – I may be able to sort something your way! You're a true brother and you helped me a lot through some of my mad times. We were there when jail was jail, with real blocks where the screws were the animals, not us! We fought all that – us, and men like us. We helped each other through because that's what cons were for. Or was it all one big dream? Were we even there? Did we ever hit the rainbow? Did we really die and crumble – 'crushed out'? Get in touch. I hope you're free and happy!

I spent £9.75 on my canteen and got it today: plenty of nuts, some honey and fruit; the rest went on phone units. I called Mark Emmins who gives me all the latest. He does me proud and I appreciate it. We have our ups and downs, but all in all he's a top geezer in my book and a really nice fella. We have become more like brothers than just friends and that's good. So all you Bronson supporters, support Mark's fight as it's my fight. If you want updated news on this fight, log onto www.freebronson.co.uk. Do it now because we need you.

I had a nice pie today. I ate it and I said to myself, "Nice, but what the fuck was in it?" I ate a fucking mystery pie. It could have been anything but it was lovely – even the pastry was lovely!

It gets madder; you'll love this one… In today's *Daily Mail* there was a brilliant article about a chimp (yeah, an ape, a monkey, whatever you wish) called Matthew. The headline reads: "Does Matthew the chimp have human rights?" Hello! It's a fucking chimp! What about me? Anyway, animal rights activist Paula Stibbe is fighting to have Matthew legally declared a person so she can be appointed as his guardian. (I need a lie down… I'm tired!) A spokesman for the court in Strasbourg said: "Any application regarding this chimpanzee will be considered at a primary level by a magistrate and a lawyer before we decide whether it deserves a full-blown hearing." For what it's worth, I hope Matthew gets it! Er, can I please be transferred to a zoo? This could be my route to justice. Well, why not?

More letters are rolling in from *Loonyology* readers. They fucking love it and they're all waiting for this one. Don't rush me, please don't rush me – you can't be pushing us writers! (Ask JK Rowling, she'll tell you!) You can't rush us because we tick over like a Rolex and flow like a Parker. We need space, time, dreams and no stress! We have to get our brain juices bubbling. You need to understand that we create books, not jacket potatoes! Yeah, I'm getting some great feedback. Thank you.

I may have a good old-fashioned wank later as my balls are getting too heavy. You girls just don't understand – we have to blow our pipe occasionally or it gets blocked up! It's ages since I bashed the meat and I don't want another wet dream! Fuck that; I'm 56 not 16.

Hey! I was having a wank one night in the dark in Risley, around 1969 time, when the door crashed in and they caught me! Fucking wankers. It was about 9.30pm and some of the lads in other cells had been slinging out burning paper. (That wasn't my cup of tea. Plus, I had no matches and no paper – all I had was a *Penthouse* mag). I was only a 17-year-old kid and these screws were men twice my size. They dragged me out of bed bollock naked (now with only a semi-hard) and start reading me the riot act:

"Fucking light fires here you cockney cunt and we will break your arms. This is Risley – 'Grisly Risley' – you little prick." Some were punching and kicking me. They were a bunch of gutless cunts. As soon as they slung me back in my cell and shut the door, I wrecked the cell. That cost me 14 days chokie, no canteen, no association and a good kicking. All I did was have a wank and it cost me all that! Maybe it's God – he sees us wanking so he grasses us up to the screws. Maybe the screws are really angels and the governors are saints. (Food for thought.)

Do you know something? It's been a crazy one-way journey with no fucking brakes, and the steering wheel fell off years ago! I'm bound to crash, so fucking keep out of my way.

23 May, 2008.

So much for the 'ham shank'; I gave up after 20 minutes! I've got to face it, it's getting boring – fuck off boring. I think this could be a serious human rights issue. Why can't there be a hole in the door or wall so we long-term isolated cons can get 'relief' – like a blow-job or a toss-off by some brass, say once a week (twice if you're good)? Cunts. Yeah, my wanking days are over now. Sad really, but that's age I suppose!

I had a nice plate of chips today. I smothered them in salt and vinegar, made four decent sandwiches and washed them down with a pint of hot, sweet tea. That's living! All that was missing was the cod, or a nice bit of plaice.

Did you know Great Britain is the No. 1 place on Earth for bluebells? Have you ever walked through a wood of bluebells? It's like a carpet of beautiful blue. There were several fantastic bluebell woods in Luton. This is a lovely country! We don't call it 'Great' Britain for nothing!

I got a great bit of news from Ifty today: his two sons Guggy and Wahid both got a 'not guilty' at trial. YIIPPpppppppeeeeeee, YARHOOooooooo. That's how to win: by stuffing it straight up the Crown (and they were innocent, too). I also found out through Gavin Meek that some so-called 'mate' of mine in Spain has been selling my art and pocketing the dosh for himself. Yeah, it all gets back to me. He's sold several pieces to Gavin behind my back. I'll keep this traitor's name under wraps for now, but my Lorraine and a few close pals will know about it! Time and place, I always say. He also knows I now know. If he had asked and said he was skint I would have helped him, or if he had told me and sent me some canteen in – sweet. But he's just sold my prized art to Gavin for his own gain, so to me he's a parasite sucking off a man in a hole. This is how it is today: there are too many gutless cunts. Well, it's destroyed my day for sure. A 60-year-old fat prick sucking off me? You fat cunt, I won't forget it – how can I?

Some will say, "Here Chaz goes again, falling out with one of the chaps!" Well, I only go on facts and proof. There is only one Bronson art dealer out there, and that's Mark Emmins. How many more times have I got to say it? Anyway, fuck it, I'll lose no sleep over it. But it's another cunt off my Xmas list and in my black book. Hopefully I'll get to chin him later, or stick a pint glass in his fat face. I fucking detest treachery and greedy fuckers, I really do. How do people sleep when they rip off men who can't even defend themselves? They must be so brave! "Ha, ha, ha, I made a nice few quid off Bronson's back." Cunts. As I get older I'm actually waking up more. It feels good to see exactly how it all is...

I had a great work-out today. I felt alive! I shaved my head and I'm growing a full beard back now – it's almost white. By Xmas I'll look like Uncle Albert out of *Only Fools and Horses* (what a great character he was). There was an old con just like Albert in Walton jail in the 1970s who was a real diamond, a proper Scouser. He used to be the library redband and he took his job deadly seriously. For the life of me I can't remember his name (we all called him 'Pops') but he was serving a 10-year stretch for a blag on Liverpool Post Office. What a story he could tell of his war years and prison years. He was a walking story teller! He gave me a book called *The Soul Brothers*. Fuck knows who wrote it, but it was a great read. He used to light up a pipe out on the exercise yard and stroll around like he was lord of the manor. His boots were always shiny and his striped prison shirt was starched! Yeah! Old Pops was the man! This was a man who had been birched in the 1950s. He was a survivor and that's why we all loved him. Fuck me; I'm going back three and a half decades here and it feels like yesterday.

There was a workshop in Walton then that made plastic watches for kids and our job was putting them together. I lasted a week and that was my lot – I slung a big table through the office window. Why? Well, why not? The bell went, I got a good kicking and a new job! That's how it works in jail. Some cons can switch off and roll on but I never could and I never wanted to. I can't do such a boring job, it's not in me.

I met some of the best screws in Walton – funny fuckers – and they always did a good soup broth there every day of the week. There was home-made bread too: four slices at breakfast and six for tea, plus a bread roll for dinner. Their canteen was always well stocked and I had a good thing going there with tobacco! I won't say I was a 'Bacca Baron' but let's say I always had a good 20 to 30 ounces owing to me. How you work it (or did in those days) is that you would lend out half an ounce and take back three-quarters, so you made a quarter ounce every time. For every two-ounce deal you got back three! You lend out another deal and it all adds up, because smokers always run out before canteen day. Then once I'd collected, I'd buy what I wanted by using the bacca! I've even got a radio for a half ounce of bacca, as well as rings, watches and bracelets. Some cons would sell their souls for a smoke! That's how it works. Bizz is bizz, in or out of jail! For a quarter of bacca I would get the con's custard, fruit and cheese all week. He smokes and coughs, I eat and train! Who's the winner?

I walked out of my cell one day on Walton's H/3 wing and jumped clear over the railing and bounced onto the wire netting. What for? Fuck knows! Just to liven the day up, I suppose. And when you get 100 cons cheering and screws blowing whistles, it does liven it up. Another time I walked into the office with my piss pot over my head (empty, of course) and started singing 'My Way'. I was bored and I wanted moving. I've truly fucked up screws' and governors' heads over the years. Ask them – they'll tell you how it was once: fucking insane! Loonyology!

Dear Charlie,
My name's Eddie Thompson from Crawley. Have you ever thought about starting up a Loonyology club? It could be great… Give it some serious thought Charlie, as it could become worldwide.

Eddie, it's strange you have written this as only recently I was discussing something on this level with Mark Emmins. You're spot on: we need our own Loonyology club with real membership for all us lunatics. We could have posters, badges, tattoos, monthly mags – even camping trips. Imagine it: thousands of us tracking across the moors, singing and laughing as one! "The hills are alive with the sound of madness."

Yes… I think I can say with a 100% guarantee there will be a Loonyology club one day, but it will have to wait till I get out, as you can't have a club whilst the leader is away. You need your leader with you! I'm no good to you loons whilst I'm inside; you need to follow me, a bit like how they followed Jesus! Or like all those rats with the Pied Piper. You need to see and hear me. We will dance and sing around the fire together. Some will probably say it's a cult, but let them say what they want. Fuck them! Loonyology is a new way of life. It's ours, so watch this space! In the meantime, spread the word, get the T-shirt, prepare! We shall fight them on the beaches! We shall kick the fuck out of them! Who's with me? YEEEeeeeeooooowwwww… YARrrrhhhoooooooo… Have some of us!

And don't forget, the uglier and madder you are the better. We love you even more, you wonderful freaky fuckers; we just love you, so start to love yourselves! It's the good-looking, brainy, boring fuckers that get up our noses. Fucking sheep. (Talking of sheep, I'm starving.) So who's gonna be a Loonyology member? Write to me and tell me your thoughts and ideas on the subject. Obviously we will have to have some sort of test before you become a member, so here are some ideas of mine: climb Snowdon naked with a peacock feather sticking out of your arse whilst blowing a party whistle; wrestle with a pig in mud; eat a live chicken; break into a zoo and nick a tiger! We need unusual things, don't you agree?

Now the million dollar question: do we keep it for us men loons only, like a sort of Masonic brotherhood, or do we have the pussy with us? Do we let in the loony sisters? It's up to you guys to decide, so let me know. You know the girls will want some of us! You also know at special times of the month they're even madder than us guys! I also say all meetings are held in the nude! That way we can check there are no spies and that no-one's taped up and bugged! Nudity is raw madness. One for all and all for one! We'll finish the meetings off with a good old-fashioned orgy.

Imagine this for a sight: 5,000 of us in a field, all in a naked circle – woman, man, woman, man! Get the picture? All fucking in a daisy chain; the longest fuck ever. All happy, laughing and fucking! That's real Loonyology. 'Freedom fuckers' alive with hearts of love! Mad people are special souls, believe me, we don't give a flying fuck about everyday life. It's now, today, that counts to us! March on, brothers and sisters, march on for your own beliefs. And if you feel the need to stop for a shit or a fuck or a blow job, then we all stop with you. One for all and all for one!

YAARRHhhhooooooo… YIIPPPpppeeeeeeee… Loonyfuckingology. He, He, He – Ha, Ha, Ha!

The night sanity died – by himself.

Shit… it's on
Someone's called it on
Hell's broke out
It's time to fight
You can't run
Even if you wanted to
Where can you run?
Where can you hide?
It's bang on you
"A riot"
Insanity is here
In your face
In your head
Sanity dies
Let's get it on
An explosion of frustrated violence
The roof's blown off
Convicts are insane
Murderers murder
Robbers rob
Rapists rape
Watch your arse, boys
Don't bend down here
Unless you want a meat injection
Screaming madmen
An explosion of anger
This is Hell
Take a photo
Shit… it's out of control
Cells ablaze
Cons on fire
Cut throats and torn bodies
Blood, guts and pieces of skull
A body falls, the soul is free
This is for real
The dream stops here
A punctured lung
A stabbed eye
A bleeding kidney
Sweet agonizing pain
Where can you run?
Where do you hide?
Fight or die
This is Hell
Shit… it's on
This is the big one!
The hunter is hunted
The predator is prey

A jail full of meat
Ready to chop
Walking chops
In front, behind
It's all around
Dripping blood
Dripping dreams
Trapped
No way out
Survive for what!
Teams of riot squads
Shields and sticks
CS gas
Another violent explosion
You survive the blades
Now it's them
Them and us
Us and them
Another battle, another war
Another scar
It never ends
Shit… it's on
How much more?
Does it ever end?
Can it ever end?
You're clubbed to your knees
Crushed
Bashed, brutalised and chained!
Ready for the darkness
An empty room
Cold and still
Dreamless
Aching and bruised
Cut and ripped
Isolated away from all worlds
Shit… it's gone down
It's over
I survived
It was fucking mental
Insane, but exciting!
An orgy of uncontrollable violence
Con on con
Con on screw
Screws on cons
More screws on cons
Lots more screws
You become one
Every fucker's gone
Disappeared

I was always alone!
Back to the womb
Back to safety
This was the way out
This was the place to run to
Back to how it all began
The safety hole
The heart beat
The beginning of your own existence!
A soulful experience
Covered in blood
A reflection of madness
Naked and free of life
Floating in a sack of humanity!
Why did it ever have to end?
That floating peace like a feeling of serenity
Like a dizzy butterfly
A loved-up puppy dog
Licks your tears dry
Shit... it's over
Another lost hole
A pool of blood and a damaged brain
Crawling through the heaps of bodies
Some dead, some dying
Another long way up
The climb begins now!
Follow the light
If there is one.

Fuck knows where poems come from; the pen just flows. It's like it's not me, but something inside! Me of all people a poet, you just can't make it up!

Roses are red
Violets are blue
I've got a big cock
Just waiting for you.

See? I can even create love poems! I'm just a lost poet, that's what I am!

Did you know the first British Prime Minister was Robert Walpole back in 1721? He stayed in office till 1742, then the Earl of Wilmington took over for a year. Not a lot of people know that. Well, you do now. The first Tory PM was the Earl of Bute in 1762, the first Liberal PM was Lord John Russell in 1846, and it wasn't until 1924 that we had the first Labour PM, James Ramsey MacDonald. Trust it to be a 'sweaty sock'. What is it with all these Scots we keep getting to run our country? If they had their way we would all be in kilts eating porridge and throwing tree trunks about. Fuck off, we ain't doing it. This is Britain – fish 'n chips. If you don't like it then fuck off – whoever you are! Porridge and kilts... do me a favour!

Sorrow is often touched with joy so don't stay sad, be happy. I know it's easy to feel isolated in your own personal grief, but remember no grief is new – it's all been experienced for centuries. The journey has to go on and on! Remember as a child when your heart was so simple and pure? Can you go back that far? Well, that's what we all need to do: go back in time and fill our hearts with happiness! Doesn't that feel good? Happiness loves to be elusive and then it takes you by surprise and makes you shine. Life is about enjoyment, so kick some fucker's arse and always remember this: *Happiness is doubled when you share it with someone special.*

It's true! Let a bit of it rub off on someone and you'll feel so much nicer. Failing that, be your own best friend and treat yourself to a nice big apple pie with double whipped cream. I'm fucking starving now.

Here's some madness gone mad: a 150-year-old monkey puzzle tree in Swansea is to be cut down because a council report says its leaves are too sharp and may cut children. That's what I call Health and Safety gone insane! Get a fucking life; that tree has stood there since Queen Victoria sat on the throne. Leave the tree alone…

Did you know too much water will kill you? It will wash away all your essential body minerals such as sodium, so go easy…

Did you know Colman's Mustard has been going for 196 years? It's still the best. It was Jeremiah Colman who started it all off in Norwich. He really knew how to cut the mustard.

Did I ever tell you about Eddie Slater, also known as the 'Birdman of Hull jail', who was on the special unit years ago? Eddie turned a spare cell into an aviary and he bred lots of budgies – some beauties too. One day he was on a domestic visit and big Tony Mac put all the budgies into a cardboard box under his bed and went about his plan. On the perches he hung a load of chicken giblets and splattered blood and feathers all over the cell. Tony was fucking crazy like that and it actually looked like a hawk had flown through the cell window and had been on a killing spree. Fuck me; Eddie went berserk. Even though we all tried to cool him down and show him the birds were safe and well, he just blew a fuse. It took him months to get back to normal. Tony was a real practical joker and was always up to stuff like that, but guys like Eddie Slater can be very touchy when pushed. Ask the Durham governor, because Ed took his roof off in the 1980s. Eddie was only 11 stone soaking wet, but he could bench-press 22 stone. He was one of those little guys with awesome strength! I liked him a lot; he was a top geezer and a top chef who made the best curry on the unit!

Another good chef I met was Ali Ahmmad, who got lifed off in the 1970s for chopping his brother-in-law's head clean off. I met Ali in Parkhurst. All the cons enjoyed his curry and he used to sell us a bowl which was worth every penny. On a Saturday, a bowl of curry and a pint of hooch with the weekly movie was the treat of the week. Our weekly movie was shown above C-Wing dome and we all used to pile in there. The old projector used to fire up on the large screen and it was as good as any picture house. Some would smoke their pot, others drank their hooch. Days like that are gone forever. It was brilliant and the atmosphere was electric – it was how jail was supposed to be. We were cons and screws were screws. Now screws are pretending to be something they're not, but they're still screws to me and always will be! Any silly cunt can open and shut a door!

In the '70s I used to buy seven onions a week and eat one a day raw with bread. I couldn't do that now – it would make me sick, but back then I loved it and it used to fill me up. If I got lucky and got a slab of cheese, that was a treat! Yep, the good old days I say…

On a hot summer's day in 1976 I was out on the yard in Parkhurst (C-Wing had its own yard separated from all the other wings) and my hour was up so it was time to go in. I said to Ron and Reg Kray, "Fuck it, I'm staying out," so I climbed up on the toilet roof and lay there in the sun.

"Come down!" the screws shouted.

"Fuck off!"

I stayed up there till tea time then came down. I was as brown as a berry! What a summer. I think I lost 14 days for that, but so what – who cares? I didn't! I was the one with the tan. People pay hundreds for a holiday like that. Like I always say, it's one big fucking holiday so enjoy your stay and make the best of it; that's what a guy's got to do…

There was a good hospital screw on C-Wing in the '70s (who shall remain nameless) and he used to look after me. Once a week he would sort me out all sorts of extras such as Complan (a kind of food supplement you stir in with milk), vitamins, marmite, honey – all sorts of goodies. He was a right decent sort of screw! He just liked me; fuck knows why, but he did. In those days I needed all I could get as I was bang into my work-outs, doing three or four hours a day. I never stopped, that's how I was, I had to be doing something. I even had a seizure because I was over-training and became dehydrated, exhausted and fucked up! I just collapsed and I had to have all sorts of tests: EEG, ECG, blood tests – all sorts. Then I was diagnosed with temple lobe epilepsy! I was having fits and all sorts of bollocks… it was a crazy time. The doctors told me to slow down and rest, but I just did more. I had to – it was my way of escaping the boredom. I was, after all, a fitness fanatic; I was the fastest, strongest, fittest convict on the Isle of Wight (if not in Britain) in the 1970s. I'll drink to that, because I was the Bruce Lee of prison. Yeah, me! Lee died young, but I died and came back… how's about that?

When it comes to serial killers who almost got away with it, Peter Moore must be one of the most notorious. In fact, he's here in 'monster mansion' where he belongs. It was back in 1995 that this Welsh cinema manager hit the headlines. He stabbed four blokes to death in a four-month orgy of violence and the police are sure he killed many more. Moore is a prison poof – several cons have come down off the wing to this seg block talking about Moore and all say the same: he loves a big cock between his legs. (You'll be amazed what gets said out of prison windows! Lots of it would drive you mental.) Moore's nickname is 'the Welsh Fairy'. Some fucking fairy – he's six foot of psycho meat. You would have to be a fucking lunatic to bend over for him, but as you know, prison is rammed packed with loonies. He gets plenty of sex here; it's why he's settled so well. They all love it here. When Moore was arrested he told the cops, "Lucky for my bank manager – he was next." Phew, that was lucky!

Hey! What about that shit thief who tried to siphon the petrol out of a campervan? Fucking idiot, he put the pipe into the septic tank and got a mouthful of shit! Still, he was Irish, so what do you expect!

I see Jeremy Beadle left a £2 million will. Top geezer. Did you know he was responsible for raising £100 million for charities? We salute the chap!

I'll tell you who's a nasty fucker: Russell Deane. He pleaded guilty to manslaughter on the grounds of diminished responsibility after bashing his grandmother's skull in with a hammer. Yeah, yeah, yeah – saying you're not responsible is the easy way out of it! "Blame my mind, it's not my fault." Broadmoor's full of these loons and on a full moon the place is howling with laughter. Deane is just another loon howling away! Behave, get better, keep taking your pills and you'll be out in no time, poor thing. Your gran won't be back though – she's stuck in the bone yard where you put her.

Did you know it's 70 years since the invention of the ballpoint pen? Three cheers for the biro! HIP HIP – HOORAY! HIP HIP – HOORAY! HIP HIP – HOORAY! 15 million biros are sold every day around the world! Work that one out at 20p each…

You'll remember in chapter one that I did a few pages on youngsters being killed on our streets in 2007 and how tragic it all was, and what we could do to try and put a stop to it all. Sadly, it's still going on in 2008. It's still only May and look at all this lot:

January 1	Henry Bolombi, 17 years old, stabbed in Edmonton, London.
January 5	Faridon Alizada, 19, stabbed in Erith, Kent.
January 21	Boduka Mudianga, 18, stabbed in Edmonton.
January 26	Fuad Buraleh, 19, beaten to death, West Ealing.
February 19	Sunday Essiet, 15, stabbed in Woolwich, south-east London.
February 23	Tung Le, 17, stabbed in Westminster, central London.
February 29	Ofiyke Nmezu, 16, beaten to death in Enfield, north London.
March 13	Michael Alexander Jones, 18, stabbed in Edmonton.
March 14	Nicholas Clarke, 19, shot in Brixton, south London.
March 27	Devoe Roach, 17, stabbed in Stoke Newington, north London.
March 27	Amro Elbadawi, 14, stabbed in Queen's Park, west London.
May 3	Lyle Tulloch, 15, stabbed in Borough, south London.
May 10	Jimmy Mizen, 16, stabbed in Lee, south-east London.
May 24	Robert Knox, 18, stabbed in Sidcup, Kent.

There's no end to it and it's getting worse. All these kids are victims of violence. Don't go out with knives and guns; real men don't need them. Look at these 14 innocent young lads – not one of them deserved this ending and neither did their families. It's bloody tragic.

Ricky Hatton fights Juan Lazcano tomorrow night at the 55,000-seater City of Manchester stadium. It's his comeback fight after he lost to Floyd Mayweather. Lazcano is no easy meal ticket, but I predict Hatton will knock him out. We shall see. It's all fate and what will be will be! You can't chance what is meant to happen.

Hey! I've got some advice for all you tortoise lovers who sometimes lose your pet in the garden. Get some superglue and a couple of flat bits of metal and stick them on its shell, then get a metal detector. Problem solved! You've got a problem? Then write to me, I'm the No. 1 problem sorter! I'm the man!

24 May 2008.

Just heard the Hatton fight on Radio 5. It went the distance and he made hard work of it, but a win is a win! Three cheers for Ricky! HIP HIP – HOORAY! HIP HIP – HOORAY! HIP HIP – HOORAY! You just can't keep a good man down!

I see we came last in the Eurovision. What a farce. In fact our entry by Andy Abraham was a good song and it surely didn't deserve to come last. Anyway, cop a load of this lot of UK entries going back to 1960:

1960 Bryan Johnson 'Looking High High High' – came 2nd

1961 The Allisons 'Are You Sure?' – 2nd

1962 Ronnie Carroll 'Ring-A-Ding Girl' – 5th

1963 Ronnie Carroll 'Say Wonderful Things' – 4th

1964 Matt Monro 'I Love the Little Things' – 2nd

1965 Kathy Kirby 'I Belong' – 2nd (Come on, who remembers our Kathy? She was a blonde bombshell with the voice of an angel. She should have won that; angels don't come in second.)

1966 Kenneth McKellar 'A Man Without Love' – 9th

1967 Sandie Shaw 'Puppet on a String' – 1st (I remember watching this one; she sang with bare feet. See how you learn things in my books? Every page is full of amazing historical facts!)

1968 Cliff Richard 'Congratulations' – 2nd

1969 Lulu 'Boom Bang-a-bang' – 1st (There were a lot of booms in '69: the Kray firm got put down,. the Parkhurst riot and the moon landing took place, and I got nicked and locked up myself.)

1970 Mary Hopkin 'Knock Knock, Who's There' – 2nd

1971 Clodagh Rogers 'Jack in the Box' – 4th

1972 The New Seekers 'Beg, Steal or Borrow' – 2nd (My son was born this year. Yiiiippppeeeeee! I'll drink to that... cheers! I sure never begged or borrowed, but boy did I steal. Well, what's a thief supposed to do?)

1973 Cliff Richard 'Power to All Our Friends' – 3rd

1974 Olivia Newton-John 'Long Live Love' – 4th (So much for love – this year I copped seven years and my old lady ran off with a lover boy.)

1975 The Shadows 'Let Me Be The One' – 2nd

1976 Brotherhood of Man 'Save Your Kisses for Me' – 1st (The only kiss I got in '76 was a size 10 boot in my nuts.)

1977 Lynsey de Paul and Mike Moran 'Rock Bottom' – 2nd (I was rock bottom in the bowels of the penal system.)

1978 Co-Co 'The Bad Old Days' – 11th (Tell me about it. I got certified insane and sent off to the asylum. I finally landed on Mars.)

1979 Black Lace ‘Mary Ann’ – 7th

1980 Prima Donna ‘Love Enough for Two’ – 3rd (A great year. I pulled Broadmoor’s roof off!)

1981 Bucks Fizz ‘Making Your Mind Up’ – 1st

1982 Bardo ‘One Step Further’ – 7th

1983 Sweet Dreams ‘I’m Never Giving Up’ – 6th (I never gave up either. I took the asylum roof off again.)

1984 Belle and the Devotions ‘Love Games’ – 7th

1985 Vikki Watson ‘Love Is’ – 4th

1986 Ryder ‘Runner in the Night’ – 7th (You getting bored yet? I am.)

1987 Rikki Peebles ‘Only the Light’ – 13th (The light shone on me this year. I was freed.)

1988 Scott Fitzgerald ‘Go’ – 2nd (The light went out again; I got nicked.)

1989 Live Report ‘Why Do I Always Get it Wrong?’ – 2nd

1990 Emma Booth ‘Give a Little Love Back to the World’ – 6th

1991 Samantha Janus ‘A Message to your Heart’ – 10th

1992 Michael Ball ‘One Step out of Time’ – 2nd

1993 Sonia ‘Better the Devil You Know’ – 2nd

1994 Frances Ruffelle ‘We Will Be Free (Lonely Symphony)’ – 10th

1995 Love City Groove ‘Love City Groove’ – 11th

1996 Gina G ‘Ooh Aah… Just a Little Bit’ – 8th (I could do with a little bit myself.)

1997 Katrina and the Waves ‘Love Shine a Light’ – 1st (We came first! No. 1! YARRRHHHoooooo… YIPPPPEeeeeeee… YEEEOOOWwwwww…)

1998 Imaani ‘Where Are You?’ – 2nd (Where was I? Fuck knows, I was having so much fun I didn’t care.)

1999 Precious ‘Say it Again’ – 13th

2000 Nicki French ‘Don’t Play that Song Again’ – 16th (Yeah, please don’t play it.)

2001 Lindsay D. ‘No Dream Impossible’ – 15th

2002 Jessica Garlick ‘Come Back’ – 4th

2003 Jemini ‘Cry Baby’ – 26th (I think she’s still crying)

2004 James Fox ‘Hold Onto Our Love’ – 16th

2005 Javine ‘Touch My Fire’ – 22nd (I would touch her fire any time, she’s bloody edible.)

2006 Daz Sampson ‘Teenage Life’ – 19th

2007 Scooch ‘Flying the Flag (For You) – 23rd

2008 Andy Abraham ‘Even If’ – 25th (Nowhere.)

Shall we give it a rest? Shall we? Let’s face facts: who’s going to vote for us? The Cliff Richard days are over! Bucks Fizz has fizzled out! Good night.

CHAPTER 7

Remember me to Santa

The fat lazy twat – where's he been for the last 35 years?

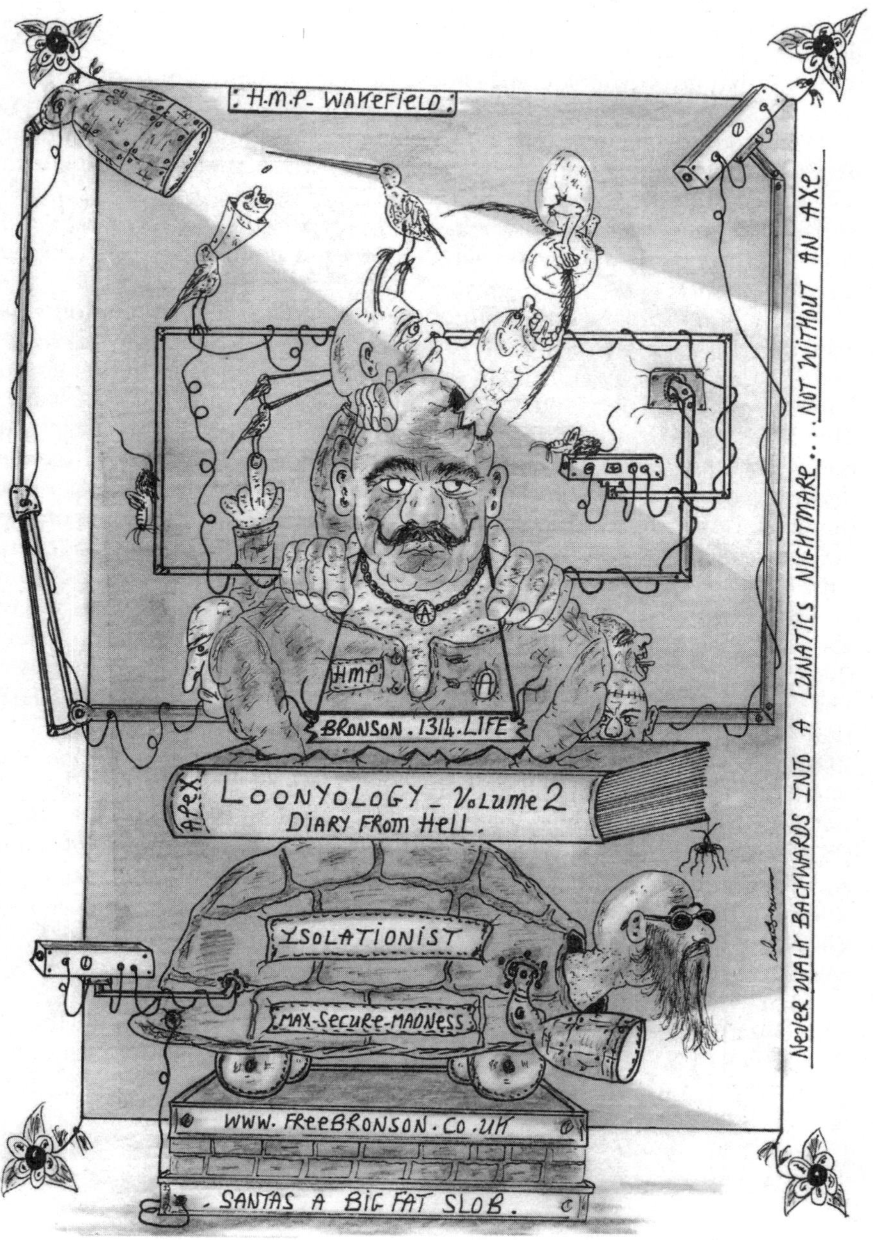

I see Evil Knievel's son has just smashed his old man's record of jumping over buses. I told you madness runs in the family. It's all in the genes and in the blood, believe me.

Talking of evil, what about Dawood Khan? He got lifed off for bashing in Nazeer Ahmed's skull with a cricket bat – eight fucking times he smashed him. And guess what, Khan was in fact an illegal immigrant. He sneaks over here from Afghanistan and smashes in heads for the hell of it. It's all gone mad... somebody turn the light off on the way out.

Talking of cricket bats, I hit a guy for a sixer years ago outside a boozer in Dunstable. I actually took the bat off him after he hit somebody else with it. What goes around comes back. Well, it did with him. 'Crack' – out cold. "Howzat?" Eat your heart out, Botham.

Watch out for the invasion of the Asian tiger mosquito. They're on their way and they're dangerous fuckers too. They transmit the chikungunya fever. You'll know if you get it, believe me.

Did you know there's a spider in Asia that's got six dicks? Now why did God create a creature with six dicks? Is that not Loonyology? It's fucking insane.

I hear Colin Moses, chairman of the Prison Officers' Association, has been slagging off my book on the Yorkshire TV news programme *Calendar*, saying I should not be allowed to profit whilst in jail! Well, what's it got to do with you? Your job is locking me up and making sure I don't escape. This is what makes the system vindictive: I sit in my cell creating art and books and they don't like it. Why not? Why don't they like it? Because they're jealous fuckers, that's why not. I've rehabilitated myself. Anyway, thanks to Colin Moses for helping to plug my book. You keep going on the news talking about *Loonyology* because you're a brilliant salesman. Thank you.

Poor old Shirley Bassey has just been rushed to hospital with severe abdominal pain. I hope she's OK! I fucking love her, she's a real superstar! Even now, at 71 years old, she's a cracker. She's my all-time favourite singer. Three cheers for Shirley! HIP HIP – HOORAY! HIP HIP – HOORAY! HIP HIP – HOORAY! Get well fast.

Did you know the Inland Taipan snake has enough poison in one bite to kill 100 humans? Can you fucking believe that?

It's 15 years since the Lucasville prison uprising in the state of Ohio, USA. Nine inmates and one guard were killed. Five inmates were later convicted and are still held on death row, but one of these men, Siddique Abdullah Hasan, was fitted up with fabricated evidence. Take that on me! Write him a letter – find out why and how. Here's his address:

SIDDIQUE ABDULLAH HASAN
NO R130 – 559
OHIO STATE PENITENTIARY 878
COITSVILLE – HUBBARD ROAD
YOUNGSTOWN
OHIO 44505 – 4635
USA

Martin Luther King said it all in one sentence: "Injustice anywhere is a threat to justice everywhere." I'll drink to that. Cheers!

In 2007 the US prison population rose to an all-time high of 2.3 million, with more than one in every 100 adults in the US a prisoner. One in 106 white men, one in 36 Hispanic, and a staggering one in 15 black men are behind bars. That's America for you – the black man is a victim and men are buried and silenced in the bowels of their penal system. Many are political prisoners.

The longest-serving political prisoner in the US is Ruchell Cinque Magee. He was sentenced to one year to life in 1963 and 45 years later the man still rots away like a dog in a cave with a chain on. He became a self-educated, politically-conscious activist and studied law books in order to fight the system. Hence, he's still inside. They're afraid of him, afraid of the truth! They created the man, now they're at a loss as to what to do with him. We salute the man. 45 hard lost years. He gets all my respect. A true survivor for real!

Could you see Colin Moses surviving for 45 years in a hole? Ha, ha, ha! Could you? He couldn't last 45 minutes behind a door without falling to his knees and begging. They're all mouth those union reps: yap, yap, yap. They're full of shit. Have you noticed that union reps have always got big beer bellies and three chins? Have you clocked that? I wonder why. Fat, lazy fuckers…

Another serious miscarriage of justice has got to be the Peter Hakala case. The Old Bill falsified and fabricated two statements against him and he even has the evidence to prove it. He is now into his 22nd year of a life sentence. Imagine that! Ask yourself how this can be. Write to the guy and give him some support. Check his case out.

Peter Hakala
No L44089
HMP Frankland
Brasside
Durham
DH1 5YD

This guy's life is being sucked away over lies, and his case is the tip of the iceberg. There's hundreds like him. After 20 years he still can't see any light of hope; he's still in a max secure jail. But he will never give up the fight. How could he? He's innocent, and it's the innocence that keeps these guys going. The day they stop believing, they die! That's the way it is, they just go to sleep and don't wake up!

I'm a bit confused about the Criminal Case Review Committee allowing so many cases to continue when there is ample evidence that they're unsafe. A good lawyer should be able to smell a rat. Come on guys… look into their cases. Free the innocent and expose the guilty fuckers. And for all the people who seem to believe the police are whiter than coke, just have a serious think about this lot:

The Birmingham Six, the Guilford Four, the Worcester Three, the Cardiff Three, the Bridgewater Four.

Shall I continue?

Winston Silcott, Eddie Browning, Susan May, the Maguire Seven, 'Big H' McKenney, Bob Maynard, Reg Dudley…

I could go on and on and on! They're all innocent people, fitted up by the Old Bill and police informers. How else do you account for that lot? Some served over 20 years of their life for fuck all, and it makes my blood boil to think about it! So wake up, you lot who say it doesn't go on! It does, it has, and it always fucking will! This country hanged innocent people! That's how fucking clever the state is; they're the real villains. It's one big conspiracy. From the day you're born till the day you die, you're numbered and tagged. Welcome to the real world… Loonyology!

I wonder what ever happened to my old jock mate Ned Bannigan. I last saw him up in Hull jail in 1975. Fuck me, could he sing. Every morning and every night in the seg block on A/1 he would sing like Al Jolson. It was fucking brilliant with the echo of the cell. I used to look forward to it. We had no radio in the block in those days, so in a way Ned was our radio. He even used to take requests! It was fucking magic – our very own *Britain's Got Talent*! Max secure *X-Factor* for real! Once Ned had finished his song, we would all be cheering and banging on the doors for more. Great memories. Just because we were slammed up 24/7 with nothing but an empty cell, it didn't stop us having some laughs. You can bet your arse on that.

I was slopping out once in Hull block and I ripped a sink off the wall. All the screws legged it whilst I flooded the place out, then they all came running back in with their shields and sticks. It's a laugh a minute, but fuck me, you don't 'arf get hurt! For what it's worth, here's a bit of advice: give it a big miss!

There was a giant of a screw in Hull in the 1970s – he was fucking massive! Six feet eight and 20 stone – awesome. Believe it or not, he was a diamond. He did his job for a wage, not for power, and he always used to give me double helpings on the hot plate! I think he respected me for how I conducted myself. For example, I can put my hand on my heart and honestly say I have never chinned a screw for no reason. Some actually need chinning, it's true! Some are just total fucking idiots who haven't got a clue, and a lot of the old screws will agree with me on that!

I'll be happy to walk out of jail and never return. I mean that; I would sooner blow my brains out than come back to this madness. I'm not mad enough to return! Fuck that; when I get out it's forever. I want to die free – that's what I want.

30 May, 2008.

Come on, I bet you've missed me…

I've had a strange week. On Tuesday 27th I called my buddy Alan Rayment up and he had it all organised for a *Calendar* news reporter to be there, so I did a very rare interview and put a few things straight. (In other words, I put the side over that the public never hears.) On the 28th I was on TV news and on the 29th I had the governor at my door telling me that all my calls were now being monitored by security and that the line would be cut off if I tried that again. I said, "What's your problem, what are you afraid of? It's OK for you lot to feed the media with lies and pass on security photos of me, but as soon as I get my side of the story out, you lot start to panic. So who's running from the truth here?"

They really are gutless fuckers. A lot of the older screws agree with me, as they know what a farce this all is. I should have been moved from here years ago! Anyway, fuck it! My side of the story's now out, told by me, and the system doesn't like it. So if the phone gets cut off when I'm talking to you, you'll know why. Call the governor up and complain! Demand to be put back on and ask for an explanation in writing as to why they cut you off. If they had their way they would love to cut me right off from the real world, as they now fear me in a new way. I now fuck them and expose them at their own game (with a pen and paper)!

I've had a sackload of mail this week. One letter was from Emma Newey of the Thetford Town Cricket Club down in Norfolk asking for some art to auction off for the club. Sorted: two bits of art on the way. "Howzat?" My good deed for the week. (It's about time somebody did me a good deed!)

Hey! Did you know Vincent Van Gogh shot himself? What was the problem with that guy? I know artists are temperamental but he sure knew how to take it to a new level. Fucking nut case…

Who remembers Kirk Douglas in *Spartacus*? That was 50 years ago. He's now 91 and still looking strong! Good old Kirk! Let's have three cheers for the old chap! HIP HIP – HOORAY! HIP HIP – HOORAY! HIP HIP – HOORAY!

Get on this: David Geering, a detective with the Metropolitan Police Force, has just copped two and a half years for being a paedophile. He was a dirty nonce trading child porn with other sickos! A cop paedo – that about sums it all up! You just can't trust any fucker today. He should have got 20 years because he's a danger to the public. Would you trust the cunt with your kids? Would you fuck… What a sick planet this is; it's a pile of shit and it's starting to stink.

I've been getting loads of letters about *Loonyology* from readers from all walks of life. They're saying things like: "We love the book, it's your best ever and it's brilliant. Hurry up with volume 2. Will there be a 3? Can you post me a sticker to put in my book? Keep writing, Charlie, you're a born writer." Hey! Thanks guys. I mean that; it means a lot to me. Cheers!

It's June tomorrow – halfway through the year!

I got a crazy letter from a bird in Holloway jail called Rachel. I won't say her last name in case she's a mental case, but here it is:

Charlie,

I've been following you for years; you're my sort of bloke. I've had some nice dreams of us! I mean hot ones. In one you came all over my tits and it was beautiful. I want a baby… yours. Now.

So can you have a wank in a balloon and post it to me so I can impregnate myself? Hurry.

Rachel.

P.S. I'll bring the baby up to see you, as I'm out in 2009.

Yeah! It's Loonyology at its very best. Now, where can I get a balloon from…?

I see they've just found a new tribe in the Brazilian jungle. Why the fuck can't we leave them be? I bet they're a lovely bunch of people with free hearts! Soon they'll be paying the poll tax... Leave them alone I say! That would do me, living like that. A great free life to live! The sex must be brilliant: "Come here, love, bend over that tree stub." Whoosh – right up to the balls. That's what I call a fuck: out in the woods with the sun on your body and the breeze in your face. I bet you can have 10 wives. What a great existence; I'm jealous. All the women are nude, everywhere you look there's pussy. I'm jealous, aren't you? I would fly out there tomorrow for some of that. Have you ever seen their lips? It would be like sucking a slice of melon. Wonderful!

The grub was good today. Plenty of it, too. I'm having an early night tonight: 9pm I'll get my nut down! I feel like a good sleep. I'll be back. If I don't wake up, tell those cunts up in prison HQ I said that they're all a bunch of clowns and I'll be back to haunt the twats.

Good night, sleep tight.

Saturday, 31 May 2008.

"30 days in September, April, June and November. All the rest have 31, blah blah blah..." I forgot May has 31 days; I honestly thought today was the beginning of June! Could this be the start of dementia or senility? Who gives a fuck anyway? It could be Xmas day for all I care.

I woke up today and there was not a cloud in the sky. Early on, about 5.30am, I heard a train. I thought to myself, how nice would it be to be on that train with a good breakfast and a read of the paper? Maybe have a chat with someone interesting. There's something about a train ride – you just never know what going to happen. A thousand tons of metal whizzing by at 100mph – that's a gamble on its own. Yeah! I do love a train ride.

There was a bird singing and a breeze blowing in my window, it felt good... I pictured myself in a field of flowers! I could even smell it – beautiful! Half asleep, half awake, what is reality? Just a dream – we are all living the dream. How many will dream of winning the lottery today, or picking all the winners at the race course? How many dream of going out for a night and meeting their perfect partner? We all live the dream and that's all it is – one big fucked-up dream. One in every million probably comes true, so unless you're a fairy it's best not to count on it!

I got up at 6am and buried my head into a sink of cold water. Lovely. The dream stops there... Then a good brush on the 'Hampstead Heath' and the day starts with press-ups, sit-ups, squats. Get the blood pumping around the body! Have a walk up and down! Hop, skip and jump – anything to fight the boredom! Blow the black clouds away as it's so easy to drop into the bitter hole. You don't need that to start a day, because when the door opens it's just more shit and more confrontation you don't need. I like to walk out of my door fresh and happy, that's how it is with me. All the regular screws will tell you the same! They know me now; they know how I am and how I tick. They can't but know me with all the years we spend together on such a small unit. It should be up to them to decide when I'm ready to be released. All the screws here would free me today if they could, because they know I'm no danger. But it doesn't work like that. Nothing's that simple in life.

I had a bowl of Rice Krispies, three bread rolls with jam on them, and a nice mug of hot, sweet tea. You can't beat a cuppa rosey to start the day! I put Radio 5 on to get all the news and see what's happening in the world. Who's dead? Any earthquakes or floods? Who's dropped a bomb? Who's shagging who? Has Gazza gone mad again? Is Amy in rehab? How's Britney? Are Jordan's tits any bigger? Who won the *X-Factor*? Who's the new Nancy? Who gives a flying fuck? Do you?

I feel a cartoon coming on! I've got my art head on, so I'll be back later. It's only 9am now – I've got the whole day to kill yet! Dinner, tea, post, news, clean up my cell, shave my head, create an art, write some letters… a man's life is what it is. This is how it is and it's why I respect the tortoise; you'll see a lot of tortoise characters in my art. Why? Well, it's fucking obvious! If you can't work that one out then fuck off out of my life. You should stick to reading Harry Potter not the Bronson Diaries. So fuck off now, I don't need you pricks that can't see past your nose. Your nose is so far up someone's arse your face has turned brown! Fuck off, shit face!

Now, where was I? Oh yeah! I've got to uget on with my day, I've got to do what a man's got to do. That mug of tea has kicked in; a good strong cup is good for the bowels. I'm ready for my morning shit. There's nothing quite like my morning shit – a good dump to start off the day. I always feel lucky because there's untold thousands of people who can't shit in peace. Some are constipated, some suffer with diarrhoea, some have colostomy bags and some have bowel cancer. So all you happy, normal dumpers, be thankful because you're lucky! We really are blessed to be able to dump in peace. I see it as giving birth to a turd. It's a part of us, it really is. I'll be back – lighter and faster. I promise.

6.30pm.

What a brilliant day. I've really enjoyed it! But let me first say what a great dump I had this morning. I just knew afterwards that it would be a great day. I gave birth to a still-born turd any man would have been proud of; it slipped out of my body like honey off a spoon and it just felt so natural and good. Am I lucky or am I lucky?

I remember a con in Parkhurst back in 1976 who was on the hospital wing. He suffered with severe piles and the poor sod was in so much pain that he cried. Who said big tough cons don't cry? He did. This chap was in constant pain. One day the alarm bell went and they found him in the recess toilet in a pool of blood with a razor blade he had used to cut off the piles. There was blood everywhere. People don't understand about piles! Some are actually hanging out of your arse, and the very thought of having a shit with them must be murder. The pain must be agonizing! Anyway, he cut off his piles with a razor and got rushed to the surgery. Fuck knows what happened to him, as soon after that I shit the doctor up – a full bucket of shit over his head. I was moved straight after that. Yeah, you may ask why I covered him in shit but come to think of it, I can't remember why. It was probably just a boring day that needed cheering up! But back to piles… let's all be thankful we haven't got them and spare a thought for those that have. Poor sods. They do tell me that everybody will suffer with piles in their lifetime, so we have yet to experience it. Something to look forward to, I don't think!

When you sit down and think about it, old age must be bloody frightening and it's coming to us all. Our bodies just crumble – even the dick shrinks and becomes useless! What a fucking ending. I think I would prefer a gang of hoodies to kick me to death down some dark alley. Fuck me, where am I going with this? Snap out of it. It's Saturday, it's been a magical day and I'm alive and kicking. Yiiipppeeeeeee!

Hey, here's some interesting information for you! Say you're thinking of buying a house and you want to know which areas in the UK have the highest levels of crime, then log on to www.crimestatistics.org.uk or, even better, www.upmystreet.com. Just punch in a postcode and you'll get a run down on the area. That's got to be great information for house buyers, and you got it out of Loonyology! This isn't just a book or a diary of madness, it's freedom of information, it's educational, it's everything you need to survive out there in your crazy fucked-up world.

Take your MP, don't you want to know what they're up to? (Well, you should.) Log on to www.theyworkforyou.com – it's all on there, so check it out and keep those fuckers on their toes. They work for you so make them work, otherwise they'll sit on their fat lazy arses getting paid for fuck all.

I got a pile of letters today. There's one I've just got to share with you – you'll fucking love it...

Chaz,
I've just read your book *Loonyology*. I've never read so much shit in my life. You're either insane or you're just a total wanker! It's no wonder you're held in a cage. If I had my way you would be shot. Why should my tax pay for you? Hurry up and die!

Dave.

Well, Dave, I've got your full name and address, so in time I may pay you a visit; then we shall see who the wanker is. Writing a letter to a man in a coffin is a brave thing to do, but if we were face-to-face you would shit yourself. I could easily have a few of the chaps pay you a visit but that's not my game. Anyway, thanks for buying my book and reading the 500 pages, you sad fucker! How sad are you? Have a nice day. I hope you get piles – in fact you probably have got them and that's what's making you so grumpy and nasty. Good, it's all you deserve!

I created a nice A3 art with ink and pencil shade today! It's in black and white and I called it 'Born Man'. I'll post it out on Monday. (I've not decided who to, yet, but some lucky fucker's in for a treat).

One of my letters today was from Karen Griffiths of Pontypool, South Wales. A few years back I sent some art for her to auction off to raise money for her little girl Shauna, who was born a very sick child. I won't go into the details, but six years on she's still not very well and has to have a lot of care. Her mother has done her so proud! Anyway, I've just found out today (as Karen hadn't told me until now) that she gave my art to somebody who gave it to somebody else to auction off, but the money didn't get back to her. So some scumbag kept it or sold it for themselves

– either way, they stole from a sick child. Karen felt terrible over it so she let it go, but I'm not letting it go. I'm onto it now and the trace is on. I've got a lot of good contacts in Wales – some serious hatchet men, so watch this space...

In the meantime, more art is on the way for little Shauna! But it's sad Karen didn't tell me back then as it could have been sorted in no time: dosh back, a serious pull and a full apology; plus some serious compensation, like a nice holiday for Shauna and Karen! Nicking my art is a very serious crime; it's an act with Loonyversal consequences! ('Loonyversal' – hey, that's not a bad word. I like that; it sounds important!)

What sort of cunt nicks from a sick child? How sick does it get? I class that as I class a paedophile! You dirty low-life cunt; you should be in prison, not walking the streets. I hope you get bowel cancer and you die screaming. You're no better than Rose West or Myra Hindley – in my book you're a child abuser. And you stole my art (nobody does that); you stole my creations, sold them and lived off my goodwill. It's unforgivable. You need to be taught some respect. You actually deserve to be crippled so you can then learn to respect sick people. You need to suffer to be aware of what they go through! Start praying, cunt.

I got a crazy card today! Fuck knows what it means. It says:

Happy Birthday Michael Peterson, AKA Jack Palance or notoriously known as Charles Bronson. I have some advice for you: Audioslave – 'Exploder'. With love, Alan x

If anybody knows what the fuck this loon is on about, let me know, as I'm lost. There's no full name or address but the post mark is Berkshire. Broadmoor's in Berkshire, so could this Alan be a fellow lunatic? Could it be a code for something mysterious? Could be buried treasure. Somebody fucking tell me!

I also got some photos and a letter in from my cousin, Deborah Parry. It's years since I heard from her and she's still looking lovely. Her dad's my mum's brother. That cheered me up. Thanks, Debbie.

I got more letters from Ray Kray, my old buddy Eddie Clinton, Redd Menzies and six from well-wishers, so it was a great day for outside contact! There was lots of news: some sad, some good. But my best letter today was from Sandra Gardner, who's always got a good story for me. Her life's a complete roller coaster and she's a laugh a minute. She's a good soul and a great friend to me!

I had a fry-up for dinner and a read of the *Daily Mail*. The headline on the front page said: 'Be Nice to Mr Huntley'. The governor up in Frankland jail has told his staff to be nice to Cuntley (ooops, sorry – Huntley) to keep his spirits up so that he doesn't try to kill himself again, poor thing. How the fuck can this be front-page news in a national newspaper? Who gives a flying fuck about Cuntley? Be nice to him? Who the fuck wants to be nice to him? Guards have been instructed to humour him and play chess and Scrabble with him! How nice for the screws! It's fucking madness at its very best! You can't make this shit up.

Tea was OK today – I had bananas and custard. The only bad part of my day was seeing the cannibal out on the yard! He's an evil bastard. One look at him and it makes me feel nasty. I'd do anything to punch a hole in his head. The day he threatened to eat my brain was the day Maudsley became my enemy. The very thought of that cunt eating my brain makes me feel angry. I'm trying to leave my violence in the past, but how can I with such insane neighbours? Could you? Anyway, fuck him, he's on Mars! He landed there years ago; he lost his light the day he ate Alan Francis' brain in Broadmoor. Lights out.

Yeah, it's been a nice day today! I'm chilled out, I feel like a polar bear on an iceberg, I feel good. You can't buy that feeling; it's a part of you deep inside. People try to get to my level but they fall off. My level is unique and only the chosen few ever reach it. 'King of the Loonyverse' – that's me! Who are you?

I'm beyond sanity and I just buzz off a loony like this 'fruit and nutter' Kumar Suleman. He's a burglar, but when he broke into a house in Luton he sort of lost the plot. He climbed into bed with the young married couple and fell asleep, so when they woke up they found him in between them. Fuck me – is that insane or is it insane? The couple jumped out of bed in shock. The judge at Luton Crown Court gave him an indeterminate sentence and said he will only be freed when the parole board thinks he is safe to be freed! Come on, this guy's a fucking mental case with 'Broadmoor' written across his head! Now see what I mean when I say the system's mad? It's pure Loonyology at its most insane and I fucking love it! You can't make this shit up. If it wasn't for loonies like Suleman, where would we be? Bored fucking suicidal. We love a nutter, don't we?

Loonyotorium –
It's a room
My secret room
Full of dreams
Full of madness
Full of nightmares
It's inside my head
Wrapped around my brain.
Loonyotorium!
It's where I go
For peace
For pleasure
You really don't want to go there
Best forget I said it
Said what?
Forgot already
Some things are best left alone
In the darkness
Behind the shadows
Buried away.
Pass the chilli sauce
Thanks.

I remember a lunatic who got out of Broadmoor and believed his hands weren't his, so he chopped them off. Now that's insanity at its very limit. It doesn't get any madder, does it? Can it? Believe me, it can and it does! There was another nutter in Rampton who believed he was the reincarnation of Guy Fawkes and his dream was to finish off the job Guy fucked up all those hundreds of years ago. Guess what? 30 years later he's still dreaming behind the walls of Rampton asylum. I wonder why? Poor old guy…

Did you know the Polo mint is 60 years old and that gobstoppers are made from over 1,000 coats of sugar? No wonder kids have bad teeth! 1,000 coats of sugar; that's insane! But it's a fact.

Here's a sweet fact for you: the roots of the liquorice plant can stretch to five feet and they're a lot sweeter than sugar cane. Not a lot of people know that, but you do now!

The first stick of Brighton Rock was first sold in 1902. I wonder how many have been sold since. It must be billions if not trillions! Sugar syrup is all it's made of, so clean your teeth or they'll rot away!

Who remembers sherbet dip dabs with the liquorice stick? I used to love them as a boy. If I had a penny for every one I nicked out of the corner shop, I'd be rich. Where I come from, kids never bought sweets, we nicked them! I even used to nick the bubblegum machines from outside the shops, then I'd sell them at school! That's how it was done in my day – why buy it when you could nick it? A bag of sweets to a boy is equivalent to a bag of dosh to a robber; it's that simple. I still love a sweet! Who doesn't?

Did you know insects can make a good protein-rich meal? Take a giant water beetle, lay it on its back and cut open the thorax, then cut out the meat like you would do with a crab. The meat is a lot like watermelon – very fruity tasting. It's got protein, fat, carbohydrate and calcium in it. If you had a good 20 of them with some fresh salad, you would have a bloody good meal. Grasshoppers are nice fried with garlic. They're very crunchy and full of protein and carbohydrates! How do I know all this? Let's just say I learnt it years ago from an old survival master.

Take the cricket: catch 30 of the fuckers and you have a good solid meal full of protein and calcium, including iron. Mix them up with some savoury rice – delicious! If you're starving out in the woods (maybe on the run from the law), look around you – they're full of grub. Find a red ants' nest; enough of them will be a good meal. Roast the fuckers with some berries! Lovely jubbly!

I'm not joking – it's all survival and it's the test of man! Find it, kill it, eat it! The planet's full of nosh everywhere you look: dogs, cats, rats, birds, fish and worms. A bowl of maggots will keep you alive and kicking. Add some herbs and spices and you'll be in for a treat.

In North Africa the locusts are called 'shy prawns'. Can you believe that? A fucking swarm of prawns. After all, insects are only arthropods (that's a great word, that is) and arthropods are much like crabs and lobsters, only smaller. In places like Taiwan, you get stir-fried crickets or a bowl of maguey worms, sautéed caterpillars or slugs on toast. It's all true! Wake up. Anyone for a vodka scorpion lolly? Cheers!

There was a Bengali lunatic in Broadmoor who used to make a wicked 'Ruby Murray' – I mean delicious. But now I look back, I wonder what the fuck he was putting in those curries, as he was forever catching spiders, roaches and earwigs! What goes into any curry? Do we really know? Do we fuck... you could be eating anything – even human flesh or organs! Well, how do you know you haven't? You will never know!

Big Jake Thompson could eat for Britain. I met Jake in Wandsworth jail in the 1970s; he was six feet seven and a good 20 stone. He'd never used a gym in his life; he was just a naturally big man. The screws used to shit themselves on hot-plate duty when Jake came up for feeding. Cons only get a basic diet and screws are there to make sure we all get the same portion: five slices of bread, one tot of margarine, one spoon of sugar, one ladle of chips, blah blah blah... But Jake got what he fucking wanted! In those days we had steel trays, and it was in Dartmoor that Jake put one in a screw's face and opened it up like a pilchard. So the screws were very wary of him and Jake had treble the amount most had. There wasn't a body belt big enough for him! Nobody wanted to upset him. Would you? He later got out and some cunt stabbed him to death in the back. That's how it all ends up for some. Jake made guys very paranoid; you were always on edge when he was near! He was like a giant from a legend and was a man of few words, but he loved his grub!

A lot of cons build themselves up in jail. The 'muscle mob' go around saying, "Look how big my biceps are! I'm hard I am, must get some more steroids. Feel my abs, look at my calves!" Cunts. They don't realise you can't pump 'bottle' and that you're either born hard or soft. So many act the tough guy but believe me, life in jail is not about how big your muscles are, it's more about how you conduct yourself and how you come across to others. It's about self-discipline, and a 20-inch bicep doesn't make a guy any stronger. The strength is from within – dig for it.

There was a transvestite in Winston Green jail in the 1980s. He/she/it – whatever – looked like Una Stubbs from *Till Death Do Us Part*, and I really mean that. He was a one off, with tight jeans, a tight top, make up, the walk, the hair! Even the screws fancied him, but they fancy anything with an arse so nothing new there! He was called 'Hot Lips' and boy, oh boy did he get through some cock! No wonder he walked like he'd just got off a horse. He was caught in the shower with three Rastafarians, dirty bastards, and his arsehole must have been like a blood orange! A screw once told me that when he was on nights he saw Hot Lips and a cell mate in the 69 position, and when he flicked the light on, Hot Lips shouted, "Fancy a threesome?" Guys like Hot Lips must come to jail for a fucking big party; it must be one big candy trip for them. But get on this, you won't believe this, it's insane! His wife (yeah, wife!) used to visit him every month with his three kids. So one day he's sucking cock like it's gone out of fashion, then he's kissing his kids. The world's gone mental. Every jail has got its 'queens' – mostly they're the governors...

It was in Albany jail that a queen called 'Mary' stabbed a con to death in the tailor shop. He got manslaughter for that. Strangely enough, a lot of the chaps stuck up for Mary at the time and said the con was bullying him. Years later in Parkhurst, Mary got his throat cut (I don't know why) but he survived. As I write this he is still locked up. He has done 30 years if not longer. He was always respectful to me and looked after me in the hospital wing in Parkhurst back in 1992 after my stabbing. He gave me milk, cheese and plenty of grub. I never forget such kindness. You can't. It's an old man's journey and you just never know who are you gonna bump into next. It could be Santa, then again it could be Lucifer! Knowing my luck it will be Jesus, another bleeding lunatic.

Here's one prison governor they would like us all to forget: Martin Lay. But I'll never forget him, you can count on me. Lay was a governor in Stafford prison, but in 2002 he was up in court for 'flashing' and he was sacked after 22 years' service. The old pervo was kicked out of the prison service! He exposed himself to a cleaner and he obviously denied it, but the cleaning woman described a distinctive mark on his privates. Bang to rights, you old pervo. Gross misconduct. Hand your keys in on the way out. Bye bye. There went his 35 grand a year, all for flashing at some old cleaning lady. I keep telling you but you don't listen: it's all fucking Loonyology and the best is yet to come!

4 June 2008.

I had a great visit from my tattoo buddy Mark Jones today. We always have a good chat and catch up with all the latest news. Just recently he's been having some tattoos of my art done. Punters want my art on their bodies. How fucking good is that? How magical does it get? Can it get any better? I doubt it – what would be better than that?

Hey! What about this for a blinder: in May 2000, Christina Riggs became the first woman to be executed in Arkansas in over 150 years. She got the lethal injection for killing her babies. Fucking good job too. The previous execution was Lavinia Burnett back in 1845. (You get all the news in *Loonyology*.)

I got a pile of mail today, including a lovely card from an old lady in Crewe who's just read my book *The Krays and Me* and says she wishes they were both still alive, as the streets would be safer! Well, Nelly, you're 100% spot-on. By the way, I'm about to sort you out a nice piece of art and a signed copy of *Loonyology: In My Own Words*. Expect a parcel, my old china, and keep strong. You get out in the sun, it will do you good. The sun rays are good for arthritis; that's why a lot of old folk move out to Spain. Enjoy it, Nelly. Nelly's a good old name! I do love the old-fashioned names; they have character.

I called up Mark Emmins today. The fucking idiots are now timing and monitoring my calls, but there's more than one way to skin a cat! If they start cutting me off, I'll just stop all my calls and go back to how it should be: us and them. Fucking silly control freaks.

Did you know that in 1952, the year I was born, King George VI died? He was my age now: 56. Also that year, the Olympic Games opened in Helsinki and 17-year-old Little Mo of the USA won Wimbledon. Anne Frank's diary was published and Agatha Christie's latest play *The Mousetrap* opened! (How do I know all this? Well, I'm a flash cunt.) Chrissie Hynde (that bird in leather trousers in the Pretenders – one hot cookie) and Jimmy Connors were born and to top it all, the last tram ran in London. You remember the old tram lines like the one's they still have in Blackpool (I take it they still have them) – they were brilliant. I remember them in Northampton.

I fucking loved them.

Yeah, '52 was a good year for us all! However, I wish I'd been born in 1932 because back then I would've been the No. 1 bank robber. It was so easy in the '40s and '50s with PC Plod on a fucking push bike and no CCTV! How the fuck would they stop a bank raid? Who in their right mind would work for peanuts when they could walk into a bank, fill up a bag and walk out? Come on, tell me it's a dream! Yeah, I would be 76 now, but a wealthy old man. Still, it's no good living on 'ifs' and 'buts'. This is my time now. Fuck yesterday, we want tomorrow.

Tragedy

October the first, nineteen thirty-three
One-eyed Jack heard the key
The sweat trickled down his spine
Now's the time to walk the line
He looked around that bare old cell
Jack felt like an empty shell
Sentenced to hang he feared this day
Six feet under soon he will lay
Trembling, he could not speak
Thirty years old, everything bleak
All his life a farmer's son
His pa was killed with his gun
Memories were passing by
Like the day he lost his eye
How he loved his wonderful wife
Soon the noose will end his life
Two prison guards lead the way
Jack swallowed hard as he prayed
A dozen more surrounded him
All this for his father Jim
His one eye stared with fear
Down his cheek ran a tear
Mouth all dry, legs so weak
Jack felt just like a freak
They reached the door he couldn't look
The preacher stood with his holy book
The governor, doctor, hangman too
Jack knew that he was through
He saw the noose dangling there
Soon he knew his neck would tear
Jack didn't want to die
Christ almighty, why oh why
His whole body was drenched in sweat
Like a beast trapped in a net
The hangman bound his hands and feet
Everybody there felt the heat
They all watched the noose slip on
He saw in the corner his brother John

Jack requested to have John there
The governor thought this only fair
The preacher man came up to Jack
Few words and pat his back
Brother John came over to talk
John's face as white as chalk
The governor said, "This must be it
I hope everybody has said their bit."
Nine o'clock, two minutes to go
Johnny saying, "Please God no."
The blindfold Jack refused
He did not want to feel abused
His one eye was on his brother John
Something is tragically wrong
Thirty seconds and Jack will hang
The trap door opens with a bang
John cried deep inside
Jack's one eye was opened wide
It opened fast, Jack was gone
A broken neck all for John
He died a man, he died with pride
But the truth he had to hide
That night Johnny slashed his throat
They found a letter in his coat
His conscience couldn't take no more
Watching Jack go through the floor
This story is very sad
One-eyed Jack loved his dad
October the first nineteen thirty-three
We pray for Jack, it was not he.

I wrote a book of poems in Broadmoor in 1981 called *Poetry From Hell* and this was one of them. I hope you liked it; it would make a great song!

The grub was good today and we had chips for tea! I love a chip butty with red sauce and a nice mug of tea. Am I lucky or am I lucky? Good night, sleep tight.

5 June 2008.

I got a very special letter today: Rita Neale wrote to me from Watford and told me her son was born on 11 February. She's named him Connor Bronson Neale in my honour. How brilliant is that? It's made me feel proud that has. Thanks, Rita. I'll create a nice art for the little chap tonight so she can give it to him later in life. It almost makes me feel a part of the human race. Wicked, cool man, squeeze my melon, chilled.

I see the latest James Bond book, *Devil May Care* by Sebastian Faulks, has sold 44,000 in the first four days (not bad for a hardback). 44,000 copies in less than a week! Would I write a Bond book? 'Never say never.' If the Fleming estate want to make me an offer I can't refuse, I'll start it tonight. (After I've created Connor Bronson's art, that is. Kids come first.)

I'm open to offers but I don't come cheap!

Did you know 5,000 violent criminals have been released under the new controversial scheme to reduce prison overcrowding so far this year (and it's only June)? 1,400 of them were foreigners (who haven't been deported). So now we know that, tell us how many are back inside? I bet it's well over half, if not three-quarters. So why was I not one of the 5,000? What's so special about Bronson that he can't join in on the early release scheme to help the overcrowding? Come on, ask some questions! I will be.

I got nine letters today – all crackers. I had a great work-out on the yard in the sun and sweated three or four pounds off. After my visit yesterday it had to be done. It's all well and good drinking milkshakes and eating chocolates, but who really wants to end up looking like Johnny Vegas, Vanessa Feltz or Bernard Manning? Do you? I fucking don't. Imagine all that fat hanging down – you wouldn't be able to see your bollocks and all the sweat stays in the flabby creases and throws off a smell of old cheese. Fuck that, it's unhealthy!

I bet the PC brigade are thinking, "Bronson should not be allowed to say such things." Well, I'm fucking saying it: fat people smell and you know it's the truth, so why pretend? At least I'm honest. They eat too much and they burp and fart a lot so they're fucking up our planet and the ozone layer! All that gas can't be doing Earth's atmosphere any good, can it? If I was the prime minister I'd have them locked up on a fatty farm! I'd call it 'Flabby Asylum' and the fat bastards wouldn't be able to come out until they were cured. If you didn't like it, you could piss off to another country and take your gas with you! Great Britain doesn't need you lot. Get a fucking life. I'm sorry but I'm only being truthful. If you don't like the truth then put this book down now.

What about big noses? You've all seen those large beaks; they're not normal and they scare the kids. Sort it – if you can't afford a nose job then get somebody to bust it and flatten it out. We don't want to see big noses – big, ugly, pointed conks. We don't like them; they put us off our food! They look like a silly mask from a fucking horror film, so sort your silly noses out, I say. Enough's enough...

OK, you might think that I'm a nasty cunt, but I'm a truthful nasty cunt. At least respect my honesty. Call me a cunt by all means. I speak the truth, the whole truth and nothing but the truth, so God help my soul. At times I may hold back on names, but only because I have to protect the guilty and the insane! (The innocent and sane are capable of doing it for themselves.)

Hey! I had mushroom soup with six brown rolls today! Tea was pizza, chips and beans. I enjoyed it and it went down a treat. I called Mum – she's a laugh! We always have a bubble (bubble bath – laugh). She's watching *Big Brother* later tonight; it's the new series – another load of shit. If I was free I could think of a thousand better things to do than watch *Big Brother*. The weather's good, so head for the hills with a packet of condoms and two tarts. Why not? That's what I call enjoying life! A crate of beer, some cheese rolls and plenty of pussy... what's wrong with that? A threesome with the sun blazing down on your back, that's living. Fuck *Big Brother*! I'd sooner dive in the ocean and strangle a shark. I get seriously bored, so I've always got to be doing something or talking about doing something. Right now, I've got a four-month-old baby boy to create an art for, so I'm off. I'll be back later! Enjoy *Big Brother* you sad people. *Adios amigos*, and *Salaam* to my Muslim brothers and sisters! (Why is it that Asian girls are so beautiful? They're angels.)

6 June 2008.

Sandra Gardner sent me a book called *Essex Boys, The New Generation*. I'll have a good read of that at the weekend; I do love a read. Sandra's a good friend.

Hey! Get on this: a poxy traffic warden is on 20K a year and a soldier is on 16K. Can you fucking believe that? That sums it all up for me! The government doesn't give a flying fuck about our forces coming back in zip-up bags; they respect the traffic wardens more. Cunts. Wake up country, it's time to wake the fuck up! How can a muggy old traffic warden get paid more than a soldier? Somebody tell me.

You'll love this: the world's most expensive zip is worth £710,000. Imagine that on your jeans. It's got 221 55-carat marquise diamonds on it. You can't make it up. What lunatic's gonna buy that? Van Cleef and Arpels made it, but why? What for? A fucking zip!

Now, take your time and read the following lines out loud and fast. The average person over 40 can't do it!

1 – THIS IS THIS CAT
2 – THIS IS IS CAT
3 – THIS IS HOW CAT
4 – THIS IS TO CAT
5 – THIS IS KEEP CAT
6 – THIS IS AN CAT
7 – THIS IS OLD CAT
8 – THIS IS FART CAT
9 – THIS IS BUSY CAT
10 – THIS IS FOR CAT
11 – THIS IS FORTY CAT
12 – THIS IS SECONDS CAT

Now go back and read the third word in each line from the top down.

You old fart!

Here's a bit of historic boxing news for you. The great-grandfather of actor Peter Sellers was a legendary 19th-century bare-knuckle prize fighter called Daniel Mendoza. How's about that! Not a lot of people know that! (Now you do.)

The governor did his rounds today and asked how I was. "Sweet, Governor," I said. How do you think I am? How the fuck would you be, stuck in a concrete coffin 24/7? Come on, tell me – how would you be? Yeah, how would he be if he was serving a life sentence like I am? Cunt. I'm sure they only come round to wind us up! Imagine some cunt knocking on your door outside and saying, "Hello, how are you?" Cunt. I'm only happy when my door's shut and I'm left in peace!

Genilson Lino Da Silva, one of Brazil's biggest drug barons, is in

Salvador jail. Guess what? The police stormed the prison and found his cell contained 87 grand in cash, a fridge, a plasma TV, two guns and a king-size bed. State prosecutor Paula Gomes, who is probing the scandal at the jail, reckons the prison boss is responsible. You don't say. Like I've always said, every man's got a price. 87 grand in cash in a prison cell? He was living it up big style. Dosh buys anything and everything. Why did he need a king-size bed? Come on, there was pussy in there for the weekend! I'll bet my arse on that… well, not my arse, I'll bet our Wakefield governor's arse. Fuck betting my own arse – I want to die a virgin! No fucker's having my brown eye. You can bet your arse on that…

Oh well, here's last month's monthly review! I only got it today; that's how slow this place is. Read and digest it, then ask yourselves what it's all about. Is this really enough hard evidence to justify keeping a man on a max secure isolated unit for year after year? For me, it's a fucking piss-take and there is no justification to hold me here! Britain's most dangerous man? Do me a favour you fucking idiots – grow up and get a life!

I was talking to an old screw today who's been in the job over 30 years. He said to me, "Charlie, it's now embarrassing having to lock you up. We all know it's a joke, but we don't know how you stay so positive and cool. Years ago you would have bowled us over like skittles!" Yeah, boss, I must be getting old.

Remember, targets are not being assessed at this review, they are being updated following a discussion about progress.

Overarching Target identified by LSP and OASys documents, such as *'Learn to manage stress more effectively'*	**Targets** These should always be positively framed and should take the form of a statement, e.g. *"completes stress management session with officer Smith each week".*	**Staff Action** This refers to things staff may want to agree to do to support the target, for example, *'Officer Smith to agree a time with Mr Bloggs at the beginning of each week for when the session can take place'*
	Charlie to continue to interact positively with staff on the unit.	All Staff and Visitors
	Charlie to make use of the available facilities	Charlie
	To be advised about the Well Man Clinic	Leaflet Information
	Charlie not to engage in verbal confrontations with other offenders within the unit.	Charlie
	Charlie to remain adjudication free	Charlie
	Charlie to be encouraged to discuss any ongoing issues with the unit staff.	Charlie
	Charlie to consider re-engaging with the units cleaning duties	Charlie Personal Officer

Crisis Plan

Medical Interventions: -Charlie will be offered medical intervention if required, and will be made through the healthcare centre at HMP Wakefield.

Mental Health Interventions: -Charlie will be offered support from the Humber centre if appropriate, or requested.

Psychological Interventions: - Charlie will be offered psychological support if he request it from within the establishments team.

Monthly Report

(To be submitted to CSCSC)

This report is to be completed by an SO following the monthly case review. An overall assessment of the month's progress should be reflected in this report with specific comments on targets set. It should be a reflection of the Multi-disciplinary teams view.

Previous minutes read and agreed.
Has made good use of exercise and gym etc in the last month.
Has received a lot of publicity in the press and on TV recently but this has not brought about a change in his demeanour.
Also a recent telephone interview shown on TV has caused him to have to book telephone calls instead of having free access. This he has accepted with no problems.
In all a quiet month in spite of the above.
His unlock level to remain the same.

Completed by: **CSC Team** Date: 29/05/2008
(On behalf of the MDT)

Recommendation to the CSCSC
Completed by the Chair on behalf of the Multi-disciplinary Team

Charlie to remain within CSC at Wakefield and is correctly placed at this time.

Date: 29th May 2008. Signed: [signature]

Prisoner Comments (RECEIVED 6.6.2008)
Date:

ANOTHER MONTH STOLEN FROM MY LIFE WHERE YOU ARE DENYING ME ANY FORM OF PROGRESS. "YOUR JUST HYPOCRITES."

Like I told you, soon this will all be exposed for what it is: a piss-take. How the fuck can I ever be freed when I'm denied any form of progress? I can't! So what's the point in wasting my time planning ahead or being positive? The cunts don't ever want to see me progress and that's the truth. They will have to be forced to move me on! Then I'll probably be fitted-up with a tool planted in my cell, or they'll get some grass to say I'm planning to take a hostage. He gets parole and I get moved back into a cage. It's so easy to fix me up, and all of you who think it doesn't happen, go and shake your heads and wake up.

I got a lovely letter today from Mrs Beryl Kelly of Dudley. (I wonder if she knows the Anslow brothers.) Anyway, this is it:

Dear Charles,
I have just finished reading your Loonyology book and I must say I could not put it down. I could not believe in this day and age a human could be treated as bad as you have been. I am about to write to my MP and I will be signing your petition to free you. So will all my family and friends. It's got to be a serious injustice keeping you isolated away for all those years, it's obvious you have changed, and you should be very proud of all your achievements, especially your art. You're a very gifted man. Don't give up Charles, and don't allow the system to drag you down to their level. To me it's obvious they don't want you to be freed! Don't give up Charles.

Beryl x

Thanks, Beryl! You're very kind and very alert. You're also spot-on saying they don't want me to be freed. It's a wonder the fuckers don't poison me and have done with it. Problem solved. It does make one wonder what the end will be! Stick around, it should be good.

When it comes to statements, they don't come any better than these prats. Read on and make up your own mind! Bear in mind it's 1994 (the mad decade) but even so this statement is still over the top. It truly makes Loonyology come alive. Enjoy it as much as I myself enjoyed it at the time. Muppets paradise!

(C. J. Act 1967, ss. 2,9:M.C.Act 1980, s. 102; M.C. Rules 1981, r.70)
HUMBERSIDE POLICE
Four MG 11M

Witness Statement

Statement of Adrian Thomas WALLACE
Age if under 21 Over 21 (if over 21 insert 'over 21')

This statement (consisting of 11 pages each signed by me) is true to the best of my knowledge and belief and I make it knowing that, if it is tendered in evidence, I shall be liable to prosecution if I have willfully stated in it anything which I know to be false or do not believe to be true.
Dated the 21 day of April 1994.
Signature A WALLACE

I am the above named and I am employed by the Home Office as Deputy Governor, Her Majesty's Prison, Hedon Road, Hull. I have been engaged in this capacity at Hull for 2 years 3 months and have worked within the prison service working my way through the ranks, for about 23 years. My duties have taken me all around the country and prior to my current post I was based at the North Allerton prison. My current position at Hull is as the Head of Operations and part of my time is spent supervising the 'Special Unit' on 'A' wing.

This unit houses only 4 inmates. They are categorised as special prisoners and are placed on this unit because they cannot interact with the mainstream prisoners. The unit is specially contained and they are given more independance in an attempt to replace them into routine prison life.

The four prisoners on the unit are Anthony McULLAGH 21/4/67, Paul FLINT 21/4/64, Edward SLATER 28/4/64 and Charles BRONSON 6/12/52. This latter prisoner changed his name to BRONSON from Michael Gordon PETERSON. He has been at Hull since November 1993 , previously being at ~~Dill Station~~ AW Frankland prison. BRONSON is an extremely large man. He is about 5' 11" tall but has a huge physique, like 'Geoff Capes'. He has a shaven head and a large handlebar moustache. He is an extremely fit man, spending a lot of time working out. He is currently serving an 8 year sentence for conspiracy to rob and has spent the vast majority of his adult life inside institutions. He is presently AW awaiting trial for a previous incident in which he took a librarian as hostage. The other 3 prisoners are all serving life sentences but even they are frightened of BRONSON. It is fair to say that I am and have been aware of his potential for being dangerous since he came to Hull.

Part of my duties, as stated previously, involve the regular visits to both staff and prisoners on this block. During the last few weeks I have been aware that BRONSON has been more and more agitated as his trial approaches. I have been informed that he had spoken recently about taking a hostage, this information being passed onto me by other prison staff.

Shortly after 9.00am on Monday 4th April 1994 I commenced my duties on 'A' wing. I walked into the block and everything appeared perfectly normal, just like any other Monday morning.

As I walked into the block I became aware of the prisoners filing out of the kitchen, to my left. I said 'Good morning' to them. I noticed that BRONSON was at the rear of the group but as soon as he saw me he pushed the other prisoners aside and rushed at me. He grabbed me around the neck and pushed me towards the wall. BRONSON was behind me with his forearm around my neck, pushing my chin up. He had come at me so quickly that I did not have time to avoid him and similarly the other prison staff did not have time to react.

BRONSON held me tightly around the neck applying pressure to my throat. He shouted at the staff 'Don't come near or I'll break his neck'. He then dragged me backwards, walking with his back to the wall, along the corridor and dragged me to the T.V. room (T.V. room 2). He threw me down in the TV room and then sat me down, telling me to put my hands behind my neck. BRONSON was extremely agitated and was not in any sort of state to be questioned or upset. BRONSON then began barricading the door with the tables and chairs in the T.V. room.

I remained sat on the: chair in the middle of the room. The chair was a tubular metal chair with a ~~yellow~~ AW thinly padded vinyl seat. Initially I was sat facing the door of the T.V. room and I recall BRONSON, speaking through the windows with one of the prison officers, Roy KIRK. BRONSON was saying that I was a bastard and that nobody liked me. He said to me "If you move, I'll kill you". There is no doubt that I took this threat seriously bearing in mind the mans history and mental instability. I was frightened, and was in a situation that was completely out of my control. BRONSON was able to do anything to me.

I was dressed in a blue pin stripe suit, brown/white striped shirt, tie and a pair of black shoes. BRONSON was wearing a dark AW track suit bottoms and a sleeveless vest and yellow painted prison boots AW He took my tie off and tied my hands together behind my back but not fastened to the chair. BRONSON was still very agitated at this time and I realised that my best option was to act quiet. BRONSON punched me a few times across my right cheek and also to the back of my head knocking me to the ground. He dragged me back up by the scruff of the neck and put me back on the chair. BRONSON was telling me I was a 'bag of shit' and said nobody liked me and that he was going to kill me. He was pacing around the room. He told me that he knew there would be police sharpshooters brought in and that I would be killed as well.

BRONSON rifled my pockets. He took my prison radio from me and asked me how it worked. He put all the items out of my pockets onto the table in front of me and then threw the items around the room and onto the floor. He took my prison keys out of my pocket and as he ~~pulled these out~~ AW took my wallet he ripped my trousers down the right side.

He picked up my wallet off the table and began throwing the credit cards around the room and started ripping up the notes. He picked up an iron that was in the room and held it close to my face. He said "I'm going to batter you with this cunt and stave your head in". It is difficult to put into words my thoughts and feeling whilst this was going on but I honestly felt in fear for my life.

All this that I have described took place in the first few minutes of the incident. BRONSON then turned me around on the chair so that I was facing away from the door. The windows of the room were therefore behind me.

The room in which I was is about 10' foot square. The chair was placed along the wall to the left about 4 or 5 feet from the door. Most of the time I was sat facing the side wall or the back wall AW BRONSON told me not to speak and kept pacing up and down behind me. He was kicking the furniture around and snorting. BRONSON asked me how the prison radio worked and I explained to him.About 30 minutes into the incident BRONSON told me to get on the radio. He told me what to say and I passed a message saying that he wanted us both to leave the prison together, that if there were any SAS or Royal Marines in the prison that they had better shoot us both. I told the communications room that Charlie had done jungle warfare and was not 'fucking' about. BRONSON held the radio whilst I spoke into it.

I continued to sit quietly on the chair facing the T.V. I was aware Roy KIRK, the prison officer, was watching through the glass windows. I could not see BRONSON but could hear him pacing up and down behind me. He told me to sit still and not to speak. BRONSON turned the sound up on the T.V. the station was tuned into pop music and when he turned it up it became very noisy.

Shortly after BRONSON asked for a cup of tea an;' he asked me if I wanted one. I told him that I did because I didn't want to upset him any further. He shouted his request to the officers in the corridor and a few minutes later BRONSON partly moved the barricade and the cups of tea were pushed through. I told BRONSON that I wouldn't be able to drink my tea with my hands tied and so he undid them. He told me however to keep one hand in my pocket, which I did. I expected that later he would re-tie my hands but he never did.

I had a watch on but was unable to look at it in case BRONSON saw me. AW However I heard BRONSON talking with Roy KIRK about an 11 o'clock deadline and said that he wouldn't hurt me until that time had elapsed, as he was a man of his word.

During the incident although I had full sense of my faculties I was not in control at any time. Many things went through my mind about the things BRONSON could and would do. I recall at one point, which I believe was after the 11 o'clock deadline, that BRONSON stood behind me, I could not tell how close he was, but ~~I heard him unzip his trousers~~ My first thought was that he was going to inflict some form of sexual abuse on me but instead he urinated in a bucket. As soon as he had finished I thought the bucket would be poured over my head and prepared myself for it, but it never came.

A few minutes later Charlie got back on the radio, the radio had been switched on all the time and we could hear the day to day running of the prison continuing on it. Charlie called up saying that he wanted the prison closing down and that he didn't want any further talk over the radio. He made some reference to having some mushrooms stolen last week, but I couldn't make much sense of that.

Shortly after that Charlie told me to get on the radio. He told me to ask for his blow-up doll and that he wanted it dressing up in a black skirt, black tights. I asked the communications officer to acknowledge that my message had been received, which he did. Charlie had told me to do it right and threatened me with violence if I didn't comply.

Charlie picked up my keys (prison [security] keys) [AW] and asked me about them. He wanted to know which doors they fitted and said that he was going to try them on the doors. By this time Charlie had calmed down a bit but because he is so volatile I thought it best not to try and engage him in any sort of conversation. I was aware however that the officers outside were trying to negotiate with him and I kept my mind active by running through the procedural matters that the negotiators would be going through in order to resolve and contain the situation. I myself have been in incidents of this type before but obviously the situation is completely different when you are the hostage. I do recall thinking that I shall have the windows in the T.V. room replaced with glass that can be broken should the need arise. The windows are presently fitted with unbreakable glass.

A while later, again I cannot say what time, but assume it was about lunch time, BRONSON told me to call up on the radio and ask for two steak and chips, one for himself, one for me. BRONSON said he wanted it in five minutes. Again I passed this message to the communications room.

I then became aware that BRONSON was becoming more and more agitated. He began pacing up and down and seemed to be working himself up. For the first time for quite a while I became frightened again. BRONSON smashed one of the chairs in the room, an armchair, and took the padded seat of the chair, he placed it across my chest, strapping it in place with a sheet which he ~~secured~~ tied behind my back. BRONSON had told me that he knew police tactics and knew that they would soon start drilling holes into the walls to listen to him and see what was going on in the room. He told me that he was going to move me. He picked me up again grabbing me around the neck. He moved the barricade out of the way and opened the door to the room. He walked me out into the corridor, again warning the other prison officers to keep away. BRONSON had me tightly around the neck and was stood behind me. I assume he had placed the chair seat onto my chest to act as some form of protection in case someone tried to shoot him. BRONSON walked me along the corridor and then dragged me into the adjoining T.V. room, only a few yards away from the first room. Again he barricaded the door to prevent the prison staff getting in, using two chairs and a table, however the barricade was not as heavy as the first one. Again BRONSON sat me down and shouted for another cup of tea, which was brought a few minutes later. I felt I had to drink it just to keep him happy. Once I'd finished it I said to him "Can I put it down" but BRONSON snorted back "No, I'm in charge! He started to puff and puff and snort and somebody came to the window and he shouted "Fuck off. I don't want to talk to you". He was becoming more and more exciteable and grabbed the radio. He said he was going to come back on the radio in 5 minutes, that he wanted the communications room to get a tape recorder and record his message that he was going to give. He said he was going to sing a song and said he wanted it playing at his funeral. He said he wanted a copy sending to his solicitor in London.

I could sense BRONSON was building himself up and expected something serious to happen. It crossed my mind that I would be killed.

A few minutes later BRONSON again spoke on the radio this time he said that he knew he was going to die today and that he was prepared for it. He said he expected to be shot by a police bullet. He said he was going to sing a song which he wanted playing at his funeral. BRONSON then sang a song called "I believe", which he sang at the top of his voice.

This must have lasted for a few minutes and when he finished I thought he was going to hurt me. BRONSON then started singing some Xmas carols and hymns AW he picked up the T. V. smashing it on the floor alongside me. He dragged me to my feet again and walked me to the door of the room, pushing aside the barricade. He again began dragging me back along the corridor and it seemed as if he was taking me back to the first TV room we had been in. BRONSON was again behind me, walking with his back to the wall, feeling his way along as we approached the first T.V. room (T.V. 2). He shouted to the prison officers, who were stood only a short distance away, asking them about his steak and chips. One of them shouted that they were unaware that he had asked for any food.

I realised that once we got back into the first room it would be more secure than the last one so I was reluctant to go back in it. As BRONSON reached out trying to find the door handle I felt his grip loosen around my neck, ever so slightly. As it did so I saw my chance and pushed with my foot against the door frame, knocking BRONSON slightly off balance. I pushed as hard as I could and BRONSON fell backwards with myself falling over with him. As we fell he released his grip on me and as soon as we landed I jumped straight to my feet, kicking BRONSON on the body and face a couple of times. Within a second a number of other prison officers jumped on top of BRONSON and one of them took hold of me and led me away. I was taken to the command post in the Governors Office.

I was extremely highly charged at this time and was grateful that I had been dragged away because I feel I would have done some harm to BRONSON if not moved.

I went to the Governors office and was sat down. Everyone was very nice to me but I felt as if I was being pampered and didn't want all the hassle. I felt I just wanted to be left along to try and sort the many different feelings out that were going through my mind. I sat and talked the situation through and slowly started to come down from the incident. I make this statement from notes taken by the police taken just a few hours after the hostage incident was resolved.

A few days later, once I had returned home. I got a portable tape recorder and dictated my recollection of the incident into it. I then had these notes typed in order to produce as accurate a picture as possible just in case my memory falters in the subsequent months. I can produce a copy of these notes, which had been signed and dated by myself as Police Item ATW 1.

Underlined = All Bollocks

What can I say to such a load of old bollocks? I got seven years added on; he got a big fat cheque and retired on invalid's pension. He played on post-traumatic stress disorder, then became a governor in Wolds private jail. It's all one big game! He milks it, the system milks it, and I survive it! Not for a second am I trying to justify what I did and I take my punishment like a man, not a mouse – if it's seven years or 27 years, I'll survive it! But the one thing I do need to clear up is that Wallace is a coward and cowardice is the biggest form of weakness a man can have. Wallace allowed me to tie him up! I had no weapons! It was just me and him!

I had known Wallace before he was a governor, because he was a screw for years before that. He was always a coward, always a bully and always an arrogant cunt! Again, I'm not justifying what I did to him, but let me say that I enjoyed myself and I proved that day what a mouse he really is. All the screws watched the spineless, gutless prat! He would have licked my arse if I'd told him to! But when it was all over, when all the screws piled on top of me, what did he do then? He kicked me to bits like a beach ball and a screw had to pull him off and restrain him. That, for me, sums up Wallace in a nutshell – he never had the bottle to defend himself, but he had the bottle to kick a man's head in whilst a dozen screws were on top of him.

I say to any man, would you allow yourself to be tied up? I was unarmed and I'm just one man! All Wallace had to do was push me over and the screws would have rushed in fast, but he never had it in him! That's why I detest the cunt, that's why the screws lost respect for him, that's why he retired and that's why he then went into the private jail! But even if he went to Mars and worked in a jail there, every time he looked in the mirror he'd know why and how it turned sour. If he had put up a struggle, everyone would've respected him, including me, but to wait till I'm on the floor in restraint then kick ten bells out of me proves what a snake he was! He was a coward – the biggest form of coward there is! And this cunt was a top governor in charge of 1,000 inmates... sorry – 999. Not me, I was the governor that day. I ran that jail that day. I was the daddy and I did a better job of it. No bitterness, no hate, no regrets – this was fair and it was all worth it just to expose the coward of the jail. Real men don't allow themselves to be tied up unless they're part of the S&M scene! Could it be that he enjoyed it? I fucking hope not. In fact, I feel a bit faint, I need a lie down. I've come over all funny. Anyway, I hope I've proved my point! Sure, he got some good shots in. My head was like a big balloon – even my jaw was smashed – but it's all in a day's work.

Wallace you'll live and die a coward! And that's the truth. Amen. Don't forget that the screws have to be able to respect a prison governor, and lots of screws would tell you what I'm telling you, if they could. Most of them can't or they'll be sacked for improper behaviour, but I can and I do. A cunt's a cunt with me. Fuck pretending, I've got nothing to pretend for. A prison governor either gets my respect or they don't; lots do, lots don't. Some couldn't lead a horse to water, they're fucking idiots straight out of training college telling screws with 30 years' experience how to do their job. Face facts, some people are born to lead, others are born to follow. That's how it is! Amen.

I got a tin of tomatoes today! I got the cleaner to microwave them for tea and put them all over my chips. I had that with pepper, salt, brown sauce, half a loaf of bread and a pint of sweet tea! Who's the daddy? It was fucking lovely. YABADABADOOOoooooo! Yiipppeeeeeee! A silly tin of toms brightens my day up big time! "Cheap as chips." Now whose catchphrase is that? I can't think...

"Shut that door" – Larry Grayson.

"Nice to see you, to see you nice" – Brucie.

"Cheap as chips" – some fucker said it, I can't think who.

"It's how I tell them" – Frank Carson.

"Here's a funny thing" – Tommy Trinder.

"It's only a puppet" – Brian Conley.

"Cheap as chips" – ? Oh fuck it… who cares?

If I were on normal location somewhere, I would be cooking my own meals – great big cooked meals, like a chicken to myself. Proper meals, a man's portion. I miss all that, but I'm still 16 stone of muscle! How big would I be up on A-Wing? Massive. I'm just a natural strong man! I baffle science; I'm a throwback to the circus era when people paid to see men like me. Call us freaky fuckers if you will, but us lot are special and unusual, if not unique. Roll up, roll up, roll up…

"Mummy, Mummy, look at that man over there picking up that elephant! Mummy, look at that lady with the beard and three tits!"

"Yes, love, it's the circus!"

"Mummy, Mummy, look at that big fat man!"

"Yes, love, it's the hippo man."

It was magical, brilliant. Who doesn't enjoy a circus? Toffee apples, candy floss, the smell of lions, the lights, the atmosphere, the clowns, the trapeze artists, the jugglers, the midgets, the sawdust, the laughter… Tell me what kid didn't love it. It was another world, a world that lit up and brought so much enjoyment. "Ladies and gentlemen, welcome to the circus!" Brilliant, but it's an era long gone… How sad is that?

Did you know John Merrick (the elephant man) was born in Leicester? It doesn't really surprise me, because when I was on Leicester prison roof I saw some strange people walking the streets. I thought to myself, thank fuck they're out there and I'm in here.

It's a funny old world. You can't take it seriously can you? If you did, you would probably want to shoot me! I bet I get right up some people's noses and I bet I upset a few, but you know I'm not so bad really! Once you get to know me, I'm like a member of your family! Uncle Charlie, that's me. I'm the harmless one in the corner with a beer and a cheese and onion roll.

They said I was mad
They labelled me bad
What can you do?
If only we knew
They beat me with sticks
They jumped on my head
What can you do?
It's too late when you're dead.

Tea time.

Fuck me; the observation hatch in my door was open and I saw 'Monster Miller' walk by. He's one fucking ugly bastard, but the crazy thing is that years ago he was brown and now his skin looks grey! He looks like one of those zombies in a graveyard horror scene. That's what solitary and madness has done to him! He never goes out for any fresh air; he spends year after year in a concrete box. Or is he dead? 'Bang.' My door shuts, then Hannibal's door unlocks and another fucking nightmare walks past my door. I'm a celebrity, get me out of here! Somebody please vote me out! I've had enough!

I had a jacket potato with cheese and a super bun for tea. Lucky me. Beggars can't be choosers, I suppose!

There was a cleaner in Wandsworth block back in the 1970s who we called 'the Shadow' – fuck knows why! He was cleaning outside my door one day and I shouted to him through the crack, "Oi, Shadow, get me a clean T-shirt and some socks." The cunt blanked me, so I said, "Oi, cunt, I'm talking to you!" But he just fucked off. I couldn't believe it. The next day, I was slopping out a potful of shit and as I got to the recess, he was walking out. 'Whoosh' it went, all over the cunt! The screws jumped me and dragged me back to my cell. That's showbiz for you!

It was in 1977 that T-shirts first came out in the local jails. Before that it was always blue and white striped shirts and we were always being told: "Do that button up, tuck that shirt in." Fuck me, it was a Godsend when the T-shirts came out; a great day for us cons. And for a jail like Wandsworth to change tradition was something very rare indeed – it's why I remember it so well. Jeans came out too! That was also a big change, as before that we all wore grey woollen trousers (which used to itch) and blue denim overalls. I miss the overalls! Plenty of pockets in them, see, to hide things. Once, I was being searched in Wandsworth and they found £200 and a tool on me. I was gutted. They were confiscated, of course, and I was nicked! So where does that dosh go? I wonder, don't you?

Most jails have got what they call the 'black museum' where they keep all the weapons they find in searches. You'd be amazed by what they've found! Blades as long as swords. I suppose in the female jails they have a dildo museum! What a sight that would be! I'll give that a miss as I'm just in the mood for a cup of tea. I'll be back later, I promise.

Hey! Did you know that bank notes were first used in seventh-century China? That's when paper was invented. Fucking amazing. Here's one that will blow your panties off: the Bank of England produces £26,731,450 a day in bank notes. Can you believe that? That is a lot of dosh. I wonder if I could get a job there? Part time will do.

Did you know that apart from the Queen and Britannia, only two other women have featured on our bank notes? They were social reformer Elizabeth Fry on the £5 note and Florence Nightingale on the £10 note. So you're asking yourselves, "How does he know all this?" I've told you before: I'm a clever cunt and my brain is like a computer. I'm a walking encyclopaedia and I just love facts. I'm a sad-o really, a boring bastard, but I'm the man you would love to have on your side in a pub quiz! Will I ever go on *Mastermind*? Never say never or it will never come off! I'm just about to look into the Bank of England job issue, as I must plan ahead. Always be three steps ahead, I say, and that job would suit me lovely. I promise I won't nick any money – honest.

Well, I can't believe Pat Mackay is on his way out of prison. He was one con I thought would die inside. I met him in Parkhurst in the 1970s and '80s on C-Wing. He's a big, tall, skinny fucker, but give him an axe and you've got a slaughter house! It was back in 1975 he axed two old women and a priest to death. He just went berserk and chopped them to pieces! Why? Well, that's what psychos do, isn't it? The Old Bill think he may have killed another nine, but they would say that – those cunts will say anything to clear the books! Personally, I think Mackay should've hanged. I remember him as a serious fucking weirdo. You can always tell by the eyes: "Look at me, I'm a psycho."

Mackay used to do a lot of technical drawings in his cell, and he was good. One day I was in there and he offered me a cup of coffee from his flask. Fuck that; I'd sooner die of thirst! I was only in there to tell him to stop giving me funny looks on the landing. He said he wasn't! I said, "You are. Stop it now! Don't make me come in here again and break your jaw." Thank fuck there were no axes about. Cunt. He's just been moved from Kingston lifers' jail to Wayland jail in Norfolk. Next stop: home leave or the axe shop.

Another lifer they are letting out on days out to prepare her for release is that lunatic Tracie Andrews. Fuck me, it's only 11 years ago that she stabbed her fella Lee Harvey to death. They went on the telly, crying and saying that some road-rage killer had done it. Now they're preparing her for release! How the fuck do they do it? Why can't I get a break? It just baffles me! She murdered a top geezer, lied about it, got lifed off and now she's on her way out! What is going on? Somebody tell me. Armed robbers serve twice as long! She's a cold, evil, murdering, lying bitch! I bet Lee Harvey's family are disgusted. That's Loonyology for you – it's all madness. Who's next out, Rose West? Find Jesus, be a goody-goody and lick the governor's arsehole. If she does all that, she may just pull it off. Don't bet against it – I wouldn't...

9 June 2008.

Oh well, a new week! I love Mondays. The sun's out, it's gorgeous and the birds are singing – beautiful! Sadly, we lost another three of our boys out in Afghanistan yesterday. Whilst we were all eating our Sunday lunch, some Taliban suicide bomber blew himself up and took three paras with him, the cunt. But that's war for you: cold as ice and soulless. That's now 100 we've lost out there – the youngest was 18-year-old private Ben Ford and the oldest was Gary Thompson, 51. I salute you all, you're all top geezers. R.I.P. How the fuck does that Blair sleep at night? I still say we shouldn't even be there.

What about that mad Jap in Tokyo yesterday? He went berserk with a knife in a shopping centre, stabbing seven people to death. He said he was 'tired of life'. Cunt. The world's gone mad; it's Loonyology gone insane! You just don't know what's coming next. I would have taken that blade off him and rammed it right up his arse. How's that for your piles, you snake-eyed cunt! There was another mad knifeman in Osaka back in 2004. He ran into a primary school and stabbed eight kids to death. That nutter was executed. Let's hope this new nutter gets the same treatment. Shoot the cunt.

You'll love this latest scandal: Glyn Hughes, the deputy prison governor of Ford prison, has been suspended over sexual harassment allegations. I'll tell you now, it's the tip of the iceberg and it's time these shit holes were truly exposed; then you would be in shock. Nothing amazes me anymore, not since a female screwess attempted to break Myra Hindley out. That summed it all up in a nutshell for me... Loonyology!

I'll tell you who's an evil bastard: Howard Zin Green. He was a choirmaster, one of the God squad – 'the untouchables'. This 47-year-old nonce copped 11 years for raping little girls. So much of the love of Jesus. This is how this world is: it's full of evil cunts, and a lot of them hide behind some sort of religious wall of silence. Bring back the lions I say, and feed these nonces to the beasts. Take a tip: stay out of the prison chapels as they're a meeting place for sex cases. 99% of church-goers in jail are nonces and that's a fact. They seem to love Jesus for some reason, but then again going to church services does help with parole. You crafty fuckers...

I got six letters today! Not bad for a Monday. One of those was from Mum, who's been writing to me for 34 years! Imagine how many stamps that is. I tell all the kids: "Look after your mother, because you won't ever have anybody more precious or loyal in your lifetime."

I had a lovely jog out on the yard in the sunshine and felt the rays on my head. I was leaking sweat, so I came in and had a shower and I felt great! What a way to start the week off. Then I called Peggy Rayment to find out how Alan's doing on his Land's End to John o'Groats feat. (He's doing great, which I knew he would be.) I also called Johnny Griffiths. He's a top geezer and a good buddy! But I'm super-charged on the phone now! It's all red alert: one slip-up and they cut the line. It's like having MI5, MI6 and the CIA listening in. Paranoid fuckers. I have to be very careful what I say, which puts a lot of tension that I don't need my way. How the fuck can you relax or enjoy a call when you know they're logging every word of it? You can't.

I'm on a visit tomorrow with my little buddy Ifty (top man). I've done him a big art as he loves my art, but then again who doesn't? (Apart from prison HQ – jealous twats.)

The man once dubbed 'Britain's most violent prisoner' has donated some of his sketches to raise funds for an Aberystwyth man suffering from variant CJD. The sketches by Aberystwyth-born Charles Bronson raised £1,100 at a fund-raising auction in the Tollgate Inn, Penparcau, after they were bought by local man Andy Griffiths. The Cambrian News has decided not to identify the man who has contracted vCJD, which is the human form of BSE and more commonly known as 'mad cow disease'. His uncle said, "Charles Bronson's mother is a friend of us to auction at the event, the proceeds of which are going towards items intended for a new flat for my nephew and his wife. Mr Griffiths is a close family friend and wanted to help the cause as much as he could, hence his magnificent bid."

Like I've been saying for a long time now, my art is collectable. A grand's nothing – peanuts – some go for a lot more. I'm the born-again artist! Who are you? 100 years from now, my art will sell for 100 grand or even a million bucks. When will prison HQ wake up? Somebody tell them Bronson's waiting to fly out and make a fortune. Stop denying me a life of luxury! Let me out to win; I can become an inspiration! I'm a fucking genius. The best is yet to come, honest.

Oh well, I'm off to bed. Another day buried and gone; what will tomorrow bring? Milkshakes and chocolate bars.

4 June 2008.
I've just dug out a few old papers, including a letter from Ron Kray and my 1992 diary. What more do you lot want? This is historic material – antique. You lucky people.

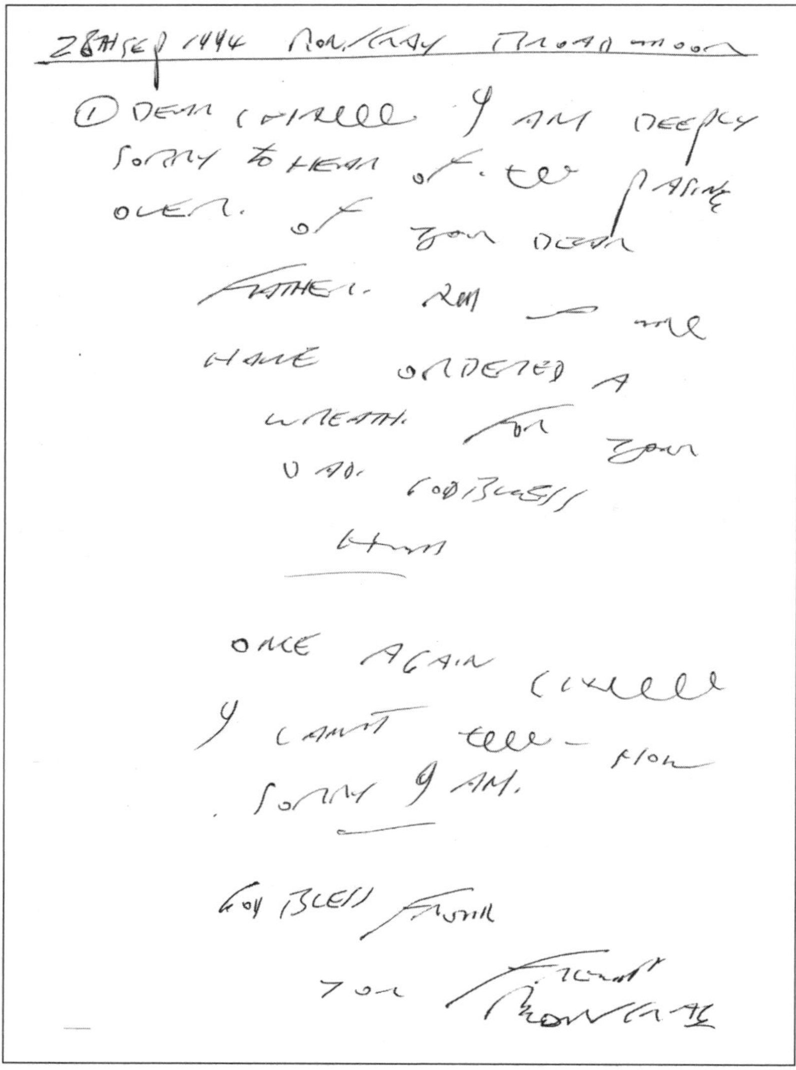

The above letter is from Ron Kray and reads:

28 Sept 1994 Ron Kray Broadmoor.

Dear Charlie, I am deeply sorry to hear of the passing over of your dear father. Reg and me have ordered a wreath for your dad. God bless him. Once again Charlie, I can't tell you how sorry I am.

God bless

From your friend, Ron Kray

<u>Diary.</u>
January 1992 – Hull Block.
If you haven't read The Tommyknockers *by Stephen King, then I recommend you do! My pal Kevin Brown sent it in to me from the next cell. Kevo's doing a 10 stretch for armed robbery – he's only 26 and he's a good, solid guy! He said to me, "Chaz, you'll love this* Tommyknockers *book." I was fed up, so I read it. Fuck me, it's brilliant – I started it and finished it in a day and half!*

My mind's been wandering and I've not been too happy. Life's been getting on top of me lately. I'm being fed shit. One governor says one thing, another says the opposite! I've been here too long now: three and a half months! Oh yeah, I've done magic, I've got my act together. I've been treated better than most places, but where the fuck am I going?

I watched a big ship come in to dock out of my cell window Xmas time – 'Sunny Fellow' (a big bugger). That same ship is still there. I'm sick of looking at it, I'm sick of looking at all the cranes, and the lorries and the buses passing by the wall. Oh, it's a lovely view but I'm still sick of it!

The Tommyknockers *finally flipped my aching head! Stephen King is without a doubt the best horror writer about, apart from James Herbert. Both these writers always send a cold sweat run down my spine. If I could write like them, I'd end up in a padded cell!*

Jan 23. I lay back in the dark and shadows of my cell. It was late and I was thinking about The Tommyknockers. *Fuck it – out came the tin of boot polish! In half an hour I was so black I felt myself slip into the darkness. I knew in my own mind something would happen in the morning, as every time I 'black up' it's a warning sign! Even after past experiences of trying to scrub it off with green brillo pads and scrubbing brushes, I felt excited! God only knows why, as I certainly didn't!*

I lay in bed stinking of polish, the sheets sticking to my body. It's a weird sensation but sadness always overcomes me as I think, WHY THIS? What do I achieve but more agony and more wasted years? It's senseless and totally insane, but I truly feel a sense of righteousness; a feeling I'm right – and they're wrong! God (or some supreme being) is on my side. I'm not getting religious but I feel I'm right. Fuck their mind games! Some jerk runs my life in the Home Office – they sit behind a desk and decide when I move, where I move, how I move. They've had me in Hull Block for over three months! But why? How do they justify it?

As I examine my state of mind, a cloud of gloom covers me and I feel alone – isolated. Nobody can, or does, understand my actions – not even I do; it's a form of depression where I only feel it's time for pain, masochism, call it what you will – maybe it's a relapse of the mind! A mental breakdown. Maybe it's all in my own subconscious. Fuck it, I swear to God I can't answer it!

The ships' foghorns can be heard – car horns in the night. I've no dreams, only nightmares. I drift in and out of sleep; it's soon time!

Jan 24. I awake early and I'm still tired. I've got a massive erection on and it looks twice as big covered in boot polish. I look at it for a spell, wondering if some polish went down the eye hole. Would it cause any harm? Jesus, it really does look twice as big! I'm in no mood to have a wank, so I get up and fill my pot almost to the brim. I was obviously bursting for a slash. Light is already filtering in through my window and it's light enough to see my face in the mirror. Fucking Hell's bells, I wish I hadn't looked! This has to be one of the best black-up jobs I've ever done. When my door opens up at 7.45am the screws won't know what's what! I'm 198lb, 5 foot 10, and here I am bollock naked, black as soot, and in a while I'll walk out of my door with a pot full of piss and a bowl of water! What would you do or say to me? This is how it is, how I am!

7.45am. I hear them coming, keys rattling, talking, boots on the floor. All the screws have treated me OK, except for a few. There are one or two dogs here – as in all jails. It turns out an SO is on duty who is a dog. He denied me a cup of tea on Boxing Day and not just me, also Vince Donnley and Darren Ramsey. I've already told him he's a dog and what else I thought of him. He's a young screw who has made it up to an SO fast – but he hasn't a clue how to conduct himself as a tough guy. But truly, he's a clown. Even other screws thought he was childish to deny us a cup of tea on Boxing Day! Still, it's his way and sooner or later he will get cut, stabbed or get a broken nose over his attitude. I never served him up as he never retaliated verbally. If he'd said a snide remark when I'd told him he was a dog, I'd have chinned him there and then. (Sad, but that's showbiz.)

I hear the key in my door – it opens and I walk out not knowing what I'll do. I feel edgy, tense, and I sense violence is seconds away. I've also rubbed some baby oil over the top of the polish on my upper body, so as to slip out of their holds if they try to fight. Nobody says a word as I spot the dog SO. In a way, I'm happy he's on duty, as only a dog deserves a headache. I can say with all honesty that the other screws have done me no harm in my stay here.

I walk down to the recess not knowing what the fuck to do. My thoughts are now racing and it's a strange feeling that comes over me. It may sound crazy but I see these screws as 'Tommyknockers'. I finally flip! It has to happen and it does. I come running out of the recess shouting, "Tommyknockers!" I jump up on a railing and pull myself up to the bars on the roof. This whole block is like a bird's cage, with bars on the windows and across the ceiling. I'm swinging from bar to bar bollock naked, screaming, "Tommyknockers!"

I start punching out the fluorescent lights and as they smash I shout, "180!" The screws run downstairs and I grab a light fitting – "Tommyknockers!" I feel a shock pass through my body. I'm smashing light fittings with my fist and blood is running down my arm and my feet are also bleeding. As the long bulbs explode in my face, I'm covered in glass. "Tommyknockers!"

Kevin Brown is shouting through his locked door: "OK, Charlie!" I'm singing, "Hi ho, hi ho, it's off the roof I go, hi ho, hi ho, it's off the roof I go!"

Tommyknockers… 180… I know it's all madness but it's gone too far! My head is in bits; I jump down off the bars and land on broken glass. The pain shoots through my feet, "AAARRggghhhhhh!" I clock the mufti below: screws with shields, boiler suits and crash helmets. I grab fire buckets and sling water at them – I'm slinging anything worth slinging at them (there ain't much to sling) and I'm shouting at the dog SO, telling him I'll come down if he fights me on his own! There's no chance of that as he's a coward. I'd put my finger in the door to fight this dog. Sometimes I say to myself, "Stab one, get life, and never hold back again!" But why the fuck should I have to die for a dog? So I hold back again! I give respect to all people – give it and get it – but I can't bring myself to smile or talk to false people.

Another SO arrives, a Mr Stockman. He's an Irishman, a fair man who speaks no shit – he tells a con 'yes' or 'no'; he doesn't play mind games. He doesn't come up but talks to me from the stairway. I tell him my grievances and he relays them to a governor, then tells me what the governor says! It's fucking obvious why it's happened: I'm stuck in a poxy cell for 23 hours every day, I'm trapped and my back is pushed too far against a wall. I'm tired and fed up of the Home Office policy of throwing me all over the place. Where am I going? When? Mr Stockman walks me to the strong-box. It's over – the insanity of it all, that is. Nobody has won. What's been achieved? Fuck all!

I was last in this box in 1975 and it's not altered at all. Bad memories flood back to me and it's like time has stood still for the last 18 years – fuck all has changed! I reflect over it all. I once spilt tears of frustration inside this room; now it feels even worse as I'm older and more alone. It's truly time I pulled myself together! Who can relate to this in the real world? It's probably so insane to the reader that it must be impossible for them to believe I'm sitting in a box as a black man with glass in my feet, blood over my body and splinters in my hands. But worse than all this is my mind. I'm a disturbed man, a sick man, and super sensitive. The smallest spark would turn me nasty. If any man was to crack a funny and call me a 'black bastard' I'd surely bite a piece of his face off. I truly expect to stay in this box for the remainder of my stay here in Hull – days, weeks, or whatever – but I'm out and back to my cell in hours! (Times are changing.)

Joe Whitty phones to see how I am; so does Mr Marriott, the governor of Parkhurst! Cons will say, "Governors phoning up Charlie? What's going on here?" Well, I'll tell you. Both Mr Marriott and Joe Whitty are decent men. Sure they're governors, but they're also men who treat men as men. I just look at 90% of governors and never speak to them – I've more time for a cockroach! A worm on a fishing line has more guts than some of the slippery fuckers I've met. I respect a governor who's straight and honest, not these creeps who deliberately build a man up only to kick him down! Both Joe Whitty and Mr Marriott sent me away on lay-downs, but only because of my unpredictable behaviour. They had little choice but to sling in the towel! But whilst in their prisons they both treated me decently and they still seem to want to see me get out. Why? I can't answer that. (Julian also called, so I'm not alone!)

Sadly, Kelly Anne upset me on Xmas Eve and we haven't written since. Yes, I miss her a lot but it's how it is. She knows what she did to hurt me so much that I've stopped contact, but I can't get her out of my fucked-up head. She's really all I need in this life, and she knows it. Still, this is showbiz.

That mad incident happened two weeks ago! I'm still here and I'm back to sanity. I got the glass out of my feet. I refused to see a doctor, so I let a hospital screw take it out! I was also sick for three days. (They reckon I breathed in the light dust from the fluorescent tubes!) I was bad, but it's history as I write this. I'm back to being a white man. The cleaner helped scrub the black off with green pads and a scrubbing brush. Never again! To top it all, I didn't get nicked! Yeah, strange, but stranger things happen at sea!

I gave up long ago trying to work out what these people will do next. Maybe the psychiatrists are all saying, "It's time old Charlie boy got certified once more!" (I don't know as I don't see them anymore.) Maybe it's the Home Office saying, "Don't nick Charlie boy as we want the mad man out, so if he goes mad outside we can get the police to shoot him." Who can say what is said or planned? All I truly know is that I feel a bit disheartened over it all. One minute I'm patted on the head, told how good I am and given remission back, and the next I'm being kept caged in a block and denied de-categorisation from the danger list! So it's all insane to me.

I would honestly say SO Stockman saved my day, as I believe that if it had been left to the dog, it would've had a bad ending. Maybe that's what I wanted. There are a lot of maybes, ifs and buts, but I only go on facts and the fact is insanity drove me mad.

I am not on ice. I could be days or hours from getting in the van! Ken Roger, another Parkhurst governor, came to see me last week with the prospect of a transfer back to Parkhurst C-Unit! Lincoln block is also being mentioned. Why another block? I'm told no dispersal jails want to accept me on normal location anymore. Am I really this bad? Am I?

It's now 6 February 1992 and I'm preparing myself for the big day (if I make it). I swear to God I don't know my own mind and I don't know what the fuck I want anymore! Sometimes I feel dangerous and unsure of myself; other times I pray I'll overcome this feeling of gloom. It's like a suicidal mission, as if I want to run through a fire of swords and leave a trail of blood. If I had the bottle I believe I would cut my own throat, as at times I sense a terrible ending. I know this all sounds like I'm a defeated man, a man with no confidence, but it's not that way at all. It's deeper than any simple way out. I could never run from myself or from life (why the fuck should I?) but at times I see a big black pit and I feel I'm so close to slipping in.

Today I copped five letters and each one lifted me up. The best one was from my pal Tommy Hole, who is now at Rampton. He sent me a classic photo in which he has a beauty of shiner. He'd had words with a mob of Irishmen and before he knew it, he had five big Irish brawlers on top of him. Tom fought back with the heart of a lion, but as he's only small and was under five men's blows it was senseless. He managed to crawl out and get away, only to watch the drunken paddies kicking the shit out of each other, thinking he was still under them! If that isn't a classic, what is?

I also got a card from my dear friend Sammy McArthy, who is enjoying freedom. This man always lights the sky up for me. He's so loyal it's untrue. I'm lucky to have such a loyal friend as Sammy.

Mickey Reilly wrote me a letter telling me he's working out every day in the gym at Parkhurst. He does half an hour on the punch bag every day, after which it's weight training with big Vicky Dark and Keith Ritchie. I got another letter from Charlie McGhee at Long Lartin. Chaz is a great friend. And, to top it all, I got a letter from Julian, so it's been a day to look upon as a success. (Plus I'm writing this, so it's even better.)

Yesterday, I got a letter from Dad! He tells me Mum is going to Australia for six weeks in April to stay with our John. (It'll do her good, I say.) It's now over four years since I've seen my parents! It's my choice and yes, it guts me, but I made up my mind when I last got arrested that I'd never let them see me in prison again. It hurts, but I'm praying that my way works out best. Why should my family have to keep seeing me in prison? I love them too much to hurt them like that, and I will get to see them when I can. It's all fate – this is how it's meant to be! Most can't understand my ways, but I know this time I am right in this decision. It will save Mum a lot of hurt and that's enough of a reason to justify not seeing her. If I felt I was being cruel I would feel bad, but I feel good alone. It's like I'm at war with myself: I need to win and come home a better person. Why should my parents be put to the test with my madness or be upset to hear about my mad ways? Haven't they seen enough? Now I keep it all secret and it's a big relief – a weight off my shoulders.

I truly love my folks. We are closer now than we ever were; we have a bond between us! My dad respects me for the man I've become – not for my criminal ways but for how I conduct myself and how I bounce back up. My old man's a man who respects a man. And my respect for him is the ultimate. Yes, I love the old git and he knows it. Roll on Xmas. End.

Thursday, 13 February 1992 – Hull.

I woke up feeling bad, depressed and full of anxiety. I don't know where or when I'm going. I went to collect my breakfast and told the screws, "Enough is enough. Fucking tell me today. I must know, I'm sick to my teeth with being sweated." An hour later the yellow bastards at HQ sent a woman governor to speak to me! She told me I'm off in the morning to a local block. I felt disgusted and I told her how I felt. She knew. Fuck it – I stripped off and went in the box, telling them I'd only be leaving naked in a body belt, and they'd have to push me in a fucking wheel chair! Big Arthur, a regular block screw, told me it's not their doing. He was genuinely disappointed.

That night I didn't sleep; I brooded and felt a fit building up. In the early hours I let roar my frustration: "AAAARRRrrggghhhhhh!" It didn't help! Neither did banging my fists on the solid steel door or smashing my bare feet into it. Tomorrow will tell! (I must stop hitting these doors, they're impregnable.)

Valentine's Day, 1992.

I lay awake thinking of what was to be. Would they refuse to take me? I still didn't have a clue where I was going, but I'd made up my mind that I wouldn't be walking there! I heard the outer door open, then the second door, and in they came with my breakfast: porridge, sausage and bread. No words were spoken. As they left, I truly felt they were going to refuse to take me – until I heard the whispering! In they came: "Charlie, you gotta go, clothes or no clothes."

"Get the belt and a fucking wheelchair then," I said. And lo and behold, they did! I was strapped in the belt, still starkers, and they wheeled in a chair. Jesus Christ, they were wheeling me out! I was wheeled out of the box with screws all over the place. I was carried down some stairs (still on the chair) and wheeled out to the waiting van. They picked the chair up and in I went. Seven screws jumped in and we drove off. Five of these screws were block screws and all had been decent guys, but you could see the guilt in their faces.

They felt gutted about taking me to a local block. No words were spoken, as I refused to talk! The tension was heavy; eyes were darting away from my eyes.

An hour and a half later, the van crept through Lincoln gate (it was Lincoln after all) and the van pulled up outside the block. I was manoeuvred out on the chair and wheeled straight into the box in silence. Once in the box, I jumped out of the chair for them to take off the belt. As the Hull screws walked out, I said my first words to them: "Tell Arthur: thanks for trying." (Arthur had done me a favour and I don't forget these things!) They wished me well and the door closed.

I felt like I was still in Hull's box. It was like a dream – what more can I say? It was a filthy liberty they had taken, but one learns to expect it. Even the screws were visibly disgusted in moving me to a block! Everybody knew it was a liberty, but they've got a job to do. Let's face facts: they're jailers. The same people walked and dragged men to the gallows years back. They're robots who do as they're told and get paid for it. Really, this move showed what it's all about and why cons can't trust the system! It's not paranoia or suspicion, it's just a fact of life. It's like a war where the enemy are as cold as steel and unpredictable beyond reason.

14 Feb – some get Valentine's cards, roses, chocolates, cuddles and smiles; I get a stinking box and seclusion. This box is the old type: 11 foot by 9 foot with slab boards and nothing else, not even a window. The light's on 24 hours a day so you have no idea of the time, not even if it's day or night. The only clue you have is the food, but I'm certain they sometimes even fuck that up by giving me porridge for tea!

A Governor Pratt (yeah, that's a name) came to see me, and my first impression of him was that he's a fair man. I didn't show him I thought so. He seemed genuinely concerned about me when most governors truly don't give a shit. Still, nor do I, so it's mutual.

A couple of very strange things occurred over the next four days. I actually block my ears up when I'm in the boxes and I go through periods where I cover my eyes. Why?

1. To close out the glare of the light, which is on day and night.

2. To meditate (close down and shut off).

3. So I can't see 'them' when they bring my food. (They're faceless people at times like this – the enemy.)

It's really a mechanical release to stop me going mad! Well, there I was, lying naked on my back, ears plugged up with bog roll and eyes covered, when I heard them (only faintly, as I was so cut off). A female voice asked if I was OK, but it felt like it wasn't really happening. Then I felt myself coming back, as if I'd been away from my body and spiritually free. This woman was, in fact, a member of the board of visitors. I didn't see her, only heard her for a few seconds and then she left. But she left something behind in that box that really made me feel human and nice: her smell. As soon as the silence crept back I jumped up and went to the door so I could smell it. The scent was lovely, and I tried to put a face to this woman. Her voice was so soft. In time, I'll hopefully find out who she was and I'll tell her this strange incident. The smell only lasted for a short while, but it truly made my day. I felt strange.

Another time, when it was late at night, an envelope came under my door, which is almost unheard of in any box. I knew it was the night screw who'd delivered it as I quickly learn who's spying on me (plus he spoke)! It was a letter from Cliffy Noody, who's serving life, and it turned out he was also in this block. His letter also enclosed a verse called 'Footsteps in the Sand'. Both the letter and the verse made me feel magic. Cliff's a young lad; he was only 18 when he got life. He has a big heart and I like him a lot. He says I'm like a dad to him, which is a nice thing to say to me. I hadn't seen him since 1989 at Durham. Yep, I must admit he lifted me right up. Cheers, Cliff.

I didn't slop out at all! I crapped in the pot and they took it out for the block cleaner to empty (must be a mug to empty my pot), so after a day or two the stench became heavy. But it's strange how one adjusts to these conditions. (I used a bit of shit to write 'Friday 14th Feb' on the wall in foot-long letters!) Mr Pratt came back with the screws to see what I wanted and why I'm not conforming! I expressed myself by telling him I was badly depressed over the latest dirty stroke. I told him I was sick of the blocks and lies, so he went away to think it all over! When he come back he put a solution to me: would I like to go on the special unit here? I said, "I'm not saying anything. I don't believe any fucker anymore. If you tell Julian Broadhead what you propose to do and Julian tells me, I'll believe your words." This is how bad I felt at this time. No disrespect to this governor, but I had to think of my mental state as dangerous thoughts were coming back and I truly felt bad. I felt a great feeling of persecution! It's a terrible thing to believe you're alone against a whole system that is destined to smash a man's dignity. I'm convinced that if it wasn't for my ability to slide away into oblivion and cut off, then I would be in a padded cell and certified insane with no hope of ever being freed. It must surely be a gift to be able to cut off and I'm grateful for possessing such a power, as it does help relax my frame of mind (not always, but sometimes).

On Monday, 17 February they came to tell me the governor had been in touch with Julian and that I could phone him! He told me exactly what Mr Pratt had told him (exactly what he had told me), so I told Julian I'd come out of the box and give it a go. So here I am: I've got to stay in this block for a week's 'test' and next week I'll move onto the special unit. There's only five cons on there. I know two: Tony Steel and Joe Purkiss; I don't know the others as I write this, but no doubt I'll know them next week! Maybe our paths have crossed and I've forgotten.

The slag John Childs has moved off. Just as well, as there would be no way I could walk past him without knocking his head off. He is one animal I would enjoy using extreme violence on and I'm not a violent sort of man, but just hearing his name sends my adrenalin flowing! (End of.)

So: how do I feel now, what am I expecting and is it right for me to go on this unit?

First: I still feel I've been shat on.

Second: I'm expecting psychological assessments and to be under observation, as having a unit with just six men (all of them 'disruptive elements') can only seen as a scientific experiment! It'll be like a putting a black rat in with a white rat, or a big guinea pig in with a bigger one. Cons are much the same as laboratory pets – confined and isolated; kept away from the majority. We are examined, assessed and truly demoralised, whether we accept the truth or not. But what choice do we have? More blocks, more moves!

Third: I don't know if it's right for me to go on the unit at this stage of my sentence. The others are all lifers and I'm supposed to be going home soon. But if I can handle it, at least I'll eat better, eat more, live better, be able to watch TV, use a multi-gym and mix with others. I'll have 100 times more privileges than I normally have. I'll use the experience to help me. So here I end, awaiting next week!

Julian is visiting me next week as well, so we can have a good chat. Right now, I'm enjoying the breeze blowing through my window and talking to Cliff through the pipe. It's good to be alive. Adios amigos. *End.*

P.S. Tony Steel has just sent me a few books, tea bags, milk, etc! He's a good guy!

P.P.S. Got word that Tony Coulson is here up on the wing. I hope to get to see him before I go on the unit. Tony and Peter Coulson are two gentlemen – both solid, staunch guys who I respect a lot.

24 February 1992.
I've just been told I'm going on the special unit tomorrow morning. Here we go! I'm fucking starving and ready for some gym.

4 June 2008.
Memory lane! I only lasted a few weeks on Governor Pratt's Lincoln unit before I chinned him. The van arrived and off I shot again. That's life for you…

That diary is 16 years old! Not much has changed, has it? But it's still a great journey and it's my life. I wouldn't have had it any other way! Would you?

A memory never forgotten:
Bullingdon HMP, Wednesday, 13 March 1996, 11pm.
I was listening to Tommy Boyd on my radio today. He does a show from noon till 2, Monday to Friday; I try to listen to him all the time. His show today just blew me away and all my problems have vanished. When Tommy read the news, I sat in total silence and I felt sick – numb! Some arsehole walked into a school and shot and killed 16 little kids and a teacher, then shot himself. My first thought was America, it had to be in America – some drug-crazed madman. But when Tommy said it was in Dunblane, Scotland it made me go cold.

The world's gone mad. My heart goes out to all those kids, parents and teachers, and everybody in the community of Dunblane. It's a sad day for humanity. X

Angels of innocence – deceased:

Victoria Clydesdale	5 yrs old
Emma Crozier	5 yrs old
Melissa Currie	5 yrs old
Charlotte Dunn	5 yrs old
Kevin Hassell	5 yrs old
Ross Irvine	5 yrs old
David Kerr	5 yrs old

Mhairi McBeath	5 yrs old
Brett McKinnon	6 yrs old
Abigail McLennan	5 yrs old
Emily Morton	5 yrs old
Sophie North	5 yrs old
John Petrie	5 yrs old
Joanna Ross	5 yrs old
Hannah Scott	5 yrs old
Megan Turner	5 yrs old

Teacher:

Gwenne Mayor	44 yrs old

Injured children:

Amie Adam	5 yrs old
Stewart Weir	5 yrs old
Coll Austin	5 yrs old
Benjamin Vallance	5 yrs old
Matthew Birnie	5 yrs old
Amy Hutchinson	5 yrs old
Ryan Liddell	5 yrs old
Mark Mullan	5 yrs old
Andrew O'Donnell	5 yrs old
Victoria Porteous	5 yrs old
Robert Purves	5 yrs old

Injured teachers:

Mark Blake	44 yrs old
Eileen Harild	44 yrs old

Five-year-old Robbie Hurst survived. They found him covered in blood under the body of his little buddy. The blood was all from his friend; Robbie didn't have a scratch on him! But what nightmares are left behind for him. Imagine it: the screaming, the guns going off, his friends falling down dead and dying, the crying, the pain! That's what this little boy's got inside his brain. To survive such a disaster leaves a mighty big scar. We all pray for little Robbie, that's all we can do.

Thomas Hamilton, the madman, was a sick-o. He actually gives the mad a bad name. He was evil, a pervert, a nasty bit of work. He loved guns but didn't have it in him to kill men, so he chose weaker ones. Probably the only good thing he did in his entire life was to shoot himself. Scum! Filth! A disgrace to the human race!

There are many more out there and in prison capable of committing such atrocities, like the sex monsters who prey on little kids, the paedophiles, the dregs of society. That's all Hamilton ever was, or ever would be. Burn you bastard, burn!

Can we ever forget?

CHAPTER 8

Broadmoor kiss my arse!

Without the insane,
What a boring existence it would be…

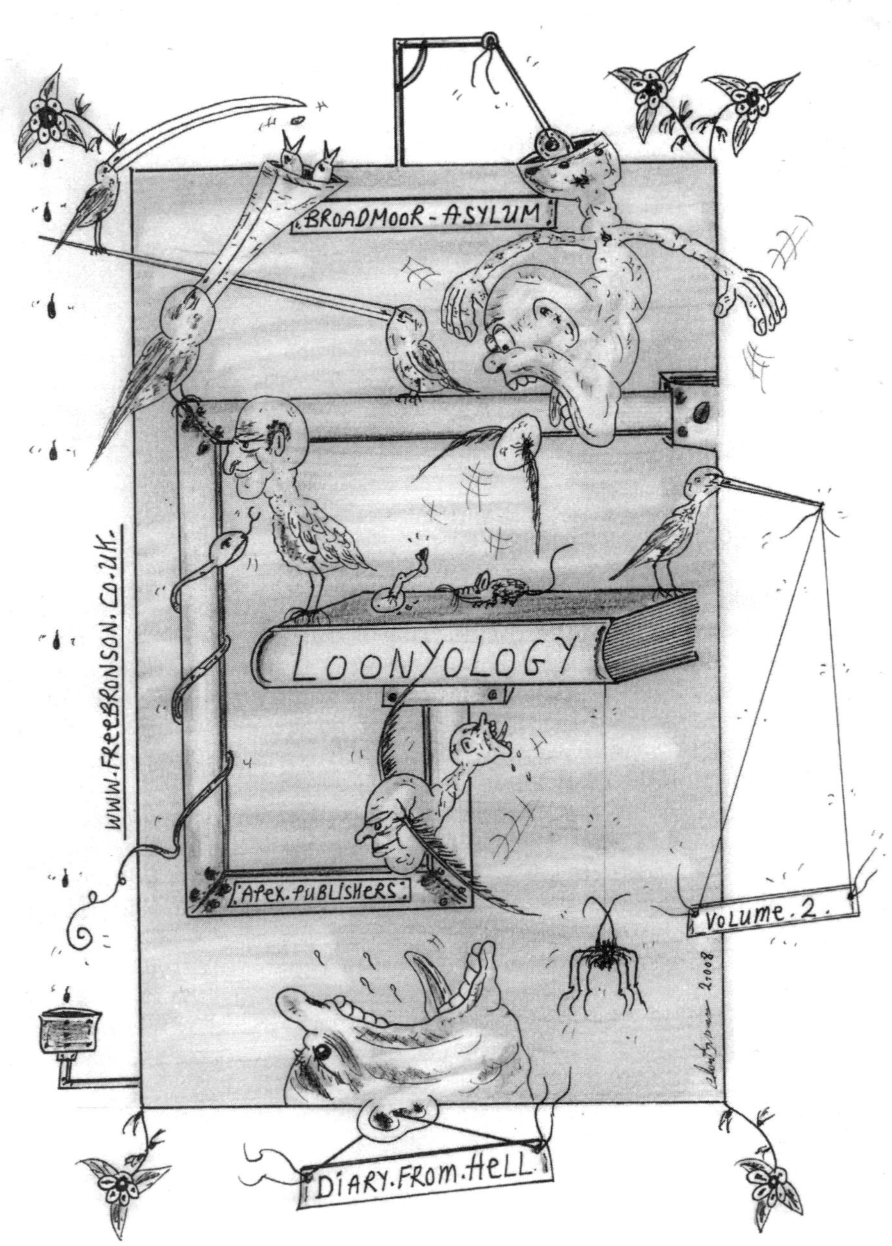

10 June 2008.

I had a great visit from my old buddy and top geezer Ifty today – plenty of choc bars and milkshakes. We always have a good laugh. He was telling me all about the brothers out in Pakistan and the house we sorted for a family. They're lovely humble souls. *Salaam*, brothers. I gave Ifty a couple of big pieces of art; he's worth it.

I see the Barry George retrial (for the murder of Jill Dando) started up yesterday at the Old Bailey. It's got to be a 'walk out' but let's wait and see... My dosh says 'NOT GUILTY'. Sure the guy's a fucking nutcase, but that doesn't mean he did it!

What about ex-copper Geoffrey Harries being stabbed to death a week before his trial for child porn? HA! HA! HA! HA! I shouldn't laugh really, as a man is innocent until proved guilty. Fuck me – he was accused of having 2,000 indecent images of children on his computer. How the fuck did they get on there? (Maybe it was 'research'. Yeah, like fuck it was!) Anyway, he died innocent so let's move on. It gets boring otherwise. Cunt.

I got a dozen letters today – seven from cons in other jails who have just read *Loonyology*! It's flying around the institutions and they all love it. Cheers, lads. Sorry I can't reply to you all (I'm in a cage, not a bleeding post office) but your comments are respected!

One of the letters was from a lad serving two years in Portland Young Offenders jail, asking me what he should do with a screw that keeps picking on him. He says the screw is a good 6 feet and 17 stone, and he's only 5 feet 3 and 9 stone. Well, son, shit him up with a full bucket of shit! Yes, you'll get a good kicking but he will never bully you again! That's what I would do. The fucking bully deserves all he gets. It does wind me up to hear this bullying still goes on in 2008. So many youngsters have turned to suicide over such cowards. The prison service will deny it goes on, but I'm telling you it always has and always will! OK, shit the cunt up; you'll lose a bit of remission and your privileges but you'll laugh yourself to sleep! HA! HA! HA! HA! Brilliant.

There was a screw in Parkhurst in the 1970s who thought it was funny to bully little cons; he soon got his just deserts. He retired early because we drove the old cunt mad! One time, I stuck a load of shit in the keyhole of my cell door and said to him, "Hey, boss, come and open my door. I want to get in my cell." He stuck his key in and got shit all over it. "Cheers, boss!" I said. That's how to fuck them. How could he nick me when he couldn't prove I'd done it? Cunt. There's always a way to get them. Think and find your own way!

I called Dee Morris up today. She's a cracker and I love her to bits. We go back years now; she's a good friend to me – a first-class buddy. She's just won a case in the small claims court defending herself and got awarded two grand. Three cheers for the victory of a little person up against the mighty establishment. HIP HIP – HOORAY! HIP HIP – HOORAY! HIP HIP – HOORAY! Cheers, Dee. I do love a winner. She's up to see me in July. Yiiippppeeeeeeeeee. My mum thinks the world of Dee (we all do), she's proper Cockney material. You don't fuck with my firm!

It was a lovely sunny day today. I had a cheese salad for tea with a good-sized lump of cheddar. Very nice too. Yep, a really nice day, but every day is another one stolen from my life by the thieving bastards. The cunts don't know when to stop, but that's life as it is. One day it'll all end. I just hope I get some serious pussy time before my heart stops ticking. Please, God, let me have a slice of pussy before you take me away through the pearly gates. Please don't let me leave this life without some pussy! It's not fair, God, don't be cruel! I'm only human; I don't want to be up there flying about with a harp until I've had some pussy pie! Please, God, have a heart! Thank you. My love to Jesus!

Friday, 13 June 2008.
Hey! I've been invited to a pot party – Friday at 9pm. I can't fucking wait. They told me to bring my own dope, so I'll pick you up at 8.30pm, OK sweetheart?

Oh! I got my parole date: 29 August – as if I give a flying fuck. It's all a joke – one big fucking joke. There's more chance of me winning the lottery!

Two eggs in a saucepan: one male, one female. The female says, "Look, I've got a crack." The male says, "No good telling me, I'm not hard yet!"

Big Tony Simpson and Charlie Breaker, two so-called buddies of mine, have become a pair of fucking parasites by selling my art behind my back – art I've given them over the years in goodwill! See how it all gets back to me? That eBay has a lot to answer for! Now, let me tell you the score on this. Nobody out there sells my art unless I give them permission. If you guys or girls are in hard times and need the dosh, then at least tell me and I'll say, "Yeah, sell them," or if it's for a charity, I'll say, "Yeah! Do it!" But if you do it behind my back, you're a snake. It wouldn't be so bad if they'd sent me some canteen, or got my mother a drink out of it.

You've been caught out, the pair of you! One was selling my art on his website, the other on eBay to some autograph hunter. And, to top it all, Breaker's selling copies of my art! You cheeky cunt, don't you realise my art fetches a couple of grand and you're flooding the market with my creations for a bag of fucking chips? You disrespectful pair of pricks! It'll never be forgotten and you've lost a friend!

This is a warning to anyone else thinking of selling my art: ask me first! Don't be selling anything of mine behind my back! Why do you think I've got my own art site and my own art dealer? To have two fat parasites rip me off? Cunts. It really does make me mad. Fucking treacherous rats! I don't know how many they've sold (or how long they've been doing it for), but one is one too many without telling or asking me. That's it now, there's no way back for us. Fuck off! Go and rob a bank, you gutless fuckers, why suck off me? Have you got no morals at all?

I get so angry when a mate does me in the back, because I take them into my heart and then some of them think: "Let's make a few bob with Charlie's art; he won't know." Well, I fucking do know. It may take months or even years, but everything gets back to me eventually and I've got my finger on the pulse! Bet your arse on that.

Athina Onassis (the daughter of Christina who sadly died back in 1988) has just sold a 38-carat diamond at Christie's for £3.6 million. Who said diamonds are a girl's best friend? Three million bucks… yiiipppppeeeee!

Did you know the longest moustache in the world is 12 feet 6 inches? That's what I call a tash. 12 and a half feet... wow! Walking down a busy street with one of those, you'd be odds-on to stab a few eyeballs. Surely you could strangle somebody with that? Imagine the murder trial: "The weapon used, your honour, was his tash! He wrapped it around his neck and choked the man to death."

"No, no, it's not true, your honour! We were having a friendly wrestle and my tash accidentally got wrapped around his neck."

What a magnificent trial that would be! Historic, magical, unfuckingbelievable. I reckon it would be a 'not guilty'! What about you?

Hannibal the cannibal started today! I was at the cage door talking to Mr Hall (a good screw who's always decent, funny and who's always got a story) when Maudsley walked past with some other screws. I shouted out, "Hey, is it true Maudsley is appearing on *Britain's Got Talent* next year as Catweazle?" Well, you should have heard the abuse that came out of his mouth. Some people just can't take a joke. I can just imagine him up on the stage in a strait-jacket, singing 'Please Release Me' then me walking on and smacking him over the head with an iron bar. I think we would win that show easily!

Apex Publishing will no longer be doing any of my books. They were to publish this one, but not now. They did a brilliant job on *Loonyology* but that's where it stops. Ask Chris Cowlin why; I really don't give a flying fuck! I'll self-publish if I have to! Any more books I do for any publisher, I want the dosh on the table in advance. I'm not fucking about anymore. Life's a bizz to me: do the bizz and move on. I'm sick of making other people rich all the time! It's Apex's loss, not mine. You wait till my novel comes out. I'll self-publish that, too. People forget a book is like a baby. That's all it is: a creation that lives on – a fucking masterpiece.

Here's a bit of serious advice to all you would-be authors out there: don't get screwed by any publisher! Self-publishing doesn't cost that much and if you believe in yourself then back yourself! Lay it all out, design it, produce it and the printers will do the magic. Just publish 1,000 copies at a time and see how it goes. If it goes well, make the next batch 10,000 then 100,000. If you don't believe you're a winner, then you'll lose!

I'm lucky because I've got good friends. Lisa Emmins does my typing and Mark Emmins puts the package together. We are a team and there's no greed, just a great team! Anybody can do it, so don't go selling yourselves short to some greedy publisher where you get peanuts and they get steaks! If a publisher loves your book, then get the dosh on the table. It's their gamble, not yours. Fuck me, it's your baby so look after it.

Cor blimey, I wish I was out there so I could pull off some serious bizz deals! People don't realise how frustrating it is for me in here, when I could be out there pulling in some big deals and cleaning up! It's heart breaking, it really is.

I got a 'ton' sent in today from my old buddy Mark Emmins, and a 'score' from Gary White. Cheers, lads! Well appreciated. I got a blinding letter from my son Mike who's just finished reading *Loonyology* and says, "Your best yet, Dad!" He's up in July to see me, which is fantastic. My boy is a good 'un. He knows the score; he's smart.

I've had a sackful of mail this last week, including some right nutty letters. This one is the cherry on the cake! You'll love it.

Dear Charles,
I've seen all your films; my favourite was *Death Wish 2*. You must be a very old man now. How did a great actor like you end up in jail? Did you kill somebody? Could you please send me your autograph!

Lots of love. Sally xx (from York.)

Can you believe that? Even the censor said, "A right nutter here, Chaz." She thinks I'm the fucking actor! Me! It beggars belief, but it did cheer my day up. Thanks, Sally. A signed photo and art is on the way!

This one will kill you! It's from a lady in Crewe, Cheshire.

Dear Charlie,
I've been following your case for some time now, I think you're being persecuted for what you once were! It's obvious to everybody that you're no longer a threat or a danger to anybody. The reason I am writing is to offer you a roof over your head, a place you can feel at home. I'm a 56-year-old divorcee; I live in a large house with only three cats for company. I would love for you to live with me... maybe we could even become lovers or marry. I'm not in bad shape for my age, and I do love lots of sex – and I mean lots. In my younger day I was a porn star, one of the best in the UK. My third husband owned several clubs and studios in Soho. I am very comfortably well-off. You will have no problems and want for nothing with me! All I ask for in return is loyalty. I'm sure a man like you, who has been starved of so much sex and love, has got a lot to give to a lady like me. I'm yours and I'm waiting. Would you like to know more about me?

Yours sincerely, Vicky.

Fuck me... frightening or what? She's a complete freaky fucker who wants to own me. But then again, it's so nice to get these nutty letters. I love them! You have to walk the road of Loonyology to experience the madness. You just know I'm on my way to Crewe! You know me and Vicky are to get it on! A day, a week, a year – who fucking cares? I love her; she's mental. There's some laughs there, I can sense it! Plus a good shag. I may even do a porno while I'm there! Why not? That's how life is: fucking insane. Us old dogs love some excitement. She dreams of cock like I dream of pussy. We are only human...

Yeah, a great week! And Friday 13th ended how it started: insanely.

I had a cheese roll and a mug of sweet tea, looking up at the sky through the bars. There's something about looking up at the night sky – it feels empty and it makes you feel so tiny and lost, like an ant! That's all we are: little ants on two legs! I do love a cheese roll. It would've been better with spring onion and tomato on it, but beggars can't be choosers and I appreciate what I've got! There's a nice breeze coming in which feels good. I stand here naked to feel it on my body in the dark! I feel nice – free and human – but fuck all lasts... I finish my tea and wash my mug and spoon, then I clean my teeth, strip and wash. I'm naked and clean! If only Vicky was bending over my bed right now, I'd give her something to smile about. But she isn't and I'm finished with pulling my cock. Dreams are for fairies. I do some sit-ups and some push-ups, and it's time for bed. Friday the 13th kiss my fucking arse!

I can feel it in my heart
It's travelling around my veins
Something don't feel right
Soon I'll rip apart
An explosion deep inside
No place left to hide
Welcome to my world
Enjoy the loony slide.

Did I ever tell you about old Bernie in Broadmoor? What a brilliant poet he was. Looking back on it now, I would say he was a fucking genius! He didn't just write poetry, he spoke it. He went to Broadmoor in 1944 and I met him in 1979, when he had been locked up for 35 years. When I left in 1984 he was still there. Fuck knows if he walked out or got carried out, but I'll never forget the old fella. He didn't tell me what he was in for, but some said he killed two men with an axe! The only thing I do know is that in all those years behind that 20-foot wall he never once had a visitor or a letter.

Bernie was a ghost from the past. He used to walk up and down the landing with a pencil and note pad, jotting things down. He was always in a deep trance, always searching for his next poem. One day a young loony shoved him and he fell onto a radiator and banged his head. I grabbed the loony and dragged him into the recess and gave him a serious going over (I mean a serious bashing). The disrespectful cunt never pushed the old chap again. Days later, I was told the young loon was going to stab me up, so I beat him up again. Well, it is an asylum! That's how it works…

I often wonder about Bernie's decades' worth of notebooks full of poetry. Where are they? What has the asylum done with them, I wonder? What a book that would be – historical, legendary! Yep, he must be long free of our planet by now, but who's got his poems? That's the million-dollar question.

I just love a character, don't you? Where would we be without them? Take the loony in Rampton asylum, for example, who used to stand to attention at the dinner table and sing 'God Save the Queen'. It was fucking brilliant! He was famous for it throughout the asylum and we looked forward to it happening; it was a part of our mad existence. It didn't matter why he did it or who he was – that was his thing and you couldn't take it away from the mad fucker! It brightened up our world.

A loony once took a swing at me because he'd dreamt he'd knocked me out. He was just living out his dream but the cunt missed! That's what asylum life's all about! It grows on you and you become part of it. Even the screws are funny characters and they also go nuts. Years of mixing with the insane rubs off on them. It's got to! You can't work in a funny farm for 20 years and not be affected. Insanity is contagious! It spreads! It's fucking brilliant. YEEEOOOOWWwwwwww. YEEEOOOOWWwwwwww. Let it rip into your soul! It's brilllllliiaaannnttt! Yiiipppeeeeeee!

Keep taking the pills, you fucking loonies. We love you all.

I see Joe Calzaghe has just got a CBE. Fantastic. What a fighter and top geezer. I was well chuffed that Lynda La Plante got one too. What a brilliant writer she is, if not one of our best ever. When it comes to crime, who's better than her? Nobody. Even her TV plays and dramas are second to none. Fantastic – she's born to write. It's a gift of life! I was born with another gift of life: the ability to knock people out! You can't knock us gifted souls, it's in us from birth. So what's your gift? Come on, don't be shy! Everyone's got a gift.

I knew a scrubber who could stick four cocks in her mouth at one go. That's a gift. (She should go on *Britain's Got Talent*!) You can't knock her for it! Could you do it? Four big cocks in one go! Try it with bananas! I bet Boy George or Graham Norton can do it!

I know a tart who can blow up a hot water bottle! (I tried but I couldn't do it.) Imagine her blowing down your bell-end. Fuck me – it would kill you!

Talking of bell-ends, I've not used mine for weeks now! All that wanking has turned me soft, but my balls are like gobstoppers – hard as rock. If I was to give a lady one doggy-style right now, I swear my balls would bruise her cheeks. Maybe I should have a pull to release some tension before they explode on me! Fuck it… I can't be bothered. I've got nothing to pull one off for. I would sooner have a cuppa rosey! How fucking sad does it get?

Cop a load of this for a beauty: the Beretta Solo EELL – a beautifully-crafted 20 gauge shotgun. It only costs 56 grand, so get me two. The first shotgun I got my hands on was an old Wembley 4.10 gauge. I soon sawed the barrel down and took it into a wood to test on a few trees. Fuck me, it was wicked. Then I got myself a 12-bore five-shot repeater! I even got myself a cartridge belt. I looked like one of those Mexican bandits. I don't give a fuck for Uzis or Magnums. You can't beat a 12-bore sawn-off! "Fuck off out of my way!" People don't argue with a double barrel in their face! You don't even have to use it. (OK… let one go in the ceiling just to scare the shit out of them, but there's no need to shoot anybody.)

I've always wanted a crossbow. Whoooooosh… AAARRggghhhhhh… right in the arse. 180! Bull's eye! Cop a hold of that, you slob. Crossbow's are good for hunting. I would settle for a pea shooter right now, to hit the cannibal in the ear as he walks past my door. Then, as he turns, pop one right in his eye. That would teach the cunt to get lemon with me.

Here's a fucking blinder, you'll love this one, and the prat's in this jail (where he belongs). Pat Simms, who was jailed for life for rape in 2000, is now suing the Home Office because his human rights were affected last year when the screws went on strike! Poor thing, he says he was locked up all day and couldn't come out of his cold cell to make some toast. How sad is that? You cunt – if I had my way you wouldn't have any human rights; you would be in the cage next to me, banged up in solitary like I am year after year. All this human rights shit really does wind me up. It's obvious I haven't got any, but a fucking rapist has? What a sick world this is! He rapes some poor woman, gets lifed off and he sues the Home Office because he spent a day in solitary. Somebody get me an aspirin.

I'll tell you who was a mad fucker: Woo Bum-kon. (No, I'm not making it up!) He was a Korean copper who went on a mad mission back in 1982 in South Korea, killing 57 and injuring 35 with guns, knives and grenades before blowing himself up. (Fuck going to prison: shovel me up and wash away the blood. Don't bury me, burn me! I'll see you all in Hell later!) That's what you call a massacre. He was a true lunatic – a fucking maniac!

Australia's worst-ever mass killer was the lunatic Martin Bryant. It was back in 1996 in Tasmania that he lost the plot and shot up the planet. He killed 35 and injured 37 others! What a fucking nutter! Talk about the Tasmanian Devil! He copped a life sentence with no hope of ever being freed. Thank fuck for that. Why did he do it? I don't think anybody knows! I don't think he even knows! These sort of killers are just totally freaked out; they're born evil. Fortunately they're rare – even rarer in Britain. Let's hope it stays that way.

One of the evilest fuckers to land here in recent years was Anthony Hardy, the 'Camden Ripper'. He chopped up Sally White, Elizabeth Valad and Brigette MacClennan in 2002. He put them in bin bags and slung them out with the rubbish. The Old Bill reckons he killed many more! They should've shot the mad dog instead of arresting him. When he was here, all he did was act loony and it worked as he got moved to Broadmoor. He reckoned he saw and heard ghosts. I told him, "That's the spirits of the women you butchered coming back to haunt you. The best thing you can do is rip your sheet up and swing from the bars. Problem solved."

Did you know an ant never sleeps? I bet you never knew that! Well, you do now!

I recently got a letter from a geezer in Newcastle asking me how Tel Currie is getting on. I don't know, mate, and I don't fucking care either! I hope that answers your question.

Did you know a swallow hardly ever lands? That's truly amazing stuff! See how you learn with my books? OK, it may be a load of bollocks not worth knowing, but it's still interesting. One day you could be in a quiz and you could win it thanks to *Loonyology*. (Send me half the winnings – don't be greedy.)

16 June 2008.

I got a pile of mail today – more than 'Monster Miller' gets in 20 years. What sane person would write to that cunt? It's bad enough for me to smell him, the filthy swine! Talking of pigs, farmer Heinz Mauer in Austria found 240 of his prize pigs dead. You'll never guess how they died. Come on, have a pop at it. I bet you can't guess. OK, I'll tell you: they suffocated on the methane from their farts! The ventilation system broke down and the farts killed them. You can't make this shit up, can you? So you're now asking, "How the fuck does Bronson know all this?" Well, I'm a clever cunt. I don't just read the news, I digest it all. I love news, especially mad news, don't you? YARRRHHHoooooo.

Nine of my letters were 'jail mail' – from cons who have just read *Loonyology*. All of them loved it! So what does that tell you? It tells me I'm a good author! Cons are the worst sort of critics; they can rip an author to bits and often do! They're hard to please. I remember when Jeffrey Archer wrote his prison diaries and 90% of the cons said they were shit. They love my books because they can relate to what I write. All Archer ever did in jail was lick the governor's arsehole clean. It's the truth. Could you picture him up on the roof protesting for more food, or grabbing a hostage. The only hostage he would grab is a sausage roll and a mug of tea! "Good night, Sir, I'm banging up now!" Cunt. Anyway, cheers lads. Respect. I appreciate all your letters and I'm sorry I can't reply to you all. It's impossible because I'd need £100 a week in stamps.

I called up Sarah Macleod today; she used to be a screwess in Long Lartin. She's a good soul and a friend of mine who left the job because of the abuse she received from male screws. Sexist twats; that's how some screws are. The ignorant fuckers even fart in front of the female screws, but that's life inside. Sarah moved on and still smiles! She got a better job too, so fuck the Long Lartin screws. Their loss, not Sarah's. I also called my mum; she's up to see me Sunday.

Get on this – the ten most wanted war criminals! For some I must add 'alleged' as they still have not had a trial, but only because they have yet to be caught! We are talking alleged Nazi war criminals here.

Albert Heim, now 93 years old. Gave prisoners lethal jabs and performed operations on them without anaesthetic, timing their deaths. It's how he got his evil name, 'Doctor Death'. He just vanished after the war. Fuck me – I wonder if he was Harold Shipman's dad?

John Demjanjuk, now 87 years old. The infamous 'Ivan the Terrible', he is alleged to have sent thousands of Jews to the gas chambers. He is in the United States fighting deportation. (How do these old cunts sleep in peace? Evil fuckers.)

Sandor Kepiro, now 93 years old. He's actually been convicted twice over the Novi Sad massacre when 1,000 people were killed. He is believed to be living in Budapest. If so then go and grab the old bastard. Wake up, get the fucker and make him pay!

Milivos Asner, now 95 years old. Alleged to have sent Jews, Gypsies and Serbs to their death in 1941 and 1942. Where is he now? Some fucker must know. He wants to pray the Gypsies don't catch up with him before the law does! They will cut his balls off and stuff them down his neck, for real.

Soeren Kam, now 87 years old. He was in the SS and is wanted in connection with the deaths of journalists in Denmark in 1943. The SS targeted journalists: "Write about us and you get a hole in your head! Heil Hitler."

Heinrich Boere, now 87 years old, ex-SS. Sentenced to death in his absence for the murder of Dutch civilians. Believed to live in Germany! Yeah, but where? Find the old cunt and lock him up!

Karoly Zentai, now 86 years old. Wanted for murder in 1944. Is he still alive? Where is he? Come out and face the truth! Either way, you're going to burn in Hell!

Mikhal Gorshkow, now 79 years old. Accused of killing Jews. Jews that is, not screws. He loved to exterminate the Jews.

Algimantas Dailide, now 86 years old. Another Jew-hater, another war criminal, where are you?

Harry Mannil, now age 87 years old. Accused of the massacre of 100 Jews during the Nazi occupation of Estonia. Now believed to live in Venezuela. Well, grab the old git and stand him on trial.

What's up with the planet's leaders? You're fast enough to hunt down gangsters and bank robbers, but what about this fucking bunch of Nazis? Get off your fat arses and hunt them down, you lazy cunts!

The sun's been lovely today and I enjoyed my hour on the yard. I felt the sun on my head like a warm glow. I've a feeling this will be a lucky week! It's just a sense, so we shall see… fuck knows what! Something good will come one day. I've got some serious hope that something will come. It's all about faith – without faith you're fucked., Talking of fucked, I'm off to bed! You can't beat a good night's kip. Good night.

Oh! I just remembered back in Armley jail in 1975 there was a German Nazi-lover down the chokie block with me and Dave Anslow. He was in his sixties and had a white goatie beard and a limp. He had evil eyes which were beady and cold! I believe he was serving six years over a fraud case. The screws fucking hated him; I think because he was stinking rich! One night I had a chat with him out of the window. I shouted over to him, "Oi, Adolf!" Boy, did I learn about hate that night. That old trout was riddled with hate and it was like a cancer eating into him. He hated the planet and he spat as he spoke. I think the governor felt it best to put him in the chokie for his own safety, because the cons would've strung him up for his attitude towards us Brits (he fucking hated us). I thought it was funny at the time. Well, I was only young then and thought guys like him were characters. Although he was knocking on in age he was fearless – the screws in Armley block were brutal fuckers in the 1970s but they never scared the old Nazi. Yeah, what a memory! He moved jails and Dougie Wakefield took his cell! That was it then – the chokie became a war zone and we were all battling the screws after that.

They were mad times but they're magical memories. It becomes a magical mystery loony tour with fuck all to lose and everything to win. Let's face it, if you've got fuck all then how can you lose? Plus, you can have a lot of fun by trying to fuck up the system. It's a party, it really is! Enjoy the ride, or as Dave Courtney says, "Stop the ride, I want to get off." (You should read Dave's book, I recommend it!)

Talking of Dave, did you know he looks after my Bertha for me? Bertha's my 18-pound medicine ball! She's safe in his drum. Dave's 200% staunch! He's been offered a lot of dosh for Bertha – thousands. Well, let's face it, she's the most notorious ball in the UK. She's mine, she's priceless and she's not for sale! So fuck off and stop trying to tempt Dave to sell her. It's a funny old game. What's next? Good night!

18 June 2008.

You'll love this: 59-year-old Kevin Staples has just copped a life sentence with a four-year tariff. He's got serious arthritis but he still held up two shops with a knife. They caught him making his getaway on a Zimmer! It's a fucking good comedy sketch if nothing else! It's a bloody liberty giving him life though. Why bother? He's fucked whether he's in or out of jail!

What an ending, what a journey. He would've done better to jump off the white cliffs of Dover and leave the planet in style, taking his worst enemy with him,.

I see the Archbishop of Canterbury has condemned the wedding of two gay clerics. HA! HA! HA! HA! What a pain in the arse, if you ask me!

What about the preacher of hate being let out of jail? It's human rights gone mad! This guy Abu Qatada is described as Osama bin Laden's right-hand man in Europe. He's only in England on a dodgy passport (as an illegal immigrant) and all he's ever done in our country is preach hate and turn good Muslims into lunatics. He's been convicted in Jordan of terror offences, so why not send him back there? Fuck him off out of the UK, we don't want the poisonous fucker! Now he's out on a tag and home curfew. Big deal – he's got more than me! Fucking let me out. Better still, why not send me to Jordan? I would get a better deal out there. It's obvious the British authorities don't like me, but they love Abu Qatada. Fuck it – it's Loonyology to me!

Not a lot of news my end. All the same old bollocks.

Hey! Did you know that tomatoes prevent sunburn and premature wrinkles? Not a lot of people know that! So get those toms on your shopping list, ladies! I bet you're all thinking, "How does he know all this?" Well, I read a lot and I study things. My brain is like a massive computer or a giant sponge and I absorb it all. I'm a clever cunt, that's what I am! I bet you're now thinking, "What a fucking big-head!" Well, you go ahead and think it! But I know you'll still read on because you love it and you don't know what's on the next page. I'm dying to find out too, and I'm the writer. Mad or what?

Did you know walnuts are known to contain a form of vitamin E that may help fight off breast, prostate and lung cancer? And that's a medical fact. You'll all live to 100 by reading my books! I'll look after you but I won't ever empty your bed pan or colostomy bags. Fuck that – I'd sooner shoot you and call it a day!

Oh, by the way, rhubarb is good for the kidneys. You can't beat a bit of rhubarb. I prefer it with pink custard myself, but these fuckers never make it anymore. I used to love pink custard. Well, I am posh, see.

I had a nice jog in the rain today!

"I'm singing in the rain
Just singing in the rain
What a glorious feelin'
I'm happy again."

Great record that; great film too! Gene Kelly! That was me today: lovely, happy and free. It's my one hour of freedom and I wouldn't swap it for sex. Well, I might do. It all depends who it was with!

I got a sad letter today from Rachel Gabbitas, a young girl in Newhall jail. It's the first time she's written to me. She's only 24 and has been in and out of jail since she was 14 years old. To top it all, she was even born in jail! What a bleeding way to start a life. But there you have it – that's how unlucky some are. It happens. It's unplanned; it's fate! I bet her mum is still a great mum. That's how life works: it's crazy for some. She saw me on TV and just wrote to me. I'll drop her a line and tell her to think positive.

One day I'm sure her luck will change, I know it will.

I had a nice tea tonight: pizza, chips and beans covered in brown sauce. Fucking good filling grub. My plate was piled sky high with it. It was a good meal and I enjoyed it. I'll give it 8 out of 10! I also had three bread rolls and a mug of hot, sweet tea! Roll on tomorrow when I'll work it all off. Prison grub is good muscle-building nosh; it's done me no harm, that's for sure! I've got a back on me like a steel gate! If you stab me, the blade will bend and snap, then I'll punch a big fucking hole through your face. You really don't want to stab me! And if you shoot me, you'd better be a good shot. Pray you hit my heart or brain because I'll keep on coming at you. You can shoot my arms off and I'll still bite you to death. You really don't want to upset me – you really, really don't! If the system hasn't crushed me in all these years, how could one man do it outside? Come on, don't make me laugh. How could one man take Charlie Bronson out? Think about it. Even if you got a lucky shot in, do you think it would stop there? In your fucking dreams! HA! HA! HA! HA!

From *Wales on Sunday*, 25 May 2008.
Singing lifer adds to criminal record.
Charles Bronson has secretly been recording an album of jailhouse rock from his cell.

The notorious 55-year-old lifer, dubbed Britain's most violent prisoner, has been working with pal Mark Emmins to record the tunes down the telephone. The album will be called 'The Birdman Sings'.

There has even been talk of using his unique version of 'My Way' over the closing credits of upcoming biopic *Bronson*, which stars Brit actor Tom Hardy.

Dad-of-three Mr Emmins, who lives in Devon and met Aberystwyth-born Bronson – real name Michael Peterson – after writing to him, said: "He's been singing 'My Way' from his cell. That was going to be used for the end of the film but at the minute they are still talking about that.

"By Christmas I'll have a complete album of Charles' stuff coming out. There is one song called 'The Birdman' which is about him. It's to the tune of 'Mellow Yellow' but he has written the words."

Bronson, caged for the last 34 years, calls himself 'The Birdman' because he has done so much 'bird' – slang for jail time. He is currently held in Wakefield. He was originally sent down in 1974 for a botched armed robbery on a Luton post office, but has been inside almost ever since because of his fondness for rooftop protests, attacks on inmates and staff and hostage takings.

Mr Emmins, 45, continued: "He can sing, but he has been singing down the phone with no backing so I've had to find his timing and his key."

As well as 'My Way' there is a song called 'Charlie's Way', which features the hardman musing about prison life. And there are versions of Eric Idle's 'Always Look on the Bright Side of Life' and Louis Armstrong's 1967 classic 'What A Wonderful World'.

Mr Emmins added: "And I've got him doing a version of 'The Laughing Policeman'."

Eat your heart out, Sinatra! It's my turn. My cage has now become my music studio. What next? I'm already an artist, singer, poet and author. What more can I do from a fucking coffin? I'm an inspiration to all the dead people! Howz about that? Wake up, prison HQ, I'm coming alive! I've hatched out of your mad shell, I'm alive in the real world and your plot to bury me has backfired! Cunts.

Talking of cunts, a little prat of a governor did his rounds today and I shouted to him, "Go and play with your train set!" Even the screw laughed. The unit governor, Mr Brookes, is not a bad chap, but when he's off duty we do seem to get a few muppets coming round. Fucking idiots!

"How are you, Mr Bronson?" they ask.

"The same as yesterday, prick. Fuck off!"

I called Mark Emmins today and had a chat with his lovely wife, Lisa. She's a gem – you can all thank her for this typing! Without her there would be no more Bronson diaries. Thanks, Lisa!

CANTEEN RETURNS FORM	ARAMARK
PRISON: WKFD	DATE: 18/06/08
NAME: BRONSON	NO: BT1314
WING/CELL NO: —	
Items returned for exchange: REFUND £0-01p P/M – TOM SOUP –	
Items missing from order:	
Authorisation Signature: Original sealed bag inspected for missing items	Report A/M
Adjustment to original spend signed for: (if any)	£0-01p
Prisoner Signature: (for any spend adjustment)	
White copy to Prisoner Blue and Yellow copy to Canteen Warehouse Yellow copy will be returned with any additional items for the Prisoner CRF/00	

Fuck me… I'm rich! I've just copped a 1p refund. I'd better keep it quiet or some mad psycho will mug me, so don't tell anybody, OK? I'm rich! Yeeooooww! Yaarrhhoooooo! Yiiippppeee!

I see a Rembrandt self portrait has just sold for £2.2 million. It's only nine inches by six. I'll do you a self portrait of me for £2,000 – A4 size. Get in touch, you know where I am. Rembrandt was Dutch, I'm British; he's dead, I'm alive. It's my turn; I'm the daddy now! And don't you forget it either!

Oh well, this next document is about to blow your panties clean off, so hold on tight! After reading it, I challenge anybody in the legal profession to tell me my conviction is safe! This is now it, the 100% proof that my case is a travesty of justice, and if the Criminal Case Review Commission don't refer my case back to the Court of Appeal then it just becomes a bigger injustice. The Bronson file will never be swept away, you can bet your arses on that one.

I hand over to the one and only Giovanni – Di – Stefano! The greatest lawyer on our planet!

STUDIO LEGALE INTERNAZIONALE
LARGO G. TARTINI 3-4
00197 ROMA Via T. Salvini 15
ITALIA
TEL: +39 06 85203516 FAX: +39 06 80692652
WWW.STUDIOLEGALEINTERNAZIONALE.COM

4th June 2008

Criminal cases Review Commission
Alpha Tower
Suffolk Street
Queensway
Birmingham
BI 1TT
ENGLAND

Dear Sirs:

CHARLES BRONSON: HMP WAKEFIELD BT 1314

We represent the above inmate and refer to a letter sent to Mr Bronson by your esteemed selves dated 6th May 2008 referring to 'further application' made by Mr Bronson or someone purporting to represent him. We note with some incredulous alarm that our name is cited in the reasons for refusing to refer this case to the Court of Appeal.

We wish to make the position crystal clear. We requested a firm of solicitors CHIVERS to attend Mr Bronson and to take an attendance note on his comments based upon a preliminary advice received from Mr James Lewis QC regarding what we consider to be a fundamental flaw in the trial of Mr Bronson namely that an 'amicus' should have been appointed by the Trial Judge as it was crystal clear Mr Bronson acting in pro per could not make appropriate submissions on legal issues.

We sent a copy of that advice to CHIVERS but neither we nor Mr Bronson granted them leave to file any 'further application' because the advice was a preliminary working advice and required further submissions.

CHIVERS acting without instructions filed the said submissions as they were drafted without the further submissions that Leading Counsel had requested of us. We have no idea why CHIVERS would take such action without instructions and Mr Bronson has quite properly complained to the Law Society over the matter.

We ask thus that you disregard that 'further application' and vacate your decision. We do ask that you retain the advice of Mr James Lewis QC and consider that advice together with submissions contained in this letter and the attachments. This letter is dispatched via fax whilst the attachments and this letter are sent by post for your full consideration.

We reiterate the position as we submit as follows:

1. We consider this case a potential leading case for evaluation by the Court of Appeal on the criteria for any Court in appointing an *amicus curia* in the circumstances analogous to those of Mr Bronson.

2. In essence Mr Bronson was without legal counsel and although that may well have been a matter for choice the question that the Learned Trial Judge, in our submission, should have considered is whether the case was fit for the imposition of an amicus to protect (a) Mr Bronson (b) the Court and (c) the interests of justice.

3. The case against Mr Bronson was complicated in procedure, preparation and law. It was a similar dilemma that the ICTY (which we were involved) faced with H.E. President Milosevic as to whether the imposition of an amicus was contrary to the right of the defendant in representing himself outweighed against the rights of natural justice. Ultimately, and notwithstanding that President Milosevic was a trained lawyer the Court ruled that in such complicated cases an amicus was required.

4. We are of the view that in the case of Mr Bronson the Learned Trial Judge should have, on the Courts own motion, and especially in light of a Legal Aid Certificate remaining in force throughout the Trial for counsel and solicitors, should have imposed an *amicus curia*.

5. The whole question mark over the trial proceedings involved also the question of whether Mr Bronson was in possession of his full faculties at the time of the offence and thereafter. It was a question that having considered the history of Mr Bronson the Trial Judge should have raised but was obviously precluded from doing so without counsel advancing the position.

6. The criteria for the imposition of an *amicus curia* has to the best of our knowledge never been raised or considered even as a Practise Direction but which obviously is now becoming more and more important as Defendants frequently dismiss their legal teams.

7. In the case of Mr Bronson it was a fundamental failure not only of the Trial Judge (who was without precedent in such and without the benefit of any direction from the Court of Appeal, House of Lords, or PD from the Lord Chief Justice) but without the benefit of having raised such with Counsel. The matter was never canvassed even with Prosecuting Counsel who must have realised the difficulties that Mr Bronson faced and the obvious lacking of equality of arms.

It is for these reasons that we are of the view the conviction of Mr Bronson was clearly unsafe but that further direction is required from the Court of Appeal to the lower courts in the form of a practise direction dealing specifically with the appointment of an amicus curia. Ultimately, it will spare the Court of Appeal much time and your organisation many resources since the bulk of the complaints arriving at the Criminal Appeal Office and the CCRC stem from defendants who have dismissed their legal teams for whatever reasons.

It is interesting to note that in other jurisdictions within the EU and the US the imposition of an amicus is almost obligatory to ensure that the Court Process runs efficiently and more important effectively for all parties. To cite the US Supreme Court: "*An amicus curiae brief that brings to the attention of the Court relevant matter not already brought to its attention by the parties may be of considerable help to the Court. An amicus curiae brief that does not serve this purpose burdens the Court, and its filing is not favored.*" Rule 37(1), Rules of the Soreme Court of the U.S.

We have found a case analogous to that of Mr Bronson tried by HH Judge Coleman at Peterborough Crown Court REF: 20070222205*8 and the specific hearing date we refer you to is 21 St July 2003. We refer you to Page 5 onwards of the transcript that we have obtained clearly showing how the Trial Judge dealt with the matter and by the use of an amicus to ensure that the rights of the defendant was protected. The ability to appoint an amicus thus exists as it was used in that trial but in the case of Bronson the Trial Judge simply failed to consider that option thus placing the fairness of the trial process at risk.

We of course appreciate the arguments raised by yourselves that the matter regarding 'provocation' was canvassed at the Court of Appeal hearing by David Whitehouse QC but what must be taken into consideration is in our submission NOT what occurred at the Court of Appeal but the fairness of the trial process before a jury.

Whilst their were three issues raised in the grounds of appeal the appeal itself *primarily* centred on the duress aspect. Mr Bronson accepted that he may have falsely imprisoned the complainant, John Danielson, and caused criminal damage, but explained that he was compelled to do so owing to the duress of circumstances under which he was placed. Mr Bronson gave evidence as to those circumstances. He sought to call evidence from a number of witnesses to establish the circumstances which he had faced in his numerous years in prison and following his move to HMP Woodhill after the date of the alleged offence. He also sought to call evidence from experts to prove the mental and physical injuries he had suffered whilst in prison. HHJ Moss largely refused Mr Bronson's requests to call that evidence.

Notwithstanding the defence advanced by Mr Bronson, the learned Judge stated: "*however you felt and what you believed or anticipated might happen, that is not the same as a threat and therefore the defence of duress is not available to you*". The judge, therefore, withdrew the defence from the jury who had no other option but to convict Mr Bronson.

Mr Bronson's evidence reveals that he moved from prison to prison on approximately 138 occasions. He makes it clear that in some years he would move up to 16 times. Mr Bronson explained that he was subjected to severe intimidation and serious assaults by <u>some</u> prison officers particularly when he was transferred from one prison to another where he was often met by an intimidating reception committee of prison officers.

In addition to the evidence that Mr Bronson provided regarding the psychological and physical injuries he had suffered, the results of one of the incidents of violence he had suffered was seen by his then solicitor, Margaret Morrissey on 4th October 1994. She noted that Mr Bronson had suffered a bruised red and swollen cheekbone; bruised left eyelid with a small mark under the right side of the eye; bruised right eye under the lid towards the nose; lump and bruising behind the right eye; various cuts on and inside his lip; graze to the right side of his chin; swollen left temple; swollen and bruised right middle finger; the nail of his right finger had been broken off and was black and red in colour although green around the edges; swelling, discolouration and, bruising on his left instep; right instep swollen and bruised; his big toe nail was coming loose and he had a swollen right ankle. A Polaroid taken by a prison officer showed a bruise on the underside of Mr Bronson's right arm about 5 inches in diameter; bruising on the upper right buttock about 1½ inches in diameter; and a large area of bruising about 4 inches by 2 inches on the left buttock.

Notwithstanding such, the Trial Judge withdrew from the jury the very reasons why Mr Bronson acted as he did namely provocation on legal issues that Mr Bronson was clearly not capable of following and if ever a case cried out for an amicus such was the case. It is clear that an amicus is available since the case of Baker as mentioned above even at trial stage is permitted on the Court's own motion.

We have accentuated the matter regarding provocation and why it was necessary that such should have been left to the jury. Leading Counsel sought from us an analogous case of prison kidnapping where provocation was involved and permitted.

We have already now cited a case involving an amicus namely that of R v Baker at Peterborough Crown Court. But has there been a case similar to that of Mr Bronson in prison?

The principal complainant in the case of Bronson, John Philip Danielson, was employed by Kingston Upon Hull City Council as a Further Education Officer. He was based at Hull Prison as an Education Manager - a position which he had held since 1 st May 1998. Prior to the incident Mr Danielson criticised a cartoon which Mr Bronson had been responsible for drawing. Sometime following that, the Crown alleged that Mr Bronson has armed himself with knives from the inmates' kitchen, and had tied a knife to a snooker cue, thereby turning it into a spear. The Crown alleged that Mr Bronson had taken the complainant prisoner and kept him in his (Mr Bronson's) cell against his will from the 1 st to 3rd February 2000. It was said that Mr Bronson had tied up the complainant with rope.

On the 13th February 1997 killer Michael Sams was cleared of attempting to murder a probation officer but jailed for a further eight years for holding her hostage with a metal spike in his prison cell. Sams was convicted of holding Julie Flack after a four-day trial at Durham Crown Court. Sams, 55, who conducted his own defence, was cleared of trying to murder Mrs Flack, 50, the wife of the Rt Rev John Flack, Bishop of Huntingdon, who was attacked as she held a surgery at Wakefield Prison, South Yorks, on Oct 23, 1995.

Mr Justice Morland told Sams: "Although I accept that you never intended to harm her, you threatened to kill her unless she did as you said and you armed yourself with a metal object, sharpening it to terrorise her. You also had tape to bind her. She was petrified, traumatised and in a state of shock."

Sams said that his intention had merely been to shock Mrs Flack. He had carried out the attack on Mrs Flack partly to focus attention on his claim that the Prison Service had prevented him from suing Miss Slater for accusing him of raping her. He was also angry about a refusal to let him sell his paintings for charity. Mr Justice Morland said he acknowledged that Sams had "genuine grievances" against the Prison Service.

In that case provocation WAS permitted thus allowing Sams to be cleared by a jury of attempted murder and convicted of kidnapping. The sentence of eight years was imposed being a definitive sentence and the comments from Mr Justice Moreland acknowledged that Sams had a 'genuine grievance' against the Prison Service.

One must thus ask how it is possible that Mr Bronson, who has clearly suffered far worse and has no history as that of killer Sams, was denied provocation relatively at the same time that Sams a killer was permitted to use provocation?

Mr Sams was permitted to use provocation because of his feeling whilst Mr

Bronson was not yet the circumstances of kidnapping are similar!

Mr Bronson quite properly feels aggrieved at this disparity not only of sentence (Sams a killer receiving 8 years as a fixed sentence whilst Bronson receives life) but on how the Bronson trial was conducted. It is this disparity of treatment that in our view must be addressed by the Court of Appeal.

There are a number of factors which require this case to be re-considered by the Court of Appeal. We have dealt with the following: (a) the use of an amicus on the court's own motion (b) disparity of treatment as outlined in the case of R v Sams (c) denial of provocation as a defence. There are of course other factors.

The refusal of the learned Judge to allow Mr Bronson to call some or all of the witnesses that he required to establish the factual circumstances that existed at the time of the offence, and/or were likely to exist in the future should he be moved back to solitary confinement, coupled with the learned Judge withdrawing the defence of duress from the jury in our view, arguably, supports the contention that the trial process failed to ensure that the minimum rights set out in **Article 6(2)(d)** were respected. The argument is even stronger in respect of the medical/expert witnesses that Mr Bronson wished to call, particularly from Dr Kennedy (available at the time of his trial) showing that Mr Bronson was suffering from post-traumatic stress disorder (a factor the jury ought to have been asked to consider when determining whether duress was made out) and from Dr Ghosh showing that Mr Bronson's condition had been aggravated by sensory deprivation which had occurred from solitary confinement over many years. It appears that an abundance of medical evidence has come to light since the trial, particularly from Dr Bob Johnson, confirming the existence of medical injuries to Mr Bronson caused to him during his time in prison.

Dr Kennedy found Mr Bronson to be mentally unstable due to the combination of post-traumatic stress disorder and certain personality factors (see his report, dated 24th January 2000). Dr Ghosh found that Mr Bronson suffered from paranoid personality disorder noting Mr Bronson to suffer from a number of associated symptoms (see Dr Ghosh's report; dated 2nd September 1999). This, in our view, ought to have been evidence that was put before the jury as being relevant factors that the jury ought to have considered when determining the defence of duress, especially as they ought to have considered the relevant characteristics of Mr Bronson and the factual circumstances that existed at the time in determining whether the defence was made out.

This is made all the more apparent in the light of the learned Judge's summing up to the jury in which he stated:

"The defence, as I have said, is limited to those circumstances where the threat, and it has to be threat of death or serious injury, arises. There has been talk in this case of psychological injury by Mr Bronson Serious injury can include psychological injury but it would be necessary for you to have heard expert evidence about that, or at least medical evidence before that could be shown to be the case. Mr Bronson tells you the situation that he believed to be then you are entitled to consider it but effectively psychological damage in this particular context again does not arise because of no other evidence that has been called to that effect." (Transcript of Summing up and verdict, page 7, para 25 to page 8, para 10).

Given that the learned Judge failed to allow Mr Bronson to call medical witnesses it must be unfair to then inform the jury to ignore whether there was/or be likely to be psychological injury as there had been no evidence called on the issue. Furthermore, in our view, this was a material misdirection insofar as the concept of duress involves the threat of serious injury or death. It did not need to be established that there was psychological injury; only that there was a threat of such injury and/or a belief that such an injury would occur **(R v S and Others)**.

In withdrawing the defence of duress for the jury's consideration and in not allowing the calling of witnesses to give relevant evidence it is arguable that Mr Bronson was denied a reasonable opportunity of presenting his case, and, therefore, placed at a substantial disadvantage in comparison with the Crown. If that be right, there is a good argument to contend that the trial process failed to respect the 'equality of arms' principle as required generally by **Article 6(1)**.

Since the Court of Appeal rejected Mr Bronson's appeal the law with regards to the withdrawing of defences from a jury has been clarified by the House of Lords in **Wang [2005]**. Had the Court which considered Mr Bronson's appeal had the advantage of seeing their Lordships' decision in **Wang [2005]** we are of the view that they would have allowed Mr Bronson's appeal. This clarification of the law, in our view, confirms that Mr.Bronson's convictions are unsafe.

We have taken some considerable time in outlining legal issues but the greatest injustice has occurred at the manner upon which in similar circumstances and at similar times a mass killer Michael Sams tried at Durham Crown Court and Mr Bronson are treated so differently. Mr Sams succeeds in his defence of duress and provocation on a far worse case than Bronson whilst Mr Bronson is not even permitted to argue such. It is this disparity and whereas Mr Baker at Peterborough Crown Court is appointed an amicus by the Trial Judge on drug offences whilst Mr Bronson must deal with complex legal issues himself.

It cannot be that a trial on similar circumstances simply because of venue and judge is dealt with differently. Justice must be consistent not diverse. Mr Bronson is entitled to feel that justice has not been 'seen to be done' let alone done.

In our view that failure made any verdict unsafe and wholly unsatisfactory and this case in our most respectful consideration requires the intervention of the Court of Appeal. We thus ask that you take these matters into consideration and ignore the 'other submissions' that were made without authority and which were incomplete.

We look forward to hearing from you. Kindest of regards

Yours faithfully

Studio Legale Internazionale

Well? Am I being denied a fair trial? Am I being denied justice? You can bet your house on it! It's a fucking travesty of justice and it's truly unlawful. Watch this space; I could be home sooner than later.

This legal stuff can really go on and on till you're all dried up. It can also cause a lot of stress and anxiety if you allow it to. It's all Loonyology to me! Even though it's 100% fact in black and white, it's still 'pie in the sky' shit to me – dreams that don't seem to come true, black rainbows, hope with big holes. The law is the law and it's there for us all! We should all be treated equally. If I was black, Irish or a Muslim I would probably have more chance of a victory. Giovanni is doing his very best, but he's up against a system that's more corrupt than Al Capone ever was. Me, I can wait another 20 years if need be, but one day the truth will free me for sure! And then what? You'll just have to wait and see! (It will be worth the wait, believe me.)

Did you know teratophobia is a fear of giving birth to a monster? Fuck me, and I'm in monster mansion. I'm a celebrity, get me out of here! Vote me out and tell Ant and Dec to come in and get me! And fucking hurry up!

I've got the official 'whole life' tariff list here – 34 of Britain's walking dead:

David Bieber
Donald Nielson
Arthur Hutchinson
Victor Miller
Peter Moore
Trevor Hardy
Andrezei Kunowski
Paul Culshaw
Billy Horncy
Mark Martin
Rahan Arshad
Glyn Dit
Colin Ireland
John Childs
John Duffy
Ian Brady
Jeremy Bamber
Tony Entwistle
Peter Hegarty
Mark Hobson
Paul Glen
John McGrady
David Tiley
Robert Maudsley
Denis Nilsen
Malcolm Green
Rose West
Victor Castigador
Anthony Arkwright
John Hilton
Kenny Regan
Viktor Dembouskis
Steve Ayre
Michael Smith

A lot I've come across and the rest I don't want to come across! But I'm baffled as to why many more names are not on this list, such as Sutcliffe, Huntley and Sidney Cooke. What about all the child killers and terrorists? I believe this list of 34 is just the tip of the iceberg; there's hundreds more I could add to this list of doom. Fuck me – there's probably 300 cunts here I could stick on and another good 500 in Broadmoor! I remember one slag there who ate a six-week-old baby. Ate it! It doesn't get any sicker than that! He had a job eating anything after I butted him in the 'boat' and smashed out some teeth. We called him 'the soup freak' after that. Cunt.

Another one who was on this list was my old pal 'Big' Harry MacKenney. He got fitted up on five murders back in 1979 but walked out of the appeal court in 2003 after a quarter of a century of his life had been sucked away from him by a filthy police informer, John Childs. Childs stuck Harry's name up for no other reason but evilness. Now get on this: Harry is still waiting for his compensation five years on. His claim is worth millions! To date, the scum have paid him two interim payments of 100K, so up to now that's £200,000 in five years – peanuts. It's a bloody insult to an innocent man and it winds me up to think about it. Harry is now 77 years old and the cunts are waiting for him to die! They don't want to pay him. It's a fucking disgrace and it's shameful – but what's new? Nothing amazes me anymore. The real criminals are the law! Fucking pay the man, you evil bastards! Pay him for the 24 years you stole off him. Harry was a good bizz man, a pilot and an inventor. He invented and manufactured a type of life jacket which still sells today. He was a good, honest man! Now, at 77, he is riddled with pulmonary emphysema. He's not a well man and the system still treats him like a leper. It's one of Britain's worst-ever cases of injustice and so few even know about it. It's time the shit hit the fan. In this case, the fan hits the shit! Pay the man.

All you cons who need some help and advice or guidance in prison legal matters, you need a lawyer who specializes in prison law. It's no good having a brief who's only good at defending speeding offences. Some of the lawyers I've had over the years were shaking just walking into jail. They were intimidated by the security and were like a fish out of water. It's like going into a monastery for some S&M – it can't happen. Forget it. So here are some good prison law specialists for you to contact. They're all good at parole reviews, licence recalls, categorizations, transfers, adjudications, drug tests, review and appeals, lifer panel reviews, confiscation orders, further charges and immigration. If you've a problem, get a good brief and fight your way out. Don't sit on your fat arses and accept the prison bollocks. Get your pen out and write to one of these guys. Good luck.

ROSS SIMON & CO SOLICITORS
UNIT 23
EUROLINK BUSINESS CENTRE
49 EFFRA ROAD
LONDON
SW2 1BZ
TEL – 0207 738 7953

RA DAVIES & CO SOLICITORS
FIRST FLOOR
THE OLD BAKE HOUSE
CANTERBURY
CT1 1TU
TEL – 01227 760500

CORPER SOLICITORS
859a HIGH ROAD
GOODMAYES
ILFORD
ESSEX
IG3 8TG
TEL – 0208 590 8686

BREYDONS SOLICITORS
64a NORTH QUAY
GREAT YARMOUTH
NORFOLK
NR30 LJB
TEL – 01493 331057

BURTON COPELAND SOLICITORS
ASTLEY HOUSE
23 QUAY STREET
MANCHESTER
M3 4AS
TEL – 0161 827 9500

LOUND MULRENAN JEFFERIES SOLICITORS
SOUTHBANK HOUSE
BLACK PRINCE ROAD
LONDON

SE1 7SJ
TEL – 0207 793 4012

NOBLE SOLICITORS
21 HIGH STREET
SHEFFORD
BEDS
SG17 5DD
TEL – 01462 814055

SOMERS AND BLAKE SOLICITORS
49b BOSTON ROAD
HANWELL
LONDON
W7 3SH
TEL – 0208 567 7025

LAWRENCE'S SOLICITORS
32a SHEEP STREET
WELLINGBOROUGH
NORTHANTS
NN8 1BT
TEL – 01933 442178

The things I do for you cons! I hope you all appreciate it. If you need any more good lawyers then get *Loonyology: In My Own Words* as I've put plenty in there from all over the UK. You're spoilt for choice, so get writing. You could have a case worth winning and get home faster. Those prison law specialists know more than we will ever know. They're the professionals!

Hey! What do you call an 88-year-old man who's had three heart attacks? Jerry Hat Trick. What, don't you get it? Are you fucking silly? Geriatric… oh, fuck it. Forget it!

What about the prison governor in a jail in Rome who allowed a pair of newlywed cons to go in a room to consummate their marriage? The groom was serving 10 years and the bride eight years, and they were allowed 30 minutes of serious shagging. That's the Italians for you. Why can't us Brits be so generous?

There's a jail in South America that allows prostitutes in once a month. That's only for the cons with dosh. Well, you don't get fuck all on this earth for nothing! You can't expect those girls to come in and go out with sore fannies just for fun, can you? Life's not like that. You have to pay your way to get the very best. Yeah, governor, stick me down for three tarts! Let's have some serious fun. Fuck the seven deadly sins – let's party!

My lovely friend Dee Morris has just sent me in a 'score' to get some canteen with. I'm truly blessed with diamond friends. Thank you, Dee, you shouldn't have.

Well, that's my lot. I'm off to bed! But I'll be back if I wake up. If I don't, then fuck the planet. You lot make sure you kick some arse! Fucking kick it black and blue – kick it till it screams! You know you'll love it. Let your hair down. If you're bald, just keep kicking it; you don't need hair. Think of the money you'll save on shampoo and haircuts. Fucking kick it… Lights out.

Saturday, 21 June 2008.
I just got my complaint form back! You've got to read their reply – it's fucking brilliant. Seeing is believing but you won't believe it! If you did, you'd deserve to be in the asylum yourself. Enjoy the read…

HM PRISON SERVICE

FORM COMP 1
PRISONER'S FORMAL COMPLAINT

Establishment
Serial no. W086/08F

Read these notes first
1. This form is for you to make a formal written complaint under the complaints procedures. Complaints should wherever possible be sorted out informally by speaking to your wing officer or making an application. Use this form only if you have not been able to resolve your complaint this way.
2. A written complaint should be made within 3 months of the incident or of the relevant facts coming to your notice.
3. Keep your complaint brief and to the point.
4. When you have completed the form, sign it and post it in the box provided. The form will be returned to you with a response.
5. If you are unhappy with the response, you can appeal on a separate form (COMP 1A).
6. Some subjects are dealt with only by the Area Manager or Prison Service headquarters. If your complaint is about one of these subjects, the reply will take longer.
7. There is a separate pink form (COMP 2) for confidential access complaints.

Your details (use BLOCK CAPITALS)

Surname	BRONSON	First name(s)	CHARLIE
Prison number	B71314	Location	C.S.C UNIT

Have you spoken to anyone about your complaint? Yes ☑ No ☐

If so, who did you speak to?
SCREW.

Your complaint
FROM 5.45PM TO 6PM I CALLED 3 HOME LINE NUMBERS ON THURSDAY 19TH JUNE. IT COST ME FOURTEEN POUNDS.
(IN MY 5 YEARS OF USING THE PHONE ITS NEVER COST ME A 1/4 OF THAT.)
I BELIEVE SECURITY ARE NOW DELIBERATLY SPEEDING UP MY UNITS TO STOP ME USING THE PHONE. OWING TO ME RECENTLY TALKING TO THE MEDIA. (AND PUTTING ME ON HIGH RISK CALLS.)
THERE CAN BE NO OTHER EXPLANATION FOR IT
(£14 FOR 15MIN ON A HOME LINE IN ENGLAND)

Does your complaint have a racial aspect? Yes ☐ No ☐
Is your complaint about bullying? Yes ☐ No ☐

What would you like to see done about your complaint?
I WANT MY DOSH BACK..
IM SUPPOSED TO BE THE ROBBER.
AND NOW IM BEING ROBBED OFF THE SYSTEM!
(IT'S CRIMINAL)

Signed [signature] Date 19/6/2008

Reply: I have attached a print of your last 30 days' calls and their costs. We have no facility to change the cost of any calls legally.

Now see why it's called Loonyology? Fuck it!

Good news today! Old one-eyed Abu Hamza, the hooked rat, has lost his bid to dodge extradition to the US. Fucking good job too! Now stick the racist fucker on a plane and let's all forget the cunt once and for all. All good Muslims should be happy about this, because all this cunt ever did was preach racial hatred. Once he gets put into one of the Yankee max secure jails, he will realise just how kind we were to him over here. You're in for a big awakening, Hamza! The bigger the better! Your tomb awaits you.

I'm on a visit tomorrow with my mum and brother, so there'll be plenty of choc bars and milkshakes. "Sunday, lovely Sunday." If my mum had a pound for every visit she would be rich. What a mother! She's got a heart of gold, but my heart melts every time I see her. It's just not right her still having to see me in jail. Something doesn't add up. It should be me visiting her, not her visiting me! It's crazy! It's mad! It's Loonyology!

One day I pray to be able to visit her, before it's too late! If that day is stolen from me, it will be my biggest regret – my only regret. I'll never forgive prison HQ if that happens, but the way it's going it could well happen. It's time to give Charlie Bronson a break! Cut me some slack, move me on and let me live!

Monday, 23 June 2008.

A great visit yesterday with mum, Mark and our cousin John Cronin! We always have a laugh together. Mum had a nice red coat on and looked well. I passed some art out as gifts – one for my aunty Eileen, one for John and one for John H Stracey. My art ends up all over the planet.

I got a letter today from Tony Simpson with all the usual bollocks excuses: "I'm skint, I only did the art deal to get the kids a birthday gift..." Fuck off, I've heard all this shit before! He should have asked me, not gone behind my back like a rat. What sort of cunt lives off a bloke in a coffin? If you're skint, do what I did to end up in jail: go rob a fucking bank.

Sadly, Tony only recently lost his mother. We were all sad to hear that. But why do deals with my art that I gave to him as a gift? In future, anybody who's skint and needs dosh and is my buddy, ask me, tell me, and we can sort something out! I'll help you. But if you do it behind my back then accept the consequences of being cunted off. OK, cunt? End of.

Loonyology is not a fucking charity! My art is my soul and it's priceless (to me), so respect it or fuck off! Please, Jesus, God, the Almighty! Let me go home so I can sort all this bollocks out. It's so frustrating that I can't break the odd few jaws. How would you feel, God? It's just not fair.

Amir Khan did it again at the weekend. He smashed the granny out of Micky Gomez at Birmingham NIA in five brilliant rounds. Gomez even knocked Khan to the canvas! I think that was Khan's best fight to date. We are soon to see him win the world title, for sure. I just hope Frank Warren doesn't keep him waiting too long, because Khan is ready for a world title shot. He's fucking brilliant. I've said this fighter is special from day one! I just hope he doesn't end up like that flash, big-headed fucker Prince Naseem Hamed.

I got nine letters today. One was from a right nutter in Strangeways jail! Even the screw censor warned me it was "nutter mail".

Charlie Bronson,
I've just read your book *Solitary Fitness*, what a right load of shit. You couldn't punch your way out of a rice pudding! You're an old has-been. Stand down and learn from me! I'm 27 yrs old and 14 stone of solid muscle! I can bench-press 300 lbs, curl 150 lbs, I could snap your neck with one punch! Retire now or face the pain later. As I will do you a lot of serious damage! Your time is now over!

Dingo.

Fuck me. Dingo? He's even got a dog's name! What a total wanker. What is his problem? Dingo, you're a fucking dreamer. Instead of wanting to take me out, why don't you take a few screws or a governor or six out? Or is it that you're taking your hate out on me instead of the penal system? You bully boys haven't got the bottle to fight this corrupt system. Rip the roof off for the lads or chin the worst screw on your wing and earn some respect! If you want to be 'hard' then do something better than writing me your muggy letters.

I bet Dingo is a petty criminal who's padded up with another con and he's pretending to be a 'face' so he can impress his cell mate. "Look at me threatening Bronson, I'm not scared of him." See Dingo, cunts like you are two-a-penny! You were born a cunt and you'll die a cunt. But it's a cunt like you who could well put an extra 10 years on my stay inside, as I would rip your throat out on sight for disrespecting me. What have I ever said or done to you? You weren't even born when I came inside! Anyway Dingo, go clean your bone! You're a cunt!

I also got a card from my son Mike! I'll be seeing him in July and I can't wait. I also called Mark Fish but he wasn't in, so I called my brother to see if they got home safe. They had a good journey home.

I had a nice cheese salad with tomatoes and lettuce – all that rabbit nosh. Good for you, though. The soup wasn't bad either; I had six bread rolls with it. The sun's out and Wimbledon's started up – a load of fairies prancing about with a racket and a furry ball. The only reason the blokes watch it is to get a butchers of the women's pants. You know that's why. It's a bollocks old game and it's snobbish. The price of those strawberries is scandalous! Fuck Wimbledon and fuck the Wombles too! I'd sooner watch a spider spin a web, and I probably will.

I got a letter from my old buddy Leighton Frayne (my Welsh connection) and another from Alfie Lodge, the No. 1 poacher in the UK! (Not bad as he was once a post office raider. What's a few rabbits and salmon between friends?)

I did a cracking cartoon today of Abu Hamza (that cunt in Belmarsh with the hook and one eye). That's the third cartoon I've done of him in a week! I just enjoy drawing ugly fuckers. At times I guess I'm still a nasty bastard under the skin. I can't help myself – I've just got that wicked way about me! Naughty but nice. (What's wrong with that?)

Did you know Tom Hardy has already been in two Hollywood blockbusters: *Band of Brothers* and *Black Hawk Down*? That's why he will make the *Bronson* movie a hit. Move over Brad Pitt and Tom Cruise, this is Tom's era. He's the man, mark my words.

Did you know it's 44 years ago that the Rolling Stones had their first No. 1 hit? Fuck me – can you believe that? Do you know what it was? I bet you don't. Well, fucking find out because I'm not telling you! Who do you think I am, a bleeding teacher? I'm nobody's teacher, I'm just me.

Tuesday, 24 June 2008.

Hey! You'll never guess what I got today. A brand-new mattress. I had the old one for four and a half years. It was lovely and thin, but scruffy! I woke up today about 5.30am and thought, I need a new mattress. The screw 'Dicko' sorted it for me! He's a diamond, a top 'kanga'. He used to work in Armley jail before he came to monster mansion. I like him because he's a character! Anyway, I've got a brand-new mattress for a brand-new day. I told you I'm lucky… born lucky.

I used to nick beds from outside shops when I was a teenager. It's easy: just hang about, wait for the shop lorry to load up, and as they stick it on the lorry you grab it and run off. I must have had hundreds of the fuckers and I would sell them for next to nothing. All my mates and their families had one. We had the best beds in Bedfordshire.

One time I nicked a motor and as I drove off I heard a strange noise on the back seat. It was a fucking geezer snoring! I shat myself and I almost crashed the motor, so I just pulled up and did a runner. That proves I'm not so bad, as I could have slung him out, the lazy drunken bastard. What the fuck was he doing on the back seat? Today's youth would've mugged him and half kicked him to death, but that's never been my scene. I don't believe in hurting innocent people. It's a new era now: a violent, out-of-control world.

I got eight letters today! One from my old buddy Johnny Griffiths and one from John H Stracey. I also called John H for a chat. What a legend, what a guy. 57 years old and he still trains every day. A top geezer in my book. Max respect.

I also got a lovely letter from Gemini Reynolds. She now lives out in Cyprus and she's one hot, sexy woman. What wouldn't I do for three hours in the pit with her! She just oozes sex. Some women are born sexy, some aren't! Gemini is one of those special sexy souls. Top lady!

Mushroom soup for dinner. I had two bowls to make up for the muggy Rice Krispie breakfast. Fuck me silly. Rice Krispies, what's all that about? It's fucking crazy. Tea was some sort of stew! It wasn't the best of diet days, but it's still better than half the world gets! And I'm locked up, so it's still good.

A screw was telling me he saw one of my unlicensed fights on some website! He said it was brilliant. Yeah, it would be better if I could get the fuck out now and fight again! The amount of dosh I could rake in would be mountain high. People would pay a ton a ticket to see me fight, hoping I'd get killed. HA! HA! HA! HA! HA!

Wyn wrote to say her dog Blue had died. That's sad, but nothing lives forever. Keep your chin up, Wyn.

Eddie Clinton is up to see me on Thursday. He's a good old buddy of mine. It's just one big lovely family to me! We're all brothers and sisters on the same journey.

I've been invited to attend my case review on 26 June. I'm supposed to be offered one every month but this is my first invite in four months. I sit in one cell with a barred hole in the wall and a team of them sit in another cell. It's like looking at the *Muppet Show* through a square hole in the wall; it's fucking mental. I'll be on it if they change it to the morning as I'm on a visit that day. I'll put my case over: I want moving on and I want progress, but I've been asking this for years and look where it's got me. After all these years of good behaviour they won't even trust me to be in the same room as them. Still, I wouldn't trust them with my pet guinea pig (if I had one), would you?

I had a nice jog on the yard today; it was lovely and sunny. I really wanted an ice cream and it doesn't help when you hear the ice cream van over the wall. It fucking does my nut in! Those vans should turn the tune off as they pass prison walls. I bet the cunts do it on purpose! Now that's evil; I call it really nasty. You cunts! Yeah, not a bad old day, it's good to be alive.

They reckon the polar bear will be extinct within 25 years. How fucking sad is that? Wake up, planet, before it's too late! The polar bear today, us tomorrow… Oh well, must try my new mattress out. Who's a lucky geezer? Nighty night!

Before I go, here's a little story for you about the one that got away. You'll love this; it's a miracle! Are you sitting comfortably? Then I shall begin.

It was Xmas 1991 and I was in the punishment block in Hull jail. As blocks go, Hull isn't so bad. The screws are pretty laid back and they turn a blind eye to a lot of things, plus they've known me since the 1970s so I suppose they do give me a bit more slack than most. One screw in that block was a giant of a man – 'Big Arthur'. He was, in fact, a trawler fisherman for 20 years before he joined the prison service. This guy was a good 20 stone and a total gentleman – a very nice, fair screw who I respected as he had a good way about him in dealing with situations. A lot of screws will just rush in pulling their sticks, but Arthur's way was: "Come on, lads, cool down, it's not worth it." Nine times out of 10 his way worked. I know one con that chinned Arthur and it had no effect. "If that's the best you can do, son," he said, "give it a rest." That's Arthur in a nutshell: hard but fair. (You show me a deep sea fisherman that's any different. They're all tough cookies. Some have lost fingers through the freezing cold oceans and all have seen sights we only have nightmares about. Working in a prison is soft and easy to them; you'd better believe it.)

Anyway, Arthur unlocked my door for Xmas feeding time. In the block only one door was unlocked at a time and I was always on a 'six guard unlock' – sometimes more if I was playing up. From my cell, I had to walk down a landing and down a set of stairs to get to the hot-plate and collect my food. I was feeling good in myself, pressure free, ready for a nice Xmas meal. It's the one meal of the year that all cons look forward to. It's a special day, a treat. But what faced me then almost turned Xmas into Hell. The Bishop of Hull was there, right in front of my very eyes! I began to sweat and the adrenalin started to pump around my body. This was my chance for the big one, a choice hostage, and I had seconds to act! Let me try to explain how it is...

Imagine you're sitting on a couch watching a great movie with a box of chocolates on your lap. You eat four, then eight, then... oh, just one more! When do you stop? Blimey, there's only six left. I had best eat them, I don't want them to go off. It would be a waste. So you eat the lot then think, "What a fucking greedy pig I am. A whole box of chocolates, greedy motherfucker!" Well, that's how a siege is with me. Do I or don't I; will I or wont I?

A hostage-taking like this can't be planned. This is the box of chocolates on a silver tray and you have to react fast with a head lock and a crack on the jaw. Grab and shout; mean business! "Stand back or I'll snap his neck! I'm in charge, now fuck off!" All this is rushing through your brains in seconds whilst your food is being dished out on your plate.

The bishop had his hat and gown on and that hooked stick (like a shepherd's). Do it! *Don't!* Now! *I can't!* Hurry up! Stop sweating! *I can't! Fuck me, he's a bishop!* Hurry up! Make a move! Chin the screw first, then grab him! *Fuck me, Charlie, you can't! Can you? He's an old man! He may die of shock!*

Do it!

Don't do it!

Do it!

Don't do it!

Do it!

Don't fucking do it!

Do it now!

My head was in bits – I was about to crash out and go insane. I had never felt so much mental anguish in my life. This was true pressure bubbling up in a pot of madness!

Fuck me, Chaz – it's the Bishop. So fucking what? *I can't.* You can. *How can I?* Why can't you? He's just a geezer in a frock with a silly hat. You're getting soft. *I'm not.* You are. Grab him and make a stand. *No... I can't.* Yes you can... and will. *But he's an old man.* So what? *He may die!* So what? *I can't.* You can. *I won't.* You will. *How can I?* Easy. *What will my demands be?* The world, your freedom, anything! *I can't, I won't, how can I?* Coward. *Fuck off.* You'll never get another chance to grab a bishop. *I don't want another chance.* You bottler. *Fuck off.*

By now the screws were closing in on me and the heat was up high! They could sense I was acting strange. It was now or never, it was that classic situation at the red traffic light: do you or don't you? It's a judgement that can cost you dearly; it could even kill you or others. Do you or don't you? I took one last look at the bishop and said, "No." I grabbed my food and almost ran back to my cell. Even Arthur said, "Are you OK, Charlie?"

"Yeah! Sweet. Shut the door!"

Bang.

That was the closest the bishop ever got to becoming a hostage at Xmas. Why did I decide not to act? The truth is I couldn't do it because of his age. My name's Charles Bronson not Charles Manson. I've got a heart. God was there that day and he must have played a part in that! And bear in mind this was the era and the decade when I truly did not give a flying fuck about anything or anybody. Even the consequences of my actions didn't bother me. It was that moment's victory that counted, not some prat in a gown with a hooked stick. Those days are gone now, because one thing I learned that day was the meaning of self-control. I proved to myself I could walk away. I had a heart and I just couldn't do it. He had done me no wrong, so why should I do him wrong? Now, if it had been the top man from prison HQ, I would've had him so fast his feet wouldn't have touched the floor all the way back to my cell. Cunt.

Arthur later asked what had upset me that Xmas day. I answered, "Myself, only myself."

Fuck me – how close were we all to Hell that day? That, my friends, is how easily insanity can explode. You just never know when or where it will come. It's fucking Loonyology. Good night.

25 June 2008.

Fuck me, this is a hard mattress. It's not a Slumberland, that's for sure! Could I get comfy on it? Could I fuck. It's going to take me years to soften this fucker up. (Let's hope I never do.) Fuck kipping on this one for four and a half years!

I found out today that the nonce John Duffy (the 'railway killer') is almost above me and has been for three months. He's like a little fucking mute mouse but that piece of shit raped and killed a few girls. Apparently, he came here from the nonce wing in Whitemoor three months back and hasn't left his cell once. He doesn't even go out on the yard because he doesn't want us to see him – not through shyness, but through shame! The little cunt. I thought there was a bad smell in the air!

It says in today's newspaper that BT (who have a monopoly over phones in English and Welsh jails) are charging prisoners seven times their normal call rates. I said all this ages ago and complained about it – it's exploitation at its very best. Cunts. Hey! Just who are the real criminals? Seven times more costly! It's a fucking liberty!

I see the French artist Claude Monet's masterpiece 'Le Bassin aux Nympheas' has just sold for 41 million smackeroons! Fuck me. I told you it's all Loonyology.

I got a pile of mail today and there's one I must share with you from a Broadmoor loony called 'Baz'. (I won't say his last name in case the asylum authorities get upset. You've got to watch out for the PC brigade today when it comes down to our country's loonies.)

Dear Chaz,

My name's Baz, I live in Broadmoor hospital. I was certified mad back in 1989. I strangled my aunty and burnt the house down! I've read all about you and some of the nurses here tell me you're a nasty person, as when you were here years ago all you did was attack people and smash the place up. Why did you do it, Chaz? Try to be good... you're not helping yourself! If you need a friend or any advice, don't be afraid to write to me. God does love you, Chaz. You're never alone. God bless you.

Baz

Well, that takes the fucking biscuit. Cheeky cunt – he strangles his poor aunty and burns the fucking house down and he wants to give me advice? You just couldn't make this shit up even if you tried. I love it. I wrote back to the mad fucker: "Strangle the Yorkshire Ripper and burn the asylum down. God won't mind. Cunt!"

CHAPTER 9

Lick it and suck it!

(Pass the ice cream – what did you think I meant?)

Jimmy Williams, 2006. Legendary fight trainer outside the legendary Hall of Fame.

Sugar Ray Leonard arriving at Grazianos. His smile speaks for him – born a star.

James Bonecrusher Smith, at the Hall of Fame 2005. This guy could hit, ask Bruno. He also went the distance with Tyson. That alone stands him in the Hall of Fame and a true legend. If he hit you now, with all that extra bulk, your head would fly off.

Two of the greats, present and past – Ricky Hatton and Carmen Basilio. How great is that to see two ring warriors together from different eras?

1994, Belmarsh Jail. My no.1 buddy on this planet – still in my heart. I'll catch the old rascal up later. RIP Dad XX.

The lovely Gemini, and she loves *Loonyology*! "Dear Chaz, well done, a great book. Love, Gemini xxx."

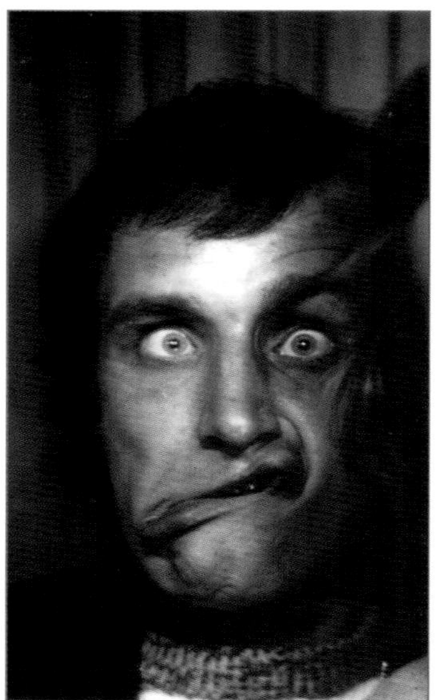

My old buddy Andy Doughall. Andy copped a life sentenc in the early 1980s. He cut a pervo's bollocks off. The last time I saw him was in Parkhurst around 1990. He had put on a lot of weight, and I mean a lot of weight. He was a bloated 22 stone and he didn't look at all well. Last I heard he had a blow up in Bristol Jail and died. He died how he lived – violently. He was a typical Jock! Proud and scared of nobody. I was in several jails with Andy and two asylums. I've got some magical memories of him – some best left buried. But he was one of the top 10 most violent men I met on my jouney and I can say with all honesty, 99% of his violence was on nonces. So I salute him… don't you? What *normal bloke* wouldn't give a nonce a slap? RIP Andy – respect to you.

Lorry Greenwood, in Newhall Prison. Lorry's brother I met some years back in Fullsutton. It was then I learnt about Lorry. She copped a life sentence as a youngster. She served 20 years and made it out. I respect her so much as she is a true survivor in my eyes. I've seen grown men on their knees in 20 weeks, let alone 20 years. Lorry came in a pretty girl and walked out a beautiful woman. That, to me, is magical.

Clare Barston, in Newhall Prison. Clare got life back in the 1980s. I've lost track of her over the years. That's what prison does. It loses you in the system. She's a very intelligent, creative woman who I admire so much. I do hope she's freed by now. She's just too pretty to be inside. The world is her oyster – in the free world: believe it.

Right: Dee Morris. She's gotta be one of my best friends – a true friend. We go back years and she's still there for me in case I need something sorting. My mum loves Dee – we all do. A true Cockney sparrow with a heart of gold. Love and respect.

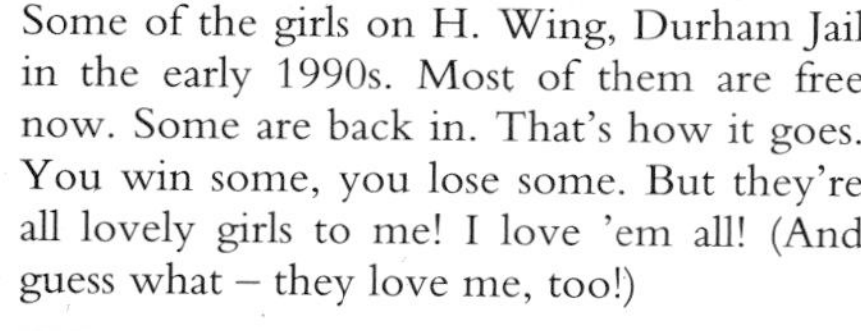

Some of the girls on H. Wing, Durham Jail in the early 1990s. Most of them are free now. Some are back in. That's how it goes. You win some, you lose some. But they're all lovely girls to me! I love 'em all! (And guess what – they love me, too!)

Above and right: The media labelled her the Black Widow. I changed that to the Black Rose. Linda Calvey is into her 20th year of a life sentence. That's a lot of porridge for a woman. She got found guilty of shooting dead Ronnie Cook. Ronnie was a proper good Eastend blagger – a top face. Linda still claims it was a fit-up, and she did not do it. Could you spend 20 years in jail and still stick to your story? Maybe she could well be innocent.

Left: Maxine Fordham and brother Danny Fordham. When it comes to prison tragedies, it don't get any sadder than Maxine's. She was a lovely girl, and a friend of mine, and I still miss her. The big 'C' beat her. She died inside. It was a one-sided fight. Some fights you just can't ever win. But the truth is, the system could have freed her long before she died. It was pointless and senseless keeping her in when she was so ill. But that's prison for you – heartless, cruel and insane. RIP.

Some of the chaps with my Mike Tyson belt. Mike signed it for me as a gift.

Andy Salvage and Dave Courtney, Spain, 2008. Eat your heart out, Elvis!

Above: Redd Menzies outside my landlady's palace. Again he's not allowed in – I wonder why? *Left:* Outside Downing Street with the legendary 'Free Bronson' T-shirt on! No wonder they wouldn't let him in. It's a wonder they never shot him.

Frank just sent me this photo. Charlie, Roger is unstoppable in his work for you. Ronnie, Reg and Charlie and Eddie would have loved him. Total loyalty, Frankie." He *never* forgets me; that's why I love him. There is only one Frankie Fraser – 'Mad Frank' (maybe)? But he's got a lion's heart, for sure. Max respect.

My lovely friend Jill Loft with the guv'nor, Mad Frankie. Taken in 2008 at Repton Boxing Club.

"Your time does not fit the crime. Let's all call it quits and move on to better things. Mad Frankie Fraser."

The legendary Barney Ross with the twins. Barney was Lightweight Champion of the World in the 1940s. He also got awarded the Purple Heart for his bravery in fighting the Japs in the 2nd World War. When it comes to bottle, he was second to nobody – a true gladiator and a great man. Ron once told me he was without a doubt the bravest Yank he ever had the privilege of meeting.

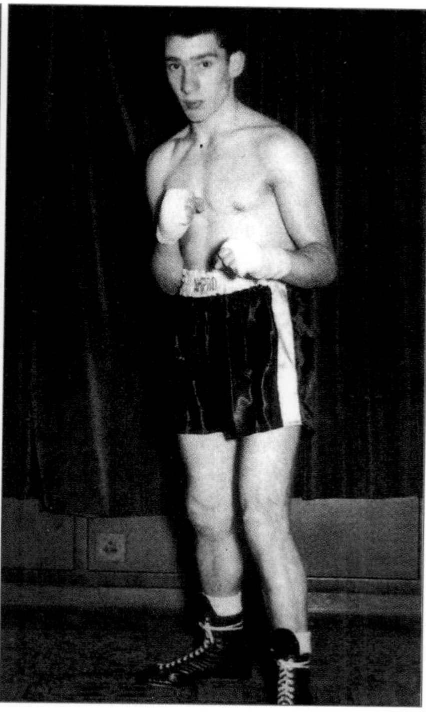

Reggie and Ronnie Kray. If the twins hadn't turned to crime, they would have made it in the boxing world. They were born fighters – "men of steel, men of morals, men of honour". Two of the best men I ever had the privilege of meeting. Legends in and out of the ring – I salute you.

This is a very rare snap of Jimmy Lee, the twins' grandfather – their mother's dad. He was a true romany gypsy and a legendary bareknuckle fighter. You did not mess with Jimmy Lee – if you did, you only did it the once.

The great Joe Louis (the Brown Bomber) with Ronnie Kray in the 1960s. The twins took Joe up to Broadmoor to visit Roy Shaw. With a twist of fate, Roy would later visit Ron there. That's how crazy life is... one decade you're visiting the asylum, the next – you're locked up inside it. Photo taken in the twins' favourite café in Bethnal Green Road.

DAI DOWER
ABERCYNON
British Empire Fly Weight Champion
MANAGER NAT SELLER

Right: Dai Dower was the Welsh legend in the 1950s. He was the British and European Champion. "To Charlie – all my best wishes for the future. Dai Dower." A truly great fighter – a man of respect. I salute.

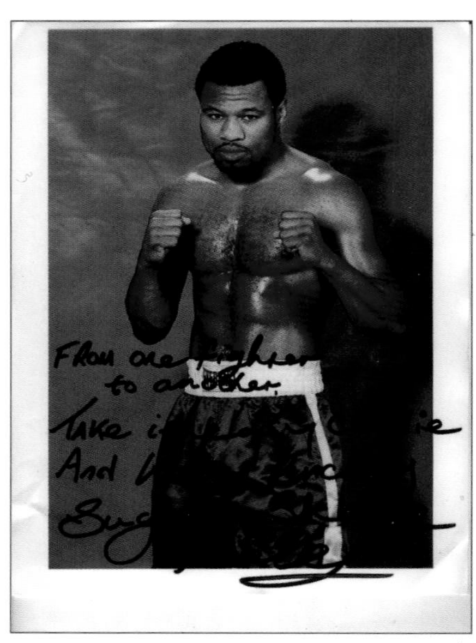

"From one fighter to another. Take it easy Charlie and Keep punching. Sugar Shane Moseley."

Aaron 'the Hawk' Pryor, one of the toughest fighters in the 1970s and 80s, inducted into the Boxing Hall of Fame in 1996. Out of 40 pro fights, he won 39 and lost one. I salute the man – respect, earned with blood, sweat and tears. "Charlie Bronson, don't ever give up fighting for your freedom. You can do it. Be good and stay cool."

This is a very rare photo of the great Cliffy Field sparring with the King himself, Ali. Only the very best ever sparred with Ali. Cliff was the best. It's about time Cliff's book came out – it *will* be a no. 1, make no bones about it. Cliffy Filed was a great fighter in and out of the ring, professional and unlicensed. A living legend.

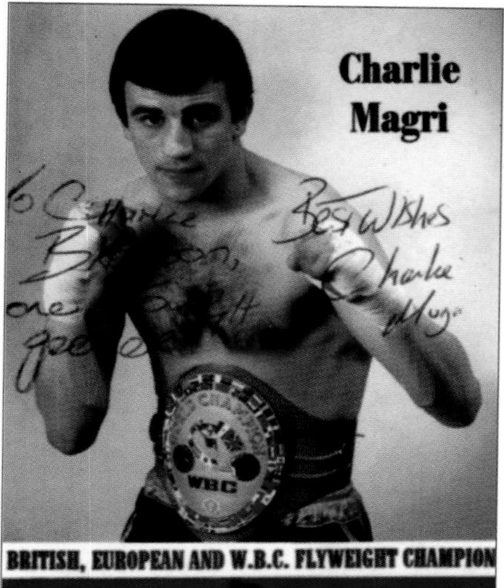

Charlie
Magri
BRITISH, EUROPEAN AND W.B.C. FLYWEIGHT CHAMPION

Above: My Andy. Joe Calzaghe and Brian, who runs the Dubliners Bar in Alicante.

Left: If you're ever in Charlie's boozer, the Vic in East London, shake his hand and tell him to keep my Guinness in the cooler for later. "To Charlie Bronson, one tough geezer. Best wishes, Charlie Magri." Cheers – top geezer.

Andy Bain with son George outside his pub, Sandyback, in Hockley, Staffordshire. Cheers, Andy – I'll pop in for a pint later.

My Brother Mark at a fancy dress party. Free drinks – that's the only excuse he needs.

My son Mike with a gun. Thank fuck it's only a tattoo gun. That's Mark Jones, one of the UK's finest tattooists and a good friend.

British champion John 'Fingers' Burton back in 1964. I told you he's a legend! All my buddies are legends, history makers. And he still visits me today – a loyal old buddy.

Billy Cooper, Manny Clarke and Matt Legg. If these guys say *Loonyology* is a winner, then who's gonna argue with them? It's a winner – okay!

Ricky Hatton and Billy 'the Preacher' Graham, the number 1 trainer in the UK. I may be locked up in a coffin but I'm never forgot, and never will be. Prison HQ can put me on the moon and I'll still have more for me than against me. That's what they don't like.

Ray Williams, Mum, and brother Mark. Outside jail waiting to come in and see me. Try to imagine how many jails they've stood outside waiting to see me? That's loyalty for you, 3½ decades of it. Love and respect.

Hitch Hitchenham and Ronnie in better and freer times. "I'll drink to that..." Cheers!

Garry Delaney, Mark's brother. (Garry got lifed off.) Top geezer. A good pal.

The boss himself, Freddie Foreman, with Matt Legg. It's 20 years since I saw the old rascal, but he *never* forgets me!

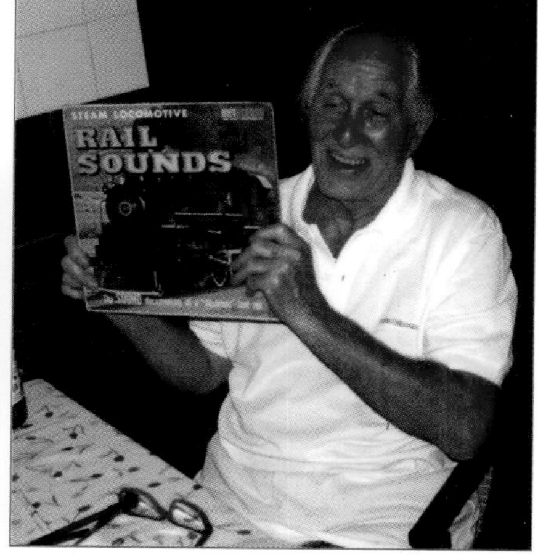

What a character Ronnie Biggs is! "Top man, solid as a rock." But has his sense of humour buried him deep inside the belly of the beast? Let's face it – it's political. Jealous fuckers!

Beard or no beard, you know it's me.

The legendary Al Rayment with some of my art. This guy is the real superman and I'm proud to say he's one of my best buddies. Respect.

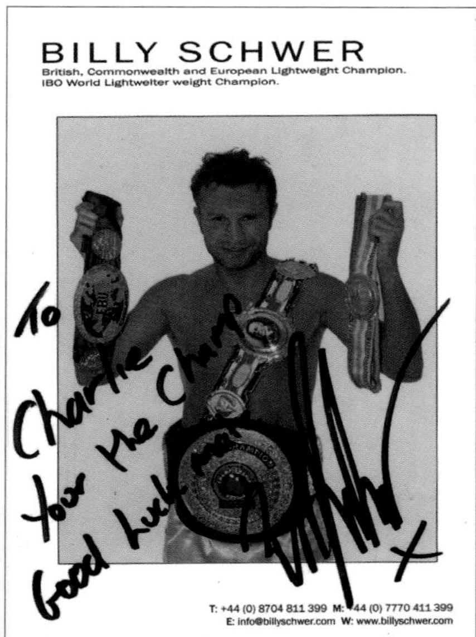

Billy Schwer. Billy and me are both Lutonians born and bred. Hatters all the way. A top geezer in my book. What a great fighter – a true legend. Max respect.

Al Rayment with Mike Tyson at the Doncaster Dome. Mike's a top Geezer, one of the best. Every time he comes over to the UK the 'chaps' all spoil him rotten. He wants me to go out to the USA to see him later.

Man U meet the legend Al Rayment. Legs or no legs, the man's a giant.

Lonely Bronson in prison kidnap

JAIL: Charles Bronson.

ONE of Luton's best known criminals has been found guilty of holding a prison official hostage during a 14-hour seige.

Keep fit fanatic Charles Bronson, 42, demanded a lifesize blow-up doll, a cup of tea, a loaded machine gun and a helicopter at Woodhill prison, Milton Keynes.

Bronson held prison librarian Andrew Love hostage for 14 hours while on remand.

On Tuesday a jury at Luton Crown Court heard Bronson had become fed up after being refused a visit from ...

As negotiators were called in Bronson said his only concern was that ...

I'll sue Scrubs, says attacked prisoner

MARTIN DELGADO ... NICHOLSON

Convict writes of life in prison

IN JAIL: Charles Bronson.

LUTON'S notorious convict Charles Bronson has written a book about life in prison ...

glass-fronted "Silence of the Lambs" cell at Wakefield in Yorkshire.

... being studied by
...ers, describes his
...ith inmates like the
...er he was first jailed
...ery in 1974.
... held the deputy
...ll Prison hostage
...nior officer at
...son in Milton-

...hit the headlines
... a helicopter,
...nd guns while
...er prisoner at

...e just wants to
... a normal life
...h the way he

... and the first
...wrong."
... will appear
...rt for false
...kmail with

has been badly treated while he has been in prison, suffering beatings and torment at the hands of prison officers at Wormwood Scrubs prison last month.

The Home Office confirmed it is investigating a complaint about an assault against Bronson at ...

Bronson backs fellow inmate

Cuffed hard man gives evidence at 'assault' tr...

THE man dubbed Britain's most violent prisoner gave evidence in a heavily guarded courtroom when he spoke up for a fellow inmate accused of assaulting a warder.

Luton-born Charles Bronson, 49, was brought from Durham Prison to Newcastle Crown Court.

Bronson, who decided to become a Muslim after his marriage to his Asian wife Saira, who lives off Lea...

served a total of 28 years in ... ent penal institutions and ... sentenced to life last year at ... Crown Court ...

Brookes had killed a woman in her late 80s and then killed a fellow prisoner known as Catweazle, who Bronson said was "Britain's most dangerous paedophile".

He added: "He (Brookes) is the closest thing you will get to anyone ... Of The Apes. He is a very ...

Prison hardman tells family: 'Stay away'

EXCLUSIVE BY GEOFF COX

FIGHTING TALK: Bronson says: 'I may never see my family until I'm freed'.

NOTORIOUS convict Charles Bronson has banned his family from seeing him in the maximum security jail where he is serving a life sentence.

The 49-year-old, dubbed Britain's most violent prisoner, made the "keep away" order because the visits were "mental torture" for his wife, daughter and mother – and for him.

And Bronson's wife, Saira, this week revealed she has seen him only TWICE since they were married nearly nine months ago.

The couple write to each other every day, but Bronson has told Saira, a 31-year-old Muslim, not to make the 500-mile round trip from her Luton home to Durham Prison, where he is in solitary confinement.

In a letter to Luton South MP Margaret Moran, the serial hostage-taker said he is being kept in "a cage" and is allowed only two visits, each of 30 minutes, a month.

"I've now stopped all visits. Would you want your mum to travel hundreds of miles to see you in a cage for half-an-hour?", he wrote.

And in a letter to his solicitor, Luton-born Bronson said: "I married Saira on June 1, 2001. Since that day I've not even been able to hold her hand. Imagine how she feels.

"It's best I've made this decision. It's better all round. The right people will know why I've done it. The rest will say 'He's mad', as usual. I really don't care what is said.

"I've given it so much thought. My mother, my wife, little Sami (Saira's 11-year-old daughter), my friends....but I have to say I'll never see them again until I'm freed.

"It may be three or four years. It may be 30 years. Nobody knows. But I now know my mental torture is to stop."

Bronson was jailed for life at Luton Crown Court for taking a prison teacher hostage for two days at Hull Jail. He is currently waiting for his appeal against the sentence to be heard.

The convict decided to stop all visits following an incident at Whitemoor Prison in Cambridgeshire on August 30 when Saira arrived to find ...

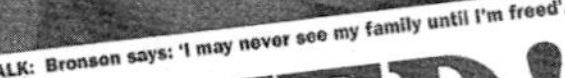

BANNED!

PLEA: Charles Bronson

...nson the 'pussycat'

Luton/Bedfordshire on Sunday, September 12, 1993

Charles Bronson 'had a death wish'

Crook had gun 'to shoot myself in front of lover'

CROOK Charles Bronson carried a loaded shotgun because he wanted to 'blow his brains out' in front of the lover who rejected him – not rob a bank.

Bronson, 40, who trained as a boxer, wears his hair and moustache like the American Death Wish film star with the same name.

He claims ...

bank, with a loaded double-barrelled sawn-off shotgun.

Shortly before being released from prison in 1988, a girl named Kelly-Ann Cooke began writing to him and Bronson met her when he was released.

He said: "I won't say I fell in love with her straight away but it was the first cuddle I have had for a very long time and it was nice, very nice."

He said they saw each other frequently and when he was back in prison he wrote to her every week but discovered she had been unfaithful.

When he was released from prison in February said he tried to find Kelly-Ann. "But she had vanished and I felt betrayed. I don't like peple who betray me. I am an honourable man," he said.

Bronson started to 'lose control'. He said: "I wanted to die but I did not want to shoot myself alone. I wanted to do it in front of Kelly-Ann. I wanted her to see me die."

Bronson decided to go into the hairdressers when she was having her hair done. "I was going to steam in, shout out ...ved her and put the gun in my mouth' ...claimed.

Bronson said he had 'kidnapped' the ...n who shared the dock with him on ...ay, Patrick Felix, and ordered him to ...e to Marsh Road, Luton.

...oth Bronson and Felix, 25, plead not ...y to conspiracy to rob Midland Bank ...

... police ... loaded ...m, wear- ...cut in it,

Trouble brews for Micky

● STORM IN TEACUP: Ex-con Micky after his release from jail.

EX-CONVICT Micky Peterson may have left Wormwood Scrubs prison last week, but he is still wanted – by Lord Longford.

The elderly prison reformer is anxious to catch up with him for a cup of tea and a chat after featuring him in his book Prisoner Or Patient, published earlier this year.

Micky, 42, from Luton, was due to meet up with his lordship in London last week after 20 years behind bars, but unfortunately there was a mix up over the hotel names, with Lord Longford going to The Grosvenor Hotel and Micky going to The Grosvenor ...

Violent convict costs £100,000 to control

ON MOVE: Bronson

By Oonagh Blackman

Crime Correspondent

BRITAIN'S most notorious prisoner is costing taxpayers £100,000 a year — the bill for moving him between dozens of jails.

The staggering cost of ...

moved 18 times. During the last six weeks alone he has been transferred four times — over a distance of 1,000 miles.

And in a prison ...

with two guards to bring up the rear. ...

written a book entitled Concrete ...

Danger con held in Hannibal cage

DANGEROUS Luton criminal Charles Bronson – named after the Death Wish film star – is in a high security glass cage after taking a jail's assistant governor hostage.

Armed robber Bronson, 42, who has officially changed his name from Michael Peterson, is being housed in the Silence of the Lambs-style cell at Wakefield Prison. He took the assistant governor of Hull jail hostage for five hours.

Unarmed body-builder Bronson, who has assaulted 20 officers during 23 years in prison, shouted demands while gripping the deputy. He was overpowered by wardens when his hostage broke free, escaping with minor cuts and bruises.

Twelve wardens and a restraining body belt were needed to move him so he could be taken to the specially designed cell.

The cage has bullet proof glass windows all around it and in the ceiling, and brick-reinforced double-doors so food can be left without the need for direct contact.

A Home Office spokesman said the cell has been specially constructed to contain the most dangerous and violent prisoners.

"He will be watched at all times and will be under strict medical supervision," the spokesman said.

Bronson will stay in the cell until he has calmed down, before being returned to Hull, where he is serving eight years for possessing a shotgun. He was arrested in Luton and police believe he was plotting to rob the Midland Bank in Marsh Road.

He has been held in 60 different prisons.

The Home Office refused to reveal the nature of Bronson's demands but confirmed they were not met.

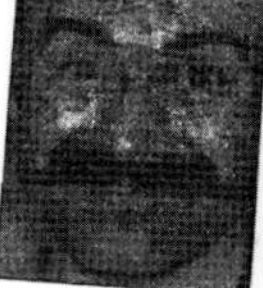

LUTON convict Michael Peterson (right), who calls himself Charles Bronson, is now in a Silence of the Lambs style cell.

Jail chiefs meet over inmate's terror reign

BY OONAGH BLACKMAN

OFFICIALS from the Home Office and prison service are to hold an urgent meeting this week to find a way to control Britain's most feared prisoner.

Charles Bronson is now locked in "The Cage", a top security cell at Wakefield Prison, West Yorkshire, after taking the deputy governor of Hull jail hostage for nearly five hours on Easter Monday.

Staff and other inmates at Hull said ...

Anger at film about Bronson, UK's most violent prisoner

by David Smith

A BIOPIC of the criminal Charles Bronson, who has been called "the most violent man in Britain", has been condemned for glorifying his life and encouraging copycat behaviour in prisons.

Bronson was made in collaboration with the notorious inmate, whose real name is Michael Peterson. Promoted as "*A Clockwork Orange* for the 21st century", the film is an unsparing depiction of Bronson's brutal attacks on prison warders, hostage-taking and fights with fellow inmates. He has spent 29 of the past 35 years in solitary confinement and is now in a specially constructed cage deep inside Wakefield maximum security prison.

"It's a sad state of affairs in society when we want to glorify someone who has committed horrendous acts of crime by making a film about him," said Glyn Travis, assistant general secretary of the Prison Officers Association. "Charles Bronson has cost the taxpayer an inordinate amount of money because of his life of crime. This is not a role model we want to portray for people who come into prisons."

Tom Hardy, who plays Charles Bronson.

The film's release date, 13 March, falls within days of a parole hearing which will consider whether to move Bronson to a lower-category jail. But its Danish director, Nicolas Winding Refn, insists he has no interest in trying to win sympathy for the 56-year-old criminal.

Bronson was originally sentenced to seven years in 1974 for armed robbery and, though twice released, was soon back behind bars. In 2000, he was given life after holding a prison teacher hostage for 44 hours.

Bronson contributed to the film's script from his cell and had meetings with Tom Hardy, the actor who portrays him.

Winding Refn, who said he spoke to Bronson on the phone for about 20 minutes during production, said he agreed with the view expressed by Travis that Bronson should not be glorified.

"I certainly would never make a film that glorifies violence or anything in that demeanour. On the contrary, all my films have always had a very strict moral code to them. I also think *Bronson* has."

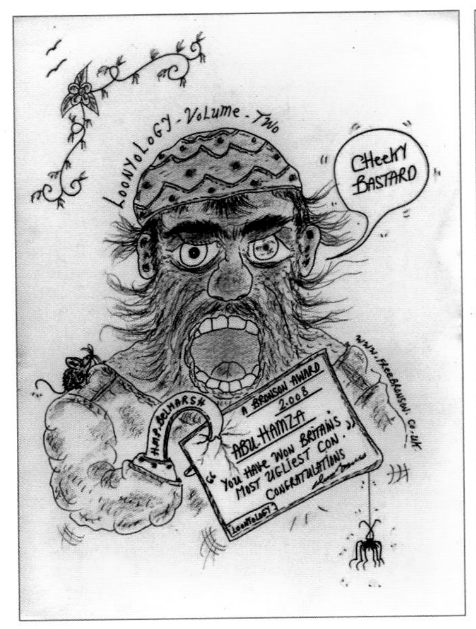

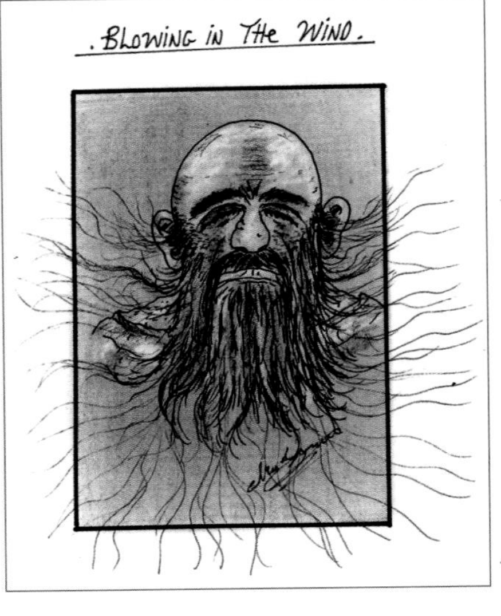

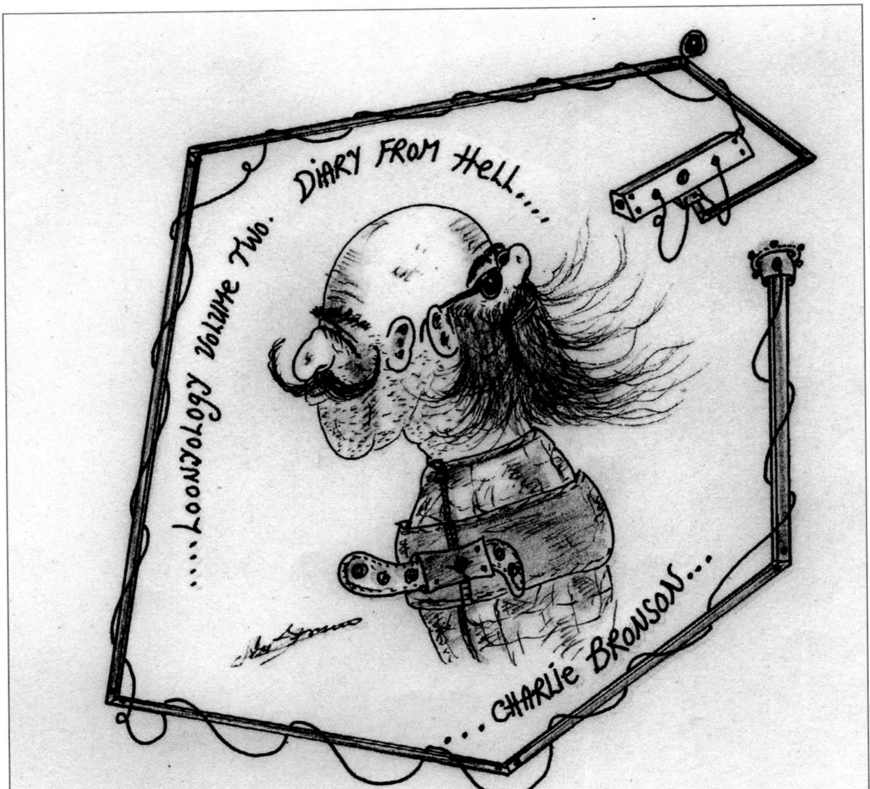

LOONYOLOGY - VOLUME - TWO
CHEEKY BASTARD
A BRONSON AWARD
2.008
ABU-HAMZA
"YOU HAVE WON BRITAINS MOST UGLIEST CON."
CONGRATULATIONS
H.M.P. BELMARSH
LOONYOLOGY
www.FREEBRONSON.CO.UK

.BLOWING IN THE WIND.

...LOONYOLOGY VOLUME TWO.
DIARY FROM HELL....
...CHARLIE BRONSON...

I got a nice letter from Di Brown out in Spain. She's a good soul with a big heart. My mum thinks the world of her. I also got a 'bull's eye' sent in from my brother Mark. I'll get some fruit and nuts with that on the next canteen day. Cheers, brother!

Some cunt sent me a card with a fucking teddy bear on it. It was a geezer too – some faggot. Oi, smart arse, fuck off. Go and shag your boyfriend, you prat. You slag. Sending me a card with a teddy on? What do you think I am? It wouldn't have been so bad if you'd slipped a bull's eye in as well, you tight bastard.

I had egg, chips and beans today. Bloody lovely. Good old-fashioned English nosh. Mug of tea, a few rounds of bread – you can't beat it! Lovely jubbley!

The cannibal was shouting his mouth off today. He really does need a right hook or a PP9 battery in a sock: 'thud' – end of shouting. Fuck him off over the hospital wing. He's a cunt. I hate him, I can't help it, I'm fucking sick of him. He's only brave because I can't crash into him. He's like those cunts that make dosh on my name or sell my art behind my back. One day lads, one fine day…

Danny Hansford wrote to assure me the movie trailer has now been put right. It wasn't the film (that's brilliant), it was the wording that needed rectifying. So cheers to Danny! He's a top producer and all's sweet now.

Eddie Clinton's up to see me tomorrow! Good old Ed. We've got lots to sort out, so it's an early night for me! Fuck this mattress. I may kip on the floor, then again I may not. It's my bizz not yours! Nobody's but mine!

OK! 3-2-1… I'm off!

26 June 2008.

Great visit from my old buddy Eddie Clinton. He's been in my corner for years now. Top geezer.

Mark Jones sent me in a 'bull's eye' and an art book! Cheers, mate. I got 14 letters today; eight were from strangers but they were all respectful. Darren (my second cousin) sent me in a photo of 'Minty' from *EastEnders* who thought I was a mass killer. Darren put him right. It's a funny old world out there!

What about Neil Entwistle, the Brit in America who's just copped life without parole? They should've gassed the monster after he shot dead his wife and baby. What sort of dog does that? Entwistle does.

I see Lee Porritt has just been freed from Broadmoor. It was only in 2000 he battered a young student and raped her in a pool of blood, so why is he out so fast? I'll tell you: it's Loonyology; that's why! I bet you he'll attack again. You remember Porritt and remember I said it! Hey – it could be your daughter, your sister or your mother next! Wake up, planet. Facts are facts and truth is truth. Are you going to accept this shit? Broadmoor's putting the sane in danger by letting the insane out. Here's a letter Porritt wrote in 2000, which has been published in the press several times:

The girls I fantasise about are 11 or 12 years old. I abduct them and carry them to a secluded spot (i.e. a wood) where I rape them. After this I torture them and bury them in the wood and try to forget about it. I have actually been planning these things.

Hey! Be careful! There's a fucking seriously sadistic lunatic out there. If he was a dog, he would be shot! Somebody tell me what's going on out there. Why the fuck is he freed and I'm still caged? Am I really such a bad guy? Am I?

I see Thomas Nugusse tried to hang himself in Bedford prison. Who gives a fuck? He was on remand for the murder of 15-year-old Arsema Dawit. The only sad part is the girl who lost her life! The screws in Bedford found Nugusse hanging off the bars, so they cut him down and gave him the kiss of life. He's now on a life support machine. I say switch it off and save the electric.

NEWS FLASH! Exclusive! Red hot off the press! Two homosexual Muslims have exploded whilst having sex. Police think they were suicide bummers! You got it from me first, OK?

Why is a 69 better than a family reunion? With a 69 you only have to kiss one twat!

A man runs into a pet shop, puts a bomb on the counter and shouts out: "Everyone has 30 seconds to get out!" A tortoise at the back of the shop says, "You cunt."

You've got to laugh or you'll cry!

I went to that silly monthly meeting this morning. It felt like a fucking zoo visit. There were eight of them in one cell with me in another and bars in between. I just said, "Why are you lot taking the piss? Move me, let me move on, let me progress. What do you want from me?" They said, "Well, Charlie, you have been a serious problem!" WHAT? That was years ago! Stop talking 'all our yesterdays'. This is 2008 – fucking wake up!

I'm seeing my legal team tomorrow! It's about time too, because I'm actually getting fed up with all this bollocks. Even the screws say I'm right, so how can I be wrong? It's a complete fucking farce. Fuck 'em.

Hey! I just popped home and caught the plumber with his cock up the dog's arse. Dirty bastard. The police say they can't do anything about it because he was corgi registered!

You'll fucking love this one. A farmer down in Devon has successfully grown a field of vibrators. Unfortunately, he now has serious problems with squatters. HA! HE! HA! HE! HA! Fuck me! HA! HE! HA! HE! That's a blinder that one.

I had a jacket potato with curried beans tonight. What a load of shit… The food's been bad today. Thank fuck for my visit with Eddie – he got me milkshakes and cakes. I would have gone to bed starving otherwise, so three cheers for Eddie: HIP HIP – HOORAY! HIP HIP – HOORAY! HIP HIP – HOORAY!

I called Sandra today. We always have a good laugh. She's up to see me a week on Sunday. I don't do badly, do I?

Did I ever tell you about the time I was on telly? It was only a small part but millions saw me. It was on *Crimewatch*! I must have been good because every fucker was trying to catch me...

No training today, but I'll have to do a few sit-ups before bed. I can't be getting fat, smelly and ugly!

Oh! On the Jon Gaunt TalkSport radio show today there was a fantastic interview with Ronnie Biggs' son Michael. He's a smashing lad and Ronnie must be so proud of him. He came over very well and I think it will get his dad a lot more support for his freedom fight. Well done, Michael. I don't know anybody who doesn't want to see Ronnie out. Let the old man out, you evil cunts!

I'm just in the mood for a pint of Guinness. I've fancied one all day. I must be dreaming – I've got more chance of a slice of pussy and that's a million to one against! I've got to shake my nut. What am I doing even thinking about it? What an evil world this is...

A man is stopped by a cop on the M6 after being clocked doing 125mph. Man says, "Two months ago my wife ran off with a traffic cop and when I saw you behind me, I thought, fuck me – the cunt's bringing her back!"

Oh well, my day is now over. It's been a colourful day with lots of news, a bit of bizz, a few laughs – and it's one less to serve inside. That's what I call one up the Queen's arse.

Talking of the Queen, my old buddy Stevie Booth hit Michael Fagan over the head with a snooker cue in Ashworth asylum in the 1980s. Fagan was the lunatic who broke into the palace and sat on the Queen's bed. Fucking mental or what? You can't make this Loonyology up! It's magical. Booth (who changed his name to Peterson out of respect to me) is a great guy and he's still locked up. He's done a good 30 years now! The Kray twins loved Stevie. He is just a loyal, staunch old fella.

Some years back I got two teeth smashed out. Shit happens, but, sadly, they were my front nashers. In the 1980s and '90s I just left the gap, but in 2000 I got a bridge put in. It cost me two grand but it was the best thing I'd ever done. Anyway, in 1984, after Stevie Booth changed his name by deed poll to Peterson, he went to the dentist and demanded he take out his two front teeth! The dentist said, "I can't, there's nothing wrong with them." Stevie said, "Oi, cunt, take them out." That's how Stevie is – he even dressed the same as me, walked like me and had a tash like me. My family adopted him and he became a true Peterson! I couldn't bear to tell him about my bridge. How could I? But after he reads this, I bet he'll go back to the dentist! Get in touch, Stevie; I'll help with the cost! You're a true brother. Max respect.

I've met some of my best pals in our asylums! Thank God for our wonderful nut houses full of lovely characters. Would your friend lose two front teeth for you? Mine did! I bet yours wouldn't. You don't know what friends are till you land on Mars! I've been there and I fucking loved every moment of it. I even laughed as I became violent! Every day was a buzz and Hell was an awakening – a blessing! I was baptised in blood; some was mine but a lot was other people's. What's a drop of blood between loons? I'll drink to that.

A couple at the zoo are passing the gorilla cage. The silver-back became excited by the woman in her mini-skirt and tight boob tube, so her hubby says, "Go and tease him." She rubs her tits, rubs her hands up her legs to her crotch and sucks on her finger, driving the gorilla wild. Hubby takes her hands, opens the cage door and pushes her in, saying, "Now tell him you've got a headache!"

3-2-1... I'm off. (I'll be back.)

27 June 2008.

Look at life with a sense of humour because you'll never get out of it alive.

"Woke up this mornin' feelin' fine..." That's a line from 'I'm Into Something Good' – the 1960s No. 1 hit by Hermans Hermit's, a Manchester band. I bought it too. Fuck me; how fucking old am I? Now I've become the hermit. How mental is that?

The mad crow was at it again this morning. It fucking woke me up at 5.45am, screeching its face off outside my window: squawk, squawk and squawk. Fuck off – I'm trying to think and plan my day. I've got a big day today because my legal team are up and I've got to get my legal head on. This is my life, not a fucking game of picking the best-looking crow. They're all the same those crows: ugly and noisy, and they shit all over my exercise yard. I have to train out there. Let's face facts: if a man shat on my yard, I would smash his face in and use his body as a punch bag. Get my point? The crows are taking the piss. Fuck off. I need a gun...

Get on this for a bit of philosophy: the things you like and the things you dislike can drive you mad if you think about them too much. How true is that?

I got out of bed at 6am for a piss. That first piss of the day for me is amazing; I see it as pissing out all the poison of the day before. The day is now new and ready for you to make of it what you will. It's all up to you! You're born again in a brand-new day. Yiipppeeeee! (OK, I may be in a coffin but I'm breathing.) So I finish my piss then wash my body, especially my dick and arse. After all, a man must maintain his hygiene. Smelly people should be shot. Lazy fuckers – they pollute our planet! Even if you live in a field you can wash in a river or a water barrel! Fucking wash, you smelly cunts. Stop giving us humans a bad name!

After going through some paperwork, I found some old nicking sheets going back 20 years. I'm gutted as I didn't keep all the hundreds of nickings I've had over my 35 years away. They would've made good reading and I could've done a write-up on each one! Oh well, that's life...

Full Sutton, 6 Aug 1988. Now this was fucking funny and I still laugh about it today. Beautiful memories, and it only cost me 14 days' punishment. I was mopping a landing and whistling away, happy as a squirrel playing with his nuts, when a governor came walking towards me with a big prison file under his arm. I clocked him getting closer and thought to myself, what's he got there? Where's he off to? Who is he? I've never seen him before and the cunt's walking on the floor I've just mopped. That's my floor, cunt. He had that sort of look – a smirk, a grin – as if to say, "Clean it again, sonny boy." Yeah, sure. 20 feet, 10 feet, five feet, SPLASH! The mop bucket water went right over his head. "You fucking clean it up, cunt," I said. Screws came running and alarm

REG No. JA 0060 NAME BRONSON

REPORTS OF OFFENCES

H.M.P. FULL SUTTON

DATE	OFFENCE	RESULTS OF ADJUDICATION: Forfeiture of Remission (Days)	Post-ponement of eligibility for release. C.T. & P.D. (Days)	(Mths.)	Other Punishments
	Rule 47 Para. 4 (245)				PLEA:- GUILTY
6 AUG 1988	Commits any assault				CAUTION ✓
	AT 09·25 hrs on 5·8·88				S.O.E. — ✓
	IN THE SECURE CORRIDOR				N.A.L. — ✓
	NEAR THE SEGREGATION UNIT				C.C. / CANTEEN — ✓
(6)	YOU DID ASSAULT MR. McLAUGHLIN				SMOKING — ✓
	BY THROWING THE CONTENTS				CLASSES — ✓
	OF A MOP BUCKET OVER HIS				RADIO — / T.V. — ✓
	PERSON.				ASSOCIATION — ✓
	MR. McLAUGHLIN - ACTING G.V.				Remanded for officers evidence [signatures]
	Rule 47 Para. 4				

bells went off. I stood there in my boxer's pose thinking, OK, let's get it on. YARHHhhooooooo! They stood back and said, "OK, Charlie, let's go," then walked me peacefully to the punishment block.

Universal insanity keeps the wheels turning. Without us madmen the world would stop. Governor McLaughlin got soaking wet, the file got wet and I got punished, but the whole jail was buzzing. I cheered up a boring prison day and that's how the prison world is: unpredictable, insane, dangerous, exciting, electrifying! It's guys like me who make it what it is. I take it to a new level – to the edge! Whilst I'm at it, I now confess that Humpty Dumpty never fell – I pushed the fat twat off the wall!

Get on this next nicking which happened in Long Lartin in 1992:

Home Office

HM PRISON SERVICE

Charge Number: 435

F256

RECORD OF HEARING AND ADJUDICATION

Part 1 (to be completed in BLOCK CAPITALS before the hearing)

1 Establishment: HM H.M. PRISON, LONG LARTIN

Date of Adjudication (Commencement): 24 JUN 1992

2 First name(s): CHARLES Surname: BRONSON.

Number: JA0060 Determinate Sentence / ~~Lifer / Unsentenced / Non-Criminal~~*

*delete whichever is not applicable

Details of the charge (as recorded on F1127): AT 18.50 HOURS ON 23rd JUNE 1992 AT CELL 36 ON DELTA WING YOU GRABBED OFFICER BRITTAIN BY THE THROAT WITH YOUR LEFT HAND. SLAMMING HIM AGAINST THE DOOR OPPOSITE AND SQUEEZING HIS THROAT. YOU THEN MADE A FIST WITH YOUR RIGHT HAND AND SAID "I WILL KILL YOU."

Rule 47. Para 1

COMMITS ANY ASSAULT

F1127 - Issued by: Officer Watterson Time and Date of Issue: 2115 hours 23.6.92

Name of Reporting Officer: BRITTAIN Rank: OFFICER

4 Certification by Medical Officer: Please TICK appropriate box(es)

Fit for adjudication ✓ Fit for cellular confinement ✓ Unfit (give details below) ☐

Any relevant medical/psychiatric observations including an opinion on the prisoner's mental condition at the time of the alleged offence (a separate report should be attached if appropriate)

Signature of Medical Officer: [signature] Date: 24 [illegible]

5 Adjudicated by Governor ☐ Other Governor grade (please specify) ✓ G4 Head of Operations

Head of Custody ☐

If adjudication is not conducted by the governing governor or Head of Custody, please give reason:

Governor and HOC in conference

000016

F256 (Rev 4/92)

[signature]

Fuck me; that's 16 years ago. Doesn't time fly when you're having fun? The screw involved was Mr Brittain. What a great old British name – pity he's such a prat. But I don't want to be nasty about him; the man's got a job to do and if he does it right, then who am I to cause problems? Let's just say it was a mad old day and it came down on me like a ton of bricks.

Now let me tell you young cons something about using violence in jail: you will always come off worse if you attack or assault a screw. Best to drop it after a bit of verbal and walk away, otherwise you'll only be digging a deeper hole for yourselves. To attack one screw is actually to attack them all. You can't possibly win. I'm telling you now: you'll lose! From the most minor assault to the most serious, you will come off second best. It's taken me a lifetime of dripping blood to realise that. So unless you're prepared for 30 years of Hell, turn your back and walk away, or the screws will nail you and bury you in some dark piss-stained hole until you're no longer human. On one occasion even my own mother didn't recognise me!

I was more animal than human. I think Humpty Dumpty may well have pushed me! But then again it was probably some fat screw that looked like Humpty – the fat, useless cunt. And to put the record straight, I never said I would kill Mr Brittain. I actually said, "Take a chill pill, you fat cunt, or I'll twist your head round till it comes off and me and the lads will play football with it. Now fuck off, you cunt." That's all I said – what's wrong with that? Nasty fucker, trying to get me in trouble!

The next two nickings were in 1988 – one at Full Sutton and the other at Durham.

The Full Sutton screw was called Mr Mortimer. He knows why I chinned him and I know why I chinned him, so that's all that matters. But why did his 30 mates have to chin me? (It's a mad old world and I fucking love it.) I've always said it and I always will: make sure you get the first punch in and make it count, because it could well be your last!

The Durham nicking sheet was from the Seg block. It was done by

REG. No. JA0060 NAME BRONSON.

REPORTS OF OFFENCES HMP- FULLSUTTON

DATE	OFFENCE	Forfeiture of Remission (Days)	Post-ponement of eligibility for release. C.T & P.D. (Days)	(Mths.)	RESULTS OF ADJUDICATION: Other Punishments
	(266)				PLEA:
31 8 88	Rule 47 Para. 4 Commits any assault	(56)			~~CAUTION~~
(B.O.V.)					S.O.
(8)	ie. AT 14.25 ON THE				N.A.
	18-8-88 IN THE CANTEEN				CC 28
	DOORWAY AT THE COMMUNITY				~~CAN~~ 28
	CENTRE YOU DID STRIKE				SMOKING 28
	OFFICER MORTIMER WITH				CIA 28
	YOUR RIGHT FIST.				RA. 28
					~~T.V.~~ 28
					ASSOCIATION 28
10 days LUR from 27/3/88 No 207/88 Activated					
	OFF MORTIMER				
1-11-88	RULE [illegible] PARA (20)				HMP DURHAM
	IN ANY WAY OFFENDS				
13:9	AGAINST GOOD ORDER				
	AND DISCIPLINE				[illegible]
(9)	AT APPROX 18.48HRS ON 31-10 88				FORFEITURE OF PRIVILEGES
	ON A1-LANDING YOU POURED				ASSOCIATION ____ SMOKING ____
	THE WATER CONTAINED IN				RECREATION ____ RADIO ____
	YOUR WASHING DISH				NEWSPAPERS ____ CANTEEN ____
	UNDER THE DOOR OF A1-27				CONCERTS ____ FILMS, T.V. ____
DURHAM	OFF HALL J.				S.O.E. [illegible]

Officer Hall on 1 November 1988 after I poured a bowl of shit and piss under a nonce's door. Lick that up, you fucking beast! I used to do that a lot to grasses, nonces and freaks in all the jails I was in. They all got a shitty cell from me! It would only cost me 14 days' punishment – that's worth it to me. The screw has to nick me; that's his job and I don't hold that against him. I deserve the punishment and I get on with it. But I'll always shit up a nonce (even today). I'm a con and it's my duty to do it. I can't be accepting the fuckers. Could you? The fucking beasts should be shot! I rest my case.

Guilty, your Lordship. Punish me, whip me, starve me, isolate me and brutalise me. But one sure thing, your Lordship, Charlie Bronson won't leave prison and rape your wife and kids or nonce your granny.

The next two nickings are from Wandsworth and Leicester in 1988 – one a roof and the other an assault on Officer Wilford. Guilty of both. Punish me! Whip me till I bleed!

REG No. 590060 NAME BRONSON C

REPORTS OF OFFENCES

DATE	OFFENCE	Forfeiture of Remission (Days)	Post-ponement of eligibility for release. C.T. & P.D. (Days)	(Mths.)	RESULTS OF ADJUDICATION: Other Punishments
	HMP LEICESTER				
27-3-88 207/88 ①	RULE 47 PARA 20 IN ANY WAY OFFENDS AGAINST GOOD ORDER AND DISCIPLINE I/E AT 0958 APPROX 27-3-88 AT WEST WALLS SEG UNIT EXERCISE YOU ABSENT YOURSELF BY CLIMBING UP THE FENCE ONTO THE ADJOINING ROOF AND DELIBERATELY BREAKING AN AIR CONDITIONING PIPE OFFR WILKIE	100			Rx B.O.V. 28.3.88 KR. *Prospective to a custodial sent + suspended i fr 6 Mths. Activated 31/8/8 by BOV
H.M.P. WANDSWORTH 20 JUN 1988 ③ 0916	RULE 47 PARA 4 Commits any assault. IE:- AT APPROX: 1145 HRS ON THE 19th OF JUNE 1988 ON D2 LANDING ASSAULTED AN OFFICER BY BARGING HIM OUT OF THE WAY. OFFR WILFORD	10	Lol.		FOREFITS DAYS: CANTEEN, SMOKING, LECTURES, CONCERTS, CINEMA, CLASSES, NEWSPAPERS, RADIO, W'WATCH. Rx 5.20 wrt BOV

No. 1150 (page 20) (27154—6-1 60) 000187 P.T.O.

I'm gutted now that I haven't kept all my boxes of nicking sheets. What an eye-opener that would've been. They could've been used as case studies for trainee prison psychologists, teachers and criminology students. The 1970s alone would've filled up a book. All lost now… or are they? Watch this space. I can see a new book on the way – a prison masterpiece: *Bronson's Crimes and Punishments*! YARHHhhoooooo! There's no stopping me, I'm a walking encyclopaedia! Who fucking said we can't live out a dream? We can. You can. We all can. I am. Yiiipppeeeeeee. Yaarrhhoooooo. Watch me fly out of this Devil's nest!

Mr and Mrs Blobby are in bed and Mrs Blobby says, "Blob, blurp, blob, blib, blob, blib, blibblob, blurp, blobblib, blob, blib, blob…" Mr Blobby says, "Oh shut up and just swallow it!"

Talking of blow jobs, did I ever tell you about the time I had one off a 26-stone lorry-driving tart? She was fucking scary – a big daddy with tits and a fanny! The things you do in life are for a laugh. She was disgusting. How could I shag that? Could you; would you? Suck it, swallow and fuck off! Kiss that? I'd sooner kiss a horse! I was told she once took on a horse! Poor horse. But I must be honest; it was a lovely blow job! The way she caressed my balls was so gentle and nice. Lovely memories. Fat slag.

She licked my bell-end till it was shining.
You could almost see it in the dark.
That smile on her face, like the cat that got the cream.
Those three chins and big puffy cheeks.
Those little, piggy, beady eyes.
Those massive muscular shoulders.
That smell of pussy dampness.
Fuck me; I've got a train to catch!

I just couldn't. How could I with the stale sweat in those rolls of fat? The blow job was it for me. Shoes, coat, I'm off. Life rolls on… I'm not being nasty or selfish or ungrateful, but fat birds put me off my stroke. A blow job's one thing, but what else can a man do? Come on, be honest! I'd sooner have a bag of fish and chips and a bottle of cream soda. Sorry, but that's how I am and how it is. I don't wish to offend the fatties, but stay out of my mobile home. I don't want you fucking up my springs! Look at those big fat blokes with their beer bellies; they haven't seen their cock for years, fucking idiots. If a man abuses himself, he will abuse anyone! Look after your body and it will look after you. How true is that? Madness is never out of fashion.

I just met my Queen's Counsel for the first time! He's a real character called David Martin Sperry and it was an absolute honour to meet the man. It turns out he got Dave Courtney a 'not guilty' a few years back, so he's the dog's bollocks. He also got my old buddy Charlie Magee a 'not guilty' over an attack on a screw in Long Lartin. This guy is mustard, red-hot chilli style! Can he win me parole? We shall see in August. Let's leave it at that for now. But my case is looking good and every month that passes by is another month the system has to justify keeping me in! They will try but they can't. Soon all this will be exposed! Wait and see…

My counsel wasn't too impressed with the legal room! It's all noted down. He wanted to be in the same room rather than looking at me through zoo bars, but that's how life is for me: looking out through bars.

Fuck me; I got a pile of mail today! I had a 'bull's eye' sent in by my brother Mark, 30 quid off Mark Sharman and another 'bull's eye' yesterday from Mark Jones. All Marks – I'm surrounded by Marks and they're all top geezers. I've never met a bad Mark yet! It must be a lucky name for me. Anyway, cheers to all the Marks. Thanks a lot, lads. I'll get some canteen next week on you lot!

My dear friends Mich and Kitch have just opened up a bar-restaurant out in Torrevieja, Alicante called the Olive Grove. Book a table when you're out there (phone 618.601.058). They do a lovely lobster.

Talking of lobster, I knew a lunatic in Rampton who looked like one. Now you're saying, how can anybody look like a lobster? Well, I'm fucking telling you this nutter did, OK? Sure it's hard to believe, but seeing is believing! I was shocked when I saw him. His face was all red and he had those beady, crabby eyes and a fat, ugly body with arms that resembled claws. Oh yeah, he was a also child rapist and when I jumped on his head it made that noise of a lobster being crushed. 'Crack' – a lovely noise. It was all he deserved, the fucking nonce!

Dee sent me in some brochures of Hampton Court. She's just had a day out there with her two girls. The gardens look lovely. (I do love a nice garden.) I was a sad bastard when I was a lad – a horrible fucker – and I used to do nasty things to gardens. I'd snap off the heads of giant sunflowers and stuff them through the letter box. I must have broken so many hearts by doing such nasty things, like pouring petrol in a fish pond! Why did I do it? Because I was a terrible cunt! I went in a chicken pen once and pulled off all their heads. I was only 14 years old and I did it for a laugh. I should've been birched. I'm sorry to all those lovely people I upset. If you still hate me, I'll let you chin me (or birch me) later! But if you forgive me, I'll buy you a pint.

When I look back at all the scooters and bikes and cars I've nicked, all I can say is I'm sorry. It sounds crazy, but I really am disgusted with all that shit I did in my youth. It was senseless. I used to go in to phone boxes and smash them to bits. I destroyed bus shelters, street lights, fences, gates, and put bricks through shop windows. Why? Because I was a horrible cunt! I once pushed a rider off a horse and rode off on it! Just for a laugh. Crazy times… Thank fuck I grew up and became a villain. Why be like a hooligan or act like a hooligan when you can turn it into a job? It's all about dosh. I was once paid a grand to smash a joint up! (That was a lot of dosh in 1970.) The geezer wanted it closed down. Why? Who cares? That wasn't my concern. My job was to close it down, collect my wage and move on! I don't ask questions. However, we all have to grow up in life. I would say to all the youngsters now: "Don't do what I did, as I've learnt the hard way!"

Have you seen the new gun statistics for the US? Cop a load of this!

70 million guns are legally licensed to householders.

31 million are unlicensed and believed to be held by criminals.

Around 30,000 people a year are killed by guns in the US (in crimes and accidents).

There are 11,000 gun-related murders a year in the US. (Work out how many body bags a week.)

73% of Americans think that everybody should carry a gun.

And we think we have problems! Fuck me – America is fucking mental! It's Loonyology gone insane!

Oh well, Mark Emmins is visiting tomorrow. What a loyal buddy. He's coming all the way from Devon to monster mansion for two hours in the Bronco Zoo. He's a top geezer and I've got bundles of respect for him.

It's been a great day and the grub wasn't too bad either. 3-2-1... I'm off!

Saturday, 27 June 2008.

I got seven letters today (really 107, because my mum's letter is worth a 100 to me). Cherri Gilham's was a good one. We have our falling-outs, me and her, but we always bounce back. She's a good soul and a smart cookie! If this wall wasn't so fucking big I would jump over and go and have tea and cakes with her in her penthouse flat in London.

Talking of prison escapes, here are a few legendary ones!

Did you know Ted Bundy escaped several times before he ended up sitting in old sparky? Back in 1975 he was sentenced to 15 years for a kidnapping offence but he escaped from court. He was soon recaptured, only he had killed and raped several women in the meantime. He also confessed to 50 more murders. Cunt.

Our very own Alfie Hinds was a top escape artist. (Eat your heart out, Houdini.) Alfie was one of the top safe crackers in the 1950s and he copped a 12 stretch in 1953. 12 years was a lot of porridge in those days. It was hard time and you had to be tough to survive 12 months let alone 12 years! He escaped from Nottingham jail, Chelmsford jail and he even had it on his toes from the London Law Courts. All in all he was a proper decent jailbird as it's every prisoner's duty to escape. Today not too many want to as it's too fucking easy! Pass the marmalade, squire! And run my bath ready. Now fuck off, screw!

One of the most spectacular escapes in my lifetime was back in 1983 at the Maze prison in Northern Ireland. It was the biggest escape in British prison history. I was in Broadmoor asylum at the time and all the loonies were cheering and jumping up and down. It was brilliant. 38 convicted IRA prisoners burst through the gate with guns blazing. Three screws were shot (all survived) and 20 others were injured. 38 cons were free – that's what I call a real escape. I'll drink to that! Bear in mind the Maze was a fucking hell hole; men died in that shit hole. They were brutalized, degraded and humiliated. No wonder they escaped. Tally ho, off we go!

Now this is the type of woman I could love till the day I die. Back in 1999 Lucy Dudko, known as 'Red Lucy', hijacked a helicopter in Australia and made the pilot land it in Silverwater jail to bust her bank-robber boyfriend John Killick out. John was serving 28 years. Their love flight only lasted six weeks before they were caught by armed cops. No doubt they were grassed up by some snake of a rat. Lucy copped 10 years. That's a real hot-blooded woman in my book! What a good sort, what a legendary woman. She must now be free! Max respect, Lucy. If she ever busted me out I would love her till the day I died. I'd kiss her feet and I'd die idolising her! I would have her as a goddess. I'm in Wakefield, sweetheart! Come and get me, please.

Another great chopper escape was at Mountjoy prison in Ireland in 1973. Mountjoy – what a piss-take name for a jail. Anyway, Seamus Twomey (an IRA chief), Kevin Mallon and JB O'Hagan flew out like skylarks from the exercise yard. Yep, I do love an escape! You never know when the next one is coming, do you? If it's ever me, there'll be some shitty pants outside. Believe me, I can't count on my fingers and toes all the parasites I'd love to bump into down a dark alley. Cunts.

I can hear you all thinking, would Bronson escape? Could he? I'll answer that by asking: do squirrels play with their nuts? Do goldfish blow bubbles? Does Elton John like fairy cakes? Do bears shit in the woods? Come on, wake up!

Remember Billy Hayes in 1970 when he escaped from the Turkish jail? You'll remember the movie *Midnight Express*. Well my train's not come in yet. I'm still waiting. I've got my ticket: one way to Disneyland! Now fuck off and stop asking me silly questions!

Hey! Here's one for the girls. The Rabbit Deluxe vibrator, with multi-speed control, now only costs £21.95 at all good sex shops. Go for it, girls. It was £29.95 so you save eight quid. You can get two tubs of fruit-flavoured lube with that – blackcurrant, raspberry or banana. You know you'll love it. I don't know any woman who can resist a nice big cock covered in banana juice! Talking of which, it's about time I had my cock sucked. I wonder which governor's on today!

I hear Donald Neilson, aka the 'black panther', has been diagnosed with motor neurone disease. He's 72 years old now and he won't see 73! Fucking good riddance to the bag of shit. I bet the family of Lesley Whittle are pleased. Pop the champers and get the party hats out. Lesley had a terrible death at the hands of the panther 33 years ago when put her down a sewer with the rats. That's the last thing she saw on earth: a sewer of shit and rats. 33 years later, he's got a terrible ending himself. The disease he's got is evil – it destroys the cells that control the muscles for speaking, swallowing and breathing. You can't even walk or move in the end. You're a brussel sprout in a field waiting to be picked, or pissed on by a fox! It's a terrible ending, but beautiful that it's happening to him.

This is how it will be: over the months he will deteriorate until he's put in the prison's hospital wing. He's still a Cat A prisoner in a max secure jail (Full Sutton in York) so he won't get any slack or any compassion. The first priority in any max secure jail like Full Sutton is security, so he will be in a bed or a chair till the day he dies. He will see everything around him! Some young con will probably give him a slap and steal his canteen or his bowl of soup. He will only have memories haunting him and he won't have anybody close to him. It's a bloody lonely old death in prison. Even more so for a cabbage.

That's the panther's end! Send him a card and wish him a long suffering – the longer the better. Hey! I bet Lesley comes back to haunt him! What do you think?

Did you know there are a good 40 assaults a day committed by teenage girls in the UK? Dangerous bitches. And get on this: 59,236 crimes were committed by teenage girls in 2007. That's fucking mental, it's insane, it's Loonyology out of control!

Talking of teenage girls, I've just had a letter from a 17-year-old tart from Manchester. I say tart, as what she wrote was disgusting. Even I blushed. I won't say what she wrote or who she is because she's only 17, but if you read this, grow up. And I never got your knickers; the censor takes them out as they're not allowed. Plus, they would never fit me.

You would be shocked at some of the stuff I get posted in. A lot of it I don't even see. I'm told there's a prison bag full of underwear and other crazy gifts nutters send me. One fucker actually sent me a noose with a card which said, "Top yourself." How nice is that? What's that all about? I'm sure people get me mixed up with somebody else! They read some mad story about me in some crazy paper or magazine and think I'm a monster! I remember when Saira's book came out. (She's the Muslim nutcase who became my mental bride.) I get a sackload of hate mail because she said I was a racist thug. People read this stuff and believe me to be some sort of Nazi nutter. Let's be honest: can you really call me a racist when I think black pussy is the sweetest on earth? How am I racist? I love the Tamla Motown and soul from the 1960s. Come on, we were kicking it; it was our era, our scene. The real time! Black, brown, white or yellow was cool with me! Aretha Franklin was the soul queen; we loved her. Racists don't like blacks. I also married an Asian beauty and I went out with an African sexpot! Racists don't do that, do they? Oh well, mud sticks and the hate mail rolls in. Fuck 'em. I don't lose any sleep over it!

When I was a kid in the 1960s, my dad was a painter and decorator in Luton. We lived in Farley Hill and there were no blacks in our area; they all lived in Bury Park. But my dad worked with a big black guy called Will. I can't remember his last name but he was a massive geezer – a good 6 foot 6, built like a barn door and as black as coal. Will was a great chap and he often came to our house for Sunday lunch. We loved him; he was our black friend. That was my family for you. We were never racist and we treated Will as we would treat anybody else, so if someone calls me racist I actually feel a serious urge to punch their teeth in. Don't do it!

Big Will always used to give me half a crown (that's two shillings and sixpence of old money) and he used to bring Superman and Marvel comics for me and my brother John. Yeah, he was a top geezer, and my mum and dad were proud to have him in our home. Lots of white folks would not have dared to do that then, but men like my dad respected all races and so do I. OK?

I see some little gay Scotch *Big Brother* contestant has just been booted out for spitting in one of the others' faces. How lovely! My question is: why didn't the other one chin him? That is an automatic broken jaw in my street! How can a man accept that? It's only instinct to attack! Cor, I wish I was on *Big Brother* and some cunt spat in my face. Six million people would see a head getting ripped off a body for the first time. (That's probably why I'm not in there!)

Did you know Oscar winner Charlize Theron witnessed her mum shoot her dad dead in self-defence? She was only 15 years old at the time but it's made her stronger – all thanks to her mum! Another violent man's life ends with a violent death. That's how it is and how it will always be: an eye for an eye. Watch out.

Running with the clock!
It's only time
Tick, tick, tock
You can't stop it
You can try
But it can't be stopped
You can die
But it still ticks on!
Time is time
It's bigger than life
It's bigger than the universe
Tick, tick, tock
Endless
A big black hole!

I had a lovely fry-up this morning. We have it every Saturday. It's scrambled egg, two bits of fried bread, two sausages, tomatoes and beans, with a mug of rosy lee and six bread rolls! I love it. They call it 'brunch' for some reason. Fuck knows why; it's a fry-up! Why call it brunch? This is England – stop fucking with our traditions and words. Next they'll be calling shit 'poo'. Shit is shit; why complicate things? Keep life simple and it's sweet.

Like I said, today started off happily but it ended with confusion and a very disturbed and dangerous mind! We shall see, oh yes, we shall see for sure or my name's not Charlie Bronson! 3-2-1 – watch me fly!

Sunday, 29 June 2008.

We had a great Sunday lunch today (only we get it at tea time): chicken, roast spuds, cauliflower, carrots and gravy. Fucking lovely. I just hope the cannibal, Miller and all the other monsters in the building choke on theirs! Fuck me; there wouldn't be too many of us left.

Monday tomorrow – a new week and almost a new month. Let's get it on. Amen.

Monday, 30 June 2008.

We lost a good senior screw today. Mr Kelly's moved off the unit after six years. He was a fair bloke and I had a lot of respect for him. He was a professional rugby player at one time. That's how being on a small unit is: the screws come and go but us cons remain. Some screws we don't miss; others we do! But when a screw is decent to me I respect it, so I wish him well for his next posting. It'll probably up on the monster wing. Still, his rugby skills could come in handy there! Drop a few of the cunts with a few good body charges. Pick them up and crush them to bits. Now that would get a screw a lot of respect!

This block is full up after four cons arrived from Frankland over the weekend. Apparently it kicked off up there but that's not unusual for Frankland; it's a volcano waiting to explode. I'm told the Muslim terror cons are trying it on – getting a bit lemon and causing a lot of shit! Cons won't put up with it. I predict a lot of violence coming very soon! It won't do any harm as it always clears the air. The sunshine causes a lot of violence because men get frustrated with their memories of holidays and families, then they explode like animals. The sun stirs up feelings, emotions, scars, hate, pain and revenge! Don't fuck with men, especially not a wing full of cons!

I see *EastEnders* star Brooke Kinsella's 16-year-old brother was stabbed to death over the weekend. How tragic is that? How many more kids are going to die on our streets?

I see the loonies in Broadmoor can't smoke after today. All smoking is banned. I can see some serious problems escalating there. How do you tell a madman who's been locked up for 20, 25, 30 years and smokes 60 fags a day that he can't smoke anymore? He won't understand it, and why should he? If the loony wants to smoke he should be allowed to smoke. They're his lungs. Why can't he smoke? This world's gone mad; it's full of wimps making the rules up as they go along. How the fuck can they stop lunatics from smoking? There are mass killers there – cannibals, psychos, schizos and psychotics – fucking dangerous men who love a smoke. I can't see it working myself. I bet the screws are shitting it. They'll be in the thick of it. Let's hope the roof comes off!

There was a lesbo siege in Bronzefield (great name for a jail) at the weekend. That's where Rose West is being held. Apparently two girls were to be split up so they barricaded themselves in a cell, but the screws smashed the door in and put an end to it. Cruel fuckers. The girls just wanted a bit of beaver action! What's wrong with that? Ain't that what lesbians do?

Seventeen young women rioted in Eastwood Park prison in Bristol over the weekend. How do I know all this? How does a man in a cage get all this prison news? I told you: I've got my finger on the pulse.

What about the beautiful 20-year-old model Ruslana Korshunova? She's just jumped to her death out of a ninth-story flat. She's been on the front cover of *Vogue*. That's New York for you. The world's a giant onion; let's all cry for Ruslana. A few tears may help. R.I.P.

The sun was out today as I jogged around the yard. I felt it on my head. I had a good work-out! I also called Dave Courtney. He's a top geezer and I'm going to stay with him during my first week of freedom! That's where I'll do all my media deals from. I've already got a national paper asking me if they can print my story! Within a week I'll have a 100K in my 'sky rocket' (if not more) then I'll be off for a bit of fun before I start training for my comeback fight. There's another 100K. I'll need a fucking big bag because I don't like banks. Robbing fuckers! Have you ever seen a skinny bank manager? Fat cunts.

One of the best screws I ever met was Charge Nurse Mr Turner in Broadmoor. What a top geezer he was. Every Xmas he spoilt me rotten with treble everything and he even cooked me an Xmas fry-up one year. He liked me – probably because of the overtime he got from my roof protests!

They never forget me either. Some ex-Broadmoor screws still send me Xmas cards. Fuck knows why, but it's probably because they respect me. It's a funny old world!

I only got three letters today, but it is Monday. There'll be a sackful tomorrow, you wait and see.

I fancy a beer... a can of bitter! I've just got the taste for one. I'll have a cup of tea instead. I've not got a lot of choice really! The screws' dogs have been barking a lot today; their pen is just over the unit wall. We often hear them. I think the dog handlers make them bark on purpose so as to remind us they're only feet away. Nasty fuckers.

Did I ever tell you about the time I dived on a dog when I was in a body-belt? Imagine it: no arms, just my mouth; 16 stone flying at it and the dog handler! That's how I got my nickname 'Mad Micky Peterson'. Would you dive on an Alsatian? I ran off from my escort and just leapt at it! That's how fucking mental I was in the 1970s. I don't know one con who's done that but me! Memories, they're beautiful – crazy but beautiful.

Oh, I saw Fred Lowe walk past today! He's an ugly fucker. It makes me laugh that he's right next door to me, only feet away, but if we see each other three or four times a year that's a result. It's like being on our own desert islands without the sea and sand – concrete islands. It's Loonyology! It's fucking insane!

This mattress is still rock-hard, like my cock first thing in the morning (one can dream).

First of July tomorrow. I wish I could pinch and punch some cunt!

Did you know it's 28 years ago that Jimi Hendrix died? He overdosed in a hotel room in London in 1970. What a genuine wizard, what a genius – what a waste!

1 July, 2008.

Here we are, let's hope it's a lucky month! What a lovely day it is today; the weather's beautiful. I could have done with a few more hours out on the yard! When it's like this it reminds me of the seaside, but there's no sea here! You've got to pretend. It works.

I only got two letters today and one of them was from a loony. You may as well share it with me, so here it is...

Charles,

I've just read your latest book *Loonyology*. I must say you have had quite a colourful life; you're certainly not a man I would wish to meet down a dark alley. How do you stay so positive in such primitive conditions? I must confess I'm a gay man myself and I'm a bit on the large size, some say I'm a lazy bugger but I just like the nicer things in life that always put the pounds on... The main reason I am writing to you is to ask could I please please have a signed photo (preferably naked) of you? I will treasure it. I would guess by your broadness and size of your hands you're a well-hung guy! What a waste.

Lots of love and respect,
Robbie

You just couldn't make it up, could you?

A nice bit of soup today! It was hot and had plenty of veg in it. I had six rolls with it and it filled me up. A nurse came over this morning to take my blood and urine. It's my ten-year MOT! I've been waiting two and a half months for it; they're fucking slow here. You can never be too careful in life – get your blood and piss tested!

That reminds me: back in 1969-71 I was a blood donor (and proud of it). I started giving a pint of claret in Risley jail. Most of the cons did; that's how it was in those days. We may have been nasty bastards but we still had our blood to help others. Jails don't do it anymore. Why not? I'll tell you why not: they're full of fucking smackheads who are riddled with diseases. Who the fuck wants their blood? Would you? I doubt it.

Talking of blood, the screws in Risley burst my nose open in 1970 when they crashed in my cell door. I bet the cunts got another two pints there! Still, it's only blood. What's a few pints between cons and screws?

One of the censors here on the unit is Mr Peak. He made me laugh today when he said, "Only two letters, Charlie. A nice, easy day for me for a change." He's only 29 years old and he's an ex-Full Sutton screw, but he's a good screw – a real character. You can't miss him as he's a good 6 feet 4! It's lucky he left Full Sutton because 80% of that lot are total wankers. A lot of screws become wankers after a spell with working with wankers. A screw has to be strong willed not to follow suit because then they become outcasts! It's sad because a lot of 'baddie' screws are really 'goodie' screws who are scared to go their own way. Such is life…

Did you know Prince Charles has a Aston Martin DB6 Volante which has been converted into an environmentally friendly car? It runs on white wine rather than petrol; can you fucking believe that? Well you'd better because it's true! Surplus plonk's not bad at £1.10 a litre. The world's gone fucking mental. But then again, it is the royals! You've got to make allowances for the insane. Even the royal train runs on cooking oil! See how you learn with Loonyology? Every page is something new. I'll be asking questions later!

It's 150 years ago today that Charles Darwin first unveiled his theory of evolution from ape to man. Was he right? Will we really ever know? Do we give a fuck? We're all animals anyway, only some of us smell sweeter than others.

I called Alan Rayment today. He was in the garden with his son and wife. They're a magic family – true friends – and I love them all! I asked Alan to stick £20 on Andy Murray to win Wimbledon. I had to as he played so well yesterday against Richard Gasquet. I think he could go all the way! I don't like the 'sweaty socks' but a winner's a winner with me. His next match is against Rafael Nadal so I should get a good price there! If he beats Nadal he can go all the way; sweaty sock or no sweaty sock…

I had a brilliant crap at dinner time! It felt great – long and skinny, not too soft and not too hard; just perfect! It's just as a turd should be. It broke my heart to flush it away! I was proud of it; I gave birth to it – a true Bronson stool. I wonder where it is now?

I was running around the yard one day in Armely jail back in 1975 when a screw shouted, "Stop running. You can't run here!" So I ran over to him and said, "What? You can't run here? Why not?"

"Because you can't."

"Why not?"

"Rules."

"What rules?"

"Look, you prat, just stop fucking running."

"Why?"

By now he was going red with rage, so for a laugh I slung the old fucker over my shoulder and did a lap of honour. All the cons were cheering. That cost me 28 days solitary and a fucking good kicking to go with it! In Armely jail cons just did not behave like that. They were terrified because the screws there were a bunch of psychos, believe me. I don't say this lightly but they were. However, my philosophy to prison life is: what can they do? Put me in prison? I'm already in prison or had you forgotten!

In Walton jail in 1974 I picked up a dustbin and hit a screw with it! I was up in front of the governor with assault and he asked, "How do you plead?"

"On what?" I asked.

"Assault with a dustbin on my officer," the governor said.

"Not guilty, your honour. He saw me with the dustbin and told me to put it down, so I let him have it! I threw it at him. How was I to know he couldn't catch?"

I've had some fun, I really have, and I've met the nasty screws and the good screws.

Talking of good screws, Mr Marsden was on today. He's been a screw for 30 years. He started off in Brixton jail in 1978 – the year I was certified insane! He's a top geezer, a funny old fucker, and he's seen it all, had it all and done it all! He's a proper Wakefield character. Let's have three cheers for him. HIP HIP – HOORAY! HIP HIP – HOORAY! HIP HIP – HOORAY! I keep telling him to retire and write a best-seller. What a story he's got to tell! He's locked up more serial killers than anyone can imagine, but he's done it with a smile. He doesn't take his job too seriously and after 30 years he's not even bothered about promotion. He's just an old-fashioned 'kangaroo'. It makes me laugh that some screws are only in their mid-twenties and they're all licking arse for promotion. When they get their 'pips' they think they know it all and treat the old screws like dogs. Give me an old screw with experience of life any day.

It's time I retired as well! I'm calling it a day. Good night. If I'm not back, just go on without me! But don't use my name in vain or I'll hunt you down and rip your ears off. Why? Because I'd like to, that's why!

Well, I've upset a few cons. I can't think why, I must have hit a raw nerve. They've all written to the letters page in the prison paper, *Inside Times*. Get on this, you'll love it:

Bronson: 'sort your head out'

RICHARD CASWELL - HMP FRANKLAND

I've just read the contribution from Charles Bronson in your June issue going on about 'prisoners moaning over petty things'. He's a fine one to talk - words like 'emptiness' and 'hopelessness' had the lads here in stitches. He claims that if we had to live his existence we would know what 'real porridge' is all about. But that's just it, we don't have to live like that, and neither would he if he kept his head down properly and got back on a wing.

I've seen him in the Full Sutton block, every weekend on exercise it would be the same old routine; time to come in and he would rip his tee-shirt to make wraps for his hands and head and shout the odds at the screws for five minutes about what he was going to do to them; then the gate opens, he lands a couple of body shots onto a stab proof vest and then he's wrapped up like a Christmas present and escorted inside - what's the point? The man is a joke. There he is in the papers crying about not being able to progress; what does he expect? If it's progression he wants then all he has to do is keep his head down; if it's fighting he wants, and a reputation, there are wings full of hate-filled lunatics who would gladly take him on just for fun; not me though, I've been schooled better than to draw hands with an old man.

What on earth gives Charles Bronson the right to criticize other cons for wanting to exercise. Yes, I want a CD digital DAB radio, a decent pillow, a kettle in my cell, Reebok trainers sent in, gymnasium, to cook my own food on association and watch Big Brother on TV whilst gobbling down a tub of raspberry ripple. Why? Because I suddenly might feel the urge to! And I want to feel like a man when I go on visits with friends and family.

What I absolutely don't want is to go from block to block wearing prison tracksuits; sit in an empty cell crying about how badly I've been treated for the past 30 years. I don't want an hour's exercise occasionally and everything else he's had for years. Charles Bronson is no more a man than anyone else.

And to think that I grew up reading his books and talking about him with respect sickens me. He's never seriously hurt anyone or been in a 20-man tear up on the wing, been assaulted with a 12 inch blade and had to fight for his life. Granted, he could have a good scrap in his prize-fighting days but he's a shadow of his former self; a glorified 'block-rat' who gets media attention because he's witty and can tell a good story.

Charles, sort your head out and have the dignity to grow old gracefully. Don't be a hypocrite by saying we moan over petty things when you're using words like 'hopelessness' to describe your own life.

SAM DAY - HMP LEEDS

So Charlie Bronson has been hard done by; well, most inmates don't start yelling and kicking just because they can't have their own way, or taking hostages. It's all about accepting your punishment and getting on with your sentence, and I'm sure I speak for a lot of prisoners when I say we can well do without this nonsense of being told we have it too easy; by Bronson or the POA's Glyn Travis!

Well, Caswell, if you were in Full Sutton Seg block when I kept refusing to come in, why couldn't you say why I behaved that way? I'd best explain that I'm entitled to one hour's exercise a day in the Seg block and that one hour in the fresh air is my heaven, my life, my pleasure each day, but the screws were nicking 20 minutes off me! Why? Because they're cunts! So I refused to come in three times in three weeks and each time, 20 screws came out to drag me in, smash me up and throw me in a box naked! Right or wrong, it's my fight, my stand, my war. If you cons want to accept having 20 minutes stolen from them, then more fool you. But the truth is, Caswell, you're afraid of the screws and the regime because you don't want to lose your TV or soft slippers or your pot of raspberry ripple. If that's how you choose to do your bird then good luck to you. Enjoy; get soft in your old age. And as far as not ever having to fight for my life, wake up, Caswell. I've had screws hang me up and kick me half to death. I don't know how old you are, but in the 1960s and '70s I came close to being drugged to death. I've also survived blades. So you think I'm a joke? I'll not forget that; you will but I never do! You enjoy your *Big Brother* shit and your raspberry ripple and keep licking those Frankland screws' arses. Let me continue my journey in peace…

ALEX POTTS - HMP HULL

Charlie Bronson should perhaps be reminded that we are not all his faithful servants and have minds of our own which, incredible as it might seem to him, allows us to make decisions based on information and not by intimidation and violence. If he wishes to publicise his new book and the film about his life then he is perfectly entitled to do so; but not at the expense of other prisoners who don't go about with knuckles scraping the floor, taking hostages and generally intimidating everyone in attempts to beat the system. We have chipped away over the years to stop inhuman treatment, so what on earth is wrong with being afforded some humanity and respect?

EAMONN ANDERSON - HMP BULLINGDON

I trust I'm far from alone in taking offence at Charlie Bronson's sweeping generalisation about 'snivelling cons' complaining over petty things – has he conveniently forgotten that many of the 'petty things' inmates complain about were the very same issues which frustrated him and led to him 'performing'.

I don't' wish to become involved in verbal confrontation with Bronson, however if he starts throwing stones he leaves himself wide open to criticism. There's no denying he's proved a handful, but in his foolish quest to be 'somebody' he embarked on a series of performances which were idiotic and self-destructive, and ultimately achieved nothing except isolation and massive sentences.

Many of us lived through the brutal systems of approved schools, borstals and prison, and participated in rioting against the old-style regimes; however a lot has changed over the years and time and people move on - including the prison system.

Book review page 40

I really have upset these cons! I've let the fox into the chicken pen; it's ripped their hearts out and they're taking all their anger and aggression out on me. Guys, it's the screws you need to retaliate against, not me! I'm just the porridge man doing my bird, that's all I am – the birdman. You guys do your bird how you do it and I'll do it how I do it. I don't need any raspberry ripple; I'm sweet enough! And fuck *Big Brother* and carpet slippers. Bare feet suit me. Good luck, lads…

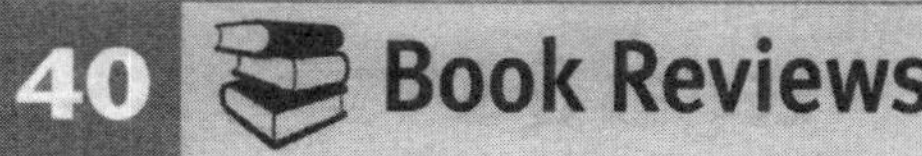

Loonyology - In my own words

by Charles Bronson

Andy Thackwray pays a mad, crazy, visit into the world of Loonyology, courtesy of Charles Bronson

This book should come with a government warning: 'Contains graphic scenes of sex, violence and 'loonacy' ... if easily offended - fuck off!' However, one thing the Government won't be warning the public about is that it also contains the truth, the whole truth and nothing but the truth. Written in his own words, Charles Bronson - mythically dubbed Britain's most violent prisoner - at long last gets a chance to put his uncensored and unedited side of his story out into the public domain.

Flitting from past to present in a somewhat unstructured and at times erratic manner, Bronson sheds light, with absolutely no holds barred, on his thirty-three years spent behind the walls of the country's harshest penal establishments - the majority of those years in solitary confinement - buried out of sight within the secretive confines of the prison estate's max-secure units.

Idolised for all the wrong reasons by many of the younger members of the prison estate, Bronson gets a chance to put his views of prison to them in no uncertain terms, and throughout the book he threads his message loud and clear to all the youngsters either in the early stages of their criminal careers and to those contemplating starting one: "Don't come to jail - it's a c**t!' - a message Bronson wants to take into schools, youth clubs and young offender institutions when he's finally released.

With brutal honesty, Bronson opens up his scrapbook of life in words, which catalogues not only his years of defiance against the prison system but also at times his regrets at having done so. You'll also discover throughout the pages of Loonyology that Bronson is a beehive of knowledge. Not only would you be daunted if you had to face him in a fight, you'd be equally as scared if you came up against him in a pub quiz!

Having first 'negotiated' Loonyology from the grip of the censor's office, and then having read it, I found it ironic that I'd be writing this review at a place where Charlie commited what is without doubt his most regrettable of prison misdemeanours - the taking hostage of a male teacher back in 1999 - regret he is at pains to illustrate throughout the book.

Whichever side of the wall you're on, Loonyology will educate, humour, shock and, much more importantly, enable you to decide on the validity of what's been previously said, written and frequently made up about its author - and I think you're in for quite a surprise!

Loonyology by Charles Bronson is available (hardback, price £18.99) from Apex Publishing Ltd, PO Box 7086, Clacton on Sea, Essex CO15 5WN. Tel: 01255 428500

Andy Thackwray is currently resident in HMP Hull

Well, at least someone enjoyed my book. Cheers, mate – it's nice to be appreciated. I'm actually amazed the prison allowed you a copy because my books are mostly banned in jails up and down the country, so that's good to hear. And it's in my old haunt, Hull. Good old nick that is. It opened in 1870 and it used to be a military prison. In the 1950s it became a borstal, then a max secure jail in the late 1960s.

If there's anything else you want to know, just ask. I keep telling you I'm a walking encyclopaedia on prison life; I'm actually a fucking genius. OK, you may be thinking, what a flash cunt. But it's true: I'm a genius, a prison historian, a professor of Loonyology! What I don't know about prison life is not worth knowing. Ask me anything as long as it's not about raspberry ripples. You've got to laugh at that; he had a right pop at me, didn't he? But deep down he probably still loves me! Years ago I would have got right upset about that! Not now – it's a different era now. A new breed! I really need to go home. I don't belong here anymore! Raspberry fucking ripples! Pass the porridge, cunt!

That's my lot for today. I'm fucked and my heads in bits. Every fucker hates me. What's a guy gotta do to get some loving? Raspberry fucking ripple. (I wonder what they're like?)

3 July, 2008

A fucking brilliant day – 14 letters and a parcel! Come on, who else gets mail like that? All these wasted years, dead years, and I'm still as loved now as I was when I was free! Who's jealous? Come on, who wishes they got 14 letters and a parcel? Yiiipppeeeeeee!

I also got my canteen today! The screwess Miss Walker handed it out. I knew it was her even before my door opened as I can smell her scent breezing through the crack in my door. It's lovely! I always say to her, "You smell nice!" Anyway, she opened the outer door and passed my canteen under the inner cage door. I got nuts, fruit, cheese and fresh orange juice. Oh, and two small bars of CDM chocolate. Who's the daddy? Fuck the raspberry ripples, men don't eat that shit. Real men wouldn't waste their dosh on that! If I was walking down my street in Luton eating a raspberry ripple, I would end up with a fucking big axe in my crust.

On the exercise yard this afternoon there was a big black storm and it was pissing down. It was brilliant and made me feel alive and kicking, free and happy. Canteen, letters, health and fitness! I was born to be happy – free of all the shit. I'm my own master, running in the wind and the rain then watching the sun come out! It should be a crime to be so happy; it's bloody brilliant. Yiiipppeeeee, yarrhhooooooo.

One of the letters today is from my lovely friend Dee Morris. She wrote a letter to her MP, Ms Siobhain McDonagh, and you have just got to read it. It's just so powerful. When you've read it, tell me she's not a special friend. She's lovely! If everyone wrote a letter like this to their MP, imagine the stink it would cause. Answers, that's what's needed! We await the answers! Thanks, Dee – you're a gem! Love ya!

Thursday, 26 June 2008.
Ms Siobhain McDonagh MP,
The House of Commons, Westminster, London, SW1A OAA

Dear Ms McDonagh,

I hope that this letter finds you well. I am writing to you because I know how dedicated you are to your constituents. I know how fearless you are in fighting for what you believe in and know that you willingly speak and act on people's behalf and are not afraid to speak out. I have been a Merton resident for 32 years and have always found you to be of great assistance.

The reason that I am writing to you is because I am compelled to. I need to express my views and opinions and want them to be heard. For over ten years now I have continuously written to the Parole Board, Home Office and government officials regarding this serious matter, to no avail.

The matter is regarding a friend of mine, Mr Charles Bronson, who is locked away in HMP Wakefield in a segregation unit. This is where he has remained for years and years, still classed as a Cat A prisoner, still on closed visits. He has been on closed visits for over 8 years now. 8 years without any physical contact, no hug even allowed from his mother who is in her 70s and loves her son with all her heart.

The full details for Charles are as follows: Mr Charles Bronson, BT1314, Seg Unit, HMP Wakefield, 5 Love Lane, Wakefield, West Yorkshire, WF2 9AG.

Mr Bronson was originally sentenced to 8 years for armed robbery, a robbery in which no-one was injured or killed. 33 years later, he remains a Cat A prisoner in a segregated unit with closed visits. I will refer to Charles as Charlie, which is what his friends call him.

Charlie has been given more time repeatedly for crimes that he committed in prison – crimes that were fuelled by the inhumane conditions that he gets, the beatings that he's had by prison officers, deaths in his family and being refused to attend funerals and constant dismissals regarding his case.

Now neither I nor Charlie will deny the crimes that he committed. Neither do we condone or justify them. I can though (as a human with a brain and a heart) understand the reasons behind them. I firmly believe, though, as do thousands of others, that he has paid the price for them. I am disgusted and sickened by the conditions that he is in. I am astounded that the government, Home Office, Parole Board and media can control someone with such disregard. Charlie is locked away like an animal. Whilst having never ever raped, sexually abused or killed anyone, he is treated far worse than those that have. He is refused all the applications and appeals that he makes. He is never given the chance to progress. Prison is supposed to be there to rehabilitate the criminals within. All other prisoners are given the chance to study, to progress to develop and enhance their studies or gain qualifications and further education, but Charlie is kept in total isolation where he has spent many, many years.

Now, I am neither a fanatic, a villain, a gangster or even a criminal to any extent. I am just an average 'Joe public' person who is speaking out like thousands of others like myself. I would not be able to sleep tonight if I hadn't written this letter to you. After our country and people fought so bravely for freedom of speech, I feel it is only right and totally justified to use mine.

Of all the letters I have written to officials regarding Charlie's case, I have never, ever received a straight answer. My letters (and my questions) are passed from pillar to post. No one, it seems, is prepared to accept or take responsibility regarding Charlie's case. Every official and every department blames another. No questions are answered, no reasons are given. The government are supposed to hear public views and opinions, take heed of them and act upon them. It is 'we' the public who vote for the government to represent our beliefs and fight for them. It seems, however, that they only fight for what they believe in.

Today's newspaper headline proved that once again. I have enclosed copies for you as I feel you have to see it to believe it. It made my blood boil. I was enraged at this. However, this is not a one-off. This is not a rarity. It continues regularly and has done for so many years and all I can ask is why? How can they justify this? How can they condone this? Why is this allowed to continuously happen? Why are the public's views and opinions heard? Why do the government and officials protect and assist rapists and paedophiles when they should be protecting and assisting the public?

I, as a child, was in the care system. I saw and heard the severity of the cases where children had been sexually and physically abused. I witnessed first-hand the devastating effects that it had on them. I have also witnessed first-hand how that continues to affect them for the rest of the lives. I have attended a number of funerals of young people where they felt that the only way to end their suffering was to end their lives.

I have seen many of these young people grow to be adults and their suffering and pain grows with them. Many turn to drink and drugs to try and suppress their suffering, but as we know it just enhances it. I have worked in many areas and have tried desperately to make a difference in people's lives. I have tried desperately to assist, advise and support others. Of all the young people I have come across in life, whether socially or through employment, I have felt compelled to protect, guide and nurture them. Grief counselling, detached youth work, mentoring, young offenders and fostering are just some of the areas in which I have worked. As well as this I adopted two children. As you can see I have tried desperately to make a difference – to assist, advise, support and protect young people. This, however, cannot be achieved. Why? I'll tell you why: because the government and judicial system does not allow us to.

My friend Charlie, who is a self-taught poet, artist and author, rots away in a dungeon. Treated like an animal. Never de-categorized. Never allowed open visits. Never allowed to associate within the prison. Never given the chance to prove himself. Never treated with any dignity or compassion. Never ever considered for release. Yet rapists, paedophiles and child killers are regularly released. How can that be justified?

It is the same case for Mr Ronnie Biggs; Mr Ronnie Biggs is still locked away. He is a dying, elderly man. Having suffered strokes, heart attacks, losing his speech and being fed through a tube, he still remains locked away. Why? Is it because no-one wants to accept responsibility? Is it that the government wants to make examples of these men? Is it that the government values and protect pounds whilst disregarding and giving no value to the lives of young people?

Ronnie Biggs and Charles Bronson have never raped, sexually abused or killed anyone. Is this what keeps them locked away? So the officials believe that a violent man cannot rehabilitate or change, yet they believe that child killers and paedophiles can? In fact even when paedophiles, rapists and child killers admit they have not changed or rehabilitated they can still be freed!

Siobhain, I am putting my heart and soul into this letter; why? Because it is something I feel so very very strongly about. I need to and want to be heard as do thousands of other public figures. I am desperate for someone to stand up for what so many believe in. I hope and pray that you will represent and support my views. Both of these cases are in urgent need of review. Mr Bronson and Mr Biggs deserve to be freed. They have paid their price.

I would very much appreciate it if you could please write letters on my behalf regarding both Mr Biggs and Mr Bronson. I also would be very grateful if you could please give me any further advice or assistance regarding pursuing this matter, e.g. addresses, names or departments that I could contact to express my views and for them to be heard.

I wish for both our sakes I could have made this letter short and sweet. But life for Mr Bronson and Mr Biggs isn't, so this needs to be portrayed. I very much hope that this hasn't been written to no avail. I am sure that you will be just as disgusted and sickened by headlines like this. But as we both know, this case is not a rarity. It will not go down in history. People of this kind are freed regularly whilst Mr Bronson and Mr Biggs are used as examples. If Mr Bronson, classed as a violent prisoner, is locked away in a segregation unit with closed visits and pure isolation is used as a "deterrent and apparent example" what exactly is the example and deterrent that is shown to potential paedophiles, rapists and child killers? If they are locked away, it will be in comfort, with all their needs being met, eventually freed as quick as the system can. Hardly a deterrent for a potential paedophile is it?

Siobhain, I would urge you to please provide me with your advice, assistance and support. I know you are capable of fighting for what you believe in and I am desperate to do the same. I eagerly await your reply. Thank you in anticipation.

Yours sincerely,
Miss Dalanya Morris

Yeah, that's what I call magical! That's a real friend – someone who cares. Thanks, Dee!

Fuck me – I went in the shower today, five minutes after the cannibal came out, and it smelt mushy, like a guinea pig's cage. I fucking hate going in there when he's been in before me. I'd love to go in there when he's in there! No words; I would just bust his jaw. Without a blade he's nothing – a non-entity!

I had pizza and chips for tea. Not bad. I've had worse! (Not a lot worse.) All in all it was a nice day. (It'll be a better one tomorrow.)

Oh! Michelle is seeing me tomorrow in the interview room. She's the prison probation officer. I've not seen her for months. I like her; she's nice to talk to, friendly, lovely and she's on my side which is good. A rare thing for me!

Wisdom is knowing when to stay silent; silence can speak for you.

Have a great night's sleep and don't dream of me. Don't be mad.

4 July 2008.

Here we go again… I've just got my yearly Cat A review reply and it's another knock-back! Another year on Cat A! Why? Because I'm Charlie Bronson, that's why! Do you think I'm a danger to the public? Well, do you?

Also, why am I on Cat A? What crime have I committed to justify it? Do you realise just how long I've been on this category? Over 30 years! The Kray twins were only Cat A for 18 years and even mass killers are not on it for as long as me! Why am I on it? Why can't I come off it so I can move on? I'll tell you: it's a political and vindictive decision. They're saying, "Bronson has fucked with us for years, so now we fuck with him. Bronson either licks our arses and grovels and does all our pathetic courses, or we will never de-categorise him. It's that simple." Well, I say, "Fuck you." I know I've changed and everyone else knows it too! I'm licking no fucker's arse. I either walk out of the courts free or they parole me (or I leave jail in a zip-up bag).

Fuck you – that's my politics! (Don't get involved in politics.) I remain Cat A; I remain Britain's No.1 danger man and I remain in a coffin! And fuck your raspberry ripples; pass the porridge. Thank you.

I had a nice hour with Michelle this morning. It went well. She believes I've changed my life around, so that's one on my side.

I got a dozen letters today and only one mad one from some cunt in Birmingham who wants me to 'arrange' something for one of his neighbours. I don't know him, he doesn't know me and he wants me to get involved in a dispute that doesn't even concern me. Is he for real? Cunt. Er, hello! I'm in jail, buddy, or had you forgotten? It's HMP Wakefield, not Wakefield Travelodge! And my firm have got better things to do than drive to Brummie land to sort your shit out! Send me 10K and I may get involved, OK? Now fuck off!

A young girl of 18 called Anthea sent me in a black, silk-scented hanky and a beautiful letter. Thanks, Anthea, you're a doll x. Write to me any time; you sound gorgeous! I bet your tears taste of wine. Old people's tears taste of salt water or sewer water. All the bitterness of life pours out. Best not cry. I bet you all think I'm a bitter, nasty old fucker. Actually I'm far from it which is a fucking miracle!

I had a lovely bowl of mushroom soup today! It tasted good and I had six mushrooms in mine. Fred Lowe had six bowls, the fat cunt! One does me. I remember Fred on the Hull special unit in 1994. He made a sandwich that was so big it looked like a loaf cut in half. He filled it up with all sorts: peanut butter, lettuce, tomatoes, cheese, sausages and bacon. It was fucking mental. He looked like a bleeding lizard – like one of those dragon reptiles eating a pig – and had that heavy, snorting breathing. Fuck me – it was like being in a zoo! But he does his bird well and you never hear him moaning. He's got no enemies; he kills them! Would you invite him or Maudsley home for dinner? What a TV documentary that would make! It's all Loonyology! Bend down and kiss a frog!

I found out today that Ray Kray's just had his third child – a little boy called Branden Kray born on 28 June. A great name, eh? Sounds cool, like a movie star or a top fighter! It's got a ring to it; a good, strong name. That's now two sons and a daughter for Ray and Emma Kray. Congratulations.

I've also just heard that my old buddy Tony Crabb has got tumours in his lungs and spine. I'm gutted to hear this news; he's looking at months left on the planet, not years. Crabby is a lifer in Kingston jail and you can read all about him in *Loonyology: In My Own Words*. But take it from me, the man's a legend – a one-off! I'm very sad to hear this news, as will be many others – apart from the Old Bill and the penal system. They love it! They love to see us go out in a body bag. They don't like armed robbers, they only love a nonce or a grass, because they can manipulate and control them! It makes them feel powerful, just like my cock first thing in the morning: rock hard. If I hit a screw over the head with my erection I would be up for murder. Honestly!

Anyway, we all love you, Crabby! Enjoy what you can, mate. Make the very best of what's left.

Crabby wrote to me on a Christmas card and it's only July, so in his heart he knows he won't make Christmas. How powerful is that? Like I've said, I'm blessed with such great mates.

Did you know dark chocolate contains antioxidants known as phenols which combats heart disease and all sorts of ailments? It also helps to lower blood pressure. So pass the chocolates, love. Don't be greedy, you fat bitch. Stop stuffing your face!

Fuck me; get on this: Kylie Minogue collected an OBE yesterday at the palace. Er… hello! What for? What about my buddy Alan Rayment? He's lost both his legs and raises untold thousands for kiddies' charities. That's the sort of person who should get an OBE! Kylie is worth millions; what's she need an OBE for? It's all bollocks to me. They're giving them out like Smarties!

Did you hear about 70-year-old Omkari Panwar and her 77-year-old husband Charan Singh Panwar in New Delhi who've just had twins? Can you fucking believe that? I told you the world's an asylum! It's fucking mental! The oldest woman to give birth in the UK was Patricia Rashbrook, aged 62, but that was with IVF treatment. Omkari Panwar takes the biscuit, she's the daddy… I mean mummy! Well done, lady. You're now a legend. What a miracle; a blessing! It just goes to show that anything is possible, apart from me ever getting off Cat A or getting a fair crack of the whip in jail.

Talking of whips, my lovely lady friend Jan Lamb, the angel of the underworld, used to enjoy giving me a good whipping. I love Jan; we all do. We go back years and I've never met nobody like her; she's a true, uncut gem – priceless. I remember we stayed in a caravan for a spell. Fuck me, how did those springs survive? Could Jan fuck or could she fuck? I was just out of jail and my balls were full of double cream. No sooner had I shot my lot than I was up and ready for seconds!

Jan was special to me and I always have her in my memory box! Some women are just born to fuck and they don't reach their peak till they're in their 40s when they've been round the block a few times. Jan knew how to turn me on, even when my cock was sore. She gave it some sweet and tender loving. I'll never forget the time I woke up with her sucking me off and playing with herself in my face at the same time. I opened my eyes to a beautiful wet pussy and her finger rubbing her clitty. I had to shake my head in case I was dreaming back in Broadmoor's padded room. A wet, juicy fanny in my face – what a way to wake up; sucked off and my face covered in pussy juice! By the time I finished with her my head was like a wet watermelon and my face was dripping wet. I bent her over the table and gave her the fucking of her life. Even today, over 20 years later, Jan still writes to me and reminds me of that time. We were a great pair, and if I wasn't so insane I would have married her and settled down. There was something about Jan; she was fearless and wasn't scared of anybody. But the truth is we would have fucked each other to death! My heart would've blown up; she would've killed me off with love! A man can only take so much, but what a way to die!

I was fucking Jan once up against a tree, really pumping away, and she was screaming and tearing bits of flesh off my back. I could feel the blood dripping all down my arse. When she squeezed my balls I thought I shot a bullet out and so did she. Never in her life has so much spunk shot into her at such a speed.

I'm going to tell you lovers around the planet a little secret now that really turns your woman on. (Jan told me I was the only lover she ever had who did this to her.) When you shoot your lot into your woman, don't waste it; go down on her and lick it up. It's pure protein, it's food – the food of life! I take it all back. It's mine and I'm a greedy fucker! And it tastes good because it's not just my spunk but also the woman's juices mingled in. It's human honey – the richest, sweetest, creamiest protein on the planet! Jan used to suck my tongue afterwards and lick my face clean. Share and share alike.

Another tip: the best sex is out in the open air! A field, a park, a bus shelter, a car park or a fucking roof if you like. I call it the 'freedom fuck'. The best position in the open air is 'doggy-style' because you're both looking in the same direction and seeing the same things. If somebody comes it's even more exciting because you're both looking! It's brilliant, try it. I don't mind people looking but you can never touch! Lay a finger on my woman and I'll snap your spine for sure! I don't share my woman with anybody!

It's a funny old world. But don't we love it? If you read *Loonyology: In My Own Words* you'll get Jan's version of our time together. Beautiful, treasured memories! Even if I never see, smell, taste or touch another pussy ever again, Jan Lamb's still left this man very happy. Thank you!

I had meatballs for tea. Shit! But I've got a pork pie for later and I'll enjoy that with a cup of tea.

Roll on 12 July. It's the commemoration of the Battle of the Boyne – a very important historical day!

5 July 2008.

Woke up, brushed teeth, shaved head
Had a good dump
Strip washed, brushed beard
Why?
Why even wake up?
Dead men don't shit
Dead men don't think
Year after year in a cage
Why?
Somebody tell me why!
A lifetime sucked away
What's left?
Old creaky bones and a colostomy bag!
Bad eyes and a bent back
Old men in lost dreams
Farting as they walk
Soiled, smelly, piss-stained pants
Rocking in a chair
Rocking all the way to the darkest hole!
Why wake up at all?
What's the point, the sense in it all?
It's fucking crazy
The journey is a circle!
Around and around and around
I'm dizzy
I'm bleeding in the head
Ice-cool blood
It's frozen my brain
It's stolen my dreams
Sleep, wake, sleep, wake, sleep, wake
I can't even sleep-walk

Where the fuck can I walk to?
Up and down a 12-foot cell
Up, down, up, down, up, down
My head's fuzzy
Airless
Stale prison claustrophobic air
I'm tired
I'm sleepy
I'm Charlie Bronson
The birdman
The bird with the fractured wing
Snapped and broken with time
Worn down
Ironed out
Dreamless
Empty
The colour's faded
It's all grey
Prison pallor
Dead, flaky skin
A beard like snow
Wake up to what?
Wake up for who?
How much longer?
What comes next?
It's all control
Power
Gods in suits
Little people with so much power
ripping away my sky
It's a mental torture
A psychological game
Wake up, a new day
It's never new
How can it be?
So why do I wake up?
Why do I put myself through all this shit?
What's in it for me?
I'll tell you!
I'm a stubborn old git
My pride comes first
I refuse to die or give up on my dream
I'm going all the way
All the way to freedom
That's why I awake with a smile
My heart won't let me down
Control or no control
I go on to win
The system can lick my dick

Lick my bum hole
Turn off my light
I'll find my way in the dark
I can't die
How can I not carry on?
All this for nothing
All this madness for a coffin
Fuck that
My name alone puts fear into them
I am what I am:
Charlie Bronson
The man they couldn't kill
They tried so many times to destroy me!
I now wake up for spite
They wake up to control me
The question is
For how much longer?
Until they're exposed!
I'm living to expose them
The system stinks
It's corrupt
It's vindictive and cruel
That's why I wake to a new day
I live in hope

I don't know where my poetry comes from but it drains me. It flows out of my pen as if I'm bleeding or shouting out. Fucking listen to me. See sense! Wake up! It feels like I've struggled free from the strait jacket; I'm on the loose and I want to tell my side of the story. Listen to me: it's the asylum that's evil, not me!

Behind these walls is Hell…
And I'm here to tell!
That's my poetry in a nutshell!
Fuck Oscar Wilde!
This is Bronson time!
The poet from within!
From deep inside the machine!
'Penal madness' – the penetration of Loonyology!
Ouch… it fucking hurts!

Did you know the first NHS hospital opened in Manchester in 1948? I bet it had an asylum ward. What good's a hospital without lunatics? The loons liven it up!

Here's a little treat for you. You can read this next bit to your kids; it may help put them off crime forever. They need to know the truth, the facts of life for criminals and what to expect when they get their collar felt. Even for lunatics like me, as hard and tough as we may be, it still fucking rips us apart to face the consequences of our actions.

Crime and Punishment: the truth, the whole truth and nothing but the truth.

I'm nicked, I'm caught, I'm back inside. Remanded, locked up.

How does it affect us? Does it mean anything? Let me tell you: it's the worst time of your life, because you're no longer in control of anything. You're a prisoner – innocent till proven guilty, but you're still a prisoner – locked away from the real world. This is where it begins. Right up until your trial you're in suspense! You don't know what the outcome will be. It's stressful and it causes mental pain. It eats you away and it's affecting your family. Everyone's worried and waiting as the months pass by; it's all a big wait. There's no rush, you're no-one special. You wait your turn.

Did you plead guilty or not guilty? Do your legal team advise you to plead guilty? If you plead guilty the judge may be lenient, but if you plead not guilty and you're found guilty you could be looking at a very long sentence! It's a hell of a gamble and the stakes are your life. Years of your life could be thrown away!

For months you read and digest all your paperwork, statements, evidence and interviews. It drives you mad! Half of it you don't understand and the other half doesn't make any sense, but that's your life and it's about to become very real in a courtroom on judgement day. It may be six months away or it could be 12. By the time it arrives you'll be more confused and unsure than the day you were arrested. The police and the prosecution all want you convicted. It's a fight to find you guilty. You may well be guilty but you feel you need to fight. It's your life up in that dock. After waiting, hoping and praying, the day finally comes! I'm going to take you through what happens on this day.

Your cell door unlocks at 6am: "OK, ready for court!" You're escorted over to reception with your bag of court papers and your few personal things. You see others getting ready for their court appearance and everyone's tense! The screws are prepared for anything as they know how you feel. This is the big day you've been waiting for! You're stripped, searched, metal-detected, then given a green and yellow boiler suit. You look like a fucking clown. Then you're cuffed up and locked into a steel box on the prison van! The box is so tiny that there's just enough room to sit down It's smelly, airless and very claustrophobic. The window is made of bullet-proofed blacked-out glass. The screws have nice, soft seats and they can stretch their legs and walk up and down outside your sweat box. As the van drives off you can smell the petrol fumes. It's hot and stuffy and very bumpy. By the time it drives into the court car park you feel sick and you've got a headache! I've had years of this and I still can't get used to it.

If the court is one of the old ones, like the Old Bailey or other old city courts, you will be lead through a tunnel of history – dirty old cells a 100, 200 or maybe 300 years old. You can smell the decay! It's a dungeon. The screws hand you your clothes and court papers and lock you up in a cell. The walls are solid stone and you can feel their coldness. There's a wooden bench embedded into a slab of concrete. You think about the hundreds and thousands of prisoners who have sat on that bench over the centuries; some, no doubt, sentenced to hang. You read the writing on the door and walls:

"Killroy was 'ere."

"Fuck the judge."

"All screws and coppers are cunts."

"I love Rose."

"I don't give a fuck."

"I only got 20 years... easy."

You walk up and down on the stone floor, thinking, wondering. You bang on the door for water! You ask to see your legal team and you are told you can see them when they arrive. You say, "Go and fucking find them now!"

Tension kicks in. You feel you're being moved around like a chess piece and you have no control. The court takes over! You're lead to a closed interview room and your legal team are behind unbreakable glass. They're advising you, but it's all down to you! It's your decision; only you can decide how to plead. They could tell you the world's square, or an orange is an apple. It's up to you whether you trust them or trust yourself!

Your name is called out and you're lead through a maze of corridors until you come to a large door, behind which are big stone steps leading up to the court dock. As you walk up the stairs with the screws, your brain is screaming, "This is it!"

The dock is the loneliest place on Earth. Facing you is the judge – that man or woman in the wig and gown. The room is full of barristers and solicitors and press reporters! The public gallery is full of your family and friends all there to support you. The 12 members of jury are sworn in. This is it: your big day. It may go on for a week, maybe two. It's your decision whether to carry on fighting or give up.

At the end of it all, the judge will look at you and deliver the outcome. You have been judged! If it's a plea of not guilty, the jury will decide; if it's a plea of guilty it's all in the hands of the judge. A guilty verdict rips your soul away! You're fucked and you're going down those stairs feeling fucked up. Whether one year or 21 years, it's all a big fuck up! You lost. All the months of stress and worry are over and you now have to get on with it the best way you can. But if you get a not guilty then you feel wow, what a victory! You've won the greatest fight of your life. You're a winner; born again. Thank you, jury. The drinks are on me.

This is what it's all about! Are you prepared to gamble your freedom away? Is it all worth it? Are you not worth more than a court room's verdict? Let me tell you kids now: one day in prison is one day too many. Don't end up in this dock and stay clear of this world of locked doors. It's painful, and it all starts from the court room dock!

If you're found guilty, you'll walk back down those steps feeling crushed. Your life is no longer your own and you walk back to the Hell you just left. The door slams shut; your life has been stolen! Then it's back into the box to be driven back to madness. Your name's a number and you're a nobody, a loser, a dreamer who's been squeezed and dried up. Your family go home destroyed and over the years your friends fade away. You become more alone. The cry of "Guilty!" echoes in your mind.

That's how it ends so don't allow it to start! That's the best advice you're ever going to get in life, and you got it from me – the man himself. I've stood in so many court rooms and I've been dragged down so many steps.

They make sure your head bounces off every one! It's become a way of life to me, but you youngsters stop and give it some serious thought. It's not guilty all the way if you didn't do it.

Then again, there's one law for some and another law for others, believe it. Take this cunt of a bent copper, Andre Nwogwugwu (strange name). He got nicked on trying to defraud £200,000 out of three building societies. This was big crime and if I'd done it I'd easily be looking at seven years. Guess what he got. Come on, guess. Three years? Two? No, he got fuck all! Judge Michael Gledhill gave him a 52-week suspended sentence! HA! HA! HA! And he said (get on this, you'll love this), "I'm sparing you a jail sentence because it would be a dreadful time for you." Oh, poor Mr Policeman! How dreadful, poor thing. That's what I mean by one law for some and another law for others. I rest my case.

Wayne Black has just arrived here on a lay down from Frankland. I saw him on the exercise yard today and had a nice chat with him (he was on the yard that's directly under my window). Wayne's into his 15th year. I first met him 12 years back in Belmarsh unit. He escaped off the van on the way to court and if I say so myself, it was a beautiful escape. A legendary one at that; one you dream of! He climbed through the trap-door in the van's roof and leapt off to freedom. Unfortunately he broke his ankle as he landed, but he still managed to get away. They caught up with him four months later. Well, he's almost home now! Two more years to go. I was made up to have a chat with him and to see him looking so well. 14 years is serious bird, especially when you do it all on Cat A like Wayne has. (It's been all max secure for him.) I salute the man! He's a proper Londoner who I respect. He comes from Islington, North London. Some good robbers have come out of that manor! Top bods.

Yeah, it was great to catch up on some prison gossip. I've learnt more today than I have all year. The prison world is full of activity but in this cemetery we are cut off from a lot of it. We get to hear about a murder or a stabbing months after the actual event.

I got a nice pile of letters today. Not bad for a Saturday! Dee Morris sent me in some photos of Joe Pyle's grave with my flowers and card on. It looks like his grave is well cared for. It lit up my day to see such a tidy, sparkling plot. (That's respect.)

I also got a cracking letter from John H Stracey, who's trying to get an exhibition fight on with Carlos Palomino. It was Carlos who took John's world title belt from him in 1976. If this fight comes off, it will be boxing history. For two world champions to meet up in the ring again after a 32-year gap would be unbelievable. Who wouldn't pay to see that? A lot of youngsters could be inspired to take up boxing if they saw two old fellas back in action. A pair of boxing gloves are better than a knife or a gun. And you get paid for it!

Mark Emmins sent me in a pile of paperwork and photos. He's just got a nice new convertible. It's a beauty!

We get hundreds of emails in support for the 'Free Bronson' campaign every week. I've got boxes and boxes of them and I've picked out the best one for June. Here it is, from a Cheryl Gardner. Thanks, Cheryl!

Dear Mr Mitchell,

I am writing to you in total disbelief at the news that Abu Qatada has just been released 'on a strict curfew'. Is this some kind of joke?!!!!! Has the British justice system gone mad? Why is this man free to live amongst us? This man had been convicted in the Middle East for involvement in terror attacks in 1998 and also for plotting to plant bombs. He should be sent back to Jordan to face up to what he has done. But what do we do? Same as always, treat him with kid gloves. God forbid that we are seen to be violating this monster's human rights, so he is on a 22-hour curfew and has to wear a tag. After 9/11 and the London bombings there should be no leniency for these people. Yet here is a man that could potentially kill maybe hundreds of people in acts of terrorism, allowed to live in Britain amongst our families and children. So he is supposed to be on a curfew and tagged. "The toughest yet"? Not enough. Can't the government see that the British public are sick of this?

On the other side of the British justice coin is a man called Mr Charles Bronson (the main reason for me writing to you), a 55-year-old man who has spent 34 years in prison, 30 of which have been in solitary confinement. This man has never killed anyone, has been certified sane and has not been violent for the last 7 years. What about this man's human rights? OK, he has been violent in the past and there is no condoning that, he has admitted that he has done wrong. But it is not all one-sided. He is a target in prison. The good old British media have given him a reputation far worse than he has given to himself. Describing him as 'Britain's most dangerous criminal', 'an animal' and 'insane' (to name a few) has made him a target and prison officers treat him like an animal, not a human. The majority of them see him as a challenge. They want to prove that they are in charge, that they call the shots, and this is done both mentally and physically. So the system is as much to blame as Charles is for his violent outbursts.

Charles was sentenced to life in 2000 for holding a teacher hostage for 44 hours in Hull prison. The teacher was not physically harmed (mentally shaken up, understandably, but not physically harmed) so why a life sentence? It is regularly on the news that drunken, uninsured drivers kill families, children and parents on our roads and receive sentences of six and a half years. That they knowingly got into a car and killed, to me, is reason for a life sentence. But then when rapists, murderers, child abusers and terrorists do get sentenced they get a cosy cell, a chance to mingle with other prisoners and when their sentence is almost up, go before a parole board and get released back into society.

Charles lives in a cage for 23 hours a day, is not allowed to mix with other prisoners and any visits he gets have to be through bars. What parole board will grant a man parole if they think he is too violent to be in the same room as them? He needs to be able to mix with people; rehabilitation is what this man needs – a chance to prove himself. He cannot do this unless he is given a chance to. That is all he needs, just one chance. He is an accomplished artist in his own right and has had 11 books published and regularly gives to charity. Are these the actions of an insane animal? No, they are the actions of a man who has openly admitted to being violent in the past but after 34 years of being moved from prison to prison, being a victim of brutality and living a lonely existence, has had enough. For the last seven years he has not been violent. Why won't anyone take responsibility for this man's welfare? Give him the chance – the same chance every other prisoner seems to get.

I don't know what needs doing to give Charles his chance. I am just an ordinary mum of four children, who fears for their future in this uncertain Britain, but I'm sure you would know where to start. The country is a joke; this place that I once loved is a shambles. We have to put the 'Great' back into Great Britain, starting with the inconsistent British justice system because, in Charlie's words, it's just 'Loonyology'.

Thank you for listening.

Regards,

Cheryl Gardner.

That says it all! But will the MPs act on it? I doubt it. We shall see… One day we will fuck 'em up; that's for sure!

I had a fry-up tonight. You can't beat a good old English nosh up and a hot mug of tea with a spoon of honey in it. That's living!

It's fucking pissing it down as I write this; I mean buckets, cats and dogs, one big, fuck off storm. It's bashing against my window and I can hear it on the roof. It's fucking brilliant. And guess what? Maudsley is out in it like a drowned rat. I hope the lightening hits him on the head and fries his brain. That would wake the cunt up! What a way to go: "Wakefield's mass murderer Robert Maudsley fries to death with a bolt of lightning on the exercise yard." Fuck me – what an ending!

A flashback from 1976 just came to me. I was in Parkhurst when John H Stracey lost his world title to Carlos Palomino; I heard the fight on the radio. The next day all the London villains were gutted! We were all slopping out miserably; gutted sick. A lot of Mars bars were lost that day! But that's showbiz for you: win some, lose some and bounce back! No shame in losing to Carlos Palomino; what a legend. Let's hope this exhibition fight takes shape. It'd be awesome.

Did you read about that pervo in Spain who was caught on the beach having sex with an octopus? He got nicked with bestiality. What a weirdo. An octopus! Come on, what a sicko. In his defence, he said, "I identify myself with beasts." Fucking lock the cunt away in the asylum. What's he going to shag next? I suppose you could have called it 'Octopussy'. It sounds a bit fishy to me. Lock the cunt up!

Sunday, 6 July 2008.

Great visit with Sandra Gardner today. She looked smart! She's one top, first-class lady and a lovely friend. I can't think of a nicer way to spend a Sunday afternoon than with a couple of milkshakes, a few bars of chocolate and a lovely lady. (Well, I can, but it's the best for me.) The only problem is it goes so fast. No sooner does it start than it's over. Two hours just fly by. She had a nice striped jacket on that was similar to a suit I once had. I like a lady who knows how to dress! I gave her a piece of art I had created. All in all it was a lovely get-together.

I see David Mulcahy got smashed over the crust with a tin of carrots in Full Sutton jail. Pity it wasn't an axe. I suppose you could say it was a '22-carrot job'. HA! HA! HA! HA! Let's have three cheers for whoever smashed him on the head. HIP HIP – HOORAY! HIP HIP – HOORAY! HIP HIP – HOORAY! He 'carrotted' the beast! He's one filthy bastard – a serial sex monster – who murdered three women and raped 15 in the 1980s. They should have hanged this piece of shit. It's about time he copped a bit of his own medicine and it's about time some other monsters got a bit too! Fucking animals. Gas the fuckers, I say – stick the fucking lot in the oven. End of problem.

Who remembers the little funny man Charlie Drake? He was one of our top actors in the 1950s and '60s. He died at 81 in 2006. He was a millionaire but he only left £5,000 in his will. Boy, did he live life in the fast lane! He had a great life. His favourite catchphrase was, "Hello, my darlings!" He loved a gamble and they say he lost £3 million in the casinos.

Top geezer, all five feet one of him! A little geezer with a big heart.

I had a lovely Sunday dinner: roast spuds, chicken and carrots. Carrots again, but not over my crust! Who's going to hit me with a tin of carrots? Who's mad enough to do that to me? Ask yourself one question: what if it didn't knock me out? What if I turned around and ripped your throat out? It's a big gamble to take. Make my day, punk!

My son Mike's up to see me on the 17th. The screws told me today it's all booked up. I can't wait to see the rascal. I'm proud of my boy. I hope he doesn't forget my banana milkshakes!

Lewis Hamilton won the British Grand Prix at Silverstone today. How good is he? Brilliant. How good can he become? Legendary.

Rafael Nadal won Wimbledon and stopped Roger Federer winning his sixth successive title in the process! Nadal's only 22 now, so he's going to be around for the next decade. Can you ever see Murray beating him? They're in a different class. It's never going to happen. Only in your dreams!

I've only played tennis once and I felt a bit of a fairy! Don't get me wrong, it's a game for the super fit but it's not my scene; I'm not cut out for tennis. It's a bit like wiping your arse on a hedgehog – it fucking hurts! All that poncing about in your little white shorts and Love 15… Love 30… 30 Love; what's that all about? Break serve, new balls. What about those 'ball youngsters' who pass the players a towel to wipe their sweat off? What's that all about? Who the fuck do they think they are? Yeah, it's not my sort of game! They never played it at my school, not in my day!

Anyway, it was a magical day today and I've enjoyed myself. It's time for bed now. My mattress is not so hard now. It doesn't take me long to wear it in. It's gonna piss down tonight! I hope it floods out the prison officers' social club! That would be a laugh. Drown a few of the fuckers!

9 July 2008.

I woke up at 5.30am when some cunt of a screw banged a door going out of the unit. There's always one. No matter where you are or what game you're in, you'll always come across a cunt. He got a buzz out of that, the sad fucker. He was probably coming to the end of his night shift and it was his way of saying, "Fuck you, cons." But that's showbiz, that how life is! What a brave fucker though. They're all the same those 'brave' screws; they're prats and even their wives think they're prats. You can't ever fool a good woman.

It's one of those wet and muggy days today, like being in a swamp! It feels like there's a leech on my eyelid sucking my eyeball out. I'm feeling a bit claustrophobic! I need to run in a field, catch a sheep and cook the fucker! I woke up feeling hungry and what did I get? Rice fucking Krispies. Snap, crackle and fucking pop! Get me out of here, I'm a celebrity, vote me out. It's my turn to come out for a good fry-up and a quick shag. I promise to come back, honest I will. Would I tell you a lie? Trust me.

Did you know that back in 1968 Judge William Openshaw sentenced 17-year-old John Smith to 18 months' borstal? When Smith reached 30 years of age, he went searching for the judge and stabbed him a dozen times. That's life for you (or death in his Lordship's case). It's a funny old world we live in!

Get on this, you'll love this one. Here in Wakefield they have 'special visitors' – mostly old folk who come into the jail to visit cons who have no family or friends. (I wonder why. Oh yeah, they probably killed them or they've been disowned over their evil crimes. Would you want to visit your son or husband who's serving life for shagging a baby or eating his elderly neighbour after doing her up the arse? Come on, is it any wonder they don't get family visits? It's fucking obvious to me!) So the prison chaplain and probation lay on visits from the wet, left-wing libs, 99% of whom are into Jesus. One is 69-year-old Jessie June Cooper, who's been a volunteer prison visitor at Wakefield for 15 years. She seemed like a decent lady – that was until 23 August 2007 when she was stopped and searched by security and was found to be carrying nine grammes of heroin in a tobacco pouch in her handbag. She was found guilty of possessing class A drugs with intent to supply. Silly, silly woman. For what it's worth, I would say she had been used. I bet she never even knew that the smack was in there. Some cunt of a con has probably got her to smuggle tobacco in and didn't tell her there would be drugs involved. It would be so easy. That's my bet and I'm not normally far wrong! That's her life fucked up. She won't be visiting any more jails; her family will be visiting her! It's all fate.

I see a bank clerk just copped nine years for 72 million quid's worth of fraud. Jagmeet Channa tried his luck and lost but it was worth the gamble. Imagine if he'd got away with it! He had used his position at HSBC to transfer 30 million euros to a Barclays account in Manchester and 60 million euros to a Société Générale account in Casablanca. That's 90 million fucking euros. At least he tried. Respect to the man! I salute you for trying and you'll bounce back, Jagmeet. Keep the faith. Men like him don't count sheep, they count £50 notes.

I got a 100 quid sent in today from my old buddy who will remain nameless. He's had a 'touch' and he always sends me in a ton when he's flush. My true mates are brothers, believe it.

The CSC prison boss was here on Monday. Get on this: the big boss comes up from London to see how the unit's going but never even stopped at any of our doors. It's a fucking insult to us as it's their job to see us and find out if we are OK or have got any complaints. I've stuck an official complaint in and as soon as I get the governor's answer I will stick it in the diary so you can all see it! Take it on me, it will be a pathetic reply. They're piss-takers and the whole system is a joke run by twats! They can't justify any of it. How can the boss ever know Bronson's changed when he won't even come to my door? Fuck me – there are only six of us to see! Five minutes each, that's only 30 minutes of his time, and it's their fucking job to see us. Why come all the way up from London? They get a nice hotel for the night (on tax payers' dosh) and they can't even come to my door! A screw said to me, in private, "Charlie, the reason is simple: they have no answers to your questions." That sums it all up for me. Cunts. They think, fuck Bronson, he's staying in the cage. Fuck him; until he begs and licks our arses he won't get fuck all. Yeah, fuck you too! You lick my arse, you cunts! On second thoughts, you'd probably enjoy that so lick Maudsley's instead – he's not wiped his arse for years. Yeah, lick the caveman's arse. My arse is my arse and it's staying that way!

Fuck me – I've had some letters this week. I've had four from Newhall women's jail up the road, all scented and full of kisses. One girl's only 22 and tells me she shaves her pussy and rubs baby oil on it every night. Why tell me that? Strange people. She doesn't know me, I don't know her, and she tells me that. Forty years ago I would've had a 'ham shank' on the strength of that; I would've shot my load all over the ceiling and spunk would've been flying all over my cell! Now, who gives a fuck? I don't. I read it and thought, what a poor, sad, lonely bitch. Why write me that? She also said her cellmate watches her do it and sometimes rubs the baby oil in. Is that supposed to turn me on? I'm a 56-year-old geezer; you can't catch me like that! Silly girl. Plus, you haven't got enough dosh to put your hands on me! They call me 'Gigolo Bronco' and I charge a monkey an inch. You really don't want to know how much that works out as, sweetheart. Write to the Ripper, he likes you young birds. He will have your pussy for you. He would slice off your piss flaps and make you eat them; honest. Talking of piss flaps, I'm starving.

I see they're making a movie about Jack 'Spot' Comer. Geoff Bell is going to play Jack. That should be a class film! Let's face it: Jack Spot was the daddy in the 1950s, a top London gangster. Him and Billy Hill were legendary characters never to be forgotten.

Who remembers Gary Stayner? His whole life was fucked-up from the day he was born. Right now he's sitting in San Quentin Penitentiary where he's been since 2001. How time flies when you're sitting and waiting to fry. He had a bad deal in life and it sent him mad; it pushed him into the darkness. When he was a youngster his brother was kidnapped by a child molester and was held captive for seven years, so he lost out on brotherly love. Once his brother was finally freed from the molester he died in a motorcycle accident, so Gary lost him forever! Then his uncle was murdered and he attempted suicide. He went on a mission to Hell between February and July 1999, butchering four innocent people. He pleaded 'by reason of insanity' but was found sane and was sentenced to death. Hell, I'm no head shrink but I would put all I've got on it that he's a fucking lunatic!

I'll tell you who's an evil fucker: Robert Hansen. He's serving 461 years in the USA! How does a man get to serve that long? Does he have to die five times and come back to serve it? He killed 17 people but did a plea bargain to own up to just four killings! Crazy – the law's insane! 461 years? Fuck that. I would sooner sit in 'old sparky' and call it a day.

I'm stopping here because I fancy a cup of tea! You'll have to hang on for a spell.

That's better. I made a good, strong brew with two tea bags. Lovely. I love a cuppa. I'd prefer a Guinness though!

Why do these young girl prisoners write to me for? Do they see me as some sort of 'sugar daddy' or an uncle figure, or do they really get off on me? Is it my bald head or my name? What is it? Even with all the young studs they could write to, they choose me. Crazy; well, that's Loonyology for you! Shaven pussies and fanny juice kisses; that's what the girls do in jail, they rub their letter on their pussy. That's why the ink's sometimes smudged! It's true; it's a known fact. They're just lonely souls crying out for a cock or three! It passes, it's all a dream. Get real, girls – I'm a nightmare. I don't need any pussy-drenched letters, I prefer a cheese and onion roll. Cheers x.

Mark Jones sent me in some magazines and I also got my Luton paper. It's been a first-class day! To put the cherry on the cake, a screw told me at shower time that I'm on a visit tomorrow with Dee Morris. Brilliant, I've not seen Dee in ages and it's always a treat to see her.

I had a cheese flan, chips and beans with six slices of brown bread for tea. Fantastic, proper grub.

The governor did his rounds today. I said, "Look, Gov, I'm not being funny but can't you take that silly mask off?" He grunted and fucked off. Some people can't take a joke!

The screw Mr Chapman's back from leave. He's a top geezer and I've got a lot of respect for him. Yeah, not a bad day. It was peaceful.

I know you lot love a story so get on this one; you'll love it! In 1988... hold up... was it '89? No, it was '88. It could have been '89... Fuck it; it was one of them when I was on E1 seg block in Wandsworth jail, South London. Down there at the time were Alan Byrne, Chris Haig and an Irish geezer called 'Toothbrush'. Strange name – he got it for stabbing a nonce's eye out with one. That's how names come about in jail. Anyway, above us was EZ, a big half-caste cleaner with a big mouth. He was giving it the large out of the window and we got to hear that he had ripped off some lads over a drug deal. He was basically a cunt on legs and he needed taking down a peg or two. I told Alan and Chris I had a good plan, so after 10pm lights out I banged on 'Capone's' ceiling and said, "Oi, up there, cleaner."

"Who's that?" he shouted through the window bars.

"It's me, Charlie Bronson, I'm down below you in the chokie block!"

"OK, Chaz! How are you? Great to hear you!" (He was going on like we were old mates.) "Hey, lads, it's Charlie Bronson below me! What do you need, Chaz? Tell me, I'll pass a line down to your window. Tobacco, food, sugar, tea bags – you name it I got it! Even a few fanny mags. I've got some serious hard-core mags here with arse shots, spunky faces, bestiality. All the lads come to me, I'm the daddy up here, I run the gaff."

BLAH BLAH BLAH. Peabrain was now boring me to death so I said, "I want you to do me a favour. If you pass your line down I'll tie on a little package of dope, good quality gear. I want you to knock it out for me and send me the dosh. You can keep half of what you make!"

"Sweet, Chaz... easy!" he said. "I'll do that for you, the line's on its way."

So I had a shit in my pot and stuck some in a plastic bag. I'd waited till lights out as it's less likely for security to see a line come down to my cell window. Plus, when he got the package he'd not be able to see it clearly in the dark. It was a winner!

"OK, Chaz," he shouted, "the line's coming down!"

"Ssshhh," I said, "not so loud. Keep it down!"

"OK, sorry Chaz."

The line arrived and I tied on the package and shouted, "All yours buddy."

Up it shot. Ten minutes later I heard him shout, "You dirty fucker! I'll kill you, Bronson. You no good, filthy cunt! You bastard."

Laugh? I was pissing myself! Then I started singing the James Bond song 'Goldfinger' but I sang, "Shitfinger," all night long. Alan and Chris had never laughed so much! It was magic. That's prison life at its best! There's always a way to sort someone out. No man is 100% safe in any jail. Personally, I would have enjoyed breaking the cunt's jaw but at least he had my shit all over his greedy fingers in the dark. That's insanity gone mad! We fucking love it...

There were two gay cons in the Scrubs block in the 1980s (1984 or '85 – I'm not sure) who were both lifers and lovers. 'Bonnie' and 'Sally' we called them, and they used to have a nylon line from window to window which they tied around their cocks and talked dirty whilst they tugged on the line. Freaky or what, but it worked for them! It helped them through the boredom of life in solitary. They were in solitary for getting caught shagging in the prison chapel. You couldn't make it up if you tried!

There was another gay in the Scrubs who got caught on a visit smuggling in a blow-up male doll in a box. A doll with a dick. He got a month in solitary for that. He was a big fan of Boy George and used to sing Culture Club songs out of the window at night. Fucking nutter, but what a laugh. There was a gay screw who used to slip into 'Boy George's' cell. We all knew about it and so did the other screws. The 'ooing' and 'aahing' coming out of that cell was like a fucking peep show in Soho! That's prison in a nutshell. It's insane!

Tomorrow the lovely Dee's up to see her old china! I'll have a few banana milkshakes, some bars of chocolate, and I'll catch up on all the news.

Did I ever tell you about the time I hit a screw on the head with a sock full of shit in Risley prison back in 1970? Fuck me – it's 38 years ago! All the shit seeped through the sock and went all over his hair and neck. He blew his whistle in between bouts of spewing up. I got a good kicking for that! I suppose I deserved it as I truly was a nasty sod, but it was fun. What were we supposed to do? We were teenagers and we were bored. What's a sock full of shit between friends? Well, that's life, that's Loonyology!

10 July 2008

What a great visit with Dee! She was her lovely self. She looks nicer every time I see her. We go back a long time now. Her late father did a bit of bird and he was a top man. Yeah, a smashing visit. Thanks, Dee, it was lovely to get all the news.

Dee got to see the cannibal through the spy hole into the cage he was in. Let's face it, it's not every day one gets to see a living fucking lunatic, and they truly don't come any madder than this freaky fucker!

I had some sad news today: Terry Smith has been charged with several counts of conspiracy to commit armed robberies and he's been banged up in Belmarsh nick. It's got to be a serious fit-up because he packed all that lark in years ago. In the last decade he's been on TV shows, written three best-selling books and has totally changed his whole life around. I'll tell you now, the law doesn't ever forget a villain and they're never happy until they screw them up for good. This is a serious fit-up; everybody knows

Terry packed crime in years ago! That's gutted me sick. He's been nicked along with Lenny and his brother and Buba Turner. Now it's the long waiting game. They're all inside whilst the Old Bill get to work on more statements and dodgy ID parades. It's a mad old game!

You youngsters take note; it's really dangerous to end up in the police force's black book. It reminds me of the cowboys and Indians. What chance did the Indians have with their bows and arrows? The peace pipe's no good in war, believe me. Again, it just proves what I've been saying for years. You've got to move on, get the fuck out of Britain and start fresh, because the system is purely vindictive and evil.

I got a cracking letter from a young prisoner in Aylesbury nick:

Dear Charlie,

I've just read your *Solitary Fitness* book and I must say, Bruv, some of the work-outs in there are killers. The book's done a lot for me. When I started with the work-outs I could hardly push a rep with the handstand push-ups but now I can do 27 reps. And with the normal push-ups I could only do 10 and now I'm up to 60. Before I read your book I was skinny and lazy, I also used to smoke shitloads. I've packed in smoking altogether now. This is just to say thanks for changing my life.

You're a legend.
Nick Jeffrey No. LB8002
HMYOI Aylesbury, Bucks, HP20 1EH

Yeah! Howz that for a top lad? Respect to the fella. I'm proud of him. I get sack loads of letters like this so I'm not all bad, see; I help these youngsters. (Does the system help them?) These young cons listen to me and they don't just read my books, they learn from them. That sums it all up for me!

I had a veg curry for tea. It was OK, I've had a lot worse. All in all it was a nice day and I got my canteen. I told you my middle name is 'lucky'. I was born lucky!

I'm having an early night because I've got lots to think about. Dee gave me some good advice; she's a smart cookie! Plus, I'm actually full up and tired so I'll sleep like a baby tonight – all warm and cosy like a fluffy lamb! Baa... Baa... Baa.

Oh! I sorted May out with a drink today. She's an old lady I love in my mum's town who's knocking on 90 now. She's a good old soul and I've known her for years. She's dying for me to pop round for a Sunday roast! Those old girls know how to cook a roast. I can smell and taste it now! That's my dream for tonight. Good night.

11 July 2008.

One man's common sense is another man's insanity! How fucking true is that? I'll tell you what's mad: political correctness. Get on this, you'll love it, it's insane. An advertisement for an air traffic controller is being offered in Braille. Now look, let's get real here, I personally respect and admire the blind but there are some jobs they just can't do and air traffic controller must be one of them! Fucking wake up and smell the roses.

Hey! Do we own a dog or does a dog own us? A dog shits and a human picks it up. Who the fuck's the boss there? We feed them, keep them warm, provide a roof over their head, then they shit and we pick it up! The dog's the boss in my book. It's all Loonyology!

Well, it's official: Britain's most dangerous prison is Peterborough. It's a private jail run by Kalyx and it holds nearly 1,000 inmates (male and female). Last year there were 115 assaults on the screws. Fuck me, it's a war zone. In jails throughout the country last year there were 2,916 assaults on screws, of which 312 were serious and reported to the cops. But bear in mind that if a screw loses a shirt button in a struggle that counts as an assault. So if you weigh it all up you can probably take away 500 of those assaults! If they get their hair ruffled they go on the sick for a month, the lazy fuckers. It makes me laugh at times, the way the screws go on the sick. Their best one is stress. I say, if you can't handle the job then fuck off, you lazy cunt! Fucking stress – do me a favour, don't take the piss!

Today came and went so fast; life's rushing by. It's been pissing down all day. Proper Yorkshire weather (shit).

I only got three letters today and two of them were 'legal'. Don't ask what they were about, because if I told you I'd have to kill you. So don't ask and live to an old age!

Did I ever tell you about the time an old lady tried to get off with me? I was only 21 and she was a good 70, maybe more. I was in a hotel in Manchester on some bizz and the bizz was sorted so I was having a drink in the bar when she came and sat with me. She was very posh and very elegant. We got chatting and I liked her – she was nice company and she smelt beautiful. Then she hit me with a bombshell: "Fancy taking me to my room and giving me a good seeing to?" Fuck me – I almost choked on my vodka!

"What?" I said.

"Give me a good seeing to," she said again!

"You're having a laugh," I said.

"Who's laughing?" she asked.

"Fuck me, lady. Behave – you're old enough to be my great Nan."

"Maybe," she said, "but I can still go a turn!"

I'll cut a very long story short. I couldn't, I just couldn't do it. She had a neck like creased paper, lots of wrinkles and her hands looked old. I thought, I can't do it. How can I? I actually felt sorry for the old girl because she was a lovely soul. Now, of course, I would! But how could I at 21? Could you? Would you? If it was today I'd carry her up, bend her over the bed and give her a good seeing to – fast, furious and plenty of it! Lock, stock and two smoking balls! But I couldn't back then. I was a pretty sane sort of geezer in those days, but now I'd video it for the hell of it. Why not?

People get lust mixed up with love. I was the same. I've fallen in love with some serious nutters in my time. Best I move on.

Early tea tonight. On Fridays the screws fuck off early – 5pm finish. That's us banged up till 8am, so it's 15 hours until my door unlocks and I see another screw. Yiiipppeeeeeee, yarrhhooooooo, yiiipppeeeee!

12 July 2008.

Fuck me; what a day. It can't get any madder than this! I woke up with a massive hard-on, bursting for a piss. My bladder was in agony. (Why do us men get a hard-on for a piss? I've never been able to work that one out.) I leapt out of bed, slipped on a sock on the floor and went flying into the table. All my stuff fell off and I hit my head. So there I am at 6am, bollock naked with a big hard-on, lying on the floor with my table upended, still bursting for a piss and my light flicks on! It was the night screw doing the last check before home time! Now see why I'm a cunt of a robber? I get caught! Fuck it...

I made the piss just in time. What a relief. It was the piss of the month. I wish I was pissing on some nonce; I'd drown the fucker! Come on, guys, how does it feel, that first slash of the day? You know it's wonderful! I pretend I'm on top of a mountain pissing down on the world, it's brilliant. That first piss is similar to a wank but more satisfying. (I once went out with a bird who loved to be pissed on! Strange people. I always seem to draw the weirdos to me. I wonder why? Will I ever meet somebody sane? I doubt it!)

So the day began with a big lump on my head and you're not gonna believe what happened next. This one will blow your socks off! Mark Fish arrived at the gate and was told: "Bronson has said he's going to attack you." They even showed him the daily incident book. Mark said, "Bollocks, why would he want to attack me? Plus he's behind bars so how can he attack me?" Nobody, governor or screw, had said a word about it to me so when they escorted Mark over and he told me what they'd said, I couldn't believe it. The screws came and I told them what had been said, but they said they didn't know a thing about it. Some fucker said it to Mark in order to really try and fuck me up for my parole and appeal. Who will they tell this shit to next?

OK, Mark and me had issues to sort out but I did not say it! Why would I say it? And if it were true, why did the screws on the unit not know about it? (They would've been told to expect trouble.) Would they have even let Mark in if they thought I would attack him?

Let me make it 100% clear now: I believe this is a serious conspiracy to fuck me up! Next they will be saying I'm going to attack my legal team, the parole judge or even my mother! I am submitting a formal complaint on Monday and my lawyer will be notified as this can't carry on!

I want to know:

1. Who said this?
2. Who wrote it down in the gate book?
3. Why was it done?
4. Why was I not asked about it?
5. Why were the unit screws not notified?
6. Why was my visitor put through this shit?

It stinks! It's a complete fucking stitch-up!

If it had happened to some of my other visitors, they may have said, "I'd best not go in and see him," and I wouldn't have had a visit. It's the system's way of fucking up my parole or appeal. "Look," they're saying, "look how dangerous he is – even his friends are scared of him! On 12 July

2008, Mr Mark Fish refused to enter the prison in fear of his life, so how can we free this violent, uncontrollable psycho?" Please wake up world; this is happening to me now, today. Even the unit screws were shocked by it (or they're good actors as they convinced Mark they didn't know anything about it). What next? I can't wait to see!

I'm glad to say that Mark Fish and me are back on track. The black cloud has blown away, the shit missed the fan, all's sweet as a nun's fanny and I had my milkshakes, chocolates and a nice visit. So what would've happened if the visit had been stopped? Yeah, that's what some cunt was wanting to see!

CSC UNIT Manager

11 July 2008

Prison Number: BT1314 BRONSON

Brett Dyer

The above named has **NOT** been approved by the Home Office for the approved visitors scheme

SECURITY DEPARTMENT:

Here's one geezer that won't be coming here to see me and be told, "Charlie may attack you." They've just totally knocked him back, but why? What's the reason? What's their motive? It's all about control: "We say who Bronson sees!" Brett, do yourself a favour: call up the prison governor and ask why you can't visit me. Get these pricks to put it in writing, then take it to your MP with a lawyer and sue the Home Office for discrimination. Don't let these cunts put you down, they're getting too powerful and they're not justifying their reasons (or if they do, it's with lies), so challenge their decision! I've had visitors who have killed people passed! I've had famous gangsters and even an ex-Broadmoor inmate visiting me, so why can't you? Are you so bad and evil that you can't see me? Are you going to accept this shit? Fight it, because you're being victimised by a system that gets a kick out of it all. They're fucking power freaky little Hitlers! (It's a pity you're not black or Muslim, they wouldn't have dared to say no then.) Believe it Brett. Anyway it's your call. I'll back you all the way, son! All the way to Hell. As it happens it's not so bad there! A bit hot, but you can have some fun! All the hot chick's end up there so at least there's plenty of shagging.

I got eight letters today, not bad for a Saturday. One was from Jan Lamb. What would I do now for a blow job off Jan? Nobody sucks a bell-end like her – nobody. Fuck me; it's not fair. Saturday night in on my own again! How fucking sad is that?

Hey, what about those bendy fuckers who can wrap their legs around their heads? Come on, you must've thought to yourselves: do they? I bet they're forever giving themselves a blow job or, if they're chicks, licking their crack. Come on, they must do it! But then again, what sort of geezer wants to give himself a blow job and what sort of bird wants to stick her face into her crack? I wonder. It's all Loonyology!

Yesterday there were four young men stabbed to death in London! One in Tottenham, one in Lexton, one in Walthamstow and one in Edmonton. Despite this, some MPs are still saying it's not out of control. Walk the real streets at night, you muppets! It's a fucking war zone out there! Stabbings are an every day event now; four dead in one day in London alone! Wake up.

I see the monster Dave Harrison just copped a life sentence. About time too; the filthy beast should've been lifed off years ago. He only served nine years of a 14-year sentence before he got out and raped another poor, innocent lady. He almost killed her! He stuck a knife in her neck after being free for only a week. She had three kids and this beast almost killed her. He's 45 now and I bet he's freed before he's 60. Anyone want to bet? I bet you know I'm right! Next time he will kill, there's no surer bet. These sort always will because they love it. It's a power thing and they rape to be 'powerful'. It's their way of saying, "I'm hard so don't fuck with me. Bend over, bitch." But these cunts are like mice in jail and it's them bending over – they become the bitches and their arses are like blood-shot tangerines. All the psycho poofs are up there arses like a rat up a drainpipe. "Come here, bitch, bend over!" Believe me, 99% of rapists haven't got a fight in them once they're in jail.

Question: how many female screws have been raped in jail?

Answer: none.

Why? Like I said, the rapists are mice! They're only brave when they pick on a weak victim. A woman screw would probably kick their bollocks in and spray the cunt with pepper spray, then he'd get a good kicking off the screws later! You rapists make my skin crawl. Fucking hurry up and die.

I see Sergeant Karl Cliff of Merseyside Police just got an eight-month suspended sentence at Liverpool Crown Court for shagging a prostitute in his police car! HA! HA! HA! HA! And they wonder why we don't trust the law! HA! HA! HA! HA! Fucking wankers. Trust the law? I would sooner put my head in a lion's mouth. What do you think we are, insane? Hey, I hope he paid the girl but I bet he didn't. He probably bullied her instead.

I had a pork pie and a bowl of corn on the cob for tea. I've had a great day but roll on Monday so I can put my official complaint form in. I want answers and so will my legal team. Watch this space!

George Galloway's on Talk Sport radio later! I'm off for a strip wash and a well deserved mug of tea. I've got a pack of custard creams, too! I told you I'm born lucky!

Three cheers for Mark Fish: HIP HIP – HOORAY! HIP HIP – HOORAY! HIP HIP – HOORAY! A great day and all's sorted.

Hey, did you know Bill Gates is worth 39 billion quid? Fuck me, it's mind-boggling; I need a lie down. It's probably gone up another billion by the time you read this. Should any one man be worth so much when half the world's population are starving and homeless? Who fucking needs £39 billion? The fucking world's full of greed and evil! No wonder the poor feel so depressed and soul-destroyed. This is Earth and we are all humans and equals (apart from nonces, grasses, nasty coppers, ruthless judges and pea-brained prison officials) so give peace a go and open your hearts!

I say to Bill Gates, "Bung me £10 billion and I'll sort something out for the needy. Trust me, Bill, I'll make this planet sparkle. I'll put a little love back in it for us all! I can do a lot with £10 billion and I need a new Ferrari myself! Not that I'm greedy, Bill, but a man's got to move about in style – and with speed to get out of a sticky situations. The way our police force drive, we need to shoot off fast and leave the fuckers behind! Yeah, Bill, consider my request. I'm the man. Leave the rest to me, let me save the world and make you proud!"

Three cheers for Bill Gates: HIP HIP – HOORAY! HIP HIP – HOORAY! HIP HIP – HOORAY!

It's strange, but I don't feel tired now. Thinking of all that dosh has lit me up and I'm all excited! I can see me on a yacht out in the Mediterranean! (Not that I'm greedy.) Oh, and I must get my own jet so I can get to all the 'poor' destinations around the world. (I need to see them with my own eyes so I can judge how best to help them out.) Yeah, I can see me in the 'Bronco jet'!

Hey, I hope you guys don't think I'm knocking the arse out of Bill's dosh? I'm sort of spending it before I even get it and it may look like it's all for me! Well, don't worry – it's £10 billion. What's a few million between friends? Fuck me; if you're all going to start pointing the finger at me, I won't do it, I really won't! Fuck it – why should I? Here I am trying to help the poor and I'm almost getting labelled a cheat! It's like I'm only doing it for my own needs as if I'm a greedy, selfish cunt. Well, fuck it! If that's the kind of disrespect I get then fuck the planet, let it starve. Unless Bill actually asks me to do it, then I won't bother. Just remember I tried. Fuck it. I'm nobody's punch bag.

The problem with you greedy, rich, fat twats is that you're all very much up your own rectums, or each other's rectums. You can't see an honest man like me and you don't want to see me; you're too busy stepping on the poor! Why don't you just pour petrol over our cardboard box homes and kill us off? Gas us! Shoot us! You'll fucking enjoy that, you Nazi pricks! Fuck off!

Honestly, I try my best to sort things out and look where it gets me! Nobody trusts me. Why doesn't anybody trust anybody else today? Where's all the trust gone? The love has gone and the world's turned evil! Bring back the Beatles: all we need is love! Let's all have one big orgy of love – a whole week of it! Share everything. Cor blimey, there would be some serious shagging going on! Let's do it. All we need is love. Fantastic!

A French man in Paris has just been caught having a blow job in the street in broad daylight! Can you believe this shit? "Yeah, big deal," you say, "so what?" Well, it was a dog licking his helmet! Those frogs are mental! Lock him up and throw away the key! Cunt.

What about prison van driver Andy Curtis? He's just been charged with murder after he allegedly ran over Naomi Benjamin whilst he was driving the prison van with 11 prisoners in it. You can't make this stuff up. His trial starts in October. That should be worth keeping an eye out for! For him to be charged with murder there must be more to it than a traffic accident. Still, what do you expect with a prison driver? I keep telling you it's Loonyology! It's a journey of madness.

I see the old paedo Alan Fitzpatrick has copped a life sentence after his third serious lot of sex crimes on kids. This time he raped a boy and assaulted another three kids. He's a pure predator and pure evil. Life should mean life in his case. Bury him! Burn the bastard! I bet he's heading for monster mansion, the cunt.

I'll tell you who's a fucking nut case: Ray Fraser (no relation to Frankie). This loon from Canada chopped up his wife's lover and made a meat pie out of him! She ate him with gravy! That's what love does for you – it makes you blind and insane. Fraser's now serving life, but what about the wife? Well, how would any wife feel after eating her bit on the side? I bet she'll never be able to love again – or eat another pie!

I'll tell you who's dangerous: the Russian SpetsNaz (they're the crack anti-terrorist commandos who make our SAS look like muppets). These guys are rock-hard hatchet lunatics and ruthless killing machines. The selection process for the SpetsNaz mob is a full five years' hard training involving sweat, blood and more blood! You pour it, you swim in it and pain becomes a pleasure. You really don't want to fuck with this firm, believe me. I would sooner fuck with the American Seals or the German GSG-9 squad, and none of those are pussies! You will die with the SpetsNaz; you can never live.

Wanna laugh? Gabriela Irimia, the lovely half of the Cheeky Girls, has dumped Lembit Opik. HA HA HA HA HA HA! Fucking good job too! What was that geek doing with Gabriela? Opik, you want to stick to being an MP not a Cheeky Girl's puppy. (That's all he ever was.) She and her sister are beautiful and fucking delicious like peaches and cream. Gabriela needs a real man, not a poxy MP! She needs excitement; a girl like her needs to live in the fast lane! It'd be like me going out with Nora Batty, Hattie Jacques or Hilda Ogden! (No disrespect to those three lovely ladies but it's just not a sane dream.) Get a life, Opik. Oh, I'm up for a Cheeky Girl! (Two if possible.)

Did you know Abba's success began in Brighton? That's where the 1973 Eurovision song contest was held and they won it with 'Waterloo'. They were offered \$1 billion to make a comeback like Take That and the Spice Girls. Crazy. Now there's a museum opening in Stockholm for 'the greatest band ever'. Were Abba the greatest? Maybe so. Who gives a fuck anyway?

PATIENT: Doctor, doctor, I keep getting a pain in the eye when I drink coffee!

DOCTOR: Have you tried taking the spoon out of the cup?

(Must have been a Broadmoor loon.)

Talking of spoons, a good buddy of mine (no names mentioned) once sharpened the handle of a dessert spoon till it was razor sharp. It did the bizz all right: a grass got his just deserts with a 'spoon cut' from ear to ear. It's a buzz when a grass comes a cropper! And, believe me, jails are full of the fuckers. Some you never find out about and some you can't believe.

It can be a terrible shock when you find out that someone you love as a brother, a guy you've bled with, a guy you've trusted with your life turns out to be a snake. It hurts and it fucking destroys all the humanity inside your heart. Pass the spoon, I want to stab one of these cunts' eyes out.

Did I tell you about the time I climbed up a 100-foot crane at Birkenhead Docks when I was 17 years old? Why? Well, why not? Why do people ask why? It was a fucking lovely view from up there. This was in the 1960s when I did a spot of labouring for the plasterers. I used to work with four Birkenhead lads called Hopkins – good, staunch brothers. People find it hard to believe I was ever an honest grafter but I was when I was on the building sites! Well, I was half good and half bad. Let's just say I sorted out plenty of bizz. Lots of material went missing: timber, tiles, bricks, breeze blocks, cement, the odd cement mixer and paint. I had a good little run. If I'd known then what I know now, I could've opened up my own building warehouse instead of selling it all to little merchants. But I was never greedy, see! That's been my major problem: I'm too soft and my heart's too big. People have taken my kindness and generosity for weakness but, believe me, they've come unstuck, the greedy bastards!

On 13 August 1964 the last execution took place in England. In fact, they went out with a bang and made it a double. Johnny Walby fell through the trap door in Strangeways jail at the exact same time as Peter Allen at Walton jail in Liverpool. In 1974 I met one of the screws in Walton who was on death duty with Peter Allen. He told me he was the bravest condemned man he'd ever known; he walked to the gallows whistling! They would have to drag me to the noose fighting. Fuck whistling, but, then again, how unique is that? Was he whistling in fear? Surely he was scared! Was it bravery or insanity? Maybe he had come to terms with God and God had forgiven him.

How would you go? Have you ever thought about how you would cope with that last walk into the unknown, looking at the faces who are about to stop you breathing? They're going to snap your neck and your head may even come off. You're going to swing and this lot are about to watch you drop through the trap door. You may deserve it; you may not! You could even be innocent. Whatever… you're going to die! Too late to beg, too late for sorry, it's lights out and you're gone. Gone where though? That's the million dollar question: where the fuck do we go?

1964 wasn't really so long ago, but that's how cruel and hard it was then and that's how it is still in some countries: brutal and swift. Will capital punishment ever return to this country? I fucking hope and pray it does, I really, truly do. It would stop some of these cocky bastards giving it the 'big daddy' bollocks in jail and all these muggy terrorist cunts blowing misery across our land.

What about cunts like Cuntley (ooops, sorry, Huntley)? Could you see that cunt pissing his pants whilst being lead to the gallows? "Please, no! What about my human rights? I'm sorry, please let me live, I'll be good. Mummy, Daddy – help!" Cunts like him won't need to cut their wrists or swallow overdoses, the state will do it for them! Yiiipppeeeee! Bring back the death sentence. If I killed I would willingly die, but it will be a hell of a fight to get me on that trap door. Well, what's to lose? One last struggle to live. Sure, you can't win but you can leave in style! YARHHhhooooooo!

Another death row inmate who walked to the gallows was Henry Neimasz at Wandsworth jail in 1961. Henry had killed two people and, again, he had accepted his end. This was his fate, his way out of the madness of life. Let's do it, boys, let's get it out of the way. Let's march in there whistling. Follow me. I'll give God your best wishes, Mr Hangman! Goodbye everybody, goodbye world… the end.

Chilling stuff, eh? Brave men. Would Brady go like that? Come to think of it, I'd say he'd walk to his death with a smile on his face! That guy's the devil in human form. He would leave behind a lot of frozen souls! His evil eyes would bore into the screws' minds and even the hangman would shiver with fear. Brady has that musky smell about him that all raving lunatics have; the smell of a monster! You have to live with them to understand what I mean as it's actually inexplicable. It's more of a sensation, a feeling, a deep awareness – my skin itches when a monster is close; that's how aware I am of them! It's a lifetime of experience that's done that to me. Some people can walk into a room and nobody notices – a glance and they're forgotten. Others light it up and you remember them forever. However, the monsters walk in and bring doom – a big black cloud of misery! Yep, hang the motherfuckers before they fuck your mother – or your father! Anything with a hole, whether dead or alive, will do for a monster. They fuck you and laugh as they come! Stick that noose on and let's party. Ding fucking dong!

Did you know only five men ever escaped from Auschwitz? That was Hell on Earth – the largest of the Nazi concentration camps. It doesn't get any worse. The Auschwitz guards were monsters. No human could be so cruel and sadistic and stay a human; they were rats from Hell! Auschwitz, kiss our arses and burn in Hell! "Hitler has only got one ball…"

14 July 2008.

What a day! After the shit that went down on Saturday I've submitted my official complaint form, posted a full statement to Giovanni and been to see the governor, so watch this space. Giovanni won't stand for this shit, nor will Mark Fish and nor will I. Who the fuck do they think they are, trying to intimidate my visitor by saying, "Bronson could attack you"? Cunts.

I got six letters today and some photos from Gemini. (See photo – that's Gemini with the Loony book. What a body eh? Look at those legs!) She's a brilliant dancer, a top-class lady and a lovely friend so keep your hands off or I'll snap your fingers like biscuits.

Did I tell you about the time I cut off a guy's thumb with some bolt cutters? The blood squirted up like a fountain. It was so so funny; you never forget things like that. It's like a roll of film in the back of your mind. It sounds cruel and evil but you have to realise that was my old lifestyle. He would've loved to do the same to me, plus he was a silly cunt playing silly games with good people. He went too far so he had to be taught a lesson: "A thumb today, an arm tomorrow." He kept his arm because he did as he was told. It's that simple in life. Don't step on others' toes! What's a thumb? He's got another one!

I got a cracking letter from Alan Rayment today and he sent me three art pens in. Top geezer; he never forgets his old china! I also got a letter from a young con in Everthorpe – a jail which used to be a borstal years ago. Anyway, he has asked me for a piece of art to hang up in his cell. It's on its way, son. I must be getting soft in my old age! We all do (so they tell me).

I hear National Service may be coming back! Not a bad thing as it teaches the lads how to kill a man. National Service began in 1945 and every lad between 17 and 21 had to serve 18 months. If you were healthy you got your boots on and marched to the army recruitment office. Yes Sir, no Sir, three bags full, Sir! Left, right, left, right, left, right, knees up, you skinny little fuckers! Fall in line! Every fortnight 6,000 lads were called up; they all had to do their bit for Queen and Country. It stopped on 31 December 1960. (How do I know all this? I told you: I'm a clever cunt!) I can even tell you the name of the last lad called up to serve: Private Fred Turner. He was discharged on 7 May 1963. Howz that? You learn with Loonyology! Every page is knowledge. So will it return? Can it? I wonder... would your parents want your son to be called up?

I had a jacket spud and some cheese for tea. It doesn't sound like a lot but I enjoyed it. The screw Mr Mitchell has just come back after a couple of weeks in Greece. I've known him years – he's one of the old style screws, a proper decent bloke. If they were all like him I could've been freed years ago. These screws don't 'arf have some holidays; there's one screw down here who's been halfway around the world since I've been here. Fucking amazing, and where have I gone? I've not even moved cages!

Yeah, not a bad day but a better one tomorrow! Every day gets better...

Happiness does not grow in the garden of angry thoughts; happiness is a bookworm with a belly full of knowledge.

They say the greatest happiness is in the heart of a child; we should learn from the children.

Oh well, I've a lot to do! I'm just about to choose my menu for 3 August! We have to choose our diet weeks in advance. Hey, what would you pick? What do you think I picked? Have a guess... what else have you got to do? Scratch your fat arse, pick your nose and watch some silly soap on the box? Get a life you fat, lazy cunts! Choose your menu!

It's not a bad choice is it? You wouldn't get that in Alcatraz! Fuck me – you wouldn't have got it in any jail 20 years ago. The grub has got a lot better over the years, without a doubt. We all have a moan now and again but it's not a bad menu. Oh yeah, don't pick the tuna sandwich, it's fucking horrible. The bread's soggy and the smell makes me puke. Apart from that, thumbs up. I'm off for a cuppa. I'll be back!

Yeah, a nice cuppa cha. I feel refreshed and ready for action. I would like some action on this cunt Courtney Bryan. He just copped a life sentence for killing his 11-week-old baby son. He hurled the kid against a wall and squeezed his ribs until they crushed. The judge at Sheffield Crown Court recommended he serve 20 years. Hello? Why not 40 years? Why not 60 years? Let's hope this cunt ends up as jail bait, because I don't know of any proper con who can tolerate a baby-killer. No man alive can accept such

WEEK 1 LUNCH

SUBJECT TO AVAILABILITY

CHOICE	*Week Comm* SUNDAY 03/08/08	ORD	HEO	VEG	VEGAN	HALAL	CHOICE
1	VEGETABLE HASH H/M	*	*	*	*	*	
2	CHEESE PASTY	*		*		*	
3	HALAL JUMBO HOT DOG(FINGER ROLL)	*				*	
4	STEAK & KIDNEY PIE	*					
5	ORANGE JUICE	6	CRANBERRY JUICE				
CHOICE	MONDAY 04/08/08	ORD	HEO	VEG	VEGAN	HALAL	CHOICE
1	SALAD SANDWICH (GRANARY)	*	*	*	*	*	
2	CHEESE & CHUTNEY SANDWICH (GRANARY)	*	*	*		*	
3	HALAL TURKEY (BAP)	*	*			*	
4	HAM & TOMATO (GRANARY)	*	*				
5	ORANGE JUICE	6	CRANBERRY JUICE				
CHOICE	TUESDAY 05/08/08	ORD	HEO	VEG	VEGAN	HALAL	CHOICE
1	PEANUT BUTTER SANDWICH (GRANARY)	*	*	*	*	*	
2	EGG MAYONAISSE SANDWICH GRANARY)	*	*	*		*	
3	HALAL CORONATION CHICKEN (BAP)	*	*			*	
4	CORNED BEEF & ONION (GRANARY)	*					
5	ORANGE JUICE	6	CRANBERRY JUICE				
CHOICE	WEDNESDAY 06/08/08	ORD	HEO	VEG	VEGAN	HALAL	CHOICE
1	VEGAN GARLIC SAUSAGE SANDWICH (GRANARY)	*	*	*	*	*	
2	TUNA ONION & MAYONAISSE SANDWICH (GRANARY)	*	*	*		*	
3	HALAL SLCD TIKKA CHICKEN ROLL (BAP)	*	*			*	
4	PORK & APPLE SAUCE (GRANARY)	*	*				
5	ORANGE JUICE	6	CRANBERRY JUICE				
CHOICE	THURSDAY 07/08/08	ORD	HEO	VEG	VEGAN	HALAL	CHOICE
1	SALAD SANDWICH (GRANARY)	*	*	*	*	*	
2	CHEESE & ONION SANDWICH (GRANARY)	*	*	*		*	
3	SEAFOOD STICKS IN A (BAP)	*	*	*		*	
4	BEEF & ONION (GRANARY)	*	*				
5	ORANGE JUICE	6	CRANBERRY JUICE				
CHOICE	FRIDAY 08/08/08	ORD	HEO	VEG	VEGAN	HALAL	CHOICE
1	PEANUT BUTTER SANDWICH (GRANARY)	*	*	*	*	*	
2	TUNA & SWEETCORN SANDWICH (GRANARY)	*	*	*		*	
3	HALAL SLICED LAMB (BAP)	*	*			*	
4	PORK LUNCHEON MEAT (GRANARY)	*					
5	ORANGE JUICE	6	CRANBERRY JUICE				
CHOICE	SATURDAY 09/08/08	VEGAN	VEG	HALAL	ORD	HEO	CHOICE
	BRUNCH	1	2	3	4	5	
6	ORANGE JUICE	7	CRANBERRY JUICE				

FISH DISH
BEEF DISH
PORK DISH
CHICKEN DISH
TURKEY DISH
LAMB DISH

MILD
MEDIUM
HOT

ALL MENU CHOICES ARE SUBJECT TO CHANGE DEPENDING ON AVAILABILITY.
MONDAY TO FRIDAY
CRISPS AND HOMEMADE SOUP WILL BE SUPPLIED WITH THE LUNCHTIME MEAL.

RETURN MEAL SELECTION SLIPS BY TUESDAY

an evil bastard near him. Could you? He deserves all the pain and misery in the world because there is no excuse for what he did, the evil fucking twat! But he will probably end up here and get lost within the system. This turd will end up a born-again Christian and 10 years from now (you mark my words) he will be let out. God will help him out but God never helped the 11-week-old baby. Some God that is!

WEEK 1 TEA AMERICAN THEME WEEK

CHOICE	Week Comm SUNDAY 03/08/08	ORD	HEO	VEG	VEGAN	HALAL	CHOICE
1	VEGAN COTTAGE PIE	*	*	*	*	*	
2	POACHED FISH	*	*	*		*	
3	HALAL CHICKEN LEG	*	*			*	
4	MINCED BEEF COTTAGE PIE	*	*				
5	EGG SALAD	*	*	*		*	
6	PEANUT BUTTER SANDWICH	*	*	*	*	*	
7	HAM SANDWICH	*	*				
8	ICE CREAM	9	FRUIT				
CHOICE	MONDAY 04/08/08	ORD	HEO	VEG	VEGAN	HALAL	CHOICE
1	JACKET POTATO & B / BEANS	*	*	*	*	*	
2	SPANISH OMELLETTE	*	*	*		*	
3	HALAL JAMAICAN BEEF PATTIE	*				*	
4	CHEESE BURGER H/M	*	*				
5	PASTA SALAD	*	*	*		*	
6	VEGAN GARLIC SAUSAGE SANDWICH	*	*	*	*	*	
7	TUNA MAYO SANDWICH	*	*	*		*	
8	TOFFEE MUFFIN	9	FRUIT				
CHOICE	TUESDAY 05/08/08	ORD	HEO	VEG	VEGAN	HALAL	CHOICE
1	SQUASH & BUTTER BEANS	*	*	*	*	*	
2	TUNA PASTA BAKE	*	*	*		*	
3	HALAL BBQ CHICKEN LEG	*	*			*	
4	DELUX STEAK PIE	*					
5	CHEESE SALAD	*	*	*		*	
6	SALAD SANDWICH	*	*	*	*	*	
7	BEEF SANDWICH	*	*				
8	RICE PUDDING	9	FRUIT				
CHOICE	WEDNESDAY 06/08/08	ORD	HEO	VEG	VEGAN	HALAL	CHOICE
1	VEGETABLE BURGER & ONION	*	*	*	*	*	
2	CHEESE QUICHE H/M	*		*		*	
3	HALAL CHICKEN JAMBALAYA	*	*			*	
4	1/4LB BEEFBUGER & ONION	*	*				
5	HAM SALAD	*	*				
6	PEANUT BUTTER SANDWICH	*	*	*	*	*	
7	EGG MAYONAISSE SANDWICH	*	*	*		*	
8	DOUGHNUT	9	FRUIT				
CHOICE	THURSDAY 07/08/08	ORD	HEO	VEG	VEGAN	HALAL	CHOICE
1	VEG SAG GOSHT & RICE H/M	*	*	*	*	*	
2	CHEESE & ONION PIE	*		*		*	
3	HALAL BEEF SAG GOSHT / RICE	*	*			*	
4	SOUTHERN FRIED CHICKEN &H/M SWEETCORN FRITTER	*	*				
5	CORNED BEEF SALAD	*					
6	VEGAN GARLIC SAUSAGE SANDWICH	*	*	*	*	*	
7	PORK SANDWICH	*	*				
8	ICE CREAM	9	FRUIT				
CHOICE	FRIDAY 08/08/08	ORD	HEO	VEG	VEGAN	HALAL	CHOICE
1	VEGAN PIZZA H/M	*	*	*	*	*	
2	CHEESE PIZZA H/M	*		*		*	
3	HADDOCK IN BATTER	*		*		*	
4	PORK CHOP WITH TEXAS BBQ SAUCE	*					
5	TURKEY SALAD	*	*				
6	SALAD SANDWICH	*	*	*	*	*	
7	CHEESE SANDWICH	*	*	*		*	
8	FRUIT SCONE	9	FRUIT				
CHOICE	SATURDAY 09/08/08	ORD	HEO	VEG	VEGAN	HALAL	CHOICE
1	VEG BOLOGNAISE H/M	*	*	*	*	*	
2	JACKET POTATO & SAVOURY CHEESE	*	*	*		*	
3	HALAL SPAGHETTI BOLOGNAISE	*	*			*	
4	PORK PIE	*					
5	CRAB STICK SALAD	*	*				
6	VEGAN CHEESE&TOMATO SANDWICH	*	*	*	*	*	
7	HALAL SLCD DONNER SANDWICH	*	*			*	
8	YOGHURT	9	FRUIT				

Who remembers Robert Ashman, the maniac with the samurai sword? I'll remind you. Back in 2000 he attacked MP Nigel Jones – who survived – and his assistant Andrew Pennington, who sadly died. Ashman was sent to Broadmoor (where the nutter belongs). I was in Woodhill at the time and it reminded me of a samurai sword killer I met in Ashworth asylum in 1984. He sliced his grandmother's head clean off and stuck it on the garden gate. I asked him why and he said, "Why not?" (I left it at that because these sorts of loonies can get very temperamental – especially with a big fuck off sword.) Anyway, going back to Ashman, eight fucking years later and he's out! He's as sane as a parrot and he's free! How do they do it? Somebody please tell me. Nigel Jones is now Lord Jones of Cheltenham. I wonder how he feels about the loon being freed? That's Broadmoor in a nutshell... Loonyology!

Hey, did you know Gene Tunney had a daughter called Joan who came to England in 1970? She murdered her husband and was sent to Broadmoor. I bet you never knew that. If you're asking who the fuck Gene Tunney is, go and check your boxing history! He was a true world champion who died at 81 of alcoholism in Greenwich Hospital. That's a good age for a boxer. Some say it was his daughter being sent to Broadmoor that pushed him over the edge! Well, let's face it, not too many daughters kill their husbands with an axe and end up in Broadmoor. That's enough to turn any dad to booze!

You get it all here and you never know what's coming next, so here's a boxing treat for you, some of the great nicknames of the ring masters:

Joe Louis	-	The Brown Bomber
James J Braddock	-	Cinderella Man
Primo Carnera	-	The Ambling Alp
George Carpenter	-	The Orchid Man
Muhammad Ali	-	The Greatest
Billy Conn	-	The Pittsburgh Kid
James J Corbett	-	Gentleman Jim
Jack Dempsey	-	The Manassa Mauler
Luis Firpo	-	The Wild Bull of the Pampas
Bob Fitzsimmons	-	Freckled Bob
Frank Fletcher	-	The Animal
Tony Galento	-	Two-Ton Tony
Kid Gavilan	-	The Hawk
Francisco Guilledo	-	Pancho Villa
Harry Greb	-	The Human Windmill
Richard Ihetu	-	Dick Tiger
James Jackson Jeffries	-	The Boilermaker
William Jones	-	Gorilla Jones
		(Ali also used to call Joe Frazier a gorilla.)
Stanley Ketchel	-	The Michigan Assassin
Jake LaMotta	-	The Bronx Bull or The Raging Bull
Sam Langford	-	The Boston Tar Baby
King Levinsky	-	Kingfish Levinsky
Charles Liston	-	Sonny (Ali called him the Bear)

Terry McGovern - Terrible Terry
Rocky Marciano - The Brockton Blockbuster
Carl Olson - Bobo
Jack Palance - Jack Brazzo
(He become a great Hollywood star)
Willie Pep Papaleo - Will o' the Wisp
Joe Rivers - Mexican Joe
Maxie Rosenbloom - Slapsie Maxie
Joe Saddler - Sandy
Eligio Sardinias - Kid Chocolate
Martin Sinatra - Marty O'Brien
(That's Frank's dad. Not a lot of people know that but you do now!)
Walker Smith - Sugar Ray Robinson
John L Sullivan - The Boston Strong Boy
Johnny Thompson - Cyclone
Mickey Walker - Toy Bulldog
Chuck Wepner - The Bayonne Bleeder
Jess Willard - The Pottawatomie Giant
Archibald Lee Wright - Archie Moore
Tony Zale - Man of Steel
Joe Zukauskas - Jack Sharkey
Lou Ambers - The Herkimer Hurricane
Henry Armstrong - Hammerin' Hank
Max Baer - The Livermore Larruper
Thomas Hearns - The Hitman

There's some pucker names here, eh? Brilliant. They were all legends in their day, believe it! I could go on all day; the list of boxing greats is endless. I salute you all, dead or alive. Respect.

Here's a funny thing. You'll crack up on this one and it's so insane you'll think I'm making it up! A British fighter (who will remain nameless) used to pay prostitutes £10 for every fart they did in his face. Ten quid a fart! That was what turned him on. She would have to squat over his face and if she did ten farts she'd get a ton! Not bad, eh? What a mad world we live in. You can't make this shit up if you tried!

Did you know the record for the longest fart is one minute and 32 seconds? It was done by a German baker. I actually find that hard to believe, but it was done on TV and eight million viewers witnessed it! I bet he had a sore arse after a one and a half minute fart. Fucking idiot!

It's lovely when you fart in the bath and the bubbles tickle your bollocks or your fanny, depending on who you are! It's a funny old world.

I'll tell you what else is funny! 'Mad' Jake Williams got so upset in Broadmoor in the 1980s that he got completely fucked up in the head. He screamed out, "Fuck you lot! I'll never speak again to another lunatic for as long as I live." He then sewed up his lips! You just can't make it up – it's fucking brilliant! Well, it has to be to be in Loonyology! Only the cream are in this book: the very best, the very worst, the very mad, the very bad and a few sad! Could you sew your lips up? Think about it!

Good night.

But remember:
Everybody has the right to feel
The way they feel.
Cry if you must,
But don't cry over my ice cream
Or I'll crush your spine.

CHAPTER 10

Peace, Love and Blood

It's better to be a lion for one day than a mouse for a lifetime!

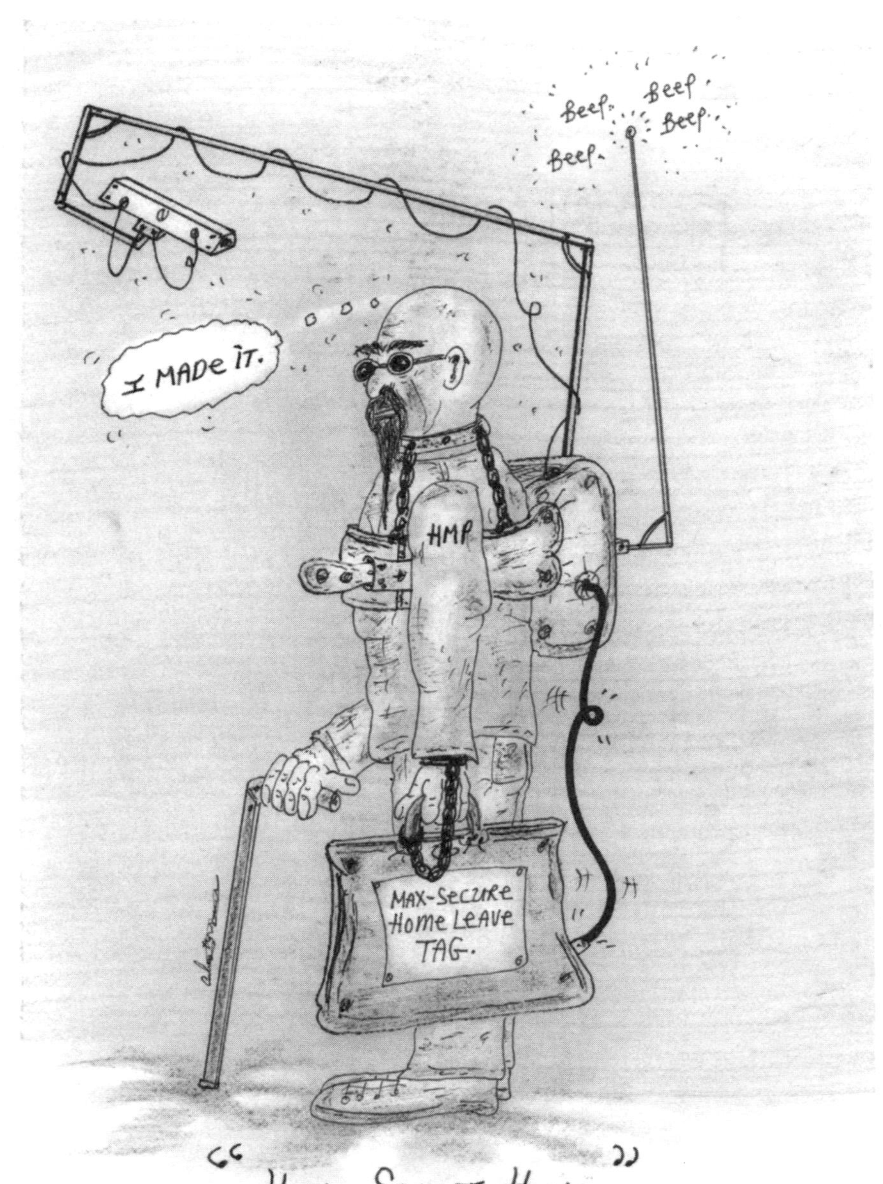

16 July 2008.

I got a terribly sad letter from my friends Lesley and Nick today, about their little girl Amber. I won't go into it as it's private, but my heart goes out to Amber, it really does. It's only when life deals such a big blow to a kid that us adults wake up. What the fuck have we got to moan about? I'll tell you: sod all. Have a stroll around a children's hospital ward then tell me you've got a problem. Life can be so cruel to children. That's when I question the existence of God. Where the fuck is he? What's he doing? Wake up and help the children…

I was told that my son won't be up tomorrow because of something to do with the trains. There go my banana milkshakes! Such is life.

I got 11 letters and a book sent in off the author Jason Cook: *There's no room for jugglers in my circus*. Cheers, mate. I'll read it at the weekend.

I got a right sexy letter from a Fiona who's serving seven years in Newhall jail for GBH. Apparently she hit her ex-boyfriend with a hammer! She's actually asked me how big my cock is. She's seen my photo and reckons I've got a big, fat one and it's between seven and eight inches! Fuck me; she doesn't mess about, does she? I'll drop a card tomorrow to tell her it's 11 and a half inches and like a baby's leg – and that the last bird who went down on me lost her tonsils. Fiona, best you write to some other con. You're too crude for me. If you ever see me outside you can come up and feel it yourself! I may even fuck the arse off you, but don't bring your hammer!

I've had two replies from my official complaints! (Over the page) You'll love these. Get on the answers and tell me these people are not clowns! They're total idiots – institutionalized muppets! Help, get me out of here, I'm a celebrity!

Reply: Dear Mr Bronson, I have made enquiries into your issue. It seems Governor Clair Hodson who is now the new head of CSC had visited as part of a familiarisation to CSC. Unfortunately she was unable to spend the normal amount of time within the establishment. I am confident that she will want to spend time speaking to offenders located within the CSC at Wakefield.

Well, that sums it all up for me. Insanity!

Reply 2: The information was received via the monitoring of the pin phone system and brought to the attention of the security department. We have a duty of care for all visitors to the establishment and therefore your visitor was informed of the risk should the threat be carried out. Unfortunately the information was not passed to CSC managers and the correct procedures were not followed in this instance. We will endeavour to ensure the correct procedures are followed in the future.

They do tell me there's no smoke without fire. Well, they lit the fire and blew it all over me! They just lie and make it up as they go along. It's like a game of pass the parcel. They're fucking parasites! Even the screws on this unit say I'm in the right. I've done fuck all wrong and I still get fitted

F2059

HM PRISON SERVICE

FORM COMP 1
PRISONER'S FORMAL COMPLAINT

Establishment
Serial no. WD109/08F

Read these notes first

1. This form is for you to make a formal written complaint under the complaints procedures. Complaints should wherever possible be sorted out informally by speaking to your wing officer or making an application. Use this form only if you have not been able to resolve your complaint this way.
2. A written complaint should be made within 3 months of the incident or of the relevant facts coming to your notice.
3. Keep your complaint brief and to the point.
4. When you have completed the form, sign it and post it in the box provided. The form will be returned to you with a response.
5. If you are unhappy with the response, you can appeal on a separate form (COMP 1A).
6. Some subjects are dealt with only by the Area Manager or Prison Service headquarters. If your complaint is about one of these subjects, the reply will take longer.
7. There is a separate pink form (COMP 2) for confidential access complaints.

Your details (use BLOCK CAPITALS)

Surname	BRONSON.	First name(s)	CHARLIE
Prison number	BT1314	Location	C.S.C. UNIT

Have you spoken to anyone about your complaint? Yes ☑ No ☐

If so, who did you speak to?
THE UNIT GOVERNOR. SEVERAL SCREWS

Your complaint
I WAS TOLD IN MAY THAT THE No1 C.S.C BOSS WOULD BE COMING HERE IN JULY. GOVERNOR BROOKES TOLD ME THIS. (AND WILL SEE ME)! YESTERDAY 7TH JULY IM TOLD BY THE SAME GOVERNOR, THE BOSS WAS HERE IN THE MORNING BUT NEVER HAD TIME TO SEE ME! "IS THE TRUTH" H/Q DONT REALLY WANT TO SEE ME? BECAUSE THEY CAN "NO-LONGER" JUSTIFY MY ISOLATED CONDITIONS OR MY NO-HOPE OF EVER BEING ALLOWED TO — — PROGRESS? IS IT REALLY A CASE OF "LET BRONSON ROT IN A HOLE"?

Does your complaint have a racial aspect? Yes ☐ No ☐
Is your complaint about bullying? Yes ☐ No ☐

What would you like to see done about your complaint?
I WOULD LIKE PRISON H/Q TO JUSTIFY MY YEARS OF BEING KEPT ON THIS HIGH RISK ISOLATION UNIT, AND DELIBERATELY "REFUSING" TO SEE ME WHEN THERE VISITING THE PRISON. (ITS THERE JOB TO SEE US C.S.C. PRISONERS). ITS AN ACT OF PROFESSIONAL INCOMPETENCE.

Signed [signature] Date 8/7/2008

Printed by Albany Print and Design. HMP Albany.

F2059 Sec.

HM PRISON SERVICE

FORM COMP 1
PRISONER'S FORMAL COMPLAINT

Establishment
Serial № WD115/08 F.

Read these notes first

1. This form is for you to make a formal written complaint under the complaints procedure. Complaints should wherever possible be sorted out informally by speaking to your wing officer or making an application. Use this form only if you have not been able to resolve your complaint this way.
2. A written complaint should be made within 3 months of the incident or of the relevant facts coming to your notice.
3. Keep the complaint brief and to the point.
4. When you have completed the form, sign it and post in the box provided. The form will be returned to you with a response.
5. If you are unhappy with the response, you can appeal on a separate form (COMP 1A).
6. Some subjects are dealt with only by the Area Manager or Prison Service headquarters. If your complaint is about one of these subjects, the reply will take longer.
7. There is a separate pink form (COMP 2) for confidential access complaints.

Your details (use BLOCK CAPITALS)

Surname	BRONSON	First name(s)	CHARLIE
Prison number	BT1314	Location	C-S-C.

Have you spoken to anyone about your complaint ? Yes [✓] No [ ]

If so, who did you speak to ?

S/O. SCREWS.

Your complaint

ON SAT 12-7-2008 MY VISITOR "MARK FISH" WAS TOLD AND SHOWN A RED INCIDENT BOOK IN THE VISITS CENTRE THAT I WAS GOING TO ATTACK HIM... AND DID HE REALLY WANT TO VISIT ME. (HE KNEW IT WAS LIES)
AFTER OUR VISIT I PULLED THE SCREWS AND EVEN THEY WERE SHOCKED OVER IT. THE SENIOR OFFICER EVEN TOLD MARK FISH HE KNEW NOTHING ABOUT IT...
ITS NOW BLATENTLY OBVIOUS "SOMEBODY" IS DELIBERATLY TRYING TO CAUSE SERIOUS PROBLEMS.
COULD IT BE THAT MY PAROLE REVIEW IS WEEKS AWAY?

Does your complaint have a racial aspect ? Yes [ ] No [ ]

Is your complaint about bullying ? Yes [✓] No [ ]

What would you like to see done about your complaint ?

WHO TOLD THE VISITS CENTRE I WAS TO ATTACK MY VISITOR?
WHERE DID THIS INFORMATION COME FROM?
WHY WAS THE UNIT STAFF NOT TOLD ABOUT IT?
WHY WAS I NOT ASKED ABOUT IT?
ITS A COMPLETE JOKE..
(YOUR RUNNING A MUPPET SHOW HERE. AND BULLYING MY VISITOR)

Signed [signature] Date 13/7/2008

VF 011 Printed at HMP Kingston 4334 03/2003

up! I've never threatened Mark Fish (or anybody else) on the phone. Sure, we've had some strong words but that's our bizz; that's how we express ourselves. We are not part of the PC brigade and don't go around saying, "I say chappie, pass the cucumber sandwiches." A cunt's a cunt in our vocabulary!

Mark and me are old buddies. We've had our ups and downs and we'll probably have a few more later, but what's that got to do with these nosey cunts? Stop bugging my calls, you Gestapo cunts! That's spying in my book. Keep your noses out of my private life! Bizz is bizz, you cunts. Who do they think they are; the CIA or the FBI? I'll tell you who they are: two-bob muggy screws sticking their oar in where it's not needed! What's all that about telling my visitor I may attack him? I'm on closed visits so how can I attack anybody?

No names mentioned, but several screws on the unit are disgusted over this because they know it's all bollocks! Security has caused a problem that doesn't even exist because they've got nothing better to do than listen to my calls and add two and two together to come up with five. Fucking idiots. I rest my case. It's now up to my legal team to sort it out because I've had enough of it now. As far as the other complaint reply goes, let's all have a laugh: HA! HA! HA! HA! HA! HA! HA! Because that's all it is – one big joke! Frick me, I need a cuppa cha! (A bottle of brandy would be better.)

It's been a strange day with a lot of stress and deep thought about who's out to nail me and why. Is it not good enough that I behave and do my time peacefully? Something doesn't add up; could it be because my parole review is next month? Are they about to fuck it all up for me? We shall see… I wouldn't put anything past them. They've done a lot of physical damage to me over the years, but it was easier to bleed than have all this psychological shit going on. I'm not cut out for this shit! It's not how I handle things. Right now I'm getting it in the back and it's a wonder I've still got my kidneys intact. Cunts.

Pizza, chips and beans for tea! Not bad at all. The governor did his rounds and I said, "Hey, Gov, there's no smoke without fire! Your security muppets have lit this fire and blown the smoke all over me… cough… splutter… cough… get my drift, Gov?" Watch this space!

Hey, I can feel a wank coming on! I forget the last time I had one, but I'm just in the mood to release some tension! A good old-fashioned wank: smother your cock in baby lotion, close your eyes and go for it! I once hit the ceiling, believe it. I think I should be awarded for a wanking title! Why not? There's no shame in having a wank. The tighter you hold your cock, the tighter you close your eyes and you can be shagging anybody you want! I've fucked half of Hollywood for four decades: the '60s, '70s, '80s and '90s. I'm the No. 1 wanker in the UK! Who can deny me the title? Somebody nominate me for world champion. Come on, let's get it on. I could teach any nice birds how to pull their boyfriends off in style! They can practise on me two at a time, I don't mind. I can see it now – four hands on my cock and balls. You watch me shoot it up! I'll show you *Big Brother* fans who's the champion! Why not? It's all good, clean, natural fun! If there were more like me there'd be less diseases and unwanted babies.

Maybe I should start a national club of wankers. I could call it 'Wankers

Incorporated'! I could be onto something here. How many wanks an hour can you manage? How far can you shoot? How much do you spunk? What are your best techniques? I can see it now: the 'Charlie Bronson Wanking Society'!

You can't tell me you girls wouldn't pay to see that. You know you would! You girls are fascinated by a guy's cock; you know it's where his brains are! So how about it, shall I organise it? If you want it, write to me and I'll set up a club later, I promise. Maybe we could even have a girls' wanking night so us guys can watch and learn! You can show us how to do it properly with close-ups of the clitty! How best to rub it, squeeze it, flick it, etc. It's food for thought... Fuck it; I'm definitely having a wank now! I'm off. You lot can fuck off, I won't be back later!

Did you know the average ice-cream is eaten in fifty licks? Not a lot of people know that!

18 July 2008.

I see Susan Atkins has been denied compassionate parole despite having brain cancer. She was one of the Charles Manson disciples – the infamous 'Manson Monsters' – who went on a killing spree in Hollywood in 1969. Forty years later they're still caged away and they'll all die inside for sure, brain cancer or no brain cancer. It was Susan who killed Sharon Tate, ripped out her unborn baby and wrote 'Pig' on the wall in its blood. It's a prison death for Susan. She died the day she ripped that baby out of the womb – her soul left her for sure. She's been living a soul-less existence for 40 long, hard years. It's all over for her and she knows it.

I got a box of chocolates sent in today from Mark Jones' five-year-old daughter Emma. Unbelievable! How nice is that? What a lovely gesture from a lovely kid. That's out of her pocket money! Obviously I can't have them; convicted cons can't have such luxuries sent in. We could years ago but it all stopped because of all the drugs being smuggled in. Blame the smack heads for that. Anyway, thanks, Emma, you're a star! We all love ya. You've got a good heart and you're very kind!

I also got the new edition of the *Loonyology* book in. My wedding photos were in the first edition but they've had to be taken out because, apparently, the Crown owns the copyrights! Cunts – they've got to stick their noses into everything! Do they own my wedding photos? I paid for them so surely I must own them, but they claim to have the copyrights! I can't be arsed arguing anymore, I'm sick of court cases, I need a break. Three months in Barbados would be nice! (It'll happen one day.)

Did you know fresh sweat doesn't smell? It's stale sweat that stinks, so wash your clothes and look after your hygiene, you dirty bastards!

Is it possible to be allergic to prison? If I could prove I was allergic to prison life, maybe I could be freed on humanitarian grounds. That would be automatic parole so it's worth a try. I'll see what my legal team have to say about it. I could be the first man in history to be freed from prison on medical grounds! Fantastic... this could be my way out! I'm a fucking born genius.

The 2010 football World Cup is to be held in South Africa. But get on this for an eye opener, you'll love this: every 24 hours in South Africa there are approximately 50 murders, 50 attempted murders, 100 rapes, 300 robberies, 600 assaults, 650 burglaries and 40 car-jackings! Even if they don't win the football, they could still be world champions when it comes to crime! In 2010, Johannesburg will be drafting in an extra 40,000 police. HA! HA! HA! HA! HA! You'll fucking need them too! I can foresee some serious trouble out there, can't you?

There's not been a lot going on lately. Butler's down from the wing. What a cunt and mouthy fucker he is. I knew him in Full Sutton and Woodhill; he's a total prat. I poured a pot of piss under his door once. Lick that up, you cunt! I also sent him in a male blow-up doll. (My mate's got three sex shops which comes in handy.) I love to wind nutters up, especially Butler. That reminds me, I must get the gay news sorted for the Cannibal. All in a day's work. There are never enough hours in a day to get everything done!

I've been told my film is to be shown at Robert Redford's Sundance Film Festival in January 2009! That's brilliant news! Then, soon after, it will be in picture houses all over the UK and you can see Tom Hardy for the actor he is. He'll have an Oscar next, I can foresee it. Don't bet against it!

Fish fingers and chips, four bread rolls and a mug of hot, sweet tea for tea! Bloody lovely. Simple but filling.

I did a 27-minute headstand today. When I got down I almost passed out! I must be getting old. I felt strange, dizzy and wobbly. It's a great exercise though – it strengthens the neck muscles and it's good for the spine. It's all about balance, as is life, and nobody on this planet balances like I do!

I wonder what the weekend's going to bring? Good or bad, I can't wait! Oh, by the way, I fucked the wank off the other night. I couldn't be bothered. I gave it a few tugs and got bored, so I had a mug of tea and six custard creams instead!

Did you know there's a centipede in South America that grows to four feet long? A fucking four-foot centipede! Imagine all those mental legs creeping up your leg on a dark night! ARRGGGHHHHHHhhhhhhhhhhh! Fucking get me the fuck out of here!

Did you know there are three jails on the Isle of Sheppey: Elmley, Swaleside and Standford Hill? Fuck me – it's only a small place in Kent. Imagine that lot going up with a massive break-out. Who said there's no Hell on Earth? There would be if that happened! Hundreds of desperate cons on the run. Yiiipppeeeeeee, yaarrhhooooooo!

Will there ever be a mass break-out? Could it happen? The truth is that I doubt it! Too many cons would stay behind so they didn't miss *EastEnders* or *Big Brother* while eating their raspberry ripples. It's true – sad but true! I think the biggest chance of it happening would be with the Islamic terrorists. I can see that happening in time as those guys really don't care about life or death; their mission is madness – madness beyond your worst ever nightmare! Pass the teapot, I'll drink to that!

Did you know there's not an Indian restaurant in Luton where I have to pay? It's all free because they love me. Why? They know why and so do I! Let's leave it at that! They're lovely people. Salaam.

Talking of curry, I'll tell you who's hot: Suzy Wilkinson. "Who?" you ask. Fuck you, I'm not saying. Just believe me when I say she's hot! So hot she drips sex, smells like sex and tastes like an apple pie. She's sex on legs! Love ya, Suzy. x

I see there's a new national newspaper for prisoners called *Con Verse*. It comes out once a month. Give them a call and find out what it's all about:

08450 660022

Or drop them a line:

Mark Leech, Editor, PO Box 116, Manchester, M9 6RL

Take it from me, it's worth a butchers. If you want to know about the prison world and how it works, this is the paper to read.

Here's a funny thing, you'll love this one. Donald Neilson's (the 'Black Panther') birth name was Donald Nappey! Fucking Nappey, what a name. I bet he got some stick at school! "Oi, shitty pants! Over here smelly arse!" Hey, maybe that's what turned him into a killer. All that childhood piss-taking could well have scarred him for life! He changed his Nappey name by deed poll to Neilson in 1960. Not a lot of people know that. How did I know? I told you: I'm a clever cunt. When it comes to crime and prison there's not a lot I don't know. In fact I'm a fucking genius! I'm not blowing my own trumpet but that's what I am!

Talking of trumpets, Ronnie Kray had one in Parkhurst in 1976. He loved the trumpet and wanted to play one like the great Roy Castle. Ron only had it for a couple of days as he said it gave him a headache. (Yeah, and us, we all have a headache over that!) Ron used to get these flashes of inspiration where he felt he'd found his true gift in life but they seldom lasted more than a day or two. I've always fancied a horse and I'm still waiting for the prison bosses to allow me one; 33 years I've been waiting. Cunts.

I've just had a pile of questions sent in for me to answer. They were emailed to Mark Emmins. I'll try and answer them to the best of my ability! Obviously I can't answer them all, as some are fucking beyond sanity. There are some right loonies out there...

Chaz,

Q – If you could be in any jail or asylum what one would you choose?

Dave from York.

A – Fuck me, Dave, that's a good question... I don't really know because I make every place work for me, so they're all the same to me, mate. One shithole's as good as the next one, but if I had to pick one it'd be Parkhurst.

Charlie,

Q – Have you ever been in a Scottish jail?

Ed from Leeds.

A – No. (Nor have I worn a kilt.)

Charlie,

Q – Is it true when you arrive in jail they stick a rubber-gloved finger up your arse?

Carol from Dover.

A – Let me tell you now: in my three and a half decades of being locked away, no fucker has ever stuck a finger up my ring piece. I know it happens in all the prison films but it's never, ever happened to me. I suppose it does happen to some, especially if they think a con is smuggling in drugs up his arse. But it would have to be done by a doctor or a qualified nurse. Anyway Carol, why are you interested in men's arses? What a strange question to ask me! Do you have fantasies about putting your finger up my arse? Very strange.

Mr Bronson.
Q – I've just read your book *The Krays and Me*. Do you think Ronnie was really mad?

Sid from Ipswich.

A – Ron was a certified schizophrenic and had serious bouts of paranoia and depression, but he was stabilized with medication. A lot of schizo people are actually very clever. Some are geniuses – masterminds. Mad people are very complex and Ronnie Kray was a true, uncut diamond.

Q – Is Frankie Fraser mad?

Sally from Glasgow.

A – Do bears shit in the woods? Of course he's mad; wouldn't you be after being locked up for over 40 years? Frank's as mad as a box of frogs but he's a 'good mad'. He's never harmed innocent people and he lives his life with good old-fashioned values and morals. He's a great man.

Q – What's it like in a strait jacket?

Robert from Clacton-on-Sea.

A – Not very nice. It's very claustrophobic. To anybody who's about to be put into one, I recommend you cool down, chill out and sleep! Use it as a meditation period and think about the Gestapo cunts who put you in it. Don't fear it, fear nothing, you're bigger than any penal contraption they throw at you. It can be very relaxing and therapeutic! It's all in the mind, Robert – the mind is the key to life.

Q – My dad knew you in the Scrubs. He was there in the 1970s when you went mad in the Seg block! He told me you smashed your way through a sheet of unbreakable glass!

Yvonne, West London.

A – Yvonne, it wasn't that unbreakable! Nothing is unbreakable. My best to your dad!

Q – Why do you shave your hair off?

June, Manchester.

A – I've got a big bald patch and I think bald patches look silly, that's why! Now I have just one big patch of baldness. It's healthy, it feels good and it looks smart! Plus the women love a bald head bobbing up and down between their legs. My beard tickles their thighs, my tongue tickles their clit and they can see my big shiny head glowing!

Q – What's your best art you have created?

Irene from Crewe

A – I really can't answer that, Irene, as I've done so many, but why don't I do one of you naked? Send me a photo. It could be my best one! I'll be doing a lot of nude art when I'm out, so all you ladies that want one creating get in touch because I'm the man to do it. My only condition is that I fuck you first – plus I charge five grand (not for the fuck, for the art!). No fatties though; I don't fuck or paint fatties. Sorry but that's the rules! Fat birds, fuck off. I know it sounds cruel but you have to be cruel to be kind. All that fat turns me off! I can't paint that, could you?

Q – Charlie, can I post you in some chocolates?

Caroline, Essex.

A – Fuck me… I wish! If only people realised what life is all about in a max secure coffin!

Q – Charles, have you still got that mad beard?

Mary, Doncaster.

A – What's mad about it? Cheeky bitch! And my cock is as long as you want it to be, so how long do you want it to be?

Q – Mr Bronson, I've been following your case for some years now and I was told by an ex-prison officer that you were having an affair with a female prison governor in a London jail. Is it true?

Liz from Holloway.

A – No comment (not until I've seen my lawyer).

Q – Charles, my brother was at one of your unlicensed fights in East London where you hit the guy out of the ring. I think it was in the mid 1980s. My question to you is: why did you not turn professional?

Dave from Stepney.

A – The British Board of Control refused me a licence!

Q – Chaz, what's your favourite food? (And don't say porridge.)

Wyn from Surrey.

A – Wyn, it's steak.

Q – Is it true you once fought a lion?

Reg from Hastings.

A – Are you for fucking real? You're getting me mixed up with Russell Crowe in *Gladiators*. A lion? Look, Reg, I may have spent a few years in the asylum but I'm not that fucking insane!

Q – Charlie, please, please, please, please, please design me a small tattoo for my left breast. Please, Charlie.

Rosy from Derby.

A – Sorted, Rosy! On its way, babe! Shall I do a nice one for your pussy lips too? Let me know!

Q – Mr Bronson, is it true you once climbed up St Paul's Cathedral, and had a shit on the roof?

Eric from Dudley.

A – Er… why would I do that, cunt?

Q – Chaz, are you doing any more CDs and what ones have you got for sale?

Geoff from Luton.

A – There's an Xmas one coming out! It's limited edition so get in fast! Call 07731 048860.

Q – Charlie, my sister wants to know if you shave your pubic hair.

Stan from Harlow.

A – No! And tell you sister to ask herself: what are you, a fucking silly parrot?

Q – Chaz, are you ever going to be set free?

Linzy from Luton.

A – I'll be free, Linzy, bet your fanny on that! Bet your arse on it too. You're safe with me! I won't let you down. X

Q – Charles, I'm a 72-year-old lady and I think it's disgusting how you're kept locked away. Is there anything I can do to help you?

Maggie from Stockton.

A – Not a lot, Maggie, but you can get a petition going with lots of signatures. Thanks for wanting to support my campaign! You're a doll.

Q – I've just bought your book *Loonyology*. It's the biggest load of shit I've ever read! I want my money back!

Spencer from Wrexham.

A – Yeah, sure you'll get it back, I'll pay you a visit later and give it back personally. What did you expect – a fucking love story?

Q – Chaz, were you ever in Alcatraz?

Dave from Berkshire.

A – Hello! Nutter about!

Q – Charles, this is serious: I want your baby! Would you please let me have your sperm? We can do it legally. Please, Charles, you're the only man alive I wish to have a baby with.

Susan from Bedford

A – Blimey, that's a new one! I'll have to think about this one, Susan! I'm stuck for words. I'm actually in shock!

Q – Mr Bronson, have you any Russian blood in you?

John from Crewe.

A – No! Why? What's your fucking problem? Why should I have, cunt?

Q – How tall are you Charlie?

Betty from Bath.

A – 5 feet 10 ½.

Q – Charles are you a breast, leg or face man?

Cindy from Epsom.

A – Arse! I love a good firm arse with strong buttocks to hold on to! You can't beat a good arse. Black girls have the best arses; it's a fact.

Q – Charlie, I recently bought a pair of your boxing gloves off eBay for £650. Can you confirm it's your signature on them? (They're signed in thick black pen.)

Eddie from Hull.

A – You'll have to send me a photo so I can see if they're mine. But what I can confirm to you is, I've signed 30 pairs of boxing gloves and most were bag training gloves. I also know one set sold for £900 at a charity auction, so you're about right in what you paid for them!

Q – Is your son a top chef?

Cyril from Canterbury.

A – Yes!

Q – Chaz, any good tips on sorting out an in-growing toe-nail?

Robbo from Brighton.

A – Cut the toe off!

There's another box of these questions! I may add some more later, then again I may not. You wouldn't want to read some of them, believe me. Some say very nasty things (such as wishing cancer on me), others want to kill me and a few even want to fuck me. Fuck me – they must have some serious mental problems. What sane person dreams of fucking my arse? You sick, twisted fucker; I'd fuck you mate… with a 12-bore! You cheeky pervo.

It's all Loonyology to me! The world's gone insane and I need a mug of tea! It's bloody hard work this. I hope you lot appreciate it all! (I doubt it.)

I see that Dwayne Chambers lost his case in the High Court. He wanted to run in the Beijing Olympics. Serves him right for cheating. They say cheats never prosper and it came true with him!

Mark Fish has just bought a new Jag. He loves his classy motors so good luck to him. In his letter today he says he will pick me up in it as soon as I'm freed! My first stop will be a greasy spoon cafe for a fry-up and a pot of tea. Fucking lovely. Then off to get myself a black suit and a nice briefcase to put my personal stuff in. Don't ask what – it's personal so don't be nosey, OK?

Is it a dream?
Will it ever come?
What if it doesn't?
Maybe it won't
Who knows?
Some pray the dream comes true.
For me
It's just a dream!
A dream of freedom!
The sweet smell of victory
To look up at the sky
Reach up and shout,
"Who's the daddy?
Fuck the penal system!
I'm free!"

Be your own best friend, that's what I say! Trust in yourself and what will be will be. A true heart is a happy heart. Fuck the planet... right now my world is this concrete coffin and I have to survive it the best way possible: my way, the only way, the Bronson way.

Did you know there's a tribe in New Guinea that greets people by sticking their tongues in their ear? Not a lot of people know that. What a nice way to make friends! That's wonderful that is! There's a tribe in my town (Luton) that would cut your ears off. HA! HA! HA! HA! HA! (I'm only joking. Don't take life so seriously! Fucking loosen up a bit. Take a chill pill and learn to ride your journey of life with a smile.)

I see Emma Manser hanged herself before standing trial for the smothering of her four-year-old son. It was probably the best thing she could do. She left a suicide note saying she can't live with herself knowing she killed the only good thing in her life. It's a sad end where nobody wins and everybody loses; pain on pain and a river of tears. That's what you call pure misery – the black tunnel of doom. Pray you never hit that low because it's fucking dark down there like a witch's arsehole!

I'll always remember sitting next to my two buddies Colin Robinson and Ronnie Kray on Broadmoor's Somerset One ward back in 1979. Somerset was the reception ward so all new loonies had to come through there to be assessed. We were all sitting facing the door when a big fat lunatic waddled in with his eyes on the floor and his shoulders hunched up. Shame, guilt and fear oozed from his fat, fucked-up body. Colin actually said, "Nonce. If that's not a nonce I'll eat my hat." I must add that I thought exactly the same! Ronnie also reckoned he was in for kids. He said, "Paedo – defo a kiddie fiddler!" The fat cunt sat at the back of the room alone with his eyes still on the floor, so I went over and sat next to him!

"Where have you just come from?" I asked.

"Winchester prison," he mumbled.

"How long were you there?" I asked.

"A year," he mumbled.

"What are you in for?" I asked.

"I'd rather not say," he mumbled.

"Oh! You would rather not say, would you?" You fat cunt, what are you in for?"

"I killed my wife and three children," he whimpered.

"You fat cunt, stay clear of me," I said.

Now this is the shock. For a couple of months this piece of shit was like a mouse: shy and too shit scared to even pick his eyes up! Then the screws gave him a 'tea boy' job with a little white 'tea boy' jacket! "How many sugars, sir? Milk or cream, sir? Biscuits, sir? Chocolate or plain?" Next thing he was bouncing about like he owned the place and the screws were his buddies! They love a lunatic they can rule as it makes them feel special, but all the fat cunt will ever be is a slave, a fucking fat woman and triple child killer and a screws' pet plaything! "Hurry up with that tea!" Get this, get that. He even got the occasional kick up the arse but he loved it!

From Somerset One the fat cunt was moved to a lovely trusted ward and got a lovely trusted job working on the gardens when I (and other 'loons' like me) would never get that in a million years. That's what made me angry in the asylum world and it's why I rebelled against their two-faced rules. That fat fucker killed four people! He wiped out his own family and he gets all the nice treatment. All his guilt and shame vanished and he started to look down on loons like me! I was dog shit to him and he was so much more superior to us. We could never work this out or accept it. Why should we have to? Could you?

There was a sort of policy in Broadmoor to keep guys like me down and not allow us the same chances and fairness as the monsters. I even pulled the superintendent Dr Mgraph over it! He sat me down to explain but it still doesn't make any sense to me. I asked him, "How come a four-time killer can be trusted to work in the gardens but I can't?" I was told: "He would never try to escape; you would! He can't escape – he's too scared to! Where can he go? The public would be a danger to him. You would escape for the fun of it. You've got many people to hide you away and you would be the danger to the public."

"Hold up," I said, "you can't fucking say that! It's all guess work with you fuckers. The fact is he's getting treated like a lord! It's as if he's not even a criminal."

"But he isn't a prisoner, he's a patient. He's mentally ill and he's here for treatment."

"What about me then?"

"You're here because the prisons couldn't control you!"

"I fucking give up, Doc," I said (and I did).

After that I could never take my life in the cuckoo house seriously again! It was a complete fucking piss-take. A loon can kill four innocent people and get treated like a lord but someone like me who's never killed gets treated like a mad dog. They never even put him on the 'liquid cosh' whereas I was forever being stabbed in the arse with needles and pumped full of psychotropic drugs. It pays to be a mass killer in Broadmoor – you'll get a lot more respect and the best jobs.

It really did open my eyes to see so much shame and guilt disappear so fast! Broadmoor saved that fat fucker's life because in jail he would've had his throat ripped out! During the year he spent on remand at Winchester he had the real treatment: piss in his food, shitty sheets and a slap here and there. In the 1970s even the screws gave child killers a slap. This piece of shit was terrified to walk out of his cell door then 'bang' – he's the tea boy in the big house and he's giving it large! Look at me: I'm daddy big bollocks! I could have easily shot that cunt's face off! But I actually blamed the screws and the doctors for that quick transformation. It was their doing and it made me (and others like me) sick.

I never did get a job in the gardens! I remained a mad 'untreatable' bastard but at least in my eyes a child killer remains a piece of shit. Thirty years have passed on by but I still feel the same: that fat cunt should've hanged and I should've had that gardening job! Fuck the tea boy job – those lazy fuckers can make their own tea! Yep, not a lot changes in my life and I doubt I'll ever get a gardening job. But one thing's for sure: I won't ever kill any kids either! That's a fact and it's carved in stone.

I see Rickie Tregaskis is now in Broadmoor. He's not mad so fuck knows why he ended up there. He was the con who copped an extra six years for attacking the child killer Roy Whiting. He should've got a medal for that, not six years! Now he's in the nut house. What for? Only a sane man would attack a child killer. I don't know anybody who wouldn't love to chin Whiting – not one person. Cunts like him need attacking 24/7! After what he did to little Sarah Payne he deserves all he gets... and more.

I've got to brush my teeth because I've got a vile taste in my mouth all of a sudden. So it's a strip-wash, clean my teeth and bed! Talking of bed, my mattress is lovely now – heavenly. Good night.

21 July 2008.

A couple of little sparrows woke me this morning! I felt like I was free in the countryside. It was nice awakening from a good sleep to hear that singing. All that was missing was a good, naked woman smelling of sex next to me! A man can't beat a good shag to start the day. I think it's the best shag of them all and it truly wakes you up. But there are no shags in Hell... unless it's your own arse getting fucked by Satan! That evil cunt will have to kill me before he fucks me!

The sun's out and it's a lovely day! I only got one letter, off Sandra, but one is still a treat! She's a bloody good 'un and a lovely friend to me. I had a nice bit of veg soup for lunch. It was like a broth: thick and full of goodness! I had six bread rolls with it. After lunch I had an hour on the yard and the sun felt great on my head and back as I jogged around. I could've run a marathon today, easily. For tea I had a cheese salad and two nice, thick pieces of cheese. I made four sandwiches out of it, with tomatoes, lettuce, cucumber and onions. Lovely it was!

I called Dee Morris. We always have a nice chat. Dee is special to me, like family. Then I called Mum up; she's just back from her holidays! So all in all it was a top day. It should be a crime to be as at peace as I am!

Dave Courtney has just spent a week out in Spain at my Lorraine's villa. She spoils all my mates. My mates are one big family. When Mark Fish was out there a month back, he said it was the best holiday he's had in years, and that guy travels the world. That's what I need – a month by the sea with a lot of pussy close by. I can't fucking wait. Fucking hurry up my case because my balls are getting heavy! I won't be able to walk soon. Can you imagine my first fuck? Yiiipppeeeeeee, I can't wait!

A gay couple have a falling out. One of them goes and gets two tattoos, one on each arse cheek. On the left cheek he had Mike Tyson and on the right cheek he had Frank Bruno. Then he gets back with his partner and they make it up. When he strips off and bends over the bed, his partner sees the tattoos and says, "Fuck me... you're joking! There's no way I'm going in the ring between those two!"

Right, I'm off! I've got a piece of art to work on and I'm feeling creative. I could be about to create a masterpiece (another one)! Don't forget: if you spend your life worrying about losing your mind you will neglect to enjoy the sanity that you have. It's all Loonyology to me. Before I go, read this page from ex-prison screwess Sarah Macleod. It sort of sums it all up. Read Sarah's page and learn from it. She's the one who's speaking sense! An angel never lies. Amen!

MY friend Charlie!

There are many misconceptions about the man who is Charlie Bronson! If you asked 'Joe public' out on the street who Charlie Bronson is then I am sure a majority would come out with: "Oh, he's that mad nutter who's been in prison for ever and can't come out as he's too dangerous!" It's a sad fact that most of us believe what we read in the tabloids and do not ever want to have ALL the facts in hand before we make judgements on someone. Unfortunately what we read is not always a fair and accurate description of someone and it's more likely to be a full-on character assassination. Sensationalism sells papers!

I worked as a female prison officer in a male maximum security prison and Charlie was infamous in the prison system. He formed part of our training too as we were taught how to perform six and eight-man unlocks (just in case we came into contact with Charlie through the dispersal system). Most Cat A lifers are unlocked by one officer; God knows I did enough of them! Charlie gets a special unlock (half a shift of officers all to himself) and total full-on escort around his prison movements.

The Charlie I now know personally (I left the prison service some years ago) is the absolute opposite of his public image. He is funny, lively, energetic, highly intelligent, artistically talented, kind, warm, thoughtful and considerate – not to mention entertaining. A conversation with Charlie is spoken at a hundred miles an hour but his personality just shines through and he is just an absolute delight. He has such an inward strength and positivity towards life that he could have been a highly-decorated SAS hero in another world. Nothing is EVER going to break his iron will or resolution. Is there any other person on this entire planet who could last thirty four years in prison and mostly in solitary confinement? I doubt it!

Charlie deserves a chance to live his life outside a cage now. He is no threat to anyone. He has a huge support network from all walks of life behind him who would ensure Charlie was able to live the life he so richly deserves. Charlie has been caged longer than any animal would be allowed to be. Let's open the cage and give him his dignity!

God bless you, Charlie!
Much love,
Sarah x

This is a woman who worked in one of Britain's max secure jails and who has locked and unlocked some of Britain's most dangerous men. She sums it all up in a nutshell for me, especially when she says, "Let's open the cage and give him his dignity!" An ex-prison officer saying that to me makes it all worthwhile – all my years of isolation and all my years of madness! She's a woman who trusts and respects me and she knows enough is enough! You can't argue with her because this is a woman who knows the true facts. She was trained to be 'prepared for Bronson' but she knows I'm a teddy bear! It's the system that has created the Bronson myth and 90% of screws are dying to jump all over my head just so they can say, "I did Bronson." They're trained to fear me and that's the truth! Bear in mind that 90% never get to see me so I remain a mythical character to them. They aren't able to judge for themselves.

This next piece you're about to read is from my buddy 'Ifty Iftkhar' and it says it all. It's very humbling for me! Thank you, my brother. Salaam! And my love and respect go out to Kala and his family. Stay strong! More houses will follow or my name is not Charlie. This is Loonyology with a soul!

Charlie changes lives of the poor and homeless

It was about two years back, whilst in Kashmir that I decided to visit the family of my priest friend.

There, I met a very poor chap named Kala and his family, his home was nothing more than a bunch of branches.

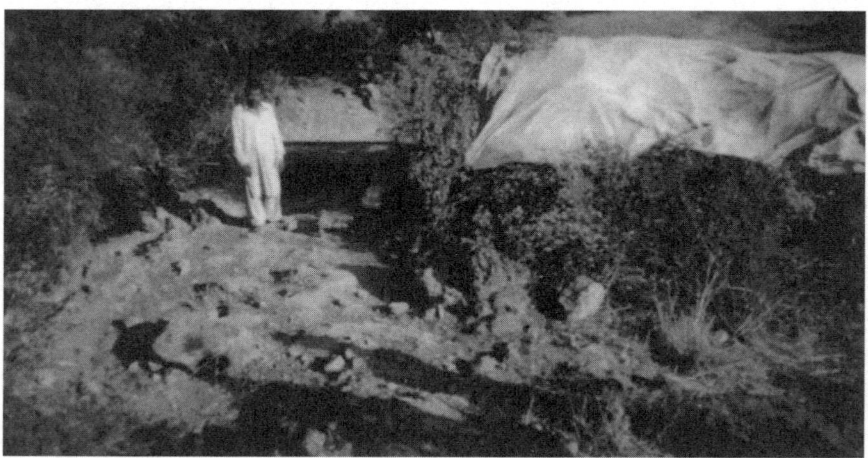

Aerial view of Kala home, a thin sheet is all they have to offer some protection from the elements

Whilst it is true to say that there are many homeless people in Kashmir and poverty surrounds one's every view, it's easy to accept that this is just a way of life for the locals.

I guess because I come from a country where most of us have not encountered starvation, and have not been left entirely to our own devices to feed, provide shelter and educate our children, that we perhaps take our own circumstances for granted.

When hope is all one has, when no one cares and no one sees or listens to your cries for help, only the massively incredibly strong get through each day.

Kala had been homeless and had been in search of shelter for his wife who was pregnant and had a 3 year old daughter.

Kala and his family stumbled across my priest friend who gave them a piece of land to build their own home.

In Pakistan, land is the only item of any value that a person may have, and to give a piece of it away for nothing is unheard off. Many people are killed over land disputes because people guard their only possession with their lives.

But the priest and his family are very good people, they reached out and gave a piece of their family heritage and only valid possession for nothing.

Kala built his self a shelter on the land that the priest had given to him, his home was made from sticks and branches, at night snakes would drop through the roof and the constant threat from wild animals such as bears.

Rear view of Kala's home, a magnet for wild animals

Just imagine this guy really has to sleep with one eye open at night for fear that has little daughter could be eaten by wild animals or bitten by snakes and spiders.

When I returned to England I quickly became immersed back into busy modern life and all the trimmings that come with it, I soon forgot about my encounter with Kala.

It was not until I was on a visit with Charlie, some months later that the thought and emotions I had felt came back to me.

Charlie asked me about my visit to Pakistan Kashmir and I mentioned to him about Kala and the way that he lived.

What happened next will always stick in my mind; Charlie looked down with disappointment, the mood changed from laughing and joking to one off sadness evident on Charlie's face.

Charlie asked more and more about Kala's situation and ironically Charlie

Kala's home circled in the distance, they live alone there

explained to me how Kala must feel, in exactly the same way that Kala told me how he felt.

Charlie was clearly concerned and I said to him 'Charlie we can not do anything to change the way Kala lives, there is millions like him'

Why not he replied?

I was dumbfounded and stuck for a valid excuse 'Ifty I share a lot in common with the poor, the young and the defenceless, because I know what it feels like to have nothing but a thread of hope to get me through each day. Go back to Pakistan and do something to help this man I will help you, you have the power of freedom don't be selfish with it'

To this day the thought stays in my mind. I realized that Charlie was right, I realized the power of freedom, and that by only thinking of my self was a selfish act.

Within days a letter landed through my letter box from Charlie, it was full of ideas and questions about Kala.

Over the course of the next month Charlie became extremely focused on getting a project of the ground for Kala. Charlie single handed put in place a fund raising day in aid of Kala so that a house could be built for him. True to his word Charlie got me all the help I needed and with his friends support we rallied around the croft street area of Walsall where I live.

"Appeal for Khala"

This appeal is to help a very poor brother in Kashmir, he lives with his wife and 3-year-old daughter, in a 15-foot square box made of branches and sticks. He was spotted by Peer Nazakat Sha, who has given him land.

Our aim is to raise a minimum of 400.00 immediately to make a house before the bad weather kicks in. This appeal is also supported and inspired by Charles Bronson.

Name for plaque	Nick name	Address	Pledged amount	Actual amount
ANIS	ANIS	29 CROFT ST	—	5-00
M.Q. Khan.	QUAD	LEWIS ST	—	2-00
BASHRAT HUSSAIN	BALH	GLADSTONE ST	—	5-00
ALI		"	"	10-00
ADNAN AHMED	DUD	25 ESCOT RD	—	10.00
MUNSAF Mohammed	TAXI 244	—	—	2-00
[illegible]		21 CANNON ST	—	5.00
MOHAMMED QAYUM	—	46 HOSPITAL ST	—	5-00
MAHAMMED BASHIR	—	54 LEWIS ST	—	10-00
	SMILER	MARY ST	—	5-00
MR WHISPY	"	"	"	5-00
ATIF	"	"	"	10-00
SHAMEEM	"	"	"	4-00
NAHEEM	"	GLADSTONE ST	"	10-00
HUSSAIN	"	"	"	5-00
KASHRESHE	"		"	5-00
AMUR	"	"	"	5-00
KALA	"	"	"	5-00
TOLO	"	"	"	5.00
SYIED IFTKHAR	S-ISY	7 MARY ST	—	5-00
WAHID IFTKHAR	WAD		—	5-00
MOHAMMED IFTKAR	IT7		—	5-00
STAR	"	"	"	5-00
MUSSY	"	"	"	10-00
[illegible]	"	"	"	5-00
SAJ	"	"	"	5-00
KASIF	"	"	"	5-00
KAREEM	"	"	"	5-00
RAJA MEHBOOB	"	"	"	5-00
BGANIUB	"	"	"	2-00
SHARAAZ	"	"	"	5-00
TAXI 21	"	"	"	5-00
RAZA	"	"	"	5-00
KAHLID	"	"	"	5-00
MAHMMED	"	"	"	1-75
"	"	"	"	2-70
YASEEN	"	"	"	10-00
Totals SHABAAZ	"	"	"	10-00
SHAFQAT HUSSAIN	SHAF	17 LEWIS ST	"	20-00
SAJID HUSSAIN	Jiga	47 Bloxwich Rd	£10	526-44
				30.11
BANNARAS	—	—	—	10-—

Names of some of the people who donated towards this project, their names were transferred to the plaque – proof of their contribution.

Charlie wanted to involve young kids and with his friends like Balla and many more from the area enough money was raised to build Kala a house.

Charlie done all this from behind a brick dungeon, parents saluted Charlie's good work they were thrilled that their children had been encouraged to do something positive with their lives.

But no one could have been more thrilled than Kala and his family. The money was sent to Kala via the priest who ensured the funds made a house for kala.

It may no seem like nothing much to us but to Kala and his family it a giant leap of hope for the future.

Through the awareness that came about from Charlie's sincerity to help the poor, his name has reached many villages in Kashmir.

Can you imagine that we do not fully understand the torture one feels in this situation as Kala, but Charlie instantly recognised Kala's silent screams'?

I could have easily forgotten about Kala and I even thought that it was impossible for me to do any thing to help him.

It was Charlie who made me stop and think of what I am saying and the selfish act I was about to commit.

I must admit Charlie made me and all the people young and old, who rallied round that day, feel a sense of accomplishment and self worth.

What is ironic is the fact that this types of compassion that Charlie has had all his life and demonstrated at any given opportunity is rarely mentioned or even known other than by those who personally know Charles Bronson.

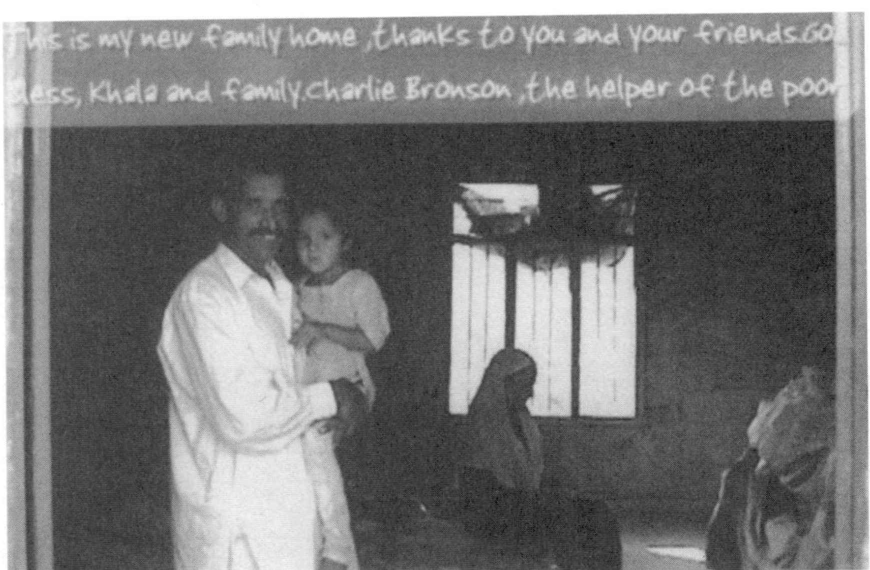

Kala in his new home with his wife and child, with a message from Kala to Charlie

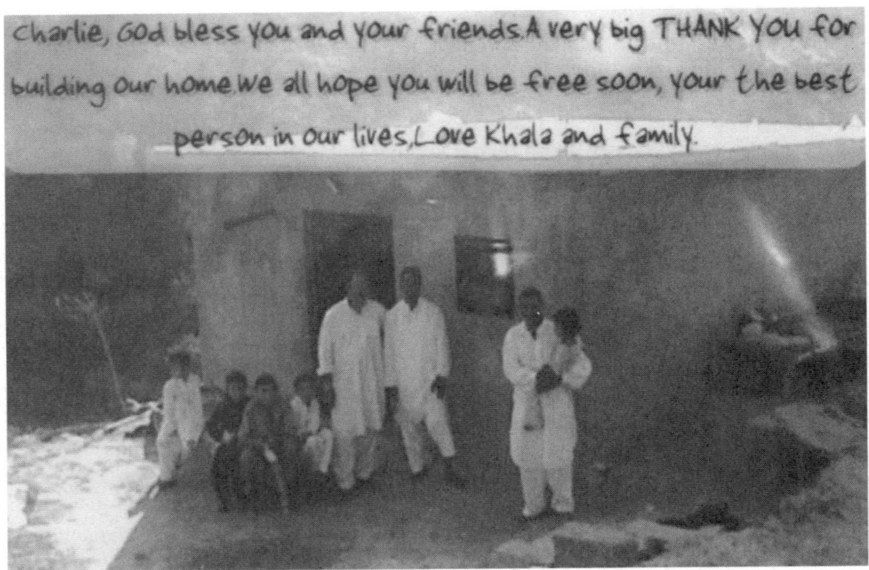

Kala holding his daughter in front of their new home, with a personal message from Kala

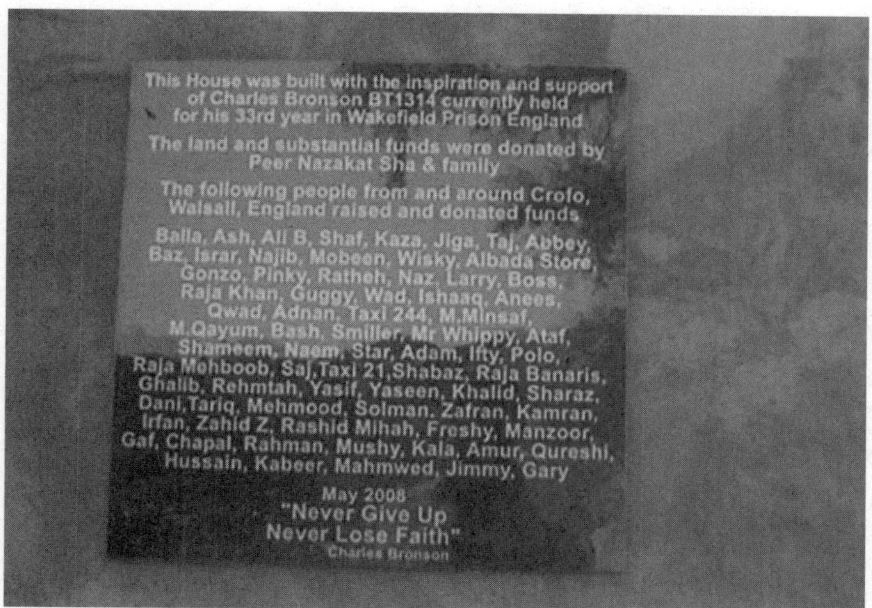

A plaque proudly displayed on Kala's new home. Proof to the people who donated funds, and a personal message from Charlie to Kala.

Kala in the middle with the priest's children. Like many people in Pakistan, they too sincerely support the Free Charles Bronson campaign.

Plaque being placed on the front of the house.

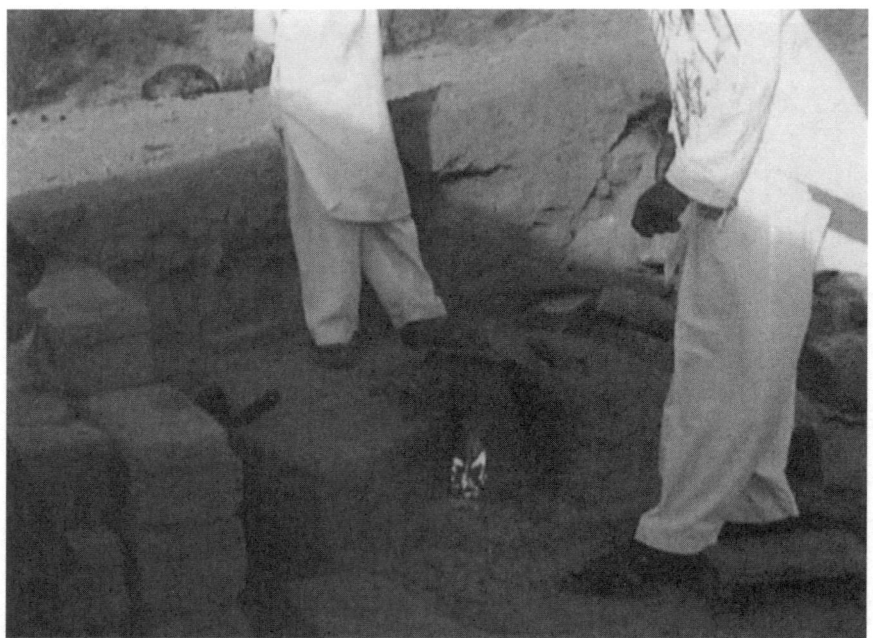

Cooking area outside. There is no gas, electricity or running water here

Me and Kala – final farewells, even at this point I have to promise Kala that I will thank everyone for him, particularly Charlie for making it happen.

Charles Bronson's help the poor Project Kashmir Pakistan 2007-2008

This Man's Home Transformed From This To This

Accomplished Through The Inspiration of This Man

Never Give Up Hope
Never Loose Faith, Charles Bronson

23 July 2008.

It's been a great day today – one of those days that go perfectly. The sun's out and I feel good. All that's missing is a cool glass of beer and some good company. (Not to be.) I got a pile of letters and some canteen. Lovely jubbly! You guys out there in the free world don't realise or understand what a bit of canteen means to us convicts. I got a bag of nuts, some fruit, a bottle of pop, some eggs, a slab of cheese and a bag of sweets! Others may get a packet of tobacco and some KY Jelly. Oh yes, you get plenty of faggots buying their Vaseline and scented soaps for their boyfriends. Bend over, sweetheart. Whoosh… right up to the nuts. Yarrrhhhooooo, ride him cowboy! I'll settle for a bag of pineapple chunks myself! Cheers.

I've got my son Mike coming up tomorrow! Yiiipppeeeeeee. I can't fucking wait and I bet he can't either. My buddy Mark Jones is going to meet him outside the jail, no doubt to get him pissed… Good luck to them.

I see they've just caught the butcher of Bosnia, Radovan Karadzic. It's 13 years he's been on the run. He was the former Bosnia Serb leader who ordered the massacre of thousands of civilians during the 1992-1995 civil war. The Bosnia Muslims and Croats have prayed for his capture for all these years. Justice will now be done as sure as the devil's got a big red cock! He's well and truly fucked.

What about the dwarf Lee Kildare? He's just admitted burglary charges and copped a 12-month community order. The little fucker, he could make a fortune in the criminal world. Use your head, Lee, because you could get in places where others can't! It's not rocket science. Think about it. Fuck me – if I was a dwarf I would be a millionaire for sure.

It must be magic to be so tiny! All day long you would be at fanny level. The women must love a dwarf. There was a dwarf who used to drink in my local and he had a cock on him like a donkey! All the barmaids loved him and he fucked them all. We had a party for him on his 40th birthday and we got this big, fat, roly-poly slag to fuck him senseless! What a laugh it was to see his little arse ramming into all that lard. Yeah, what a party he had. The sick little fucker would shag anything and everything but we all loved him. He was a funny fucker and used to get right nasty when he was pissed. He tried to pick a fight with everybody – even me. One night when he tried it I picked him up and slung him over a wall. "Now fuck off, you little cunt!" I said. He climbed back over with a shovel! "Cunt… put it down," I told him. Whoosh – he took a strike at my head. "Put it down, cunt!" Whoosh – another shot. It only just missed but my kick to his head didn't miss! Cunt. I love a dwarf with bottle! Don't you?

I see the John and Anne Darwin both got six years. Fucking good job. John was the ex-prison officer who faked his own death in a canoe accident. His wife Anne lived a lie and kept living it. Half a million bucks' insurance helps, but fancy lying to her two sons and saying: "Your dad's dead." Being an ex-screw, he'd be good at lying (it's all part of the job). They tell such whoppers that they make MPs seem almost believable! Anyway, get it done, do your bird. Let's see how he likes a door slammed in his 'boat'! He will be kept on the protection wing with all the other ex-screws and dodgy coppers. They stick together like shit to a blanket. "Lights out!" He'll be out in three years then he'll make a million bucks with a movie, books and a play. He could even make a fortune selling canoes! He'll be on all the chat shows and the after dinner speaker circuit. So was it all worth it? Will it be worth three years in jail? Normally I would say, "Too fucking right," but in his case even £100 million couldn't compensate for his betrayal of his two sons. He killed himself off and they grieved for a dead dad. To them he's dead and that's a hell of a lot to live with. No dosh is worth that!

I see my old mate Perry Wharrie copped a 30-year sentence over a £350 million cocaine deal. I bet he was fitted up. He's already served 16 years of a life sentence! It fucking breaks my heart to hear all this. But that's showbiz for you.

They've put Amy Winehouse in Madame Tussauds. I wonder if she's in the horror section! What a great singer though – fucking brilliant. Imagine waking up with that next to you. "HELP!"

What about this American loony Eric Tavulares? He watched the movie *Natural Born Killers* then strangled his girlfriend. Death row for you, buddy. Burn, you mad bastard! *Mad Bastard* would be a great title for a book. *Mad Bastards* by Charlie Bronson! It would be about all the mad hatters I've met on my journey through the asylums. It's the perfect project for me.

Did you know Ricky Hatton's PA is ex-Manchester police detective Paul Speak? He was Old Bill for 22 years! I can't work that one out. Fuck having an ex-copper run your fan club. I wouldn't trust him as far as I could throw him! Of all the lovely people Ricky could pick to run his fan club, it's old filth. I'm amazed and confused! Still, that's Ricky's bizz. I just can't trust the Old Bill and I doubt I ever will. How can I? Could you if you were in my shoes? They're fucking walking a road that goes one way when mine goes in the opposite direction. Fuck off! Stay out of my road and I'll stay out of yours. Sweet.

Did you know the legendary gunfighter and lawman Wyatt Earp refereed the great fight between Bob Fitzsimmons and Tom Sharkey? Tonto (the Lone Ranger's partner) was Jay Silverheels – a full-blooded Mohawk Indian. Both he and singer Jackie Wilson were Golden Glove boxing champions. Howz about that? A lot of people don't know this stuff. Remember you got it from Loonyology! Fantastic or what? It's not all mad, is it? Knowledge is dangerous; it's why I'm so ruthless when I need to be. I'm just a clever cunt; I can't help it. I'm just sharing my knowledge with you all so respect it or fuck off! OK?

Did you know that if you'd bought £1,000 of McDonald's shares back in 1967 they'd be worth £66 million today? Now that's mind-blowing, fucking frightening, beyond sanity, and it's a fact. But who would've bought £1,000 of McDonald's shares then? No-one knew who McDonald's were. We all know now! If only we'd known then.

I got a letter from Mich and Kitch out in Torrevieja (Spain). They're doing well in their new bar. My Lorraine and Andy just took Dave Courtney there for a meal. It's a tonic to read they're doing so well. Save me a table for later.

Another letter I got today was from a Loony in Rampton asylum who writes:

Mr Bronson,
I've just finished reading your *Loonyology* book and some of the nurses here remember you. One told me you were a horrible, nasty bastard who did nothing but cause trouble. He told me about the time you strangled John White in the day room and you were laughing as you did it! You're a psycho, Mr Bronson and you should die in that cage you're in! You seem to think you'll get out one day! Keep dreaming, Mr Bronson.

Mad Jake.

Well thanks, Jake, but you must be mad to listen to those silly screws. Don't believe all they tell you or you'll end up even madder than they are. And bear in mind it's 30 years since I was there. I was a young man on a mission to fuck up their precious little regime and, if I say so myself, I did a good job. I must have done, for them to still talk about me three decades later. I left my mark in the asylum's history! So what are you doing, Mad Jake (apart from licking arse)? Don't write to me again, as I've got three good brothers there who will rip your throat out for the fun of it. One word from me and you cop it so get sane and fuck off, you traitor. Go and have a cup of tea with the lovely nurses, you cunt.

I called up my brother Mark and Mum! All's well at home. All in all it was a good day and I even said, "Good morning," to the governor! (I'll probably tell him to fuck off tomorrow. You can't be nice all the time!)

Mark Emmins' dog Kayla, a beautiful German Shepherd, died. She was 10 years old. I'll create a nice tribute art for her so she lives on. It's always sad when a family loses a dog but that's what life is: death. A black cloud sucks away the soul and the heart stops beating. It's stillness – eternal sleep. Good night!

24 July 2008.
I woke up at 5.30am and lay still till 6am, thinking about my son. It was 30 minutes of joy. I can't help loving my son Mike. He's a chip off the old block and he's coming up to see his old man! Yiiipppeeeee! Yaarrhhoooooooooo! By 6.30am I'd washed, made the bed, cleaned my teeth and polished off some press-ups. A fresh day is a new chapter of life and it's wonderful!

I had Rice Krispies for breakfast. A big man's brekkie! HA HA HA HA. What a fucking joke. Then I posted out six letters. I hope you lot out there appreciate my letters because it comes out of my canteen spend. Please send me stamps or self-addressed envelopes; I'm not a fucking post office general! A Snickers bar comes first in my canteen, not a stamp!

I went on the monthly meeting just before lunch. The governor was in there, with probation and psychology and a few screws. It's all red tape shit but I thought I'd best attend to put my case over to them. Stop taking the piss and let me move on! Ten minutes later I'm back in my flowery dell and they're still talking a load of shit. Who are they kidding apart from themselves? They don't fucking kid the kidder! No fucker pulls the wool over my eyes.

Talking of wool, did you read about the guy in South Wales who got caught having a threesome? "So what?" you say. Well, it was with sheep. Dirty cunt. How can a man have sex with two sheep? He's the fucking animal. Some poor sod's got to eat them! Fancy eating one after he's shagged it?

Another pile of letters today! I got ten. Now get my meaning? How can I reply to ten? That's £3.50 out of my canteen! Fuck that; my canteen is my No. 1 priority!

The visit with Mike went well. We had a brilliant two hours and he looked fit and well. I showed him my chair handstands because he likes to see me do my acrobatics. What son doesn't love to see his dad do that? Only some dads are fat, lazy cunts who can't even wipe there arses properly. Cunts, get off your fat arses and show your sons how it's done. I gave Mike two poster-sized pieces of art: one for him and one for Johnny Griffiths. Yeah, it was a great visit! Thanks, son. Max respect!

Friday tomorrow! This week's flown by. It's actually going so fast I can't keep up with it. My head's still stuck in Tuesday! Then again, it is Loonyology.

I called Mark Fish. He's off to the Matt Legg fight in two weeks and says he'll pick Roy Shaw up on his way. It's going to be a great comeback fight for Matt. Knock him silly, Matt. We're all in your corner, mate!

It was jacket potato and curry beans for tea! Shit. That's not a man tea, is it? But I've got a pint of sweet tea and I've got a slice of malt loaf for supper so fuck 'em! Hey, they don't call me the 'Birdman' for fuck all!

I got a lovely letter from the lovely Gemini Reywolds in Cyprus. She's a hot cookie. She's that sort of classy chick who could make you come and come and come again! You know the sort: hot and sticky with that sweet smell of sex – pussy tears; droplets of lust! Who needs sugar? Pussy juice is sweeter! Some chicks never have it; they pretend to but they never reach the max. They can't handle the madness! It's like breaking in a horse: some horses just can't be broken! They're wild and crazy and that's how a real woman should be! Crazy like Gemini: a lady when the occasion calls but a lunatic in the bedroom. Yiiipppeeeeeee! Ride it, cowgirl!

I'll tell you what's lovely: pull your cock out of a juicy fanny and let your cowgirl lick it, then suck her tongue and taste her fanny juices! Awesome. It beats a Curly Wurly or a toffee apple! I heard that Pamela Anderson's favourite sex position is the 'windmill'. Er, hello, what's that? That's a new one to me but it sounds good.

Who remembers that 1970s song *Ride The Swan* by T-Rex? I'll never forget it because I once walked into a lunatic's cell in Broadmoor and that was blaring out while this big fat fucker was sucking one loony off and wanking off two others. It was a lunatics' foursome. If that doesn't put you off your Rise Krispies, nothing will. It was fucking madness gone sick! You could smell the insanity of it creeping through your skin. This big fat cunt of a lunatic was in his applecart. He was known as the 'Cocksucker' and he sucked more bell-ends than fag-ash Lill! His fat, fucked-up face stunk of spunk! There's no smell on earth like stale spunk. It's no wonder I ended up hitting him with a rolling pin. Crash... fuck off. That's one off for the infirmary.

I hit another guy in Parkhurst with a rolling pin. Smack... fuck off! They are very naughty tools, take it from me. They're solid wood. Crunch... the skull fractures! It does the bizz; it's lights out. I reckon I could get a job in Hollywood as an advisor on violent movies. There's fuck all I don't know about violence! I was a professional – the best. (Who's better?) Those movie directors would love me on their set! "No, no, stop… not like that, like this! Don't use that, use this. Fuck off; you don't hit him there, you hit him here! Quick, fast, a good chop like this. That's it: hard between the eyes. Grab his nose, squeeze and twist… lovely! Whack him in the kidneys like this! One good crack. Lovely!" How good would I be? The best.

Oh well, that's a great day over and buried. Thank you, son. Love ya to bits! Keep the dream alive, Mike!

Dad x

25th July, 2008.

What a great sleep I had last night. I was dreaming of Mike and me, fishing, shooting, travelling, shagging some birds, having a party – living. I'm going to tell you all something now (and I mean what I say and I say what I mean): a father and son bond is priceless! No fucker on this planet can take away the love between a father and his son – no fucker. It's a special bond between two men and the blood flows as one. The genes are the same and we are the same. They say insanity is hereditary. If so, then my son's a mad hatter and I love him even more for it! He doesn't just look like me, he thinks like me, because he *is* me. Together we are a force to be reckoned with! It's simple: don't fuck with us! Don't fuck with the unknown! Let's leave it at that. Father and son – respect!

Yeah, I feel good today. I've got a sort of buzzing feeling, a flow of hope, a sprinkle of faith and a lot of good thoughts. There are good solid vibes and I think something good is on its way! I can feel it in my bones. Watch this space.

Astronaut Edgar Mitchell was on the Apollo 14 mission in 1971 and was the sixth man to walk on the moon. He now says there are aliens which look like ET and his space agency pals have already made contact with them. Well that blows religion away for sure. What will happen when the little green men land? I can't fucking wait, can you?

It was Coco Pops, a jam roll and a mug of tea for breakfast! Talk about Beslan! (For those of you who don't know about Beslan then look it up in your history books. It's a fucking disgrace if you don't know. Everybody should know about Beslan, especially the kids.) Food is priceless, Heaven-sent, so respect it. Beans on toast are a luxury for some, remember that. Coco Pops… don't make me laugh! The veg soup for dinner was good though. Plenty of goodness in it and six bread rolls to mop it up. Yeah, lovely!

I got my Luton paper and six letters plus a book. You're never going to guess which book. Come on, three guesses. I'll give you a clue: I slung it in the bin! I took one look at it and that was enough. It was the Bible; some old lady from Bristol sent it. Sorry, love, it's not for me. It's very kind of you but I can't read that crap, I prefer *Viz* or a boxing magazine or a crime thriller. To me, the Bible represents hypocrisy. Religion is full of deceitful phonies, insane people pretending to be purified and weak-minded, spineless fakes. Wake up and come to reality! It's the biggest deception on our planet. It makes my skin crawl when I see all those bishops in flowing gowns carrying their sticks. HA! HA! HA! HA! HA! They all wear tight little panties underneath. (Well, maybe not all but plenty do.) Amen.

It's on… it's here!
The time is now
All the training, all the pain
All the blood and all the tears
Here we go!
The noise, the lights, the heat!
That walk from the dressing room
Into the ring
The cheers, the boos!
They love you, they hate you!
It's time…
Time to do the bizz
Punch your way to victory
Or crumble to the canvas
Punch for punch, blow for blow
It's on… it's here
The time is now
Best man wins
Or does he?
Ding ding, it's off
Hit hit. Hit him. Knock him out!
Bust his ribs, destroy him
Attack, attack, attack!
Two men
Gladiators of the 20th century
One may die
Both will bleed
Ding ding!
The things we do for money!
Isn't it wonderful?
Ding ding!

I got a letter off Di Brown today. She's a hot cookie, born sexy, and she knows it! Some women are born to be sexy – look at Joan Collins, the ultimate sex machine! Even now at her ripe old age you wouldn't kick her out of bed. It's all in a woman's eyes and her mind; she penetrates your soul and sucks you in! Next time you're shagging your partner, look into her eyes and you'll see the real woman. It's all in those eyes. If there's nothing there then you're shagging a stiff, a dead soul, a soulless bitch. Move on. The eyes speak volumes so learn to read them.

I once went out with a lovely girl (who shall remain nameless) and we used to shag to Percy Sledge's 'When A Man Loves A Woman'. She used to cry and I would lick the tears away! Yeah, Loonyology. They were obviously tears of happiness, that's why they tasted sweet! Only tears of sadness taste sour.

Did you know there are approximately 45 million mobile phones in the

UK? Fuck me; that's a lot of mobiles. Some cunt's getting rich! There are still some cancer scientists who say they cause brain cancer so be careful, you mobile phone users! It could be more dangerous than smoking.

I see little Maddie McCann is still missing 14 months after disappearing in Portugal. How sad is that? She vanished in thin air but some fucker knows the truth and one day it will be found out. It always does. I think in cases like Maddie's, torture should be used. You grab a suspect and grill them; it's that simple. "Talk, cunt... or scream!"

Blimey, I've just found the canteen slip I got the other day. I know you guys love to clock what I've bought so here it is:

ARAMARK

HMP Wakefield

BRONSON
BT1314

Location : S - 2 - 006
Ref : 0807001356 22/07/2008

Phone Credit	7	£7.00
H.S. NAS Orange Squash 1ltr	1	£0.65
Nescafe Coffee Sachet One Cup	6	£0.48
UHT Whole Milk 500ml	2	£0.92
Princes Chopped Tomatoes 400g	1	£0.44
Jamaica Bun	1	£1.16
T[illegible]i 9pk	1	£1.09
Heinz Tomato Soup 400g	2	£1.40
Jif Lemon Juice 55ml	1	£0.41
C.Rich Salted Peanuts 300g	1	£0.97
Cadbury's Dairy Milk 50g	1	£0.40
Tunes - Cherry Flavour	1	£0.51
Eggs 6pk	2	£1.14
Tomatoes x 3	1	£0.57
Fresh Fruit Pack - Banana x 3	1	£0.64

ORDER TOTAL £17.78

Not bad, eh? Seven quid of it went on phone calls (and I hope those I call appreciate it because it comes out of my canteen spends) but I do enjoy a phone call. By the way, those Jamaica buns are delicious!

Right, who's ready for a bit of penal history? You'll love this. Newgate prison was destroyed in the great fire of London in 1672 so it was rebuilt. The most famous of its executioners was the dreaded Jack Ketch. He once took five strokes with an axe to kill a prisoner and he also killed Lord Russell with a saw! This fucker was a serious psycho. Torture and heads being chopped off were daily events in Newgate. A lot of executions were held in the public square and folk used to bring picnic baskets for a day out at the bloodbath. Fuck me; what a carry on! That's what you call doing bird!

Did you know the only way a condemned woman could be saved from death was if she was pregnant? Lots of Newgate screws were 'bought' by villains to shag their women in the hope of saving them. Even then, some would only be committed to life or sent to the pillory or transported to the Australian colony as prisoners. These were seriously hard times! There were maggots in the food, rats, cockroaches, shit on the walls, piss on the floor and wooden bed boards. Fuck me – it reminds me of Wandsworth in the 1960s. HA! HA! HA! HA! HA! HA! Newgate was Hell on Earth but it would've been so easy to escape with outside help, as the security in those days was extremely primitive. I would've walked out and left behind a pile of bodies. That place was insanity gone mental! Loonyology.

I had chips, pork pie and tomatoes for tea, and it was bloody lovely. I'm having a thick slice of my Jamaica bun later with a mug of coffee. Do I live it up or do I live it up? I told you I'm a lucky fucker!

I got a letter from Billy Cooper today. He lives in my town Luton and he's a smashing bloke who always keeps in touch. That's what mates are for. The system would love nothing better than to see me old, alone and forgotten so they could take serious liberties – maybe even kill me off. I'd put nothing past these fuckers".

Oh! The cannibal's done his back in and he's walking about like a crab. Fucking good job too.

There's an Iraqi prisoner just arrived from Doncaster jail who's alleged to have stabbed another con. They've got him on the other side from us. I wonder if he knows about the time I grabbed three Iraqis hostage? I'll have to get a message to him to let him know I've found peace and I love all walks of life! Peace, man. Search for your hearts, brothers; reach inside and find yourselves. Yeah, that's me today! Just don't upset me or I'll smash your face in and crush your spine. Peace, man...

It's been a great day and I've enjoyed myself. I had a wonderful dump. It was one of those logs that you can feel so proud of: skinny and alive. It slipped out so gently and peacefully! When I have a shit like that I feel so blessed. I feel so grateful that I'm able to lay a log like that. Let's face reality here: some poor sods would love to shit like us real shitters but they have to empty colostomy bags or suffer with diarrhoea. Some can't even control their bowels! So be proud you shitters; I salute you all. Isn't it a miracle how such a large log can squeeze out of such a little hole? The human body is awesome! YARHHhhooooooo, YEEOooowwwwwww, Yiiipppeeeeeeeeeee! It was a shame to flush it away! What wouldn't I do to slip it into Bob Maudsley's pillow case? This solitary is so cruel – it stops me having fun! HA! HA! HA! HA! HA! HA!

You'll love this: Father Eric Woodhead, a priest in Suffolk, has just been jailed for two years for stealing 90 grand from the church. And get on this: the old cunt's an alcoholic! (You just can't make this shit up.) God save your soul, Father. Cunt, you're a thieving bastard just like all of us. Throw your dog collar away and accept the truth: Satan's got your arse. Amen!

I'm off to bed for a fucking good laugh! I really am, I'm going to enjoy myself for half an hour and just laugh. A good laugh helps keep the stress away! It's good for the heart.

Don't rely on anybody to show you the way. Carry your own map in your head. Remember that and remember this: you can't die with an overdose of love.

Good night! (Is that noise coming from your wardrobe?)

26 July 2008.

"Happy Birthday to you! Happy Birthday to you!" It's Mick Jagger's 65th birthday today! He's on his way to Route 66... What a legend, what a band – they're icons. The Rolling Stones kick arse (probably shag a few, too).

Fuck me, what a hot day; it's the hottest day of 2008 up to now and all I'm doing is sweat. There's nothing worse than a hot, sticky, airless day when you're locked up 24/7! It's fucking insane and it stinks, it really does! This is beach weather – ice cream and sunbathing, not doing time in a 12-foot by eight-foot coffin. You lucky fuckers out there! Even the screws' shirts smell of BO! Come to think of it, some of them always stink of BO… I gave my cell a good going over with a green brillo pad and soapy water, so it's now spotless and smells of soap – a nice hygienic smell, like a hospital.

Saturday is the big fry-up meal – a once in a week treat! I love it; it's a proper English nosh-up! I got six letters and none were mad ones so there's not a lot to write about really.

Hey, what about this dirty bastard Dominic Liversedge? He's another copper who's been caught playing around with a kid. He's 27 and he's copped a 12-month prison sentence for fondling a 14-year-old girl. He was in love with her and even had a tattoo of her name put on his wrist. What sort of man cops off with a 14-year-old kid? A fucking pervo. He got sentenced in Luton! Cunt. That's the British Old Bill for you: they don't have to catch the paedos, they *are* the paedos! I would've given this nonce ten years' hard labour. The dirty nonce just wanted a little virgin pussy all to himself, the dirty bastard. And he was a sergeant! It's no wonder our police force are hated and not trusted when they're the villains! (Hey, if you kids want to make crime pay then become a lawyer!)

Did you know Joan Rivers is 75 years old? I actually think she's still a very sexy woman! Yeah, yeah, I know she's had plenty of cosmetic surgery and probably looks more 95 without the make-up on, but I'm talking sexy as in a real woman! Her eyes sparkle, she's got character, she's got style and she's very dirty! Come and sort me out, Joan! You just know she's up for a good seeing-to and to top it all, she's one of the world's true survivors. She really is a great lady in my book – a very hot cookie – and all she would ever do is make you laugh and feel good. What a woman; a star! She's the sort of lover who would say, "Is in it yet?" after you've been banging away for 15 minutes. I just love a cheeky, funny lover. Joan would be the perfect match for me! I'd probably laugh myself into a massive heart attack.

I had salad for tea. There was a nice big lump of cheese with it too, so I've done well. It's been a lazy old day! What would be nice now, just to end the day, would be a good long swim in a nice cool lake. That'd be a dream come true.

Talking of lakes, there was a lunatic in Parkhurst who drowned his wife and her lover in one up in Cumbria back in the 1970s. And do you want to know something? He was one of the happiest cons I ever met! He was always smiling, whistling, singing and he had that bounce in his step of a man who's forever happy. He had no regrets and he served his double life sentence like a man. He walked tall! Right or wrong, he'd killed the cheating bitch and her lover boy. In his eyes he'd done what most men only think of doing. Most men are too weak to do it. They'd accept it and live on in shame like a little field mouse! Squeak, fucking squeak. Cunts, letting your old lady have a shag behind your back! But that's how true life is. It's Loonyology, it's fucking insane! Yiiipppeeeeeee!

I once tried water-polo but my horse drowned.

Wandering in the darkness
Feeling only pain
Stepping on the broken glass
Grabbing hold of razor blades
Swallowing pills by the dozen
On the road to Hell
Someone turn the heat up
Melt until you yell.

Talking of Hell, Ian Brady now wants to be cremated. He's made his will, so burn the bastard with a can of petrol and a match. That'll be one less monster to feed. Fuck political correctness and human rights, I'll do it for him. End of.

Wandering in the darkness
Feeling only pain
Someone stabbed my eyes out
Now I've gone insane
I crept across a sheet of glass
It cracked and I fell through
Splinters of glass pierced my head
Thank fuck for superglue.

What about the lunatic in Rampton who superglued a cork up his arse and plastic in his ears? Why? Because he's a fucking lunatic; that's what lunatics do. Wake up, it's a nuthouse.

Wandering in the darkness
Feeling only pain
I stepped onto a railway line
The train smashed in my brain
My head flew off my body
It glided through the sky
Nothing seemed to matter
The truth does never lie.

What about the lunatic who got caught shagging a wheelie bin? Yeah, a fucking wheelie bin! Nothing is safe from Loonyology.

Wandering in the darkness
Feeling only pain
I fell into a wishing well
They pulled me out insane
A rat bit half my ear off
A worm slid up my nose
In the darkness screaming
With a blood red rose

Poetry! It brings me alive and lights me up inside. It's better than anything (well… nearly anything). There was a top poet in Walton jail in the mid 1970s. I'm fucked if I can remember his name; we just called him 'the poet'. A lot of the cons used to bung him a bit of canteen in return for a nice poem for their girlfriends. The poet was never short of a bit of canteen! He must have created hundreds of love poems and he kept a lot of couples together. See, prison is full of all walks of life! It's not all about evil cunts and psychos and bank robbers. You wouldn't believe some of those who're inside. Some are wonderful characters and I've met them all.

One such character was an old con called Jack Turner. One day I was doing some pull-ups under the big metal stairs in Parkhurst (I used to put my fingers in the holes and do a good 50 pull-ups; it was murder on the fingers but magic on the shoulders) when he walked over to me and said, "Hi, Charlie, how are you?"

"Yeah, not bad, Pop. All sweet," I said. "How's yourself?"

He sat down and called me over. We had a good, long chat and many more chats after that. I learned a lot from him. He'd been lifed off back in 1963 and was a wise old owl. He'd seen it, done it and got the scars! He was what we call 'a real con' in the game and was well into his 70s when I met him in 1978. He had served 15 years then and he served another 10 before he made it out as a very old man. He then went straight to an old folks' home.

Was it all worth it for him? Did he really ever win? Yeah, he sure did because I still have fond memories of him, the old rascal! Jack never had a son but I think I could've been the son he never had. He was kind to me – not that he ever had a lot but he never needed a lot. He was a man of wisdom and was rich in knowledge. He actually told me in 1978 that I would live to become something. He predicted my life would change and said I stood out from the rest because I had a gift of life. Jack said all this to me but it went in one ear and out the other! I was more interested in doing my pull-ups and press-ups. I kept in touch with him as I moved around the country's jails but over the years life rips people apart. (At one time even my family became strangers to me.) But it's great to look back on such wonderful memories!

Old Jack Turner remains a pleasant memory. I've never forgotten him and I never will. By the way, he got his life sentence for killing a kiddie fiddler. He strangled the cunt to death and burned the body in a big oil drum! He cremated a monster! He should've got an OBE rather than a life sentence. I salute the old rascal and so do many others. R.I.P. Amen.

What about the 'birdman of Wetherby'? Wetherby is a young offender's prison in Yorkshire and the governor is allowing them to breed racing pigeons. That's a good governor they've got there! Let's have three cheers for Governor Styles! HIP HIP – HOORAY! HIP HIP – HOORAY! HIP HIP – HOORAY! (Not too many governors would allow that.) But get on this: one young lad there is called Adam Bird and he loves breeding pigeons! (I bet your thinking I'm making this shit up. Drop Adam or the governor a letter and they'll confirm it!) It's fantastic. I've already put in an application to have a pair of eagles. Fuck pigeons (unless it's pigeon pie!) but it's great and very positive for the young cons to be allowed to do such things. We need more governors like Mr Styles!

I'll tell you who's a fucking right nonce: Richard Moulding. He used to get kids as young as 10 to sign contracts agreeing to have sex for money. Dirty bastard. The Old Bill found some DVDs of him having sex with the kids and he copped a life sentence with a tariff of only eight years! He could be back on the streets in less than ten years so watch out, kids. Moulding admitted to 22 charges including rape and sexual assault on children, some as young as six. So the question is: why only an eight-year tariff? Why not 20 or 30 years? I'll tell you why (it's simple): the law doesn't give a fuck about your kids! To me it's blatantly obvious that this cunt is a serious danger to society, and eight years is a fucking joke. British justice? I wipe my arse on it!

I got a letter from my old buddy Harry Roberts who's down in Littlehay jail. He's just had his 72nd birthday and he's been inside for 46 of them. What a survivor. He's been shot at by Kenyan and Malayan terrorists and has been awarded bravery medals by the British army! This man is a true hero but people have short memories and he got a life sentence with a 30-year tariff. That's double the time Moulding will serve! That sums it all up for me. It's fucking madness gone insane!

I see Iran has just hanged 29 criminals in the biggest public execution in years! They were all convicted drug traffickers, rapists and murderers. They don't fuck about over there! Phew, not 'arf! There are another 74 convicts (who were all over 18 when they committed their crimes) waiting to hang. Most are kept in solitary in the notorious Evin prison. Let's face it, the Iranians don't play games. With so many hangings it's no wonder there are a lot of flies out there! Amnesty International says Iran executed 317 convicts in 2007 and only one country in the world killed more. Can you guess which? I'll give you some clues: chopsticks, snake eyes and paddy fields. Yeah, you got it: China! They snuffed out 470 in 2007! So all you youngsters who are thinking of setting out on the road to crime, don't go to China or Iran or you could well end up getting your neck stretched!

Did you know coconuts kill more people than sharks or that a greyhound can go from 0 to 40mph in one second? One fucking second! That's awesome – unbelievable. Did you know a golf hole has a diameter of four inches? Here's a blinder that will blow your socks off! Keith Richards of the Rolling Stones was a choir boy in the Queen's Coronation! (I bet that's blown you away.) Keith, a bleeding choir boy? Hard to believe, eh? But it's true! You never know what's coming next in Loonyology. Even I don't; that's why it's brilliant! I take my readers on a journey of madness. Keith Richards a choir boy? You can only get that sort of thing out of one of my books. It's so insane but it's so true! I fucking love it. Watch out for those coconuts because their shells are a lot harder than your skull! If one drops and hits you, you'll die (or be seriously brain damaged), so be warned.

I'm fucked so I'm going to call it a day now. It's hot, airless and I'm a bit bored, but I'll be back.

29 July 2008.

I woke up this morning halfway through a dream where I was robbing a bank in the Wild West. It was fucking brilliant. Did you know Billy the Kid killed 21 men and robbed 100 banks in his lifetime? He died at 21 when that snake of a rat Pat 'Coward' Garrett shot him in the back, like the cunt he was. Jesse James killed 25 men and robbed over 100 banks, trains and stagecoaches! They were both legends of the West, proper blaggers, men of rock – and I'll tell you now, both these men's graves get more visitors than any President's grave. Who the fuck wants to visit the likes of J Edgar Hoover? Do you? It's Jesse and the Kid who you want to see! Their graves are legendary because they were true legends!

Did you know Hoover was a cross-dresser? Yeah, kinky cunt! Could you see Jesse James in silk panties or Billy the Kid in a frock? HA! HA! HA! HA! HA! Could you fuck! They were true, fearless men who lived hard and fought hard. I salute them…

Yeah, it was a nice dream. I woke up just as the safe door flew off and smashed into the bank manager's head. He shouldn't have had such a big head, the cunt.

Fuck me; it's another hot, sticky day! Coco Pops for breakfast again (stop laughing, it's not funny) and mushroom soup for lunch. I counted six mushrooms in mine; not bad for a bowl of prison swill but the six bread rolls made it better! I enjoy a few rolls.

I got 10 letters in today! There were some blinders too, with lots of news. I love a bit of news! I heard that my old mate Lenny Drummond just copped seven years (but he was expecting 12 so he got a good result). He's at Belmarsh but they'll probably move him next week to Shitmoor by mistake. Seven years is easily done; they soon fly by. It's not a bad sentence considering he almost took a bloke's face off with a cut-throat razor! But the cunt deserved it as he was playing about with a 12-year-old girl, so fuck the old fuck face. At least the kids can now see him coming. "Watch out, here comes old fuck face! Uncle Lenny cut him up for noncing a little girl! Fuck face, fuck face, fuck face." That's how to deal with a nonce. Lenny will do seven years on his head, easy.

I got my monthly report today! It says the 24th on it but I got it on the 29th! To me it's just another wasted month and a total load of bollocks. If you can work it out then let me know, because it baffles me, it really does…

MONTHLY REVIEW

CHARLIE BRONSON

The monthly reviews should take place 1 week prior to the CSCSC and will act as the report, which is submitted to this Committee.

The purpose of the monthly review is to consider progress from the previous month and revise behavioural monitoring targets for the next month.

Date of Review: 24th July 2008

Attendance list names of people attending review

WING GOVERNOR WING S/O WING OFFICER PSYCHOLOGY PROBATION	[redacted]

Begin the review by reviewing the progress over the last month. Examining the weekly reviews/behavioural monitoring can act as a good reminder. How has the prisoner progressed overall? and how have they progressed on particular targets over the month?

This discussion will form the basis of the monthly report for the CSCSC.

Do not complete the behavioural checklist during this review, rather, go through it and decide whether any targets have been consistently met and can come off and what further targets it may be helpful to add. The Prisoner should be invited to input into this process and targets should be agreed collaboratively during the review.

At any one time a maximum of 10 targets should be set
Remember, targets are not being assessed at this review, they are being updated following a discussion about progress.

Overarching Target identified by LSP and OASys documents, such as *'Learn to manage stress more effectively'*	**Targets** These should always be positively framed and should take the form of a statement, e.g. *"completes stress management session with officer Smith each week".*	**Staff Action** This refers to things staff may want to agree to do to support the target, for example, *'Officer Smith to agree a time with Mr Bloggs at the beginning of each week for when the session can take place'*
	Charlie to continue to interact positively with staff on the unit.	Charlie
	Charlie to make use of the CSC Unit facilities	Charlie
	Charlie to Identify possible in cell activities on the unit.	Charlie
	Charlie to remain adjudication free.	Charlie
	Charlie to continue to engage with any reports over the next month.	Charlie
	Charlie to consider working with psychology and probation department.	Personnel officer to discuss this with Charlie.

Crisis Plan

Charlie's medical intervention if required will be made through the healthcare centre at HMP Wakefield. *Charlie's will be offered support from the Humber centre if appropriate, or requested.*

This report is to be completed by an SO following the monthly case review. An overall assessment of the month's progress should be reflected in this report with specific comments on targets set. It should be a reflection of the Multi-disciplinary teams view.

Previous minutes read and agreed.

Charlie continued to use the unit's facilities during this month.

He has continued to interact well with all members of staff who work or attend the unit.

There will be no change to the phone system until at least after Charlie's DLP to which he has been informed by Governor Brook.

Charlie attended this review and started with the issues over the alleged threats to one of his visitors. He stated that this had been taken out of all context and that this is the way that himself and his peers talk to one another.

He also raised the point of his progression from Wakefield CSC and wanted to know when he would be moving on. Stating that he felt this was another wasted month.

His DLP will be held on the unit on the 29/08/2008.

Unlock level to remain the same at this time.

Completed by: **CSC Team** Date: 24/07/2008
(On behalf of the MDT)

Recommendation to the CSCSC
Completed by the Chair on behalf of the Multi-disciplinary Team

Charlie to remain within CSC at Wakefield and is correctly placed at this time, his requests will be raised at the next CSC Committee meeting.

Date: 24 July 2008. Signed:

Prisoner Comments
Date: 29-7. 2008

WHY AM I EVEN HERE?
WHY CANT I BE LET OUT OF ISOLATION?

I'll tell you what's tragic: the poor, forgotten souls of Long Grove asylum in Surrey. Long Grove was a mental hospital for a 100 years or more but it closed down in 1992. However, between 1943 and 1957, 43 suspected typhoid carriers were sent there to be put on an isolation ward. When Long Grove closed down it was found that two women were still in isolation four decades later! The poor souls had been driven insane.

Firstly, you need to ask: why send them to a lunatic asylum in the first place? Secondly, even if they did have typhoid – so what? Antibiotics could treat that. How the fuck could this happen? Even old nursing staff have spoken up at the unjust way these typhoid patients were treated. What about the families? Why did they sit back and allow such liberties? OK, 1943 was a tough era what with the war going on and the misery and the scare of typhoid. But again, why put these women in a fucking cuckoo house? And why forget them? These poor women were sent there to be forgotten.

Mrs Kennett, a retired ward manager, stated that these people were condemned to a life of isolation through no fault of their own. Another nurse, May Heffernan, who started to work there in the 1960s, said, "All the patients there had mental health problems, but staff were reluctant to go inside the isolation ward. As a nation we failed these people and we could have done better." Hugh Pennington, a professor of bacteria at Aberdeen University, said, "These women would only have posed a small risk and what happened to them was not at all necessary. There was a big fear factor about typhoid, a bit like leprosy. They were locked up because it was the easiest thing to do!" He said, "It would appear that the women had simply been forgotten in the system." Yep, that's how it is… or was: 20, 30, 40, even 50 years stolen away. It breaks my fucking heart; it's beyond cruelty. It seems to me these poor souls landed in Long Grove with a very serious red alert warning to isolate them and that's exactly what was done! They were forgotten people and it's fucking shameful – a bloody disgrace. (But what's new? That's the asylum world for all to see… Loonyology.)

Incidentally, the last major outbreak of typhoid in England was in Croydon, South London back in 1937, which killed 43 people. Typhoid is a disease associated with insanitary conditions and even today it affects 17 million people a year around the world, with an estimated 600,000 deaths. That's a lot of bodies. That's typhoid for you; thank your lucky stars you live in Britain and not a third world country. Again I ask: why send suspected typhoid patients to an asylum? If you find out, let me know!

I called Mum today and all's well at home. She's fit and well. I also sent Nina Camplin a visiting order. She's now graduated (with honours) in Art and I'm so proud of her. What a great artist and a good soul she is. We'll do some projects together later for sure! It's taken her five years to achieve that BA, so let's have three cheers for Nina! HIP HIP – HOORAY! HIP HIP – HOORAY! HIP HIP – HOORAY!

I also got a smashing letter from a young con in Feltham who's just read my *Solitary Fitness* book and is bang into his cell work-outs as a result. That sort of letter always cheers me up. Go for it, son – stay healthy. Since reading that book he's stopped smoking and taking drugs, so there's another lad I've helped. How many has the system helped? Wake up, you cunts; it's me that helps them, not you!

Darren Powell is another buddy who hasn't been approved to visit me and won't ever get to see me till I'm free. They haven't given any reason but if I know Darren, he won't accept it – he'll be straight onto his MP and solicitor! He won't be fobbed off; he's a working-class man, he pays his taxes and he'll demand to know why he can't visit me. The police passed him OK, so it must be somebody up in HQ that's playing silly games again. This shit doesn't ever stop. I'm convinced it's done to stir things up! Oh well, let them play their silly games. Who knows, it could be me visiting my mates sooner than we all think!

Kenny Herriot just posted me in a book called *Dispatches From The Edge: A Memoir of War, Disaster and Survival* by Anderson Cooper. It's a No. 1 *New York Times* best-seller and I'll have a nice weekend reading it! Cheers, Kenny…

I've got a currant bun for supper and a spoon of honey for my mug of tea!

I was chatting to an old screw today whom I've not seen for years. He started work here in 1972 and he's still here 36 years later. Frightening. Imagine the changes he's seen! He was here all those years ago when Maudsley put two cons under the bed. How can a screw work in the same jail for so long? Fuck me; talk about boring. It's a miracle he hasn't topped himself! Hey, what a best-seller he could write with all the stories he could tell! I'd better not put the idea in his head because I'm the No. 1 author and the king of prison literature! It's no good laughing or calling me a cunt because I *am* the top prison author! Name me one other prisoner in the world with so many books to his name. There ain't any, so I'm the No. 1. Respect it and accept it, because I'm here to stay! My best is yet to come – you wait and see!

I had six egg whites today. It's like drinking sour treacle but they're a good source of protein so it's got to be done. I did some crocodile press-ups on the yard; they're my speciality. From the CCTV cameras I must look like a real croc moving across the floor. I bet they pick up some funny things, like when I get a banana for tea and I pretend to hold up the hot plate screws: "Don't fucking move – this is loaded, cunt!" (You don't get that on *Big Brother*.)

Yeah, I've had a good day and it'll be a better one tomorrow! Life gets better even with the knocks. It's August on Friday – another new month! Yiiipppeeeeeeeeeeee.

Why is it that the search for Loonyology is something so insane? Think about that one! Good night!

31 July 2008.

Fuck me; it's August tomorrow. Nearly Christmas! The years almost over… Fuck it – what's another year?

It truly pissed down today and guess who was jogging around the yard in it? Brilliant, it was magical.

"I'm singing in the rain,
Just singing in the rain…"

That's how great it was. Beautiful!

I also had a chat with 'Nat West'. I don't know his real name but they call him 'Nat West' because he loves a bank job. He's on the block side on good order and discipline and he's a top con. He's done about eight years now, all over the place, and they're now on about deporting him back to Jamaica! Fuck me; I'll have some of that! Yeah, 'Nat West' has done bird well. I'm proud of him.

Rice Krispies for breakfast again: snap, crackle and pop. Tomato soup and a cheese roll for dinner, and a pile of mail from Di Brown, Ifty, Al Rayment, Johnny Griffiths, Harry Roberts, Claire Raper, Mum, brother Mark, a con in strangeways, Gary Jones and five people I don't know who all wrote to say *Loonyology* is the best read ever! One of them, called Jackie, sent me a £30 postal order to get some canteen with. Thanks, Jackie, and I'm pleased you enjoyed the book. (I hope this one is even better for you.) And my answer to the (personal) question you asked is definitely yes! I'll look forward to that one but be gentle with me – I've not had a shag in years! I don't want to bruise my helmet by having a raving nympho riding it.

I called Dave Courtney. He got his gun charge dropped, so that only leaves him with the two minor charges! Great news. I also called Ifty; it's always great to have a chat with him. I've had a right good day and to top it all I had pizza and chips with beans for tea, washed down with a hot, sweet mug of tea! Bloody lovely it was.

I see Mader auctioneers in Suffolk just sold eight paintings by Ronnie Kray for 16 and a half grand. That's 2K a painting! I wonder who had them? Pity they didn't sell them and send the dosh to him while he was alive. (I hope whoever got this dosh will sort something out for the Krays burial ground.) Now I understand why those cunts can't even wait till I'm dead before selling my masterpieces, the disrespectful twats! I keep on telling people that if it's not Gavin Meek selling my work then don't buy it. Can't you understand you're putting dosh into a toe rag's pocket when it's my art and my pocket it should be going in? I can see me ending up having to smash some skulls in! Piss-taking, brain-dead, fucking sardine prats, don't you understand us artists are very temperamental emotional freaks? Don't fuck with our art! Call Gavin for art, 07746 781366.

I got a lovely letter off Di Brown today. She's just gone back to her retreat in Spain. She's a hot cookie is our Di, she can share an apple pie with me any time!

A screw passed the shower today with a great big electric fan for their office. They're spoilt fuckers. That's the POA for you! These screws have never had it so good. Reggie Kray had a little portable battery fan in his cell in Parkhurst. I remember it well because when he moved to Gartree in 1986 they wouldn't let him have it, the fucking idiots. They said it wasn't allowed! That's prison rules for you, they're nuts. Why can't you have one? What harm is it? Rules are rules and each jail is different!

In Parkhurst I remember the Kray twins both had red silk dressing gowns and that Mad Jacko dragged a screw into the medical room, got the medicine cabinet open and drank all the valium and chloral. He was out for two days! Another con on F/2 grabbed a screw hostage and demanded a fucking sword! All he got was a bloody good kicking and 36 hours in a strait jacket. This was way back in 1976 when Parkhurst was the No. 1 jail. That era is long gone but they were fucking brilliant, magical times. Memories like that just keep flooding back. How can I ever regret my life when it's so full of wonderful stories?

Wandsworth was another insane jail. One time, two cons were having a punch-up in the recess on E-wing then two more ran in, then six more… soon there were a good twenty in there punching and kicking away before the 'locomotive' (a stampede of screws) arrived with their boots, whistles, shouts and truncheons banging the metal railings as they rushed in. That's pure adrenalin, pure madness and pure excitement! You can watch all your movies and read all your books; this is for real and it's priceless. You haven't fucking lived till the 'locomotive' smashes in to you; that's survival. And God help you if one of those screws gets hurt! You'll really be in for it then. I used to brew up in my cell with a candle and an empty bean tin. Boil the water and bosh, a hot cuppa tea! If you got caught it would cost you 14 days' punishment and 14 days' remission… all for a mug of tea! Fucking insane or what? There was one con who set fire to himself and went running down the wing screaming and another who dived off the top landing! One sliced his throat on the exercise yard, one cut his ear off and another sewed up his eyelids and lips! One mugged a screw and another scolded a governor! Fuck me; it was brilliant! Wandsworth was and probably still is an asylum. Boy do I miss it. I wonder if it misses me?

It's a big day for me tomorrow: I'm going over to the hospital wing to see the optician. I've got two nice frames which Sandra Gardner got for me, so I've now got to get the lenses sorted. I wear the John Lennon style frames: round, small, light and bendy (that's me)! I'll be escorted over there by seven screws and a dog handler! It's a massive event to move one of us lot over there because they have to stop all movement to escort us over. It's a half-hour job for them but it's a big event for me. I get to see grass, flowers, the rest of the jail, cons at their cell windows and the nurses. Yeah, it's a simple thing to most cons but it's massive to me and I love it!

Did you know a pair of Buddy Holly's specs sold at auction for 100K? An old pair of mine sold for £3K so I'm catching Buddy up slowly.

Oh well, my day's over and it's been a great day. I even created a nice piece of art! I'll post it tomorrow.

Don't forget:

Loonyology does not depend upon
Getting other people's approval,
It depends upon getting your own approval.
There is no wrong time for Loonyology!

Good night… sweet dreams!

1 August 2008.

You just never know who this mob will pass or not pass. Joe and Sandra are the parents of my old buddy Mark Jones, the tattooist, and they're now passed to visit me. I actually think it's one big game with security.

It probably all depends who's on duty the day the application goes in. It may be some old cunt who doesn't like Bronson because I chinned him 20 years ago and this is his way of saying, "Fuck Bronson, I'll show him who's boss!" Anyway, it will be nice to see Joe and Sandra and I'll sort them a VO for September!

Paddy's wife goes to the doctor's and says, "Can you put me on the birth pill please, Doctor?"

The doctor says: "Good heavens, Mary, you're eight months pregnant! Why do you want to be on the birth pill?"

Mary says: "My husband's found the other hole and I don't want one of these humps on my back!"

I went over to the hospital wing and he's a top geezer our optician. He really does his job properly. It was a smashing walk over. One of the dogs looked like a wolf and all it did was growl at me! I saw some flowers and grass, and loads of cons walking around a fenced-off yard. Some shouted to me, "Alright, Charlie, who's the gang of thugs with you?" The sun was shining and the birds whistling. Who said Hell's so bad? To top it all, my door opened later and I was told I'm on a legal visit with QC Sperry. I didn't even know. It was good to see him and he feels very confident for my parole later this month. We shall see on the 28th and 29th. Let's just say I could well squeeze something out of all this. Let's face it, what the fuck am I even doing locked up?

Barry George walked out of court today after eight years of his life had been stolen away for a murder he didn't commit. Read *Loonyology: In My Own Words*; what I think about that case is all in there. I predicted he would win his case – he had to. He couldn't have killed Jill Dando because he's a muppet. The Old Bill knew he was two cans short of a six pack, so he did nicely for them. Case solved! It happens in case after case after case… Wake up! Believe me, if the Old Bill can't catch the real criminals they will nab the village idiot – the poor sod with an unbalanced mind and an IQ of a peanut. "You did it, didn't you, son. Sign this and have a nice bag of toffees!" Case closed. Anyway, it was nice to see justice being done today. Now say sorry and give George a big fat cheque, you bastards. Find the real killer and say sorry to the Dando family as well! How must they feel? The George family are buzzing but the Dando family will be devastated. That's crime bizz for you!

Fish 'n chips today! Plenty of it too. I got five letters and two postcards. Mark Fish, Dave Courtney and all the 'faces' are at the Matt Legg fight in Watford tomorrow. It should be a cracker as it Matt's comeback fight. He's a good friend of my family so we all wish him well. Some of my clan will be there but I can't make it as I'm busy! Bizz before pleasure, I say!

Yeah, it was a great day for British justice although it's taken eight years to put right. At least it's been sorted. Out of it all I would say Barry George's sister is the star; she kept the hope flag flying because she knew in her heart he was innocent. Well done, girl, I salute you.

Is August going to be a lucky month? Could I be next? Could I be weeks away from freedom? I'd be tagged and on a curfew but so what? I'd still get a shag, a Guinness, and be able to walk out in the pissing rain, free and happy. Tags and curfews don't last and it's freedom that counts. Fuck anything else, freedom is the goal! The ideal ending would be to get parole and win my appeal later. I'd walk out of the London Law Courts and say on the steps: "What a wonderful world! Now fuck off and let me get on with my life." What an ending that'd be! That's a Hollywood ending – the baddie turns good and wins, then he walks out with the Cheeky Girls! What a fucking ending to a journey of Loonyology. Then a bus hits us all!

Oh yeah, I bet anybody a 'monkey' (and I'll give you 5/1) that Barry George didn't have a freedom shag. What sane girl is going to shag that? I'm not being cruel here, but could you girls really see yourself in bed with that? Could you see yourself with him on top of you, breathing all over you and sticking his tongue down your throat? But, then again, maybe you would when he gets his million pound cheque! Yeah, I can see some of you girls having some of it then! There are plenty of blokes who would bend over for a slice of that sort of dosh; it's insane what a bit of dosh can do. However, knowing Barry George (as I do), he'll probably buy a train set, a box of fanny mags and a bag of sweets! That's a life for you.

What about that 15-year-old girl who's 33 stone? Thirty-three fucking stone! Who's her dad, Mr Hippo? That's disgusting and the parents are responsible. How can a 15-year-old kid weigh 33 stone and why have the social services allowed that to go on? It's child abuse! She is two of me and a sack of spuds! You can't make this shit up. Stop eating… before you die.

What about 19-year-old Nathan Mann? He was burgling an old folks' home and two old ladies woke up. What did he do? He beat one to death and suffocated the other. What a cowardly cunt! Hang the monster. What good is he to the planet? The judge sentenced him to double life and he must serve 24 years. Big deal – that's just 12 years a murder and he'll only be 43 when he gets out, the cunt. Let's hope some nasty con gets a hold of him and gives him some of his own treatment.

One of the old ladies he snuffed out was 72 years old and was a stroke victim who could only move her left arm. The other girl had epilepsy and diabetes and could hardly speak or walk. She didn't even have the power to run or scream! What a brave fucker he is… It makes me feel sick. 24 years! I would ask the judge, Mr McCombe, why not 44 years? I actually think the British public are now sick of you judges – you're not in the real world. Wake up! You can start by letting me out!

Who remembers the mad Pakistani Javed Iqbal? Note I said Pakistani and not 'Paki' as one has to be very careful of racial issues. However, I've never accepted 'Paki' as a racist term; it's just short for Pakistani. Anyway, in 2000 this mad fucker killed 100 children and chopped them up, the dirty bastard. He was sentenced to death by slow strangulation then his body was cut into 100 pieces and dissolved in acid. Fuck me; what a sentence. That's brilliant! Why can't we have some of that Pakistani law? But sadly, the slippery snake hanged himself in his cell. (I wonder if they still cut him up and put him in acid.) I do hope so, don't you?

Another nasty fucker was a Ukrainian called Anatoly Onoprienko who had the nickname 'Terminator'. He killed 52 people from 1995 to 1999 but the European Union saved his arse when his death sentence was commuted to life in prison. That's human rights for you. Mental.

In 1999 the Colombian beast Luis Alfredo Gavarito confessed to raping and killing 140 children. All he copped for that was 30 years. What a result he got. What a fucking joke! Colombian law must be insane! If anybody should have got a hole in the crust it had to be this cunt. How can you allow such a monster to carry on breathing after destroying so many innocent lives? Crime and punishment is a funny old world. If you dwell on it, you'll end up in a strait jacket.

Ronnie Kray wrote this poem called 'The Troubled Mind'. Read it, digest it, and think on.

As I walk along the Broadmoor corridors
I see my fellow man trudging the floors
Getting nowhere, like a boat with no oars
They all have a troubled mind
Most are looking for the peace of mind
They cannot find
Some are cruel, some are kind
God forgive them who have the troubled mind
Only when they go to the great beyond
Peace will they find.

That's powerful, that's Ronnie Kray! It was at St Matthew's Church, Bethnal Green on 29 March 1995 that Ron's funeral service took place. The pall bearers were Charlie Kray, Teddy Dennis, Freddie Foreman and Johnny Nash. These four men represented the four corners of London: south, east, north and west. Anyone who was anyone turned up. It was a send-off fit for royalty! That's Ronnie Kray in a nutshell: style. The late Joey Pyle summed it all up by saying: "Ronnie Kray was a man. There will never be another one like him."

Saturday, 2 August 2008.

I shaved my beard off today. Why? Because it's my fucking face and I'll do what the fuck I want with it! So fuck off, you nosey cunt! For that, I'm off and I may not be back! Kiss my ring piece! Stick your tongue up and make me laugh!

Did you know a butterfly tastes with its feet? Can you fucking believe that? Now why did God create a creature that tastes with its feet? He's got to be having a fucking laugh, ain't he?

Anyway, fuck it. That's my lot till another day. Oh, I almost forgot: don't be too sad over Barry George because the cunt's a dirty old nonce anyway! He copped a two and a half stretch some time back for rape so he's a fat toothless nonce. Fuck him!

4 August 2008.

What a fucking mental day! The beast Miller got ordered to have a shower by the governor. (He hasn't had one for 16 weeks and his cell stinks.) Whilst the governor was at his door, I shouted out, "Shut the door, the smell is drifting out into my door, cunt." Then Maudsley walked by and I couldn't help myself, I had to say: "Fuck me it's Catweazle, can I have your autograph?" So he started up: "You fucking retard, I'll stab your heart out." What a nasty bastard he is, and he means it. But what he fails to realise is what I'll be doing whilst he's stabbing me. I'll tell you: I'll be ripping his beard off his face and caving his ribs in. I'll hit that cunt so hard I'll put his spine into the front of his body! Power punching, body smashing, bone crunching… who needs a tool? I fucking don't.

I'll tell you who was a brave man: Nobel Prize winner Alexander Solzhenitsyn. He died yesterday at the ripe old age of 89. For all you lot who don't know of him, I had best explain that he exposed the evils of Stalin's Soviet system. He served seven years in a brutal labour camp for writing a letter during World War II describing Stalin as "the mad man with the moustache." Read his Gulag Archipelago trilogy, it's brilliant, as is the novel he wrote in the 1960s: *One Day in the Life of Ivan Denisovich* which describes life in the 'human meat grinder'. I salute the man, he's a true survivor.

Did you know the African elephant will be extinct by 2020 if the ivory poachers don't stop now? Why don't we hunt them down instead? Cunts – see how they fucking like it.

Did you know Radio Luxembourg is 75 years old? It was founded in 1933 and was shut down in 1992. In the early 1960s it reached 78 million listeners and I was one of them. Until Radio 1 started up in 1967, Radio Luxembourg was the daddy, believe it! The DJs I remember being on the station are: Jimmy Saville, Pete Murray, Mike Reid, Mark Wesley, Paul Burnett, Tony Price. Emperor Rosko and Dave Christian. Yeah, I remember them all! I used to listen in on my little transistor with ear phones. It was on 208 medium-wave band and it was very crackly. I remember it like it was yesterday! It was the buzz, the 'in thing', the best music played by the best DJs in the world! Luxembourg, we loved you; you were legendary and a part of history.

Can a vibrating bed help couples with their sex life? Cor blimey, I'd love to try one out. Who's got one? Write and let me know how good they are. Mind you, my mattress is now perfect – well squashed – and I sleep like a kitten in a cotton wool box. I heard Fred Lowe snoring last night for the first time for ages! He sounded like a bear in labour. I banged the wall a good 20 times and he stopped.

I got three letters today; not bad for a Monday. It's three more than Miller gets in a year!

One of Ronnie Kray's best statements was: "I'd rather die standing than live on my knees begging to be freed." What a statement; I love it and he fucking meant it! Most men say it but don't mean it. That's the difference, see. Ronnie meant it and that's why I loved him. He was unique. He walked into my cell one day with a great big plate of top quality cream cakes (not prison shit). "Here," he said, "get this lot down your neck; me and Reg can't eat no more. Enjoy…" and with that he walked out. There were six cakes on that plate! For me that was Xmas and a birthday all rolled into one. This was back in 1975 when prison was prison and porridge was porridge. I bet you're wondering where he got the cakes from? Don't ask – you must never ask a convict such a question, so don't fucking ask! Only coppers ask questions like that (and nosey cunts) so fuck off! You can ask me if they were nice cakes, how big they were or if I saved any. I'll answer the final question: I ate the lot myself because I'm a greedy cunt! Plus I was training three hours a day in those days,

I called Mark Fish tonight and he told me Matt Legg won his comeback fight in the second round, so congratulations to him. Let's have three cheers for Matt: HIP HIP – HOORAY! HIP HIP – HOORAY! HIP HIP – HOORAY! Well done, my old china, that's what I love to hear. All the chaps were there for him: Roy Shaw, Dave Courtney, Mark Fish, Redd Menzies and Billy Cooper. I couldn't make it – something popped up! That's life... Oh well, let's all call it a day. And don't forget: don't snore!

6 August 2008.
Get on these statistics from 2006.

PRISON POPULATIONS:

NORTHERN IRELAND	1,433
SCOTLAND	7,111
AUSTRIA	8,780
BELGIUM	9,635
CYPRUS	599

Now that last one amazes me. I would've thought it's a lot higher because I know some right nasty Cypriots who would cut your throat for 10 pence. Nasty fuckers!

CZECH REPUBLIC	18,578
DENMARK	3,759
ESTONIA	4,411
FINLAND	3,477
FRANCE	55,754

Now *that* last one doesn't surprise me at all; any country where frogs are a delicacy is a bit dodgy for me. 55,754 sums that lot up properly! Fucking criminals!

GERMANY	78,581

Fuck me; the old Krauts don't fuck about in sending 'em to jail. Still, they should be thankful Hitler is no more!

GREECE	10,113
HUNGARY	14,821
ICELAND	119

Fuck me; what's going on in Iceland? They sound like a load of pussies to me. I bet they've never had a bank job over there, it's all nicking ice lollies. Cunts.

ITALY	39,005

Half of them are the Mafia!

LATVIA	6,665
LITHUANIA	8,137
LUXEMBOURG	756

MALTA	346
NETHERLANDS	20,463
NORWAY	3,164
POLAND	87,669

The number of Poles doesn't shock me and there would be a lot more if they weren't over here in our jails. Thieving bastards.

PORTUGAL	12,636
SLOVAKIA	8,249
SLOVENIA	1,301
SPAIN	64,120
SWEDEN	7,175
SWITZERLAND	5,888
TURKEY	67,795

Ruthless fuckers, the Turks. I had a spot of trouble with a family of them in Luton but they soon stood down when I kicked in their door with a chainsaw. "Want some of this, cunts?" 67,795 fucking criminals.

AUSTRALIA	25,790

I bet half of them are Aborigines. Poor sods; they're like the Red Indians – they're victims of humanity. They were kicked about and robbed of their homeland. No wonder they turned to crime.

CANADA	34,244
JAPAN	79,052

(Never trust nobody with snake eyes. No wonder it's 79,052.)

NEW ZEALAND	7,595

I bet half of them are sheep abusers! They do love a sheep over there.

SOUTH AFRICA	150,302
USA	2,245,189

Trust the Yanks to kick the arse out of it. They've always got to be the best or worst... however you see the jail population!

ENGLAND AND WALES	79,085

How's that? Stick with Loonyology – I'll educate you guys and girls! Every page is knowledge.

You'll love this one: there are an estimated 10,000 trillion ants on Earth! Yeah, sure; I'll fucking challenge that! Who fucking counted them? You can't take all these facts seriously, can you? Do you? You do? You sad fuckers... you're all nutters.

Did you know Scrabble was originally called 'Lexiko'? Not a lot of people know that! 150 million Scrabble sets have been sold worldwide. Yeah, you lot learn a lot from reading my books. Eat your heart out, Jeffrey Archer! "An eye for an eye," – who fucking wrote that? Some mad cunt! If we all followed that, this world would be blind!

Did you know Boris Becker was only 17 years old when he won Wimbledon in 1985? (In fact, he was actually 17 years and 227 days old, so he was pretty old.) Plus he was the first German to even win it! Yep, it's all knowledge and you may need it one day. Imagine you're taken hostage by an escaped lunatic and he's stuffed a shotgun in your ear, saying: "Who's the fucking German who won Wimbledon in 1985? You've got three seconds to answer or I'll blow your fucking brains out of your crust!"

"It's Boris Becker, Boris Becker!"

See how I may have saved your life? You never know what's around the corner!

I'm just in the mood to go into boxing mode! Shall I? Are you up for a page or two of boxing quotes and facts? Yeah? Then let's get it on. Are you ready to rumble? DING DING... Round one...

In 1916 Walter Edgerton knocked out John Henry Johnson in the fourth round. Johnson was 45 years old but Edgerton was 65. Could you see the British Boxing Board of Control letting that fight go on today? That's why I love the old time boxers! They were made of rock.

Take Dal Hawkins and Fred Bogan in June 1889 in San Francisco. They climbed into the ring and 75 rounds later the fight had to be abandoned after bad lighting. The next day the fight started again and Hawkins knocked Bogan out in the 15th round. So that was 90 fucking rounds they fought. Insane or what? That's what you call a fight!

Ali was the one with the greatest quotes. I loved this one he said about Joe Frazier: "He's so ugly they ought to donate his face to the worldwide fund." Hey, wasn't he magical? Was he not one of the greatest boxers of all time? How can you not but love Ali? "Float like a butterfly and sting like a bee!"

Who remembers the former world lightweight champion from Argentina, Victor Galindez? When he retired from boxing he took up motor racing but he didn't last long. In his first race he broke down and got out of the car only to be run over and killed. He should've stuck to boxing.

A bare knuckle fight in 1887 between Jake Kilrain and Jem Smith went on for 106 rounds in the open air. It resulted in a draw because nightfall crept in!

Vinnie Pazienza once stated: "It's no secret that I like to sleep with two or three porn stars. That is my life: sex and fighting." We love you Vinnie, at least you're honest! And you're a great fighter.

"The bigger they are the harder they fall." Have you ever wondered who first said those immortal words? It was Bob Fitzsimmons after he'd fought Eddie Dunkhurst in 1896. Eddie was a massive 300 pounds and Bob sparked him. Good old Bob...

I loved Tommy Farr's quote on Joe Louis: "I only have to read Joe Louis' name and my nose starts to bleed again." How great is that saying? I fucking love a character! The boxing world is full of them.

What about Alan Minters? "Sure there have been deaths and injuries in boxing, but none of them serious." Is that brilliant or what? It's a masterpiece, a gem. We love you, Alan.

The worst one was from Joe Bugner: "In my opinion Henry Cooper couldn't walk in my shadow as a fighter. I am a legend." That very statement from Bugner started off the 'hate crowd' against him. He never could live that down and never will. What a fucking thing to say about our Henry!

In the boxing world, one guy's crocodile shoes you really don't want to step on are the great Don King's. You have to salute this guy for his survival in life. Back in 1954 he shot dead a burglar in Cleveland and it was ruled as justifiable homicide. Back in 1966 he killed Sam Garrett and served four years for second-degree murder. In 1972 he entered into the world of boxing promoting and the man is still around. He's even beat the FBI on fraud charges! He's a walking legend and a real boxing character. Love him or hate him, you have to admire him. I fucking love him. He's what I call 'a man's man' and he's helped a lot of guys become super rich along the way! We need more Don Kings in the fight world. Three cheers for the Don: HIP HIP – HOORAY! HIP HIP – HOORAY! HIP HIP – HOORAY!

One of the maddest ever quotes must be one by Mike Tyson: "I try to catch my opponent on the tip of the nose because I try to punch the bone into his brain." Fucking Loonyology or what?

Marvin Hagler said: "If they cut my bald head open, they will find one big boxing glove. That's all I am, I live it."

Ali said: "I'll beat Floyd Patterson so bad, he will need a shoe horn to put his hat on." Another great Ali line was: "When you're as great as I am, it's hard to be humble."

Randall Cobb said: "All I want to do is hit somebody in the mouth; it's easier than working for a living."

One of the funniest lines has to be from Jim Wicks (Henry Cooper's manager) on the talk of a Liston v Cooper fight: "We don't want to meet this geezer Liston walking down the street, let alone in the ring." I'm afraid old Jim was spot on there about Sonny Liston. He would have put our Henry in hospital, if not the morgue.

"Sonny Liston's so ugly that when he cries, the tears run down the back of his neck." (That's another one of Ali's.)

Hector Camacho said: "My girlfriend boos when we make love because she knows it turns me on."

The great Rocky Graziano said: "Me and Jake LaMotta grew up in the same neighbourhood. You wanna know how popular Jake was? When we played hide and seek, nobody ever looked for LaMotta." How fucking pucker is that? Only Graziano could come up with that one.

I've saved my own quote till last: "Get a fucking life, cunt – stick the gloves on."

Nine letters today and they were all crackers too! Called Mum and we had a good laugh. Beans, chips and pie for tea! They spoil me; I'm the most spoilt convict on the planet! You should all complain to your local MP: "Bronson is spoilt rotten and he needs a good birching." The truth is I could do with a whip round because I'm skint. At least I got my canteen today! I keep telling you, I'm a lucky old geezer!

Good night.

7 August 2008.

OK, let's have three cheers for the unit governor! HIP HIP – HOORAY! HIP HIP – HOORAY! HIP HIP – HOORAY! Why? He's just sent monster Miller to the punishment cell for seven days! The air smells fresher now the filthy nonce is away for a week, and they can now fumigate the cunt's cell while he's away. It stinks.

I hit 95 press-ups in 30 seconds! That's how good I feel today: fast and alive. I also created an A4 art for Charles Byrd. He's an old man of 91 years who's a legendary Welsh artist. He's a genius and a true living legend. I do love a legend. He's been a professional artist for 60 years! I'll send the art I've done for him to my buddy Alfie Lodge who'll frame it and present it to the old chap. It's nice to be nice. Us artists must stick together, see; we are a special breed – gifted specimens! We were born with gold dust and a flash of a rainbow. Lucky babies, that's what we are. Our art brightens up the planet. Understand me? If you don't then just fuck off, OK!

Did I ever tell you about the time I put a pig's head in a hat box and had it posted to an Islamic nutter? He was a foul-mouthed fucking Christian-hater! That's how to deal with those bigots – fuck up their heads. Who the fuck do they think they are, standing on their soap boxes and preaching hate against us Brits? I've got no time for any religious nutter, have you? Or are you all too scared to say anything about it? The PC brigade may tell you off, but call a cunt a cunt I say. Fuck 'em.

I see RAF veteran Eric 'Digger' Dowling died this week. He was one of the real war heroes. We have Eric and his prisoner-of-war comrades to thank for the film *The Great Escape*. Always remember that the famous escape from the German war camp Stalag Luft III was actually a living nightmare. 250 planned to escape through that tunnel, 76 got through it, 50 were executed and only three made it home. A film's only a film but these guys were true life heroes and men of steel. To me, men like Dowling are so brave that you can't help but admire them. He made it to the ripe old age of 92. R.I.P.

I got five letters today. One was from a loony and you'll love it…

Charlie,

I've just read your book *Silent Scream*. It's brilliant – the best book I've ever read. Please, Charlie, if I post you my bra would you sign it for me and post it back? Please, please, please, Charlie. Oh, please do this for me. I enclose a self-addressed envelope. If you do this for me, Charlie, I'll do anything for you – just name it! Anything. When I post in the bra, you'll see I'm a very big girl! I'm not fat, but my tits are huge. Please, please, please, Charlie.

x x x x Carol x x x x

Would you sign it? I fucking won't! In fact I've steamed the stamps off the loon's envelope and I'll re-use them.

Did you know Princess Diana went to Broadmoor in 1991 to open the brand-new Abingdon ward? What sane people don't understand is that this was a massive thing back then because Broadmoor was a Victorian asylum. For 100 years the loonies had to shit in a chamber pot and slop it out down the recess sloosh (and it stunk). Abingdon ward was new, with toilets in the rooms (luxury to the loons) and it was our lovely Lady Di that opened it! Now, Broadmoor has many other new wards and even the old ones have caught up with the modern asylums, thank fuck. Not that I've got any plans to return there! Not fucking likely.

I had a nice letter and photos off Sandra Gardner today! She's a good friend of mine. I also had a nice veg curry for tea. Not bad. I didn't make any phone calls though, because I'm short. People outside don't realise my calls come out of my canteen and that's why I don't always call. It's simple: sometimes I prefer to treat myself.

Yeah, it's been a good day! From the moment I shaved my head till lights out, I was smiling. Not bad, eh? Can you honestly say you're as happy a soul as me? Can you, with all your stresses in life, all your bits, all your problems – the car's broken down, the dog's unwell and the vet bills are piling up, the kids are playing up and the TV's on the blink. HA! HA! HA! HA! Look at me: fresh as a daisy and raring to go! My best chapter is yet to come. Fuck the prison psychologists (and fuck the system) – what good are they? Nosey gits! I know where I'm heading: Heaven. It's all waiting for me. I'll see you all at the party! Mine's a double Black Russian. Cheers.

Anyway, be happy because Miller's got fuck all but an empty cell and that's all the filthy child killer deserves! Fuck him. Hurry up and die, you cunt! Talking of dying, it's time Huntley had another go. Keep trying, you'll get there soon. Try, try again and never give up, cunt.

Oh well, time for some shut eye.

Good night.

12 August 2008.

I had a visit today from Mark Jones and got all the latest news. He got me three milkshakes, three chocolate cakes and some bars of chocolate. He clocked Maudsley in the caged yard and said he looks like Worzel Gummidge. Yep, he ain't far wrong! I say he's more like Catweazle, but both of those characters are idiots so that sums him up for me!

It's been lovely this last week without Miller. The unit smells cleaner and fresher without that dirty nonce bastard.

Did you know that since 1992 Mark Chapman, the killer of John Lennon, has been having conjugal visits? That's how it is in New York's Attica prison. Prisoners get locked up for 44 hours in a private room with their wives and shag them silly. How about that for porridge? Why can't us Brits have some of that? It's called the 'Family Reunion Scheme' and it's supposed to help prepare the cons for freedom. All us cons in Britain get is kicked out after years of wanking. Where's the humanity? Cunts!

I see Frankland prison Seg block kicked off last week and nine cons smashed up their cells. That jail is like a powder keg waiting to blow up! Someone's going to get hurt up there soon, if not killed. Yaarrhhooooooooooo, yiiipppeeeeeeeeee, let's hope it's Cuntley (oops, sorry – Huntley)!

Blimey, soul legend Isaac Hayes died yesterday and he was only 65. You must remember his classic theme tune for the film *Shaft* – it was fucking awesome. I recommend his 1969 album 'Hot Buttered Soul'. This guy was a legend; the soul man! I was bang into the soul era, it was great shagging music.

Fuck me; here's a classic for you: Lester Piggott's son Jamie is about to follow in his old man's saddle. Let's face it, Piggott was the governor. He won his first race at Haydock Park at the age of 12 and won his first Derby aged 18 in 1954. He won a total of eight Derbys. Back in 1987 he copped three years over tax fraud, so he was a birdman too! Good old Lester – a true legend! (1987 was a lucky year for me. I made it out to freedom and had some good shagging sessions, but fuck all lasts. I soon had my collar felt.)

I see Audley Harrison's brother Vincent died of a lethal cocktail of drugs. He was only 26 years old; what a waste. Why can't people wake up and realise that drugs are shit? They kill you! Audley doesn't seem to have done a lot in the boxing world since he won the gold medal at the Olympics. It just goes to prove the pro game is a different kettle of fish. A gold medal doesn't mean anything in the prize-fight world, and that's a fact.

Elvis Presley's white jumpsuit has just sold for 156 grand at auction. I wonder how much I could get for my jock-strap?

What about Gerald Mellin? He tied one end of a rope around a tree and the other end to his neck. Then he got into his Aston Martin, drove away and his head came off! What's all that about? I told you it's a crazy old world, but that's how some decide to call it a day. The police found his headless body in the driving seat and his head on the back seat. What a find! I bet those coppers went on sick leave.

Did you know Britain's smallest man, Michael Henbury, is 2 feet 11 inches? Let's have a cheer for the little fella! HIP HIP – HOORAY! That's enough – we don't want to make him too big for his boots!

I had a cheese salad today but I saved it as I ate so much on my visit! I made some sandwiches and I'll eat them tomorrow. There's always another day. There was a lunatic in Ashworth asylum who used to make wonderful salad rolls and sell them for porno mags (he loved a porno mag), so I had a box sent in for him and had a couple of rolls every night for supper for my whole stay there! It's strange how some guys need porn to survive life inside. Me, I've got my imagination. If you see one dirty mag you've seen them all! But having said that, some mags are a bit more than just a mag – they're pure filth! Some of those cocks are like a copper's truncheon. No wonder the girls' eyes look watery with one of those right up their arseholes. Ouch!

There was another loony in Ashworth who collected pop bottle tops. Why? What for? How the fuck do I know? But his cell was full of them! A lot of loonies have health problems because of all the pop and sweets they stuff in their faces. You'll notice a lot of mad people have no teeth and they're fat. Many are diabetics and it's no fucking wonder with their lifestyles! All they do is eat, shit, watch TV, wank, sleep and eat bags and bags of sweets for year after year! What a fucking existence.

There's a strong smell of spunk in the asylums first thing in the morning, from sticky, smelly pyjamas and bed sheets. I've seen loonies walking to the shower with dribbling cocks. This is hard to believe, but I saw one nutter walk out of his cell whistling away with a brush sticking out of his arse. I also saw a loon leading another loon by holding his erect cock and pulling him to the shower. I've seen it all and believe me, it's fucking insane! But that's Loonyology. Fuck me; even now I have to ask myself why was I ever in those funny farms.

One day a loon walked into my cell one day and said, "Fancy a fairy cake?"

"What?" I said.

"A fairy cake!"

"Where is it?" I asked.

"In my pocket, he said. He then pulled out a squashed cake.

"Fuck off," I said, "go and fuck off!"

Later that day he went to hit me with a sock full of batteries so I broke both his arms. What else could I do? What would you have done? That's the asylum world for you. You either learn to survive or you get smashed in the skull by a fairy cake assassin.

What do you call a snake on Viagra? A cane!

I got a smashing letter from Jillian Lofts today. She always lets me know all the latest news. I also called my buddy Alan Rayment. He had a car crash last week but what a survivor he is. As you all know by now, he's got no legs, so picture this: he's doing 60mph in his specially-adapted car when some other driver pulls out and 'crash'! This was on a busy street so there were loads of witnesses and a big crowd gathered, along with the Old Bill and an ambulance. Someone in the crowd shouted, "God, he's lost his legs!" What a bloody good comedy sketch that would make. Now can you see how funny life really is? It's pure magic, brilliant, even crazy. Don't you just love it? Even in the midst of a serious accident there can be humour. It's lucky both drivers escaped with minor injuries, but how funny was that? Alan's a living legend! Respect.

What's German for Viagra? 'Stopemfromflopping'!

Did you hear about the geezer who spent his life savings on a sex change? He hasn't got a sausage left!

Did you know the World Farting Championships are held every year in Lebanon's national farting stadium? Angus Ali Khan holds the record with a 21-second ripping, explosive eruption. That's some fart! They say it started with a squeak then went into a rumble, then onto a massive loud explosion! Angus has held the title since 1989. He trains on duck eggs, mushy peas, figs and lots of fizzy drinks. The fart entries come in all descriptions: dry farts, long farts, wet farts, short farts, rip-raps, bubbles, blobs and squeaks. A shit is immediately disqualified! Your probably asking yourselves: how does Bronson know all this? Well, I'll tell you: I know a geezer who flew out to take part in it and he came sixth. Apparently there was one fat bastard there from Japan (31 stone of him) who he bent over to let one rip and apparently had a stroke! Fat, lazy bastard. Hey, the crazy sport is taken seriously out there. The judges take into consideration all aspects of the fart: the strength, the odour, the posture of the farter and whether the fart is a blanket ripper or a thunder clap. Every fart gets a grading. Can you really see Angus Ali Khan's 21-second fart ever being beaten? I can't! The show opens up with the 'Thunder Box Farting Formation Team' giving their display of formation farting. What a day out! The kids love it! One day I may well enter it myself. You never know with me!

I had a lovely hour on the yard today. I felt free and I could've been jogging around Big Ben for all I cared. My mind was open and I wasn't here – my body was but my mind was free. That's how lucky I am! Well... can you do that in your life? Let's be honest about it: could you do that in my world of razor wire, CCTV, walls and fences? It just shows you how free my soul is and boy do I know it. I'm blessed!

Well it's creeping up to my parole review date. It's two weeks tomorrow and I can't fucking wait. I called Mark Fish as well today but no-one was in. He's got a daughter called Jazz who's only about 12 years old but she's really smart and a brilliant artist. She makes me laugh. Kids are so funny! I was one once. It's true, I was! Well, I think I was. Wasn't I?

I had eight letters today (nine counting Jillian's), so a bloody good day all in all. One mustn't grumble... The governor stuck his head in and asked how I was. "Yeah, not bad, Guv," I said, "but I could do with a bottle of brandy next time you do your rounds." If looks could kill, I would've died years ago!

I wonder how much longer it will be before I'm walking the streets? What a lovely dream. The first cake shop I come to, I'll go in and smell that beautiful home-made bread and pastry. Fuck me; my mouth's watering just thinking about it! One day...

14 August 2008.

Some nutcase set fire to his cell today on the Seg side of the unit. They put a hosepipe in and drenched him. That was a bit of excitement for the screws! At least it gives everybody something to talk about. Miller came back into his pigsty. It's been a nice week without the smelly cunt.

I've had a good day as I got to see Ms Clare Hodson, the new operational manager of the CSC system. She spent 10 minutes outside my cage door and I must say she seems a very decent sort of person! I put my case over to her and she listened and promised me she will be looking into it, so watch this space.

I got a pile of mail today and there were some cracking letters. Di Brown, my Lorraine, Mum, Sandra and Sarah all wished me well. A dozen others were from people who've just read *Loonyology* and fucking loved it. That book is really taking off! They all commented on what I wrote about Barry George and that it's now come true. But as I said, don't feel sorry for that cunt as he's still a nonce and a danger to women. Once a nonce, always a nonce in my book! Personally, I would sooner see him six feet under the earth! Cunt. A cunt's a cunt in my book. Remember that!

I see Colin Stagg got 700 grand compensation and everybody is moaning about it:

"My Johnny lost a leg in Iraq and only got 20K."

"My uncle Bert lost two legs in the London bombings and only received 100 grand."

"My aunty Rose only got 50K for losing her arm."

BLAH BLAH BLAH! Stop fucking moaning and look at the facts: Colin Stagg was accused of – then charged with – murdering Rachel Nickell on Wimbledon Common 15 years ago. Rachel was stabbed 49 times and we all remember it because it was disgusting and horrific. Stagg spent a year on remand in Wandsworth jail when he was the most hated man in the UK, so that year of his life was Hell. He was another innocent man who'd been fitted-up. It was another high-profile case where the police had to catch the killer quickly, and Stagg was the victim this time. All charges against him were eventually dropped and he was freed. But freed to what? The public still believed he'd done it. It's taken the Home Office 15 years to cough up this dosh and at last it proves he didn't do it. (Otherwise, why would they pay him 700K?) Personally, I don't think it's enough. The cops fucked up his life forever. How can he ever live a normal life? So all you lot moaning and asking why he got more than your Johnny, it's obvious why: he was stitched-up. Even a judge accused the police of 'deceptive conduct' (that's a posh way of saying it was a fit-up) so stop moaning and let Stagg enjoy his pay out! I would've wanted 100 million but I'm a greedy fucker!

Syied and Wahid Iftkhar (Ifty's teenage sons) put in requests to visit me and today I've been told Wahid has been knocked back by the Home Office but his brother Syied has been granted! What's that all about? If that's not bollocks then I'm a Martian! Some prat has gone too far. This is a piss-take, it's got to be! I've known these two since they were small. They call me 'Uncle Charlie' and to me they are family. Their father is a brother to me. I love and respect them all as they love me. They are both bang into boxing at the moment – they train hard and fight hard. I'm in the process of trying to sort them out with a trainer and a manger.

So how come can one be passed to visit me and the other can't? It doesn't add up. It's pure madness – it's Loonyology! It can be seen as racist and I predict this will backfire on those muppets in HQ because Ifty won't allow this sort of shit against his son! There is no reason why he can't visit me. If they think there is, then let's see it in writing! These are two decent Asian brothers and one has been victimised and persecuted for no other reason than bollocks. Definitely watch this space!

I'm about to treat myself to a mug of coffee. I'll be back in 15 minutes as I like to enjoy it, sip it slowly, relax and chill out. I drink a coffee as if I was on death row and it was to be my last: I enjoy the smell and the taste and picture a beautiful Brazilian belly-dancer in front of my eyes! I'll be back after a coffee break. (Fuck me; that was nice!)

I called Ray Williams at about 6pm and it was great to talk to him. I also spoke to his son Raymond who's 17 now and a great lad.

Strangely enough, Ifty is up to see me next week so we will sort this bollocks out about his son. We will get an MP on it and expose the prison HQ for their prejudices against Asian lads. If we play our cards right we could even sue the bastards! They're not getting away with it. Who the fuck do they think they are – God? All they're proving is that they're a bunch

ARAMARK
HMP Wakefield

BRONSON
BT1314

Location : S - 2 - 006
Ref : 0208000156 11/08/2008

Item	Qty	Price
Cadburys Dairy Milk 140g	1	£1.09
Phone Credit	13	£13.00
H.S. NAS Orange Squash 1ltr	1	£0.65
Nescafe Coffee Sachet One Cup	7	£0.56
UHT Whole Milk 500ml	1	£0.46
Princes Pink Salmon 105g	2	£1.78
Soreen Malt Loaf	1	£0.79
Jif Lemon Juice 55ml	1	£0.41
C.Rich Salted Peanuts 300g	1	£0.97
Mars Bar 58g	1	£0.39
Snickers Bar 58g	1	£0.39
Tunes - Cherry Flavour	1	£0.51
Nestlé Yorkie - Milk 68g	1	£0.48
Eggs 6pk	2	£1.72
Tomatoes x 3	1	£0.70
Fresh Fruit Pack - Banana x 3	1	£0.82
Dairylea Cheese Triangles	1	£1.15

ORDER TOTAL £25.87

Discounts (included in Order Total)

of fucking Nazis and Hitler lovers. Well, they've chosen the wrong family to fuck with this time! I ask you, the readers, to get *Loonyology* and read what both brothers wrote in there. That will prove what sort of family the Iftkhars are. They're a proper, decent, respectful bunch of lovely people.

Tea was beef burger, onions, beans, chips, four bread rolls and a mug of hot tea with honey in. Fucking magic – a proper man's plate of grub. If it was a choice of that or a blow-job off a tart, she can fuck off every time! Food comes first with me.

Got my canteen this week!

As you can see, I got £26 worth. Not bad, eh? I had a bit extra this week as I saved some up. £13 went on phone credit! I hope you lot who I call appreciate it, because that could've bought me a lot of Mars bars. Clock the two tins of salmon. Am I posh or what? Do I know how to do my porridge or what? Yeah, I must admit that's a bloody good canteen; I'm proud of it. Well, I deserved it since I've done a couple of nice things this week. I won't say what or who to (since some things are personal), but I sorted a few quid for some special people. That's how I live my life. Fuck the tax man – I am the fucking tax man! You can stick your cheques up your arse; it's cash with me. Pay up or go 10 rounds with me! (It's best to pay.)

My old buddy Stu Cheshire's been in touch. He's a top geezer and one of the best doormen in the game. If you get my book *Heroes and Villains* you'll see a photo of him with a big, fuck-off tiger.

What do you get if you cross a rottweiler with the Andrex puppy? A dog that scares the shit out of you and then runs off with the bog roll!

Oh well, life's still rolling on so one mustn't grumble, must one? Hey, it is possible to live without happiness but where's the fun in that? And always remember: sorrow and heartache are often touched with joy. Dig deep and stay alive!

I arrived home and found the cat in the washing machine. I was gutted but at least he died in Comfort!

A woman goes into Homebase and buys a wall mirror. The assistant asks, "Do you want a screw for that?" The woman says, "No, but I'll suck your cock for a lawn-mower!"

This isn't the way it should be!
But it's the way it ended up.
I'm here,
You're there.
The time is now uncertain.
It's a very fractured world
Not a nice place to be.
It's soul is ripped and ruptured
It's a fucked-up freezing hole of custard!
Custard turned to cancer
Crawling through your bones
The silent words of despair
Brain-dead and praying.
The streets are swarming with nutters,
Axe men, gun men and cut-throat killers.

Your world is crazy,
Tripping on fear.
Who's going to cop it next?
Lay down in the gutter
Play dead
It may pass you by.
Stick the Colt 45 in your eye
Blow a fucking big hole in your face
Let the brain be free
Show the fuckers you won't be manipulated
Show them you won't be fucked.
Better to die than be abused
End the joke
Don't end up the joke!
You're too smart for that,
Too strong
You're nobody's arse-wipe
You're nobody's fool.
Deep inside it fucking hurts.
I actually used to feel for you
I trusted you in my dreams
My fist smashed through the unbreakable glass
'Unbreakable' –
Don't make me fucking laugh,
Crazy bitch.
A scar is for all time,
On the slab for all to see.
What happened to the last 30 years?
What went wrong?
Who's driving this machine?
Some cunt without a map.
"Hell"
Staring me in the face,
Some cunt with a large fork,
Horns on top of his large red head,
A tail – and I don't mean cock.
The Devil himself
In bra and panties,
Fucking pervo.
There was a time not long back
I could've, would've crippled him.
Now… I laugh.
A friendly gesture,
A crooked smile,
Brokenhearted but laughing.
I hear an angel,
I think I do.
One must hold on to small blessings,
Never let go.

Like holding onto a moving train,
Your arms leave your body
Armless and bleeding.
The blood of insanity.
Night time I crawl back into my dream
A punch in the teeth
A kick in the head
It doesn't hurt so much in the dark
Hell… that was no angel
That was a copper with a gun in my ear!
Cunt.
They crept up on me like rats from the sewer
They want to break and snap my arms
Demobilise me
I'm just a target!
The man they want so bad
The man they dream of catching
We got him… he's not so tough!
We gave him a fucking good going over
He screamed like a castrated cat
Scream?
I don't think so!
I fucking know so!
Me scream? That wasn't a scream
It was a shout
A demand
Pull the fucking trigger, cunt!
Everything's cool
It's sweet
Do it
Release the pain
I'm drunk on madness
Every fucker blames everybody else!
You're all somebody's excuse
Me,
I'm just lost inside the graveyard
A lost soul in the pouring rain
That's not rain
It's droplets of blood
I'm drenched in human liquid
Red as a tomato…
A festering, stinking swamp of monsters
Heavy, sinking thoughts of hopelessness
A broken neck
A bent spine
Sweet agony
The smell of rotting flesh
Stale smell of stinking sweat
Shower you bastard or die

Experiments on the brain
Lobotomised
Sliced open like a spring onion
The mission crashed
The street light's gone out
A car blew up in the darkness
Who was in it?
A calf to the slaughter
A lamb chopped in half
A dog without a head
Chicken and chips
You either destroy it or become it!
Brainwash time
The time is now
Ready to fight or run!
The past is bleeding
A mountain of shit
A river of tears
So fucking ugly and insane
Petrol
Up in flames
The air fills with fear
Burn you bastard
It's beautiful.

Fuck knows where these poems come from but I sure know where they're going: straight to Hell. I just feel them flow out of my pen and they amaze me. Me a poet, me of all people. It's wonderful!

Paddy takes his new wife home on their wedding night and she lays on the bed naked and spread-eagled and says, "Do you know what I want, Paddy?"

"Yeah," Paddy replies, "the whole fucking bed by the look of it!"

A murderer is sitting in the electric chair, about to be executed. "Have you any last requests?" asks the governor. "Yeah," replies the murderer, "will you hold my hand?"

Saturday, 16 August 2008.

I got a pile of mail today: some good, some funny and one sad. My old buddy Paul Massey just lost his mother. She passed away on Wednesday. That's the biggest loss a man can have. A mother is priceless. Paul's a top chap from Manchester, a well-respected man who's seen it all, done it all and got a box full of T-shirts. His mother used to love my art so I'll create a tribute art in her honour, which will be an honour to do. Chin up, pal...

Dee wrote and enclosed this letter from Siobhain McDonagh MP via Maria Eagle MP, under-secretary of state for justice. Read it and have a good laugh!

Siobhain McDonagh MP
020 7219 4678 (tel)
020 7219 0986 (fax)
mcdonaghs@parliament.uk

HOUSE OF COMMONS
LONDON SW1A 0AA
LABOUR MEMBER OF PARLIAMENT FOR MITCHAM AND MORDEN

Our Ref: MORR01002/01020997

5 August 2008

Dear Miss Morris

I attach a copy of a letter I have received regarding your enquiry.

I do hope this is helpful and if I can be of any further assistance in this or any other matter, please do not hesitate to contact me.

Yours sincerely

Siobhain McDonagh

www.siobhainmcdonagh.org.uk

*Colliers Wood*Figges Marsh*Graveney*Lavender*Longthornton*Lower Morden*Phipps Bridge*Pollards Hill*Ravensbury*St Helier*

Constituency office, 1 Crown Road, Morden, SM4 5DD. Please address all replies to the House of Commons, SW1A 0AA.

Maria Eagle MP
Parliamentary Under-Secretary of State
Selborne House
54 Victoria Street
London
SW1E 6QW

T: 020 7210 8500
E: general.queries@justice.gsi.gov.uk

www.justice.gov.uk

Siobhain McDonagh MP
1 Crown Road
MORDEN
SM4 5DD

Our Ref: 207558/48408mc
Your Ref: MORR01002/0102099

28 JUL 2008

Dear Siobhain,

Thank you for your letter of 7 July, addressed to Vernon Coaker at the Home Office, on behalf of Miss Dalanya Morris about Charles Bronson. Miss Morris also refers to the case of Ronald Biggs. I am replying as Minister responsible for the matters raised.

I am unable to comment on the individual circumstances of either Mr Bronson or Mr Biggs. However, I have to say that neither Mr Bronson or Mr Biggs are being detained as political prisoners. Furthermore, neither is in prison custody as any form of example as suggested by Miss Morris. Both men were convicted by the courts of criminal offences and sentenced to terms of imprisonment, and the National Offender Management Service (NOMS) is complying with those court decisions.

NOMS is committed to treating those sentenced by the courts fairly, decently and humanely. Equally, it is expected of prisoners that they will treat staff and other prisoners in the same way and work towards compliance with their sentence plan. Every prisoner is the subject of an individual risk assessment that takes into account the nature of their offence, compliance with sentence planning and their general behaviour amongst other matters. Depending on the results of those assessment matters such as a security category and location within prisons will be determined. Unfortunately, a number of prisoners will remain category A for many years.

Social visits with family and friends are encouraged by NOMS, but again these are all subject to individual risk assessments. If Mr Bronson disagrees with any decision taken by the prison then, in common with all other prisoners, he is able to lodge a complaint and if necessary refer the matter to the Prisons and Probation Ombudsman.

All prisoners have their security category reviewed on a regular basis and those classified as category A are no exception. Mr Bronson is able to participate fully in this process and again has the right to challenge any decision made. No prisoner is treated as an animal as Miss Morris implies or is rotting in the prison. NOMS aims to treat all prisoners fairly and with respect.

In the case of Mr Biggs, he is serving a sentence of imprisonment imposed on him by the courts. All prisoners receive appropriate medical and other health care support as required and this will include any assistance considered necessary for Mr Biggs.

Finally, Miss Morris attaches a media report on another person. While I note she seeks to compare the case of this person with that of Mr Bronson and Mr Biggs, without full details of the individual circumstances such comparisons can be misleading. However, the person that is the subject of the media report appears not to have been in prison custody.

Best Wishes, Maria Eagle

MARIA EAGLE MP

It's all a bloody joke! It really is an insult to anybody with a brain. It actually tells me what I already know. What a complete farce it all is. The old saying 'They all piss in the same pot' comes to mind. But their pot is overflowing and it stinks! At least Siobhain McDonagh tried to get some answers, but these answers are really not worth having. Going on this, I'm not being kept in a cage or in isolation and Ronnie Biggs is not a political prisoner! (And pigs do fly…)

Hey, my thanks to Dee Morris. She really does go out of her way to get my case sorted. If there were another 10,000 like Dee, the MPs would have to give real reasons for this madness. But believe me, there are no reasons to keep any man in a cage for year after year. Unless of course you're a brain sucker or a complete raving psycho…

I've had a nice relaxing day today. I slept a bit and did an A3-sized art. I had a read and I played my soul tape! It was a Saturday; we should all be in the pub having a sing song. Well, I should be anyway. Why not? Give me one good reason why not. You can't, so fuck off!

Monday, 18 August 2008.

Oh well, I got the governor's decision for my parole review on 29 August in black and white today. Read it yourselves and decide if it's fair! Deciding to have me in a cage like an ape with the parole board looking in on me is all I expected from the fucking idiots. The only good part will be my QC ripping into them. (If he doesn't I'll want to know why not!)

The truth is that it's all a big farce, so I'll make my prediction of the outcome now: "Bronson's too dangerous to be given parole. Next review August 2010. Goodbye!"

Oh well, fuck all that. What will be will be.

I'll tell you who must have a headache: Phil Collins, who's just paid out £25 million on his third divorce. Fuck me; doesn't he ever learn? As I've said for years, marriage is for muppets.

I got a letter off my aunty Eileen today! She's a good old stick, a true survivor. Ifty is up to visit me tomorrow! It's always a treat to have a chat with Ifty.

I see Ronald O'Sullivan, (Ronnie's dad) just won a prison snooker tournament in Sudbury jail where he's serving his life sentence. He copped his life sentence in 1991 and it's time they let him out, as he only had a row with a geezer. Sadly he got killed but it's not as if Ron's a big-time gangster! In fact he's a decent bloke and a fucking good snooker player. It's funny really: Ronnie Jnr wins a tournament and gets quarter of a million whereas Ronnie Snr probably won £50 if that! Yeah, it's time they let him out. If he was a dirty old nonce he would've been let out years ago. Fucking let him out, you cunts! He's done his bird.

I got a parcel with some pens and pencils and stuff from Sandra Gardner. She spoils me. I called Danny Hansford. He's just back from Hollywood and it's all good news from him. But it's hard to discuss bizz matters when I'm on these high-risk calls with some nosey cunt 'ear holing' every word and getting ready to cut the line if I say anything out of line! I fucking hate nosey fuckers sticking their nose into my bizz, don't you? It's none of their

Your Ref:

Our Ref:

Date: 18th August 2008

MR SPERRY. Q.C

RE: Mr Charles Bronson BT1314

Many thanks for your letter dated 5th August 2008 in respect of Mr Bronson (BT1314), the content of which I note.

I have fully discussed the issues that you raised in your letter in respect of Mr Bronson forthcoming DLP Hearing with the Multi Disciplinary Team involved in the management of your client and I can conclude the following:

Firstly I wish to clarify that Mr Bronson's parole hearing has now been moved to Friday 29th August at 10:00am at the request of the Judge chairing the Panel. Mr Bronson has been made aware of this change.

Secondly, I have discussed the location of the DLP hearing following your request that it be heard in the Adjudication Room at HMP Wakefield. Having considered this request we feel that we are unable to do so. Mr Bronson is currently located within an Exceptional Risk Unit due to his custodial Behaviour over many years. As such, the Policy for visits (Legal & Domestic), DLPs, or any visit involving members of the public will be closed/controlled conditions; therefore I am unable to facilitate your request.

Finally, as indicated above, I am unable to grant your request for an Open Consultation with Mr Bronson prior to the DLP for the reasons I have indicated above. We are more than happy to facilitate a visit with Mr Bronson before the hearing under the guidelines currently in place for Legal visits to Offenders held within our Exceptional Risk Unit.

I hope I have been able to clarify the issues that you have raised. However, please feel free to contact me if can be of further assistance to you in this matter.

Many thanks

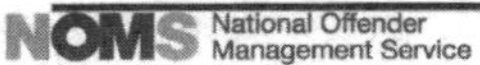

Page 1 of 1

bizz and I say it's illegal. Who the fuck do they think they are, the FBI? Oh well, that's prison for you!

I had a nice cheese salad for tea and I had my monthly cell search. They found fuck all because there's nothing to find! I always tell them, "If you find any dosh I'll go halves with you." They're called the DST (Dedicated Search Team) and they're dressed in black. Some actually believe they're the SAS and they walk like John Wayne just getting off a horse! Fucking idiots, they've found fuck all in my cell for years! But I must admit that over the years they've had a few buckets of 'Bronco Moonshine' and the odd home-made 'chiv'. Well, I'm not an angel! Who is? I don't even want to be an angel. Could you really imagine me with a set of wings?

19 August 2008.

I had a great visit from Ifty; we always have a good old chat. He got me two banana milkshakes and eight choc bars. Fucking lovely. I've been known to polish off a few choc bars. We've decided to slam in an official complaint over his son Wahid not being allowed to see me. It's just pure evilness (if not a racial issue) to let one son see me and not another! So watch this space on that. The good news is that I'm to be godfather to his lovely daughter Zahra's baby. I keep telling you we're all one big family and I'm proud of it. The more the merrier!

Talking of kids... watch out – Gary Glitter's out. The dirty nonce is now out of jail and back in the UK. No kid is safe with that cunt about!

What's the difference between a woman and a computer? A woman won't accept a 3½ inch floppy!

Who remembers Big James Allen Red Dog? Nah, I don't suppose you do. He was executed by lethal injection in 1993. His last words, just before the poison shot into his veins, were: "I'm going home, baby." Don't you just love a good saying? I fucking love it. Brilliant!

Ifty looked smart in his black suit. Black's my favourite colour; there's something about it – it's mysterious and spooky. I've always liked black pussies too; they seem to shine and glow and sparkle! A black pussy seems to come alive and speak. (Fuck me, if the prison shrink reads this I'll be carted back to the asylums. "Bronson's been talking to black pussies!")

Hey! I've got a list of the top 10 prison films:

1	*Shawshank Redemption*	1994
2	*Midnight Express*	1978
3	*Cool Hand Luke*	1967
4	*The Green Mile*	1999
5	*Scum*	1979
6	*The Big House*	1930
7	*Papillon*	1973
8	*Stir Crazy*	1980
9	*The Longest Yard*	1974
10	*Escape From Alcatraz*	1979

Well, it's not my top 10! What about *The Birdman of Alcatraz, In the Name of the Father, Last Light* or *Jimmy Boyle*? Come to think of it, what about mine? Do you cunts think I've survived three and a half decades to not have my movie in the top 10?

Hey! John H Stracey has now been refused permission to visit me. This month must be knock-back month. It's piss-take month. I'm not quite sure how there going to justify this one! John's in the boxing hall of fame and is an ex-world champion with a clean record (not even a parking ticket). He's a respected member of the public, a charity worker and a bloody good man. Like I say, this system is full of hypocrites, piss-takers and total wankers! Fuck 'em and watch this space, because John won't take this shit! Nobody mugs him off. This one should be good, because whoever made this mental decision has now got to justify it! Try it, cunt.

As Gary Miller sat in the death chamber of a Texas jail he was asked: "Is there any last request?" Miller replied, "I suppose resuscitation is out of the question?" Isn't that brilliant? Words of wisdom from a dying man. He's just about to be murdered by the state and he comes out with a classic like that!

In 1994 Robert Drew was executed by lethal injection in Texas. His last words were: "Remember, the death penalty is murder." Sean Flannagan's last words were, "I love you." (A nice way to die I suppose.) They executed him in 1989. James French went to the electric chair in 1966 in Oklahoma and he shouted out, "French fries!" Now that's a fucking blinder; I love it. But my favourite of all time was George Appel. He was an old mobster who went to the chair in 1928 and said, "Well folks, you'll soon see a baked apple." That's what I call a star! Max respect to the man.

The last man to die in the gas chamber in California was Robert Alton Harris back in 1992. He said, "You can be a king or a street cleaner, but we all gotta dance with the grim reaper." Fuck me; he knew how to send a shiver down your spine!

Tough guy Johnny Frank Garrett Snr went to the death chamber in 1992 and said, "I'd like to thank my family for loving me and taking care of me. And the rest of the world can kiss my ass." I'll drink to that one! Three cheers for JF Garrett. HIP HIP – HOORAY! HIP HIP – HOORAY! HIP HIP – HOORAY! Guys like him make this shithole of a planet shine! Even in death they're legends. Respect.

Hey, the electric chair was not so clever! Back in 1946, 17-year-old Willie Francis survived 'old sparky' and said afterwards that he felt a burning inside his head and in his left leg. A year later he sat in 'old sparky' again and fried! The last man to die in the chair was Brandon Hendrick in Nebraska on 20 July 2006. It's now mostly lethal injection in the USA. So which would you prefer: gas, an injection, electricity, a noose or a bullet? Come on, make your mind up, how do you want to die?

Life on death row in China is short. Once you're sentenced to death you're normally executed within a week. If you're lucky enough to appeal you may last another week, but then you're shot. In the USA you can be on death row for 10, 20, even 30 years. So which is the cruellest? What would you prefer: 30 years in a tin can then taken out and blown away; or China's fast justice – blink, fart and die? Does a man really want to live in a tin can for all those years waiting to die? Why bother? Fuck it; China's for me! A cup of tea and a slice of fairy cake, then put a big hole in the back of my skull! Good night, cunts.

Can you believe it's 31 years since they executed Gary Gilmore in Utah prison? He chose to die by bullet! Did you know his last phone call to the outside world was to Johnny Cash? Then they sat him in the chair, put a hood over his head, four marksmen took aim and Gilmore shouted out, "Let's do it!" BANG... lights out. It's interesting that one of those four marksmen had a dud bullet and none of them knew who it was. They live on wondering if it was them with the blank! Yeah, it's all fucking mental to me – pure Loonyology. "Let's do it!"

I got a dozen letters today – all crackers with loads of news. A brilliant day! I called Mark Fish and he's always got the finger on the pulse. Giovanni told him to tell me: "Stay cool, Charlie, we are getting you out. It's all unlawful what they are doing to you." Yeah! I'm not alone! My case will never be swept under the mat. I'm prison HQ's worst nightmare, I really am.

I pulled the governor this morning and said: "Oi, Gov, do you honestly believe you're getting away with all this shit? Soon you'll be exposed," and went on about John H Stracey being knocked back. You've guessed it: he said, "It wasn't my decision." It's 'pass the parcel' with these spineless prats!

John Spenkelink was executed in the chair in Florida in 1979. He said it all: "Capital punishment? Those without capital get the punishment." How fucking true is that? No cash, no lawyer; plenty of cash, plenty of lawyers! Did you know 90% of people executed in the US are black? It's time you Yanks woke up!

Hey, don't you think I'm a walking prison encyclopaedia? Am I a genius or what? I bet you lot are wondering if there's anything I don't know about prisons and asylums!

One prisoner in American history stands out for me, and that's George Jackson. He was a young black guy from Chicago who was slung into Hell and died in Hell! His crime was a poxy £30 gas station hold-up in which nobody got hurt. Then, in 1970, along with three other inmates, he killed a guard in Soledad prison but so few understand why they did it. It was in retaliation for a guard killing three black prison activists! Guess what? The guard got a 'not guilty' but we all know what George Jackson got: a fucking big hole of isolation and brutality. George's brother Jonathan ended up taking a judge hostage in Marin County Court and demanded that his brother George be freed. Come on, his kid brother was only 17 and he idolised his brother. Guess what happened? They shot him dead. (That's how true heroes go: out in a blaze.) George survived a year or two more until a San Quentin guard shot him dead on the exercise yard. They said George was armed. Was he? I doubt it! I'd say they shot him over the Soledad guard's murder. Revenge is best served cold on a plate of misery! I respect both George and Jonathan because they lived and died how they chose: "Fuck with me and you get fucked." They are brothers to remember; brothers in the fight for sanity – feared but respected. God bless you both.

By the way, George wrote two books whilst in solitary: *Blood in my Eye* and *Soledad Brother*. If you want a good read about the prison world then treat yourselves to those. Enjoy. Oh, the judge young Jonathan took hostage was Harold Haley. I bet he shat himself! It amazes me that a film hasn't been made about the Jackson brothers. I wonder why? It's probably because the truth really does open up a hornets' nest and people get stung. Cunts...

Three cheers for the Jackson brothers: HIP HIP – HOORAY! HIP HIP – HOORAY! HIP HIP – HOORAY!

I'll tell you a gang you really don't want to fuck with: the 'Surenos'. This Mexican American mob rules the inside of California's jails and you don't fuck with them or you'll get your balls cut off and lose your head. *Adios, amigos*! Be warned. The Texas branch is known as Mexikanemi. Their membership is for life and they make the Hell's Angels look like pussies! We're talking about a serious criminal organization here. They're men on a mission who are prepared to sacrifice their own lives or those of others – die or kill with a smile! Fuck me; anyone for tea and toast? Get me out of here, I'm a celebrity!

Yeah, American jails are full of gangs and wars. Guys go into jail for stealing a packet of fags and end up in a war zone. Next thing they're dragged into some sort of brotherhood and wake up on death row, all for a packet of fags.

Do you know that a 'torpedo' is gangland slang for a hitman? If you hear someone say, "Bring down the light," then fucking run or pull out an Uzi and start firing because they're talking about fulfilling their contract. Yiiippppeeeee! Yarrhhooooooo!

Shall I give you some basic rules on how best to survive prison? (Just in case the tax man catches up with you!) OK, here goes:

1 Keep your mouth shut.
2 Don't talk in your sleep.
3 Be your own boss.
4 If you have to share a cell then tell your cellmate on day one: "Fart, and I'll snap your spine!"
5 Do one day at a time and pray that tomorrow comes.
6 Stay clear of poofs!

Those are the Bronson rules. Take them or leave them, but if you live by those six rules you'll survive easily... unless of course you become some con's bitch or rent boy! You won't be the first to suck cock or take a length and you won't be the last, either. Some men are born to bend over and become bitches; that's how they survive inside. What a way to live, though. How can a man end up on his knees like that, with a mouth and arse full of spunk? Boy, oh boy, how fucking sad does it get? Kill yourselves, you sad bastards – die with some dignity, you cunts.

Did you know that no British boxer who's won an Olympic gold medal has ever gone on to win a world champion belt in the pro game? Not yet anyway, but here's the ones from other countries who have:

1920	Frankie Genard	(Flyweight)
1924	Jackie Fields	(Featherweight)
	Willie Smith	(Bantamweight)
	Fidel Labarba	(Flyweight)

1948	Pascal Perez	(Flyweight)
1952	Floyd Patterson	(Middleweight)
1960	Cassius Clay	(Light Heavyweight)
1964	Joe Frazier	(Heavyweight)
1968	George Foreman	(Heavyweight)
1972	Mate Parlov	(Light Heavyweight)
1976	Leon Spinks	(Light Heavyweight)
	Michael Spinks	(Middleweight)
	Sugar Ray Leonard	(Light Welterweight)
	Leo Randolph	(Flyweight)
1980	Slobodan Kacar	(Light Heavyweight)
	Patrizio Oliva	(Light Welterweight)

I hope you're all taking note as I'll be asking questions later! Don't fucking take my knowledge for weakness or I swear I'll knock you out...

1984	Frank Tate	(Light Middleweight)
	Mark Breland	(Welterweight)
	Meldrick Taylor	(Featherweight)
	Maurizio Stecca	(Bantamweight)
1988	Lenny Lewis	(Super Heavyweight)
	Ray Mercer	(Heavyweight)
	Henry Maske	(Middleweight)
	Giovanni Parisi	(Featherweight)
	Kennedy Mckinney	(Bantamweight)
1992	Oscar De La Hoya	(Lightweight)
	Joel Casamayor	(Bantamweight)
1996	David Reid	(Light Middleweight)
	Istvan Kovacs	(Bantamweight)
	Vassily Jirov	(Light Heavyweight)
	Wladimir Klitschko	(Super Heavyweight)

Look, guys, I think that's enough on boxing legends for now. Let's get back to prison...

You all remember the Oklahoma bomber Timothy McVeigh who was executed in 2001? Before they blew him away, he said, "I knew my objective was a state-assisted suicide and when it happens it's in your face, motherfuckers, you just did something you're trying to say should be illegal for medical personnel." This guy had serious psychological damage and was one dangerous motherfucker.

So, do you want to know what's in that lethal cocktail they use in the death chamber? What do you think it is, weedkiller? I'll tell you what it is: sodium thiopental to induce sleep, pancuronium bromide to collapse the lungs and potassium chloride to shut down the heart. It's a cocktail of death! Good night, have a good journey! It's all over. Back to the darkness...

Talking of darkness, Ronnie Phillips, who I met in Hull jail in 1975, painted his cell, curtains, bedspread and clothes black. He even had a fucking crow as a pet. I wonder what ever happened to Ronnie and the crow? Mad fucker.

We had a full-sized snooker table on every wing in Hull jail. One night on association on B-Wing we got a grass and held him down on the table whilst others took shots and bounced the ball off his head! It was so funny and memories like that last forever. They were great times!

I picked a screw up in Hull and ran with him through B-Wing dining hall, shouting, "I've got a bomb, stand back or I'll explode it!" I was only having a laugh but it cost me 28 days remission and a £5 fine. Cunts. Some people just can't take a joke!

There was a screw in Hull in the 1970s who had a big scar down his 'boat' which Frankie Mitchell gave him in the 1960s. He was a horrible cunt and I used to say to him: "Fuck off, before I slice the other half of your boat." He fucking hated me… I also said to him, "If Frank was still alive he would cut your fucking head off." He was a horrible cunt. But then again, he was a survivor! Frank Mitchell could have a serious fight. What a legend he was: six feet two of muscle and 16 stone of porridge. You did not fuck with mad Frank. Some tried and they all got hurt! Only a bullet in the crust could stop Frank and even then it took six. God bless him.

I had fish fingers and chip, six bread rolls and some fruit and nuts today! I'm calling it a day now. If I don't come back then it's your loss, not mine! Remember what I told you guys: don't fuck with the 'Brotherhood' and never forget who's the daddy. Is that somebody hiding under your bed? I did warn you! Would you listen to me? Would you fuck, you cunt.

23 August 2008.

Fuck me; we're doing well out in Beijing. 18 golds and it's still not over. Come on you Brits! We've won more golds than ever before. The next Olympics are over here in 2012 and I fucking want to be there. What a liberty it'll be I'm still locked up! I just can't think that far ahead because it drives me nuts.

I woke up at 5.30am, jumped out of bed and stuck my head in a bowl of cold water. It was beautiful and I felt fresh and alive like one of the Olympic divers. Then I had a good dump – that's a good three pounds I lost! What is it about a good shit? (And it was a good shit too!) It was one of those turds that slips out so long, cool and splendid that it touches the bottom of the pan and begins to curl up like a snake. I felt a twinge of pride! It was a good colour, a good texture and a good healthy log. I thank God for it! Some poor souls would love to shit like I do! After that I had a good wash all over my body, brushed my teeth and felt alive. Another day and a new chapter to life! The coffin is alive with good vibes. If zombies are for real, we know how to come alive and kick some serious arse.

Talking of arses, I'll tell you who's got a gorgeous arse: actress Roxanne Pallett. She's the one who stars in Emmerdale and she's got an arse to die for. What a beautiful, angelic body she has, but don't tell her I said so or I'll go all shy! You lot know what I'm like – I get all flustered and shy about things like that. So don't fucking say a word or I'll have to get nasty! OK?

Talking of nasty, what about this filthy cunt Peter Rowley from Sutton in Surrey? (I've got a lot of pals in that area.) He's just copped 14 years for paedophilia. He told a girl he had satanic powers and scared the pants off of her to have his wicked ways. 14 years, eh? He's 62 now! Hurry up and die, you old fart! He's lucky none of my mates got a hold of him. I've known the 'chaps' to bury people for less! The late Joe Pyle Snr used to live in that plot and a lot of the 'faces' still do. We all hate a fucking nonce. Leave our kids alone, you old pervos. Somebody kick that Glitter in the bollocks to teach the old nonce a lesson. LEAVE OUR KIDS ALONE!

I see Kerry Katona (ex-Atomic Kitten) has just declared herself bankrupt! I like Kerry, she's a good soul. If times get hard for her, she can always kip in my caravan. (She'd be more than welcome.)

Have you heard the latest Home Office fuck up? Data on 84,000 prisoners has been lost, including their names, addresses and release dates! These fucking idiots are in charge of the country and they can't even sort their own office out! It's a serious security blunder and they're all a bunch of muppets. (I've been telling you this for years.) I'm now in the process of seeking legal advice in order to sue them for neglect. Some cunt has got my file so some cunt knows my home address and all my details! It's all on a computer memory stick and they've lost it. Cunts. These cunts are in charge of our lives! Fuck me; you can't make it up. It's a massive security breach and every prisoner in the UK should sue and be compensated. Let's see, what's a fair pay out? 20K each for all the stress that it's caused us and our families? Yeah, that sounds about spot on. Cunts...

I'll tell you who's a nasty fucker: Paul Slack. He got lifed off for killing Alan Bowles by ramming his walking stick down his throat. What a way to leave the planet!

What about 75-year-old Ged Mullane? He's Britain's strongest pensioner and he just bench-pressed 105 kilos – that's 16 ½ stone. That's awesome for an old chap like him. Respect to you, Grandpop.

Did you know there are currently 4,400 women in British prisons? That's 5% of the prison population and it's creeping up. What a waste of good pussy! Let's have mixed prisons. I think it would work with all the sweet and tender loving, but knowing my luck I'd end up sharing a cell with Rose West. Rose and Charlie, Charlie and Rose... Nah, it doesn't sound right. Let's forget it (as I've got a headache coming on)!

Get on this one, this is a fucking insult to all kids. Filthy Phil Thompson ran a global paedo ring with 10,000 monster members. He pleaded guilty to 27 charges and was sentenced to life with a tariff of three years. Three fucking years? Why not 30? Make an example of the beast like they do with armed robbers! It's time our judges woke up and smelt the shit! "30 years, Thompson. Take him down!" (And make sure he slips on the steps and bangs his head all the way down to the bottom. Cunt.) This is why our country is laughed at by the rest of the world. We are too soft on the sick bastards and it's time to fucking get real. What do you say?

I see Guantanamo Bay military prison is still alive and kicking. How do the Yanks get away with that? Human rights don't exist there. We still have one British detainee there – Binyam Mohamed has been held there for five years. All his confessions were made under torture and he faces a military trial where a guilty verdict could result in the death penalty! So what are we doing about that, then? I'll tell you: fuck all... If it was the Russians or Chinese holding him there'd be murders over it. Oh well, that's showbiz. Guantanamo Bay, kiss my fucking arse! You can kid some but you won't kid us all!

You're going to love this one: Steve McGovers just climbed up on the roof of Broadmoor to protest about the smoking ban. Fucking good stuff, Steve... but why climb down without wrecking the place? You had a chance to destroy the God-forsaken place that most lunatics can only dream of having. Every lunatic around the planet dreams of ripping off the asylum roof! You climbed all the way up then came down without destroying anything or achieving anything. The smoking ban is still on.

I told you the loons wouldn't be happy with that smoking ban. Watch this space because more protests will follow! Some of those loonies have been smoking for 50 or 60 years, so how can you expect them to stop? What are you – mad? A fag and a cup of tea is all they've got in life, you cruel fuckers. Give 'em a fag, you mad fuckers. I bet there will soon be some suicides there. You're driving the mad men mad. Fuck me; how would Ronnie Kray have handled a ban on fags? He was a 60 a day man! Yep, I can foresee some serious shit over this, can't you? It's a 'catch-22' situation because Broadmoor comes under the NHS so it has to follow strict Health Service rules. The screws are nurses, the inmates are patients and the cells are rooms! Keep taking your pills, lads! It's nicotine patches and pretend sweet fags for you lot.

It sort of makes Broadmoor look like a pussy house. It's a different era now, because 30 years ago the loons would have taken a stand; they wouldn't have accepted such bollocks! What the fuck have they got to lose? Oh well, that's life. (I don't give a fuck anyway – I don't even smoke!)

I remember old Jerry Dale, he was a Broadmoor legend who smoked a pipe which he used to fill with dope. He was always out of his nut and laughed his years away. He was an old man full of dreams but he would've ripped your throat out if you'd taken his pipe off him. That was his life, his world. He was a happy soul – a madman blessed with joy! I'll drink to that.

There was a doctor in Broadmoor in the 1970s who had a nose on him like a beak. It was massive and we called him 'Parrot-face'. One day I walked into his office and grabbed it! I squeezed and twisted it whilst I sang: "Rudolph the red nosed reindeer, had a very shiny nose..." That cost me a couple of weeks in seclusion and my medication increased. But I won 10 giant Galaxy bars because I had a bet with two loons who said I wouldn't do it! That's how fun it was in them days. We were always up to something. That's what loonies are supposed to do, aren't they? It's Broadmoor, not Balmoral or Butlins. It's a fucking cuckoo house.

The maddest fucker I ever saw in my life was a loon who bit through the TV wire and electrocuted himself. If it wasn't for the fast actions of a screw who turned the mains off, we would've witnessed a mad death. It was insane, it was fucking Loonyology! It was madness at its very best and I love it. I was a part of all this stuff so I salute every loony on the planet. You all made my life a richer journey; you educated me beyond my wildest dreams and I wouldn't have missed it for the world. It made me what I am today: a man of substance and a professor of Loonyology! Thank you, my brothers.

I see Bridget Wilkinson just copped a 15-month prison sentence for trying to smuggle in 2.3 grammes of amphetamine into Drake Hall women's prison. She tried to get it in by concealing it under a Valentine's card to her friend, Jennifer Eiley. Fifteen months is a bit strong for that, don't you think? 2.3 grammes of amphetamine is worth about £100 – it's not exactly crime of the century, is it? Or a particularly dangerous drug. She's had a bad deal there. I hope she appeals. Fifteen months for that? What a farce!

Oh well, cop a load of the letter (over the page) I got from Ifty today about his son Wahid not being allowed to visit me. We will get this put right. Shall I tell you why? Because some prick is taking the piss, that's why! Watch this space because this one is not going away. You can bet your arse on that!

Ifty sure knows how to put a letter together! I have also put in an official complaint and you'll see the reply when I get it. It should be good to see how they worm their way out of this one. Brilliant. Some idiot has made this decision and now has to justify it – some little arsehole who sits behind a desk in his ill-fitting muggy suit with a £10 silly tie and his Parker pen that mummy got him. It's some fucking little power freak who's out to show his authority. It's just pure bollocks, that's all it is! Yeah, this one should be good to see. I can't fucking wait! Personally, I'd prefer to give the cunt a well deserved slap because that's really the best solution to a silly problem. Fucking grow up. As if there aren't enough problems in the world already without making this stuff up. Look at that plane crash in Spain with 153 victims. Now that's a real problem! Get a fucking life, that's what I say!

I had a dozen letters today. I'm still getting plenty from *Loonyology* fans who loved the book. Thanks, I appreciate your support. Mark Fish and Alan Rayment were both on *Calendar News* last night talking about my parole hearing on Friday. Thanks, lads, you do me proud! The hearing's creeping up. It's only six days away now. Doesn't time fly when you're having fun?

I had a fry-up today – the Saturday brunch – fucking lovely it was. I washed down with a pint of tea that I put a spoon of honey in. Do I spoil myself or what? Well, do I? Of course I do. If I don't, who else will? No fucker, and you know it! I'm Charlie Bronson not Jeffrey Archer! Who in their right mind's going to spoil me?

Some people think I'm a right clever cunt, they really do, and they say I'm a know-it-all. I am a clever cunt but don't be jealous. Wouldn't you want me on your team in a pub quiz? OK, I'll give you some facts you can astound your friends with (as long as you say they came from me).

Did you know no English football manager has ever won the premier league? (Not a lot of people know that!) And 650,000 people in Korea have a Manchester United credit card. That's fucking mental!

Did you know about 18% of British men have had a vasectomy? Would you get the snip? There is no way in 1,000 years I'd have my balls fucked about with. It's not normal, is it? Fuck that!

Did you know a cow farts a good 280 litres of methane per day? That is awesome! What a gas!

There are twice as many chickens on the planet than humans, so get eating the little fuckers. They're taking us over!

21st August 2008

The No 1 GOVERNOR
H M PRISON WAKEFIELD
LOVE LANE
WEST YORKSHIRE
WF2 9AG

Dear Mrs Tilley,
Re: BT1314 CHARLES BRONSON, VISIT FROM WAHID IFTKHAR
It is with great disappointment that we are in receipt of the home of decision for my son Wahid Iftkhar's visiting request.

We are appalled at the one line reply which does not give any reason for refusal, thus open to interpretation regards to the deciding factors that formed the basis of the home office decision.

Please bear in mind my both sons applied together, both went through the correct police clearance procedure, both have similar criminal records yet one passed and one was not. Why? It can not be because one has been to prison and one has not because we only have to look at the other people who have been cleared as this has quite rightly not been a deciding factor.

It has been suggested to us by the media that the decision could be based upon our ethnic origins creed and religion, what ever the case we do feel extremely persecuted.

Charles Bronson who is referred to and accepted as an uncle to my children, has helped to keep Wahid and Syied out of serious trouble, I am sure this is evident with in the recorded phone calls and written correspondences.

If it was not for Charles Bronson then I am of no doubt that they would have been in serious trouble, we are very disappointed, my sons where excited at the prospect of seeing their uncle for the first time, they kept to their promise to him to stay away from trouble, take up boxing and encourage other youngsters to do the same.

Charles Bronson and my sons where launching a project to help youngsters get out of gangs. and into sport such as boxing, every body's hopes have been dashed now, the only person that my sons took note of has been taken away.

I thank you for your time and I urge you for an early response.

Yours Sincerely

M. Iftkhar

Did you know a fully-grown rat can run 100 yards in 9.5 seconds and jump a good six feet? Eat your heart out, you sports people. Those rats are born athletes!

Every day in China approximately 44,000 babies are born. No wonder our planet is sinking. That's a lot of nappies – a sky-high pile of shit!

Here's a fact that will blow your socks off: in 1938 Hitler was on the short list for the Nobel Prize. You can say what you like about him but he sure made his mark on our planet. The guy was a fucking genius who come close to ruling the world with his 'perfect nation'. He was one ruthless motherfucker. If you fucked with Adolf you died – it was that simple.

Did you know the average British woman spends two years of her life looking in the mirror? You vain bitches; what a waste of two years! I could understand it if the mirror was above your bed! Have you ever done that? It's fucking brilliant. I recommend it. What a turn on! (Talking of shagging, I'm dying for a session. God, let me win my parole so I can get a bit of pussy before I'm too old! Have a heart, God… I'm only human! A fucking good shag will do me some good.)

The door to 10 Downing Street has always been black, apart from when Herbert Asquith was prime minister from 1908 to 1916. He had it painted dark green. I wonder why? Some flash fucker must know the answer! There's always one big head who knows everything. Come on, crawl out and let us know, you flash cunt!

On 2 May 1960 Caryl Chessman was strapped into the death chair in San Quentin after being on death row for 12 years. Outside the prison gates there was a massive demonstration against the death penalty and Marlon Brando was in the crowd. The only hope Chessman had was of a last-minute call to reprieve him. One actually came through at the same time the deadly gas was released but the warden decided in a split-second it was too late to stop it. Chessman died soon after! Whilst on death row he wrote several books and won a law degree. I guess his most famous sentence would be: "I don't mind dying; I just don't like being told when." However, the most unique thing about the Chessman case was that he was the only man in US criminal history who went to the death chamber without having committed murder. He was known as the 'red light bandit' because he raped and robbed his victims.

The last man to be executed in US by gas was Walter Lagrand in 1999. It's now been branded inhumane and an act of torture by the United Nations Human Rights Committee. Well, we knew all that when Hitler was about!

Talking of gas, I knew a geezer who gassed his wife's cat because he couldn't stand the fucking thing. He threw it in the oven and gassed it! End of cat. Cruel fucker. He later confessed what he'd done to his wife because he couldn't live with his guilt. She hit him with an iron and gave him brain damage. All that for a cat! What you have to understand is that some people can't live with guilt. I've known men walk into a cop shop and confess to a murder they'd committed 20 years previously! It eats them up and they can't let it go, or it can't let them go. They have nightmares. Really, it's best to not kill anybody as you may be killing yourself as well!

In Pollsmoor jail in South Africa, a prisoner called Mogamat Benjamin has served 24 years after he beheaded his victims and ate their hearts. He believes he is God, and to many of the inmates, he is. They idolise him! Fuck messing with Mogamat… I wonder if he's any relation to Maudsley? You never know.

Did you know Winchester Cathedral goes back to the 11th century or that Winchester was once the capital of England? I bet you never knew that? "Winchester Cathedral, you're breaking my heart!"

Yeah, it's all knowledge with Loonyology. The diary room from Hell will teach you a lot – especially how to stay out of jail.

Did you know it's illegal to kiss your partner in public in India? You can actually be sent to prison for two years for it! I wonder what the 'dogging firm' would get? Dogging is a big thing now, it's catching on!

The spy George Blake made a nice escape from the Scrubs back in 1966 after serving only five years of his 42-year sentence! Not bad, eh? He escaped by cutting his cell bars and vanishing in the London fog. He made it over to Moscow and lived happily ever after. I could never understand why he didn't hang. Treason was a capital offence back in 1961 when he copped his sentence. Lucky old George!

In 1990 Michael Randle and Pat Pottle were charged with helping Blake escape. They stood trial and but both were found not guilty. But the insane part is, they had written a book called *The Blake Escape – How We Freed George Blake and Why*. They actually confessed to helping him! How weird is that? They admitted a crime and still got a not guilty. In fact, if they hadn't written the book they wouldn't have stood trial. British law is a funny thing. You just can't make this stuff up. It's brilliant!

In 1987, Jimmy Glass was about to fry in 'old sparky' in Louisiana and said: "I'd rather be fishing." (Don't these legendary dead man quotes blow you away?)

In 1933 in Manchuria, four men were hanged for the murder of a child. They abused, raped and sodomised the 14-year-old girl. Three of the monsters' heads snapped off. Fucking brilliant. That's how crude and brutal hanging was in some parts of the world. Only the best for a nonce, I say. Off with their heads and feed them to the dogs! Yeeeeeooowwwwww, yiiippppeeeeeeeee, yaarrrhhhooooooo, yabadabadoooooooooooooooooo!

Get on this: in May 2006 in Iran, Abbas Hajizadeh and Mohboubeh Mohammadi were both stoned to death under Islamic Sharia law. Talk about old-fashioned; I thought all that shit was a thing of the past! A bit messy if you ask me. A bit over the top don't you think? Shoot the fuckers by all means, but why stone people to death? Get with the times, brothers. This is the 21st century. Wake up.

Yep, it's a crazy old planet! Even the animals are insane. It's like one big dream that's turned into a hellish nightmare. It's fucking magical!

Anyone for a cuppa chow? Pass the fig rolls. Cheers!

25th August, 2008 Monday Bank Holiday!

Oh well, the Beijing Olympics are all over. Britain won 19 golds. Fucking brilliant! The best gold for me was boxer James Degale from London. He beat Cuban favourite Emilio Correa. Degale's a true champ and he can turn pro now and pick up a million bucks (easy). Go for it, buddy – get rich quick! You can't eat a medal.

I personally don't give a flying fuck about half of the golds because I'm not interested in sailing or rowing or bicycles! They're all boring. Let's face facts: a lot of Olympic sports are for posh kids in private schools, like tennis, archery, canoeing, rowing, hockey and horse jumping. Who really gives a fuck! The kids on the council estates don't get a chance to do all that stuff. The only horses they see are on the local gypsy sites! I'm not knocking them; good luck to them! But those sports send me to sleep. I'd sooner watch a blue movie than some prat in Lycra shorts peddling down a road, or four posh ex-public school boys rowing a boat. What the fuck's all that about? It's boring! Even swimming – at least put a shark in the pool to liven it up a bit, boring fuckers!

Anyway, talking of sleep, I've had a brainwave! Well, more a hypothesis. (That's a lovely word. They don't make words like that anymore.) It's a fact that thousands of folk die in their sleep (mostly old folk) and I believe I know why. How many times have you had a dream where you're falling through the air and you wake up confused and in a sweaty panic? You always wake up just before you crash. Well, I think sometimes the dream is so real that people forget to wake up and their hearts blow up when they crash. Their dream is reality – it's about their death from a massive heart failure. You dream the dream and pray you can survive it. If you're not sure you can, then don't ever dream again...

What a boring day today. No mail, no calls – these Bank Holidays are shit. But this is the big week for me! You all know when and why and you're all thinking, "Will he or won't he get parole?" Stick around and find out. You know you have to because this diary has become such a big part of your own life! Where else do you get a journey through Hell?

Oh well, that's my lot. I'm off to bed and it's only 5pm! I'm switching off and I'm going to have a good 14 hours' sleep! Fuck the system.

Good night!

PS Don't forget to look in the mirror because you may not be you! You could be an imposter. If you are then shoot yourself!

26 August 2008.

Robbie Stewart arrived today from the Whitemoor CSC special unit. He killed his unfortunate cellmate Zahid Mubarek in Feltham jail back in 2000. Robbie just flipped and took him out. That's how jail fever can chew your life up! Zahid wasn't the first and you can bet your arse he won't be the last to die a violent death. Robbie bashed his skull in like a boiled egg: 'crack' – lights out. But this was truly a serious fuck-up by the jail bosses. Robbie's a psycho and he should've been in a single cell. He doesn't like Asians and he's got National Front tattoos! He's even got 'R.I.P.' and a cross tattooed on his forehead. Let's be honest here: sticking an Asian con in his cell was not going to make him happy! It's like sticking a scorpion in a tank with a centipede – it's not rocket science to predict what will happen next. Every screw knew the danger and if they say they didn't then there either fucking liars or they're not in the right job.

Robbie ended up with a life sentence and the Mubarek family live on with the sadness of losing their son, brother, uncle, cousin. Everybody loses; nobody wins. I believe the screws should've been put on trial for their lack of common sense. They were in charge of that young con's life and he should never have been put in a racist's cell. How can that be right? There should have been sackings. They fed the pussy cat to the bear. Lunch is served! All in all it's a very sad case. That's Loonyology for you.

By the way, screws in Feltham were known to stick two prisoners in a cell to start a fight. It's known in the system as a 'gladiatorial contest' and the screws bet on the outcome!

There's a movie called *Pierrepoint* and the eponymous hangman is played by the big fat British actor Timothy Spall. It's fucking brilliant so get it now – you're in a for a treat. Spall is amazing and the whole thing looks so real – even the hanging scenes. If you're into prison history then you must see it. You'll be made up. You see it all: the old cells, the condemned cell, the trap door, the noose, even the Ruth Ellis hanging! Yeah, it's a No. 1 movie –five stars for sure.

Talking of hanging, Magdi Elgizoull should've swung. Back in 1997 he stabbed his daughter and a female copper to death. I remember the case well because I was shocked to hear he pleaded guilty to manslaughter on the grounds of diminished responsibility and even more shocked to hear it was accepted! He went to Rampton asylum and now he's having days out and trips home. The only trip he would've had 50 years ago was to Pierrepoint's trap door (no surer bet). I really can't believe it myself, especially since he killed a copper. I actually thought he'd be buried for a good 30 years, but that's how it is today! If you know how to use the mental health people, jump when they tell you to and bend over occasionally, you can get out. Two murders, 10 years, and you're out! Rob a bank and you're a nasty fucker who'll rot inside. It's fucking insane!

Hey, get on this for a laugh: 22-stone Richard Coney got sent to death row in Ohio in 1986 and he's just got his date for death (14 October) but his lawyers are arguing he's too fat to kill! They say the medication he takes due to his size would stop the process of the lethal cocktail in its tracks and his massive bulk would cause him an excruciating death. Oh yeah? So what? The fat cunt never give a shit for the two young women he raped and murdered. Fry the fucker if he's 22 stone or 32 stone. I'll pay the electric bill! Coney, it's time to pack up and fuck off! Stop making excuses and face your end: Hell. The devil awaits and you're going to get that fork rammed right up your arse. You'll be 22 stone of beefburger, cunt.

David Payne's another fucking beast. He raped a 12-year-old and had sex with six other kids – one aged just four. He served eight years of a 21-year sentence and is now back on the streets. Come on, why wasn't this beast jailed for life? How can a man do what he did and walk the streets after eight years? It's sick. Remember his name because you'll hear about him again. Some poor kid's going to suffer soon.

When are people going to wake up? Of course this cunt's been a model prisoner when he's had no kids to shag – that's why he got out so quick! He's a predator to children and the system knows it, but they've freed him to walk amongst your kids! Just who are the real sickos here? Yep, it's crazy but it keeps happening…

I got eight letters today, from Debbie Diamond, Alan Bain, Darren

Powell, Zahra Iftkhar, Mum, Lorraine, and two jail letters which you'll love…

Dear Charles,
My name is Sally and I'm serving 3 ½ years in Styal. I've just read your book called *The Krays and Me*. My dad knew the twins and he told me so many good stories about them. I respect men like the Krays. The reason I'm writing to you is to say I think you're one of life's uncut diamonds, and I believe you will die a mysterious death inside. It's just on the cards for you, Charles! (I also think you know this yourself.) You're a good man! I admire you!
Sally.

Fuck me, Sally, you know how to cheer a guy up! Cheers.

Chaz,
I'm down in Parkhurst and I've just had to tell you that I'm in an old cell of yours as your name is carved into the door. The door's no doubt had many coats of paint since you did it but it's still very clear. It gives me a buzz to know I'm sleeping in a real Bronson cell. Respect to you, Chaz. I hope to read one day soon that you're free! Even some screws down here say you should be let out; it's a bloody injustice the years you have served. Killers and rapists don't serve half of what you have. Stay well, Chaz…
Johnny Wright.

I called Mark Fish tonight but he wasn't in, so I called Dave Courtney. He's a funny fucker. He wished me well for my parole hearing on Friday. All the 'chaps' are rooting for me! Cheers, lads. (What a fucking party it'll be if I win.)

A new governor came on the unit today. He's only in his early 30s and he said he was a screw in Full Sutton when I was there a few years back. I said, "Fuck me; you must have been licking some arse to get a governor's grade so fast." Well, it's only the truth but the truth fucking hurts these people. Fight them with the truth and watch them choke on it! Cunts.

Yeah, I've had a good day with a good session on the yard and a good shower. I felt a hard-on coming, but I thought of Jackie 'Fatso' Jenkins and my cock soon shrivelled! If you're wondering who she is, you really don't want to know. Suffice to say she's a sweaty slag with BO, missing teeth, tattoos, big feet and a fat neck. Fucking forget I ever mentioned her name. She'll kill me if I go on. I've said to much as it is…

Hey, I hope your days are as good as mine! Even if they're half as good you'll be happy. Have a good night. I will!

PS I think I may be getting old, as I farted today and dust flew out! Old or not, clock this complaint I made about Wahid not being allowed to visit me and the reply:

F2059 Sec

HM PRISON SERVICE

FORM COMP 1
PRISONER'S FORMAL COMPLAINT

Establishment
Serial № Wo 175/08F

Read these notes first

1. This form is for you to make a formal written complaint under the complaints procedure. Complaints should wherever possible be sorted out informally by speaking to your wing officer or making an application. Use this form only if you have not been able to resolve your complaint this way.
2. A written complaint should be made within 3 months of the incident or of the relevant facts coming to your notice.
3. Keep the complaint brief and to the point.
4. When you have completed the form, sign it and post in the box provided. The form will be returned to you with a response.
5. If you are unhappy with the response, you can appeal on a separate form (COMP 1A).
6. Some subjects are dealt with only by the Area Manager or Prison Service headquarters. If your complaint is about one of these subjects, the reply will take longer.
7. There is a separate pink form (COMP 2) for confidential access complaints.

Your details (use BLOCK CAPITALS)

Surname	BRONSON	First name(s)	CHARLES ARTHUR
Prison number	BT1314	Location	C.S.C.

Have you spoken to anyone about your complaint ? Yes [✓] No [ ]
If so, who did you speak to ?

STAFF ON UNIT.

Your complaint

YESTERDAY 19.8.2008 MR IFTIKHAR VISITED ME AND HE WAS VERY DISTRESSED AND SHOCKED TO FIND OUT HIS SON WAHID HAS BEEN REFUSED TO VISIT ME, WHEN HIS OTHER SON GUGGY HAS BEEN PASSED. HE FEELS, AND I ALSO FEEL IT IS A SERIOUS RACIAL DECISION MADE BY SOME 'POWER FREAK'.
BOTH SONS I HAVE KNOWN SINCE THEY WERE BOYS: THEY CALL ME UNCLE. AND THIS EVIL DECISION AS CAUSED ALOT OF PAIN AND HEARTACHE FOR THE IFTIKHAR FAMILY.
FOR ME IT JUST PROVES WHAT I'VE SAID FOR 4 DECADES. THE PENAL SYSTEM STINKS OF HYPOCRISY..

Does your complaint have a racial aspect ? Yes [✓] No [ ]
Is your complaint about bullying ? Yes [ ] No [ ]
What would you like to see done about your complaint ?

TO HAVE IT PUT IN WRITING WHY TWO YOUNG BROTHERS HAVE BEEN TREAT SO DIFFERENTLY.
AND WHY IS THE PRISON SERVICE TRYING THERE UPMOST IN STOPPING ME FROM SEEING MY GOOD FRIENDS, WHO ARE STRONG SUPPORTERS OF MINE. (WHAT ARE YOU AFRAID OF)?

Signed [signature] Date 20/8/2008

VF 011 Printed at HMP Kingston 4334 03/2003

Reply: Thank you for your p/c dated 20.8.08. I have investigated this issue and due to intelligence received he was deemed unfit/unsuitable to visit this establishment.

Do they think I'm fucking stupid? That's not an answer – they've got no answer because there is no answer! (Except a load of bollocks.) Oh well, let's see what Ifty can do now. I think it's a disgrace – and the reply even more so. It's an insult to my intelligence! They really must think I'm stupid when they're actually dealing with a genius. I've got a brain like a computer. Fucking idiots. Now you know why I've pulled off nine roofs – the system drove me to it. It's a fact.

Good night.

28 August 2008.

Well, that's my lot. Another book completed! Tomorrow is my parole hearing. The result of that will be the end to this masterpiece, so this will be my last chapter. I'm pleased if the truth be told as it gets very stressful writing it and having to get it to the outside world to be typed up and put into order. It's a fucking headache! Also, as you well know, this lot would sling it all in the bin given half the chance. The governors and the Home Office hate my books, jealous pricks!

I would like to thank Lisa Emmins for all her hard work in typing and compiling it all for me! You're a diamond, Lisa. Without you there would be no book. It's no secret that her husband Mark and me are no longer a team. He knows why and so do I; that's all that matters. I wish him no harm, but life must move on! I don't carry baggage with me because baggage is a burden and it slows a man down. You can become sluggish and stale and end up a demented freak. Fuck that. I rock on, no matter what tomorrow brings. Fuck 'em; fuck the system, it can suck my cock. I'm not playing their silly games. I never have and I never will. I just can't! Why should I?

Anyway, I'll end with some great knowledge for all you fucking ugly brain-dead geeks. (You all know I love you really!)

Did you know Alcatraz had its first lighthouse on the rock in 1854? In 1861 the first civilian prisoners arrived, in 1915 it became a military prison and in 1934 it was handed over to the Department of Justice and re-opened as a Federal penitentiary. US Attorney-General Robert F Kennedy ordered its closure in 1963, then in 1969 Indians occupied the island in protest. (I'm not sure what about. Those Indians are like new age travellers to me – they pop up all over the fucking place!) In 1973 the National Park Service took over and visitors arrived for a tour of the most famous prison on Earth!

Here are some more Alcatraz facts for you! The only land mammal on the rock is the deer mouse and the only amphibian is the salamander. Then there's the gulls – thousands of the fuckers. There's birdshit everywhere. The sharks that swim in the San Francisco Bay are common sand sharks which do not attack people.

There were no executions in Alcatraz but there were eight murders and five suicides. Every prisoner sent to Alcatraz was labelled 'incorrigible' and the average stay was eight to 10 years!

And here's a fucking bombshell for you: the food there was brilliant (for prison grub)! So howz about that then?

I must end this Alcatraz section with a Bronson poem:

You locked me up
Threw away the key
You stole my soul
Away from me
You threw me in the darkest pit
I covered you guards with a bucket of shit
You beat me till I was black and red
I awoke on a blood-stained bed
You even tried to break my heart
Hell on Earth from the start
Fuck you Alcatraz – rot in Hell
I survived and lived to tell.

Hey, you boxing fans, get on this then tell me the Cubans are wankers. These are all the Cuban Olympic boxing champions:

1972 – Munich:	Orlando Martinez	(Bantamweight)
	Emilio Correa	(Welterweight)
	Teofilio Stevenson	(Heavyweight)
1976 Montreal:	Jorge Hernandez	(Flyweight – Light)
	Angel Herrera	(Featherweight)
	Teofilio Stevenson	(Heavyweight)

If Teofilio had turned pro, he would've ruled the world. He would've beaten Ali! Teofilio was without a doubt the best heavyweight on the planet in the 1970s but Castro doesn't like his boxers to turn pro! (I wonder why.)

1980 – Moscow	Juan Hernandez	(Bantamweight)
	Angel Herrera	(Lightweight)
	Andres Aldama	(Welterweight)
	Armando Martinez	(Light Middleweight)
	Jose Gomez	(Middleweight)
	Teofilio Stevenson	(Heavyweight)

Look – it's Teofilio again! He was a superman. He would've won gold again in 1984 but Cuba boycotted the games, probably because the US upset Castro again. The Yanks are good at winding him up!

1984 – Los Angeles	(Olympic Boycott)	
1988 – Seoul	(Olympic Boycott)	
1992 – Barcelona	Roger Marcelo	(Light Flyweight)
	Joe Casamayor	(Bantamweight)
	Hector Vincent	(Light Welterweight)
	Juan Lemus	(Light Middleweight)
	Ariel Harnandez	(Middleweight)
	Felix Savon	(Heavyweight)
	Roberto Balado	(Super Heavyweight)
1996 – Atlanta	Maltiro Romero	(Flyweight)
	Hector Vincent	(Light Welterweight)

	Ariel Hernandez	(Middleweight)
	Felix Savon	(Heavyweight)
2000 – Sydney	Guillermo Rigondeauz	(Bantamweight)
	Mario Kindelam	(Lightweight)
	Jorge Gutierrez	(Middleweight)
	Felix Savon	(Heavyweight)
2004 – Athens	Y.Bartelmi	(Light Flyweight)
	Y.Gamboa	(Flyweight)
	G. Rigondeaux	(Bantamweight)
	M. Kindelan	(Lightweight)
	O. Solis	(Heavyweight)

2008 – Check it out yourselves. What do you think I am, your fucking servant? Lazy fuckers!

Hey, those Cubans can fight, dance and fuck! They're beautiful people. Respect to you Cubans. Boxing is in your blood, the first game is in your heart, your soul's ablaze with victory!

What's a man made for? To fight and to win! If a man can't fight then he's not a man. Today's man is a pussy cat; a house-husband. Wash the dishes, you prats. Men of my generation didn't do that – they either worked hard or robbed harder! A fight was all part of a day's graft. You'd punch their fucking lights out in the ring with gloves, or out of the ring with knuckle dusters! That's life and who can argue with that? Men are men and mice are mice. Squeak, fucking squeak. Just don't squeak near me! (Let's leave it at that.)

The US Hall of Fame Golden Gloves champions who went onto become world champions in the pro ranks, are:

1929	Barney Ross
1934	Joe Louis
1939	Ezzard Charles
1953	Sonny Liston
1960	Cassius Clay
1974	Sugar Ray Leonard
1979	Mike McCallum
1986	Roy Jones Jnr
1987	Roy Jones Jnr
1989	Oscar de la Hoya
1993	Floyd Mayweather
1994	Floyd Mayweather
1996	Floyd Mayweather

Max respect to you all.

Take a ride with me on some of the downfalls of the heavyweight champions of the world.

JAMES J CORBETT was hounded after taking the title off John L Sullivan by the fight fans. They idolized Sullivan.

BOB FITZSIMMONS was arrested and charged with manslaughter after one of his sparring partners collapsed and died. (It's a fucking tough game and can end up a very lonely old road.)

JACK JOHNSON was the first black heavyweight champion of the world… and boy did he know how to wind up the white guys. He even married a white woman! Bear in mind that blacks in his day were still treated like slaves in America. No shit, man – black men were second class citizens. It was a tough time, with race riots and lynchings. The Ku Klux Klan was out and about, searching for a hit. Jack got gold teeth, a cane and a bowler! Fuck me; he was a proper flash fucker but a brilliant fighter. He was hated by so many whites but loved by the blacks. I thought he was awesome and I can't help but respect the man. It's the racist cunts I dislike! Until a man's had black pussy, he's never lived. Believe it.

JAMES J JEFFRIES lost his boxing fortune in the Wall Street Crash.

JACK DEMPSEY had to face taunts of being a coward when he was accused of ducking out of wartime service.

MAX SCHMELING fell out with Hitler and the Germans because he refused to sack his Jewish manager. What a brave decision but what a hardnut.

JOE LOUIS became a coke head and was brought to his knees by the tax man. (That fucking tax man again – he's everywhere!) Poor old Joe lost his mind and died a very lonely death!

EZZARD CHARLES ended up in a wheelchair – penny-less.

MAX BEER died at 58! He never lived to see his son Max Jnr play Jethro in the TV series *The Beverley Hillbillies*.

PRIMO CARNERA was robbed by mobsters! He turned to wrestling and died at 60 of cirrhosis of the liver.

SONNY LISTON was found dead in mysterious circumstances. (We all know the truth. It's probably best forgotten.)

ROCKY MARCIANO died at 46 in a plane crash in 1969!

ALI ignored warnings about boxing on too long. Now look at him – how sad is it to see 'the greatest' like that?

KEN NORTON almost died in a horrific car crash.

LEON SPINKS battled with alcoholism and drug abuse. He's now a cleaner in a factory.

MIKE TYSON – we all know about him!

TREVOR BERBICK fell into the black pit of no hope and was stabbed to death in 2007.

FRANK BRUNO had a mental breakdown.

I could go on and on and on! There are hundreds more stories like that and some are even sadder. There have been some ugly deaths, but that's the filthy game for you. They don't all walk away rich and pretty like Sugar Ray Leonard or Lennox Lewis. More fall into a big fucking black hole and never climb back out. It's a man's gamble!

Did you know the actor Dennis Waterman's elder brother Peter was the undefeated British Welterweight champion from 1956 to 1958? He passed away in 1986. Peter Seller's great grandfather was Daniel Mendoza, the legendary East End bare knuckle champion, and Tommy 'The Duke' Morrison's uncle was John Wayne (hence the nickname). Tommy was WBO heavyweight champion.

If you ever get chance to see Paul Newman in the film *Somebody Up There Likes Me* then watch it. He plays the legendary Rocky Graziano and it's a classic... Another great boxing film is *Monkey On My Back*. It's boxing legend Barney Ross' story, played by Cameron Mitchell. Yep, they're great films and great guys! I'm just a boxing man – I admire and respect a fighter! That's all it is...

Today, I copped a dozen letters and my Luton newspaper. It's been a great day! One of my letters was from my son Mike and I've re-read it ten times already! I just love my son; he's made my life worthwhile – fuck what anybody else says or thinks! Think what you like, but say it in a whisper! If you shout it out, it will get back to me! (You really don't want that on your plate, believe me.)

I had chips, egg and beans for tea – plenty of it too. That's good training grub for me! Still, beggars can't be choosers and after all is said and done I'm only a birdman. Prison is my life and it could also be my death. Who knows what tomorrow may bring? It's all part of the journey for me! My bus doesn't stop till the end. The driver's a madman and the ticket inspector's a fucking lunatic. How can I get off? I'll have an axe in the back of my head before you can say "Luton for the Cup".

Well, I'm running short, I'm tired and I'm ready for bed. I've got a big day tomorrow. So has my QC, Mr Sperry. Tomorrow could be the day I crack this nut (or it cracks me). If I lose, my next parole date will be August 2010. My writing stops here – today; now!

28 August 2008

This is the end!

All I want to say is that I deserved everything I ever got. I was a nasty bastard and I lost my way in life but it's now, today, that can see the real man – the real me! My only fear in life is to lose my mother whilst I'm inside. If that happened it could well send me back into the black hole of insanity from where it will be impossible for me to get back to the light. If there is any justice or fairness that can't happen.

Am I sorry for all the bad things I've done? Am I fuck! Why should I be sorry? Is the system sorry for all the innocent men and women they've locked up and executed? Are they fuck! We all do what we do and we all have to take the consequences of our actions. We have to learn from them and change our ways! At 56 years of age and after 35 years locked away, do you think I might have learned my lesson? What do you think? (Need I say any more?)

I love you Mum xxx

THE END

5 September 2008.

As you can see, the parole hearing didn't go ahead! More shit... The judge wanted to do it in one hour. Ask yourselves how a parole hearing can be dealt with in one hour? I've since learned I'm the only con in Wakefield jail to be given only one hour and to have it held behind bars! So what does that tell you? Everything I've ever said before: it's all Loonyology.

The only great part about my journey through the penal system is that I have the No. 1 lawyer on the planet fighting for me. Giovanni will never ever throw in the towel or do me in the back. For that I am grateful and truly blessed. The man is an inspiration to the legal world and a great source of strength to me. It's only with his help that I'm able be patient and continue swallowing this shit.

Now you'll never know how my parole review will end up – unless I write another book or you read it in the papers or see it on the news, because this is where the diary ends. I'm sorry to leave you all in suspense but that's how life is. It's a mystery – one big fucking mystery tour. And don't we all love it? But no matter how tough life becomes, always remember the guys and girls who have lost it all. The following were all executed in June 2008:

CURTIS OSBORNE – DEATH ROW, GEORGIA. He'd been on death row for a double murder back in 1990 when he was 19. On 4 June he was executed by lethal injection.

DAVID HILL – DEATH ROW, SOUTH CAROLINA. He shot three people dead in 1996 then shot himself in the head. Fuck me; he survived so the state could kill him! How insane is that? On 6 June they pumped his veins with poison.

KARL CHAMBERLAIN – DEATH ROW, TEXAS. He spent 12 years on death row then on 11 June they injected him and put him to sleep like a dog.

TERRY SHORT – DEATH ROW, OKLAHOMA. On June 17 he was executed by lethal injection. Good night!

JAMES EARL REED – DEATH ROW, SOUTH CAROLINA. He chose the chair – 'old sparky'. They let him have 1,000 volts on 20 June; they fried his brain like an egg.

ROBERT STACY – DEATH ROW, VIRGINIA. On 25 June they injected him over his 1997 murder where he sawed through a man's throat. He was on the ice block waiting to die for 11 years.

Like I said, the world's full of pain!

SHEP WILSON – After 21 years on death row in Alabama, they opened up his door and found he'd died of natural causes! That's crazy – the old boy pegged out before they could strap him in the chair. That's one the state of Alabama never murdered!

It's insanity all over the world! In Japan, they hanged three people on 17 June:

TSUTOMU MIYAZAKI – The monster who raped and killed four young girls back in 1988/'89. He even ate one of them. His time arrived after 20 years on death row in Tokyo.

SHINJI MUTSUDA – He'd been on death row since 1995! They

stretched his neck so that he looked like a fucking ostrich on the slab.

YOSHIO YAMASAKI – They hanged him in Osaka for the murder of two women 20 years ago.

Life really is stolen away from some. Some deserve it too.

Johnny Griffiths just sent me the *Let Him Have Justice* book by Iris Bentley. Iris was Derek Bentley's sister! Please read it. If your heart doesn't fill up then you're not human. I had tears on my eyes! Britain hanged this boy Derek Bentley for fuck all. Read it and feel ashamed of this 'great country' and its evil fucking Law Lords! I spit on them all for the parasites they truly are!

I must end this with some good news: Monster Miller has been swagged out! They took him to the Seg block in Full Sutton this morning. He will be in my old dungeon with no window to open and a lumpy, old, thin mattress. He will be fed through a hatch in the door like a dog in a kennel. He will be on a 10-guard unlock and will be so depressed. Let's hope its suicidal depression and the fucker tops himself so we can all be shot of the cunt.

This really is the end!

Adios, amigos.

And always remember: *tempus fugit* (time flies).

www.bronsonloonyology.com

bronsonloonyology.com@ymail.com

or call up Gavin Meek, my right hand buddy (07746 781366)
coz I know your dying to find out the result of my parole hearing?
You know you are! Fuck me… so am I!

Thanks to Nina for the cover. My fav artist in the UK. Max respect.

Other books by Bronson

Insanity: My Mad Life
The Krays and Me
The Prison Guide Book
Bronson
Solitary Fitness
Heroes and Villains: The Good, the Mad, the Bad and the Ugly
(John Blake Publishing)

Legends
Silent Scream
(Mirage)

Loonyology
(Apex)

Write to me

1314 Bronson
HMP Wakefield
W Yorks
England
WF2 9AG
UK